# Purcell Manuscripts: The Principal Musical Sources

Few details are known about the life of Henry Purcell. This book provides the first in-depth analysis of the most obvious documentary evidence of Purcell's career – the music manuscripts of his own hand and those copied by his colleagues. Robert Shay and Robert Thompson offer a richly illustrated study of Purcell's sources, examining in detail the physical features of the manuscripts as well as their musical content. Their survey sheds new light on the chronology of composition and copying of Purcell's works and reassesses the place of extant autographs in his musical development. Major sources are fully catalogued, providing information about the context in which Purcell's music was collected and performed, and his handwriting is more closely examined than ever before. The book represents a significant new reference tool for scholars, applying a forensic approach that greatly enriches our knowledge of the composer and the music of his time.

Robert Shay is Academic Dean at the Longy School of Music, Cambridge, Massachusetts. As a specialist in the music of Henry Purcell, he contributed to *Purcell Studies* (Cambridge University Press, 1995). He has also edited a volume of works by Henry Aldrich, *Selected Anthems and Motet Recompositions* (1998).

Robert Thompson is Head of General Studies at Colfe's School, Lee, London. He is also a contributor to *Purcell Studies* and has written articles on seventeenth-century music manuscripts for a number of publications including *Chelys*, which he now edits. In 1995 he was curator of the Purcell Tercentenary exhibition at The British Library.

☙☙☙

# *Purcell Manuscripts*
## The Principal Musical Sources

ROBERT SHAY AND ROBERT THOMPSON

CAMBRIDGE
UNIVERSITY PRESS

CAMBRIDGE UNIVERSITY PRESS
Cambridge, New York, Melbourne, Madrid, Cape Town, Singapore, São Paulo

Cambridge University Press
The Edinburgh Building, Cambridge CB2 2RU, UK

Published in the United States of America by Cambridge University Press, New York

www.cambridge.org
Information on this title: www.cambridge.org/9780521580946

First published 2000
This digitally printed first paperback version 2006

*A catalogue record for this publication is available from the British Library*

*Library of Congress Cataloguing in Publication data*

Shay, Robert Stuart.
Purcell manuscripts: the principal musical sources / Robert Shay and
Robert Thompson.
p.   cm.
Includes bibliographical references (p.   ) and indexes.
ISBN 0 521 58094 3 (hardback)
1. Purcell, Henry, 1659–1695 – Manuscripts Catalogs.   2. Music –
Manuscripts Catalogs.   I. Thompson, Robert, 1952–.   II. Title.
ML134.P95S53   2000
780'.92 – dc21   99–38030 CIP

ISBN-13  978-0-521-58094-6 hardback
ISBN-10  0-521-58094-3 hardback

ISBN-13  978-0-521-02811-0 paperback
ISBN-10  0-521-02811-6 paperback

# Contents

# Illustrations

Illustrations are reproduced by courtesy of the following copyright holders:
1.1–1.3, 1.5–1.7, 2.1, 3.1, 3.2, 4.1, 4.2, 5.3, 6.3, 6.4, 7.1, 7.4, The British
Library; 1.4, the Victoria and Albert Museum; 2.2–2.5, the Syndics of the
Fitzwilliam Museum, Cambridge; 2.6, the University of Texas, Austin; 2.7, the
Eastman School of Music, University of Rochester; 3.3, 5.2, 5.4, 7.3, the
Governing Body of Christ Church, Oxford; 5.1, the Dean and Chapter of
Westminster Abbey; 5.5, the University of California, Los Angeles; 6.1, 6.2, the
Royal Academy of Music, London; 7.2, the Bodleian Library, Oxford.

# Tables

ix

# Preface

The origins of this book lie in separate research projects, some of which had little or nothing to do with Purcell. Enquiries into sources of the English composer George Jeffreys demonstrated that a careful examination of a manuscript's physical make-up, a process for which we later learned the ugly but succinct word 'codicology', could yield surprising and informative results; some received opinions concerning composers' handwriting seemed due for re-examination; and we both acquired a growing awareness of the activities of copyists and other relatively obscure musicians in the later seventeenth century. Our contributions to *Purcell Studies* in 1995, independently conceived and written, fortuitously complemented each other and formed the basis of this more comprehensive survey of Purcell manuscripts aiming to arrive at a better understanding of the *stemmata* of some of Purcell's works and a deeper appreciation of the place of each major manuscript source in the working life of the musicians who copied and used it. Our readers must decide whether and to what extent we have succeeded.

The task would have been unthinkable without Franklin B. Zimmerman's *Henry Purcell, 1659–1695: an Analytical Catalogue of his Music*, and readers may be surprised to find a paucity of 'Z numbers' in our text and tables. We felt that in most cases the identity of a work was made clear by its title or incipit and therefore decided to reserve Zimmerman's catalogue numbers for ambiguously titled works such as keyboard pieces: no disrespect to a great Purcellian is intended. Other decisions unlikely to be beyond criticism include a certain inconsistency in the identification of works in the tables: when we thought there was anything to be gained from it we have included literal transcriptions of 'headings' or 'incipits' (information listed under such categories is given as it appears in the source *without* inverted commas); when not, we have used the modernised 'title'. Similarly, we have given the full inclusive pagination or foliation for works contained in all autographs and certain non-autographs, while simply providing the initial page or folio number for other manuscripts. Contractions in quoted material, both in the tables and the text, are expanded except in the case of those involving the y-thorn, when it seemed absurdly pedantic to alter 'yt' to 'y[a]t'.

Most of the manuscripts discussed in this book have been examined at first hand, and we are responsible for all details of their watermarks, measurements and other physical features. A handful, which we judged not to be of the first importance, we studied only in reproductions, and codicological information is omitted from the tables of their contents unless it could be reliably obtained: the sources of such information are acknowledged at the appropriate places. We have tried to provide a reference for each identified copyist or early owner sufficient to enable any interested reader to pursue further enquiries: most such references are in footnotes, but a number of major copyists, along with a few others for whom adequate information is not readily available, are dealt with in the Appendices.

Our intention from the outset was to produce not simply a catalogue of the major manuscript sources but a relatively detailed treatment in prose, thus enabling us to explore interconnections between sources, copyists and variant versions of particular works. It is our hope, however, that those who wish to consult this book for specific information about a particular manuscript or work will find the several indexes sufficient for their purposes. For those less familiar with Purcell source material some indication of the book's overall layout should be given here: Chapter 1 explores Purcell's career as viewed from the extant manuscript sources and then provides background information on the major facets of codicological study, namely paper and handwriting. Chapters 2–4 each take as their focal point one of the three great autograph scorebooks, also encompassing closely related sources or (in Chapters 3–4) sources containing related repertories. Chapters 5–7 then cover the remaining ground: the miscellaneous sacred sources, the theatre sources, and everything else (the sources of songs, keyboard music and instrumental works not previously covered).

# Acknowledgements

Our debt to existing published material will be apparent on every page and is, we hope, adequately acknowledged. In the years in which this book has been in preparation we have both taken part in conferences, exhibitions and editorial work, all of which deepened our understanding of our subject: our obligation for specific pieces of information passed on informally or through correspondence is stated in the relevant footnotes, but our special thanks for sustained and substantial support, help and encouragement are due to Curtis Price, Principal of the Royal Academy of Music; Margaret Laurie, Chairwoman of the Purcell Society; Bruce Wood, Peter Holman, Christopher Hogwood and Keri Dexter. Correspondence and conversation with scholars pursuing lines of enquiry very different from our own, notably Martin Adams and Rebecca Herissone, produced many rewarding points of convergence but also some instructive divergences. The staff of each and every library holding our source material have far exceeded their professional obligations and have readily shared their knowledge with us: we must especially thank Chris Banks, Curator of Music Manuscripts at The British Library, not only for assisting in numerous ways but also for doing so while the Library was moving to its new premises. Finally, and above all, we must record our debt to our wives Elizabeth Shay and Janet Thompson for their support and forbearance over a long period of preoccupation with seventeenth-century matters.

# Bibliographical procedure

BOOKS, ARTICLES AND PUBLISHED MUSIC
As a rule all references to books, articles and published music are given in full on their first appearance in each chapter and thereafter in short-title form. Frequently cited books and periodicals, however, are identified by the abbreviations given on pp. xvii–xix below. Publications of the Purcell Society are identified in footnotes in the form *Works*; volume number; date (dates of publication are given in preference to the description 'revised edition').

MANUSCRIPTS

Music manuscripts are identified in full in section or table headings but by RISM sigla and abbreviated shelfmarks throughout the body of the text: in particular, the element 'MS' has been omitted unless its absence causes potential confusion. Two unfamiliar sigla have been introduced:

GB-Ktp    Knutsford, Tatton Park

US-NHb    New Haven, Yale University, Beinecke Rare Book and Manuscript Library

Unnumbered pages or folios within the main pagination or foliation sequence are designated by a Roman numeral after the previous numbered page or folio (e.g. 30/ii).

# Abbreviations

## BOOKS

| | |
|---|---|
| Adams, *Henry Purcell* | Martin Adams, *Henry Purcell: the Origins and Development of his Musical Style* (Cambridge, 1995) |
| *BDM* | Andrew Ashbee and David Lasocki, assisted by Peter Holman and Fiona Kisby, *A Biographical Dictionary of English Court Musicians, 1485–1714*, 2 vols. (Aldershot, 1998) |
| Bloxam, *Register* | J. R. Bloxam, ed., *A Register of the Presidents, Fellows, Demies . . . of St Mary Magdalen College*, 8 vols. (Oxford, 1853–85) |
| Burney, *History* | Charles Burney, *A General History of Music from the Earliest Ages to the Present Period (1789)*, 2 vols., ed. Frank Mercer (London, 1935; repr. New York, 1957) |
| Churchill | W. A. Churchill, *Watermarks in Paper . . . in the XVII and XVIII Centuries and their Interconnection* (Amsterdam, 1935) |
| Crosby, *Catalogue* | Brian Crosby, *A Catalogue of Durham Cathedral Music Manuscripts* (Oxford, 1986) |
| *CSPD* | M. A. E. Green, et al., eds., *Calendar of State Papers, Domestic Series . . . Preserved in the State Paper Department of Her Majesty's Public Record Office* (London, 1860–) |
| Dawe, *Organists* | Donovan Dawe, *Organists of the City of London* (Padstow, 1983) |
| *DNB* | Leslie Stephen et al., eds., *The Dictionary of National Biography*, 22 vols. and supplements (London and Oxford, 1917–) |
| Dodd, *Thematic Index* | Gordon Dodd, ed., *Thematic Index of Music for Viols* (London, 1980–92) |
| Foster, *Alumni* | Joseph Foster, *Alumni Oxonienses, 1500–1714*, 4 vols. (Oxford, 1891) |
| Grindle, *Irish Cathedral Music* | W. H. Grindle, *Irish Cathedral Music: a History of Music at the Cathedrals of the Church of Ireland* (Belfast, 1989) |
| *Grove* | Stanley Sadie, ed., *The New Grove Dictionary of Music and Musicians*, 20 vols. (London, 1980) |

| | |
|---|---|
| Hawkins, *History* | John Hawkins, *A General History of the Science and Practice of Music*, 2 vols. (London, 1853; repr. New York, 1963) |
| *Hearne* | C. E. Doble et al., eds., *Remarks and Collections of Thomas Hearne*, 11 vols. (Oxford, 1885–1921) |
| Heawood | Edward Heawood, *Watermarks, Mainly of the 17th and 18th Centuries* (Hilversum, 1950) |
| Holman, *Four and Twenty Fiddlers* | Peter Holman, *Four and Twenty Fiddlers: the Violin at the English Court, 1540–1690* (Oxford, 1993) |
| Holman, *Henry Purcell* | Peter Holman, *Henry Purcell* (Oxford, 1994) |
| Holst, ed., *Henry Purcell* | Imogen Holst, ed., *Henry Purcell, 1659–1695: Essays on his Music* (London, 1959) |
| King, *Some British Collectors* | A. Hyatt King, *Some British Collectors of Music, c.1600–1960* (Cambridge, 1963) |
| Lawlor, *Fasti* | H. J. Lawlor, ed., *The Fasti of St Patrick's, Dublin* (Dundalk, 1930) |
| Madan, *Summary Catalogue* | Falconer Madan, *A Summary Catalogue of Western Manuscripts in the Bodleian Library at Oxford*, III (Oxford, 1895); V (Oxford, 1905) |
| *Performing the Music* | Michael Burden, ed., *Performing the Music of Henry Purcell* (Oxford, 1996) |
| *Purcell Companion* | Michael Burden, ed., *The Purcell Companion* (London, 1995) |
| *Purcell Studies* | Curtis Price, ed., *Purcell Studies* (Cambridge, 1995) |
| *RECM* | Andrew Ashbee, ed., *Records of English Court Music*, I (Snodland, 1986); V (Aldershot, 1991); VIII (Aldershot, 1995) |
| Shaw, *The Succession* | Watkins Shaw, *The Succession of Organists of the Chapel Royal and the Cathedrals of England and Wales from c.1538* (Oxford, 1991) |
| Spink, *Restoration* | Ian Spink, *Restoration Cathedral Music, 1660–1714* (Oxford, 1995) |
| Vicars, *Index* | Arthur Edward Vicars, *Index to the Prerogative Wills of Ireland, 1536–1810* (Dublin, 1897) |
| Voorn, *De papiermolens* | Henk Voorn, *De papiermolens in de provincie Noord-Holland* (Haarlem, 1960) |
| Westrup, *Purcell* | J. A. Westrup, *Purcell*, rev. Nigel Fortune (London, 1980; repr. with new foreword by Curtis Price, Oxford, 1995) |
| *Wood* | Andrew Clark, ed., *The Life and Times of Anthony Wood*, 5 vols. (Oxford, 1891–1900) |
| Zimmerman, *Catalogue* | Franklin B. Zimmerman, *Henry Purcell 1659–1695: an Analytical Catalogue of his Music* (London, 1963) |
| Zimmerman, *Life* | Franklin B. Zimmerman, *Henry Purcell, 1659–1695: his Life and Times*, 2nd edn (Philadelphia, 1983) |

## PERIODICALS

| | |
|---|---|
| *AcM* | *Acta Musicologica* |
| *BLJ* | *British Library Journal* |

| | |
|---|---|
| *BLR* | *Bodleian Library Record* |
| *BMQ* | *British Museum Quarterly* |
| *EM* | *Early Music* |
| *FAM* | *Fontes Artis Musicae* |
| *GSJ* | *Galpin Society Journal* |
| *JAMS* | *Journal of the American Musicological Society* |
| *JRMA* | *Journal of the Royal Musical Association* |
| *MA* | *Musical Antiquary* |
| *M&L* | *Music and Letters* |
| *MQ* | *Musical Quarterly* |
| *MR* | *Music Review* |
| *MT* | *The Musical Times* |
| *PRMA* | *Proceedings of the Royal Musical Association* |
| *RMARC* | *Royal Musical Association Research Chronicle* |

## GENERAL ABBREVIATIONS

| | |
|---|---|
| bc | basso continuo |
| INV | Inverted: used when modern foliation or pagination applies to music copied with the manuscript reversed and for the reverse sequence when a manuscript has separate pagination from the front and back |
| MLE | Music for London Entertainment: a series of facsimiles issued by Richard MacNutt 1983–7 and subsequently by Stainer and Bell |
| S, A, CT, T, B | soprano, alto, countertenor, tenor, bass solo voices |
| satb | soprano, alto, tenor, bass chorus voices |
| va | viola |
| vn | violin |

## RISM LIBRARY SIGLA

*Belgium*

| | |
|---|---|
| B-Bc | Brussels, Koninklijk Conservatorium |

*Eire*

| | |
|---|---|
| EIRE-Dcc | Dublin, Christ Church Cathedral (deposited at the Representative Church Body Library, Dublin) |

*France*

| | |
|---|---|
| F-Pc | Paris, Conservatoire National (housed at F-Pn) |
| F-Pn | Paris, Bibliothèque Nationale |

*Germany*

D-Hs                 Hamburg, Staats- und Universitätsbibliothek

*Great Britain* (the national siglum 'GB' is omitted)

Bu                   Birmingham University, Barber Institute of Fine Arts

Cfm                  Cambridge, Fitzwilliam Museum

Ckc                  Cambridge, King's College, Rowe Music Library

Cmc                  Cambridge, Magdalene College

CDp                  Cardiff, Public Libraries, Central Library

CH                   Chichester, West Sussex Record Office

DRc                  Durham, Cathedral

En                   Edinburgh, National Library of Scotland

EL                   Ely, Cathedral (deposited at Cambridge University Library)

EXc                  Exeter, Cathedral

Ktp                  Knutsford, Tatton Park

Lam                  London, Royal Academy of Music

Lcm                  London, Royal College of Music

Lg                   London, Guildhall Library

Lpro                 London, Public Record Office

Lsp                  London, St Paul's Cathedral

Lwa                  London, Westminster Abbey

Ll                   Lincoln, Cathedral

Mp                   Manchester, Central Public Library, Henry Watson Music Library

Ob                   Oxford, Bodleian Library

Och                  Oxford, Christ Church

Ooc                  Oxford, Oriel College

WO                   Worcester, Cathedral

WRch                 Windsor, St George's Chapter Library

WRec                 Windsor, Eton College

Y                    York, Minster

*Japan*

J-Tn                 Tokyo, Nanki Music Library

*United States*

US-AUS               Austin, University of Texas, Harry Ransom Humanities Research Center

US-BE                Berkeley, University of California, Music Library

US-Cn                Chicago, Newberry Library

US-Cu                Chicago, University of Chicago, Joseph Regenstein Library

US-LAuc              Los Angeles, University of California, William Andrews Clark Memorial Library

| | |
|---|---|
| US-NH | New Haven, Yale University, Music Library |
| US-NHb | New Haven, Yale University, Beinecke Rare Book and Manuscript Library |
| US-NYp | New York, Public Library |
| US-R | Rochester, Eastman School of Music, Sibley Music Library |
| US-Wc | Washington, Library of Congress, Music Division |
| US-Ws | Washington, Folger Shakespeare Library |

# A note on the tables

All measurements in tables are in millimetres. Details of rastrology include the following information:

> The total number of staves on a page
> The number of staves drawn at once by a single multi-stave rastrum
> The overall span of the multi-stave rastrum
> The 'profile' of the rastrum, consisting of the width of each individual stave and (in parentheses) the width of the spaces between the staves

All rastral measurements are variable, and deviations of up to 1 mm are not unusual. For further information, see pp. 17–18 below.

# Introduction: manuscript sources and Purcell's music

## PURCELL MANUSCRIPTS: A LIFE IN MUSIC

Beyond the outline of his professional career and a few details of his private life little is known about Henry Purcell.[1] No surviving parish register records his baptism, his date of birth in 1659 being inferred from the ages given in the flyleaf portrait of the 1683 sonatas and on his memorial tablet in Westminster Abbey; subsequent documentary evidence tells us hardly more than that he was successful at his work, married in about 1680, had children and died prematurely at the age of thirty-six.[2] Against the background of this biographical anonymity, the man himself often emerges more clearly from music manuscripts than from any other kind of material.

The composer's parents are now thought to have been the elder Henry Purcell (d. 1664) and his wife Elizabeth,[3] though the younger Henry's uncle Thomas undoubtedly played a major part in his upbringing and referred to him in a surviving letter as 'my son'.[4] Both of the elder Purcells were musicians in Charles II's Restoration court,[5] and young Henry must have shown enough natural ability to gain a chorister's place in the Chapel Royal, from which he was discharged when his voice

[1] Biographical information can be found in Zimmerman, *Life*; Maureen Duffy, *Henry Purcell* (London, 1994).

[2] For details of Purcell's family life see Duffy, *Henry Purcell*, 63, and J. L. Chester, *The Marriage, Baptismal and Burial Registers of the Collegiate Church or Abbey of St Peter, Westminster* (London, 1876).

[3] Apart from biographies already cited, see J. A. Westrup, 'Purcell's Parentage', *MR* 25 (1964), 100–3, and Robert Thompson, review of Margaret Campbell, *Henry Purcell, Glory of his Age* (London, 1993), in *Chelys* 22 (1993), 49–50.

[4] In a letter to John Gostling dated 8 February 1679 preserved in the Nanki Library, Tokyo: reproduced in Westrup, *Purcell*, between pp. 80 and 81.

[5] *RECM*, I, 38–40 and passim.

broke in 1673.[6] The customary sum of £30 a year for 'keeping' him was paid to Purcell in person rather than to the Master of the Children, John Blow, so he probably lived at home while pursuing his musical studies at Whitehall until Matthew Locke's death in 1677 made the court post of Composer for the Violins available for him.[7]

A number of manuscripts in Purcell's hand date from before the end of 1677, all distinguished by a hook-shaped bass clef broadly similar to that of Pelham Humfrey, who as Master of the Children from 1672 to 1674 was responsible for some of his training. The guardbook Lbl Add. 30932, a miscellaneous collection of originally unbound scores, contains Humfrey's anthem *By the waters of Babylon*, transcribed and probably arranged by Purcell with the string symphony and ritornelli replaced by somewhat inept passages for organ;[8] in places Purcell uses a form of treble clef quite different from his characteristic pattern, and this manuscript may be the earliest surviving example of his copying (Illus. 1.1). Other autographs written in a relatively awkward, unformed style include a few bass parts bound in US-NHb Osborn 515 (not unexpectedly showing that Purcell's first attempts at instrumental composition were influenced by Locke), an anthem, *Who hath believed our report*, in Lbl Add. 30932[9] (see Illus. 5.3) and the incomplete score of the Funeral Sentences in Lbl Add. 30931.[10] This last work may be connected with Humfrey's burial in 1674, for by the time of the next major musical funeral, that of Christopher Gibbons in 1676, Purcell's writing had acquired many of its mature characteristics. Slightly later autographs featuring the reversed bass clef are the symphony anthem *My beloved spake* in Lbl Add. 30932 (Illus. 1.5) and an organ part of Blow's *God is our hope and strength*, Och 554, fol. 3, inscribed on the reverse by the Chapel Royal organist Edward Lowe (see Illus. 5.4).

Secondary sources such as the partbooks copied by William Tucker (d. 28 February 1679) for Westminster Abbey and the Chapel Royal[11] confirm that well before 1680 Purcell had a number of works to his credit including at least three symphony anthems composed for performance in the king's presence:[12] Tucker never credits John Blow with the doctorate conferred upon him on 10 December 1677, so his copying was probably completed before that date. Purcell's appointment as Composer for the Violins appears to have been a nominal one to provide him with an

---

[6] Ibid., 131–2.   [7] Ibid., 173.   [8] Fols. 52r–55v.   [9] Fols. 94r–98v.   [10] Fols. 81r–84v.
[11] Purcell works copied by Tucker are found in Lbl R.M. 27.a.1-8, Lbl Add. 50860, Lwa Triforium Set I and J-Tn N5/10.
[12] See Christopher Hogwood, 'Thomas Tudway's History of Music', in *Music in Eighteenth-Century England: Essays in Honour of Charles Cudworth*, ed. C. Hogwood and Richard Luckett (Cambridge, 1983), 25.

Illus. 1.1 Pelham Humfrey, *By the waters of Babylon*, copied by Purcell. British Library Add. MS 30932, fol. 53v

income, because hardly any of his movements for string band were composed in the late 1670s; the principal document of his work at this period, the great autograph scorebook Cfm 88, suggests that his first major responsibility at court was the editing and composition of Anglican sacred music in the distinctly conservative style that provided the mainstay of the Chapel Royal repertory on weekdays and when the king did not attend the Chapel in person.[13] It is perhaps surprising that the youthful composer of *My beloved spake* was apparently steered away from the prestigious symphony anthem, but until Purcell's twenty-first birthday his superiors in the royal service seem to have subjected him to quite rigorous discipline, at first putting him to work revising and correcting earlier music and only in 1680 allowing him to

---

[13] *RECM*, I, 162–4.

contribute a court ode, *Welcome vicegerent of the mighty king.* The perception of Purcell as a junior partner to John Blow and the late Pelham Humfrey is underlined by the contents of Och 628, a presentation manuscript copied by Blow *c.* 1678, in which the older composers are mainly represented by symphony anthems written for the court but Purcell by domestic sacred songs. At about the same time, working initially on loose sheets, Purcell began the collection of vocal and instrumental chamber music bound together in 1680 to become the volume now Lbl Add. 30930: this scorebook, which contains revised versions of the sacred partsongs copied by John Blow, emphasises the seriousness of Purcell's study of counterpoint, culminating in 1680 in his anachronistic but musically fascinating series of fantazias.[14] Though mentors such as Blow may well have encouraged Purcell to compose the partsongs and sonatas, his exploration of the outmoded fantazia form is more likely to have arisen from his own interest, inspired perhaps by some of the ancient vocal music he edited in Cfm 88.

The third of Purcell's great autograph scorebooks, Lbl R.M. 20.h.8, which was started around the beginning of 1681, marks a new stage in the composer's career. Whether on account of the attainment of his majority or because of a perceived development in his abilities, from 1680 or 1681 onwards Purcell's professional duties involved the composition of the most elaborate forms of court music: the symphony anthem, the court ode, and, for more private occasions, the symphony song. A new type of ode, the 'Welcome Song' to celebrate the king's return to Whitehall after his summer progress, appears to have been added to the established New Year and birthday odes to exploit Purcell's abilities without disadvantaging Blow and other senior composers.[15] With Purcell's appointment in 1682 to Edward Lowe's place as an organist of the Chapel Royal his status as a court musician received final confirmation,[16] and his works of the period 1681–5, mostly preserved in his own hand in R.M. 20.h.8, reflect complete absorption in his occupation as a servant of an absolutist but highly sophisticated court in which his art was evidently appreciated: Charles II's reputation as a lover of trivial and superficial music is belied by many of the works written for him by Humfrey, Blow and Purcell, and it is interesting to speculate how Purcell's career might have developed had secure Stuart rule lasted longer. But Charles died in 1685, and although at first his

---

[14] See Robert Thompson, 'The Sources of Purcell's Fantasias', *Chelys* 25 (1996–7), 88–96.
[15] Regular annual performance of welcome songs took place only from 1680 to 1687, in which period all were composed by Purcell. See Rosamond McGuinness, *English Court Odes, 1660–1820* (Oxford, 1971), 1, 12–23.
[16] *RECM*, V, 80.

Catholic brother James's accession was happily accepted by a nation eager for stability[17] Purcell's musical reaction suggests that he may have had some idea of what lay ahead.

James II's rationalisation of court musical appointments, in which Purcell was designated as harpsichordist in what was in effect a modern baroque ensemble of strings, wind players and vocal soloists,[18] cannot in itself have caused a real reduction in Purcell's status, and the Anglican Chapel Royal continued to function even though the new monarch attended Catholic devotions:[19] on 21 October 1687 Nicholas Staggins, Master of the Music, was reproached for failing to ensure that string players attended, and Purcell was named as one of the organists in the sixteenth (1687) edition of Edward Chamberlain's *Anglia Notitiae*.[20] But according to a petition submitted by Purcell on 12 February 1688 the Chapel Royal organ was by then 'so out of repair that to cleanse, tune and put in good order will cost £40',[21] and Lbl R.M. 20.h.8 reveals a change of attitude on Purcell's part after the death of Charles II: he failed to transcribe anthems he had already listed in the manuscript's index, and apart from the great coronation anthem *My heart is inditing* entered no more sacred music in the scorebook even though a number of symphony anthems were in fact composed during James II's reign. Much of the secular music copied in the scorebook from 1685 onwards is in the hands of assistants, and few works for informal occasions were added; songs and ensembles already composed for the court began to appear in print, as if Purcell no longer regarded them as belonging to a special repertory dedicated to the secular life of the court in the same way as the symphony anthem was dedicated to the king's public worship at the Chapel Royal. Two retrospective collections started by the copyist London D around 1685, Lbl Add. 33287 and Lcm 2011, suggest that the death of Charles II was seen as a watershed by at least some court musicians, and the implication of Purcell's altered approach to R.M. 20.h.8 is that security had given way to an uncertainty which can only have grown worse as the political situation deteriorated until James was finally ousted by William and Mary in 1688.

Though Purcell continued to be employed by the new Protestant monarchs, court music was never again to be the vocation it had been under Charles II. When in England William III preferred to live away from Whitehall, and the court ceased to

[17] See J. R. Jones, *Country and Court* (London, 1978), 225–7.
[18] *RECM*, II, 2–3; Holman, *Four and Twenty Fiddlers*, 415–20.
[19] Holman, *Four and Twenty Fiddlers*, 411.    [20] *RECM*, II, 15–16; V, 284–5.
[21] Lpro T27/11, p. 314. See *RECM*, VIII, 275–6 and W. A. Shaw, ed., *Calendar of Treasury Books 1685–1689*, III (London, 1923), 1763–4.

be a self-contained musical centre, drawing instead upon the range of professional expertise available in the commercial world of London music.[22] It is unlikely to be a coincidence that in 1689 Purcell undertook two ventures connected with education: the composition of the ode *Celestial Music*,[23] performed at Lewis Maidwell's progressive academy in Westminster,[24] and a production of the opera *Dido and Aeneas*, possibly a revival of an earlier work, at Josias Priest's school for young gentlewomen in Chelsea.[25] At around the same time, Purcell began a close association with the London theatres which lasted until his death, involving the composition of large numbers of songs, incidental instrumental movements and extended musical scenes as well as the four long dramatic operas *Dioclesian* (1690), *King Arthur* (1691), *The Fairy Queen* (1692, revived 1693) and *The Indian Queen* (1695). Source material for these works is often problematic, only the *Fairy Queen* score in Lam 3 containing a few passages in Purcell's own hand. Other late autographs similarly reflect a practical function rather than the partly archival purpose of the great court scorebooks of earlier years: the keyboard volume Lbl MS Mus.1 contains teaching material, and the Gresham songbook, possibly related to Purcell's court employment, appears to be a repertoire collection for an accomplished soprano. Lbl Add. 30934 includes a score of Purcell's last court ode, the birthday song for the Duke of Gloucester *Who can from joy refrain*,[26] and is clearly a composing draft: the systematic collection of court odes in a single fair-copy manuscript had been finally abandoned with the exile of James II, and none of the fine odes for the birthday of Queen Mary survives in an autograph.

Purcell's manuscripts provide considerable insight into his working methods and his thoughts about music.[27] Composing drafts show numerous corrections and

---

[22] Holman, *Henry Purcell*, 18–20.

[23] A partial autograph survives in Lbl R.M. 20.h.8, fols. 125v–117r INV.

[24] In 1687 Maidwell established a boarding school in King Street, Westminster, offering a comprehensive curriculum including modern subjects such as mathematics and European languages as well as the gentlemanly accomplishments of dancing, fencing and horsemanship. See F. H. W. Sheppard, ed., *London County Council Survey of London*, XXXI (London, 1963), 177–9.

[25] Josias Priest (d. 1734) was a leading dancer and choreographer from the mid-1670s onwards: see S. J. Cohen, 'Theory and Practice of Theatrical Dancing', *Bulletin of the New York Public Library* 63 (1959), 541–54 (reprinted in Ifan Kyrle Fletcher, Selma Jean Cohen and Roger Lonsdale, *Famed for Dance: Essays on the Theory and Practice of Theatrical Dancing in England, 1660–1740* (New York, 1960), 22–33); Richard Semmens, 'Dancing and Dance Music in Purcell's Operas', in *Performing the Music*, 180–96; Richard Ralph, *The Life and Works of John Weaver* (New York, 1985), 662–4. For Priest's school in Chelsea see W. H. Godfrey, *London County Council Survey of London*, IV (London, 1913), 45 and plates 1 and 22.

[26] Fols. 80–93.

[27] See Rebecca Herissone, 'Purcell's Revisions of his Own Works', in *Purcell Studies*, 51–86.

changes of mind, and his unfinished manuscripts, or scores completed in differently coloured ink, reveal that he composed the outer parts first. More surprisingly, the incomplete score of the anthem *Rejoice in the Lord alway* in Lbl R.M. 20.h.8 suggests that he made fair copies in the same order, either to facilitate revision or to ensure that the most important details of the music were written down first. Four R.M. 20.h.8 anthems for which closely contemporary draft copies survive are similar in both autograph sources, but in other cases, perhaps when a slightly longer period had elapsed between initial composition and fair copying, Purcell regularly made significant alterations, as in the successive versions of the Funeral Sentences.[28] In later manuscripts, most notably the *Fairy Queen* score Lam 3, he demonstrably worked closely with one or more assistants, checking and correcting their work and returning to unfinished movements to add missing sections: certain sections of *The Fairy Queen*, and a set of string parts of *My song shall be alway* in Och 1188/9, indicate that Purcell sometimes gave partially completed material to an assistant to be copied while he composed the rest of the music, added subsequently in his own hand. The later autographs imply that much of Purcell's work was carried out at the last minute, in contrast to the ordered planning generally reflected in his major scorebooks of the period 1678–85.

The difference between Purcell's manuscripts of the Stuart period and those dating from after 1688 reflects far more than a development in his own musical interests or in his approach to his work. During the period in which the three great autograph scorebooks were mostly compiled, Purcell's principal task was the glorification of a monarch who claimed to rule by Divine Right; after 1688 he lived under a monarch who ruled by the invitation of Parliament, and his role at court and in society was that of an entertainer, albeit of an elevated kind, competing with all the other distractions the capital could offer. At first a dedicated court servant whose music seems to have been consciously reserved to the precincts of Whitehall, he had to become a freelance musician in the modern sense, earning his living wherever he could find the opportunity and satisfying a constant public desire for novelty. Purcell's short career began in a world which for all Charles II's preference for modern music adopted essentially conservative values; it ended in a world that looked forward, and his continued success is a measure of his resilience and strength of character as well as of his musical genius.

---

[28] Detailed analyses of some of Purcell's revisions are contained in Adams, *Henry Purcell*: see, for example, the discussion of the Overture in G, pp. 118–19.

## PAPER, BOOKS AND BINDING IN LATE SEVENTEENTH-CENTURY MUSIC

During Purcell's lifetime English music manuscripts invariably consisted of continental paper, until the late 1680s mostly imported from the Angoumois region of southwestern France where, with the help of substantial Dutch investment, an advanced paper industry had developed, but thereafter often from Holland. Although the process of making paper by hand has been expertly described in a number of works,[29] a brief account is necessary here to provide a background to the detailed discussions of sources that follow and a justification of the use of features of paper as historical evidence.

### The craft of papermaking

In the seventeenth century, and indeed throughout the history of European hand-made paper, white paper for writing or printing was made from linen rags. These were cut into convenient sizes, left partially to decay, and then subjected to a long process of washing and beating to separate the linen fibres and reduce the rags to a pulp, known as 'stuff', from which paper could be made. Beating was traditionally carried out in a stamping mill using large hammers driven by water power, and a supply of pure water was required for the continuous washing to which the rags were subjected during the earlier stages of the process. The ideal site for a paper mill had access to a fast-flowing river for the waterwheel and a smaller stream or spring to supply the washing water, so paper industries generally developed in hilly areas, although the Zaanland of Holland lacked all such geographical advantages and its wind-powered mills pulped rags with a rotary machine known as the 'hollander'. Technical developments in the hollander were essential to the flowering of the Dutch white paper industry after 1670.

Whichever method of beating was employed, the process ended with the transfer of the now liquid stuff to a vat. Each individual sheet of paper began its life when a mould consisting of an oblong lattice of fine metal wire supported on a wooden frame was dipped into the vat by a craftsman known as the 'vatman'. To prevent the stuff from running off the mould, an oblong wooden edge or 'deckel' was fitted over it:

---

[29] See in particular Dard Hunter, *Papermaking: the History and Technique of an Ancient Craft*, 2nd edn (London, 1957); J.-L. Boithias and C. Mondin, *Les moulins à papier et les anciens papetiers d'Auvergne* (Nonette, 1981).

when mould and deckel were taken out of the vat, the vatman allowed the stuff to drain, removed the deckel, and slid the mould along a board to his colleague the 'coucher', who at the same time returned an empty mould to him. This second mould was covered with the deckel and in turn dipped into the vat, while the coucher was transferring the partly formed paper to a stack made up alternately of similar sheets and pieces of felt. When this stack, known as the 'post', was large enough, it was mechanically pressed to remove as much water as possible and the paper and felt were separated. The felts were returned to form another post and the new paper went on to be dried, sized with animal glue, pressed again, and finished by processes such as polishing with a smooth stone. When all was complete, the paper left the mill packed into a ream wrapper, which was often elaborately printed with a description of its contents.

## The characteristics of handmade paper

Each sheet of handmade paper exactly reflects the characteristics of the mould on which it was made. The oblong wooden frame of the mould had ribs running in one direction only, to which relatively heavy wires or 'chains' were attached: when the paper is lit from behind, the marks left by these wires are visible as evenly spaced 'chain lines', between *c.* 20 and 40 mm apart, parallel to the shorter edge of the sheet (see Illus. 1.2 and 1.3). In the 'antique laid' paper of the seventeenth century the chains were sewn directly to the ribs of the mould, resulting in shadows visible on either side of the chain lines. At either end of the mould there was a more closely spaced extra wire parallel with the edge: these wires, variously known as edge wires, water bar wires or tranchefiles, were not attached to wooden ribs and did not cause shadows. Their presence in a sheet of paper is a reliable indication that the edge they parallel has not been heavily trimmed. At right angles to the ribs and chain lines were the finer and much more closely spaced 'laid' wires, perhaps one millimetre apart, which created the 'laid lines' visible in paper. Finally, a watermark of some kind was almost always provided in the centre of the left half of the mould, sometimes with a countermark in the corresponding position on the right. Every handmade paper mould was unique, the complexity of its construction being such that no mould-maker could produce two identical in every respect: only sheets of paper made in the same mould can properly be described as 'identical', and even they will show changes as the mould ages, deteriorates, and is repaired. The uneven 'deckel edges' left when the stuff seeped between the mould and the deckel were not removed at the paper mill; edges might be cut by the stationer or bookbinder, but many musical sources still have all or some of their deckel edges intact. The presence or absence of such edges, the dimensions of pages relative to the original sheet size, the possible division of watermarks between different pages, and the direction of the chain lines all provide valuable evidence of the way in which a manuscript was assembled.

## Watermarks

In the finished paper, letters in the watermark and countermark can usually be read with the countermark on the left and the watermark on the right, forming a mirror image of the pattern in the mould. The presence of countermarks was to some extent a regional feature: in the Angoumois the countermark often represented the initials of the papermaker,[30] and some mills which stood on Jesuit land used the symbol 'IHS',[31] either alone or with the craftsman's initials beneath (Illus. 1.2). In Angoumois paper, any initials or monogram beneath the watermark itself belonged to the merchant or 'factor' for whom the paper was made: factors' marks do not become common in English music sources until the late 1670s, though examples can be found in Dutch archives as early as 1658.[32] The involvement of Dutch factors in the Angoumois industry ultimately went far beyond the purchase of paper when it was offered for sale and led some, notably the Janssen family, to settle in the area.[33]

Although there is considerable variation of detail between the marks in different moulds, the number of broad types of watermark found in music manuscripts of Purcell's period is relatively small. Between the Restoration and the late 1680s most

---

[30] An *Arrêt de conseil* of 21 July 1671 laid down that paper should bear a mark identifying its maker: see J. Savary de Bruslons, *Dictionaire universel de commerce* (Paris, 1723), II, 969–71. Surviving paper suggests that manufacturers often ignored this regulation in material intended for export.

[31] In *Hollandse Mercurius* (1672), p. 30, it is claimed that the return to Holland of Dutch citizens caused disruption to the paper industry of Angoulême, where the Jesuits had made 'the finest paper the world had ever seen'; quoted in W. E. J. Berg, *De réfugiés in de Nederlanden na der herroeping van het Edict van Nantes* (Amsterdam, 1845), 142.

[32] A monogram dated 1658 which may belong to the van der Ley family is shown as a factor's mark in Voorn, *De papiermolens*, no. 79, pp. 133 and 164.

[33] For evidence of the early development of this relationship see J. G. van Dillen, ed., *Bronnen tot de geschiedenis van het bedrijfsleven en het gildewesen van Amsterdam*, III (The Hague, 1974), 426; Jean Louis Guez de Balzac, *Lettres de feu Monsieur de Balzac à Monsieur Conrart* (Amsterdam, 1659), 48; Henri Lacomb, 'Guez de Balzac, fabricant de papier de l'Angoumois', in *Contribution à l'histoire de la papeterie en France*, X (Grenoble, 1945), 72–89. The industry depended on overseas business to the extent that the loss of the export trade during the Nine Years War (1688–97) caused its temporary collapse; see W. C. Scoville, *The Persecution of Huguenots and French Economic Development, 1680–1720* (Berkeley and Los Angeles, 1960), 185, 230–1.

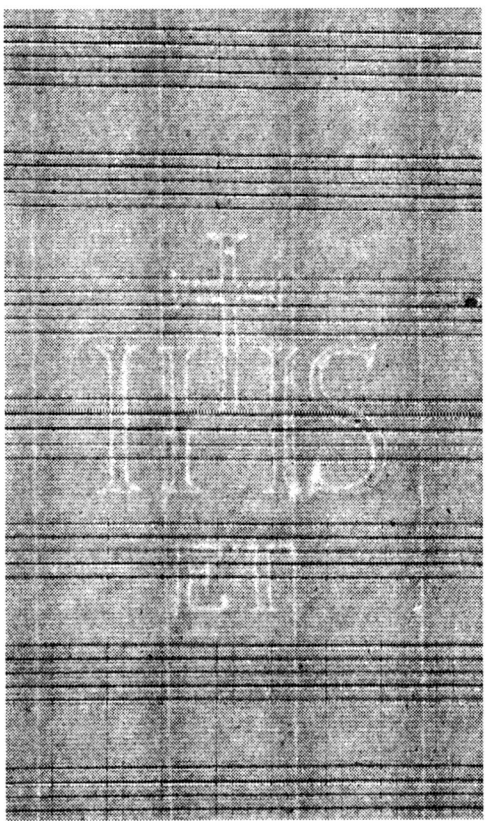

Illus. 1.2 'IHS' countermark with initials of Etienne Touzeau. British Library Add. MS 30930, fol. 29/i

English music manuscripts consist of paper from the Angoumois, often identified as 'Rochelle Paper', after the port from which it was exported, or described as 'Dutch' because it was sold by Dutch merchants or had watermarks with Dutch associations such as the arms of Amsterdam and the patriotic Dutch Lion emblem symbolising the seven United Provinces of the Netherlands. Both of these marks are found in relatively heavy foolscap-sized paper measuring about 325 mm by 415 mm. The third mark found in paper of this kind is of course the 'fool's cap' itself which, in Angoumois papers of Purcell's working lifetime, had a symmetrical seven-pointed form in which the foolscap's 'face' is shown in naturalistic profile. Foolscap-sized paper is commonly found in more functional manuscripts such as instrumental partbooks or composers' working copies: examples in Purcell's hand-writing include the organ part to John Blow's *God is our hope and strength*, Och

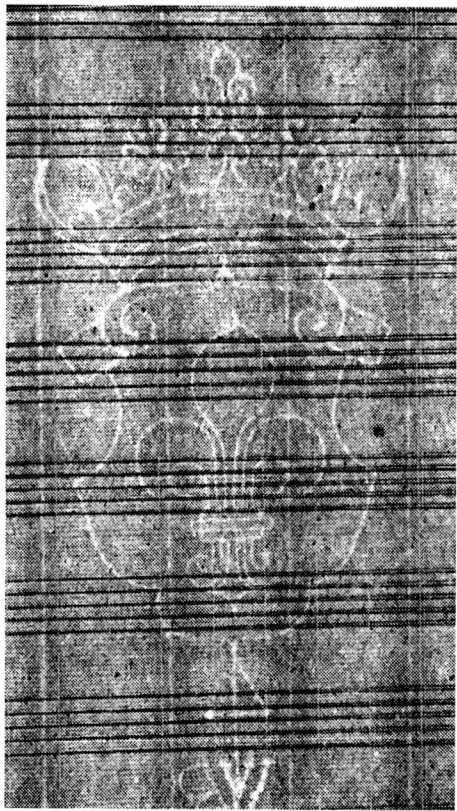

Illus. 1.3 Angoumois fleur-de-lys watermark. British Library Add. MS 30930, fol. 29/ii

554, fol. 3, and smaller autographs like the copy of *Plunged in the confines of despair* in Bu 5001.

More expensive partbooks, and scores such as Purcell's autographs Lbl Add. 30930 and R.M. 20.h.8, were made of the larger and heavier 'demy' and 'medium' sizes of paper, both of which used the watermark of a fleur-de-lys on a crowned shield (referred to herein as the Angoumois fleur-de-lys: see Illus. 1.3). Demy papers measured *c.* 350 by 485 mm; mediums up to 400 by 550 mm. 'Royal', the largest type generally found in music sources, measured 450 by 560 mm and was tradition-ally marked with the arms of Strasbourg, a bend on a shield surmounted by a large fleur-de-lys: paper of this kind is found in Cfm 88 and in the important secondary source Lbl Add. 33287. A few important craftsmen are identifiable from their initials in Angoumois paper: Claude de George, whose initials 'CDG' are found in much excellent material, ran the Nersac mill from 1674 or 1675 until his death in 1683;[34] Jean Monédière, 'IM', is known to have been working the Puy Moyen mill in the same year;[35] Etienne Touzeau, whose initials appear in both L♭! Add. 30930 and R.M. 20.h.8, was at work as a master papermaker by 1671, when he was running the St Michel mill,[36] and was clearly still active around 1680. All three, and others, worked for the paper merchant Abraham Janssen, whose initials appear as a factor's mark from *c.* 1679. The Janssen family had been involved in the Angoumois paper industry for some years,[37] and the appearance of Abraham's personal mark in the late 1670s probably reflects new confidence after the end of the Franco-Dutch war of 1672–8.[38] Another important merchant was the unidentified 'HC', active between 1676 and 1686.

Because of the substantial involvement of Dutch merchants in French papermaking and an exodus of Huguenot craftsmen to the Netherlands which began before the formal revocation of the Edict of Nantes in 1685, late seventeenth-century Dutch paper imitates Angoumois features, including the general style of watermarks and countermarks, though the new mills did not find it easy to match Angoumois standards.[39] Part of the problem may have been the need to wash the rags in water raised from a well; also the chopping action of the hollander resulted in paper less resilient than that produced in a stamping mill, where the linen fibres were separated but not cut into shorter lengths. It is perhaps significant that some early van der Ley monograms are found in paper that otherwise seems to be French,[40] and that the initials of the prominent Amsterdam papermaker and merchant Gillis van Hoven are found first in the factor's position,[41] as an importer of paper, and then in the

---

[34] See G. Babinet de Rencogne, *Recueil de documents pour servir à l'histoire de commerce et de l'industrie en Angoumois*, Bulletin de la société archéologique et historique de la Charente, 5th series, II (Angoulême, 1880), 103–14.

[35] Voorn, *De papiermolens*, 116.   [36] Rencogne, *Recueil*, 62.

[37] Abraham's brother Dericq bought the St Michel mill in 1656 and rented Tudeboeuf in 1668; see Rencogne, *Recueil*, 61, 67. In 1668 he was described as 'merchant and citizen of Angoulême'. In 1673 he rented a mill called 'L'Abbaye' for the duration of the war between France and Holland; see C. M. Briquet, *Les Filigranes* (facsimile edn), intro. by Allan Stevenson (Amsterdam, 1968), II, 701. Abraham's brothers installed de George at Nersac; see Rencogne, *Recueil*, 103–14. See also n. 51 below.

[38] Settled at the Treaty of Nijmegen on terms favourable to the Dutch: see H. Vast, *Les grands traités du règne de Louis XIV* (Paris, 1893–99), II, 66–8.

[39] Och 12 is an example of good-quality paper of the 1690s that nevertheless fails to match the highest French standards of previous decades.

[40] For example, in Bu 5001, fols. 32–51, autograph scores of Blow's New Year songs for 1681 and 1682. The countermark here appears to represent the same monogram as the 1658 factor's mark illustrated by Voorn, *De papiermolens* (see n. 32 above).

[41] The 'GVH' monogram appears as a factor's mark throughout the Lord Chamberlain's bill book for 1686, Lpro LC9/278. It later becomes a common countermark.

13

countermark position, as the craftsman-papermaker or the owner of the mill where the paper was made. The implication is that a number of Dutchmen learnt about the business, and even practised the craft of papermaking, in the Angoumois but ultimately began producing paper in Holland itself, when technical improvements and political circumstances made such a move desirable.

While the recognition of a particular watermark type or personal mark might well help in the dating of a manuscript, the principal bibliographical value of paper evidence depends on more detailed examination. Individual papermaking moulds can be identified not only by the precise features of the watermarks, and their relationship with the chain lines, but by the exact spacing of the chain lines themselves, often a helpful method when the watermark is obscured by text or lies within the binding. Proportions and relationships, rather than absolute measurements, are critical because of the slight variations caused by differing rates of paper shrinkage in manufacture. At each papermaking vat the vatman and the coucher worked together using two moulds and one deckel, so that sheets from the two moulds alternated in the original post:[42] sources of paper from the same moulds can be identified with most confidence if both marks of the pair, with the characteristic distribution of chain lines of each mould, can be distinguished. Marks which are closely similar do not necessarily form a pair in the sense just described: in the Angoumois, and probably in Holland, moulds were made by specialist 'maîtres faiseurs de formes',[43] who appear to have used a limited number of patterns for producing watermarks.[44] In its appearance, as opposed to the way it was used, a mark is no more closely related to its pair at the vat than to another made on the same pattern, so where the papermaker, stationer, or copyist have mixed papers of the same watermark type and quality it is occasionally difficult to be sure which sheets were produced by a mould pair at the vat. The tendency evident in earlier paper for watermarks to drift bodily towards chainlines does not affect most of the marks of Purcell's period, which are large enough to be secured to at least one chain-line from the outset.[45] Movement can, however, often be detected in outlying parts of a mark, such as the stem of a foolscap, and the early Purcell sources include a large enough

---

[42] See Allan Stevenson, 'Watermarks are Twins', *Studies in Bibliography* 4 (1951–2), 57–92.

[43] One Jean Delafont 'l'aisné' carried on this trade in the Angoumois parish of La Couronne; see Rencogne, *Recueil,* 96.

[44] Enquiries made by Allan Stevenson to the long-established papermaking firm of van Gelder Zonen produced an account published earlier this century describing a traditional craftsman using a pattern consisting of pins hammered into a drawing on a wooden block to make a watermark; see A. Stevenson, *The Problem of the Missale Speciale* (London, 1967), 245–7.

[45] Ibid., 248–52.

sample of paper made by Etienne Touzeau to show evidence of wear in their fleur-de-lys watermarks.

### The English trade in music paper

Paper was manufactured in a wide variety of sizes, types and qualities appropriate to the different uses for which it was intended. Only the best types of relatively heavy writing paper would meet the high standards demanded by musical use: music paper had to be capable of carrying dense, black notation on both sides without obtrusive show-through; take heavy note-heads without the ink spreading; and be sufficiently durable to stand repeated handling. The surviving material indicates that with the possible exception of some of the Dutch papers used in the 1690s most music paper was highly satisfactory.

Throughout Purcell's lifetime the publications of John and Henry Playford regularly advertise music books and music paper available from their shop.[46] The high level of standardisation of paper type, stave ruling, and format of books found in music sources of the period strongly suggests that paper was selected and prepared by a small group of stationers with a detailed knowledge of the paper trade rather than by individual copyists, and it is almost certain that Purcell and his colleagues obtained their books and paper from the Playfords, either directly or through their employment at Whitehall or Westminster Abbey. By wholesale standards, the amounts of paper prepared for music must have been small, and the stationers involved in this specialist business probably bought their paper a few reams at a time from major importers. Some indication of both the range of papers available and the identity of at least one important supplier comes from Ob MS Rawlinson D.398, fols. 156–7,[47] a list of sixty-six available paper types made in 1674 for John Fell, a delegate of the Oxford University Press.[48] The two merchants named, 'Merreatt' and 'Seward', were apparently in a position to deliver a wide variety of paper in considerable quantities: the latter is identifiable as the London merchant Thomas Seaward, a shareholder in

---

[46] See Robert Thompson, 'Manuscript Music in Purcell's London', *EM* 23 (1995), 612–13.

[47] See R. W. Chapman, 'An Inventory of Paper, 1674', *The Library*, 4th series, 7 (1927), 402–8.

[48] John Fell (1625–86), dean of Christ Church from 1660 and Bishop of Oxford from 1676, was a member of a new delegacy established in 1662 for the Oxford University Press: with three fellow delegates he held the privilege of printing from 22 August 1671 and planned to fund prestigious publications through the sale of school books and bibles produced in quantity. Such a project would require a range of paper types. See Strickland Gibson and John Johnson, eds., *The First Minute Book of the Oxford University Press, 1668–1756* (Oxford, 1943), xviii–xix; Harry Carter, *A History of the Oxford University Press I: to the Year 1780* (Oxford, 1975).

the King's Printing House who died in 1673,[49] so it is possible that the 'Seward' paper listed in the Rawlinson document represents stock being disposed of by his executors. In any event, Seaward or other merchants operating on a similar scale provide a necessary link in the chain from paper mill and factor to specialist London stationer and music copyist.

As an imported commodity, paper might be expected to reflect impediments to trade caused by wars and periods of lesser tension between England and France, England and Holland, or France and Holland, but for a variety of reasons such events seem not to be reflected in sources until the Nine Years War of 1688–97. Import prohibitions during the Second Dutch War of 1665–7 led only to the granting of a large number of licences to import paper from France;[50] the Franco-Dutch war of 1672–8 caused the rent of one Angoumois mill to be reduced from 700 livres a year to 600 but hardly seems to have ruined its trade;[51] and a subsequent ban on the importation of French goods, including paper, to England imposed on 20 March 1678[52] had so little effect that the Lord Chancellor's office continued to buy 'Fine Rochelle' paper throughout the period of prohibition, in spite of a further provision of the act which laid down that from 1 May 1679 the sale of all French goods, whenever imported, was illegal.[53] If the entries in the London Port Books are to be believed, imports of paper from France fell from 63,647 reams in 1678 to 300 in 1679, while those from Holland rose from 1,178 reams to 73,902 in the same period.[54] Clearly merchants simply redirected their ships through Dutch ports, or at the most collected their paper from Dutch warehouses.

Between 1688 and 1697, however, such convenient compromises could no longer help the Angoumois paper industry. To a greater extent than previous conflicts, the Nine Years War was an economic as well as a military contest;[55] moreover, English paper merchants could now turn to the paper industry of Holland, England's ally in the war, which had been greatly strengthened by the Huguenot workmen who fled there in the 1680s. Genuinely Dutch paper is therefore to be expected in sources of

[49] Thompson, 'Manuscript Music', 610.

[50] See Robert Steele, *Tudor and Stuart Proclamations* (Oxford, 1910), nos. 3408 and 3481; *CSPD 1666–7*, 492, 494, 512, 527, 585 and passim.

[51] The mill's tenant was Jacob Janssen, who in 1677 advanced 1,000 livres to Adam Mazure to make paper there; see Briquet, *Les Filigranes*, II, 693.

[52] Lbl 505.e.11 (2). For the response to the act, see Gilbert Burnet, *History of his own Time* (Oxford, 1833, repr. Hildesheim, 1968), II, 125.

[53] See Lpro LC9/276, fols. 75r–78r, 125v–128v, and 151v–153v.

[54] See D. C. Coleman, *The British Paper Industry, 1495–1860,* (Oxford, 1958), 121.

[55] See David Ogg, *Europe in the Seventeenth Century*, 9th edn (London, 1971), 259.

the 1690s, although stationers evidently had stocks of French material for some time; Purcell's Gresham autograph songbook, not copied until the early 1690s, consists of French paper apparently dating from the previous decade.

## Manuscript music paper and music books

Most performance and archival material in late seventeenth-century English music was handwritten. Even the Playfords, the leading publishers of printed music, also sold manuscripts, which provided a means of circulating copies in numbers too small for economical printing or of meeting individual demands: in *Choice Ayres* of 1681 John Playford stated that anyone requiring consorts by Jenkins, Locke and other older composers could have them 'fairly and true Prick'd' and Locke's *Melothesia* of 1673, published by John Carr, contains a similar advertisement for 'Songs and Airs Vocal and Instrumental ready Prick't'.[56] In general, seventeenth-century music printing was confined to material with a large potential amateur market, the few exceptions to this rule being works published for reasons of political propaganda, such as Nathaniel Thompson's edition of Grabu's *Albion and Albanius* (1685), or for self-advertisement, a category which would include Purcell's *Sonnata's of III. Parts* of 1683 and *Dioclesian* published in 1691.[57] Posthumous publications of Purcell's music exploited his reputation and the tragedy of his early death, but nevertheless tended to be of material with popular appeal, such as *A Choice Collection of Lessons* of 1696 and the *Ayres* of 1697; no one seems to have considered publishing a complete dramatic opera or court ode, though individual songs and instrumental movements were extracted from such works. Manuscripts therefore provide the primary sources for most of Purcell's music, and the characteristics of paper and books especially prepared for writing music can often cast light on the material they contain.

Once paper had been selected as suitable for music it was ruled up by or for the stationer and then sold either in separate sheets or bound into books. In 1703, Henry Playford was charged no more than a shilling for ruling four quires of twenty-four or twenty-five sheets,[58] which might have added about 15 per cent to the price of the finished paper. Rastrology – the study of stave rulings – can provide useful evidence about a manuscript's history. In the seventeenth century ruling was usually carried out

---

[56] Thompson, 'Manuscript Music', 613.

[57] The title pages of both works confirm that they were printed 'for the author' and sold on his behalf.

[58] C. L. Day and E. B. Murrie, 'Playford v. Pearson', *The Library*, 4th series, 17 (1937), 427–47; Thompson, 'Manuscript Music', 606.

on unbound paper by a complex pen or rastrum drawing between two and six staves at a time: special rulings, such as six-line staves for keyboard music or combinations of five and six lines for lute songs, were available, but most ruling seems to have been of ordinary five-line staves. Many features of a rastrum, such as individual stave widths, the spaces between staves, and the overall rastrum span, are consistent within the small range of variation to be expected as a result of wear, paper shrinkage, or of fluctuating ink flow and pressure on the pen, and so provide a good means of describing or identifying music paper,[59] up to a point even when working with microfilm.[60]

A catalogue issued by Henry Playford in 1690 contains a number of music books with prices ranging from one shilling for 'A Ruled Book, 6 lines, 8 Staves in Folio' to eight shillings for 'Another large Ruled Book of the largest and best Demy Paper, neatly bound in Calves Leather, Gilt, 5 Lines, 12 Staves, Folio',[61] but the majority of music sources were copied on loose sheets and bound subsequently, whether for a contemporary owner, an eighteenth- or nineteenth-century collector or a modern library. Even when no trace of the original binding remains, a number of significant characteristics provide evidence of a volume's collational history. Books planned by either the stationer or the initial copyist as bound volumes tend to consist entirely of a single paper type, or of a small number of related types, and to have consistent stave rulings. The deckel edges left on the paper as manufactured will have been removed, and a coloured or gilt finish will sometimes have been applied to the exposed edges of the paper. Especially in books bound before copying, collation will usually be in regular quires of four, six or eight. If the original binding survives, the presence of a large number of blank pages is a sure sign that the source left the stationer's shop as a bound volume, and a contemporary pagination or series of collation letters offers evidence that all or part of a manuscript may have been copied before it was assembled: an example is Charles Morgan's songbook Lbl Add. 33234. If, as in Lbl Add. 33287, part was copied before binding and part afterwards, a clear difference may be apparent in the handwriting or between the sections of a table of contents

[59] See Cathie Miserandino-Gaherty, 'The Codicology and Rastrology of GB-Ob Mus. Sch. MSS c.64–9: Manuscripts in Support of Transmission Theory', *Chelys* 25 (1996–7), 78–87. It is interesting that single-stave rastra were more widely used in the eighteenth century: see Jean K. and Eugene K. Wolf, 'Rastrology and its Use in Eighteenth-Century Manuscript Studies', in *Studies in Musical Sources and Style: Essays in Honor of Jan LaRue*, ed. E. K. Wolf and Edward H. Roesner (Madison, 1990), 231–91.

[60] See Owen Jander, 'Staff-Liner Identification: a Technique for the Age of Microfilm', *JAMS* 20 (1967), 112–16.

[61] Lbl Harl. 5936, nos 419–20. The catalogue in question can be dated to the earlier part of 1690 by a reference to it in *The London Gazette* of 5 June 1690; see Michael Tilmouth, 'A Calendar of References to Music in Newspapers Published in London and the Provinces (1660–1719)', *RMARC* 1 (1961), 9.

added at different stages. Irregular collation, contrasts in paper type and varied rulings sometimes reveal that a manuscript copied in a single hand grew up over a number of years, probably without any clear plan for its final contents: the most important Purcell source in this category is John Gostling's scorebook US-AUS Pre-1700 85, which in fact retains a high-quality contemporary binding. Other attractive early bindings, like that of William Croft's Lcm 2230 (1700), may only be the equivalents of modern guardbooks, providing protection for casually related material that conveniently happens to be the same size: examples dating from later in the eighteenth century include Bu 5001, possibly bound for John Barker in 1731, and a number of composite volumes assembled for the younger Richard Goodson at Christ Church, Oxford, containing music from his father's collection.

Only two formats were commonly used for music paper in Purcell's time, whether bound or loose: 'folio', in which the original sheets were folded once, along the vertical centre-line, and 'oblong quarto', in which a further horizontal fold was made so that each sheet produces four folios or eight pages. Paper intended to be made into a quarto book was ruled in advance with separate blocks of staves which emerge in the correct position when the paper is folded, no doubt what is meant by the expression 'Large Paper Rul'd in 4to' in a bill submitted by John Wilson at Oxford in 1657.[62] The folio and oblong quarto formats both preserve the maximum possible width of the paper and therefore allow for longer staves and fewer line-ends, features with self-evident advantages for both copyist and performer. For the same reason the few manuscript music books made in smaller sizes, such as the duodecimo Lbl Add. 29397, retain a narrow oblong format which would also fit easily into a deep pocket. At the opposite extreme, professional copyists such as John Walter and William Isaack sometimes joined together the separate stave blocks on flat sheets ruled normally for folio use and copied 'stratigraphically' across the entire width of the page, probably for archival purposes: in this case the reduction in the number of line ends and new systems enabled the copyists to work more quickly.

The few contemporary bindings that survive in Purcell sources are of limited historical value, as they reflect no more than the standard practices of their period. For the most part they consist of boards covered in brown calf- or sheepskin, or occasionally white vellum: patterns consisting of a double or treble rectangle framing the face of the boards and decorations at the corners or centre of the rectangle were often applied, either blind-tooled or gilt, and elaborate patterning sometimes

---

[62] Margaret Crum, 'Early Lists of the Oxford Music School Collection', *M&L* 48 (1967), 27.

decorated the top, bottom and front edges. The relative opulence of the binding may bear no relation to the character of the contents: John Blow's beautiful calligraphic autograph Och 628, for example, is bound in plain boards, but the far more elaborate covers of Ob MS Mus.Sch. E.399 protect a few keyboard pieces added at two different periods and a large number of blank pages.

## Purcell's handwriting

Not since Augustus Hughes-Hughes's 1896 study and the amplifications of Hughes-Hughes's work by G. E. P. Arkwright, published in 1910,[63] has there been any attempt to examine systematically Purcell's hand or to codify the various aspects of it that changed throughout his career, despite Arkwright's call for a 'more complete study of Purcell's autograph [to] make it possible to place in final order a few anthems of which at present the exact date is unknown'.[64] Other essays have appeared: F. H. Walker's graphological analysis is of no value here,[65] and Franklin B. Zimmerman's contribution adds only slightly to earlier studies, Zimmerman himself later directing interested readers to Hughes-Hughes's, rather than his own, work on Purcell's handwriting.[66] Perhaps some have felt that there has not been a need for such a study: there are a limited number of autographs; the problems of manuscripts once mistakenly claimed to be autograph have with few exceptions long been solved;[67] and Purcell's handwriting is in many of its features consistent throughout his career. But since his hand maintained many of its characteristics over a long period minor changes prove to be quite important, especially when connected to dates or datable works in the manuscripts themselves. While there are not enough manuscripts to produce the kind of detailed *Schriftchronologie* that has contributed significantly to Bach and Mozart studies,[68] leading at times to extremely precise information on dating, Arkwright's call

---

[63] Augustus Hughes-Hughes, 'Henry Purcell's Handwriting', *MT* 37 (1896), 81–3; G. E. P. Arkwright, 'Purcell's Church Music', *MA* 1 (1909–10), 240–8.

[64] Ibid., 240.     [65] F. H. Walker, 'Purcell's Handwriting', *Monthly Musical Record* 72 (1942), 155–7.

[66] Franklin B. Zimmerman, 'Purcell's Handwriting', in Holst, ed., *Henry Purcell*, 103–5; cf. Zimmerman, *Life*, xxx.

[67] See Hughes-Hughes, 'Henry Purcell's Handwriting', 81; and Nigel Fortune and Franklin B. Zimmerman, 'Purcell's Autographs', in Holst, ed., *Henry Purcell*, 120–1.

[68] Yoshitake Kobayashi, *Die Notenschrift Johann Sebastian Bachs: Dokumentation ihrer Entwicklung*, Neue Bach-Ausgabe (9th series) II (Kassel, 1989); Georg von Dadelsen, *Beiträge zur Chronologie der Werke Johann Sebastian Bachs*, Tübinger Bach-Studien 4–5 (Trossingen, 1958); Alan Tyson, *Mozart: Studies of the Autograph Scores* (Cambridge, Mass., 1987), esp. chaps. 1–2; Wolfgang Plath, 'Beiträge zur Mozart-Autographie II: Schriftchronologie 1770–1780', *Mozart-Jahrbuch* (1976–7), 131–73. An excellent survey

for a 'more complete study' is justified: in the case of Purcell, handwriting evidence provides a great deal of assistance in working towards an accurate and informed chronology for Purcell's autograph manuscripts and the works they contain.

The process of authenticating autograph manuscripts by means of handwriting varies from composer to composer. An important first step often entails examining apparent holograph manuscripts – those bearing the composer's signature – and then if further confirmation is required comparing these to other signed instances of the composer's hand, when available, in the form of letters or archival documents. This process normally leads to a recognition that certain aspects of the hand are unusual or, better still, idiosyncratic to the composer. Then one can approach the process of identifying unsigned autographs, including not only the composer's own works but also the composer's copies of the works of others, from a position of strength.

For the vast majority of the major autograph sources Purcell's hand has been accurately recognised at least since the time the manuscripts began to fall into various collections in the eighteenth century. Although non-autograph manuscripts have been purportedly advanced as authentic through the years (and in some cases this is explainable through a kind of familial resemblance to Purcell's hand), by the time Hughes-Hughes and others set out to identify the genuine autographs common sense normally prevailed and conclusions were drawn that hold up well today. There has thus not been need for the kind of archival documentation of the handwriting's authenticity that is often necessary when dealing with lesser composers or scribes whose work has been forgotten. There are in fact very few samples of Purcell's hand by way of non-musical documents: a letter from Purcell to the Dean of Exeter from 2 November 1686,[69] a receipt (now lost) for a rental allowance from 22 December 1682,[70] two documents surviving at Westminster Abbey bearing Purcell's signature,[71] and his ill-formed signature on his last will and testament produced on the day of his death, 21 November 1695.[72] We do, though, have a large enough body of authentic music manuscripts to form a clear picture of those features of Purcell's hand which

of writings on musical autographs, as well as a discussion of forensic methods of handwriting analysis, is found in Peter Grant Jeffery, 'The Autograph Manuscripts of Francesco Cavalli' (Ph.D. thesis, Princeton University, 1980), 30–80.

[69] EXc 6077/1; reproduced in Robert King, *Henry Purcell* (London, 1994), 143.

[70] Reproduced in J. Frederick Bridge, 'Purcell's Birthplace and Residences', *MT* 36 (1895), 734. Bridge mentions several other documents similar to the one reproduced.

[71] Lwa WAM 9834 (an agreement, which Purcell witnessed, with Bernard Smith for repair of the Abbey organ) and 47667 (a receipt dated 9 January 1691). We wish to thank Dr Tony Trowles of the Abbey Library for information on these documents.

[72] Lpro PROB 1/8; reproduced in Zimmerman, *Life*, 257.

remain consistent from manuscript to manuscript and which separate his handwriting from the work of others. The following is a summary list of musical manuscripts containing Purcell autograph material:[73]

**Birmingham, Barber Institute of Fine Arts**

Bu 5001      guardbook; includes scores of three anthems and a sacred song in Purcell's hand

**Cambridge, Fitzwilliam Museum**

Cfm 88      scorebook of anthems, mostly in Purcell's hand

Cfm 152      extracts from one or more organbooks including two items in Purcell's hand

**London, British Library**

Lbl Add. 30930      scorebook of instrumental works and sacred songs

Lbl Add. 30931      guardbook; includes scores of two anthems and the Funeral Sentences in Purcell's hand

Lbl Add. 30932      guardbook; includes scores of four anthems (one by Pelham Humfrey) and a fragment of an instrumental work in Purcell's hand

Lbl Add. 30934      composite manuscript of separate scores of odes; includes *Who can from joy refrain* in Purcell's hand

Lbl Egerton 2956      separate score of the Yorkshire Feast Song

Lbl MS Mus.1      keyboard book in the hands of Purcell and (probably) Draghi

Lbl R.M. 20.h.8      scorebook of anthems, odes and songs, mostly in Purcell's hand

**London, Guildhall Library (Gresham College)**

Lg Safe 3      songbook

**London, Royal Academy of Music**

Lam 3      performing score of *The Fairy Queen*, partially in Purcell's hand

**London, Westminster Abbey**

Lwa Triforium Set I      countertenor partbook; corrections to one anthem in Purcell's hand

**New Haven, Yale University, Beinecke Rare Book and Manuscript Library**

US-NHb Osborn 515      guardbook of instrumental bass parts; includes six movements in Purcell's hand

**Oxford, Bodleian Library**

Ob MS Mus.a.1      separate score of the Benedicite from the Service in B♭

Ob MS Mus.c.26      guardbook; includes scores of two anthems and one ode (partial autograph) in Purcell's hand

---

[73] Listed alphabetically by city. For the location of further information on each manuscript see the Index of manuscripts mentioned in the text, pp. 344–7.

**Oxford, Christ Church**

| | |
|---|---|
| Och 554 | guardbook; includes an organ part for John Blow's *God is our hope and strength* in Purcell's hand |
| Och 1188/9 | guardbook; includes string parts to *My song shall be alway* partially in Purcell's hand |
| Och 1215 | guardbook; includes a score of Daniel Roseingrave's *Lord thou art become gracious* partially in Purcell's hand |

**Tokyo, Nanki Library**

| | |
|---|---|
| J-Tn N5/10 | bass partbook; includes *Sing unto God* in Purcell's hand |

**Location unknown**

| | |
|---|---|
| 'Ord–Dart' MS | scorebook of miscellaneous items; includes John Bull's *Miserere mei Domine* in Purcell's hand[74] |

## Handwriting in late seventeenth-century England

Before discussing the specific characteristics of Purcell's hand, some explanation of the conventions in English handwriting in the seventeenth century will help place his style in context and explain some of the changes he made to particular letter forms during his career. It was not until very late in Purcell's lifetime that the form of italic cursive writing known as the English round hand or 'copperplate' became established as a basic writing style, first in England and subsequently in much of the rest of western Europe. This explains in great part both the trend towards uniformity one finds amongst eighteenth-century scribes and the diversity of hands one regularly encounters in the seventeenth century, even within fairly small provincial circles. Writing masters active around 1600 taught not just one type of penmanship but possessed a wide repertory of italic and running gothic hands that could be used for various purposes, with descriptive names like 'secretary', 'chancery' and 'court'. The fact that one's writing style could openly reflect matters of education, social standing and even political viewpoint led Commonwealth lawmakers in 1650 to ban all unusual forms of handwriting for official documents, though the diversity in hands returned quickly, if temporarily, at the Restoration.[75]

---

[74] See Thurston Dart, 'Purcell and Bull', *MT* 104 (1963), 30–1.

[75] C. H. Firth and R. S. Rait, eds., *Acts and Ordinances of the Interregnum, 1642–1660*, II, *Acts and Ordinances from 9th February, 1649, to 16th March, 1660* (London, 1911; repr. Holmes Beach, 1972), 455–6; see also L. C. Hector, *The Handwriting of English Documents*, 2nd edn (London, 1966), 22–3. Other useful studies on handwriting include Ambrose Heal, *The English Writing-Masters and Their Copy-Books, 1570–1800: a Biographical Dictionary & a Bibliography* (London, 1931; repr. Hildesheim, 1962); and Joyce Irene Whalley, *The Pen's Excellencie: a Pictorial History of Western Calligraphy* (New York, 1980).

If a single handwriting style was winning out in mid-seventeenth-century England it was the italic bastarda ('bastarda' because it borrowed elements of the secretary hand), clearly an immediate ancestor to the round hand, in which open letters (like 'o', 'd' etc.) were decidedly more open than was common in the older secretary or chancery hands, and letters with ascenders or descenders were often made with large and at times decorative loops. The engraved title page from Edward Cocker's *Arts Glory or The Pen-Man's Treasurie* (London, 1657) is particularly instructive (Illus. 1.4). The first two and the fourth lines of the subtitle (beginning 'Wherein you may be accommodated') are in italic bastarda. Most of the letter forms are produced with an eye to uniformity, with variances mostly found in loops and other non-essential decorations. The lowercase 'd', for example, may be seen with leftward and rightward loops, as well as with a straight ascender. Cocker also advocated at least two different forms of the lowercase 'h', both of which are seen here. Some variants are vestiges of secretary hand, and in fact the third line of the subtitle (beginning 'And also with') is given by Cocker in secretary, indicating that many of the specialised hands (or individual features of these hands) were still widely used. Specifically, the 'e' of Cocker's italic bastarda exhibits secretary variants. It can be found in three forms in the first line of the subtitle: (1) the standard italic form (in 'Wherein'); (2) a form with two short strokes (in 'accommodated'), a variant of the secretary 'e', which is usually made with a counterclockwise stroke from left to right with an upper loop (seen in its usual form in the third line of the subtitle, in 'Practise'); and (3) a decorated version of the two-stroke form, seen in the second 'e' in 'varietie'.

Other common acceptable variants often found in italic bastarda, which derived from secretary or other early styles, include a lowercase 'w' with two distinct loops of approximately equal width, as opposed to the version made with an up-and-down stroke followed by a single loop. The former may be seen in the third line of the subtitle in 'with', and the latter in the first line, also in 'with'. Also acceptable were at least two forms of the lowercase 'r'. The most common one was the standard italic 'r', as in 'Wherein' in the first line of the subtitle. Cocker also taught an 'r' that closely resembles the modern American cursive or Spencerian 'r', with a careful upstroke, slightly descending rightward flag and downstroke, another holdover from secretary, which remained an acceptable variant even amongst early proponents of the English round hand. An inverted version of this 'r' was used commonly in the sixteenth century and earlier periods, though Cocker still uses it in his display of the secretary hand on the title page.

Illus. 1.4  Title page of Edward Cocker, *Arts Glory or The Pen-Man's Treasurie*, London, 1657

Purcell's early career corresponds to a time when the most prominent writing masters were consolidating variant styles towards a uniform practice. Most notable amongst these masters was John Ayres, who published several copy-books between 1680 and 1700. The title and subtitle of his first work explain something of the state of English handwriting in 1680: *The A la Mode Secretarie, or Practical Penman: A New Copy Book, Wherein the Bastard Italians (commonly) called the New Ala Mode Round-hands, and Mixt Running hands and Mixt Secretary's are ... performed according to the nature, freedom and tendency of the Pen.* Variant letter forms, excluding decorative ones, still allowable in Ayres's round hand include either form of the lowercase 'w' (which Ayres himself used interchangeably), a slightly elongated lowercase 's', and the secretary 'e' and 'r', though Ayres's copy-books show that he strongly preferred the italic 'e' and 'r': these were the 'a la mode' forms of these letters, and the secretary variants, while acceptable, were becoming increasingly old-fashioned. It is not surprising, then, that Purcell began to change minor aspects of his handwriting in the late 1670s and early 1680s, the years of his early maturity and a time when England was moving decidedly towards the uniform aspects of the English round hand.

## The characteristics of Purcell's hand

A comparison of three examples from Purcell autographs from roughly the early, middle and late portions of his career helps to point out those aspects of his musical and textual script that remained constant throughout much of his life as well as those that changed either slightly or substantially. These examples are taken from Purcell's symphony anthem, *My beloved spake*, in a copy dating from no later than 1677 in Lbl Add. 30932, fol. 90v (Illus. 1.5); Purcell's welcome song, *From those serene and rapturous joys*, in a copy produced very close to the time the work was first performed for Charles II's return from Winchester in September 1684, found in Lbl R.M. 20.h.8, fol. 182r (Illus. 1.6); and Purcell's birthday song for the Duke of Gloucester, *Who can from joy refrain*, in a copy again very likely produced when the work was first given in July 1695, found in Lbl Add. 30934, fol. 88r (Illus. 1.7).

One of the most easily recognised musical symbols denoting a Purcell autograph as early is the hook- or figure-eight-shaped bass clef, of which there are five examples in Illus. 1.5. The only other autographs that use this clef type are three other separate scores (*Who hath believed our report*, the early version of the Funeral Sentences, and an arrangement of Pelham Humfrey's *By the waters of Babylon*) in Lbl Add. 30931–2; the instrumental basses in US-NHb Osborn 515; Och 554, fol. 3, Purcell's organ part for Blow's *God is our hope and strength*; and, interestingly, a single system in Purcell's later copy of the same work in his scorebook Cfm 88. Excepting the system brackets and two specific letter forms discussed below, there are few other obvious indicators of earliness in Illus. 1.5: compared to Illus. 1.6 and 1.7 there is a noticeable difference in the slant of the textual hand, but in fact there are many more similarities than differences amongst all three examples. Clefs in general are very reliable indicators of genuineness in working with Purcell autographs, especially the C clef. Like many composers and scribes from this period Purcell forms his C clef with two vertical lines and four short horizontal or diagonal strokes, two above and two below the line denoting C. Only occasionally did truly neat forms of this clef flow from Purcell's pen, such as that in the second system of Illus. 1.6. More often Purcell seems to have made these four short strokes very hastily, often without lifting the pen. This

Illus. 1.5  Henry Purcell: *My beloved spake* (*c.* 1677), autograph. British Library Add.
MS 30932, fol. 90v

Illus. 1.6  Henry Purcell: *From those serene and rapturous joys* (1684), autograph. British Library
R.M. 20.h.8, fol. 182r

Illus. 1.7  Henry Purcell: *Who can from joy refrain* (1695), autograph. British Library Add. MS 30934, fol. 88r

often resulted in a Z-shaped figure between the two verticals, seen in the first systems in both Illus. 1.6 and 1.7, and there are also many instances when the four strokes run together somewhat indiscernibly, such as in Illus. 1.5, system 3 (tenor), and Illus. 1.7, system 2. The treble clef, too, was made with great consistency throughout Purcell's career (excepting the rare early form seen in Illus. 1.1): the basic shape is the same in all three works given here, the two later ones providing especially clear examples of Purcell's mature treble clef, with its basic H shape, round upper loops, and, most characteristically, its pronounced lower-left loop. After the hook-shape is abandoned for the bass clef, Purcell settles most often, though there are occasional variants, on a form that is visible in both Illus. 1.6 and 1.7, with very full upper and lower loops resembling a reversed uppercase B. Other musical symbols are often highly consistent throughout the career: time signatures, directs (made with a small U-shaped stroke with a rightward descender), key signatures or accidentals (flats are often just slightly open at the top of the loop), and note shapes themselves, with semibreves and minims often made with a somewhat flat right side.

Textual symbols as well are often quite uniform, such as the y-thorn and ampersand. (Compare, for the latter, the second systems in Illus. 1.6 and 1.7.) As to individual letter forms themselves, Purcell is extremely consistent in the use of a large loop for his lowercase 'd' and 'h', and in the use of a slightly elongated 's' often with a slight upper loop. Many of the capitals, too, are very characteristic.[76] More generally, it should be noted that in defining the traits of a particular scribe one will regularly encounter odd variants which seem to run counter to established practice, but handwriting while visibly consistent is rarely perfectly so; the more manuscripts surveyed, however, the more reasonable it is to explain variants as minor aberrations from an otherwise consistent practice. Even the writing masters mentioned above occasionally produced letter forms that they nowhere else used or endorsed.

We believe the changes that occurred in two of Purcell's letter forms – the lowercase 'e' and 'r' – are the most meaningful in working towards an accurate chronology for the autographs.[77] It has proved especially instructive for us to study Purcell's approach to these letters in his three great scorebooks: Cfm 88, and Lbl Add. 30930 and R.M. 20.h.8, in which it is possible at times to see minor changes in handwriting from page to page. Throughout his early manuscripts Purcell used the secretary 'e': it is readily apparent in all of the manuscripts that use the hook-shaped

---

[76] Zimmerman, 'Purcell's Handwriting', 104.

[77] Hughes-Hughes first noted the existence of different 'e' forms in Purcell's autographs, without connecting them to specific dates; see 'Henry Purcell's Handwriting'.

bass clef and also in somewhat later sources such as Purcell's first phase of work in Cfm 88. Purcell abandoned the secretary 'e' in favour of the italic one absolutely no later than June 1680, though the change probably occurred about two years earlier, in the first few months of 1678. Unfortunately, there is no incontrovertible evidence for dating Purcell's autographs between December 1677, the date of Blow's Lambeth doctorate, a time by which Purcell had not yet given up the old 'e' (Purcell ascribes several works in which he uses the old 'e' to 'Dr' Blow in Cfm 88), and June 1680, when Purcell began to enter precise dates for several of the viol fantazias in Add. 30930, wherein the old 'e' is completely absent. But there is no reason to assume that the latter of these two dates is closer to the actual time when the change occurred, and circumstantial evidence gleaned particularly from our study of Cfm 88 and Lbl Add. 30930 leads us to suggest that it probably took place in 1678.

The changes Purcell made in his lowercase 'r' took place over several years in the early 1680s and can be chronicled quite precisely in Lbl R.M. 20.h.8, thanks to the fact that here (particularly in the reverse end devoted largely to welcome songs and odes) Purcell was entering dated or datable works very close to when they were first composed. Purcell's early 'r' is an upright form of the secretary 'r'. Unlike the lowercase 'e', there are numerous pages from autograph manuscripts exhibiting both the secretary and italic forms of the 'r', and it seems that Purcell was moving towards the italic form not only because it was an innovation but also since he found it more efficient to produce. This may explain why Purcell began using the new 'r' only in rubrics such as 'vers' and 'ritor' and at the ends of words in the text: it would be unnecessary to continue the 'r' downward if no other letter was to follow, and the italic 'r' runs naturally into an 's'. This practice occurs for the first time in a datable context in *What shall be done in behalf of the man*, the second piece in the reverse end of R.M. 20.h.8, a welcome song for the Duke of York's return from Scotland in May 1682. Purcell used the italic 'r' increasingly during 1683, as can be seen from later additions to R.M. 20.h.8, such as *From hardy climes*, written for the wedding of Prince George of Denmark and Princess Anne; and *Fly bold rebellion*, very likely performed in September 1683, as part of the celebrations for the overthrowing of the Rye House Plot. By about a year later, when Purcell was adding *From those serene and rapturous joys* (Illus. 1.6) to R.M. 20.h.8, the new 'r' accounts for over a third of all Purcell's lowercase 'r's. (Note, for example, in Illus. 1.6, at the second appearance of the word 'rapturous', the first 'r' is secretary while the second is italic.) The first datable work in R.M. 20.h.8 to use the italic 'r' exclusively is *If prayers and tears*, a solo song on the death of Charles II, which would reasonably date from the time between Charles's death in February 1685 and James II's coronation in April 1685. The old 'r' thus disappeared from R.M. 20.h.8 by early 1685, and there is no evidence of it in any other manuscript that can be dated later than 1685. As well as the carefully formed italic 'r', R.M. 20.h.8 contains examples of a variant made in a single looped stroke that is increasingly common in Purcell's later autographs. (Further study of the incidence of the italic 'r' in R.M. 20.h.8 is found in Chapter 4 below.)

# Fitzwilliam Museum Music MS 88
## and three principal concordances

The anthem scorebook Cfm 88 is perhaps best known for the special nature of its contents: a selection of works by Purcell's predecessors (Tallis, Byrd and Gibbons, amongst others) and contemporaries (Locke, Humfrey and Blow), which Purcell later expanded to include compositions of his own (see Table 2.1). Cfm 88 has long been recognised as the earliest of Purcell's three great autograph scorebooks,[1] though the precise date of its inception, as well as the possible presence in the manuscript of hands other than Purcell's, has been a matter of debate. We believe it was begun by John Blow no later than 1677 (though possibly a few years earlier) and that Purcell first contributed to it around the end of 1677.

Cfm 88 was part of the vast collection bequeathed to the University of Cambridge by Richard Fitzwilliam in 1816, eventually coming to reside in the Museum at its completion in 1837. Fol. 1r of the manuscript bears the inscription 'R. Fitzwilliam 1767'. The manuscript previously belonged to Bernard Gates (c. 1685–1773), one of John Blow's last pupils, who held posts at both the Chapel Royal and Westminster Abbey throughout much of the first half of the eighteenth century: his inscription appears on the front flyleaf: 'N.5. B. Gates, 13th: Jan[uar]y: 1727/8'. The mark 'N.5' would seem to refer to a cataloguing system, though we have found no evidence that this manuscript was part of an official collection at the Chapel Royal or the Abbey. It is possible that Cfm 88 remained in the circle of the Chapel Royal after Purcell's death, coming into Gates's possession just after his appointment as Master of the Children at the Chapel in 1727.

---

[1] E.g., Nigel Fortune and Franklin B. Zimmerman, 'Purcell's Autographs', in Holst, ed., *Henry Purcell*, 108.

## CODICOLOGY

The main body of Cfm 88 is composed of 'royal' size paper produced by an unidentified Angoumois craftsman, bearing the arms of Strasbourg watermark with the countermark 'RC'. Paper thus marked was the third most expensive type listed in a report to John Fell, for use at the Oxford University Press, made in 1674 (Ob MS Rawlinson D.398, fols. 156–7).[2] It is there described as 'M[erreatt's] Dutch Royall',[3] and its page dimensions of 18 by $11\frac{3}{4}$ inches are consistent with the size of Cfm 88, allowing for trimming, wear and restoration. Flyleaves at each end are of different paper types and contain both watermark and countermark, at right angles to the spine, suggesting that they have been cut down from larger sheets to match the size of a half-sheet of royal paper. The front flyleaf bears an Angoumois fleur-de-lys watermark with the countermark 'PB' and the initials 'HC', found regularly in English sources between 1676 and 1686, in the factor's position. The reverse flyleaf is also marked with a fleur-de-lys: the countermark is 'IHS' above 'ET', indicating that this sheet is the product of the Angoumois craftsman Etienne Touzeau, whose work is represented significantly in Purcell's two other great scorebooks, Lbl R.M. 20.h.8 and Add. 30930. All the music paper was ruled with three distinct five-stave systems per page. Purcell at times added up to three freehand staves per page, not always neatly, allowing him to copy (at most) three systems of a six-part work.

The leaves in Cfm 88 have been thoroughly restored and individually guarded, so that the original quiring must be ascertained by matching watermarks and countermarks. This process suggests that little has altered the structure of the manuscript since Purcell's time; in all likelihood it was originally composed of twenty-five gatherings, the first consisting of four folios and all the remaining consisting of six folios each. Three folios were removed from the third and fourth gatherings at an early stage, possibly by Blow, after the first forty-eight leaves were foliated. These are missing fols. 15, 17 and 18, which were excised from the middle of Blow's *Sing we merrily*; there is, however, no missing music, suggesting that Blow removed these pages at the time of copying the work as a result of revisions or corrections at this juncture. At the reverse end only the first twenty leaves show early foliation.[4] There is

[2] R. W. Chapman, 'An Inventory of Paper, 1674', *The Library*, 4th series, 7 (1927), 402–8; see also Heawood no. 150.

[3] For a discussion of the 1674 inventory in relation to music sources see Robert Thompson, 'Manuscript Music in Purcell's London', *EM* 23 (1995), 608–11.

[4] Modern pencil additions have completed a single foliation from beginning to end, used for references herein.

34

one missing folio from the fifteenth gathering (between fols. 83 and 84), three missing folios from the sixteenth gathering (between fols. 87 and 88) and two missing folios from the twenty-fifth gathering, all of which were likely removed at an early stage. There are currently 141 folios in the book, including the two flyleaves. A typewritten note kept inside the manuscript includes the following information about its original binding and 1979 restoration:

> Before conservation treatment this manuscript was bound in brown calf leather with patterned paper sides. The spine cover was missing, and the sewing had disintegrated in some places. The paper was stained, acid and brittle.

> During treatment the manuscript was disbound, cleaned, deacidified with magnesium bicarbonate, and repaired with Japanese hand-made paper. It was then bound in oasis niger, with vellum tips, and marbled paper sides.

The dating of Cfm 88 has normally been carried out in connection with the dates on the two flyleaves, 167[7] and 1682, but we believe work on the manuscript began before 1677 and carried on for at least three years after 1682. The front flyleaf shows carefully ruled columns for a list of the contents, with the following inscription across the top: 'A Table of all the Anthems contain'd in this book. Sep[tember] ye 13th Anno Domine 167[7]'. The last, illegible, number appears to have been written across a crease parallel to the right margin (which resulted in a visible break in the adjacent ruled line when it was unfolded) and close inspection of the manuscript reveals a tiny wedge of ink on the outer side of the opened fold which looks like the angular top of a '3' or '7'. The lower part of the figure is obviously different from the '3' earlier in the inscription, so '1677' seems the most likely interpretation.[5] The same hand then added the titles of the first six anthems of the front end. At a much later time (after the secretary 'e' and 'r' disappeared from his handwriting) Purcell continued this list, providing titles for all of the remaining front-end works, with the exception of the 'Club' anthem fragment.[6]

---

[5] Various dates have been submitted in earlier literature, including 1673 (suggested by J. A. Fuller-Maitland and A. H. Mann, *Catalogue of the Music in the Fitzwilliam Museum. Cambridge* (London, 1893), 37), 1681 and 1687. The latter two dates, stemming from Augustus Hughes-Hughes, 'Henry Purcell's Handwriting', *MT* 37 (1896), 82, cannot be accepted in any way, since the third number in the date is unequivocally '7'. The date of 1677 has generally been accepted since it was put forth by Fortune and Zimmerman, 'Purcell's Autographs', 108, though Rebecca Herissone recently suggested a reading of 1672: see 'Purcell's Revisions of his own Works', in *Purcell Studies*, 55. It is difficult to reconcile any date much earlier than 1676 with the 'HC' factor's mark of the front flyleaf.

[6] The only other markings on the front flyleaf, besides Gates's inscription, are a few stray bits of text (upside down), 'have mercy' and 'I will' (perhaps in Gates's hand) and several pen flourishes in the lower-left corner. The Fitzwilliam Museum's bookplate is centred on this page, obscuring the last few page references of the table of contents.

## CONTENTS AND HANDWRITING

For a long time it was thought that the first twenty-six folios of Cfm 88 represented the earliest samples of Purcell's handwriting and must have been produced at a time when Purcell held some sort of official copyist's post at Westminster Abbey (though no such position existed).[7] There can now no longer be any doubt that someone other than Purcell copied these early folios in Cfm 88. Another unidentified scribe contributed the first system of Humfrey, Blow and Turner's 'Club' anthem (fol. 26v). An additional five hands inscribed other textual material from close to the time of the manuscript's inception until the early nineteenth century: the compiler of the first portion of the table of contents on the front flyleaf (not one of the main music contributors), the compiler of the list of works on the reverse flyleaf (one other example of this hand may be found on fol. 9r, where it supplies a bit of missing text in the top system), Bernard Gates, Richard Fitzwilliam and Vincent Novello, who made a few pencil notes in the manuscript, mostly on the reverse flyleaf, the last of which is dated 1830.[8]

### John Blow's handwriting

The identity of the first main copyist in Cfm 88 has long proved elusive. Augustus Hughes-Hughes early on expressed caution in stating that the whole manuscript was in Purcell's hand,[9] but it was not until 1980 that Katherine Rohrer became the first to state outright that the meticulous and highly stylised calligraphy in the first part of Cfm 88 could not be the work of Purcell; it is different in nearly every respect from the overall shape of the hand to the formation of individual musical and textual characters.[10] The early copyist of Cfm 88 used a number of distinctive letter forms,

---

[7] The earlier literature on Cfm 88 includes Fuller-Maitland and Mann, *Catalogue of the Music in the Fitzwilliam Museum*, 37–8; G. E. P. Arkwright, 'Purcell's Church Music', *MA* 1 (1909–10), 243; Fortune and Zimmerman, 'Purcell's Autographs', 108–10; Eric Van Tassel, 'Fitzwilliam Museum, MS Mu 88: Score in the Hand of Henry Purcell', in *Cambridge Music Manuscripts, 900–1700*, ed. Iain Fenlon (Cambridge, 1982), 170–4; and Robert Shay, 'Purcell as Collector of "Ancient" Music: Fitzwilliam MS 88', in *Purcell Studies*, 35–50. See also Westrup, *Purcell*, 25 and passim.

[8] Across the top of the page Novello instructs that 'The whole of this very valuable Vol. is in the handwriting of Henry Purcell'; reading sideways along the right margin, he notes 'See also the other End of the Book'; and in the lower-right corner: 'NB: There are more Anthems in this Vol. than what are here enumerated; such Purcell probably wrote after this Index was made. V.N. 1830.'

[9] Hughes-Hughes, 'Henry Purcell's Handwriting', 82; see also Fortune and Zimmerman, 'Purcell's Autographs', 108.

[10] Katherine Tinley Rohrer, '"The Energy of English Words": a Linguistic Approach to Henry Purcell's Method of Setting Texts' (Ph.D. thesis, Princeton University, 1980), 112.

particularly a lowercase 'g' and 'y', both with centred descenders, and an 'l' that frequently bulges to the right, a form that has long been a recognised trait of Blow's early autographs. Both the musical and textual hands of the first Cfm 88 scribe suggest rather painstaking copying, with numerous stops of the pen. Given the likelihood that Cfm 88 was at least initially an important court manuscript, it is surprising that no other samples of this fine copying have survived. The nearest equivalent is the calligraphic hand of Blow in Och 628, which in itself is significantly different from other authoritative Blow autographs. Confirmation that Cfm 88 too is initially the work of Blow finally came with the discovery that an established Blow autograph in Lbl Add. 31458, a score of Blow's *O sing unto the Lord . . . for he hath done marvellous things*, contains at the head of fol. 1r a title in the same mannered script found in Cfm 88, identical in every respect, including the centred descenders (Illus. 2.1 and 2.2).

This work is also found in Cfm 88, and a comparison of the two versions shows that the musical hands are extremely close in many respects: note size and shape, clefs, metre signatures, directs and the placement of fermatas partially over the ending flourishes. When the two copies of the musical work are compared it can be shown further that the one in Lbl Add. 31458 was made directly from that in Cfm 88: the readings are virtually identical right down to details such as cautionary accidentals and, until well into the work, system breaks. A likely scenario is that sometime shortly after Blow made corrections to this anthem, while entering it into Cfm 88, he realised he had no personal file copy of the corrected version, which he then made rather quickly: several corrections in the Add. 31458 copy show Blow rushing ahead, apparently getting away from his copy text, only to have to slow down and correct his work, bringing it into line with the reading in Cfm 88.[11] One other detail in Add. 31458 hints that all this activity might have taken place in the early 1670s, no later than 1674: at the bottom of the final page of the anthem (fol. 5v) is an anthem fragment possibly in the hand of Pelham Humfrey, suggested through the use of an unusual C clef, made without lifting the pen, also seen in the Humfrey autograph material in Cfm 152, for example fol. 9r. Of course Blow might simply have been using paper left behind by Humfrey after his death, if this is Humfrey's hand, though it should be noted that none of the works Blow copied in Cfm 88 were composed demonstrably later than 1674.

---

[11] For example, in Lbl Add. 31458, fol. 4r, middle system, third bar, Blow mistakenly began to recopy part of a bar already copied two bars before (i.e., a third of the way through the first bar), apparently because all four starting pitches were the same as the current bar; the mistake was, however, quickly noticed and the reading corrected to conform to Cfm 88.

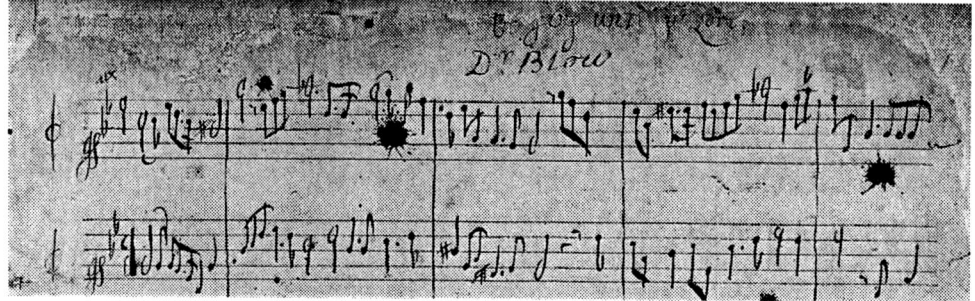

Illus. 2.1 John Blow: *O sing unto the Lord*, autograph. British Library Add. MS 31458, fol. 1r, detail

Illus. 2.2 John Blow: *O sing unto the Lord*, autograph. Fitzwilliam Museum MU MS 88, fol. 9v

Further study of Och 628 and other early Blow autographs such as Och 14 has shown that there are many more parallels between established examples of Blow's handwriting and the Cfm 88 hand; for example Blow's characteristic beamed quaver/dotted-semiquaver figure with a double flag on the second note is readily found in all three sources. A comparison of the text hands reveals that most of the letters of the Cfm 88 scribe are related in their general shape and curvature to established examples of Blow's hand, taking into account that the writing in Cfm 88 is a calligraphic style, with frequent and intentional stops of the pen. In this context Blow's idiosyncratic bulging 'l' proves especially persuasive. Also, Blow's unusual practice of (rather inconsistently) doubling a final 't' (as in 'itt' or 'trumpett'), seen in the early Christ Church autographs, is frequently in evidence in Cfm 88.[12] The ascription at the end of *O sing unto the Lord* in Cfm 88 to 'Mr Jo: Blow' might seem to provide proof that Blow himself could not have been the copyist, but the scorebook's formal purpose might have led him to make a formal self-ascription in this instance. (We have another example of such a formal self-styling in the same manuscript: Purcell's signature 'Mr Henry Purcell' on the reverse flyleaf.)

## Purcell's handwriting

Considering only the portions of Cfm 88 copied by Purcell, one easily imagines that he considered it a book of liturgical music – that is, mainly full anthems and verse anthems with organ accompaniment for use in the Anglican service. It has been a common misconception to associate Cfm 88 with Purcell's time at the Abbey because of the types of anthem it contains, but full and verse anthems were performed at the Chapel Royal as well, as is clear from the surviving partbooks, Lbl R.M. 27.a.1–8, and from the 'Catalogue' of anthems and services found amongst the Lord Chamberlain's papers from 1676.[13] In all likelihood Cfm 88 was created for the exclusive use of the Chapel Royal; indeed Purcell added to the selection of symphony anthems – works conceived for performance at Whitehall and limited in use to those times when Charles II himself was in attendance – begun by Blow.

Purcell's contributions to Cfm 88 came in several stages, identifiable through minor variants that occurred in his handwriting in the 1670s and 1680s (see Chapter 1, pp. 26–32). One of the most important indicators of an early date in a Purcell autograph is the hook-shaped bass clef, which he had abandoned by the time he began contributing to Cfm 88. He reverted to it only once in the manuscript for the first system of Blow's *God is our hope and strength*, which he perhaps copied in full score in Cfm 88 with his earlier organ score of the same work, Och 554, fol. 3 (produced at a time when the hook-shaped clef was his usual one), at hand (see Illus. 5.4). More useful for dating Purcell's work in Cfm 88 are the changes he made from the old secretary 'e' and 'r' to the modern italic versions. The first phase of Purcell's copying in Cfm 88 exhibits exclusively the secretary 'e', a letter form entirely absent

---

[12] Blow's tendency to double a final 't' shows up in later autographs as well: in Mp BRm370Bp35, for example, he titles a Purcell anthem 'Itt is a good thing' (fol. 8v), though he changes to 'it' within the work.

[13] *RECM*, I, 162–4.

from the other great scorebooks Lbl R.M. 20.h.8 and Add. 30930; we may thus conclude that Purcell abandoned it in favour of the more modern form by June 1680 at the very latest, when precise dates first appear in the latter source, though the change may well have come as early as 1678.

The first work Purcell copied in Cfm 88 was in all likelihood Blow's *O Lord I have sinned* (the 1670 funeral anthem for General Monck), which Purcell left unascribed; thus the work may have been copied before Blow received his Lambeth doctorate on 10 December 1677, though it is unlikely Purcell worked in the manuscript before September 1677 when Blow's copying was listed on the front flyleaf. Sometime shortly after Blow received his doctorate (Purcell subsequently always styles Blow 'Dr'), Purcell added the next sixteen works in the reverse end (Table 2.1, items 15–30) and two works at the front end (Blow's *Cry aloud and spare not* and *Sing unto the Lord O ye saints*). Of these only a single anthem, *Save me O God*, is by Purcell himself; he was mainly compiling a set of for the most part full anthems by Blow, Locke, Byrd, Tallis, Orlando Gibbons and others, taking as his primary source for the pre-Commonwealth works John Barnard's *First Book of Selected Church Musick*.[14] It would seem then that Purcell's role in Cfm 88 was initially less personal and more official: he appears to have been intent on producing clean, well-edited drafts in score of a number of important works by other composers, presumably library copies for the Chapel Royal.[15] His copy of his own *Save me O God*, possibly added to Cfm 88 in late 1678,[16] represents a revised version different from that found in several other non-autograph sources, and we may be justified in concluding that he himself saw *Save me O God* as his first 'adult' work, worthy of being revised and edited alongside the masterpieces of his predecessors and senior contemporaries.

It was at this stage of copying that the Windsor musician William Isaack first came in contact with Cfm 88, possibly in the summer of 1678, using it to augment and correct his vast collection of anthems in score, Cfm 117, completed for the most part by 1683.[17] The first ten works from the front end of Cfm 88 (excluding

---

[14] On the connection between Cfm 88 and Barnard's *First Book*, see Shay, 'Purcell as Collector', 44–8.

[15] On Purcell's role as editor in Cfm 88, see Shay, 'Purcell as Collector', 45–7; Robert Thompson, 'Purcell's Great Autographs', in *Purcell Studies*, 16–19; and Holman, *Henry Purcell*, 9–10.

[16] This work is dated 'by Nov 1681' in *Grove*, XV, 470, based on its inclusion in Y M1(S), where it appears in the earlier version in the hand of Stephen Bing (d. November 1681). This date can be firmly changed to no later than June 1680, because of the use of the secretary 'e' in Cfm 88, but *c.* 1677 is more likely the original date of composition, a possibility supported by the anthem's position in Y M1(S) (see Chapter 5).

[17] For further information on the relationship of Purcell's and Isaack's manuscripts see pp. 55–61; on the identification of Isaack's handwriting in Cfm 117 see Bruce Wood, 'A Note on Two Cambridge Manuscripts and their Copyists', *M&L* 56 (1975), 308–12; and Peter Holman, 'Bartholomew Isaack and "Mr Isaack" of Eton: a Confusing Tale of Restoration Musicians', *MT* 128 (1987), 381–5.

the 'Club' anthem fragment) and nineteen of the first twenty-eight items at the reverse end were either directly copied by Isaack from Cfm 88, corrected from Cfm 88, or copied by Purcell and Isaack from a common source. It seems clear that Isaack's copying from Cfm 88 took place on more than one occasion, since, amongst other things, string parts for some of the anthems were copied later than the vocal parts onto separate sheets now bound into the front of Cfm 117. This close connection between the two Fitzwilliam manuscripts provides strong circumstantial evidence that Cfm 88 was at this time a Chapel Royal manuscript, travelling with Charles II's musical entourage between London and Windsor on several occasions. Since string players were amongst those musicians that attended the King at Windsor,[18] it would thus seem that if a number of symphony anthems were performed at St George's Chapel *c.* 1678 or after Cfm 88 was a key source for the music.

In Purcell's subsequent additions to Cfm 88, the italic 'r' replaces the secretary one gradually, and by comparison with Lbl R.M. 20.h.8, in which the new 'r' similarly wins out as the favoured version in a series of dated or datable works, it is possible to identify approximately five further stages of Purcell's work in Cfm 88 (see Table 2.2). The group of works dated *c.* 1679–81 were all copied by Purcell in a hand using the italic 'e' but the secretary 'r'. Included in this stage of work is Purcell's completion of Blow's *Sing we merrily* on fol. 20r, the only place in the manuscript where Blow's calligraphic hand and a significant sample of Purcell's hand are seen on the same page (Illus. 2.3).[19] Also at this time Purcell added one new work to the front end, Locke's *When the son of man shall come*, and an additional eleven works to the reverse end (Table 2.1, items 31–41), increasingly (though by no means exclusively) focusing on his own compositions. Like *Save me O God*, some of Purcell's further copies of his own works in Cfm 88 represent edited or at times revised drafts of works that appear in demonstrably earlier, though not necessarily autograph, copies elsewhere.

It is difficult to know with certainty what events in Blow's and Purcell's lives corresponded to Cfm 88 being 'handed down' from one to the other. Much has been made along personal lines (commemoration of a possible birth, death, wedding anniversary etc.[20]) of Purcell's inscription on the reverse flyleaf, 'God bless

---

[18] Holman, *Four and Twenty Fiddlers*, 401.

[19] Possibly also dating from this stage is Purcell's addition of a few missing notes in Humfrey's *O Lord my God*, fol. 4r, top system, and two earlier minor additions to Blow's *Sing we merrily*: fols. 15r, bottom system, and 19v, bottom system.

[20] A number of speculations are mentioned by Zimmerman, *Life*, xviii, 74–5, 92.

## Table 2.1 Cambridge, Fitzwilliam Museum Music MS 88: contents

| Item | Folios | Title | Ascription | Copyist |
|------|--------|-------|------------|---------|
| 1 | 1r–3v | O praise the Lord | Pellham Humfreys | Blow |
| 2 | 4r–7r | O Lord my God | Pellham Humfreys | Blow |
| 3 | 7r–9v | Like as the hart | Mr Pelham Humfryes | Blow |
| 4 | 9v–14r | O sing unto the Lord … for he hath done | Mr Jo: Blow | Blow |
| 5 | 14v–20r | Sing we merrily | Dr Blow | Blow/Purcell |
| 6 | 21r–23v | Lord teach us to number our days | Mr Humfryes | Blow |
| 7 | 23v–26v | Lift up your heads | Mr Pelham Humphrey[a] | Blow |
| 8 | 26v | I will alway give thanks (inc.) | [Humfrey, Blow, Turner] | unidentified |
| 9 | 28v–31r | Cry aloud and spare not | Dr Blow | Purcell |
| 10 | 31r–36r | Sing unto the Lord O ye saints (inc.) | Mr Matthew Lock[b] | Purcell |
| 11 | 36v–38v | When the son of man shall come | Mr Matthew Lock | Purcell |
| 12 | 38v–40v | The Lord hear thee | Mr Lock | Purcell |
| 13 | 40v–42r | I will hear what the Lord God will say | MLock | Purcell |

[manuscript inverted]

| Item | Folios | Title | Ascription | Copyist |
|------|--------|-------|------------|---------|
| 14 | 142v–141r | O Lord I have sinned | [John Blow] | Purcell |
| 15 | 141r–138v | God is our hope and strength | Dr Blow | Purcell |
| 16 | 138r–136v | O God wherefore art thou absent | Dr Blow | Purcell |
| 17 | 136r–134v | *Hosanna to the son of David | Orlando Gibbon's | Purcell |
| 18 | 134v–133v | Save me O God | Dr Blow | Purcell |
| 19 | 133v–131r | Lord let me know mine end | Mr Matthew Lock | Purcell |
| 20 | 131r–129v | Turn thy face from my sins | Mr Mathew Lock | Purcell |
| 21 | 129r–127v | *Bow thine ear O Lord | Mr Will: Bird | Purcell |
| 22 | 127v–126v | *I call and cry | Tho: Tallis | Purcell |
| 23 | 126r–125v | *Prevent us O Lord | William Byrd | Purcell |
| 24 | 125r–124v | *O Lord make thy servant Charles | Mr Will: Bird | Purcell |
| 25 | 124r–123r | *Lift up your heads | Orlando Gibbons | Purcell |
| 26 | 122v–121r | *O Lord I bow the knees | Mr Will: Mundy | Purcell |
| 27 | 120v–119v | O Lord I have loved | Mr Tho: Tomkins | Purcell |
| 28 | 119v–118r | *O give thanks | Dr Giles | Purcell |
| 29 | 118r–116v | Hear my prayer O God | Mr Adrian Batten | Purcell |
| 30 | 116r–115r | Save me O God | HP | Purcell |
| 31 | 114v–112r | Sing we merrily | Dr Child | Purcell |
| 32 | 112r | *Almighty and everlasting God (inc.) | [Orlando Gibbons] | Purcell |
| 33 | 111r–108v | Blessed is he whose unrighteousness is forgiven | HP | Purcell |
| 34 | 108r–107r | My God my soul is vexed | Dr Blow | Purcell |
| 35 | 106v–104v | Hear me O Lord and that soon | HP | Purcell |
| 36 | 104r–102r | Bow down thine ear O Lord | [Henry Purcell] | Purcell |
| 37 | 102r–100v | Funeral Sentences (inc.) | [Henry Purcell] | Purcell |
| 38 | 99r–98v | Remember not Lord our offences | [Henry Purcell] | Purcell |
| 39 | 98r–96v | O Lord God of my salvation | Dr Blow | Purcell |
| 40 | 96r–94r | O God thou hast cast us out | HP | Purcell |
| 41 | 93v–92r | Christ being raised from the dead | Dr Blow | Purcell |
| 42 | 92r–89r | O Lord God of hosts | HP | Purcell |
| 43 | 89r–88v | O God thou art my God (inc.) | [Henry Purcell] | Purcell |

## Table 2.1 (*cont.*)

| Item | Folios | Title | Ascription | Copyist |
|------|--------|-------|------------|---------|
| 44 | 87v–86v | Lord how long wilt thou be angry | [Henry Purcell] | Purcell |
| 45 | 86r–84r | O Lord thou art my God 'Isaiah ye 25th vers ye 1st part of ye 4th & ye 7th 8th & 9th verses' | [Henry Purcell] | Purcell |
| 46 | 83v–83r | Hear my prayer O Lord (inc.) | [Henry Purcell] | Purcell |

Folio, 440 × 280. Watermarks: arms of Strasbourg with countermark 'RC'; front flyleaf, Angoumois fleur-de-lys with factor's mark 'HC' and countermark 'PB'; reverse flyleaf, Angoumois fleur-de-lys with countermark 'IHS/ET'.

Rastrology: fifteen staves in three five-stave systems throughout. Ruled with a five-stave rastrum, span: 108, profile: 11(13.5)11(13)10.5(14)11(14)10.

* In John Barnard's *First Book of Selected Church Musick* (London, 1641).

*a* Ascription in a later hand, not Blow or Purcell.

*b* Incorrect ascription in a later hand, *recte* John Blow.

Mr Henry Purcell 1682 September ye 10th 1682', made underneath the large and ornate initials 'JB' or 'IB', possibly a reference to Blow. But in 1682 Purcell joined William Child and Blow as one of three Chapel Royal organists: while the date of appointment is normally given as 14 July (three days after Edward Lowe's death), Purcell seems not to have been installed until 16 September, responsibilities at Windsor (his or, since we have no record of Purcell's presence in Windsor that summer, the court's) presumably causing the delay.[21] Thus 10 September, the exact date of the court's return to London from its summer residency in Windsor, would have been the first opportunity for Purcell to be recognised in his new post. It is possible that Cfm 88 became Purcell's property at this juncture; if nothing else, the manuscript clearly takes on a more personal character after late 1682, with Purcell's official duties being reflected thereafter in Lbl R.M. 20.h.8.

Indeed Purcell's interest in Cfm 88 waned after this time. The next works added, in late 1682 or 1683 (Locke's *The Lord hear thee*, in the front, and Purcell's *O Lord God of hosts* and *O God thou art my God*, at the reverse), are the first to exhibit the italic 'r', especially in the final consonants of words (though the secretary 'r' is still the preferred version for initial and internal consonants). Purcell's hand in these works is much the same as that found in the 1682 and 1683 works in Lbl R.M. 20.h.8. Purcell's *Lord how long wilt thou be angry* seems to have been added in 1684, as the

[21] *RECM*, V, 80; Edward F. Rimbault, ed., *The Old Cheque-Book or Book of Remembrance of the Chapel Royal from 1561 to 1744* (London, 1872; repr. New York, 1966), 17.

## Table 2.2 Probable dates of Purcell's copying in Cambridge, Fitzwilliam Museum Music MS 88

|  | *Front contents* | *Reverse contents* |
|---|---|---|
| *c.* 1678 (September 1677– no later than June 1680) |  | O Lord I have sinned (Blow) |
| *c.* 1678 (December 1677– no later than June 1680) | Cry aloud and spare not (Blow) <br> Sing unto the Lord ye saints (Blow) | God is our hope and strength (Blow) <br> O God wherefore art thou absent (Blow) <br> Hosanna to the son of David (Gibbons) <br> Save me O God (Blow) <br> Lord let me know mine end (Locke) <br> Turn thy face from my sins (Locke) <br> Bow thine ear O Lord (Byrd) <br> I call and cry (Tallis) <br> Prevent us O Lord (Byrd) <br> O Lord make thy servant (Byrd) <br> Lift up your heads (Gibbons) <br> O Lord I bow the knees (Mundy) <br> O Lord I have loved (Tomkins) <br> O give thanks (Giles) <br> Hear my prayer O God (Batten) <br> Save me O God (Purcell) |
| *c.* 1679–81 | Sing we merrily (Blow)[a] <br> When the son of man shall come (Locke) | Sing we merrily (Child) <br> Almighty and everlasting God (Gibbons) <br> Blessed is he whose unrighteousness is forgiven (Purcell) <br> My God my soul is vexed (Blow) <br> Hear me O Lord (Purcell) <br> Bow down thine ear O Lord (Purcell) <br> Funeral Sentences (Purcell) <br> Remember not Lord our offences (Purcell) <br> O Lord God of my salvation (Blow) <br> O God thou hast cast us out (Purcell) <br> Christ being raised (Blow) |
| *c.* 1682–3 | The Lord hear thee (Locke) | O Lord God of hosts (Purcell) <br> O God thou art my God (Purcell) |
| *c.* 1684 |  | Lord how long wilt thou be angry (Purcell) |
| *c.* late 1684 |  | O Lord thou art my God (Purcell) |
| *c.* 1685 or later | I will hear what the Lord God will say (Locke) | Hear my prayer O Lord (Purcell) |

[a] Completed by Purcell.

44

Illus. 2.3  John Blow: *Sing we merrily*, partly autograph and partly copied by Purcell. Fitzwilliam Museum MU MS 88, fol. 20r

use of the italic 'r' is significantly greater than in the previous work and comparable to the 1684 works in R.M. 20.h.8; and it was probably in late 1684 or early 1685 that Purcell copied the penultimate work at the reverse end, *O Lord thou art my God,* in which the high incidence of the italic 'r' would indicate a date after the 1684 welcome song, *From those serene and rapturous joys,* in R.M. 20.h.8. The final works at both the front and reverse ends (Locke's *I will hear what the Lord God will say* and Purcell's eight-part *Hear my prayer O Lord,* respectively) feature the italic 'r' exclusively and were thus added to Cfm 88 no earlier than 1685. Comparably, the 1685 works in R.M. 20.h.8, *My heart is inditing* and *If prayers and tears,* are amongst the very first in that manuscript to show a 100 per cent italic 'r' incidence.

The status of the final three works in the reverse end of Cfm 88 is particularly curious: with the exception of contemporary copies of *O Lord thou art my God* and *Lord how long wilt thou be angry* in US-R M2040/A628/Folio, a scorebook in the hand of Purcell's principal assistant in Lbl R.M. 20.h.8 (herein identified as London A), there are no seventeenth-century concordances for these works. By means of comparison, for *O God thou art my God* there are at least ten seventeenth-century concordances extant. It is possible that, despite our modern estimation that *Lord how long wilt thou be angry* and *Hear my prayer O Lord* should be considered amongst Purcell's finest works for the church, these last pieces in Cfm 88 remained largely unknown in Purcell's lifetime. It would thus seem unreasonable here to suggest that Purcell was copying these particular pieces into Cfm 88 to preserve works that had previously circulated elsewhere, as was true for much of the earlier portion of the manuscript; the copying must have taken place very close to the dates of composition. The speculative leap is thus a short one to suggest that the composition of *Hear my prayer O Lord,* previously thought to have been written about 1680, was connected with some important event of early 1685, perhaps even the death of Charles II, a possibility which helps to explain its grand conception. It is usually stated that *Hear my prayer O Lord* was left unfinished by Purcell, but it is equally possible that Purcell completed the work as a rough separate score, as was his practice, and simply never had time to enter the complete work in his fair-copy scorebook.


THREE PRINCIPAL CONCORDANCES

There are clearly two categories of concordances for Cfm 88: (1) manuscripts that feature a substantial number of works in common with Purcell's scorebook, which can be shown in all likelihood to have been copied directly from Cfm 88 at a time when (or immediately after) Purcell was still compiling the manuscript (limited to three extant sources, Cfm 117, US-AUS Pre-1700 85 and US-R M2040/A628/Folio, each of which is treated in detail below); and (2) manuscripts that share with Cfm 88 just one or at most a few works, which, though they might shed light on the status of individual compositions (dates of composition, matters of genesis, dissemination etc.), tell us decidedly less than the former category about the manuscript as a whole. Since concordances in this second category often also contain works by Purcell not found in Cfm 88 (and there are numerous other important, non-autograph sources for Purcell's anthems with no overlapping repertory), these will be discussed separately in Chapter 5, in the context of the extant materials from the major London sacred establishments of Purcell's time.

### Cambridge, Fitzwilliam Museum Music MS 117

The importance of Cfm 117, easily one of the most massive scorebooks of anthems and services from the late seventeenth century, has been recognised since the eighteenth century, when it was owned by Philip Hayes (1738–97). The first marking on the front flyleaf is 'E Libris P. Hayes', and further confirmation that this volume was in Hayes's possession comes from a signed note in Lbl Add. 30931, fol. 81r, the autograph score of Purcell's early settings of the Funeral Sentences:

> The following verses of Mr Hen[r]y Purcel's composition seem to have been alter'd, and in some instances not for the better; the first verse viz 'Man that is born of a woman' is here wanting to complete the Anthem for as such it was evidently composed, and not intended as a Funeral Service. I have the whole perfect in a large collection of Anthems transcrib'd in the year 1683 at Windsor. Phil. Hayes. August 1784[22]

This description matches Cfm 117 precisely: not only are the three tables of contents (one each for full anthems, verse anthems and service music) individually dated 1683, but recent research has shown beyond doubt that Cfm 117 has a Windsor provenance.[23] Moreover, Cfm 117 is the only contemporary source to contain all three sections of Purcell's Funeral Sentences in their final version. Cfm 117 was probably purchased by Samuel Arnold at the sale of William and Philip Hayes's library in 1798

---

[22] Hayes did not apparently realise that the version in Lbl Add. 30931 was the earlier one, nor is it clear why he felt this should be considered an anthem rather than service music.

[23] Wood, 'A Note on Two Cambridge Manuscripts', 310–12; Holman, 'Bartholomew Isaack'.

at Smart's Music Warehouse in London;[24] Arnold's signature appears below Hayes's on the front flyleaf. Arnold himself died in 1802, and a year later Richard Fitzwilliam acquired Cfm 117; below Arnold's signature is Fitzwilliam's inscription: 'Fitzwilliam 1803. This Volume is in the hand-writing of Dr Blow. Dr Blow was born in 1648, & died in 1708.' Fitzwilliam's note about Blow's handwriting initiated a long and erroneous tradition that Cfm 117 was an important Blow autograph.[25] Philip Hayes did not identify it as such, though it is possible that Arnold purchased it as a Blow autograph, since several items (including some difficult to connect with known autographs) were listed in the Hayes sale catalogue as being in Blow's hand.[26] J. A. Fuller-Maitland and A. H. Mann perpetuated the Blow misattribution in their 1896 Fitzwilliam Museum catalogue,[27] and it was not until Watkins Shaw's investigations of Blow sources that the prevalent thinking about the copyist of Cfm 117 was first questioned.[28]

Thanks to the more recent research of Bruce Wood and Peter Holman the identification of the scribe of Cfm 117 as William Isaack, one of several Windsor-connected scribes who intersected with Purcell at various points in his career, can be firmly established.[29] To summarise this research briefly, Wood discovered in two organbooks at Eton College, WRec 299, vols. 1 (pp. 17–55) and 2 (pp. 71–241), samples of the same hand as in Cfm 117, thus adding to a list of for the most part significant manuscripts in this hand.[30] In one instance in the Eton books, a work is dated by the copyist 'Jan 1701'.[31] In the same books are layers of copying by John Walter and Benjamin Lamb, Eton College organists 1681–1705 and 1705–33

---

[24] *A Catalogue of the Very Curious and Valuable Music Library of Antient and Modern Compositions . . . Collected . . . by the Late W. and P. Hayes, Doctors in Music, Oxon* (London, [1798]); Cfm 117 cannot unequivocally be identified as one of the lots in this catalogue, though there are several possibilities, the most likely of which is lot 148 (p. 11): 'Cathedral Music, in score, MS. a large folio, by different Authors, bound in rough calf, 1–1–0'. See King, *Some British Collectors*, 21–2.

[25] A tradition maintained by the modern inscription on the spine of each volume (Cfm 117 is now bound in two volumes), dating from 1974, when the manuscript was last rebound: 'John Blow's Anthem Book'.

[26] *Catalogue . . . W. and P. Hayes*, 11.

[27] Fuller-Maitland and Mann, *Catalogue of the Music in the Fitzwilliam Museum*, 62.

[28] Harold Watkins Shaw, 'John Blow's Anthems', *M&L* 19 (1938), 431, n. 16; see also John Blow, *Coronation Anthems, Anthems with Strings*, ed. Anthony Lewis and Harold Watkins Shaw, Musica Britannica 7 (London, 1953), 58; and Watkins Shaw, 'The Autographs of John Blow', *MR* 25 (1964), 93–4.

[29] See n. 23; and also Bruce Wood, 'John Blow: Anthems with Orchestra' (Ph.D. thesis, University of Cambridge, 1977), V, 399–415.

[30] Shaw, 'Autographs of John Blow', 94; Wood, 'A Note on Two Cambridge Manuscripts', 308. See also Roderick Williams, 'Manuscript Organ Books in Eton College Library', *M&L* 41 (1960), 358–9. Our thanks are due to Mr Keri Dexter for further information on these organbooks.

[31] Wood, 'A Note on Two Cambridge Manuscripts', 310.

respectively. Wood then went on to locate payments to these scribes in the Eton audit books: various payments to Walter from 1684 to 1704, and to Lamb from 1705 on; only one other scribe was paid for copying: 'to Mr Isaack for writing & pricking 156 sheets of paper for Anthems & Psalms for the Organ Loft in the year 1702'.[32] Finally, Wood noted, examining the composer ascriptions within Cfm 117, that only one composer lacked the proper style, 'Mr' or 'Dr': one 'B. Isaack', probably the minor composer Bartholomew Isaack, a few of whose works survive in contemporary sources, and thus a likely candidate for the copyist of Cfm 117. Holman followed up on this, researching the biography of Bartholomew Isaack, and concluded as a result of several inconsistencies that the 'Mr Isaack' mentioned in the Eton records could not be Bartholomew but had to be his older brother William, who held positions at both Eton and St George's Chapel from the early 1670s until his death in 1703.[33]

William Isaack's careful compilation in Cfm 117 of approximately 140 anthems and 30 services (see Table 2.3) certainly reflects the description made of him in 1671 as one of the 'most diligent' members of the St George's choir;[34] and the consistency of paper type and stave-rulings throughout much of the manuscript suggests a large collection was Isaack's aim from the outset (see Table 2.4). Much of the paper in Cfm 117 bears the marks of Abraham Janssen in both the manufacturer's and factor's positions, suggesting a date of *c.* 1678. We have earlier suggested that paper marketed by Janssen *as factor* in all likelihood does not predate the end of the Franco-Dutch War in 1678 (see p. 13), though Janssen's initials may have found their way into the watermark side of his own moulds some years earlier, a possibility supported by internal evidence in Cfm 117 itself. The reverse end of the manuscript, devoted to service music, is more suggestive of its Windsor provenance than the front, devoted to anthems: the earliest section of the reverse end (original pp. 5–102) – possibly the first copying in the manuscript – is made up entirely of William Child's services (Child was organist at St George's for the better part of the seventeenth century), all or part of twelve different works. It is easy to imagine that the eclectic nature of Cfm 117 was not Isaack's first intention and that he began by compiling the works of his esteemed Windsor colleague, later expanding his plan to include a retrospective of earlier composers and many of the best works of his contemporaries. The first work

---

[32] Eton Audit Book, 1702–15: Accounts for 1703, p. 72. See Wood, 'A Note on Two Cambridge Manuscripts', 311.

[33] Holman, 'Bartholomew Isaack', 384.

[34] Shelagh Bond, *The Chapter Acts of the Dean and Canons of Windsor, 1430, 1523–1672* (Windsor, 1966), 295.

## Table 2.3  Cambridge, Fitzwilliam Museum Music MS 117: contents

KEY:

After item number: *in original tables of contents, copied by 1683

†later addition to tables of contents, copied in 1683 or after

Ascriptions in parentheses are from the tables of contents.

Relationship with Cfm 88 (far right column)

A = concordance without evident immediate relationship

B = copy corrected from Cfm 88

C = close concordance suggesting an immediate common source

D = direct copy from Cfm 88

followed by item number from Table 2.1

| Item | Folio | Page | Title | Ascription | Relationship with Cfm 88 |
|------|-------|------|-------|------------|--------------------------|
| 1 | 1r | — | O Lord turn thy wrath (inc.) | [William Byrd] | |
| 2 | 1r | — | Wipe away my sins | Mr Tho: Tallis | |
| 3 | 3v | — | O God whom our offences have displeased | Mr Wm Bird | |
| 4 | 5r | — | Blessed be thy name O God | Mr Tho: Tallis | |
| 5 | 9r | — | Like as the hart (string parts) | [Pelham Humfrey] | D (3) |
| 6 | 10r | — | O praise the Lord (string parts) | [Pelham Humfrey] | D (1) |
| 7 | 11r | — | O Lord my God (string parts) | Mr Humphryes | D (2) |
| 8 | 12r | — | Lord teach us to number our days (string parts) | [Pelham Humfrey] | D (6) |
| 9† | 13r | — | How long wilt thou forget me | Dr Gibbons | |
| 10† | 14r | — | Let thy merciful ears O Lord | [Robert White][a] | |

[end of additional material bound before the front end]

| | | | | | |
|------|-------|------|-------|------------|--------------------------|
| 11* | 15r | 1 | The Lord said unto my lord | (Dr Gibbons) | |
| 12* | 16v | 4 | Sing unto the Lord | Dr Christopher Gibbons | |
| 13* | 19r | 9 | Teach me O Lord | Dr Christopher Gibbons | |
| 14* | 21r | 13 | O Lord I have loved | Mr Thomas Tomkins | D (27) |
| 15* | 22v | 16 | Hear my prayer O God | Mr Adrian Batten | D (29) |
| 16* | 24v | 20 | Lift up your heads | Mr Orlando Gibbons | D (25) |
| 17* | 26v | 24 | Prevent us O Lord | Mr William Bird | D (23) |
| 18* | 27v | 26 | O Lord make thy servant | Mr William Bird | D (24) |
| 19* | 29r | 29 | Hosanna to the son of David | Mr Orlando Gibbons | D (17) |
| 20* | 31v | 34 | Deliver me from mine enemies | Mr Robert Parsons | |
| 21* | 33r | 37 | The king shall rejoice | Dr Wm Childe | |
| 22* | 34r | 39 | O Lord grant the king a long life | Dr Wm Childe | |
| 23* | 36r | 43 | Save me O God | Dr Wm Childe | |
| 24* | 37v | 46 | I will be glad and rejoice | Dr Wm Childe | |
| 25* | 39r | 49 | O Lord God the heathen are come | Dr Wm Childe | |
| 26* | 41r | 53 | O Lord grant the king a long life | Mr Tho. Weelks | |
| 27* | 42r | 55 | O thou God almighty | Mr Edmund Hooper | |
| 28* | 43r | 57 | With all our hearts and mouths | Mr Thomas Tallis | |
| 29* | 44r | 59 | The Lord bless us and keep us | Mr Robert White | |
| 30* | 45v | 62 | Arise O Lord | Mr William Bird | |
| 31* | 47r | 65 | I call and cry | Mr Tallis | A (22) |
| 32* | 48r | 65bis | O Lord I bow the knees | Mr Will Mundy | A (26) |

## Table 2.3 (*cont.*)

| Item | Folio | Page | Title | Ascription | Relationship with Cfm 88 |
|------|-------|------|-------|------------|--------------------------|
| 33* | 49v | 68 | Behold it is Christ | Mr Hooper | |
| 34* | 50v | 70 | Bow thine ear O Lord | Mr Bird | B (21) |
| 35* | 52r | 73 | O clap your hands | Dr Wm Childe | |
| 36* | 52v | 74 | Sing we merrily | Dr Wm Childe | A (31) |
| 37* | 52v | 74 | O give thanks | Dr Giles | B (28) |
| 38* | 55v | 80 | Therefore with angels (to item 161) | To Dr Childs ♯ Service | |
| 39* | 56v | 82 | Sing joyfully | Mr Wm Bird | |
| 40* | 58r | 85 | Behold thou hast made my days | Mr Orlando Gibbons | |
| 41* | 59v | 88 | Holy, holy, holy (8 parts) | Dr Childe | |
| 42* | 59v | 88 | Blessed is he that considereth | Mr Michaell Wise | |
| 43* | 60v | 90 | Gloria in excelsis (8 parts) | Dr Wm Childe | |
| 44* | 62v | 94 | I will magnify thee | Dr Giles | |
| 45* | 65r | 99 | Almighty God which by the leading of a star | Dr Bull | |
| 46* | 66v | 102 | Behold how good and joyful | Dr Childe | |
| 47* | 68v | 106 | Give the king thy judgements | Dr Childe | |
| 48* | 70r | 109 | My heart is fixed | (Dr Childe) | |
| 49 | 70v | 110 | Holy, holy, holy (to item 167) | to Dr Childs Elami Sharp | |
| 50* | 71r | 111 | O how amiable | (Dr Childe) | |
| 51* | 71v | 112 | Turn thou us good Lord | (Dr Childe) | |
| 52* | 73v | 116 | O praise the Lord | Dr Wm. Child | |
| 53* | 74v | 118 | The earth is the Lord's | Dr Childe | |
| 54* | 76v | 122 | O Lord my God (strings fol. 11r) | Mr Pelham Humphryes | A (2) |
| 55* | 80r | 127 | Have mercy upon me O God | Mr Pelham Humphryes | |
| 56* | 82v | 132 | O praise the Lord (strings fol. 10r) | Mr Pelham Humphrys | A (1) |
| 57* | 84v | 136 | Lord teach us to number our days (strings fol. 12r) | Mr Pelham Humphryes | A (6) |
| 58* | 85v | 138 | God is our hope and strength | Dr John Blow | C (15) |
| 59* | 89r | 145 | O God wherefore art thou absent | (Dr Blow) | C (16) |
| 60* | 90v | 148 | Save me O God | Dr John Blow | C (18) |
| 61* | 91r | 149 | Haste thee O God (strings fol. 247v) | Mr Pelham Humphrys | |
| 62* | 93r | 153 | O be joyful | Mr Pelham Humphryes | |
| 63* | 94v | 156 | Lord what is man | Mr William Turner | |
| 64* | 96r | 159 | And I heard a great voice (strings fol. 245r) | Dr John Blow | |
| 65* | 99r | 165 | When Israel came out of Egypt (strings fol. 246r) | Dr John Blow | |
| 66* | 101v | 170 | O Lord I have sinned | (Dr Blow) | A (14) |
| 67* | 104r | 175 | O Lord rebuke me not | Dr Childe | |
| 68* | 105v | 178 | Let God arise | (Dr Childe) | |
| 69* | 107v | 182 | If the Lord himself | Dr Childe | |
| 70* | 108v | 184 | O pray for the peace of Jerusalem | Dr Childe | |
| 71* | 110v | 186 | O that the salvation | Dr Child | |
| 72* | 111r | 187 | Save me O God | Mr Henry Purcell | C (30) |
| 73* | 113r | 191 | By the waters of Babylon | Mr Pelham Humphrys | |
| 74* | 115v | 196 | Awake up my glory | Mr Michaell Wise | |
| 75* | 116v | 198 | Come unto me saith the Lord | B. Isaack | |
| 76* | 118v | 202 | Turn thy face from my sins | Mr Matthew Locke | A (20) |
| 77* | 120v | 206 | O God thou hast cast us out | Mr Purcell | C (40) |
| 78* | 122v | 210 | My God my soul is vexed | (Mr Blow) | |

## Table 2.3 (*cont.*)

| Item | Folio | Page | Title | Ascription | Relationship with Cfm 88 |
|------|-------|------|-------|------------|--------------------------|
| 79* | 124r | 213 | Remember not Lord our offences 'Vers of ye letany' | (Mr Purcell) | A (38) |
| 80* | 124v | 214 | I will sing unto the Lord | Mr Hen: Purcell | |
| 81* | 125v | 216 | O Lord God of my salvation | Dr John Blow | C (39) |
| 82* | 125v | 216 | O Lord thou hast searched me out | Dr Blow | |
| 83* | 129r | 223 | Like as the hart (strings fol. 9r) | Mr Humphryes | A (3) |
| 84* | 130v | 226 | Hear O heavens | Mr Humphryes | |
| 85* | 132r | 229 | Lord thou hast been our refuge | Mr Turner | |
| 86* | 134r | 233 | Lord who can tell | Mr Henry Purcell | |
| 87* | 135r | 235 | Blessed be the Lord my strength | Mr Hen: Purcell | |
| 88* | 137r | 239 | Let God arise | Mr Henry Purcell | |
| 89* | 138v | 242 | O Lord our governor | Mr Hen: Purcell | |
| 90* | 141v | 248 | Lord how are they increased | Dr John Blow | |
| 91* | 143v | 252 | Behold how good and joyful | Dr Blow | |
| 92* | 144v | 254 | Lord let me know mine end | Mr Matthew Locke | |
| 93* | 147v | 260 | I beheld and lo a great multitude | Dr Blow | |
| 94* | 151r | 267 | Rejoice in the Lord (strings fol. 247r) | (Mr Humphrys) | |
| 95* | 152r | 269 | Blessed is the man | Mr Michaell Wise | |
| 96* | 153r | 271 | How are the mighty fallen | Mr Michaell Wise | |
| 97* | 154v | 274 | My soul is weary of my life | Mr Henry Hall | |
| 98* | 156v | 278 | Turn thee unto me O Lord | Dr John Blow | |
| 99* | 158r | 281 | O sing unto the Lord . . . for he | Dr John Blow | D (4) |
| 100* | 162v | 288 | Sing we merrily | (Dr Blow) | D (5) |
| 101* | 164v | 294 | Lift up your heads | (Dr Blow) [*recte* Pelham Humfrey] | D (7) |
| 102* | 166r | 297 | Cry aloud and spare not | Dr Blow | D (9) |
| 103* | 170r | 305 | Sing unto the Lord O ye saints | (Dr Blow) | D (10) |
| 104* | 176r | 317 | When the son of man shall come | Mr Matthew Locke | D (11) |
| 105* | 179r | 323 | Awake put on thy strength | Mr Michael Wise | |
| 106* | 181r | 327 | Blessed is he whose unrighteousness is forgiven | Mr Henry Purcell | D (33) |
| 107* | 185r | 335 | Hear me O Lord and that soon | Mr Hen Purcell | D (35) |
| 108* | 187v | 340 | Bow down thine ear | (Mr Purcell) | D (36) |
| 109* | 190r | 345 | Funeral Sentences | [Henry Purcell] | D (37) |
| 110* | 191v | 349 | Christ being raised from the dead | Dr Blow | D (41) |
| 111 | 192 | — | Thou knowest Lord (completion of item 109 on a separate folio) | Mr Purcell | |
| 112* | 195v | 355 | The Lord is king ('Symphony to The Lord is King' on separate fol. 196) | Dr John Blow | |
| 113† | 201r | 364 | Not unto us O Lord | Mr Mathew Locke | |
| 114† | 203v | 369 | I was glad | Mr Hen: Purcell | |
| 115† | 206r | 374 | I will magnify thee | Mr Wm: Turner | |

[Cfm 117 is now bound in two volumes; fol. 206 is the last folio of vol. I.]

| Item | Folio | Page | Title | Ascription | Relationship with Cfm 88 |
|------|-------|------|-------|------------|--------------------------|
| 116† | 207r | 376 | The king shall rejoice (strings fol. 251v) | Mr Humphryes | |
| 117† | 208v | 379 | O give thanks (strings fol. 247v) | Mr Pelham Humphryes | |
| 118† | 210r | 382 | When the Lord turned again (strings fol. 248v) | Dr John Blow | |

## Table 2.3 (*cont.*)

| Item | Folio | Page | Title | Ascription | Relationship with Cfm 88 |
|------|-------|------|-------|------------|--------------------------|
| 119† | 212v | 387 | The Lord is my shepherd (strings fol. 249v) | Dr Blow | |
| 120† | 214v | 391 | I said in the cutting off of my days (strings fol. 250v) | Dr Blow | |
| 121† | 216v | 395 | The kings of Tharsis (strings fol. 252r) | (Dr Blow) | |
| 122† | 219r | 398 | Thou art my king O God | Mr Pelham Humphryes | |
| 123† | 220v | 401 | Hear my crying O God | Mr Pelham Humphryes | |
| 124† | 223r | 406 | I will alway give thanks | The Clubb anthem | A (8) |
| 125† | 224v | 409 | My beloved spake | Mr Henry Purcell | |
| 126† | 228r | 416 | Arise O Lord | (Dr Blow) | |
| 127† | 231r | 422 | I will hearken | Dr John Blow | |
| 128† | 233v | 427 | Blessed is the man | Dr John Blow | |
| 129† | 236v | 433 | O give thanks 'upon a ground' | Dr John Blow | |
| 130† | 241r | 442 | Hear my voice O God ('July ye 18th 1683', fol. 244v) | Dr Blow | |

[on fol. 245r: 'The symphonyes to some of the foregoing anthems']

| Item | Folio | Page | Title | Ascription | Relationship with Cfm 88 |
|------|-------|------|-------|------------|--------------------------|
| 131 | 245r | 450 | And I heard a great voice (string parts) | [John Blow] | |
| 132 | 246r | 452 | When Israel came out of Egypt (string parts) | [John Blow] | |
| 133 | 247r | 454 | Rejoice in the Lord (string parts) | [Pelham Humfrey] | |
| 134 | 247v | 455 | Haste thee O God (string parts) | [Pelham Humfrey] | |
| 135 | 247v | 455 | O give thanks (string parts) | Mr Humphryes | |
| 136 | 248v | 457 | When the Lord turned again (string parts) | [John Blow] | |
| 137 | 249v | 459 | The Lord is my shepherd (string parts) | [John Blow] | |
| 138 | 250v | 461 | I said in the cutting off of my days (string parts) | [John Blow] | |
| 139 | 251v | 463 | The king shall rejoice (string parts) | Mr Pelham Humphrys | |
| 140 | 252r | 464 | The kings of Tharsis (string parts) | [John Blow] | |
| 141† | 252v | 465 | Out of the deep | Dr Aldrich | |
| 142† | 253r | 466 | O give thanks | Mr John Walter | |
| 143† | 255v | 471 | Thy mercy O Lord | Dr John Blow | |
| 144† | 258v | 477 | O give thanks*b* | Dr John Blow | |
| 145† | 263v | 487 | I beheld and lo | Dr John Blow | |
| 146† | 266v | 493 | Hear me O God | Mr John Goldwin | |
| 147† | 267v | 495 | Ponder my words O Lord | Mr John Goldwin | |
| 148† | 270r | 500 | God be merciful | Mr Locke | |
| 149† | 271v | 503 | Jesus seeing the multitude | Dr John Blow | |
| 150† | 274r | 508 | I am well pleased | (Mr Goldwin) | |
| 151† | 275r | 510 | O Lord God of hosts (6 parts) | Mr Goldwin | |
| 152† | 276v | 513 | O God thou art my God | to Mr Purcells Bmi Service | A (43) |

[manuscript inverted]

| Item | Folio | Page | Title | Ascription | Relationship with Cfm 88 |
|------|-------|------|-------|------------|--------------------------|
| 153* | [448v] | 01 | *Modern Church-Musick . . . April 1, 1666* (includes Communion Service in F) | Matt. Lock | |
| 154 | 446v | 05 | Psalm 119 'to be sung on ye 24 day of ye month only att Evening Prayer' | Mr Tallis | |
| 155* | 445v | 07 | Service in d | Mr Tallis | |
| 156* | 439v | 019 | Morning and Evening Service in d | Mr Elway Bevin | |
| 157 | 434v | [029] | Evening Service in d (to item 176) | Mr Bird | |

## Table 2.3 (*cont.*)

| Item | Folio | Page | Title | Ascription | Relationship with *Cfm* 88 |
|------|-------|------|-------|------------|----------------------------|
| 158 | 432v | [033] | Service in G*<sup>c</sup>* | Dr Henry Aldrich | |

[end of additional material bound before the reverse end]

| Item | Folio | Page | Title | Ascription | Relationship with *Cfm* 88 |
|------|-------|------|-------|------------|----------------------------|
| 159* | 424v | 5 | Nunc dimittis in B♭*<sup>d</sup>* | Dr Wm Childe | |
| 160* | 424r | 6 | 'Dr Childs Service in Are' | Dr Child | |
| 161* | 419v | 17 | Morning and Evening Service in D | Dr Child | |
| 162* | 412v | 29 | Evening Service 'for 4 means' in d | Dr Child | |
| 163* | 411r | 32 | Service in d | Dr Child | |
| 164* | 405r | 42 | Evening Service (with verses) in a | Dr Childe | |
| 165* | 403r | 46 | Evening Service (with verses) in B♭ | Dr Childe | |
| 166* | 401v | 49 | Evening Service (with verses) in c | Dr Child | |
| 167* | 400r | 52 | Service (with verses) in 'Elami sharp' | Dr Child | |
| 168* | 395r | 60 | Service (with verses) in 'Elami fflatt' | Dr Child | |
| 169* | 389v | 69 | 'Dr Childs ffull Service in F ffaut' | Dr Child | |
| 170* | 385r | 77 | 'Dr Childs Service in Gamut' (includes alternative evening canticles with verses) | Dr Child | |
| 171* | 374r | 102 | Service in e | Mr John Blow/Dr Blow*<sup>e</sup>* | |
| 172† | 362v | 123 | 'Mr Orlando Gibbons Service for verses' in d | Mr Orlando Gibbons | |
| 173* | 359v | 131 | 'Mr Orlando Gibbons His full Service ffor 4 voc:' in F | Mr Orlando Gibbons | |
| 174* | 353v | 143 | 'Dr Giles Evening Service ffor verses in C ffaut' | Dr Giles | |
| 175* | 349v | 149 | 'Dr Giles new [evening] Service in Are ffor verses' | Dr Giles | |
| 176* | 345v | 157 | 'Mr Birds full Service' in d | Mr Bird | |
| 177* | 341r | 166 | Evening Service in g*<sup>f</sup>* | (Mr Bird) | |
| 178* | 329v | 181 | 'Dr Blows service in Gamut' | Dr Blow | |
| 179* | 323r | 196 | 'Dr Blows service in Are' | Dr Blow | |
| 180* | 315v | 211 | 'Mr Humphryes Service in Elami' | Mr Humphryes | |
| 181* | 308v | 225 | Communion Service (with verses) in E | Mr Michaell Wise | |
| 182* | 307r | 228 | Communion Service (with verses) in f | (Mr Wise) | |
| 183* | 305v | 231 | 'Mr Purcell's Service in Bmi' | Mr Purcell | |
| 184† | 299r | 244 | Sanctus and Gloria in G (to item 178) | Dr Blow | |
| 185† | 297v | 247 | Morning and Evening Service (alternative canticles to item 183) | Mr Henry Purcell | |
| 186† | 291r | 260 | 'Service in F ffaut' | Mr John Goldwin | |
| 187† | 286r | 269bis | Communion Service in G ('tripla') | Dr Blow | |
| 188† | 284r | 273 | 'Mr Tho: Morleys Service in Dsolre for verses' | Mr Tho: Morley | |

Folio, 339 × 215 (insertions at each end variable). Watermarks and rastrology: see Table 2.4.

Copyist: William Isaack

---

*<sup>a</sup> Let thy merciful ears O Lord* is not by Christopher Gibbons, as tentatively noted in Fuller-Maitland and Mann, *Catalogue of the Music in the Fitzwilliam Museum*, 62, but seems to be the work of Robert White; see Spink, *Restoration*, 80; John Morehen, 'The Sources of English Cathedral Music, c.1617–c.1644' (Ph.D. thesis, University of Cambridge, 1969), 352.

*b* Inscribed 'This anthem is sung some part in ye Singing loft & some part below in ye Quire' (fol. 259r) and with various annotations throughout such as '3 voc. above' and '4 voc. below'.

*c* The Sanctus and Gloria to Aldrich's service were inserted later on a smaller bifolium. The Sanctus is here inscribed 'The Lady Trelawneys', probably a reference to the wedding of Christ Church patron Jonathan Trelawney in 1684 (Spink, *Restoration*, 81), suggesting a date for some of William Isaack's final work in Cfm 117.

*d* This portion of Child's Service in B♭ is completely crossed through in the manuscript, though the entire service was once apparently present: the index suggests that the morning canticles once began on p. 029 and the evening canticles on p. 3; original pp. 029ff. and 1–4 do not survive.

*e* Isaack's several ascriptions to Blow vary between 'Mr' and 'Dr' within this service; the final ascription (fol. 362r) reads: 'Here ends Mr John Blow his Service for Morning and Evening in Elami'.

*f* As it appears in the manuscript (though listed separately in the index) item 177 is a continuation of item 176; the evening canticles which comprise item 177 are, however, from Byrd's Second Service, while item 176 is Byrd's Short Service. The missing evening canticles from the Short Service are found earlier in the manuscript, though were likely added at a later time; see item 157.

after Child's services is Blow's Service in E Minor, and there are several ascriptions to Blow within this work, varying between 'Mr' and 'Dr'. Those using 'Dr' do not appear to be later additions: Isaack, very careful to style composers correctly throughout the remainder of the manuscript (and everywhere else in the manuscript Blow appears as 'Dr'), may well have been copying this work in late 1677, just after Blow's style had changed (or shortly after news of Blow's doctorate reached Windsor), and we might infer from this that the work of compiling Child's services began several months earlier.

The ordering of the material in the manuscript, taken together with the nature of its relationship to Cfm 88 and the obviously helpful 1683 inscriptions on the tables of contents, allows the story of its further compilation to be told with some security. The main body of Cfm 117, with original pagination to 514 at the front end and to 228 at the reverse, and preceded at both ends by material copied separately, was in all likelihood worked on steadily from about 1677 to probably no later than 1684, a roughly similar period of compilation to Cfm 88, and in fact some of the first material in the anthem section was copied by Isaack directly from Purcell's manuscript. Isaack followed a loosely chronological plan in adding anthems to his scorebook,[35] emphasising at first the selection in Barnard's printed partbooks. (Interestingly, Isaack's scorebook preserves none of the four-part full anthems from Barnard but has eighteen of Barnard's nineteen full anthems for five or more voices.) Isaack began by copying Purcell's already scored versions of Barnard anthems compiled in Cfm 88. After beginning the anthem section with three works by Christopher Gibbons (not

[35] Spink, *Restoration*, 80.

## Table 2.4 Paper types, collation and rastrology in Cambridge, Fitzwilliam Museum Music MS 117

| Folios | Watermark/countermark | Quiring |
|---|---|---|
| iii–vi (tables) | Angoumois fleur-de-lys/'IHS' with 'RC' | 4 |
| 1–2 | arms of Amsterdam/'IP' | 2 |
| 3–6 | foolscap/'PT' | 4 |
| 7–8 | arms of Amsterdam/'PR'[?] | 2 |
| 9–12 | Angoumois fleur-de-lys with 'AJ'/'AI' | 4 |
| 13–14 | arms of Amsterdam/'CDG' | 2 |
| 15–46 | Angoumois fleur-de-lys with 'AJ'/'AI' | 6; 6; 6; 8; 6 |
| 47–55/i | mixed gathering: fols. 47–8, countermark 'AI'; fols. 49–54, Angoumois fleur-de-lys/'IHS'; fol. 55, Angoumois fleur-de-lys with 'AJ' | 10 (1 missing; fol. 55/i is a guard stub) |
| 56–191 | Angoumois fleur-de-lys/'IHS' except fols. 90–3 and 179–80: Angoumois fleur-de-lys with 'AJ'/'AI' | 8 (1 missing); 8; 8; 8; 8; 8 (fols. 77 and 109 are slips); 8; 8 (1 missing); 8; 8; 8; 8; 8; 8; 8 |
| 192 | arms of Amsterdam | 1 |
| 193–311 | Angoumois fleur-de-lys with 'AJ'/'AI' | 8 (1 missing; fol. 196 is an inserted single folio (no watermark)); 6; 6; 4; 4 (fol. 218 is a slip); 6; 4; 6; 6; 4; 6; 4; 4; 6; 6; 4; 4; 4; 6; 6; 6 |
| 312–329/ii | Angoumois fleur-de-lys/'IHS' | 6; 2; 6; 6 (2 missing; fols. 329/i–ii are stubs of copied music pages) |
| 330–7 (unused) | simple fleur-de-lys/'ID' | 8 |
| 337/i–367 | Angoumois fleur-de-lys/'IHS' | 8 (3 missing; fols. 337/i–iii are stubs of copied music pages); 8 (fol. 352 is a slip); 8; 8 (fol. 363 is a slip) |
| 368–369/ii | Angoumois fleur-de-lys with 'AJ'/'AI' | 4 (2 missing) |
| 370–410 | Angoumois fleur-de-lys/'IHS' except fols. 394 and 400: Angoumois fleur-de-lys with 'AJ'/'AI' | 6 (fols. 374–374/i are pasted); 10; 6; 2 (1 missing; fol. 392 is a slip); 8 (fol. 398 is a slip); 8 (fol. 407 is a slip) |
| 411–19 | Angoumois fleur-de-lys with 'AJ'/'AI' except fols. 411 and 419: Angoumois fleur-de-lys/'IHS' | 8 (fol. 416 is a slip) |
| 420 | Angoumois fleur-de-lys | collation of next five folios unclear |
| 421 | Angoumois fleur-de-lys with 'AJ' | |
| 422 | 'IHS' | |
| 422/i | | stub of copied music page |
| 423 | 'IHS' | |
| 424 | 'AI' | |
| 425–6 | arms of Amsterdam/[illegible] | 2 |
| 427–32 | simple fleur-de-lys/'ID' | 10 (fols 428/i and 430/i–iii are stubs) |
| 433–4 | fleur-de-lys (different from any other herein)/[monogram?] | 2 |
| 435–46 | Angoumois fleur-de-lys with 'AJ'/'AI' | 8; 4 |

Rastrology (main paper types only): twelve staves throughout.

| Paper type | Staves in rastrum | Rastrum span | Rastrum profile |
|---|---|---|---|
| Angoumois fleur-de-lys with 'AJ'/'AI' | 4 | 93 | 13(14.5)13(13.5)12(14.5)12.5 |
| Angoumois fleur-de-lys/'IHS' | 4 | 92 | 12(15)12.5(15)11(14.5)12 |
| simple fleur-de-iys/'ID' | 4 | 94.5 | 11.5(16)11(16)12(17)11 |

found in Cfm 88), Isaack copied six works by Tomkins, Batten, Orlando Gibbons and Byrd from Purcell's copies (Table 2.3, items 14–19). (It may not have been simply coincidence that Isaack's copying from Cfm 88 began with Tomkins's *O Lord I have loved* and Batten's *Hear my prayer O God*, the only two older works copied by Purcell not found in Barnard; Isaack may have wanted to get these two works – not otherwise available – transcribed first.) As mentioned above, Purcell's scores of these anthems required considerable editing from the copies in Barnard in order to produce consistent library copies, ones that would result in few if any problems in performance once transcribed into partbooks. It is thus easy to determine that Purcell's copies were the source for these six works, since his distinct readings are replicated by Isaack in Cfm 117.

One of these six works particularly clarifies this relationship: Byrd's *O Lord make thy servant* circulated widely in the seventeenth century in both five- and six-part versions. The six-part scoring (SAATTB) begins with the tenors in unison; while versions using only the first tenor proved widely acceptable, Barnard alone provided a version with only the second tenor, resulting in 'numerous bare and ungrammatical moments'.[36] Purcell began with this unique five-part version (confirming Barnard to be his source), supplying at a later time part of the missing material on an added stave in different ink (Cfm 88, fol. 125r).[37] The six-part version of *O Lord make thy servant* in Cfm 117 at first appears unrelated to the faulty five-part version, but Isaack undoubtedly began with Purcell's copy: he not only faithfully copied Purcell's arrangement of the text (given by Barnard as 'O Lord make thy servant Charles our King', though poorly underlaid) but also reproduced in his first stage of work the missing material added by Purcell. Possibly warned by Purcell that there was a part missing, Isaack had allowed an extra tenor stave throughout, later finding a version of the work with the complete sixth part (though texted, 'O Lord make thy servant our sovereign Lord King') and adding it, in different ink, to his copy. Finally he edited the words of the two tenor parts, preserving 'Charles' in the incipit but otherwise altering those of the tenor part copied from Purcell to conform to the one he had found elsewhere.

The nature of Purcell's copying in Cfm 88 may well have instigated Isaack to score additional works from Barnard himself; certainly from the copying Isaack completed before he encountered Cfm 88 (works by Child, Blow and Christopher Gibbons)

---

[36] Craig Monson, ed., William Byrd, *The English Anthems*, The Byrd Edition 11 (London, 1983), 210.
[37] Reproduced in Shay, 'Purcell as Collector', 46, and Robert Thompson, *The Glory of the Temple and the Stage: Henry Purcell (1659–1695)* (London, 1995), 15.

Illus. 2.4 Henry Purcell: *Save me O God*, copied by William Isaack. Fitzwilliam Museum MU MS 117, fol. 111r

there is little indication that he planned to include a selection of Tudor and early Stuart anthems. Of the next twenty-one works copied by Isaack (after the six from Cfm 88), eight are by Child, and twelve of the remaining thirteen are from Barnard's *First Book* (the exception being Byrd's *Arise O Lord*). Isaack's own copies of older works differ substantially from those reproduced from Purcell's well-edited scores, and in all likelihood Isaack scored the works from the printed partbooks himself. His copy of Tallis's *I call and cry*, for example, parallels the reading in Barnard very closely, but for this work and most of the other Barnard derivatives Isaack imposes an awkward triple-metre barring on the music. The differences between the anthems Isaack copied from Purcell and those he scored himself is striking, not just in matters of layout but in the overall musical precision as well, underscoring the exceptional care taken by Purcell.

The first of Purcell's works to appear in Cfm 117 is *Save me O God* (Illus. 2.4). The version in Isaack's scorebook is, however, not derived from Purcell's copy in Cfm 88, where it was revised from a version already in circulation. In Cfm 88 *Save me O God* is the seventeenth anthem in the reverse end and the last work to display the secretary 'e'. The first six works Isaack transcribed from Cfm 88 include the sixteenth anthem from the reverse end, Batten's *Hear my prayer O God*, and it is difficult to imagine Isaack passing on the opportunity to copy a relatively new Purcell anthem had it been available when those transcriptions were completed. It seems that *Save me O God* was not yet in Cfm 88 when Isaack first worked from it; only subsequently did he add it to Cfm 117 from another source, possibly a now-lost autograph which at the time was loosely collected together with Purcell's very early copy of Humfrey's *By the waters of Babylon* in Lbl Add. 30932. *Save me O God* and the Humfrey anthem are adjacent in Cfm 117, and the idiosyncrasies of Purcell's organ arrangement of the Humfrey are largely preserved by Isaack. The absence of the revised *Save me O God* in Cfm 117 suggests that Isaack's first stage of transcriptions from Cfm 88 took place well before 1680, by which time (at the very latest) Purcell had replaced the secretary 'e' with the italic one (proven by his dated copying in Lbl Add. 30930). Since Purcell may have originally composed the work as early as 1677[38] and the revised version may come from late 1678 or 1679 (in addition to the change in 'e' there is a noticeable overall difference in Purcell's hand between the early sections of Cfm 88 and Lbl Add. 30930 suggesting that some length of time passed), the summer of 1678 is a strong possibility for the time of Isaack's first transcriptions from Cfm 88. Probably more than once Cfm 88 accompanied court musicians to Windsor, where Isaack would have had, it seems, easy access to it.

The remainder of Isaack's transcriptions from Cfm 88 figure more towards the later stages of his work. Items 99–104 and 106–10 were copied from Purcell's scorebook nearly in one continuous effort, interrupted only by Michael Wise's *Awake put on thy strength*. It may also be at this time that Isaack made some minor corrections based on Purcell's edited scores to two Barnard works he had earlier scored himself (items 34 and 37). But his main interest at this stage seems to have been in the genre of the symphony anthem; it is certainly possible that several concerted works were performed in Windsor at about the same time Isaack produced these copies. In addition to completing six full scores of symphony anthems by Blow, Humfrey and Locke (working from both Blow's and Purcell's copying in Cfm 88),

---

[38] See n. 16.

Isaack at the same time wrote out string parts for a few additional works already reproduced from other sources (items 5–8, preceding the main body of the manuscript). The summer of 1682 is the most likely date for this stage of Isaack's work: as suggested before, Purcell probably became the owner of Cfm 88 in September 1682 and on the evidence of handwriting he added only a few works to his scorebook after that year. The last two works Isaack copied from Cfm 88, Locke's *When the son of man shall come* (from the front end), and Blow's *Christ being raised from the dead* (from the reverse), are precisely the last works in Cfm 88 that exhibit the italic 'e' together with the secretary 'r'; the works immediately following in Purcell's manuscript exhibit an italic 'r' incidence placing their copying in late 1682 or after. Isaack copied nothing from Cfm 88 that can be dated later than 1682.[39]

The other five works Isaack copied at this stage (items 106–10) came from the full and verse anthem end of Cfm 88; four of these are by Purcell: *Blessed is he whose unrighteousness is forgiven*, *Hear me O Lord and that soon*, *Bow down thine ear* and *Man that is born of a woman*. Isaack's readings of each of these works closely match Purcell's copies in Cfm 88, and the relationship between the two sources' versions of the last of these, the settings of the Funeral Sentences, provides an even tighter link. Purcell's score of the Funeral Sentences in Cfm 88 contains only two of the three sections he set, and in entering this work in his scorebook Purcell made further revisions to this material, first composed by the mid-1670s (part of his early efforts survives in Lbl Add. 30931) and revised quite heavily sometime around 1680 (a version represented in several non-autograph manuscripts).[40] Purcell's middle version is the one that circulated widely in his day, and the only contemporary concordance for his final revisions is Cfm 117; furthermore, Isaack at first copied only the two sections of the work found in Cfm 88, and then later located a source for the third section, copied it on a loose folio, and inserted it in his scorebook as near to the end of the previously copied material as possible.

After the tables in Cfm 117 were drawn up – not by Isaack; the scribe of the tables was at times rather careless about the wording of titles and correct composer attributions, in contrast to Isaack's usual meticulousness – and dated 1683, an additional thirty anthems, services by John Goldwin and Thomas Morley, and additional canticles to previously copied services by Blow and Purcell were added to

---

[39] The apparent interruption in Isaack's access to Cfm 88 between 1678 and 1682 is supported by recent research into the Chapel Royal's attendance at Windsor, which was similarly interrupted for logistical reasons; see Keri Dexter, 'The Provision of Choral Music at St George's Chapel, Windsor, and Eton College, *c.* 1640–1733' (Ph.D. thesis, Royal Holloway, University of London, in progress).

[40] See Robert Shay, 'Purcell's Revisions to the Funeral Sentences Revisited', *EM* 26 (1998), 457–67.

the manuscript (items 113–52 and 184–8). These were added to the tables in a different hand, that of Isaack himself, who also corrected a number of the mistakes in the original entries.[41] One anthem, Blow's *Hear my voice O God*, coming about midway through this later group of thirty, was inscribed by Isaack in the manuscript 'July ye 18th 1683', suggesting that the original tables were put together in early 1683 and that Isaack's remaining work in the volume continued immediately thereafter. This date may of course refer to a date of composition,[42] but it seems likely that Isaack's project was largely finished by about 1684. He added nothing to the manuscript after the original tables were made that can be dated later than this, and in fact some of the later additions are of rather early items (Purcell's *My beloved spake*, for example). Four anthems and a service by John Goldwin may be the newest music in the volume. Goldwin, organist at St George's from 1697 to 1719, may have been only in his late teens in 1685, but by July of that year he had 'sufficient skill in music to be capable of performing the duties of organist as well as the master of the choristers' in assistance to the aged Child and Matthew Green, 'for their ease'.[43] Certainly Goldwin would have been composing by then: all of the works of his in Cfm 117 are also found in a volume devoted to Goldwin's earliest works, Och 94, copied by none other than William Isaack.[44]

It remains to discuss Isaack's copies of works by Purcell not found in Cfm 88. After copying Barnard derivatives from Purcell's scores and then going on to score additional Barnard anthems himself, Isaack copied a repertory with numerous links to Chapel Royal and Westminster Abbey sources. While there are additional concordances with Cfm 88, there is no evidence of direct copying until the group of works transcribed by Isaack probably in 1682, mentioned above. All but one of items 54–60 in Cfm 117 are also in Cfm 88, but here the repertory in the two sources derives individually from probably common Chapel Royal manuscripts. There are several sequential similarities between groups of anthems in Cfm 117, Cfm 88 and the earliest extant Chapel partbooks, Lbl R.M. 27.a.1–8, as well as the 'Catalogue' of anthems and services added to the Chapel Royal books from 'Anno 1670 to Midsumer 1676'.[45] For example, items 58–60 in Cfm 117 (Blow's *God is our hope and strength*, *O God wherefore art thou absent* and *Save me O God*) are items 15, 16

---

[41] One further work added later to the original tables, a D minor service by Orlando Gibbons (Table 2.3, item 172), seems to have been omitted for a lack of space at the bottom of a page; from its position in the manuscript this work would in all likelihood have been copied before the original tables were compiled.

[42] Wood, 'A Note on Two Cambridge Manuscripts', 309.

[43] From the Chapter Acts; cited in Shaw, *The Succession*, 346. See also Spink, *Restoration*, 371–86.

[44] Spink, *Restoration*, 381.    [45] *RECM*, I, 162–4.

and 18 in Cfm 88, and the three works are listed in the same order in the 'Catalogue'. In Lbl R.M. 27.a.7, the oldest intact fragment amongst the Chapel partbooks, entirely in the hand of William Tucker, the last two of these Blow anthems are adjacent. It would thus seem that both Purcell and Isaack had access to the same Chapel Royal performing materials, each scoring some of the works for themselves at about the same time. Various works by Purcell in Cfm 117 (including items 72, 77, 79 and 86), copied not long after the three Blow anthems, may have all once been in the Chapel books: Purcell's *Lord who can tell* is the only work of his in the earliest layers of R.M. 27.a.1–8, and *O God thou hast cast us out* appears in the next oldest layers. Four further Purcell anthems from Cfm 117 (items 80 and 87–9) tend to be associated with Purcell's work at the Abbey, since they are found in two surviving Abbey partbooks, Lwa Triforium Set I, which are also in the hand of Tucker.

Another four works by Purcell (items 114, 125, 152 and 183/185) were copied by Isaack after the original tables were drawn up in the first half of 1683. The very last anthem in the main body of the manuscript is in fact by Purcell (*O God thou art my God*), and this may have been added at the same time the alternative canticles to Purcell's service were copied at the reverse end, the fourth item from the end there. Isaack inscribed the anthem 'to Mr Purcells Bmi Service', suggesting his source here too was of Chapel Royal provenance, since the anthem appears amongst canticles from Purcell's service in Lbl R.M. 27.a.1–8.[46] Two of Purcell's symphony anthems figure amongst Isaack's later work in Cfm 117. *I was glad* was copied in a reading close to that of Purcell's in Lbl R.M. 20.h.8, though the source was more likely an intermediary one: it is difficult to imagine Isaack, from the picture Cfm 117 paints of him, restricting himself to a single work should he have had access to another Purcell scorebook. Isaack's copy of *My beloved spake* (Illus. 2.5) comes near the end of a group of eleven symphony anthems (items 116–26), all but one of which are found in one or the other of two extant Chapel Royal partbooks devoted to symphony anthems, in Tucker's hand, Lbl Add. 50860 and J-Tn N5/10. *My beloved spake* is here given in its revised version, though in many respects this copy is distinct from that in Ob MS Tenbury 1031, a much later source (*c.*1705) which served as the copy-text for the Purcell Society's most recent edition of the anthem, on the grounds that the copy in Cfm 117 'shows evidence of modification of detail made probably in the process of transcription that could not possibly represent Purcell's intentions'.[47] But Philip Hayes's scorebook Ktp MR 2–5.4, pp. 108–37, contains a closely related copy of the

[46] Franklin B. Zimmerman, 'Purcell's "Service Anthem" *O God thou art my God* and the B-Flat Major Service', *MQ* 50 (1964), 208.    [47] *Works*, XIII (1988), 162.

Illus. 2.5  Henry Purcell: *My beloved spake*, copied by William Isaack. Fitzwilliam Museum MU MS 117, fol. 225r

anthem annotated 'This and the following Anthem [Purcell's arrangement of Hum-frey's *By the waters of Babylon*] were transcrib'd from Henry Purcel's Original Scores in the Possession of Mr W: Flacton at Canterbury who favor'd me with the loan of them. 1785.' Hayes's remark raises the possibility that the Flackton collection once included a revised autograph of *My beloved spake*, as well as the surviving original now in Lbl Add. 30932, at the end of which is Flackton's note 'See a fair Copy of this in Catalogue No. 72.' It cannot be ruled out that some of the distinctive characteristics (and even some of the mistakes) of the version shared by Cfm 117, Ktp MR 2–5.4 and another eighteenth-century source, Lbl Add. 17820, such as the more pervasive use of dotted rhythms in the final 'Alleluia', descend from an authoritative source. Some serious problems in the underlay of *My beloved spake* in Cfm 117, which suggest that the eighteenth-century copies are independent of it, are probably the result of Isaack working from a copy which at the time included only the incipits, adding most of the text at a later stage: for example, in Illus. 2.5, only the words 'My beloved spake' and the several instances of 'Rise' seem to have been copied with the music.

## University of Texas at Austin, Harry Ransom Humanities Research Center MS Pre-1700 85

John Gostling's first scorebook, US-AUS Pre-1700 85, has become widely known as 'The Gostling Manuscript', thanks to its publication in facsimile under that title,[48] though some caution is in order here since it is by no means the only significant manuscript copied by Gostling (*c.* 1650–1733), the renowned bass of Charles II's Chapel Royal and later subdean at St Paul's Cathedral. US-AUS Pre-1700 85, along with numerous other manuscript and printed items, passed from John Gostling to his son William, a musician and avid collector himself,[49] whose bookplate is still found on the front pastedown. Zimmerman suggests that it never left the Gostling family, since before it passed through Sotheby's in 1935 it was known to be in the possession of William Kennedy Gostling and a Miss Gostling of Folkestone,[50] though it can be

---

[48] *The Gostling Manuscript* (facsimile edn), intro. by Franklin B. Zimmerman (Austin and London, 1977); Zimmerman's introduction largely overlaps with his earlier article: 'Anthems of Purcell and Contemporaries in a Newly Rediscovered "Gostling Manuscript"', *AcM* 41 (1969), 55–70. Amongst the reviews of the facsimile see especially those by Peter le Huray, *MT* 120 (1979), 585–6; Watkins Shaw, *M&L* 60 (1979), 487–90; and Bruce Wood, *EM* 9 (1981), 117–20.

[49] King, *Some British Collectors*, 19–20.

[50] The entry from the 1935 Sotheby's catalogue is reproduced in Zimmerman, 'Anthems of Purcell', 56. Pre-1935 references to US-AUS Pre-1700 85 include Frederick Bridge, 'Purcell's Editors', *Musical News* (23 May 1903), 486–7; and Arkwright, 'Purcell's Church Music', 246.

identified with lot 79 (of the first day) in the 1777 sale catalogue of William Gostling's music collection: 'Anthems in Score, 112 in number, by Aldrich, Blow, Croft, Purcell, and others, 2 vol. Folio, finely written by Mr. John Gostling, Sub Dean of St. Paul's'.[51] The 64 anthems in US-AUS Pre-1700 85, taken together with the 48 items in Gostling's second scorebook, US-Cn Case 7A/2, comprise the 112 total referred to in the catalogue.[52] The purchaser of the scorebooks in 1777 is unknown, but US-AUS Pre-1700 85 may not have been returned to Gostling's descendants until the twentieth century; there is some evidence to suggest that it was in John S. Bumpus's hands for a time.[53] As for its more recent whereabouts, the University of Texas acquired the manuscript in December 1965, when it purchased the entire inventory of the New York rare book firm of James F. Drake, Inc., at the time of its closing.[54]

US-AUS Pre-1700 85 has long been viewed as one of the most important non-autograph manuscript sources for Purcell's music, providing the primary text for a number of works surviving elsewhere in sources less directly connected to the composer. The manuscript's true distinctiveness comes, further, from the fact that Gostling was closely acquainted with Purcell and the Chapel Royal scene, and thus the information he provided in his scorebook about the dates of composition or first performances for a number of works (information in some instances not found anywhere else) can be viewed as authoritative. Bruce Wood has pointed out that

[51] *A Catalogue of the Scarce, Valuable and Curious Collection of Music, Manuscript and Printed, of the Reverend and Learned William Gostling* ([London], 1777), 12. (The unique copy is Lbl Hirsch.IV.1083.) The sale took place on 26–7 May 1777, just over two months after William's death.

[52] US-Cn Case 7A/2 was first identified as the work of Gostling in Robert Francis Ford, 'Minor Canons at Canterbury Cathedral: the Gostlings and their Colleagues' (Ph.D. thesis, University of California at Berkeley, 1984), 288–94, 893–9. While none of Croft's anthems are found in US-AUS Pre-1700 85, they are heavily represented in US-Cn Case 7A/2, including, according to Ford, several works not found elsewhere.

[53] In *A History of English Cathedral Music, 1549–1889*, 2 vols. (London, [1908]), I, 198–9, Bumpus notes with reference to Jeremiah Clarke's *I will love thee*: 'In a contemporary MS. score book in the writer's possession there is a setting of an anthem by Clark with the same title, but the music is entirely different. The copy has the following *colophon*: "Thanksgiving Anthem, Sept. 23, 1705, at S. Paul's. The Queen present for the Victory and Success in Flanders in passing the French lines".' The inscription after this anthem in US-AUS Pre-1700 85, p. 213 INV, is the same.

[54] James F. Drake established his business in 1905, and it was continued by his sons Marston E. and James H. Drake after his death in 1933; see S.M.M., 'The House of James F. Drake', *Antiquarian Bookman* (24 January 1966), 292–3. It is not known how long the manuscript resided on the shelves of the Drake shop prior to 1965, though it seems unlikely that it was in the possession of the Drakes since the Sotheby's sale of 1935, since the University of Texas and numerous other institutions and individuals were 'regular clients of theirs prior to 1965'. The Gostling Manuscript was 'indeed listed on an inventory of misc. items that were in the shop at the time of its closing'. We are indebted to Ms Dell Anne Hollingsworth (private correspondence, 2 July 1997), Music Specialist at the Ransom Center, for providing additional information about the University of Texas's acquisition of the Gostling Manuscript.

Gostling seems to have been intent on specifically recording the repertory of the Chapel Royal, providing every known Chapel Royal anthem composed by Blow and Purcell during the period 1685 to 1696, while conspicuously omitting works, such as coronation anthems, associated with Westminster Abbey.[55] The works Gostling inscribed with dates in US-AUS Pre-1700 85 range from 1686 to 1705, but the manuscript begins at each end (like Cfm 88 it opens with symphony anthems at the front, and full and verse anthems at the reverse, though Gostling's front end eventually gives way to non-concerted works) with a series of much earlier works, for example Blow's *O Lord I have sinned* of 1670 and a number of other anthems listed in the Chapel Royal 'Catalogue' of 1670 to 1676.

The parallel organizational scheme between US-AUS Pre-1700 85 and Cfm 88, while not unusual amongst scorebooks from the period, may in this case be more than coincidence. Gostling's first eight works at the reverse end, by Blow, Locke, Purcell and Child, correspond to the first eight works in Cfm 88 written by active composers, omitting the anthems by Batten, Tomkins and those from Barnard's *First Book* (see Table 2.5). Gostling's front end opens with six of the first ten items from the front of Cfm 88, omitting only the 'Club' anthem fragment, Blow's *Sing we merrily* (which Purcell completed in the second stage of his work in Cfm 88, so the work was probably incomplete when Gostling started his scorebook), and two works by Humfrey. A comparison of the readings of works in the two sources confirms that Gostling was working directly from Cfm 88: while he occasionally makes slight changes in layout, for example halving or doubling bar lengths, all matters of substance are replicated from one manuscript to the other with great consistency. Gostling's copy of Blow's *O sing unto the Lord ... for he hath done* is typical in its correlations to the copy, in Blow's hand, in Cfm 88: for example, Gostling reproduces an abbreviated opening of a symphony repeated from earlier in the work exactly as Blow lays it out, copying five notes and three directs in the first violin, and six notes and three directs in the bass, writing over the second violin and viola staves, as Blow did, 'Symphony again as before'.[56]

Gostling's cut-off points in working from Cfm 88 allow us to suggest a date of inception for US-AUS Pre-1700 85. His copy of Blow's *Sing unto the Lord O ye saints*, the last work in the front end copied from Cfm 88, is also the last work in the front of Cfm 88 to display the secretary 'e' in Purcell's hand. The last work Gostling copied from the reverse of Purcell's scorebook, Child's *Sing we merrily*, is the very first in the

---

[55] Wood, Review of *The Gostling Manuscript*, 118.    [56] US-AUS Pre-1700 85, p. 40; Cfm 88, fol. 12r.

## Table 2.5 University of Texas at Austin, Harry Ransom Humanities Research Center MS Pre-1700 85: contents

KEY:

Ascriptions in parentheses are from the tables of contents.

Relationship to Purcell's scorebooks (far right column)

    A = direct copy from Cfm 88 (followed by item number from Table 2.1)

    B = also in Cfm 88, no direct relationship

    C = also in Lbl R.M. 20.h.8, no direct relationship

| Item | Page | Title | Ascription | Original annotations | Relationship to Purcell scorebook |
|------|------|-------|------------|----------------------|-----------------------------------|
| 1 | 1 | Like as the hart | Mr Pel: Humphreys | | A (3) |
| 2 | 6 | O Lord my God | Mr Humphreys | | A (2) |
| 3 | 12 | Lord teach us to number our days | Mr Humphrey's | | A (6) |
| 4 | 17 | Cry aloud and spare not | Dr Blow | | A (9) |
| 5 | 24 | Sing unto the Lord O ye saints | Dr Blow | | A (10) |
| 6 | 36 | O sing unto the Lord . . . for he hath done | Dr Blow | | A (4) |
| 7 | 44 | I was glad | H.P. | | C |
| 8 | 50 | God showeth me his goodness | Mr Wm. Turner (Dr Turner) | | |
| 9 | 59 | Thy mercy O Lord | Dr Blow | | |
| 10 | 68 | It is a good thing to give thanks | H.P. | | C |
| 11 | 77 | They that go down to the sea in ships | Hen: Purcell | | C |
| 12 | 86 | Preserve me O God | Mr. Wm. Turner (Dr Turner) | 'Composed by Mr. Wm. Turner Aug: 24th. 1686' | |
| 13 | 95 | Behold I bring you glad tidings | Mr Henry Purcell | 'Composed by Mr Henry Purcell For Christmas day 1687' | |
| 14 | 105 | Blessed are they that fear the Lord | Mr Henry Purcell | 'Anthem for ye Thanksgiving appointed Jan 15th 1687/8 for ye Queens being w[i]th child'; 'Composed by Mr Henry Purcell. Jan: 12. 1687. For ye Thanksgiving Appointed in London & 12 miles round upon her Majesties being w[i]th Child. & on ye 29 following over England.' | |
| 15 | 110bis | Praise the Lord . . . O Lord my God | Mr Hen: Purcel | 'Composed by Mr Hen: Purcel. 1687' | C |
| 16 | 119 | Thy way O God is holy | Mr Hen: Purcel | 'Composed by Mr Hen: Purcel 1687' | C |
| 17 | 124 | O sing unto the Lord | Mr Purcell | 'Composed by Mr Purcell 1688' | C |

## Table 2.5  (*cont.*)

| Item | Page | Title | Ascription | Original annotations | Relationship to Purcell scorebook |
|------|------|-------|------------|----------------------|-----------------------------------|
| 18 | 138 | O sing praises unto our God | Mr Turner (Dr Turner) | 'Composed by Mr Turner 1687' | |
| 19 | 146 | I am well pleased | Dr Aldrich alias Charisimi | | |
| 20 | 153 | O sing unto the Lord . . . all the whole earth | Dr Blow | 'For Mr Weedons musical meeting'; named soloists: 'Mr Barns', 'Mr Williams', 'Mr Edwards', 'Mr Howel', 'Mr Church', 'Mr Estwick' | |
| 21 | 172bis | Ponder my words O Lord | Dr Blow | | |
| 22 | 176 | Be merciful unto me O God | Dr Blow | | |
| 23 | 183 | Thy hands have made me | JBlow | | |
| 24 | 185 | Bring unto the Lord O ye mighty | Dr Blow | | |
| 25 | 190 | O how amiable | Mr Tudway (Dr Tudway) | | |
| 26 | 198 | Praise the Lord O my soul | Mr J. Clark | named soloists: 'Mr Barns or Mr Elford' | |

[manuscript inverted]

| Item | Page | Title | Ascription | Original annotations | Relationship to Purcell scorebook |
|------|------|-------|------------|----------------------|-----------------------------------|
| 27 | 1 | O Lord I have sinned | Dr Blow | | A (14) |
| 28 | 5 | Lord let me know mine end | Mr Lock | | A (19) |
| 29 | 10 | Save me O God | Dr Blow | | A (18) |
| 30 | 13 | O God wherefore art thou absent | Dr Blow's | | A (16) |
| 31 | 17 | God is our hope and strength | (Dr Blow) | | A (15) |
| 32 | 23 | Save me O God | Hen. Purcell | | A (30) |
| 33 | 26 | Turn thy face from my sins | Mr Lock | | A (20) |
| 34 | 30 | Sing we merrily | Dr Child | | A (31) |
| 35 | 38 | O Lord thou hast searched me out | (Dr Blow) | | |
| 36 | 43 | Lord how are they increased | Dr Blow | | |
| 37 | 48 | Hear O heavens | P.H. | | |
| 38 | 52 | Blessed be the Lord my strength | Dr Blow | 'Composed by Dr Blow June 30. 1688' | |
| 39 | 58 | Blessed is the man*a* | (Mr Purcell) | 'Anthem for ye Charter-house sung upon ye Founders day by Mr Barincloe & Mr Bowman' | |
| 40 | 63 | Thy righteousness O God | Dr Blow | 'Anthem composed by Dr Blow, Aug: 1693' | |
| 41 | 73 | Lord what is man | Mr. Wm. Turner (Dr Turner) | | |
| 42 | 78 | O give thanks | Mr Hen: Purcell | 'Composed by Mr Purcell. 1693' | |
| 43 | 86 | Turn us again | Dr John Blow | 'Composed by Dr John Blow Septemb: 1694' | |
| 44 | 95 | The way of God is an undefiled way | Mr Purcell | 'November ye 11th 1694 King William then return[e]d from Flanders' | |

## Table 2.5 (*cont.*)

| Item | Page | Title | Ascription | Original annotations | Relationship to Purcell scorebook |
|------|------|-------|-----------|---------------------|----------------------------------|
| 45 | 102 | We will rejoice in thy salvation | Dr Blow | '1696 Anthem made upon ye discovery of ye plot against King William Sung April 16: 1696 the Thanksgiving Day'; 'Composed by Dr Blow. Ap[ril] 9th 1696 Performed ye 16th following at Whitehall.' | |
| 46 | 109 | The Lord is king | J anonimous B | | |
| 47 | 117 | The Lord even the most mighty | Dr Blow | 'comp: 1687' | |
| 48 | 122 | Sing unto God | Hen: Purcell | 'Composuit 1687' | |
| 49 | 125 | My song shall be alway | (Mr Purcell) | | |
| 50 | 130 | O Lord thou art my God | Dr. Jo: Blow | 'Composed by Dr. Jo: Blow June 19 1688' | |
| 51 | 135 | The Lord is king the earth may be glad | Mr Hen: Purcel | 'Composed by Mr Hen: Purcel. 1688' | |
| 52 | 141 | Lord remember David | Dr Blow | '1698' | |
| 53 | 147 | Blessed is he that considereth the poor | H: Purcell | | |
| 54 | 153 | Not unto us O Lord | Mr Lock | | |
| 55 | 154 | Thy beauty O Israel | (Dr Aldrich upon Mr Wise) | | |
| 56 | 166 | Be not wroth | (Mr Bird & Dr Aldrich) | | |
| 57 | 169 | I was glad | Mr F. Piggott | | |
| 58 | 173 | Praise the Lord O Jerusalem | Mr Jer: Clark | | |
| 59 | 176 | Is it true | Mr Tudway (Dr Tudway) | 'Sung before Queen Anne at Windsor July 12. 1702. by Dr Turner. Mr Damascene & Jo: Gostling' | |
| 60 | 181 | O Lord God of my salvation | Dr Blow | | B |
| 61 | 186 | Funeral Sentences | Mr Purcell | | B |
| 62 | 190 | Sing O heavens | Mr Tudway (Dr Tudway) | | |
| 63 | 196 | I will love thee . . . my stony rock | Mr Jer: Clark | | |
| 64 | 203 | I will love thee . . . it is God | Mr Jer: Clark | 'Thanksgiving Anthem Aug: 23. 1705'; 'Thanksgiving Anthem Sept 23. 1705 at St Pauls ye Queen present for ye victory & success in fflanders, in passing ye ffrench lines. Composed By Mr Jer: Clark Organist of St Pauls' | |

Folio, 435 × 295 mm. Watermarks and rastrology: see Table 2.6.

Copyist: John Gostling

---

[a] Version for alto and bass; tenor part (different hand) inserted between pp. 62 and 63.

**Table 2.6 Paper types, collation and rastrology in University of Texas at Austin, Harry Ransom Humanities Research Center MS Pre-1700 85**

| Layer | Pages | Watermark/countermark | Quiring |
|---|---|---|---|
| 1 | 1–56 | Angoumois fleur-de-lys with 'AJ'/ 'IHS' (backwards 'S') with 'PT' | 6; 4 (2 missing); 4; 4; 8; 4 |
| 2 | 57–84 | Angoumois fleur-de-lys/'IHS' | 4; 4; 4; 2 |
| 3 | 85–108bis | Angoumois fleur-de-lys/'PB' | 4; 4 (2 missing); 4; 4 |
| 4 | 109bis–116 | same as layer 3 | 4 |
| 5 | 117–24 | same as layer 2 | 4 |
| 6 | 125–40 | Angoumois fleur-de-lys with 'AI'/'IV' | 4; 4 |
| 7 | 141–50 | Angoumois fleur-de-lys with 'HC'/'PB' | 6 (p. 140/i is a stub) |
| 8 | 151–62 | simple fleur-de-lys/'AI IC' | 6 |
| 9 | 163–74 | same as layer 7 | 8 (1 missing) |
| 10 | 175–213 INV | Angoumois fleur-de-lys/'IV' | 8; 8 |

[manuscript inverted]

| Layer | Pages | Watermark/countermark | Quiring |
|---|---|---|---|
| 11 | 1–40 INV | same as layer 1 | 4; 4; 4; 4; 4 |
| 12 | 41–56 INV | same as layer 7 | 4; 4 |
| 13 | 57–64 INV | same as layer 1 | 4 (single folio inserted between pp. 62 and 63 INV) |
| 14 | 65–80 INV | same as layer 8 | 4; 4 |
| 15 | 81–96 INV | same as layer 10 | 4; 4 |
| 16 | 97–116 INV | same as layer 8 | 4; 4 (2 missing); 4 |
| 17 | 117–24 INV | pp. 117–18 and 123–4 INV: same as layer 10; pp. 119–22 INV: same as layer 7 | 4 |
| 18 | 125–32 INV | same as layer 3 | 4 |
| 19 | 133–64 INV | same as layer 8 | 4; 6; 6 [stub visible between pp. 164 and 165 INV; its relation to the adjacent quires is unclear] |
| 20 | 165–76 INV | Angoumois fleur-de-lys with 'HC'/'IB' | 6 |
| 21 | 177–212 INV | same as layer 10 | 6; 8; 4 |

Rastrology: sixteen staves throughout.

| Layer | Staves in rastrum | Rastrum span | Rastrum profile |
|---|---|---|---|
| 1 | 4 | 85.5 | 12.5(12)13(12.5)12(11.5)12 |
| 2 | 4 | 83 | 11.5(12)12(12.5)10.5(12.5)12 |
| 3 | 4 | 84 | 11(12)11.5(13)11.5(12.5)12.5 |
| 4 | 4 | 83 | 12.5(12.5)11.5(13)11.5(11.5)10.5 |
| 5 | same as layer 2 | | |
| 6 | 4 | 81 | 11(11.5)12(11.5)12(11.5)11.5 |
| 7 | 4 | 83.5 | 11(12)11.5(13)11(12.5)12.5 |

**Table 2.6** (*cont.*)

| Layer | Staves in rastrum | Rastrum span | Rastrum profile |
|---|---|---|---|
| 8 | 4 | 82 | 11.5(11.5)12.5(10.5)12.5(11.5)12 |
| 9 | 4 | 82.5 | 11.5(12.5)11.5(12)12(12)11 |
| 10 | 4 | 82 | 11.5(11.5)12.5(11.5)12(11)12 |
| 11 | same as layer 1 | | |
| 12 | same as layer 7 | | |
| 13 | 4 | 82 | 11.5(12)12(12)11.5(12)11 |
| 14 | same as layer 8 | | |
| 15 | same as layer 10 | | |
| 16 | same as layer 8 | | |
| 17 | same as layers 10 and 7 | | |
| 18 | 4 | 82.5 | 11(12)11.5(12.5)12(12)11.5 |
| 19 | same as layer 8 | | |
| 20 | same as layer 18 | | |
| 21 | same as layer 10 | | |

reverse of Cfm 88 to feature the italic 'e' in Purcell's hand. This suggests that Gostling began his own Chapel Royal scorebook, starting from the well-edited scores in Cfm 88, sometime in *c.*1678–79, at the time Purcell changed to the italic 'e'. He did not copy the works in Cfm 88 that follow Blow's *Sing unto the Lord O ye saints* and Child's *Sing we merrily* because they were not in the manuscript when he began his copying. Gostling's appointment on 28 February 1679 as a Gentleman of the Chapel Royal[57] may then have served as impetus for the inception of US-AUS Pre-1700 85, his own collection of Chapel Royal repertory.

A date of *c.*1679 for Gostling's earliest copying in US-AUS Pre-1700 85 is well supported by watermark evidence. Zimmerman mentions the presence of a single common watermark in the scorebook,[58] and in fact the fleur-de-lys, usually in its elaborate, Angoumois form, is found throughout; but there are many more variations in the makers' and factors' marks than he suggests. These are consistent, along with the stave rulings (produced with four-stave rastra throughout), within the various layers of the manuscript, some of which consist only of a single four-folio quire and suggest that Gostling at times acquired paper in small quantities (see Table 2.6). Each end of the manuscript begins with a comparatively large supply of paper featuring the fleur-de-lys watermark with a cursive 'AJ' below, the work of Abraham Janssen as factor, especially common in English sources *c.* 1679 and after. All of Gostling's copies made directly

[57] *RECM*, V, 76.   [58] Zimmerman, 'Anthems of Purcell', 59–60.

from Cfm 88 are found in these first layers. There are no contradictions between paper types and Gostling's dates in the manuscript, though the presence of newer counter-marks, such as the 'IV' of Jean Villedary, in its later layers supports the idea that the copying took place over a fairly broad timespan, from *c.* 1679 to 1705.

The presence of so many distinguishable layers of paper in US-AUS Pre-1700 85, together with the fact that a cancelled copy of Humfrey's *Like as the hart* was incorporated upside down as p. 40 INV, points to an unbound origin for the manuscript.[59] The ends of layers only occasionally correspond with the ends of particular works; apparently Gostling kept on copying, adding a new supply of paper whenever necessary. There is nothing in the front end of US-AUS Pre-1700 85 to suggest anything other than a chronological approach: after the anthems copied from Cfm 88 come five undated works (Table 2.5, items 7–11), including Purcell's *I was glad*, *It is a good thing to give thanks* and *They that go down to the sea in ships*, all composed and probably copied here in the early to mid 1680s. Then follow seven works (items 12–18), including five by Purcell, all inscribed by Gostling with dates of composition between 1686 and 1688, and all probably copied at about the same time, sometime after 1688 but before the early 1690s. The remaining eight works at the front (items 19–26) are undated and include only one symphony anthem, Blow's *O sing unto the Lord . . . all the whole earth*, inscribed for 'Mr Weedons musical meeting', a reference to Cavendish Weedon's Sacred Concert at Stationers' Hall on 31 January 1702.[60] These last anthems all exhibit an increased tendency in Gostling's hand to form open notes with a teardrop shape, a change that occurred in the mid-1690s in connection with his preparation of materials for the opening of the new St Paul's Cathedral, the choir of which opened for services in December 1697: in that task he was using Stephen Bing's partbooks Y M1(S) and some older books of services copied by Bing for St Paul's as sources and exemplars, and at times Gostling mimicked Bing's hand rather conspicuously.[61] Even after other Bing traits disappear from Gostling's copying the teardrop-shaped notes remain, though with some

---

[59] Ibid., 60. The manuscript survives in its original brown calf binding, which features modestly decorated panels on either side. 'Jo: Gostling' is inscribed above the panel on one side (that which opens to the symphony anthems).

[60] Spink, *Restoration*, 132. Cavendish Weedon was a lawyer admitted to Gray's Inn on 10 August 1677; in 1702 he promoted a series of concerts of sacred music 'for the better Encouragement of Piety and Morality and Discountenance of Vice'. See Michael Tilmouth, 'A Calendar of References to Music in Newspapers Published in London and the Provinces (1660–1719)', *RMARC* 1 (1961), 40–2; Joseph Foster, *The Register of Admissions to Gray's Inn, 1521–1889* (London, 1889), 325; Rosamond McGuinness and H. Diack Johnstone, 'Concert Life in England I', in *The Blackwell History of Music in Britain, IV: The Eighteenth Century*, ed. H. D. Johnstone and Roger Fiske, (Oxford, 1990), 32.

[61] Watkins Shaw, *The Bing-Gostling Part-books at York Minster: a Catalogue with Introduction* (Croydon, 1986), 112–14. See also Chapter 5 below.

inconsistency. The fact that the teardrop shape is present in this final group, while other Bing characteristics are not so much in evidence, suggests that a date of *c.* 1701–5 is about right for this stage of Gostling's work.

The reverse end of US-AUS Pre-1700 85 unfolds in a similar fashion, though with one or two easily explained inconsistencies. After the eight pieces copied from Cfm 88 follow three undated works (items 35–7) by Blow and Humfrey, probably copied not much later than the first group. Blow's *Blessed be the Lord my strength* comes next, inscribed 'Composed by Dr Blow June 30. 1688', and is followed by Purcell's probably contemporaneous *Blessed is the man* and then Blow's *Thy righteousness O God* composed in 'Aug: 1693'. The last of these is the first work in the reverse end to feature Gostling's 'Bing' hand, appropriately so given its date. The next work, however, William Turner's *Lord what is man*, exhibits Gostling's older hand, but Turner's anthem begins on the opening recto of a new gathering. Here and at one other point in the reverse of US-AUS Pre-1700 85 Gostling had to allow his final ordering to break from an otherwise chronological sequence because he had at times gone back and, apparently not wanting to waste paper, copied newer works beginning at the ends of unfinished quires. After Turner's anthem come five works (items 42–6), including Purcell's *O give thanks* and *The way of God is an undefiled way*, four of which are inscribed with dates of composition between 1693 and 1696, and all of which exhibit a pronounced use of the 'Bing' hand (see Illus. 2.6). The next four works (items 47–50), three of which are by Purcell, were all probably composed between 1687 and 1688 (only Purcell's *My song shall be alway* is undated here) and were copied (using the pre-'Bing' hand) onto three four-folio quires of varying paper types (pp. 117–40 INV); when it came time to order the pages for binding the only earlier position in which Gostling could have placed these gatherings was before Turner's undated *Lord what is man*, which would have confused the ordering of the manuscript even more, interrupting the early-1690s sequence with a group of dated works from the late 1680s. The reverse end concludes with fourteen works, the emphasis on Blow and Purcell (only two of the latter's works are in this group) giving way to figures like Henry Aldrich, Jeremiah Clarke and Thomas Tudway. Three are dated, ranging from 1698 to 1705, and this group was copied with the less-pronounced version of the 'Bing' hand and, for the last six works, on the same paper type used for the final copying at the front end.

Some measure of the value of US-AUS Pre-1700 85 as a source of Purcell's music can be made by surveying Gostling's copies of Purcell's works as they fall into two categories: those also found in the autograph scorebooks, Cfm 88 and Lbl R.M. 20.h.8 (see Table 2.4), and those found only in other, primarily non-autograph manuscripts. Seven of the seventeen of Purcell's works copied in US-AUS Pre-1700

Illus. 2.6 Henry Purcell: *O give thanks*, copied by John Gostling. University of Texas, Austin, Harry Ransom Humanities Research Center MS Pre-1700 85, p. 78 INV

85 may be found in one of the two Purcell scorebooks. While the relationship between US-AUS Pre-1700 85 and Cfm 88 is obviously a close one, shedding light on the former manuscript's earliest history, Gostling only copied two of Purcell's works found in Cfm 88. The first, *Save me O God*, copied by Gostling in his earliest phase of work, is, as has already been noted, a direct copy from Cfm 88, Gostling preserving Purcell's revised version of the anthem with its dotted rhythms at 'and avenge me in thy strength' and missing tenor parts at 'Behold God is my helper'.[62] The other is *Man that is born of a woman*, added to US-AUS Pre-1700 85 in the last stage of its compilation, sometime after 1698, and definitely not copied from Cfm 88, since Gostling's copy represents the middle stage of Purcell's work on the Funeral Sentences, whereas Cfm 88 contains Purcell's final thoughts.

[62] Gostling did, however, fill in one of the missing parts at a later time (US-AUS Pre-1700 85, p. 24).

Five more of Gostling's Purcell copies are found in Lbl R.M. 20.h.8, Purcell's scorebook devoted to symphony anthems, welcome songs and other secular works, three in Purcell's hand (*I was glad, It is a good thing to give thanks* and an incomplete version of *They that go down to the sea in ships*) and two (*O sing unto the Lord* and an incomplete copy of *Praise the Lord . . . O Lord my God*) in the hand of London A. Gostling's copies of *I was glad* and *It is a good thing to give thanks*, stemming from the early 1680s, were probably copied from Purcell's rough drafts such as those in Bu 5001, rather than from Lbl R.M. 20.h.8.[63] In *I was glad*, where direct comparison is possible, Gostling follows the rough draft's practice of indicating each *petite reprise* with repeat signs instead of writing them out in full with contrasting dynamics, as happens in R.M. 20.h.8; a minor variant in bar 175, making the last two notes of the solo alto part quavers rather than a dotted quaver and semiquaver, is also common to Bu 5001 and US-AUS Pre-1700 85. Alterations of time signatures, for example from '3' to '31', a tendency to double the length of Purcell's 3/4 bars, and slight changes in the position of clef changes seem to be ingrained and sometimes very sensible habits in Gostling's copying, but three minor variants in *It is a good thing to give thanks* again suggest that he was working from an earlier Purcell autograph than R.M. 20.h.8: in bar 92 he makes the last two notes of the bass part match the rhythm of the alto imitation; in bar 106 he gives the bass a different underlay; and in bar 137 he makes the last two notes of the vocal bass even crotchets. In bar 273 he corrects a minor slip in the alto part followed by Purcell in transcribing the copy in R.M. 20.h.8. The textual evidence offered by *I was glad* and *It is a good thing to give thanks* that Gostling copied his scores from Purcell's draft autographs gives his other transcriptions a special authority. *They that go down to the sea in ships* (unfinished by Purcell in Lbl R.M. 20.h.8) occupies an undated portion of US-AUS Pre-1700 85 between *It is a good thing to give thanks* and the first work of the 1686–88 series of symphony anthems: a date of *c.* 1682 is by no means impossible (see pp. 145–50), and the score certainly lacks the detailed annotation given to works written for specific occasions from 1686 onwards. For this and many of the subsequent anthems copied by Gostling, US-AUS Pre-1700 85 must be considered the primary source, and Gostling's scores of *Praise the Lord . . . O Lord my God* and *O sing unto the Lord* are almost certainly earlier than the London A copies in R.M. 20.h.8.

US-AUS Pre-1700 85 is of equal if not greater value as a source for several of Purcell's symphony anthems not in Lbl R.M. 20.h.8. Gostling's annotations to his copy of *Blessed are they that fear the Lord* suggest an immediate relationship to the

---

[63] *Works*, XIV (1973), vii, ix, xv, xvii, 1–20, 97–111.

autograph in Lbl Add. 30931: 'Anthem for ye Thanksgiving appointed Jan: 15th 1687/8 for ye Queens being w[i]th child' (p. 105) and 'Composed by Mr Henry Purcell. Jan: 12. 1687. For ye Thanksgiving Appointed in London & 12 miles round, upon her Majesties being w[i]th Child, & on ye 29 following over England' (p. 109bis). Gostling not only provides the date of the first performance but the precise date of composition, which is not found in the autograph. He must have made his copy immediately after Purcell produced his in Lbl Add. 30931, knowing exactly when Purcell wrote it. Similarly, Gostling's copy of *Behold I bring you glad tidings* is the source of the work most closely connected to Purcell and the earliest as well, and Gostling provides the unique source for the symphony anthem version of *Thy way O God is holy.* This work, like two others Gostling provides in the reverse end, without strings, *O give thanks* – this seems never to have been a symphony anthem[64] – and *My song shall be alway,* survive most commonly as organ verse anthems. Gostling's copy of *My song shall be alway,* lacking the extended string introduction and interludes found in the partially autograph performing material in Och 1188/9 and other Oxford sources (see Chapter 4), may represent an original version composed *c.* 1688 for the Chapel Royal (perhaps the only instance of Purcell revising an organ verse anthem as a symphony anthem).

US-AUS Pre-1700 85 also provides the primary text for four other non-symphony anthems by Purcell, for which no autographs (with one incomplete exception) survive. Gostling's is the earliest score of *Sing unto God,* inscribed 'Hen: Purcell Composuit 1687' (p. 124 INV), the only other roughly contemporary sources being the Chapel Royal partbooks, Lbl R.M. 27.a.1–6 and 8, and J-Tn N5/10, the latter an autograph (for this particular work only) with an errant title in Purcell's hand 'Sing unto the Lord'. Of similar vintage is Gostling's copy of *The Lord is king the earth may be glad* dated '1688', the next earliest being John Blow's of *c.*1698 in Mp BRm370Bp35,[65] a source with close repertorial ties to US-AUS Pre-1700 85. Another important source for *The Lord is king the earth may be glad,* though a late one probably from 1776, is William Flackton's copy in Lbl Add. 30931, fols. 75r–78r, which is inscribed on fol. 78r 'NB. This Copied from an original Copy of Mr Purcell's own handwriting'. Flackton's reading of this anthem is extremely close to Gostling's, but some slight differences in the figured bass together with Flackton's

---

[64] Gostling labels one of the ritornelli for organ, and in fact there is no source that provides string parts indicated as such. In *Works*, XXIX (1960), 197, Anthony Lewis and Nigel Fortune note that the string parts are shown in Henry Playford, ed., *Harmonia Sacra*, Book I, 2nd edn (London, 1703) 'on separate lines with treble clefs. The style of [the] ritornelli in this anthem suggests that they were intended for strings, though there is no specific indication to that effect.'

[65] Shaw, 'Autographs of John Blow', 87.

spelling of 'Halleluja' versus Gostling's 'Alleluia' (as well as several other spellings in Flackton's copy which seem more likely to be Purcell's than either Gostling's or Flackton's) suggest that both copied from the same draft autograph and that Flackton was here producing a kind of diplomatic copy.[66] The last Purcell anthem Gostling added to US-AUS Pre-1700 85 before the composer's death was *The way of God is an undefiled way*, which was composed on 'November ye 11th 1694 King William then return[e]d from Flanders' (p. 102 INV). For this work and *Blessed is he that considereth the poor*, entered in US-AUS Pre-1700 85 in *c.* 1698, Gostling again provides the earliest and most important text, with Mp BRm370Bp35 serving once more, for both works, as the next earliest corroborative source.

The complex origins of *Blessed is the man*, the last of this group of four, are made clearer by the material Gostling provides in US-AUS Pre-1700 85, easily the work's earliest source, inscribed 'Anthem for ye Charter-house sung upon ye Founders day by Mr Barincloe & Mr Bowman' (p. 58 INV). Zimmerman suggests that this was for 12 December 1688,[67] which is in accord with the style of Gostling's handwriting and the anthem's position in the manuscript, though one or two years later is equally possible. The Charterhouse, a former Carthusian monastery north of St Paul's, was in Purcell's time a charitable hospital and school, which conducted regular chapel services and employed an organist whose duties included 'teaching the poor Scholars to Sing'.[68] Its preacher was then John Patrick, whose metrical psalms served as Purcell's main source of texts for the sacred partsongs in Lbl Add. 30930, and Nigel Fortune has put forth the possibility that 'in his earliest years as a composer Purcell enjoyed a professional relationship with the Charterhouse', the sacred partsongs perhaps having been composed as a result of that relationship.[69] The so-called

---

[66] Further evidence of Flackton's desire to reproduce Purcell's handwriting comes from the reverse of the final page of this anthem (fol. 78v), where Flackton writes 'A Specimen of Mr Purcell's hand writing [the following made to resemble Purcell's hand] Arm–Heavns–Chorus–Earth Lord Gods. R R T H H K C E O F' and 'This Copied from a MS in The Revd Mr Jon. Gostling posession [sic] & of Mr Purcells hand writing. 1776 W. F.' An additional inscription notes 'Now in my possession Phil. Hayes.'

[67] Zimmerman, *Catalogue*, 8.

[68] Samuel Herne, *Domus Carthusiana, or an Account of the Most Noble Foundation of the Charter-House near Smithfield in London* (London, 1677); cited in Nigel Fortune, 'The Domestic Sacred Music', in *Essays on Opera and English Music in Honour of Sir Jack Westrup*, ed. F. W. Sternfeld et al. (Oxford, 1975), 64. See also Jonathan Keates, *Purcell* (London, 1995), 72–3; and Holman, *Henry Purcell*, 49. Stephen Porter (in 'Henry Purcell and the Charterhouse: Composer in Residence', *MT* 79 (1998), 14–17) suggests that *Blessed is the man* dates from the 1687 Founder's Day, but his argument is not well supported; nonetheless the work could have been used for that year's ceremonies, Gostling adding it to his scorebook in 1688 or after, perhaps explaining his omission of any indication of date.

[69] Fortune, 'Domestic Sacred Music', 64. For new evidence of Patrick's musical interests and identification of his music hand see Richard Charteris, 'A Newly Discovered Songbook in Poland with Works by Henry Lawes and his Contemporaries', *English Manuscript Studies 1100–1700* 8, forthcoming.

'Charterhouse' anthem was probably first a trio for alto, tenor and bass with continuo[70] (Thomas Tudway preserved this version in Lbl Harley 7340) composed several years before the version Gostling provides, possibly contemporaneously with the sacred partsongs on Patrick texts, which hints that the work may have had a Charterhouse connection since its inception. In preparing to reuse the work for the Founder's Day occasion Purcell probably felt that the tenor was unsatisfactory (it is often redundant with the bass or alto), and so he incorporated its most salient features into either the alto or bass in the version in US-AUS Pre-1700 85, with the result that the two solo lines given by Gostling are distinctly different from those in all other sources, except for Gostling's later copy in Ob MSS Tenbury 1176–80. At a later time the alto–bass duet was turned into an anthem when the final 'Alleluia' was expanded to four parts. Gostling initially copied only the duet in US-AUS Pre-1700 85, and then after a gap of several years (his change to teardrop-shaped notes indicates in *c.* 1693–4) added the final chorus mixing his usual spelling 'Alleluia' with the more Purcellian 'Halleluja', suggesting that he may have had a draft autograph of the chorus at hand. Sometime before Gostling had his scorebook bound he inserted a copy in someone else's hand of the original tenor solo (which was now unusable with the revised duet). In another scorebook, US-LAuc fC6966/M4/A627/1700, mostly copied by Daniel Henstridge (see Chapter 5), the final chorus is given alone, with the inscription 'To Blessed is the Man &c. The Charterhouse Anthem' (p. 230), implying that the chorus was disseminated separately and that others would know what to do with it. It is entirely possible that the version for three soloists and chorus is an early eighteenth-century conflation of the various material Purcell left behind.

### Rochester, Eastman School of Music, Sibley Music Library
### MS M2040/A628/Folio

The last of three manuscripts with an immediate, contemporary relationship to Cfm 88 is US-R M2040/A628/Folio, a scorebook mainly containing anthems by Purcell and Blow (Table 2.7), copied by London A, Purcell's chief assistant in Lbl R.M. 20.h.8, whose identity is explored in Chapter 4. Hughes-Hughes recognised a century ago that the R.M. 20.h.8 assistant and the copyist of US-R M2040/A628/Folio were one and the same,[71] when the latter source belonged to W. H. Cummings

---

[70] Zimmerman notes that 'Evidence from several MSS suggests that Purcell wrote an earlier version ... that required only two solo voices (tenor and bass) and no four-part chorus' (*Catalogue*, 9), but we have not found any manuscripts that support this claim.

[71] Hughes-Hughes, 'Henry Purcell's Handwriting', 81. We are grateful to Dr Peter Holman for the identification of Cummings's volume with US-R M2040/A628/Folio.

**Table 2.7** Rochester, Eastman School of Music, Sibley Music Library MS M2040/A628/Folio: contents

| Pages | (earlier pp.) | Title (Cfm 88 item no.) | Ascription | Copyist |
|---|---|---|---|---|
| 1–7 | | Hosanna to the son of David (17) | Orlando Gibbons | London A |
| 7–12 | | Lift up your heads (25) | Or Gibbons | London A |
| 13–20 | (21–8) | O God thou hast cast us out (40) | Mr H Pursell | London A |
| 21–4 | (35–8) | Save me O God (18) | Dr Blow | London A |
| 25–8 | (55–8) | Save me O God (30) | Mr H Pursells | London A |
| 29–38 | (59–68) | O sing unto the Lord . . . for he hath done (4) | Dr John Blow | London A |
| 39–42 | (83–[86]) | How long wilt thou forget me | Dr Gibbons | London A |
| 43–50 | (87–94) | O Lord thou art my God (45) 'Isaiah ye 25th vers 1st part ye 4th ye 7th 8th & 9th verses' | Mr H Pursell | London A |
| 51–66 | (105–[120]) | Sing unto the Lord O ye saints (inc.) (10) | Dr Blow[a] | London A |
| 67–70 | (121–4) | My God my soul is vexed (34) | Dr Blow | London A |
| 71–8 | (125–32) | Out of the deep | Mr H Pursell | London A |
| 79–82 | (149–52) | Thy way O God is holy | Dr Blow | London A |
| 83–6 | (153–6) | Lord how long wilt thou be angry (44) | HP | London A |
| 87–96 | (181–90) | Cry aloud and spare not (9) | [John Blow] | London A |
| 97–102 | (191–6) | O Lord God of my salvation (39) | Dr Blows | London A[b] |
| 103–10 | | The king shall rejoice | Mr Pelham Humphreyes | John Playford |

Folio, 456 × 338. Watermarks: Angoumois fleur-de-lys with countermark 'IHS/RC' (pp. 1–10, 17–20, 39–46, 51–2, 55–66 and 69–86); Angoumois fleur-de-lys and cursive 'AJ' with countermark 'IHS/PT' (pp. 11–16, 21–38, 47–50, 53–4, 67–8 and 87–102); arms of Strasbourg (pp. 103–10).

Rastrology: fifteen staves, ruled with a five-stave rastrum throughout.

| Pages | Rastrum span | Rastrum profile |
|---|---|---|
| 1–20, 39–50, 55–66, 71–86 | 123.5 | 13(15.5)13(16)13(13)13.5(13)13.5 |
| 21–4, 29–38, 67–70, 87–102 | 125.5 | 13(14.5)14(16.5)13(13.5)13.5(13.5)14 |
| 25–8, 51–4 | 122.5 | 12.5(14)13(13.5)12.5(16.5)12(16.5)12 |
| 103–10 | 107 | 11(11.5)12(12)11.5(13)11.5(12.5)12 |

[a] Written on top of 'Mr Locke'; cf. Cfm 88.     [b] With a correction slip in W. H. Husk's hand.

(1831–1915). Previous owners include W. H. Husk (1814–87), who inserted a correction in the midst of Blow's *O Lord God of my salvation*, and E. T. Warren-Horne (1730–94), whose signature (along with Cummings's signature and book-plate) appears on fol. [iii]r, though Warren-Horne's is on a small rectangular slip pasted to this folio. The recent pencil inscription '10/6/53 Gottlieb 85.00', on the table of contents page, fol. [iv]r (which was probably drawn up in the late eighteenth century, to judge by cross-references to Boyce and the presence of a 'J WHATMAN' countermark), refers to the Sibley Music Library's 1953 acquisition of the manuscript from the music publisher and rare book dealer Ernest E. Gottlieb of Beverly Hills, California, for $85.00.[72]

[72] Information kindly provided by Ms Mary Wallace Davidson, Librarian at the Sibley Music Library.

In all likelihood US-R M2040/A628/Folio came into its present form in the nineteenth century, during Husk's ownership. The last anthem in the book, Pelham Humfrey's *The king shall rejoice*, is on smaller, differently ruled paper and is in a different hand, that of John Playford.[73] Each page of the Humfrey has been guarded into the binding on stubs showing portions of a Fortune-on-globe watermark and 'VAN GELDER' countermark, a combination also seen on the flyleaves fol. [iii] and pp. [111–12]; this paper type was widely available during the first half of the nineteenth century.[74] Husk's correction to Blow's *O Lord God of my salvation* is also guarded into the volume, and the stub looks to be of the same material as the other 'VAN GELDER' pages, though here traces of the watermark are not present. The lacquered parchment binding may come from this time as well or possibly later; four additional flyleaves, fols. [i-ii] and pp. [113–16], are of apparently newer, unmarked paper. Embossed on the spine is the inscription 'Anthems in Purcell's Autograph', which must have led Hughes-Hughes to consider the volume amongst purported autographs.[75] It is unlikely that Cummings would have described the volume as such given his careful assessment of Purcell's hand in US-NHb Osborn 515, fol. iir.

The super-royal size paper (456 × 338 mm) of the main body of the manuscript (the material copied by London A) all bears the Angoumois fleur-de-lys watermark, occasionally with Janssen's cursive 'AJ' factor's mark, and the 'IHS' countermark with two different makers' marks in evidence, 'RC' or 'PT' (see Table 2.7). This slight variety in paper type, taken together with the rastrology (all of the pages were ruled with one of three similar and recurring five-stave rastra), suggest that London A acquired leftover paper in a few small batches or perhaps from an extensive stock. The first and last pages of London A's copying (pp. 1 and 102) are considerably darker than the rest of the volume and have frayed edges, indicating that these were the outside pages of an unbound collection for some time. US-R M2040/A628/Folio may have once been a much larger volume: an earlier pagination is readable at various points, running to p. 196 (= p. 102). It may be that a later owner discarded works by composers less interesting than Purcell, Blow or the Gibbonses, though the current pagination looks as if it was added at an early stage as well, so the precise nature of what once comprised the volume is beyond speculation.

Twelve of the fifteen works copied by London A in US-R M2040/A628/Folio are also found in Cfm 88, and there is no shortage of evidence to suggest that these derive

---

[73] On Playford's hand see Thompson, 'Manuscript Music in Purcell's London'.
[74] See Churchill, p. 14; Heawood no. 1365; and J. S. G. Simmons, *Addenda and Corrigenda to Heawood's Watermarks* (Amsterdam, 1970), p. v.     [75] Hughes-Hughes, 'Henry Purcell's Handwriting', 81.

directly from Purcell's scorebook. London A reproduces the barring and text under-lay in the works by Orlando Gibbons, which Purcell edited from the Barnard partbooks; he tries to replicate the unusual scripture reference (and its orthography) Purcell provided for *O Lord thou art my God* in Cfm 88 (see Tables 2.1 and 2.7); and he even mimics some of the calligraphic features of Blow's handwriting in Cfm 88: for example, on p. 32 of US-R M2040/A628/Folio London A matches the bulging double 'l' in 'Israell', found in Blow's copy of *O sing unto the Lord . . . for he hath done* (Cfm 88, fol. 11r), quite precisely, though A reverts to his usual double 'l' in the next system in the word 'all'. Also, A's copy of Blow's *Sing unto the Lord O ye saints* is incomplete, like Purcell's; Purcell gave no ascription, but from the table in Cfm 88 the work appears to be by Locke, to whom A initally misattributes it.

Although London A's copy of Purcell's *Save me O God*[76] has the tenor parts complete at bars 27–35 (these were left unfinished by Purcell in Cfm 88), here too A's work descends from Purcell's autograph and may be of far greater importance than previously recognised: London A provides all of the revised dotted rhythms at 'and avenge me in thy strength' (bars 6–9), which were new to the Cfm 88 copy, and his barring and layout throughout match Purcell's almost exactly (Illus. 2.7; cf. Illus. 2.4). London A also gives Purcell's revised version of the cadential material in the alto at bars 33–4, a passage which shows far greater melodic motion than Purcell's earlier effort with its reiteration of G above middle C, seen in William Isaack's copy in Cfm 117. This is significant in light of London A's readings of the omitted tenor parts, which match those in Cfm 117 with the exception of one important detail: in the tenor cantoris part (labelled as such in Isaack's, Purcell's and London A's copies), at the same place where Purcell revised the alto, London A supplies a G, five notes before the cadence, where Isaack had given an E♭. This change prevents parallel octaves with the *revised* alto material, and thus suggests that the version in US-R M2040/A628/Folio may represent Purcell's final thoughts on *Save me O God*, in the handwriting of a copyist working in close proximity or perhaps even under his supervision.

The broad consistency in stave ruling, paper type and handwriting in US-R M2040/A628/Folio implies a relatively brief period of copying, probably, as in-dicated by the repertory it contains, in *c.*1685. US-R M2040/A628/Folio, as noted above, is the only contemporary concordance for two Purcell anthems in Cfm 88, *Lord how long wilt thou be angry* and *O Lord thou art my God*, which, given the

---

[76] *Works*, XIII (1988), 133–41, 164–5; it should be noted that US-R M2040/A628/Folio was not amongst the sources consulted for this edition, nor were Purcell's earlier variants in sources such as Cfm 117 or Y M1(S) listed in the critical commentary.

Illus. 2.7  Henry Purcell: *Save me O God*, copied by London A. Rochester, Eastman School of Music, Sibley Music Library MS M2040/A628/Folio, p. 25

increasingly limited incidence of the secretary 'r' in Purcell's hand, could not have been copied before *c.*1684 (see Table 2.2). Another Purcell anthem copied by London A, *Out of the deep*, seems to have been composed too late for inclusion in Cfm 88: stylistic and calligraphic considerations suggest a date of 1685 or after. But a separate draft autograph exists in Lbl Add. 30931, fols. 67–70, and this in all likelihood served as A's exemplar: there are few discrepancies between the two copies, London A largely preserving Purcell's figuring, indications of ornamentation and, for the most part, barring (including the latter's irregular barring at 'But there is mercy with thee'). While the music in US-R M2040/A628/Folio could have all been performed in the Chapel Royal in the 1680s, the manuscript has a decidedly different character from that of the other scorebooks discussed in this chapter (even if we consider the possibility that it was once twice as large): it lacks the depth of repertory of the other sources, and there is no clear organisational plan in its contents, perhaps indicating that this is the work of an apprentice musician eager to learn from his elders rather than material copied for an immediate practical purpose.

# 3

## *British Library Additional MS 30930 and its repertories*

The main contents of Lbl Add. 30930 are fantazias, sonatas and devotional songs for three, four and five voices and continuo (Tables 3.1–3). The manuscript therefore contains a primarily domestic repertory different in overall character from that of the other major autograph scorebooks Cfm 88 and Lbl R.M. 20.h.8.

Ownership of Add. 30930 can be traced back to the mid-eighteenth century, when it seems to have belonged to Philip Hayes. Four partsongs in Lbl Add. 33235, which Hayes owned in 1757, were altered by him to conform with the readings of Add. 30930, and Hayes states on fol. 14v of Add. 33235 that he has made corrections 'from Henry Purcell's own copy in my possession'. Later the manuscript was owned by E. T. Warren-Horne, whose list of contents pasted to fol. 72 is written on the reverse of a pamphlet issued between 1779 and 1789.[1] For some reason Add. 30930 was not sold immediately after Warren-Horne's death in 1797 but formed lot 180 in 'the Entire Reserved Part of Vocal and Instrumental Music in Score of Edmund Tho. Warren Horne' auctioned by Leigh and Sotheby in January 1810 (S.C.S. 66 (5))[2] and was bought for £2 5s by John Parker, Rector of St George's, Botolph Lane. The manuscript then appears in Parker's sale of 1813 (S.C. 1076 (5)), where it was sold to T. Jones; the catalogue of Jones's sale in 1826 (S.C. 1077 (3)) describes it as 'in Purcell's own hand-writing bound in one thick volume'. By 1849 Add. 30930 belonged to Joseph Warren, who gave a detailed account of it in his edition of Boyce's *Cathedral Music*.[3]

---

[1] *A Short State of the Case respecting the intended Canal from Cromford in the County of Derby to communicate with the River Trent through the Erewash canal.* The Cromford canal was constructed between 1789 and 1795; the Erewash, which clearly pre-dated the pamphlet, between 1777 and 1779. See J. R. Ward, *The Finance of Canal Building in Eighteenth-Century England* (London, 1974), 38, 39.

[2] References are to the British Library's collection of sale catalogues.

[3] William Boyce, *Cathedral Music*, ed. Joseph Warren (London, 1849), II, 18.

Table 3.1 London, British Library Additional MS 30930: vocal music. Contents and concordances

| Folio | Title | Och 628 page | Ob MS Mus.c.28 fol. | Ob MS Tenbury 1175 page | Lbl Add. 33234 fol. | Lbl Add. 33235 fol. | Bu 5002 page | J-Tn 0–1–54 page |
|---|---|---|---|---|---|---|---|---|
| 3r | Plunged in the confines[a] | 39 | 100r | 264 | 154r | 80r | | |
| 4r | O all ye people | 3 | 103v | 258 | 156v | 17v | | 6 |
| 6r | When on my sick bed | 130 | 106r | 272 | 151r | 14v | 147 | 122 |
| 7v | Gloria Patri et Filio | 1 | | 254 | | | | |
| 8v | Jehova quam multi sunt hostes | 135 | | 248 | | | | |
| 11r | Beati omnes | 141 | | 242 | | | | |
| 13r | Domine non est exaltatum (inc.) | | | | | | | |
| 14r | Lord not to us (inc.) | | | 270 | | | | |
| 15v | Ah! few and full (inc.) | | 115v | 297 | | | | |
| 18r | O Lord our governor | 125 | 107v | 290 | | | | |
| 20v | O I'm sick of life | 121 | 109v | 302 | | | 153 | |
| 22r | Lord I can suffer | | 111v | 306 | | | | |
| 23v | Hear me O Lord and that soon (inc.) | | | 268 | | | | |
| 24v | Since God so tender a regard | 111 | 119r | 312 | | 7v | 141 | 117 |
| 26r | Early O Lord my fainting soul | 116 | 113v | 283 | | 10v | | |
| 28r | Hear me O Lord the great support | | 120v | 277 | | | | |

[a] Also in Bu 5001, fol. 172r (autograph).

Thereafter it came into the possession of Julian Marshall, who in 1878 sold it to the British Museum.[4] The current pencil foliation dates from September 1878, when a note was made on fol. 72v giving the present number of 'ii + 72' copied folios, and the binding from 1895, after several detached folios had been exhibited in commemoration of Purcell's bicentenary. The unused folios which now interrupt several works were not mentioned by Joseph Warren in 1849; they must reflect the condition in which the volume was acquired from Julian Marshall and a decision by the Museum's staff at the time not to attempt to restore the original collation.

CONTENTS

The sacred partsongs are copied from one end of the manuscript, where the flyleaf bears the date '1680', and instrumental music from the other. No page or folio

[4] Arthur Searle, 'Julian Marshall and the British Museum: Music Collecting in the Later Nineteenth Century', *BLJ* 11 (1985), 80.

Table 3.2 London, British Library Additional MS 30930: instrumental music other than sonatas. Contents and concordances

| Folio | Work* | US-NYp Drexel 5061 page | Lbl Add. 31435 folios | Lbl Add. 33236 folio | Och 620 page |
|---|---|---|---|---|---|
| 71r | Fantazia 1 | 92 | | 65v† | |
| 70v | Fantazia 2 | | 17v; 34v; 51v; 68v | 66r | |
| 69v | Fantazia 3 | | | 67r | |
| 67r | Fantazia 4 | 14 | | | |
| 66r | Fantazia 5 | 17 | | | |
| 65r | Fantazia 6 | 20 | | | |
| 64r | Fantazia 7 | 23 | | | |
| 63r | Fantazia 8 | 26 | | | |
| 62r | Fantazia 9 | 32 | | | |
| 61r | Fantazia 10 | 29 | | | |
| 60r | Fantazia 11 | 35 | | | |
| 59r | Fantazia 12 | 38 | | | |
| 58r | Fantazia 13§ | | | | |
| 57r | Pavan of Four Parts | 40 | | | |
| 56r | Chacony | | | 65r† | |
| | Suite in G major: | | | | |
| 54r | Overture | | | | |
| 53v | [Air] | | | | |
| 53r | [Borry, Minuet]‡ | | | | |
| 52v | [Jigg]‡ | | | | |
| 50r | Fantazia upon One Note | 55 | | | 129 |
| 48r | In Nomine of Six Parts | 57 | | | |
| 46r | In Nomine of Seven Parts | 59 | | | |

* Titles as given in *Works*, XXXI (1990).

† Most of this folio has been torn out, but the Chacony could not in any case have been completed on a single page before Fantazia 1 on fol. 65v.

§ Dated 24 February 1683 and abandoned by Purcell after thirty-one bars.

‡ Outer parts only: space left at the top of fol. 52v for another movement.

numbering was applied in the seventeenth century, and Tables 3.1–4 follow the current British Library pencil foliation, which treats the vocal section as the 'front' of the book and omits all folios on which nothing has been written. Such folios are identified here by reference to the previous copied folio, for example [15/iii].

   With the possible exception of the incomplete suite in G major[5] none of the music in Add. 30930 is likely to have been composed in connection with Purcell's court

[5] Holman, *Henry Purcell*, 13, 66–8.

Table 3.3 London, British Library Additional MS 30930: sonatas. Contents and concordances

| Folio | Sonatas 1697 | Ob MSS Mus.Sch. E.400–3 no. | Och 3 fol. | Och 620 page | J-Tn N2/15 no. |
|---|---|---|---|---|---|
| 43v | I | 42 | | | 32 |
| 41v | II[a] | 41 | | | 33 |
| 39v | III[b] | 43 | | | 34 |
| 37v | IX[c] | | 47r | 87 | 40 |
| 35v | VII | | 49v | | 39 |
| 34r | VIII | | 51v | | |
| 31r | X | | | 23 | 38 |

[a] first violin also in Lbl Add. 63627, fol. 14v.
[b] first violin also in Lbl Add. 63627, fol. 16v.
[c] also in Cfm 652, fol. 42 inv; US-Cu 959, no. 32; CH Cap. VI/I/I, p. 1; US-LAuc *M401.P98s, no. 2 of MS section; J-Tn N3/35, fols. 35v–38r; Y M57/1–4(S).

appointments, the contrapuntal Chacony being in some ways more akin to the fantazias than to the ceremonial chaconnes of Lully or Purcell's own later movements in the same form. The Pavan of Four Parts, perhaps composed as a tribute to John Jenkins after his death on 27 October 1678, is obliquely related to the court through its reference to the three-violin-and-bass texture used by Jenkins and Baltzar in the early 1660s,[6] but belongs with the fantazias in the realm of domestic chamber music. Similarly, with the exception of *Hear me O Lord and that soon*, which exists in a different version as a full-scale anthem,[7] the vocal music is essentially of a private devotional character with many points of resemblance to William and Henry Lawes's *Choice Psalms*.[8]

John Patrick's *A Century of Select Psalms*, the source of many of Purcell's partsong texts, was listed in the Stationers' Company *Term Catalogue* for November 1679, apparently confirming the evidence of the flyleaf inscription 'The Work's of Hen: Purcell Anno Dom. 1680' and the individual dates of the four-part fantazias that most of the manuscript's contents were composed in 1680. But the *imprimatur* of Patrick's book is dated 21 November 1678, so it is possible that Purcell composed much of the vocal repertory of Add. 30930 in 1678 or 1679, perhaps using pre-publication prints or a final manuscript copy of the text. Certain codicological

[6] Ibid., 72–3, and Holman, *Four and Twenty Fiddlers*, 276–81.
[7] See Robert Manning, 'Revisions and Reworkings in Purcell's Anthems', *Soundings* 9 (1982), 33–5.
[8] Holman, *Henry Purcell*, 49.

features (see below) also suggest that the history of Add. 30930 might be much more complex than the inscribed dates reveal.

## CODICOLOGY

The paper of Add. 30930, of 'medium' size and marked with an Angoumois fleur-de-lys, was made by Etienne Touzeau, whose initials 'ET' appear in the countermark beneath the symbol 'IHS' (see Illus. 1.2 and 1.3). The same watermarks appear in Lbl R.M. 20.h.8 and other manuscripts listed below, including CH Cap. VI/I/I, in which copying may have been started in 1677, and Och 628, probably completed in unbound form in 1678.

| | |
|---|---|
| Lbl Add. 30930 | 'The Work's of Hen: Purcell Anno Dom. 1680' |
| Lbl R.M. 20.h.8 | |
| CH Cap. VI/I/I | 'Jo: Walter his Book Anno Domino 1680':* ruled as R.M. 20.h.8 |
| Och 628 | This paper up to p. 80 only: Blow autograph |
| Lbl Harl. 1501 | 'Scritto a richesta di Monsieur Didie in Londra Anno Domini 1681'. Reggio autograph |

*Binding date; probably started in 1677

The consistent paper type and stave ruling throughout Add. 30930 would normally indicate that the source had always been used as a bound volume. A marked variation in Purcell's hand, some of which might result from copying before and after binding, and the irregularity of the probable seventeenth-century collation (Table 3.4) nevertheless suggest that at first Purcell worked upon separate pages, although further works were undoubtedly entered after the volume was bound. The manuscript offers enough internal evidence to enable its first collation to be reconstructed with some confidence: whatever arrangement existed must have allowed the pieces now interrupted by blank pages to have been continuous; the watermark and countermark sides of the 'a' and 'b' moulds must correspond in type and orientation, and the ruling pattern, in which the sixteen staves, though evenly spaced, are drawn in two blocks of six and one of four, must similarly match in conjunct folios. Much of the visible stitching appears to mark the centre of original gatherings, and a number of individual sheets have unusually clear or opaque textures which enable their opposite halves to be related. In the following discussion and in Table 3.4 gatherings are lettered A–Y omitting I, O, U and W: existing gatherings are identified by plain letters and hypothetical originals, where they differ from the present gatherings, in italics.

The folios containing vocal music appear to have been quired thus: $A^8$ $B^6$ *C2*$^6$ $D^8$ *E1*$^6$ *E2*$^4$ $F^4$, though there is sometimes no means of knowing whether blank sheets have been removed from gatherings containing fewer than eight folios. Two groups of partsongs and one individual work (items 1–3, 10–12 and 15), which begin at or near the first folio of four separate gatherings and are completed within the same gathering, were copied consecutively in that order by John Walter in Ob MS Mus.c.28, fols. 100–24, followed by three further partsongs, Add. 30930, items 9, 14 and 16, which extend across successive gatherings of the autograph. Walter's manuscript implies that the seven works contained within separate gatherings of Add. 30930 were available to him earlier than those extending from one gathering to the next, either because he had access to the unbound quires or because he began his transcription from the bound autograph before the later works had been composed. The first page of the sonata section of Add. 30930, fol. 43v, is discoloured, as though it was an exposed outer leaf for some time, so some gatherings could have had a prior independent existence.

The order of copying of the various genres of instrumental music in Add. 30930 is less obvious than that of the vocal music because of the absence of a revealing concordance such as Ob MS Mus.c.28. The fact that Purcell began the four-part fantazia sequence on 10 June 1680 in the middle of Gathering X, rather than across the first opening or on the first page, suggests that he intended the gathering to follow a three-part section, the extent of which was already approximately decided and included Gathering Y. If the obviously misplaced blank sheet forming fols. 64/v and 68/ii is disregarded, it can be seen that Gathering X is of six folios while *TV* is of ten: unlike the ten-folio gatherings in the vocal music section, all of which could result from the misplacement of unused sheets, *TV* must have consisted of ten folios from the time of copying. This irregularity, more likely to be caused by Purcell than by a binder assembling blank pages, suggests that the four-part fantazias were copied before the manuscript was bound, though with allowance for binding in the near future revealed by the room left for further three-part compositions.

The earliest copying in Add. 30930 might be represented by the Pavan (fol. 57r), which begins in the first opening (inverted) of Gathering S. Purcell may not have realised he would be able to copy the whole movement on a single page and so started inside the gathering rather than on the first recto, now 57v: the gathering then contains three unused pages before the Chacony on fols. 56r–55r, perhaps because Purcell intended the Pavan as the first movement of a three-violin suite modelled on the works for the same combination of instruments by John Jenkins.

## Table 3.4 London, British Library Additional MS 30930: current and possible original collation

KEY:

Unwritten folios are not numbered in the manuscript and are here indicated thus: 62/i. Torn-out pages of which there is any evidence are shown in the same way.

Folios tabulated within square brackets [57/i] are hypothetical; original gatherings that no longer exist are identified in italics, e.g. *Original Gathering E1*.

-------- = visible stitching

Up = block of four staves at the top of the page
Lo = block of four staves at the bottom of the page

Where the stave ruling is the same throughout a gathering the description is given for the first folio only.

a = Fleur-de-lys watermark a       IHSa = Countermark a
b = Fleur-de-lys watermark b       IHSb = Countermark b

References to 'top' or 'bottom' or to inverted watermarks (↓) assume that the manuscript is viewed the right way up for the vocal music and inverted for the instrumental, following the current British Library foliation.

| Folio | Watermark | Ruling | | Contents and comments |
|-------|-----------|--------|---|-----------------------|
| **Gathering A** | | | | |
| 3 | IHSa | Up | 3r–4r | *Plunged in the confines* (1) |
| 4 | a↓ | | 4r–5v | *O all ye people* (2) |
| 5 | b | | | |
| 6 | b↓ | | 6r–7r | *When on my sick bed* (3) |
| 7 | IHSb↓ | | 7v–8r | *Gloria Patri* (4) |
| 8 | IHSb | | 8v–11r | *Jehova quam multi sunt hostes* (5) |
| 9 | IHSa↓ | | | |
| 10 | a | | | |
| **Gathering B** | | | | |
| 11 | IHSb | Lo | 11r–12v | *Beati omnes* (6) |
| 12 | IHSb | Up | | |
| 13 | IHSb | Up | 13r | *Domine non est exaltatum* (inc.; 7) |
| 13/i | b | Up | | |
| 13/ii | b | Up | | |
| [13/iii | b] | | | guard stub |
| **Gathering C** | | | | |
| [13/iv | IHSb] | Lo | | guard stub |
| 13/v | IHSb | Lo | | |
| 13/vi | b↓ | Lo | | |
| 13/vii | IHSb | Lo | | |
| 13/viii | IHSa | Lo | | |
| 13/ix | IHSb | Up | | |

## Table 3.4 (*cont.*)

| Folio | Watermark | Ruling | | Contents and comments |
|---|---|---|---|---|
| 13/x | b | Up | | |
| 13/xi | a | Lo | | |
| 14 | b | Lo | 14r | *Lord not to us* (inc.; 8); 14v–15r blank |
| 15 | IHSb↓ | Lo | 15v | *Ah! few and full of sorrows* (inc.; 9) |
| 15/i | b | Lo | | blank; clearly misplaced |
| 16 | b | Lo | 16r–16v | continuation of *Ah! few and full* |

The evident disarrangement here is best considered after the following gathering.

Gathering D

| | | | | |
|---|---|---|---|---|
| 17 | b | Lo | 17r | last part of *Ah! few and full* (inc.) |
| | | | | 17v blank |
| 18 | b↓ | | 18r–20r | *O Lord our Governor* (10) |
| 19 | IHSb | | | |
| 20 | IHSb | | 20v–21v | *O I'm sick of life* (11) |
| - - - - - - - - - - - - - - - - - - - - | | | | |
| 21 | b | | | |
| 22 | b | | 22r–23r | *Lord I can suffer* (12) |
| 23 | IHSb↓ | | 23v–24r | *Hear me O Lord and that soon* (inc.; 13) |
| 24 | IHSb | | 24v–26r | *Since God so tender a regard* (14) |

Continuity of the music shows that fols. 14–17 were originally consecutive. Gathering D might thus have been preceded by a six-folio gathering as follows:

*Original Gathering C2*

| | | | | |
|---|---|---|---|---|
| [13/iv | IHSb] | | | |
| 13/vi | b↓ | | | |
| 13/vii | IHSb | | | |
| 14 | b | | 14r | *Lord not to us* (8) |
| 15 | IHSb↓ | | 15v–17r | *Ah! few and full* (9) |
| 16 | b | | | |

The three blank bifolia may have made up a separate, unused, six-folio gathering:

*Original Gathering C1*

| | | | |
|---|---|---|---|
| 13/v | IHSb | Lo | |
| 13/viii | IHSa | Lo | |
| 13/ix | IHSb | Up | |
| 13/x | b | Up | |
| 13/xi | a | Lo | |
| 15/i | b | Lo | |

Gathering E

| | | | | |
|---|---|---|---|---|
| 25 | b↓ | Up | 25r–26r | continuation of *Since God so tender a regard*; 25 guarded |
| 26 | IHSa | Lo | 26r–27v | *Early O Lord* (15) |

## Table 3.4  (*cont.*)

| | Folio | Watermark | Ruling | Contents and comments | |
|---|---|---|---|---|---|
| **Gathering E** (*cont.*) | | | | | |
| | 26/i | IHSb | Lo | | |
| | 26/ii | IHSa | Lo | | |
| | 27 | IHSa↓ | Up | 27r–27v | continuation of *Early O Lord* |
| | 27/i | [a↓] | | stub visible | |
| | 28 | a | Lo | 28r–29v | *Hear me O Lord the great support* (16) |
| | 28/i | a | Lo | | |
| | 28/ii | b | Lo | guarded | |
| | 28/iii | IHSb | Lo | guarded | |

*Early O Lord* must have run consecutively from 26r to 27, and *Hear me O Lord* from 28 to 29. These requirements are met by the following hypothetical structure:

*Original Gathering E1*

| | | | |
|---|---|---|---|
| 25 | b↓ | Up | |
| 26 | IHSa | Lo | |
| 27 | IHSa↓ | Lo | |
| 27/i | [a↓] | | stub visible |
| 28/i | a | Lo | |
| 28/iii | IHSb | Lo | |

28/iii does not match 25, but is guarded and could be pasted in the wrong way up.

*Original Gathering E2*

| | | | |
|---|---|---|---|
| 26/ii | IHSa | Lo | |
| 26/i | IHSb | Lo | |
| 28/ii | b | Lo | |
| 28 | a | Lo | |

| | Folio | Watermark | Ruling | Contents and comments |
|---|---|---|---|---|
| **Gathering F** | | | | |
| | 29 | IHSa | Lo | 29r–29v    conclusion of *Hear me O Lord* |
| | 29/i | IHSa | | |
| | 29/ii | a | | |
| | 29/iii | a | | |
| **Gathering G** | | | | |
| | 29/iv | b↓ | Lo | |
| | 29/v | b | | |
| | 29/vi | IHSb | | |
| | 30 | IHSb↓ | | 30v–30r    end of Sonata X (inverted) |
| **Gathering H** | | | | |
| | 30/i | | | guard stub |
| | 30/ii | IHSb | Up | |

## Table 3.4 *(cont.)*

| Folio | Watermark | Ruling | | Contents and comments |
|-------|-----------|--------|--|-----------------------|
| 30/iii | b↓ | Lo | | misplaced unused gathering |
| 30/iv | IHSb↓ | Lo | | |
| 30/v | b | Up | | |
| 30/vi | IHSa | Up | | |
| **Gathering J** | | | | |
| 31 | b | Lo | 31r–30r | Sonata X |
| 32 | b↓ | | 32r | Sonata IV (fragment; second copy) |
| 33 | b↓ | | | |
| 34 | b↓ | | 34r–32v | Sonata VIII |
| 35 | IHSb↓ | | 35v–34r | Sonata VII |
| 36 | IHSb↓ | | | |
| 37 | IHSb↓ | | 37v–36r | Sonata IX |
| [37/i | IHSb] | | | |
| **Gathering K** | | | | |
| 37* | [b↓] | [incomplete page] | 37*r | part of Sonata IV |
| 38 | IHSb | Up | | |
| 39 | b | Up | 39v–37*v | Sonata III |
| 40 | IHSa | Up | | |
| 41 | a | Up | 41v–40r | Sonata II |
| 41/i | [IHSb] | | | stub visible |
| 42 | b | Up | | |
| 43 | IHSb↓ | Up | 43v–42r | Sonata I |
| | | | 43v | discoloured; heading 'Sonnata's' |
| **Gathering L** | | | | |
| 43/i | a↓ | Up | | |
| 43/ii | IHSa | Lo | | |
| 44 | b↓ | Lo | 44r | fragments, not in Purcell's hand |
| 44/i | IHSb↓ | Lo | | |
| 44/ii | a | Lo | | |
| 45 | IHSa↓ | Up | 45r | end of In Nomine [7 parts] |
| **Gathering M** | | | | |
| 46 | a | Lo | 46r–45r | In Nomine [7 parts]; 46v blank |
| 47 | IHSa | Lo | 47v | end of In Nomine [6 parts] |
| 47/i | IHSa | Lo | | |
| 47/ii | a | Lo | | |
| 47/iii | a | Lo | | |
| 47/iv | IHSa | Lo | | |

## Table 3.4 (*cont.*)

| Folio | Watermark | Ruling | | Contents and comments |
|-------|-----------|--------|---|-----------------------|

The bifolium 48–48/ii has been misplaced, this gathering probably originally being:

*Original Gathering M1*

| | Folio | Watermark | Ruling | | Contents and comments |
|--|-------|-----------|--------|---|-----------------------|
| | 46 | a | Lo | 46r–45r | In Nomine [7 parts] |
| | 47 | IHSa | Lo | | |
| | 48 | b | Lo | 48r–47v | In Nomine [6 parts]; 48r: 'Here Begineth ye 6, 7, & 8 part Fantazia's' |
| | 47/ii | a | Lo | | |
| | 47/i | IHSa | Lo | | |
| | 48/ii | IHSb | Lo | | |
| | 47/iii | a | Lo | | |
| | 47/iv | IHSa | Lo | | |

The reasons for matching 48 with 48/ii are given after Gathering P below.

Gathering N

| | Folio | Watermark | Ruling | | Contents and comments |
|--|-------|-----------|--------|---|-----------------------|
| | 47/v | a↓ | Up | | |
| | 47/vi | IHSa | Lo | | |
| | 47/vii | a↓ | Lo | | |
| | 47/viii | IHSa | Lo | | |
| | 47/ix | a | Lo | | |
| | 47/x | IHSa↓ | Lo | | |
| | 47/xi | a | Lo | | |
| | 47/xii | IHSa↓ | Up | | |

Gathering P

| | Folio | Watermark | Ruling | | Contents and comments |
|--|-------|-----------|--------|---|-----------------------|
| | 48 | b | Lo | 48r–47v | In Nomine [6 parts]: 'Here Begineth ye 6, 7, & 8 part Fantazia's' |
| | 48/i | b | | | 48 and 48/ii guarded |
| | 48/ii | IHSb | | | |
| | 49 | IHSa | | | |
| | 50 | a | | 50r–49v | Fantazia upon One Note; 50r: 'Fantazias of 5 Parts' |
| | 50/i | a | | | guarded |
| | [50/ii] | | | | |
| | 50/iii | a | | | guarded |

Gathering P mainly consists of artificial bifolia, with 48–50/iii and 48/ii–50/i mounted on guard stubs. 48 and 48/ii may in fact have been an original bifolium belonging in the previous written gathering after 47, as shown above. 49 and 50 are certainly an original bifolium, the implications of which are shown below.

Gathering Q

| | Folio | Watermark | Ruling | | Contents and comments |
|--|-------|-----------|--------|---|-----------------------|
| | 51 | IHSa | Lo | 51r | 'Here Begineth ye 5 part: Fantazies' |
| | [51/i] | | | | |
| | 51/ii | IHSb | | | |
| | 51/iii | b↓ | | | 51/iii–52 form an artificial bifolium |

Table 3.4 (*cont.*)

| | Folio | Watermark | Ruling | | Contents and comments |
|---|---|---|---|---|---|
| | 51/iv | a↓ | | | |
| | 52 | b | | 52v | [Jigg] in G (outer parts) |
| | 52/i | IHSa↓ | | | |
| | 52/ii | IHSb↓ | | | |
| | 53 | IHSa | | 53r | [Borry, Minuet (outer parts)]; 53v: end of Overture in G; [Air] |
| | 53/i | a | | | |

The bifolium 51–53/i must be misplaced as it interrupts the overture; 52 and 53 need to be continuous for the dances. The original arrangement may have been:

*Original Gathering P1*

| | 48/i | b | Lo | | |
|---|---|---|---|---|---|
| | 49 | IHSa | | 49v | end of Fantazia upon One Note |
| | 50 | a | | 50r | beginning of Fantazia upon One Note |
| | [50/ii] | | | | |

*Original Gathering Q1*

| | 51 | IHSa | Lo | 51r | 'Here Begineth ye 5 part: Fantazies' |
|---|---|---|---|---|---|
| | 51/iii | b↓ | | | |
| | 51/iv | a↓ | | | |
| | 52/i | IHSa↓ | | | |
| | 52/ii | IHSb↓ | | | |
| | 53/i | a | | | |

*Original Gathering Q2*

| | [51/i | a] | Lo | | |
|---|---|---|---|---|---|
| | 51/ii | IHSb | | | |
| | 52 | b | | 52v | [Jigg] |
| | 53 | IHSa | | 53r | [Borry; Minuet] |
| | | | | 53v | end of Overture; [Air] |

*Gathering R*

| | 54 | IHSb | Lo | 54r–53v | Overture |
|---|---|---|---|---|---|
| | 54/i | IHSa | | | |
| | 54/ii | b↓ | | | |
| | 54/iii | a↓ | | | |
| | 54/iv | IHSa↓ | | | |
| | 54/v | IHSb↓ | | | |
| | 54/vi | a | | | |
| | 54/vii | b | | | |

*Gathering S*

| | 55 | a↓ | Up | 55r | end of Chacony |
|---|---|---|---|---|---|
| | 56 | b↓ | Lo | 56r–55r | Chacony |
| | 56/i | IHSb↓ | Lo | | |
| | 57 | IHSa↓ | Up | 57r | Pavan |

## Table 3.4 (*cont.*)

| Folio | Watermark | Ruling | Contents and comments | |
|---|---|---|---|---|
| **Gathering T** | | | | |
| [57/i | b↓] | | | |
| 58 | b↓ | Up | 58r | Fantazia (inc.): 'Feb. ye 24th 1682/3' |
| 59 | a↓ | Up | 59r–58v | Fantazia: 'August ye 31 1680' |
| 60 | IHSa↓ | Up | 60r–59v | Fantazia: 'August ye 18 [16]80' |
| 61 | IHSb↓ | Up | 61r–60v | Fantazia: 'June ye 30 [16]80' |
| 62 | IHSb↓ | Lo | 62r–61v | Fantazia: 'June ye 23 [16]80' |
| | | | | 62v: end of June 22 fantazia |
| **Gathering V** | | | | |
| 62/i | b↓ | Lo | | |
| 62/ii | IHSb | Up | | |
| 63 | IHSb↓ | Lo | 63r–62v | Fantazia: 'June ye 22 1680' |
| 64 | IHSb | Lo | 64r–63v | Fantazia: 'June ye 19 1680' |
| 64/i | b | Up | | |
| 64/ii | IHSb↓ | Lo | | |
| 64/iii | b↓ | Lo | | |
| 64/iv | b | Lo | | |

The bifolia 62/i–64/ii and 62/ii–64/i appear to be original. 63–4 is an artificial bifolium; the two folios match the isolated folios 64/iii and iv. The most satisfactory interpretation of the original structure is the following complete re-ordering into a ten-folio gathering:

*Original Gathering TV*

| | | | | |
|---|---|---|---|---|
| 64/iv | b | Lo | | |
| 64/iii | b↓ | Lo | | |
| [57/i | b↓] | | | |
| 58 | b↓ | Up | 58r | 'Feb. ye 24 1682/3' |
| 59 | a↓ | Up | 59r–58v | 'August ye 31 1680' |
| 60 | IHSa↓ | Up | 60r–59v | 'August ye 19 [16]80' |
| 61 | IHSb↓ | Up | 61r–60v | 'June ye 30 [16]80' |
| 62 | IHSb↓ | Lo | 62r–61v | 'June ye 23 [16]80' |
| 63 | IHSb↓ | Lo | 63r–62v | 'June ye 22 1680' |
| 64 | IHSb | Lo | 64r–63v | 'June ye 19 1680' |
| **Gathering X** | | | | |
| 64/v | IHSb | Up | | |
| 65 | IHSb | Lo | 65r–64v | Fantazia: 'June ye 14 1680' |
| 66 | a↓ | Lo | 66r–65v | Fantazia: 'June ye 11 1680' |
| 67 | IHSa | Lo | 67r–66v | Fantazia: 'June ye 10 1680' |
| 68 | a | Lo | 68r | 'Here begineth ye 4 part Fantazia's' |
| 68/i | IHSa↓ | Lo | | |
| 68/ii | b | Lo | | |
| 68/iii | b | Up | | 64/v–68/iii misplaced |

**Table 3.4** (*cont.*)

|  | Folio | Watermark | Ruling | Contents and comments |  |
|---|---|---|---|---|---|
| Gathering Y |  |  |  |  |  |
|  | 68/iv | b↓ | Lo |  |  |
|  | 69 | b↓ |  | 69v–69r | [Fantazia 3] |
|  | [69/i | a] |  |  |  |
|  | 70 | IHSa |  | 70v | Fantazia [2] |
|  | 71 | IHSb↓ |  | 71r | 'Here begineth ye 3 part Fantazia's' |
|  | 72 | IHSb↓ |  |  |  |

Folio, 408 × 260. Watermarks: Angoumois fleur-de-lys with countermark 'IHS/ET'.

Rastrology: sixteen staves, ruled with a six-stave and a four-stave rastrum. Six-stave rastrum, span: 132, profile: 10(13.5)11.5(13.5)11(13.5)11(13)12(13)11. Four-stave rastrum, span: 83.5, profile: 11(13.5)10.5(13)13(13)11. (Evenly spaced staves ruled in two blocks of six and one of four.)

The inclusion of the atypical Pavan and Chacony within a distinct gathering suggests that Purcell extracted the two sheets involved from the supply that later became Add. 30930 and copied them before the score was bound. The five-part Fantazia upon One Note is copied on one side of a single sheet of paper which formed the centre of *P1*, so Purcell planned his five-part section around a copy which already existed; the rubric 'Here Begineth ye 5 part: Fantazies' on fol. 51r presumably post-dates the binding as it lies in the previous gathering and there is nothing to tell the binder in what order the gatherings should be put together. The rubric 'Here Begineth ye 6, 7 & 8 part Fantazia's' (48r), in contrast, is immediately followed by the six-part In Nomine (Illus. 3.1). The seven-part In Nomine extended from *M1* to L and, like the later vocal works, is likely to have been copied after binding.

The surviving sonatas occupy two eight-folio gatherings, K and J, and one of four folios, Gathering G. The final leaf of Gathering K, fol. 37*, survives only as a fragment bearing the conclusion of Sonata III and enough of Sonata IV to show that this work began on the same page: Sonata IV must also have taken up some of the missing fol. 37/i, in the next gathering, and so is likely to have been added after the manuscript was bound. The same is true of Sonata X, which extends from J to G. There are marked differences of hand between Sonatas I–III, which begin on the discoloured fol. 43v, and Sonatas IX, VII and VIII; Sonata X introduces a further variety of hand and appears to have been copied later than the three previous works.

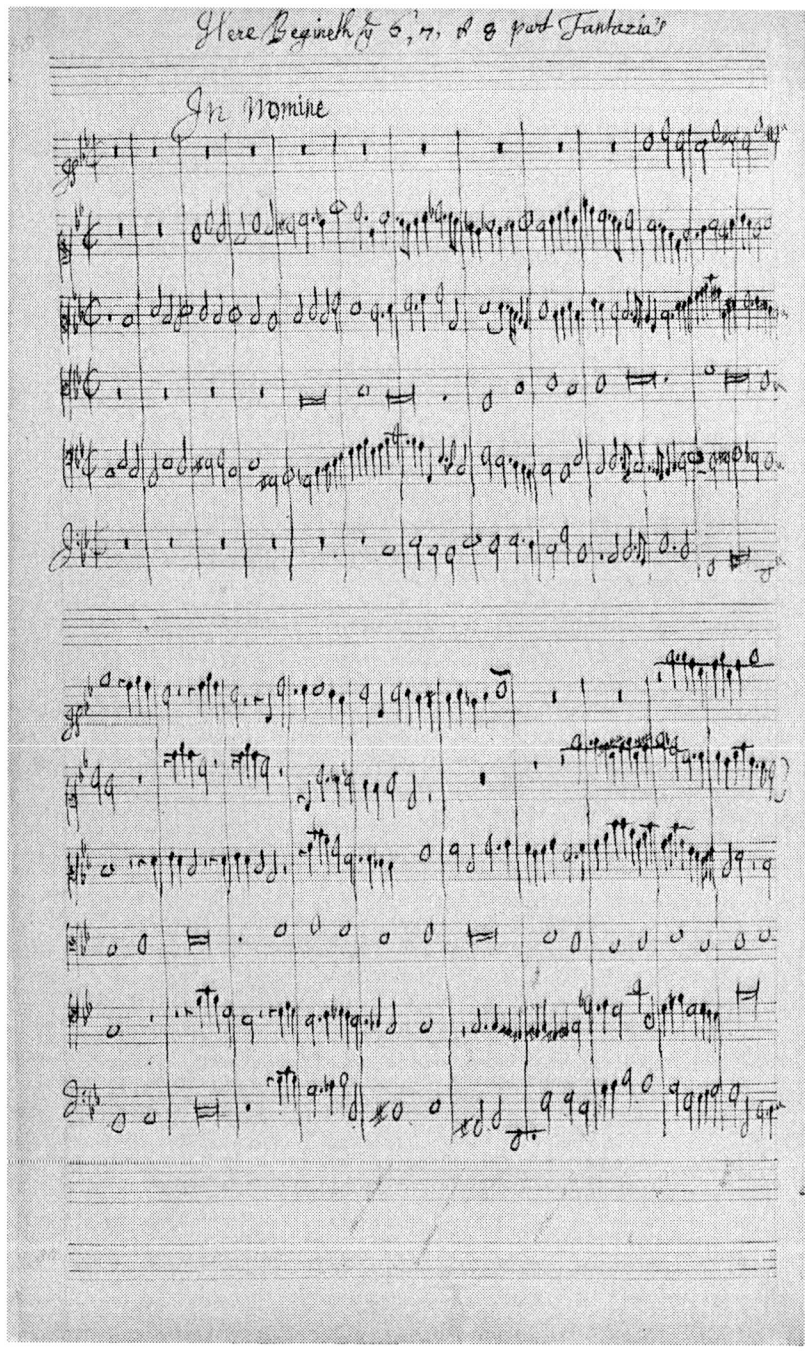

Illus. 3.1  Henry Purcell: 'Here Begineth ye 6, 7, & 8 part Fantazia's', autograph. British Library Add. MS 30930, fol. 48r

The evidence of the Ob MS Mus.c.28 concordances, the discoloration of fol. 43v and the irregularity of some of the quiring all indicate that Add. 30930 had a significant pre-binding history. Yet it contains no pagination or other binder's scheme, which would have been essential for copied quires to be assembled in the correct order, so some of the vocal works, Sonata X and the excised Sonata IV, the overture in G, the seven-part In Nomine and the heading to the five-part fantazias must have been copied into an already-bound volume. Similarly, the mid-gathering beginning of the four-part fantazias falls in an odd position unless the binding of the manuscript had at least been planned. The sheets Purcell took to the binder might therefore have contained the seven English sacred songs lying within separate gatherings and possibly some of the Latin music; the Pavan and Chacony; the first three-part fantazia; the dated series of four-part fantazias; the five-part fantazia; and the first three sonatas, which had perhaps lain on the top of a pile of unbound quires for some time: only one of these works, a four-part fantazia, extends from one gathering to another, and oral instructions to the binder would have sufficed. A lack of precision in the binder's directions is reflected in the apparent misplacement of Gathering S, containing the Pavan and Chacony, which might have been expected to follow the orderly sequence of fantazias rather than to interrupt it.

Although many pages of Add. 30930 are elegantly written, instances of rushed and messy copying or of subsequent alterations make it unlikely that the whole manuscript was intended as a fair copy. The differences between one page and another usually seem to have more to do with the speed at which Purcell was working or his attitude to the text being copied than with any consistent development or degeneration of his hand over a period of time, though the handwriting does provide a few more positive indications of date: Purcell's hook-shaped bass clef, which he had abandoned by 1678, and the secretary 'e' characteristic of his earlier manuscripts are nowhere to be found, although the titles and annotations of the instrumental music of course provide only limited samples of text. Handwriting offers no reason why the Pavan should not have been copied in late 1678 or 1679 and, as suggested, be the earliest work in the present manuscript. The absence of the secretary 'e' from the texts of the vocal pieces shows that they are all later than Purcell's first stage of work in Cfm 88, carried out in late 1677 or 1678, and the separate autograph of *Behold now praise the Lord* which followed soon afterwards. Another feature of Purcell's earlier manuscripts, the secretary 'r', confirms that all the vocal music in Add. 30930 except possibly *Domine non est exaltatum* had been copied by 1683 and marks a distinction between Sonatas I–III and Sonatas VII–X, in which an italic 'r' is used in tempo directions. Internal evidence therefore suggests that Add. 30930 was acquired by Purcell as unbound paper and partially copied some time before binding *c.* 1680, perhaps in late 1678 or 1679, a hypothesis supported by the manuscript's close concordances.

## CONCORDANCES: VOCAL MUSIC

Concordances of the vocal music in Add. 30930 follow one of two major lines of filiation. The first, which appears to descend from a source or sources earlier than Add. 30930, is represented by John Blow's score Och 628, a separate autograph copy of *Plunged in the confines of despair* in Bu 5001 and individual works in Bu 5002, J-Tn 0–1–54, Lbl Add. 33234 and Lbl Add. 33235 (see pp. 266–72). The second line of filiation descends directly from Add. 30930 to Ob MSS Mus.c.28 and Tenbury 1175: Mus.c.28 was copied by John Walter, a younger contemporary of Purcell as a Chapel Royal chorister, and Tenbury 1175 appears to have been started *c.* 1696 in circles close to the Purcell family (see p. 241), though the sacred partsongs were transcribed from Add. 30930 many years later and are of no value as independent texts. The majority of secondary sources belong to the first filiation, reinforcing the impression that Add. 30930 was regarded by Purcell as a private manuscript for his personal use: its apparent simplifications of rhythm and figuration may therefore be no more than Purcell's shorthand rather than definitive revisions.

## Oxford, Christ Church Mus. 628

Och 628, copied by John Blow in an unusually elegant form of his early hand,[9] contains most of Purcell's completed sacred partsongs, symphony anthems by Blow and Humfrey, and Blow's symphony song *Go perjured man.* The manuscript's appearance and varied repertory suggest that it was a presentation volume representing the copyist's own recent achievements alongside the work of his predecessor Humfrey and his pupil Purcell (Table 3.5). Two of the Blow anthems appear in Lbl Add. 50860, a Chapel Royal bass partbook copied before the end of 1677 (see below, p. 144), and Och 628 might also have been completed at about the same time, its texts of the Purcell sacred partsongs, which display many variants from Add. 30930, representing versions subsequently altered by Purcell in compiling the

---

[9] See Watkins Shaw, 'The Autographs of John Blow', *MR* 25 (1964), 89–90.

## Table 3.5 Oxford, Christ Church Mus. 628: contents

| Pages* | Title | Ascription |
|---|---|---|
| 1–3 | Gloria Patri | Henry Purcell |
| 3–7 | O all ye people clap your hands | Henry Purcell |
| 8–11 | Go perjured man† | Jo: Blow |
| 11–19 | O praise the Lord§ | Pellham Humfreys |
| 19–25 | I said in the cutting off of my days§ | Jo: Blow |
| 26–32 | Thou art my king O God§ | Pelham Humfrey |
| 32–9 | The kings of Tharsis§ | Jo: Blow |
| 39–42 | Plunged in the confines of despair | Henry Purcell |
| 43–52 | The king shall rejoice§ | Pelham Humfrey |
| 52–63 | When the Lord turned again§ | Jo: Blow |
| 63–74 | Hear my crying O God§ | Pelham Humfrey |
| 74–86 | The Lord is my shepherd§ | Jo: Blow |
| 86–96 | O give thanks unto the Lord§ | Pelham Humfreys |
| 96–110 | O give thanks unto the Lord§ | Jo: Blow |
| 111–15 | Since God so tender a regard | Henry Purcell |
| 116–20 | Early O Lord my fainting soul | Henry Purcell |
| 121–4 | O I'm sick of life | Henry Purcell |
| 125–30 | O Lord our governor | Henry Purcell |
| 130–5 | When on my sick bed I languish | Henry Purcell |
| 135–40 | Jehova quam multi sunt hostes | [Henry Purcell] |
| 141–6 | Beati omnes | Henry Purcell |

Folio, 417 × 270. Watermarks: Angoumois fleurs-de-lys with countermark 'IHS/ET' (pp. 1–80) or 'IHS/RC' (p. 81 onwards).

Rastrology: fifteen staves in discrete blocks of five, ruled with a five-stave rastrum: 'IHS/ET' paper, span: 107, profile: 11(12)12(12)11.5(13)11(13)11; 'IHS/RC' paper, span: 109, profile 12(13)12(13)11(14)11 (13)11

Copyist: John Blow

* Page nos. 133 and 144 were omitted.
† Symphony song with two violins.
§ Symphony anthem.

great scorebook: one such change is to the vocal bass of *Plunged in the confines of despair* at the first appearance of the words 'and pardons' (Illus. 3.2 and 3.3). Pages 1–80 of Och 628 consist of the same Etienne Touzeau paper as Add. 30930 and the rastrology of the latter part of the volume, on paper countermarked 'IHS/RC', is very similar to that of Cfm 88. Collation is regular and there is a contemporary pagination for the whole volume from p. '1st' to p. 146, a necessary feature if sheets copied before binding, as was probably the case here, were to be assembled in the right order.

Illus. 3.2  Henry Purcell: *Plunged in the confines of despair*, autograph. British Library Add. MS 30930, fol 4r

Birmingham University, Barber Institute of Fine Arts MS 5001, fols. 172–4

The folio guardbook Bu 5001, purchased by the University of Birmingham in an auction at Hodgson & Co. of London in 1949,[10] contains a collection of separate autographs of works by Cooke, Blow, Humfrey, Purcell and Turner.[11] The present volume had been bound by 1731, when John Barker, organist of Holy Trinity Church, Coventry, from 1731 to 1752, signed the back flyleaf.[12] *Plunged in the*

[10] Iain Fenlon, *Catalogue of the Printed Music and Music Manuscripts before 1801 in the Music Library of the University of Birmingham, Barber Institute of Fine Arts* (London, 1976), 113–14. A microfiche of the manuscript was issued with this catalogue.

[11] Watkins Shaw, 'A Collection of Musical Manuscripts in the Autographs of Henry Purcell and Other English Composers, c.1665–85', *The Library*, 5th series, 14 (1959), 126–31.

[12] See p. 143.

Illus. 3.3  Henry Purcell: *Plunged in the confines of despair*, copied by John Blow. Christ Church, Oxford, Mus. 628, p. 42

*confines of despair* covers the complete recto and verso sides of fols. 172 and 173 and extends onto the upper section of fol. 174r; the rest of this folio has been torn away, removing the watermark. Fol. 172 has a conventional Angoumois seven-pointed foolscap with the factor's mark 'HC' beneath, inverted in relation to the music copying. Fol. 173 has the countermark 'IP' the other way up, so it is virtually certain that fols. 172 and 173 are not the two halves of the same sheet of paper. All three folios measure 320 by 197 mm: they are ruled with twelve staves, drawn by a four-stave rastrum of span 85 mm and profile 12(13)12(13)11(13)11.5 mm, closely resembling that of Lbl R.M. 20.h.8.

The 'HC' factor's mark appears in combination with the countermark 'IP' in the 1680s,[13] though the factor's mark itself is found as early as 1676 and Purcell used other paper made by 'IP' for his score of *Behold now praise the Lord* (Lbl Add. 30932, fols. 121–5) in 1678 or 1679. Paper evidence is therefore inconclusive: the text of the Bu 5001 copy of *Plunged in the confines* predates Add. 30930,[14] but its handwriting so closely resembles that of the great autograph as to suggest that the two sources are nearly contemporary.[15]

## Oxford, Bodleian Library MS Mus.c.28, fols. 100–24

The final section of the composite scorebook Ob MS Mus.c.28 contains most of Purcell's English sacred partsongs in the hand of John Walter. On fols. 101v and 102r is a textless, incomplete and very compressed score of *In a deep vision's intellectual scene*, perhaps using up an opening inadvertently left blank: its details generally correspond to Bu 5002, Lbl Add. 33235 and Och 1150 rather than the copy entered in Lbl R.M. 20.h.8 in the summer of 1683. The separate parts of Ob MS Mus.c.28 (Table 3.6) were bound together well before it was purchased by the Bodleian Library at an auction at Puttick and Simpson's on 22 December 1869:[16] its complete contents are described as '1 vol MS' in William Dowding's sale catalogue of 1823[17] and a flyleaf inscription by W. Russell records a purchase at Samuel Arnold's sale on 24 May 1803, presumably of the entire manuscript.[18]

[13] Heawood no. 1784 shows an example of this combination dated 1683.

[14] *Works*, XXX (1965), 218.    [15] For a facsimile see Fenlon, *Catalogue*, [127].

[16] The manuscript was lot 613 in this sale: Madan, *A Summary Catalogue*, V, 536. The sale is not mentioned in King, *Some British Collectors*.

[17] 12–13 February 1823: Lbl S.C. 1078(5), lot 156.

[18] No catalogue of the 1803 Arnold sale is listed in King, *Some British Collectors*. Another identified owner, James Pears, seems to have owned a number of manuscripts in the first half of the nineteenth century: ibid., 148.

## Table 3.6 Oxford, Bodleian Library MS Mus.c.28: contents

| Folio | Headings, incipits and titles | Ascription | Copyist[a] |
|---|---|---|---|
| 3r | First Song in ye 2d Act of Don Quixote; 'Sing all ye muses' | [Purcell] | W |
| 6v | 7th Song in ye first part of Don Quixote in ye 5th Act; 'With this sacred charming wand' (inc.) | | W |
| 12r | [Part of 'Let the dreadful engines'] | | W |
| 13v | A Dialogue in ye 4th Act of ye 2d part of Don Quixote for a Clown and his Wife; 'Since Times are so bad' | | W |
| 19r | An Ode written for the Birthday of Queen Mary set to music by Hen[r]y Purcell; 'Now does the Glorious Day appear' | | 1 |
| 40r | Ode on St Cecilia's Day set to music by Mr Norris late Master of ye Children & one of the Cathedral at Lincoln; 'Begin the noble song' | [William Norris] | 1 |
| 64r | 'Hear us great Rugwith' [*Bonduca*] | Mr Henry Purcell | 2 |
| 67v | 'Hear, ye Gods of Brittain' | | 2 |
| 69v | 'Sing ye Druids all' | | 2 |
| 72v | 'Divine Andate' | | 2 |
| 73r | [Symphony] (Z.574/15a) | | 2 |
| 74r | 'To Armes y[ou]r Ensings strait display' | | 2 |
| 75v | 'Brittains strike home' | Mr Henry Purcell | 2 |
| 78r | Celebrate this Festivall | [Purcell] | W/Is |
| 100r | 'Plung'd in ye confines of despair' | Mr Henry Purcell | W |
| 101v | [In a deep vision's intellectual scene]; textless | | W |
| 103v | 'O all ye people' | Mr Purcell | W |
| 106r | 'When on my sick bed I languish' | | W |
| 107v | [O Lord our governor] | | W |
| 109v | O I'm sick [of life] | | W |
| 111v | [Lord I can suffer thy rebuke] | | W |
| 113v | 'Early O L[or]d my fainting soul' | | W |
| 115v | Ah! few and full of sorrows[b] | | W |
| 119r | Since God so tender [a regard] | | W |
| 120v | [Hear me O Lord the great support][c] | | W |
| 122v | O happy man[d] | | W |
| 124r | Fragments | | W |
| 124v | Fragments | | W? |

Measurements of fols. 100–24: folio, 325 × 208. Watermarks: seven-pointed Angoumois foolscap without countermark.

Rastrology: twelve staves ruled with a six-stave rastrum, span: 137.5, profile: 12.5(11)13.5(12.5)13(11.5)14(12)12.5(11.5)13.

[a] Copyists: W = John Walter; Is = William Isaack; 1, 2 unidentified.
[b] Incomplete here as in the autograph Lbl Add. 30930.
[c] Ends at bar 24, which begins with a new triple time signature.
[d] Unfinished: not in Lbl Add. 30930.

**Table 3.7 Purcell's sacred partsongs in London, British Library Additional MS 30930 and Oxford, Bodleian Library MS Mus.c.28**

| Gathering in Lbl Add. 30930* | Title | Position in Lbl Add. 30930 | Position in Mus.c.28 |
|---|---|---|---|
| A | Plunged in the confines | 1 | 1 |
| | O all ye people | 2 | 2 |
| | When on my sick bed | 3 | 3 |
| [C2]† | Ah! few and full (beginning) | 9 | 8 |
| D | Ah! few and full (end) | | |
| | O Lord our governor | 10 | 4 |
| | O I'm sick of life | 11 | 5 |
| | Lord I can suffer | 12 | 6 |
| | Since God so tender a regard (beginning) | 14 | 9 |
| [E1]† | Since God so tender a regard (end) | | |
| | Early O Lord | 15 | 7 |
| [E2]† | Hear me, O Lord the great support (beginning) | 16 | 10 |
| F | Hear me O Lord the great support (end) | | |

* See Table 3.4.

† Gatherings no longer in their original collation: see Table 3.4.

Ob MS Mus.c.28 preserves a text of the sacred songs closely related to the autograph score, its order of copying reflecting the likely copying order in Add. 30930 (see Table 3.7). Words are not underlaid but, apart from cursory cues, written in the margins, suggesting that the score was used as an organ part. The manuscript provides evidence of performing material being prepared alongside the autograph score, implying that there was also a set of vocal partbooks from which musicians in Purcell's circle sang the songs in their revised version.

## CONCORDANCES: FANTAZIAS AND RELATED FORMS

With the exception of a three-part fantazia in Lbl Add. 31435 all copies of Purcell's music in archaic forms prove to derive from the autograph score.

### New York Public Library, Drexel MS 5061

Much the most extensive secondary source of Purcell's polyphonic chamber music is US-NYp Drexel 5061 (Table 3.8). The manuscript consists of a single type of music paper but seems to have had a complex history: there are two stave rulings, and

## Table 3.8 New York Public Library, Drexel MS 5061: contents

| Ink pagination | Pencil pagination | Staves in block | Contents and ascription |
|---|---|---|---|
| 1–13 | | 4 | 'Gamut. Mr Mat: Lock' [15 four-part movements in G minor]* |
| 14–39 | | 4 | '4 prt Fantazia. Mr Purcell' [p. 14: subsequent works headed 'Fantazia' without ascription] |
| | 40–1 | 4 | Pavan [Purcell] |
| | 42–3 unused | 4 | |
| | 44–9 | 4 | 'Gamut. Mr Rob Smith' [seven movements in G minor] |
| | 50–4 unused | 4 | |
| | 55–6 | 3 | 'Fantazia 5 Parts upon one Note. Mr Purcell' |
| | 57–8 | 3 | '6 Parts. In Nomine Mr Purcell' |
| | 59–61 | 3 | '7 Parts In Nomine' [Purcell] |
| | 62 | 3 | [correction to In Nomine a7] |
| | 63–8 unused | 3 | |
| | 69 unused | 4 | |
| | 70–9 | 4 | 'Ground B mi Mr Francis Forcer' |
| | 80 unused | 4 | |
| 1–11 | 81–91 | 3 | 'Mr Locks Little Consort of 3 Parts' [movements 1–17] |
| 14–15 | 92–3 | 3 | 'Mr Purcell. Fantazia 3 Parts' |
| | 94–6 unused | 3 | |
| 1 | 97–8 | 3 | 'Ground: Mr Bartholmew Isaack' |
| | 21–2 | | Unruled: fleur-de-lys watermark |
| 1 | 23–4 | 4 | 'Mr Bartholmew Isaack' [incipit 'Once more the mouth of heav'n'] |
| | 24–7 | 4 | 'Song 3 voc' [incipit 'Lament, lament, look, look what thou hast done']† |
| | 28–31 | 4 | 'Vers Anthem: Compos'd 1677' [incipit 'Lord thou art become gracious']† |
| | 32–5 | 4 | 'Vers Anthem' [incipit 'Turn thou us, good Lord']† |
| | 36–9 | 4 | 'Psalme 51st' [verses 1–6. Incipit 'Gratiam fac mihi'; S,S,B, 2vn, bc]† |
| | 40 unused | 4 | |

Folio, 403 × 255. Watermarks: Angoumois fleur–de–lys with countermark 'IHS/AI'; one front flyleaf, countermark 'IHS/IM'.

Rastrology: twelve ruled staves in discrete blocks of three or four. Three–stave rastrum, span: 74, profile: 14.5(15)14.5(15)15; four–stave rastrum, span: 104, profile: 13.5(16.5)14(15.5)14(16.5)14.

---

* See R. E. M. Harding, *A Thematic Catalogue of the Works of Matthew Locke* (Oxford, 1971), 117–18.
† Possibly by Bartholomew Isaack.

duplicate or incomplete paginations indicate that various sections once existed independently. Pages 1–13 and 43–9 perhaps belonged to the G minor section of a collection of dance movements from the repertory of the royal violin band related to the lost 'Gamut' section of US-NYp Drexel 3976, which is copied in the same hand.[19] Most of the composers represented in the manuscript were connected with the court. Like Purcell, both Matthew Locke (d. 1677) and Robert Smith (d. 1675) were court musicians, and Bartholomew Isaack was a Chapel Royal choirboy until 1676: his ground in Drexel 5061, which incorporates some ingenious canonic passages, is clearly modelled on Purcell's own Three Parts on a Ground, and the inclusion in the manuscript of music by this relatively obscure composer suggests that its copyist must have been a close colleague or even a member of the Isaack family.[20]

Contrasts in handwriting reflect the repertorial divisions in the manuscript. The music by Locke, the Smith dances, the ground by Bartholomew Isaack and the vocal music are all written in a plain but workmanlike late seventeenth-century manner, whereas the Purcell copying is not only heavier in appearance but also deliberately archaic, featuring an old-fashioned two-piece G clef and, sometimes, minim and crotchet stems descending from the centre of the notehead. The initial impression is that the manuscript was copied by two different scribes, but the Forcer ground combines elements of both styles, and several details confirm that the whole is the work of one man: the central descending stems, for example, often give way in the Purcell fantazias to the copyist's more conventional right-hand stems, suggesting that his archaic style was self-conscious rather than natural. The same variation of hand appears in US-NYp Drexel 3976.

The main watermark of US-NYp Drexel 5061 is a fleur-de-lys countermarked with the initials 'AI', probably identifying Abraham Janssen as maker rather than factor, beneath the Jesuit emblem 'IHS'.[21] The 'AI' maker's mark suggests that initial copying in these sections took place in the 1670s, an appropriate date for the music by Locke and Smith, but both Purcell sequences are evidently additions to earlier material and offer no more evidence of the date of the fantazias' composition than is available from the autograph score itself. As well as displaying a close textual

---

[19] See Matthew Locke, *The Rare Theatrical: New York Public Library, Drexel MS 3976* (facsimile edn), intro. by Peter Holman, MLE A4 (London, 1989); Holman, *Four and Twenty Fiddlers*, 318.

[20] Peter Holman, 'Bartholomew Isaack and "Mr Isaack" of Eton: a Confusing Tale of Restoration Musicians', MT 128 (1987), 381–5.

[21] We are grateful to John Shepard of the New York Public Library, whose information and watermark tracing enabled us substantially to complete this section before we had seen the manuscript.

similarity with Add. 30930, predominantly transmitting its corrected readings, the Drexel score adopts many incidental features of Purcell's autograph: titles such as 'Fantazia 5 Parts upon One Note' reflect Purcell's spellings or phraseology, and with the exception of Fantazias 6 and 12, where Purcell uses 4/4 rather than 4/2 bars, the Drexel scribe follows Purcell's barring pattern, for example reproducing the autograph's halving of bar lengths in the active final section of Fantazia 4. An extra terminal flourish after the Drexel score of Fantazia 10, dated 30 June in Add. 30930, suggests that it was regarded as the final work of a sequence and was therefore copied from the autograph before Purcell began the fantazias bearing dates in August, nos 11 and 12. The few genuine variants in Drexel 5061 do not result from any lack of clarity in Purcell's autograph, and the close relationship between the two manuscripts rules out any possibility that the Drexel fantazias might represent an earlier version comparable to the sacred partsongs in Och 628.

### London, British Library Additional MS 33236

Lbl Add. 33236, the unique source of Purcell's four early three-part pavans and a secondary source of the three-part fantazias, contains a variety of instrumental and vocal music ranging from Locke's *Consort for Several Friends*[22] to an extensive sonata repertory also found in other English sources of the 1680s (Tables 3.9 and 3.10). The watermark, a Strasbourg bend with the initials of Abraham Janssen beneath and the countermark of Etienne Touzeau, indicates that the paper was obtained between 1679 and 1683, and three distinct rulings, distributed as shown in Table 3.9, suggest that the scorebook was divided into sections for different types of music. Each folio is now mounted individually, but watermark and rastral correspondences show that the present fols. 11–12 and 70–3 formed a single six-folio quire so that fol. 12v was once followed by 70r. The latest music added by the principal copyist, Purcell's *Fly swift ye hours* (*c.* 1692), is in a hand differing markedly from most of his work but *With sick and famished eyes* (fols. 70r–70v), entered in Lbl R.M. 20.h.8 in the summer of 1683, is in the characteristic main hand and would originally have followed the Lanier dialogue *Nor com'st thou yet*. The suggestion that Add. 33236 might date from the early 1680s is therefore consistent with the general repertory copied in the manuscript's principal hand as well as with the unique version it contains of the second Purcell three-part fantazia.

[22] Robert Thompson, 'The Sources of Locke's Consort "for seaverall freinds"', *Chelys* 19 (1990), 25–6.

**Table 3.9 London, British Library Additional MS 33236: contents**

| Folio | Ascription and contents | Comments |
|---|---|---|
| 3r | [Locke: *Consort for Several Friends*] | 11r: 'Finis Mr Matthew Lock 2 pts' |
| 11v | Nic. Laniere: 'Nor com'st thou yet' | |
| 13r | Lelio Colista: [ten sonatas; see Table 3.10] | headed 'Sympho: 1', 'Symphonia 2da' etc. |
| 30v | Archangelo Corelli: 'Opera 1a' | 'Scor'd from the printed copy' |
| 50v | Carolo Ruggiero: Sonata | |
| 52r | 'Sonata del Sen[io]r Lelicolista' | |
| 53v | J. Blow: Sonata | |
| 55r | Anon.: Sonata | |
| 56v | Archangelo Corelli: two sonatas | |
| 60r | Mr Henry Purcell: [four pavans a3] | |
| 61r | 'Mons[ieur] Baptiste' [Draghi]: 'Sonata in Gamut ♭' | |
| 63r | Locke: Little Consort | three movements only |
| 63v | Dr John Blow: A Ground for 2 violins | |
| 64v | 'J. Blow' [*recte* Purcell]: Symphony for flutes | from *How pleasant is this flowery plain* |
| 65r | [Purcell] Chacony | fragmentary: most of the page is torn out |
| 65v | Henry Purcell: three fantazias a3 | the first fragmentary |
| 67v | Dialogue by Mr Henry Purcell: 'You say 'tis love' | |
| 70r | H. Purcell: 'With sick and famished eyes' | |
| 71r | Henry Purcell: 'How long, great God' | |
| 71v | Henry Purcell: 'O solitude' | |
| 72v | Mr Henry Purcell: 'Fly swift, ye hours' | |

Folio, 428 × 279. Watermarks: arms of Strasbourg with factor's initials 'AJ' and countermark 'ET'.

Rastrology (staves ruled in discrete blocks of two, three and four)

| Staves on page | Staves in rastrum | Rastrum span | Rastrum profile | Folios |
|---|---|---|---|---|
| 14 | 2 | 36 | 12(12.5)11.5 | 3–12; 70–3 |
| 16 | 4 | 85 | 11(12.5)12(12.5)12(13)12 | 13–59 |
| 15 | 3 | 60.5 | 12(12.5)12.5(12.5)11.5 | 60–9 |

The Purcell fantazias on fols. 65v–67r, at the end of the section ruled for three-part music, appear after the symphony for flutes from *How pleasant is this flowery plain* which was entered in Lbl R.M. 20.h.8 some time after 21 October 1682. The pages of this part of the manuscript do not seem to have been disarranged, and the apparently rather late date of the Lbl Add. 33236 copies of the three-part fantazias could provide evidence for the history of the autograph score. Much of the first fantazia has been torn out of Add. 33236, but what remains corresponds with Add. 30930, as does Fantazia 3, which in the autograph shares a bifolium with Fantazia 1. The end of Fantazia 2 is incomplete in Add. 33236, as in

## Table 3.10 Related English sources of sonatas

| Composer | Work | J-Tn N2/15 no. | Ob MS Mus. Sch. D.256 no. | Ob MSS Mus.Sch. E.400–403 no. | Lbl Add. 33236 fols. (no.) | Ob MS Mus.Sch. D.254 no. | US-Cu 959 no. |
|---|---|---|---|---|---|---|---|
| Corelli | Op. 1 nos. 1–12 | 1–12 | | 10–21 | 30v–50r | | 1–12 |
| Lonati A4[a] | W-K 20[b] | 13 | 4 | 3 | 18r (4) | | 25 |
| Lonati A3 | W-K 23 | 14 | 3 | 7 | 16v (3) | | |
| Anon. | | 15 | | | | 12 | |
| G. B. Vitali | Op. 2 no. 6 | 16 | | | | | |
| G. B. Vitali | Op. 2 no. 3 | 17 | | | | | |
| G. B. Vitali | Op. 2 no. 1 | 18 | | | | | |
| Lonati A6 | W-K 34 | 19 | 1 | 1 | 13r (1) | | |
| Colista | W-K 33 | 20 | 10 | 2 | 28r (10) | | |
| Colista | W-K 22 | 21 | 2 | 4 | 14v (2) | | |
| Lonati A2 | W-K 35 | 22 | 6 | 5 | 22v (6) | | |
| Lonati A8 | W-K 11 | 23 | 5 | 6 | 20v (5) | | |
| Lonati A1 | W-K 36 | 24 | 9 | 8 | 26v (9) | | |
| Colista | W-K 15 | | 8 | | 24v (7) | | |
| Colista | W-K 10 | | 7 | | 25v (8) | | |
| Colista | W-K 16 | 25 | | 9 | 52r | | |
| G. B. Draghi | | 26 | | | 61r | | |
| Matteis | | 27 | | 22 | | | |
| Matteis[c] | | 28 | | 23 | | | |
| Anon. | | 29 | | 38 | 55r (3) | 3 | 24 |
| Corelli[d] | | 30 | | 39 | 56v (4) | 4 | 20 |
| Corelli[e] | | 31 | | 40 | 58r (5) | 5 | 19 |
| Purcell | 1697 no. 1 | 32 | | 42 | | 7 | |
| Purcell | 1697 no. 2 | 33 | | 41 | | 6 | |
| Purcell | 1697 no. 3 | 34 | | 43 | | 8 | |
| Ruggiero | | 35 | | 36 | 50v (1) | 1 | |
| Blow[f] | | 36 | | 37 | 53v (2) | 2 | |
| Anon.[g] | | 37 | | 44 | | 10 | 18 |
| G. M. Bononcini[h] | | | | 45 | | 9 | |
| G. Legrenzi[i] | | | | 47 | | 11 | 23 |
| Anon. | | | | 46 | | | |
| Purcell | 1697 no. 10 | 38 | | | | | |
| Purcell | 1697 no. 7 | 39 | | | | | |
| Purcell | 1697 no. 9 | 40 | | | | | 32 |

[a] Numbering of Lonati sonatas according to Peter Allsop, 'Problems of Ascription in the Roman *Simfonia* of the late Seventeenth Century: Colista and Lonati', *MR* 50 (1989), 34–44.

[b] References from Helene Wessely-Kropik, *Lelio Colista: ein Römischer Meister vor Corelli. Leben und Umwelt* (Vienna, 1961).

[c] Ground in D minor for three trebles and bass: bass part also in US-NHb Osborn 515.

[d] Ascr. 'L. Calista' in US-Cu 959; in Ob MS Mus.Sch. D.249, fol. 172, entitled 'La Rospa', anon. See Hans Joachim Marx, *Die Überlieferung der Werke Archangelo Corellis. Catalogue raisonné* (Cologne, 1980), 237–8.

[e] Published in Archangelo Corelli, *Sonate a tre, due violini col basso per l'organo*, ouvrage posthume (Amsterdam, Estienne Roger, [1714]): also in Italian sources. See Marx, *Die Überlieferung der Werke Archangelo Corellis*, 218–20.

[f] Also in Lbl R.M. 20.h.9, fols. 108r–105r INV.

[g] Ascr. Corelli in US-Cu 959: see Marx, *Die Überlieferung der Werke Archangelo Corellis*, 239–40.

[h] Published in Marino Silvano, *Scielta della Suonate* (Bologna, 1680), Sonata 7: serious mistakes in the edition are not apparent in the manuscript sources listed here. See William Klenz, *Giovanni Maria Bononcini of Modena* (Durham, NC, 1962), 255–61.

[i] G. Legrenzi, Op. 1, no. 10, 'La Bentivoglia'.

the autograph, and Add. 33236 gives a reading for the treble of bars 28–9 that Purcell initially wrote in Add. 30930. It seems likely that the three-part fantazias were transcribed from the autograph before these bars were altered, and as the Add. 33236 fantazias were apparently copied later than the symphony from *How pleasant is this flowery plain*, Purcell's final changes to the second fantazia might therefore have been contemporary with the incomplete four-part fantazia in Add. 30930 dated 24 February 1683.

## London, British Library Additional MS 31435

The guardbook Lbl Add. 31435 contains two separate sets of fantazia parts. The first, beginning at fols. 2, 19, 35 and 52, contains Locke's *The First Part of the Broken Consort* and some similar works by Christopher Gibbons, all with a duplicate bass part for organ; the second, beginning at fols. 70, 78, 86, 94 and 103, contains the fantazias only from Locke's *Consort of Four Parts*. A copy of Purcell's second three-part fantazia, in an early version lacking the whole of the concluding slow section, has been added on the unused final verso of each book in the first set. Both sets bear inscriptions such as 'All the Fanta: in this book of Mr Locks I exa[mined] by Mr Purcells Score Book', an apparent reference to Locke's autograph score Lbl Add. 17801.

These partbooks have sometimes been thought to provide evidence that Fantazia 2 was composed some years before the date *c.* 1680 implied by the autograph score, but this claim does not stand up to inspection. The string parts of the first set are made of paper with a fleur-de-lys watermark and the countermark of Jean Monédière, which could indeed date from the mid-1670s but might equally have been made a few years later. The duplicate bass part, in which Purcell's fantazia seems to have been added at the same time as in the string parts, contains several folios with the factor's mark of Abraham Janssen and is unlikely to have been copied before 1679. The two sets of partbooks nevertheless have an important bearing on Purcell's interest in the fantazia form: the anonymous examiner and annotator of both sets, identified as 'F. T.', had access to a score belonging to Purcell; and in the four-part music the principal copyist included only fantazias, foreshadowing Purcell's own practice of writing such movements independently rather than as the first movements of suites. The whole collection suggests an active interest in the fantazia amongst Purcell's acquaintances in or after 1679.

## Oxford, Christ Church Mus. 620

The flyleaf inscription in Och 620, 'Liber Richardi Goodson Jun[ior] ex dono Reverendi Viri Gulielmi Dingle Collegi Corporis Christi Socii ac Philo-musici 1702', records the gift to the younger Richard Goodson, then a chorister at Christ Church aged about fourteen, of a manuscript score of some of Purcell's *Ayres* (1697) followed by more than eighty unused pages.[23] This volume was later bound with two older books in the hand of the senior Richard Goodson containing fantazia and dance sets by Christopher Gibbons and John Coprario. On pp. 129–31, at the end of the Gibbons volume, is Purcell's *Fantazia upon One Note*, apparently copied directly from Add. 30930. Together with the sonata copies in Och 3 this score raises the possibility that all or part of Purcell's autograph made the journey to Oxford and that some of his chamber music was played at the Music School. The later part of the manuscript contains Sonata X from Purcell's 1697 set (pp. 23–8), written in what seems to be a youthful form of the younger Goodson's writing: on pp. 87–9 he made an incomplete copy of Sonata IX.

### SECONDARY SOURCES OF THE AUTOGRAPH SONATAS

At first sight the sonatas of Purcell's '1697' set seem better represented in secondary sources than the fantazias, but three of the manuscripts containing more than one work, the partbook sets J-Tn N2/15, Ob MSS Mus.Sch. E.400–403 and Ob MS Mus.Sch. D.254, are interrelated and the most significant score copy, Och 3, is a transcription from Add. 30930. In Sonatas VII and VIII, where there are major differences between the autograph and printed versions of the music, all early secondary manuscripts invariably follow the autograph rather than the text published in 1697. The same is not true of Sonatas I–III, though in these works the differences are usually minor, and fols. 14v–17r of Lbl Add. 63627, 'The First Treble Book 1686', contain a single part of Sonatas II and III with some variants found in neither the autograph nor the print. The sonatas missing from the autograph have no seventeenth-century concordances, despite the evidence of fragments in Add. 30930 that Sonata IV was composed at about the same time as Sonatas I–III.

---

[23] William Dingley (*c.* 1673–1735), clergyman, was elected a fellow of Corpus Christi College on 26 February 1698.

### Three interrelated partbook sets

J-Tn N2/15, which contains six of the seven complete Purcell sonatas present in Add. 30930, comprises the printed second violin and bass partbooks of Purcell's 1683 sonatas followed by a further forty works in manuscript. These additions are related to a number of other English partbook sets containing Corelli's Op. 1, unpublished sonatas by Colista and Lonati, and a miscellaneous series of sonatas including Purcell's '1697' sonatas I–III. Table 3.10 shows the contents of these sources, amongst which Ob MSS Mus.Sch. D.254 and 256 were copied by the English amateur composer James Sherard (1666–1738).[24] A further set in Sherard's hand, Ob MS Mus.Sch. D.255, contains Corelli's Op. 1.

J-Tn N2/15 and Ob MSS Mus.Sch. E.400–403 share an important copyist who seems to have worked with Sherard because his work includes Ob MS Mus.Sch. D.252, a manuscript set of parts of Sherard's Op. 2 eventually published *c.* 1711, and other sources at Oxford, not all necessarily from Sherard's library.[25] Three sets of partbooks copied by Sherard himself, Ob MSS Mus.Sch. D.254, 255 and 256, have the 'PVL' monogram countermark of Peter van der Ley which first appears in paper used in England in the mid-1680s,[26] and in D.255 Sherard identifies himself by an early form of his name, 'Sharwood', suggesting that all three sources were copied relatively early in the long period from *c.* 1686 onwards during which paper with the 'PVL' monogram was available. Repertorial connections with D.254 and 256, as well as with the score Lbl Add. 33236, therefore suggest that the related partbooks J-Tn N2/15 and Ob MS Mus.Sch. E.400–403 are earlier than some of their principal copyist's other work.

The two partbooks of J-Tn MS N2/15 were purchased by Yorisada Tokugawa, founder of the Nanki Music Library, at W. H. Cummings's sale in 1917.[27] Microfilm shows the covers of both volumes fully open, revealing a late seventeenth-century

---

[24] Sherard became wealthy as an apothecary in London and in later life devoted himself to botany, which he pursued in his gardens at Eltham in Kent; early in the eighteenth century he issued two collections of trio sonatas. Unpublished research by Margaret Crum, much incorporated in the typescript 'Revised Descriptions' at the Bodleian Music Room, has identified Sherard's hand in a large number of manuscripts. See also Michael Tilmouth, 'James Sherard: an English Amateur Composer', *M&L* 47 (1966), 313–22.

[25] The principal hand of Ob MSS Mus.Sch. E.400–403 also appears in Sonata VII of Ob MS Mus.Sch. C.78 a–c and in Och 1141A, Och 1154 and Ob MS Mus.Sch. D.249: the last source definitely belonged to Sherard's collection.

[26] Examples of the 'PVL' monogram in Heawood nos 151, 1781A and 1782 date from 1686. The countermark was first used in 1675: see Voorn, *De papiermolens*, 131.

[27] See description and bibliography by James Siddons in Rita Benton, ed., *Directory of Music Research Libraries*, IV (Kassel, 1979), 138–40.

gilt-tooled binding and apparently contemporary spines. The manuscript paper, cut to match the dimensions of the 1683 printed partbooks, is consistently ruled with ten rather closely-spaced staves on pages whose size and proportions differ from those of most contemporary English manuscript books. The set seems therefore to have been designed as a single collection of printed and manuscript material, a torn-out page in the bass part of the tenth sonata suggesting that copying took place after the books were bound.

Two copyists worked on the manuscript section, the first (hand 1) contributing sonatas 1–18 and the second, Sherard's collaborator (hand 2), 19–40, including all the Purcell. The first copyist consistently heads the works he copies 'Sonnata', numbers such as 'Primo' and 'Seconda' being added to the Corelli sonatas by hand 2, who also added performance directions in various places. Hand 1's idiosyncratic spellings 'pianna' and 'fort' suggest limited familiarity with Italian sources. The involvement of hand 2 does not mean that Sherard owned the J-Tn N2/15 partbooks, but he probably had access to them because the last sonata he copied in Ob MS Mus.Sch. D.254, which otherwise reproduces the miscellaneous series found in Ob MSS Mus.Sch. E.400–403, is sonata 15 from the Nanki set.

The manuscript repertory of J-Tn N2/15 is likely to have been compiled within a few years of the publication of the 1683 sonatas, which the manuscript paper was prepared to match. Printed or manuscript copies of Corelli's Op. 1 (1681) were certainly available in England by 1684, when Francis Withy scored several extracts in Och 337;[28] sonatas from Vitali's Op. 2 (1667) and Op. 5 (1669) appear in an English source dated 1680, Lbl Add. 31431.[29] The works by Lelio Colista (d. 1680) and Carlo Ambrogio Lonati are all attributed to the former composer in English manuscripts: Colista is of course 'the famous Lelio Calista' praised by Purcell in his 1694 revision of Playford's *Introduction*,[30] although the passage of triple counterpoint he quotes is in fact by Lonati. Two Colista sonatas in Add. 31431 suggest that English musicians might have encountered this Roman repertory, which circulated in manuscript rather than in print, before 1680. The miscellaneous series of sonatas similarly contains nothing demonstrably later than *c.* 1680, but music undoubtedly known in England a few years later, such as Bassani's Op. 5, is absent.

The partbooks Ob MSS Mus.Sch. E.400–403 (Table 3.11) were acquired by the

---

[28] Robert Thompson, '"Francis Withie of Oxon" and his Commonplace Book, Christ Church, Oxford, MS 337', *Chelys* 20 (1991), 10. One extract is dated 18 September 1684.

[29] Other published sonatas in Lbl Add. 31431 are from Cazzati's Op. 18 and Legrenzi's Op. 2.

[30] John Playford, *An Introduction to the Skill of Musick*, 12th edn (London, 1694), 124.

**Table 3.11 Oxford, Bodleian Library MSS Mus.Sch. E.400-403: contents**

| Pages in E.400 | Numbers | Contents | Comments |
|---|---|---|---|
| 3–19 | [I]–IX | ['Colista']: nine sonatas (see Table 3.10) | pp. 1–2 lacking in this part; p. 19: 'hier endeth Lelli Colista his sonates' |
| 20–45 | X–XXI | Corelli: [Op. 1] | |
| 46–7 | XXII | 'Nicolla Mathise': [Sonata] | |
| 47–8 | XXIII | 'Nicolla Mathise': [Ground in d] | |
| 50–73 | XXIV–XXXV | Corelli: [Op. 2] | p. 51: 'hir Begineth Corelli his last sonates in 1685' |
| 74–97 | XXXVI–XLVII | [Anthology of twelve sonatas] (see Table 3.10) | |
| 98–121 | XLVII–[LIX] | 'Battista Bassani': [Op. 5] | Roman numbering ends at XLIX |
| 122–3 | | Anon: 'Sonata 1' | Incomplete: blank pages in E.401–2 |
| 124–5 | | Antonio Biffi: [Sonata] | |
| 126–7 | | [Exercises for the violin] | |
| 128 | | Unused | |

Oblong quarto, 214 × 284. Binding: contemporary blind-tooled reversed calf, 221 × 285.
Watermarks: MS Mus.Sch. E.400, arms of Strasbourg with factor's mark 'AJ'; no countermark; MSS Mus. Sch. E.401–3, Angoumois fleur-de-lys with factor's mark 'HC' and countermark 'IP'.

Rastrology: eight staves ruled with a four-stave rastrum; E.400 span: 82.5, profile: 12(12)11.5(13)11.5(12) 11; E.401–403: span: 83.5, profile: 12(12.5)11(13)11.5(12)11.5.

Music School as part of Richard Rawlinson's bequest in 1755.[31] Most occurrences of the 'HC' factor's mark which appears in the three lower parts fall between 1676 and 1686, and an example of the same watermark and countermark combination is dated 1683.[32] As far as the second Bassani sonata (the last to be included in the basso continuo book, MS Mus.Sch. E.403) the principal copyist was Sherard's collaborator, hand 2 of J-Tn N2/15, who probably carried out his work in the mid-1680s. The Bodleian and Nanki sets are related though additions appear to have been made to Ob MSS Mus.Sch. E.400–403 over a rather longer period: contents and readings are closely similar, and the J-Tn N2/15 bass part contains cross-references to Mus.Sch. E.400–403.

The Purcell sonatas in J-Tn N2/15 clearly fall into two groups: Sonatas I–III, which form part of the series of works by different composers in Ob MSS Mus.Sch.

[31] Richard Rawlinson (1690–1755) bequeathed his extensive collection of books and manuscripts to the Bodleian Library but made a separate bequest of his music books to the Music School. As Margaret Crum suggested (in typescript notes kept at the Bodleian Music Room), the latter bequest cannot have consisted only of the three items now identifiable as his, MSS Mus.Sch. C.95, D.222 and E.400–403. See Madan, *Summary Catalogue*, III, 177–8; V, 259.
[32] Heawood no. 1784.

E.400–403 and D.254, and Sonatas X, VII and IX, in that order, which have no concordances amongst the other manuscripts listed in Table 3.10.[33] A major difference between the Nanki and Oxford manuscripts is that in Mus.Sch. E.400–403 and D.256 Sonata I is transposed down a tone to A minor, though in other respects the text of this sonata varies no more from the Nanki parts than is inevitable because of the altered pitch. As the Nanki source is the earliest of the related partbook sets, it is unlikely that A minor was the work's original key. Throughout Sonatas I–III the related sets share distinctive variants not only with each other but also with the printed edition of 1697, in only one instance (Sonata I, bar 96) giving the tempo direction from the autograph score when the print has a different one. Otherwise, the following variants are common to Ob MSS Mus.Sch. E.400–403, J-Tn N2/15 and *Ten Sonata's in Four Parts*:

| Sonata | Bar | Variant from Add. 30930 |
|--------|-----|-------------------------|
| I | 11 | time signature ¢ |
| II | 1 | tempo direction 'Adagio' |
| | 19 | time signature ¢ |
| | 71 | tempo direction 'Grave' |
| | 73 | string bass matches continuo |
| | 164 | vn 2, note 2, g" |
| III | 1 | tempo direction 'Grave' |
| | 19 | time signature 3/1 |
| | 106 | time signature in two parts 9/6 |
| | 136 | vn 2, note 2, b' |
| | 148 | tempo direction 'Grave' |

The version of Sonatas I–III found in these manuscript partbooks probably derives from a secondary autograph score or set of parts on which the 1697 print was itself eventually based. In contrast, Sonatas VII, IX and X in J-Tn N2/15 generally preserve readings much closer to those of Add. 30930: Sonata VII appears in its manuscript rather than printed version, and there are none of the contrasts of tempo direction and time signature that differentiate the autograph and J-Tn N2/15 texts of the first three works. Some minor variants suggest that the Nanki parts of the later sonatas were not copied directly from Add. 30930 but they could well have been transcribed from an earlier set of parts based on the autograph score.

---

[33] The otherwise very helpful *stemma* printed in *Works*, VII (1981), xii, overlooks the different relationship between either sequence of Purcell sonatas in J-Tn N2/15 and the autograph.

## Oxford, Christ Church Mus. 3

The predominantly eighteenth-century manuscript Och 3 incorporates two earlier sections copied by the elder Richard Goodson: fols. 39–42, containing a score of the first sonata from Bassani's Op. 5, and fols. 47–58, in which Purcell's sonatas IX, VII and VIII, following both the order and the textual details of Add. 30930 rather than the 1697 print, occupy fols. 47r–53r. Both sections are made of similar paper with a Strasbourg bend watermark and countermarks 'RC' or 'AI'. Goodson appears to have transcribed the three Purcell sonatas from Add. 30930, in which they were entered *c.* 1683 or later.

## Further concordances of the 'Golden Sonata':
### University of Chicago, Joseph Regenstein Library MS 959
### York, Minster Library MSS M57/1–4(S)
### Chichester, West Sussex Record Office MS Cap. VI/I/I
### Tokyo, Nanki Library MS N3/35

It is not immediately obvious why Sonata IX of the 1697 set acquired an early popularity far beyond that of the other works in the set. The modern Italianate style especially apparent in the last movement might offer an explanation,[34] but Sonata X, which has comparable qualities, appears in relatively few sources.[35] Textual comparison of manuscripts containing isolated copies of Sonata IX indicates that most descend from a single original differing from both the 1697 print and the extant autograph.[36]

Only US-Cu 959 presents the complete text of all four parts. Y M57/1–4(S), a similar though inferior source, lacks the last page of the first violin part and the two scores, CH Cap. VI/I/I and J-Tn N3/35, each have a single bass part, the former conflating the string bass with the thorough-bass of the lost original, the latter generally disregarding the continuo. These sources effectively prove that Purcell produced a separate autograph of Sonata IX in the early or mid-1680s with many minor variants and some, such as interchanged violin parts in bars 96–7[37] and a varied second violin in bar 143, of more importance. The continuo of this version appears from the York and Chicago sources to have followed the

---

[34] Adams, *Henry Purcell*, 34.    [35] Holman, *Henry Purcell*, 89–90.
[36] See *Works*, VII (1981), xix–xxii.    [37] Not noted in *Works*, VII (1981).

string bass rather more closely than that of the 1697 print, in this respect perhaps showing an affinity with Add. 30930. The separate autograph is unlikely to have pre-dated Add. 30930 not only because its derivatives were copied well into the 1680s or later but also because they do not contain the scorebook's initial reading of bars 106–8.

The four partbooks of US-Cu 959 have obvious similarities of presentation and repertory with Ob MSS Mus.Sch. E.400–403 and share a number of works with the related sources outlined in Table 3.10. As in Mus.Sch. E.400–403 the sonatas are presented in a continuous roman-numbered sequence and the calligraphic style of the several copyists broadly resembles the work of Sherard's associate in E.400–403, though the Chicago partbooks apparently date from a slightly later period (Table 3.12).[38] Each volume begins with an elaborate copy of the title page of Corelli's Op. 1 sonatas, the first works in the collection.[39] Inscriptions in the partbooks identifying later owners, 'Chas A. Wheelwright' of Tansor and William Bure of Allesley, cast little light on their origins.

Italian names, musical terms and annotations are accurately spelt and two of the music copyists, hands 6 and 7, as well as the calligrapher of the title pages and the scribe who wrote the part names at the head of each page, use the German 'ß' symbol for the double 's', but English provenance can be established on repertorial and other grounds. Several of the sonatas included are familiar from the English repertory of J-Tn N2/15 and related sources, and English performance directions are used in Sonata 24. The paper, characteristic of English music manuscripts of the mid-1680s,[40] is the work of the three papermakers represented in Lbl Add. 33287, copied *c.*1685, and a four-stave rastrum was used to rule the eight staves on each page, again a typically English procedure.

Circumstantial evidence tends to link the Chicago partbooks with the Catholic court of James II. Three of the sonatas by Godfrey Finger are the trio sonatas from his *Sonatae XII, pro diversis instrumentis* (London, 1688), music said in its dedication to have been performed in the Catholic Chapel Royal. The partbooks include two sonatas, otherwise unknown in English sources, by Roman composers: one by Hippolito Bocaletti, not belonging to his Op. 1 of 1692, and Carlo Manelli's Op. 2, no. 2, 'La Fede', presumably dedicated to a member of the family of Innocenzo

---

[38] Joan Wasson, 'Three Corelli Attributions in an Eighteenth Century Manuscript of Trio Sonatas' (M.A. thesis, University of Chicago, 1966).    [39] Ibid., 15–16.
[40] Ibid., 2–5. The date suggested, *c.*1710, is at least twenty years too late, a date *c.*1685–90 being more appropriate both for the paper and for the collection's repertory.

## Table 3.12  University of Chicago, Joseph Regenstein Library MS 959: contents

| Numbers | Ascription | Work | Comments | Copyist |
|---|---|---|---|---|
| I–XII | Arcangelo Corelli | Op. 1 | each headed 'Sonata Prima', etc. | 1 |
| XIII | [Anonymous] | | | 2 |
| XIV | [Anonymous] | | | 2 |
| XV, XVI | Antonius Poole | | | 2 |
| XVII | L. Calista | G. B. Vitali: Op. 5/7 | not found in other English sources | 2 |
| XVIII | A. Corelli | | see Table 3.10 | 2 |
| XIX | Arcangelo Corelli | | see Table 3.10 | 2 |
| XX | L. Calista | | see Table 3.10 | 2 |
| XXI | [Anonymous] | | | 3 |
| XXII | [Anonymous] | G. B. Vitali: Op. 5/8 | also in Lbl R.M. 20.h.9 | 2 |
| XXIII | Gio: Legrenzi | G. Legrenzi: Op. 1/10 | see Table 3.10 | 2 |
| XXIV | [Anonymous] | | see Table 3.10 | 2 |
| XXV | L. Calista | C. Lonati | see Table 3.10 | 2 |
| XXVI | [Anonymous] | | | 2 |
| XXVII | [Anonymous] | | | 2 |
| XXVIII | Carlo Mannelli | Op. 2/2, 'La Fede' | | 2 |
| XXIX | A. Corelli | | undoubtedly spurious | 2 |
| XXX | [Anonymous] | | | 4 |
| XXXI | Hippolito Bocaletti | | not in *Sonate a tre* (Venice, 1692) | 4 |
| XXXII | Hen: Purcell | Sonata IX (1697) | | 5 |
| XXXIII–XLIV | Gio: Battista Bassani | Op. 5 | each headed 'Sonata Prima' etc. | 6 |
| XLV–LVI | A. Corelli | Op. 3 | each headed 'Sonata 1ma', etc. Not in the published sequence but in order of tonality from G to F. | 6 |
| LVII | G. Finger | Op. 1/4[a] | | 7 |
| LVIII | G. Finger | Op. 5/2[b] | | 7 |
| LIX | G. Finger | Op. 1/5 | | 7 |
| LX | G. Finger | Op. 5/1 | | 7 |
| LXI | G. Finger | Op. 1/6 | | 7 |
| LXII | G. Finger | Op. 5/5 | | 7 |
| LXIII–LXXIV | Johan Philip Kruger | Op. 1 | | 5 |

Oblong folio, 224 × 328.[c] Watermarks: Angoumois fleurs-de-lys with factors' marks 'AJ' or 'TJ', countermarked 'IHS' with initials 'PT', 'CDG' or 'RC'.

Rastrology: eight staves ruled with a four-stave rastrum, span: 76.5, profile: 11(10)11.5(10.5)12(10)11.5.

[a] *Sonatae XII, pro diversis instrumentis*, Op. 1 (1688).

[b] *X Suonate a tre*, Op. 5 (*c.* 1705).

[c] We are grateful to Russell Stinson for supplying much information about the manuscript's measurements, watermarks, rastrology and other details.

Fede,[41] who came to England in 1686 to serve as Master of the Music in James II's Catholic chapel.[42] The obscure English composer Anthony Poole, here called 'Antonius', is possibly to be identified with a Jesuit of that name who died in 1692.[43] Hand 1 of US-Cu 959 was also responsible for Ob MSS Mus.Sch. C.77a and b, beautifully written partbooks containing bass viol music by John Jenkins and Christopher Simpson, himself possibly a Jesuit:[44] these manuscripts have a fleur-de-lys watermark countermarked 'IHS/RC', a combination also found in the Chicago books. Taken together, these details suggest that US-Cu 959 was started at Whitehall in the late 1680s, though later additions were made for the exiled court at Saint-Germain. Despite their varied order, Corelli's Op. 3 sonatas appear to have been copied from the edition of 1689 so they and the subsequent music in the collection must have been added after the Glorious Revolution.

CH Cap. VI/I/I, deposited in the West Sussex Record Office by the Dean and Chapter of Chichester Cathedral, is partly in the hand of John Walter (Table 3.13). Pasted inside its front cover are the Cathedral bookplate and two cut-out labels, one bearing the inscription 'Io: Walter Ano 1630' inside an ornamental outline and the other, larger but less elegant, 'Jo Walter: His Book Anno Domino 1680'. To the right of the date is the scribble 'Walr'. The labels were probably attached to the cover at the same time as the nineteenth-century bookplate, and although the second is undoubtedly in Walter's handwriting there is no absolute proof that it ever formed an integral part of the following volume; the first, half a century older, obviously came from elsewhere.

The paper and ruling of the music pages are identical to those of Lbl R.M. 20.h.8. Walter's own contributions to his manuscript are limited to a small number of songs and vocal ensembles, mainly by Blow and Purcell (see pp. 260–1); all attributions to Blow refer to his doctorate and the year 1680 is mentioned in the heading of *She loves and she confesses too* (p. 411 INV). At the reverse of the manuscript Walter's text hand

[41] Edward Corp suggests that the dedication is probably to Innocenzo Fede's uncle Giuseppe: see 'The Musical Manuscripts of "Copiste Z"', *Revue de Musicologie* 84 (1998), 58.

[42] Edward T. Corp, 'The Exiled Court of James II and James III: a Centre of Italian Music in France, 1689–1712', *JRMA* 120 (1995), 218–19.

[43] For the Jesuit Anthony Poole (1627–92) see Anthony Kenny, ed., *The Responsa Scholarum of the English College, Rome, Part II: 1622–1685*, Catholic Record Society 55 (1963), 500; Godfrey Anstruther, *The Seminary Priests II: Early Stuarts 1603–1659* (Great Wakering, 1975), 248. For works of the composer see Dodd, *Thematic Index*; Robert Ford, 'Osborn MS 515: a Guardbook of Restoration Instrumental Music', *FAM* 30 (1983), 174–84; Corp, 'The Musical Manuscripts of "Copiste Z"', 56.

[44] Margaret Urquhart, 'Was Christopher Simpson a Jesuit?', *Chelys* 21 (1992), 3–26.

## Table 3.13 Chichester, West Sussex Record Office, MS Cap. VI/I/I: contents

| Page | Headings and incipits | Ascription | Copyist[a] |
|---|---|---|---|
| 1 | Sonnata [Purcell: 1697 Sonata IX] | Mr Hen: Purcell | 1 |
| 8 | Song: 'And art y[o]u griev'd' | Dr Blow | W |
| 10 | Song: 'O y[o]u yt didst Create ye Light | Dr Blow | W |
| 12 | Song: 'Peacefull is he' | 'Composed by Docr Blow' | W |
| 14 | Song: 'The Angell Gabriel' | 'Composed by Dr Blow' | W |
| 17 | Song: 'Stay stay gentle Eccho' | 'Composed by Dr Blow' | W |
| 19 | Song: 'How I have serv'd' | 'Composed by Dr Jo: Blow' | W |
| 22 | A Dialouge between Christian and Death [inc.] | [Blow] | W |
| 24 | 'From harmony, from heav'nly harmony' | 'Senior Baptist' | 1 |
| 64 | O Sing unto God [inc.] | Dr Blows | 1 |
| 79 | (Song) 'Enough my muse' | [Blow] | W |
| 82 | 'Sonatas Mr Fingers' [Op. 1, no. 1 (1688) only, inc.] | [Godfrey Finger] | 1 |
| 88 | Masque in Timon of Athens | Set by Mr H: Purcell | 1 |
| 104 | 'Aligeri amores' [inc.] | Bassani | 1 |
| 106 | Mr Henry Purcell's Cecilia's, Novbr ye 22. 1692 [inc.] | [Purcell] | 1 |
| 118 | 'I will lift up mine eyes' [inc.] | [anon.] | 1 |
| 144 | 'Nominativo his hac hoc' | by Sigr Merula | 1 |
| 149 | 'Nominativo quis' | [Merula] | 1 |
| 154 | 'Lord what love have I unto thy law' [inc.] | [anon.] | 1 |
| 156 | O Be Joyfull & c. Psalm ye 100 ye 2 first verses | [anon.] | 1 |
| 160 | 'O Lord rebuke me not' | Dr Crofts | 1 |
| 161 | Sanctus | [anon.] | 2 |
| 164 | 'The ways of Sion do mourn' | [Wise] | 2 |
| 167 | 'Open me the Gates of Righteousness' | Mr Wise | 2 |
| 174 | 'O God wherefore art thou absent' | Dr John Blow | 2 |
| 180 | 'My God my God look upon me' | Dr Tudway | 2 |
| 184 | 'Hear me O God in the multitude' | Mr John Goldwin | 2 |
| 189 | 'Hast ye O God to deliver me' | [anon.] | 2 |
| 195 | 'I was in the Spirit' | Dr John Blow | 2 |
| 201 | 'Lord how are they increased' | Dr John Blow | 2 |
| 207 | 'I beheld & lo a great multitude' | Dr Blow | 2 |

[manuscript inverted]

| | | | |
|---|---|---|---|
| 414 | Song: 'Sleep Adam sleep' | Mr Henry: Purcell | W |
| 413 | 'What hope for us remains' [inc.] | 'Composed by Mr Henry: Purcell' | W |
| 411 | A Song upon A Ground Made 1680 'She Loves and she confesses too' | 'Composed by Mr Henry: Purcell' | W |
| 410 | 'Urge me no more' | 'Composed by Mr Henry: Purcell' | W |
| 408 | 'In a deep visions intellectual scene' [mostly text only] | [Purcell] | W |
| 400 | Vers Anthem psalm ye 47th 'O Clap yo[u]r hands' [clefs, k-s, t-s, text incipit only] | [anon.] | 1 |
| 399 | Te Deum in Gamut [inc.: continued p. 389] | [Hall] | 1 |
| 397 | The Soules of ye Righteous | Mr Hen: Hall | 1 |
| 392 | O sing unto ye Lord [inc.] | [Blow] | 1 |
| 389 | Te Deum [continued from p. 398]; Jubilate; Magnificat [inc.] | | 1 |

Folio, 418 × 262. Watermarks: Angoumois fleur-de-lys with countermark 'IHS/ET'; pp. 225–7 only: a different fleur-de-lys with countermark 'IS'.

Rastrology (both paper types): sixteen staves ruled with a four-stave rastrum, span: 86, profile: 12(13)11.5(13)11(13)11.

[a] Copyists: W = John Walter; 1, 2 unidentified.

in *Sleep, Adam, sleep* and *What hope for us remains now he has gone* shares two features with Purcell's early handwriting, the secretary forms of the lowercase 'e' and 'r', though by the time he copied the song dated 1680 and wrote the signature now in the front of the book Walter had adopted modern italic patterns. These changes in Walter's handwriting offer further evidence that the Touzeau paper of Add. 30930 and Lbl R.M. 20.h.8 was available some time before 1680. The manuscript must, however, have been started in or after August 1677 as the second song in Walter's earlier style of writing is Purcell's elegy for Matthew Locke, who died in that month.

Walter's copying appears to have been carried out before the volume was bound. For most of its 414 pages collation is in regular eight-folio quires but a number of pages are missing from the sections in Walter's hand and the isolated Blow song *Enough my muse* (p. 79), at the beginning of a gathering, may have been separated from the rest of the series by mistake. Much other late seventeenth-century music, including Purcell's Sonata IX, was copied by a second hand, and further additions were made into the eighteenth century. The second copyist began Draghi's 1687 ode *From harmony, from heavenly harmony* on the first complete opening after the end of Walter's initial series of songs, and his datable work elsewhere in the manuscript including *Timon*, part of Purcell's 1692 St Cecilia ode and the beginning of Croft's *O Lord rebuke me not* points to a period of activity from 1687 onwards. The Purcell sonata, written on pp. 1–5 left unused by Walter at the beginning of the first gathering, is therefore unlikely to be an especially early source; it was clearly derived from an original resembling US-Cu 959, the Chichester copyist conflating the two bass parts into one and omitting much of the figuring.

The four folio partbooks Y M57/1–4(S) contain Corelli's Op. 1 and Bassani's Op. 5 in the hand of Matthew Hutton (1638–1711).[45] The Purcell sonata was added by a different copyist on spare pages following the Bassani. Each book consists of two gatherings, though the division does not correspond with the end of the Corelli sonatas. The main watermark of the latter gathering is a fleur-de-lys with the factor's mark 'AJ' and the countermark 'ET', but the outermost folios of the second gathering in the bassus book Y M57/3 are formed of a sheet of fleur-de-lys paper countermarked with the monogram 'PVL'. The combination of these makers' initials suggests

[45] Hutton was elected to a fellowship at Brasenose College, Oxford, in 1659; he was appointed rector of Aynho in Northamptonshire in 1677 and resigned his fellowship two years later. Manuscripts in his hand include Purcell's 'Behold the man that with gigantic might' (*The Richmond Heiress*, 1693) in Y M32/1(S), though some copying has been mistakenly attributed to him. See Richard Charteris, 'Matthew Hutton (1638–1711) and his Manuscripts in York Minster Library', *GSJ* 28 (1975), 2–6; John Irving, 'Matthew Hutton and York Minster MSS M.3/1–4(S)', *MR* 44 (1983), 163–77.

that the partbooks date from the mid-1680s, though the Purcell need not have been added for some time. The last page of the first violin book, which contained Sonata IX from bar 81 onwards, has been lost and the source is in other respects slightly inferior to US-Cu 959.

In J-Tn N3/35 'Mr Henry Purcells Golden Sonata in F fa ut' occupies fols. 35v–38r, preceded on fol. 34r by Handel's famous air from *Rinaldo* (1711) and followed by an arrangement of his concerto, Op. 3, no. 4, dated 1716. Most of the later material in the book, including the Purcell, was copied by William Raylton, organist of Canterbury Cathedral from 1736 to 1757. The version of Sonata IX copied by John Harris[46] in Cfm 652 is related to the 1697 publication, which must have been its primary source; a bass part in US-LAuc *M401.P98s also lies outside the group of manuscripts descended from the independent autograph, although in places it was evidently influenced by this tradition.

## EARLY MANUSCRIPT SOURCES OF THE *SONNATA'S OF III. PARTS*

The primary source of the 1683 sonatas is the printed edition, from which several manuscript scores were soon derived, although in some cases the printed parts from which they were copied appear to have been altered in minor detail. The calligraphic score Och 39, copied by Edward Hull, is listed in John Malchair's catalogue of Henry Aldrich's music library, Lcm 2125: its watermarks are conventional Angoumois fleurs-de-lys but the distinctive countermark, which seems to depict a flower between two pillars, resembles that of Lbl Add. 31430, a set of parts copied by John Playford (d. 1686–7).[47] Unusually for an open score the paper is ruled with six-line staves. Another Oxford source, Och 1174, is in the same hand as the final section of Och 8 which is otherwise the work of Francis Withy. It consists of two kinds of foolscap paper, one, countermarked 'IM', resembling paper found in Lbl Add. 33234, an Oxford manuscript dated 1682. Each of the Christ Church scores derives from a different set of parts with distinctive manuscript alterations: unlike the presentation volume Och 39, Och 1174 includes only the basic text of the music, leaving out much of the thorough-bass part and most tempo directions. A score copied by the Winchester organist John Read-

---

[46] A son of Renatus Harris, the famous organ builder, who had another son also named Renatus. An inscription on fol. ii reads 'This Book was given me by my Brother Renatus for some other things which I gave for it.'

[47] See Robert Thompson, 'Manuscript Music in Purcell's London', *EM* 23 (1995), 607, 615–16.

ing, Lbl R.M. 20.h.9, is discussed at greater length in Chapter 6: the twelve sonatas (fols. 98v–52r INV) were evidently transcribed from the printed edition, and at two points (fols. 90v and 62v) Reading imitates the engraver's trefoil terminal flourish. The last of the early scores, Ob MS Tenbury 1011, consists of three originally loose foolscap sheets on which the veteran composer George Jeffreys (*c*. 1610–85) copied sonatas I, II and IX.[48]

---

[48] For Jeffreys's life and works see Peter Aston, 'George Jeffreys', *MT* 110 (1969), 772–6; Aston, 'Tradition and Experiment in the Works of George Jeffreys', *PRMA* 99 (1972–3), 105–15; Jonathan Wainwright, *Musical Patronage in Seventeenth-Century England: Christopher, First Baron Hatton (1605–1670)* (Aldershot, 1997).

# British Library Royal Music 20.h.8
## and its repertories

The third of Purcell's great autograph scorebooks, Lbl R.M. 20.h.8, contains a series of Chapel Royal symphony anthems at one end and at the other a sequence of mainly secular vocal works ranging from court odes to solo songs (Table 4.1). The manuscript is the only major autograph in which Purcell employed assistants to copy some of the music, perhaps suggesting that he regarded it less as a personal document than as a formal record and master copy of music performed at Whitehall in the Chapel Royal, at semi-public ceremonial occasions, and privately in the royal apartments. Flyleaf inscriptions identifying the composer's son Edward Purcell (1689–1740) and his grandson Edward Henry Purcell (1716–65) show that R.M. 20.h.8 remained in the Purcell family for some years, but by 1781 it belonged to Philip Hayes, who transcribed from it the manuscripts now Ktp MR 2–5.1 and 2. In MR 2–5.2 Hayes records that he then presented R.M. 20.h.8 to King George III,[1] and in 1911 King George V deposited it in the British Museum, on permanent loan as part of the Royal Music Library.[2]

## CODICOLOGY

The 269 music folios of R.M. 20.h.8 are arranged in forty-six quires, mostly of six folios though one of four begins at fol. 84/v and one of eight at fol. 180. A leaf is

[1] 'The greatest part of the Odes &c &c contained in this book were carefully transcrib'd from Hen[r]y Purcel's original Score, which I presented to my Royal Master King George the third, in June 1781 at the Queen's House at Windsor. Phil. Hayes'. See *Works*, XVII (1996), xi, xvii–xviii; Nigel Fortune, 'A New Purcell Source', *MR* 25 (1964), 109–13.
[2] 'The King's Music: Loan to the British Museum', *The Times*, 13 February 1911, 8. The anonymous article is by William Barclay Squire: see King, *Some British Collectors*, 110n.

missing after fols. 62, 84, 113, 117 and 241 and two after fol. 169. The British Library foliation starts at the anthem end and runs from 1 to 245 ignoring unwritten folios: fols. 1–3 are the original front flyleaves and three similar flyleaves at the back are unnumbered. Sheets forming pastedowns and endpapers date from the volume's late eighteenth-century rebinding for the royal library.[3]

Although R.M. 20.h.8 and Lbl Add. 30930 consist of identical Etienne Touzeau paper (see p. 88) the two sources have dissimilar histories, the regular collation of R.M. 20.h.8 leaving no doubt that unlike Add. 30930 it was made as a bound manuscript book. In Add. 30930 the flyleaves are unruled sheets of the main paper type, but those of R.M. 20.h.8, some bearing writing in Purcell's hand, have a different fleur-de-lys watermark with the 'GP' countermark adopted by Gerrit Pieterszoon van der Ley between 1673 and 1677.[4] Collation offers no evidence concerning the manuscript's general history but three places where pages have been removed from works in Purcell's hand may indicate passages he found difficult or decided to revise: in the 1685 coronation anthem *My heart is inditing*, apparently written in some haste, the missing folio after fol. 62 corresponds with the beginning of the chorus 'Praise the Lord O Jerusalem' (bar 386); at the reverse, the loss of two folios between fols. 170 and 169 indicates that Purcell made major alterations to the opening of *Awake and with attention hear*, which begins halfway down fol. 169r INV, and in consequence had to rewrite *In some kind dream* (fols. 169v–169r INV). Apart from an excision between fols. 242 and 241 in *Swifter Isis swifter flow* the other missing folios are in sections copied by Purcell's assistants.

Purcell probably took charge of R.M. 20.h.8 after October 1680 as it omits *Welcome vicegerent*, his welcome song for that year.[5] It is uncertain whether *Swifter Isis* was composed for March or August of 1681, but from 1682 to 1687 a key to the manuscript's chronology is provided by the welcome songs and other odes, for which the year of performance is usually in the heading. Only one welcome song is given a precise performance date, *The summer's absence unconcerned we bear* of 21 October 1682, but most works without more specific titles celebrated the court's return to Whitehall after the summer progress,[6] an event invariably recorded in

[3] King, *Some British Collectors*, 110n.    [4] See Voorn, *De papiermolens*, 117, 131, 143, 145.

[5] The suggestion in *Works*, XV (1905), ii, that *Welcome vicegerent* was omitted as 'an early work not worthy of preservation' is inconsistent with Purcell's general practice around 1680 and the personal significance of his first royal ode.

[6] Ian Spink, 'Purcell's Odes: Propaganda and Panegyric', in *Purcell Studies*, 146. The published text of the 1684 welcome song *From those serene and rapturous joys* is headed 'On the King's Return to White-hall after his Summer's Progress, 1684' (Thomas Flatman, *Poems and Songs* (London, 1686)); Spink, 'Purcell's Odes', 169.

## Table 4.1 London, British Library Royal Music 20.h.8: contents

| Folios | Headings, incipits and inscriptions[a] | Copyist (P = Purcell; A–C = London A–C) |
|---|---|---|
| 1r | Flyleaf inscribed 'Ed H. Purcell Grandson to the Author of this Book' | E. H. Purcell |
| 2r | Flyleaf inscribed 'A Score Book Containing Severall Anthems w[i]th Symphonies' | P, after 1683 |
| 3r | Flyleaf; 'The Table' (incomplete) | P, after 1683 |
| 4r | Heading; 'Anthems' | P |
| 4r–7v | It is a good thing to give thanks [incipit; no heading] | P |
| 7v–13r | O praise God in his holiness 'ye 150 Psl' | P |
| 13v–15v | Awake, put on thy strength 'Isaiah ye 51st' (inc.) | A (1st violin and a few notes of the bass of bars 1–4, P) |
| 16v–17r | O pray for ye peace of Jerusalem 'ye 122 Psl': Dr Blow | P |
| 17v–22r | In thee O Lord do I put my trust 'ye 71st Pslm 1st 4th 5th 9th 18th 20th 21st verses'[b] | P |
| 22v–25v | The Lord is my light and my salvation 'Psalm ye 27th' | P |
| 25v–28v | I was glad when they said unto me 'Psl ye 122' | P |
| 28v–32r | My heart is fixed O God 'Pslm ye 57th vers ye 8th 9th 10th 11th & 12th' | P |
| 32v–37r | Praise the Lord O my soul [incipit; no heading] | P |
| 37v–39v | Rejoice in the Lord alway [incipit; no heading] | P |
| 39v–43r | Why do the heathen so furiously rage 'Psalm ye 2d' | P |
| 43r–48r | Unto thee will I cry 'The 28th Psalm' | P |
| 48r–51v | I will give thanks unto thee O Lord | P |
| 52r | They that go down to the sea in ships (inc.) | P |
| | I will give thanks unto the Lord | Index only |
| | O Lord grant the king a long life | Index only |
| 53v–66v | My heart is inditing [incipit; no heading]: 'One of the Anthems Sung at ye Coronation of King James the 2d' | P, 1685 |
| 67r–74v | O sing unto ye Lord | A |
| 75r–81r | Praise ye Lord O Jerusalem | A |
| 81r–84v | Praise the Lord O my soul (inc.) | A |

[manuscript inverted]

| Folios | Headings, incipits and inscriptions[a] | Copyist (P = Purcell; A–C = London A–C) |
|---|---|---|
| 246v | Flyleaf: 'Score Booke' | P |
| | 'Anthems and Welcome Songs and other Songs all by my father' | ?Edward Purcell |
| 245v–238v | (1) A Welcome Song in ye Year 1681 For ye King; 'Swifter, Isis' | P |
| 238r–233r | (2) A Welcome Song for his Royall Highness at his return from Scotland in the yeare 1682; 'What shal be done in behalf of the man' | P |
| 232v–226v | (3) A Welcome Song for his Majesty at his return from New Market October ye 21 1682; 'The summers absence unconcern'd we beare' | P |
| 226r–224v | (4) 'How pleasant is this flow'ry plain' | P |
| 224r–223v | (5) 'Wee reap all ye pleasures' (inc.) | P |

Table 4.1 (*cont.*)

| Folios | Headings, incipits and inscriptions[a] | Copyist (P = Purcell; A–C = London A–C) |
|---|---|---|
| 222v–218v | (6) 'Heark how ye wild Musitians sing' | P |
| 218r–217r | (7) 'Heark Damon heark' | P |
| 217r–216r | 'Above ye Tumults of a buisy state' | P |
| 216r–215r | (The 9th Ode of Horrace imitated) (A Dialouge betwixt ye Poet & Lydia); 'While you for me alone had Charmes' | P |
| 215r–214r | (A dialouge between Charon & Orpheus); 'Hast, gentle Charon' | P |
| 213v–212v | (ye Epicure); 'Underneath this Mirtle shade' | P |
| 212v–211v | (The Concealment); 'No: to what purpose shou'd I speak' | P |
| 211v–211r | 'Draw neare you Lovers that complaine' | P |
| 211r–210r | (Jobs Curse); 'Let ye Night perish' | P |
| 210r–209v | (Song.) 'Amidst ye shades' | P |
| 209r–207v | (14) 'See where she sits' | P |
| 207r–201v | (15) A Song yt was perform'd to Prince George upon his marriage wth ye Lady Ann; 'From hardy Climes & dangerous toyles of Warr' | P; 28 July 1683 |
| 201r–199r | (16) (Mr Cowley's complaint); 'In a deep visions intelectuall scene' | P |
| 198v–198r | (17) (Song) out of Mr Herbert; 'With sick and famish'd Eyes' | P |
| 197v–190v | (18) ye Welcome Song perform'd to his Majesty in ye Year 1683; 'Fly bold Rebellion' | P |
| 190r–188r | (19) A Latine Song made upon St Cecilia whoes day is commerated yearly by all Musitians made in ye year 1683; 'Laudate Cecilliam' | P |
| 188r–186v | 'Oh; what a Scene do's entertain my sight' | P |
| 186r–185v | 'Tho' my Mistriss be fair' | P |
| 185r–184v | (A Serandeing Song). 'Soft notes & gentely rais'd' | P |
| 184r–183v | A Seranading Song: 'Silvia, thou brighter eye of Night' | P |
| 183v–183r | 'Goe tell Aminta gentle Swain' | P |
| 182v–175v | (23) The Welcome Song perform'd to his Majesty in ye Year 1684; 'From those serene & rapturous joyes' | P |
| 175r–174v | (24) (Song on a Ground) 'Cease Anxious World your fruitless pain' | P; last line A |
| 174v–174r | (25) The Rich Rivall out of Mr Cowly; 'They say you're angry' | A |
| 174r–173v | 'O solitude my sweetest choice' | A to end of 174; P |
| 173r–172r | (26) 'When Teucer from his Father fled' | P |
| 172r–171r | (Sighs for our Late Sov'raign King Charles ye 2d); 'If Pray'rs & Teares' | P |
| 170v | (28) (The Thraldome out of Mr Cowley) | P; title only |
| 169v–169r | 'In some kind dream' | P |
| 169r–166v | (The 34 chapter of Isaiah paraphras'd by Mr Cowley); 'Awake and w[i]th attention hear' | P |
| 166r–157r | (30) Welcome Song 1685 being ye first Song perform'd to King James ye 2d; 'Why are all ye Muses mute' | P to end of 162v, then B |
| 157r–155v | The words by Mr Cowley; 'Here's to ye Dick' | A |

## Table 4.1 (*cont.*)

| Folios | Headings, incipits and inscriptions[a] | Copyist (P = Purcell; A–C = London A–C) |
|---|---|---|
| 155r–145r | (32) Welcome Song 1686; 'Yee tunefull Muses' | B |
| 144v–140r | (33) 'If ever I more riches did desire' | P |
| 140r–139v | (34) (Anacreon's Defeat); 'This Poet sings the Trojan Warrs' | P |
| 139r–128v | (35) Welcome Song 1687; 'Sound the Trumpet, Beat ye Drum' | P |
| 128r | The Resurrection: out of Cowley's Pindaricks; 'Begin ye Song' | P; outline of beginning only |
| 127r–125v | (36) [Cazzati]; 'Crucior in hâc flâma' | P |
| 125v–117r | (37) A Song that was perform'd at Mr Maidwells a schoolmaster on ye 5th of August 1689 ye words by one of his scholars; 'Celestial Music' | P to middle of 124, then C |
| 116v–106r | (38) 'Now does ye Glorious day Appear' [1689] | A |
| 105v–90v | (39) 'Of old when Heroes thought it base'; 'Mr H Pursell 1690' | A |
| 90r–85v | (40) 'Arise my muse arise' [inc., 1690] | A |

Folio, 410 × 250. Watermarks: Angoumois fleur-de-lys with countermark 'IHS/ET'.

Rastrology: sixteen staves ruled with a four-stave rastrum, span: 85, profile: 12(13)11.5(12.5)11.5(13)11.

[a] No attempt has been made to record minor differences between the headings and incipits of anthems or to reproduce Purcell's orthography in them. For the works copied from the reverse of the manuscript Purcell's headings (if any) are transcribed literally, including his item numbers and parentheses. Other annotations and incipits are given between inverted commas.    [b] Verse 9 is not in fact set.

Luttrell's *Brief Relation of State Affairs*.[7] In addition, *My heart is inditing* was composed for James II's coronation on 23 April 1685, *If prayers and tears* refers to the death of Charles II, and *Celestial Music* was performed on 5 August 1689. The transformation from secretary to italic as Purcell's principal form of the lowercase 'r' (see pp. 31–2) is therefore a genuine if not entirely progressive chronological development likely to be replicated in other manuscripts (Table 4.2). The handwriting of the anthem sequence indicates a chronology more or less parallel to that of the odes (Table 4.3), though *Awake put on thy strength*, which is mostly not in Purcell's hand, is followed by five anthems in which the incidence of the italic lowercase 'r' lies in the range between 10 per cent and 20 per cent characteristic of the English odes of 1682 and 1683. The evidence of Purcell's handwriting is therefore that his anthems were not transcribed at an even rate but rather that a concentrated period of activity followed his appointment in 1682 as one of the three organists of the Chapel Royal. Four of Purcell's anthem copies in R.M. 20.h.8 can be compared with their rough drafts in Bu 5001 and Ob MS Mus.c.26 (see pp. 142–3): the similar incidence of secretary and italic forms of the lowercase 'r' and the close relationship of text in the two copies of

[7] Narcissus Luttrell, *A Brief Relation of State Affairs from September 1678 to April 1714* (Oxford, 1857).

Table 4.2 London, British Library Royal Music 20.h.8: incidence of secretary and italic forms of the lowercase 'r' in odes and welcome songs

| Work | Performance date | Secretary | Italic | Total | Percentage of italic |
|---|---|---|---|---|---|
| Swifter Isis[a] | March or August 1681 | 567 | 10 | 577 | 1.7 |
| What shall be done | 27 May 1682 | 312 | 89 | 401 | 22.2[b] |
| The summer's absence | 21 October 1682 | 373 | 43 | 416 | 10.3 |
| From hardy climes | 28 July 1683 | 355 | 61 | 416 | 14.7 |
| Fly bold rebellion | 25 September 1683 | 469 | 109 | 578 | 18.9 |
| Laudate Ceciliam | 22 November 1683 | 79 | 2 | 81 | 2.5 |
| From those serene and rapturous joys | 25 September 1684 | 198 | 109 | 307 | 35.5 |
| Why are all the muses mute[c] | 6 October 1685 | 0 | 335 | 335 | 100.0 |

[a] Probably copied in March.

[b] The unusually high proportion of italic letters in *What shall be done in behalf of the man* is partly explained by a homophonic setting of the words 'that York, Royall York is ye next in succession' on fol. 236, where text appears to have been added to the lower voices at a later date. If these additions had corresponded with the style of the original text the overall proportion of italic forms of 'r' would have been 17 per cent.

[c] Numbers refer to the section in Purcell's hand only.

each work suggesting that Purcell proceeded from the composing stage to the finished version almost immediately. A number of secondary sources nevertheless represent earlier versions of certain anthems, symphony songs and smaller-scale works, in some cases with significant variation, and the chronology of transcription into the great scorebook should not be uncritically extended to dates of initial composition.

Three copyists assisted Purcell in the compilation of R.M. 20.h.8 (see Table 4.1). London B and London C are each represented in one or two works only, the former copying about half of *Why are all the muses mute* and the whole of *Ye tuneful muses*, the welcome songs for 1685 and 1686, and the latter completing *Celestial Music*. London A, in contrast, was responsible for all or part of eleven works, including several lengthy odes: like B and C, he completed works Purcell had left unfinished (Illus. 4.1), and on either side of fol. 174 supplied the beginning and end of otherwise autograph songs. London A's variable hand has been identified in many manuscripts connected with the Purcells and the Chapel Royal circle of John Blow, Jeremiah Clarke and William Croft (Table 4.4),[8] and the relationship with Purcell apparent in

[8] See *Works*, II (1994), xiv, xvi; Peter Holman, 'Purcell and Roseingrave: a New Autograph', in *Purcell Studies*, 94–5; *Works*, XIX (1994), xxiv. See also *The Island Princess* (facsimile edn), intro. by Curtis Price and Robert Hume, MLE C2 (Tunbridge Wells, 1985); *Instrumental Music for London Theatres, 1690–99: Royal College of Music MS 1172* (facsimile edn), intro. by Curtis Price, MLE A3 (Withyham, 1987).

Illus. 4.1 Henry Purcell: *Awake put on thy strength*, mostly copied by London A. British Library R.M. 20.h.8, fol. 13v

Table 4.3 **London, British Library Royal Music 20.h.8: incidence of secretary and italic forms of the lowercase 'r' in anthems**

| Work | Secretary | Italic | Total | Percentage of italic |
|------|-----------|--------|-------|----------------------|
| It is a good thing to give thanks | 151 | 2 | 153 | 1.3 |
| O praise God in his holiness | 326 | 0 | 326 | 0.0 |
| In thee O Lord do I put my trust | 155 | 30 | 185 | 16.2 |
| The Lord is my light | 88 | 15 | 103 | 14.6 |
| I was glad | 104 | 32 | 136 | 23.5 |
| My heart is fixed | 97 | 12 | 109 | 11.0 |
| Praise the Lord O my soul | 221 | 55 | 276 | 19.9 |
| Rejoice in the Lord | 104 | 35 | 139 | 25.2 |
| Why do the heathen | 149 | 64 | 213 | 30.0 |
| Unto thee will I cry | 24 | 181 | 205 | 88.3 |
| I will give thanks | 0 | 225 | 225 | 100.0 |

R.M. 20.h.8 and US-R M2040/A628/Folio indicates that he might have been a former Chapel Royal chorister retained as an apprentice after his voice changed. His copying in R.M. 20.h.8 began rather later than the manuscript's overall chronology seems to suggest: if *Awake put on thy strength* of *c*. 1681–2 had been in its present, substantially complete, form by 1685 it might be expected to appear with other contemporary works in Lcm 2011, so its continuation is more likely to have taken place in or after 1689, when London A copied three odes dating from 1689 or 1690 and the three final anthems in the scorebook: these transcriptions were probably made soon after the music was composed and some details of London A's hand still resemble the earlier manuscript US-R M2040/A628/Folio rather than later sources such as Lbl Add. 31449. Around the same time he made corrections to several copies of *Dioclesian* (published 1691).[9] London A's earliest contribution to R.M. 20.h.8 is probably fol. 174, an entire leaf integral to the structure of the manuscript which includes the last line of *Cease anxious world*, the whole of *They say you're angry* and the beginning of *O solitude*. This folio lies between the welcome song for 1684 and *If prayers and tears*, composed in memory of Charles II, so in late 1684 or 1685 London A must have been working very closely with Purcell; the duet *Here's to ye Dick* was added between the welcome songs for 1685 and 1686, when London B was Purcell's principal assistant.

[9] See *Works*, IX (1961), xiv. London A's corrections and annotations in one of the two copies at the Royal Academy of Music seem broadly to resemble the style of his writing in R.M. 20.h.8.

### Table 4.4 Manuscripts copied by London A

| *Library and shelfmark* | *Contents* |
| --- | --- |
| Lbl R.M. 20.h.8 | songs, odes and anthems by Purcell (Table 4.1) |
| Lbl R.M. 24.e.13, fols. 62–110 | Henry Purcell: *Timon of Athens*, score |
| Lbl Add. 30934, fols. 3–34; fols. 94v–95r | Jeremiah Clarke: *Come, come along for a dance and a song*, score |
| | Daniel Purcell: *The loud-tongued warlike thunder*, score of overture |
| Lbl Add. 31449 | Henry Purcell: *The Indian Queen*, theatre score |
| Lbl Add. 15318 | *The Island Princess* (1699): music by Daniel Purcell, Richard Leveridge and Jeremiah Clarke |
| Lbl Add. 31452, fols. 82v–100r | Jeremiah Clarke: *The Barbadoes Song*, score |
| Lcm 862 | *The Virgin Prophetess* (1701): music by Godfrey Finger |
| Lcm 1106, fols. 1r–28r | Jeremiah Clarke: *The Barbadoes Song*, score |
| Lcm 1172 | theatre tunes in score by various composers, all in G minor, originally copied on loose sheets |
| Ob MS Mus.c.26, fols. 71–94 | Henry Purcell: *Arise my muse*, score |
| Ob MS Tenbury 345, fols. 11v–18v | MS songs, including two by Purcell, bound at the end of *Harmonia Sacra* (1693) |
| Ob MS Tenbury 1232 | songs by Croft and anon.; odes by Clarke and Henry Hall (*Yes my Aminta 'tis too true*: 'A Peace of Musicke upon ye Death of Mr H. Purcell') |
| Och 1141A, fols. 30–43 | parts of an anonymous sonata in C for trumpet, two oboes and four-part strings |
| Och 1215, no. 11 | Daniel Purcell: dialogue, *In spite of despair*. One of a number of unrelated manuscripts in a modern guardbook |
| US-R M2040/A628/Folio | anthems by Blow, Purcell, Orlando Gibbons and Christopher Gibbons: see Table 2.7 |
| US-NYp Drexel 4285.6 | Henry Purcell: *Oedipus*, score |
| US-Wc M21/M185/Case | keyboard music by Pasquini, Draghi, Purcell, Forcer, Kuhnau and others |

The identity of London A may never be known for certain, but his manuscripts provide enough evidence for an informed guess. In late 1684 or early 1685 he seems to have been working under Purcell's direction, copying music into US-R M2040/A628/Folio from Cfm 88 and beginning to contribute to R.M. 20.h.8 itself, and although in later years Purcell taught pupils from other backgrounds any young musician in his charge at that time is likely to have been a former Chapel Royal chorister or an apprentice sent from another choral foundation. The difficult and varied harpsichord music in US-Wc M21/M185/Case is evidence that London A became a keyboard player of the first rank, and the theatre music in his hand shows that he cannot have died before 1702, for he copied music written in that year. He is unlikely to have worked for long outside London, a restriction which disqualifies

Purcell's pupil Robert Hodge. Jeremiah Clarke is ruled out by his youth in 1685 and by the identification of the hand in his *Song on the Assumption* (Ob MS Tenbury 1226, fols. 102r–124v)[10] with Clarke's signatures at St Paul's Cathedral.[11] The most promising candidate is Francis Pigott, who left the Chapel at Michaelmas 1683, succeeded to Purcell's place as organist in 1695 and died in 1704. From 1686 to 1688 Pigott was organist of Magdalen College, Oxford, having previously held a similar post at St John's[12] which he perhaps took up in late 1684 or early 1685, after copying fol. 174 of R.M. 20.h.8. *Here's to ye Dick* could have been transcribed during a brief visit in 1685 or 1686, but Pigott's Oxford appointments would explain why it was only after 1688, when he returned to London to become organist of the Temple Church, that he was entrusted with the copying of major works. London B, who acted as Purcell's principal assistant in his absence, may in fact be Hodge, who left for Wells around the end of 1688.

CONTENTS: THE ANTHEMS

Purcell's list of fifteen anthems in 'The Table' on fol. 3r appears to have been drawn up in late 1684 or 1685, the last page reference, '39', being for the eleventh anthem, *Unto thee will I cry.* Four more anthems included in the table but without page numbers were evidently intended to form part of the same sequence, but only *I will give thanks unto thee O Lord* and the first few bars of *They that go down to the sea in ships* were completed. The interruption in transcription was presumably caused by the king's death on 6 February 1685, so the last five anthems in the table must have been composed by that date. Up to this point only two works interrupt the autograph sequence of Purcell's own anthems: *Awake put on thy strength*, in 1685 still in the vestigial state in which it had been left by Purcell, and Blow's verse anthem *O pray for the peace of Jerusalem.* With the incomplete copy of *They that go*

---

[10] This score is described as autograph in the manuscript's table of contents (fol. 1r) and in Edmund H. Fellowes, *The Catalogue of the Manuscripts in the Library of St Michael's College, Tenbury* (Paris, 1934), 268. Even without the evidence of the signatures listed in n. 11 below it would be a strong contender to represent Clarke's hand: some supposed autographs were in fact copied by London A and the sonata parts inscribed 'J Clark' in Ckc 228 and 229 were probably copied by their composer, Charles Rosier.

[11] Lg 25650/4 (Acquittance Book, 1699–1705); 22 December 1699; 25 March, 24 June, 30 September 1700 etc. After 20 December 1701 Clarke's signatures adopt a different form.

[12] Zimmerman refers to an early Magdalen College organ book written in a hand 'somewhat similar to that of Daniel Purcell', a description which suggests it may have been copied by London A: see Zimmerman, *Catalogue*, 414. A thorough search failed to bring this manuscript to light.

*down* on fol. 52r Purcell's intended plan was abandoned, and the coronation anthem *My heart is inditing* is the last sacred work Purcell entered in the manuscript, the last three anthems being added by London A. Since the first and last of these three are respectively dated 1688 and 1687 in US-AUS Pre-1700 85, and the second was almost certainly composed for William and Mary's coronation in 1689,[13] it is likely that all were copied in 1689 or later, and despite London A's close relationship with Purcell, these scores are not necessarily more authoritative than manuscripts in other hands. Although Purcell continued to compose anthems after 1685, the fact that no more were transcribed into R.M. 20.h.8 in his autograph, and none at all between 1685 and, at the earliest, 1688, tells its own story about the status of the Anglican Chapel Royal. The work of London A at the end of the anthem sequence, and the near-completion of *Awake put on thy strength*, may well have been carried out in the belief that William and Mary would restore the Chapel to its former glory, but such hopes were soon disappointed and under the new Protestant monarchs even the most elaborate anthems were normally performed with organ accompaniment.[14]

Two anthems in Purcell's hand raise significant textual difficulties, *Rejoice in the Lord alway* and *I will give thanks unto thee O Lord*. In *Rejoice in the Lord* the inner parts of both chorus and instrumental passages are omitted, though a number of precise performance directions are given and all the verse parts are present apart from interjections in the choruses. Complete secondary sources such as Lbl Add. 17840 presumably descend from a preliminary version which Purcell intended to revise in detail. *I will give thanks unto thee O Lord*, which in R.M. 20.h.8 omits all the music of bars 194–203, differs more extensively from its other principal source, Lbl Add. 47845,[15] and may therefore be a rather earlier work for some reason not entered in R.M. 20.h.8 at the time of its composition.

---

[13] Eric Van Tassel, 'Music for the Church', in *Purcell Companion*, 187–9, 199n; Anselm Hughes, 'Music of the Coronation over a Thousand Years', *PRMA* 79 (1952–3), 94. See also correspondence from Maurice Bevan and Robert Manning, *MT* 119 (1978), 938; *MT* 120 (1979), 1, 22, 114.

[14] This must be the implication of an order of 1691 that 'the King's Chapel shall be all the year through kept both morning and evening with solemn musick like a collegiate church': see Henry Cart de Lafontaine, *The King's Musick* (London, 1909), 407. The document cannot now be traced, but Paul Hopkins has recently discovered an order dated 23 February 1689 banning the use of instruments in the Chapel Royal: Lpro RG8/110, fols. 24r–25v.

[15] *Works*, XVII (1996), 54–77.

## CONTENTS: SECULAR AND DOMESTIC MUSIC

The secular and domestic repertory copied in R.M. 20.h.8 includes odes for formal occasions, symphony songs for varied ensembles of voices and instruments, music for smaller vocal groups and solo songs. The distinctive nature of the symphony song, a genre as closely linked to the court as the symphony anthem was to the Chapel Royal,[16] is underlined by the principal concordance of the longer works in R.M. 20.h.8, Lbl Add. 33287, in which the first section is devoted to symphony songs and the second to court odes (see Table 4.21 below). The remaining vocal music generally has a different set of concordances from the symphony songs (Table 4.5). There are also two Latin works: Purcell's *Laudate Ceciliam* and the duet *Crucior in hac flamma* by Cazzati.

Though New Year and birthday odes were already well established, regular performance of welcome songs appears to have commenced with Purcell's *Welcome vicegerent of the mighty king* of 1680[17] and was possibly intended to provide a showcase for Purcell's talents without disadvantaging Blow and other senior composers. The performance date of *Swifter Isis* is uncertain, if it was performed at all:[18] several features of the text make little sense unless the ode was intended to welcome the king back from the Oxford parliament, opened on 21 March 1681, but Charles's abrupt dissolution of the parliament on 27 March and immediate return to London seem to have taken his courtiers by surprise.[19] Purcell's copying of this work may reflect a rushed attempt to complete it, for at first his writing is careful and elegant but the last chorus is much less tidy and lacks most of its inner parts. Dating of *Swifter Isis* to March 1681 allows its ground and pseudo-ground movements to be a prompt response to their apparent model, Blow's 1681 New Year Song *Great Sir the joy of all our hearts*,[20] so the anthems *It is a good thing* and *O praise God in his holiness*, which appear from their handwriting to predate *Swifter Isis*, may therefore have been entered in R.M. 20.h.8 between October 1680 and March 1681. The secular contents of the manuscript were initially confined to court odes, but after the 1682

---

[16] The status of the symphony song as an independent genre is discussed in Holman, *Henry Purcell*, 45–7.

[17] 9 September or 9 October 1680. See Spink, 'Purcell's Odes', 149–50, 168.

[18] A performance date of 27 August is suggested in Zimmerman, *Catalogue*, 162; in *Works*, XV (1905), iv, Ralph Vaughan Williams put forward 12 October 1681, when Charles returned from Newmarket, but this event is inconsistent with the text's repeated references to the river. See Spink, 'Purcell's Odes', 150–2.

[19] Spink, 'Purcell's Odes', 151; Luttrell, *A Brief Relation*, I, 72.

[20] Bruce Wood, 'Purcell's Odes: a Reappraisal', in *Purcell Companion*, 203–6; Wood, 'Only Purcell e're shall equal Blow', in *Purcell Studies*, 113–14 and 144: 'the two composers borrowed almost exclusively from each other's recent music, allowing a lapse of only a few months at most'.

**Table 4.5 London, British Library Royal Music 20.h.8: solo songs and duets**

| Title | Print[a] | Author | Manuscript concordances[b] |
|---|---|---|---|
| Above the tumults of a busy state | – | anon. | Bu 5002; Lbl Add. 33235 |
| Amidst the shades | TM4 | anon. | Bu 5002 |
| Awake and with attention hear | HS | Cowley | Lbl Add. 31460 |
| Cease anxious world | TM4 | Etheredge | |
| Draw near, you lovers | – | Stanley | |
| Go tell Aminta | – | Dryden | Bu 5002; Lbl Add. 30382 |
| Haste gentle Charon | – | anon. | B-Bc 1035.g; Lbl Add. 22100, 33234 |
| Here's to ye Dick | BM1 | Cowley | |
| If prayers and tears | OB | anon. | B-Bc 1035.g |
| In some kind dream | TM4 | Etheredge | Lbl Add. 30382; J-Tn 0–1–54 |
| Let the night perish | HS | Taylor | Bu 5002; Lbl Add. 31460, 33235 |
| No, to what purpose | – | Cowley | B-Bc 1035.g |
| O solitude | CA | Phillips | Lbl Add. 22099, 29397, 33235/6 |
| Silvia, thou brighter eye | – | anon. | Bu 5002 |
| They say you're angry | TM2 | Cowley | |
| This poet sings the Trojan wars | BM1 | anon. | |
| Though my mistress be fair | CCC | anon. | |
| Underneath this Mirtle shade | BM6 | Cowley | |
| When Teucer from his father fled | PMC2 | Kenrick | |
| While you for me alone had charms | – | Oldham | B-Bc 1035.g |
| With sick and famished eyes | HS | Herbert | Bu 5002; Lbl Add. 33236 |

[a] Earliest printed editions:

| | |
|---|---|
| BM1 | *The Banquet of Music...the first book*, 1688 |
| BM6 | *The Banquet of Music...the sixth and last book*, 1692 |
| CA | *Comes Amoris; or the Companion of Love*, 1687 |
| CCC | *Catch that Catch Can: or the Second Part of the Musical Companion*, 1685 |
| HS | *Harmonia Sacra; or Divine Hymns and Dialogues*, 1688 |
| OB | *Orpheus Britannicus*, 1698 |
| PMC2 | *The Second Book of the Pleasant Musical Companion*, 1686 |
| TM2 | *The Theater of Music...the second book*, 1685 |
| TM4 | *The Theater of Music...the fourth and last book*, 1687 |

[b] Principal early manuscript concordances only.

welcome song *The summer's absence unconcerned we bear* Purcell began to enter a sophisticated and varied repertory for less formal entertainment.

R.M. 20.h.8 is essentially a document of musical life at Whitehall in the last few years of Charles II's reign: Purcell provided three late summer welcome songs for James II, but only *Sound the trumpet* of 1687 is entirely in his autograph and he copied few other works in the manuscript after 1685. *Celestial Music*, composed in

1689 for the schoolmaster Lewis Maidwell (*c.* 1650–1716),[21] marks a further change in the function of the manuscript, for although Maidwell's school was patronised by aristocratic families this ode has no direct connection with the court. London A's copy of the Yorkshire Feast Song, another major work not composed for the court, further underlines the manuscript's altered status.

OTHER AUTOGRAPH SOURCES OF SYMPHONY ANTHEMS

By no means all of Purcell's symphony anthems are contained in R.M. 20.h.8, and the primary sources include several other autographs as well as scribal copies (Tables 4.6 and 4.7). Two early works, *My beloved spake* and *Behold now praise the Lord*, survive in separate autographs bound into Lbl Add. 30932, part of a collection assembled by the Canterbury bookseller William Flackton in the late eighteenth century. Each of the three volumes (Lbl Add. 30931–3) has a title page identifying Flackton as its compiler and consists of varied material obtained from different sources: much is in the hand of Daniel Henstridge, organist of Canterbury Cathedral, and other material may have been collected by him.[22] *My beloved spake* extends from fol. 87r to fol. 93v of Add. 30932, on what appears to be an eight-folio gathering of foolscap paper from which the blank final leaf has been removed. Purcell's hand-writing features the reversed bass clef found only in his earliest manuscripts and in general appearance is less mature than even the first stage of his work in Cfm 88. The Add. 30932 score represents an early form of *My beloved spake* supplanted in other sources by a significantly modified second version: the oldest complete copy of the revised anthem is amongst the later additions to Cfm 117 (*c.* 1683), though one part appears in Lbl Add. 50860, a Chapel Royal bass partbook copied before December 1677 (see p. 144). A further score of the revised anthem in Ktp MR 2–5.4 pp. 118–37 is said in an annotation to have been transcribed in 1785 'from Henry Purcells original [score] in the Possession of Mr W: Flacton at Canterbury': it is clearly related to Cfm 117, but either derives from a superior lost source or was produced by careful collation of Cfm 117 with the surviving autograph.[23]

---

[21] See p. 6, n. 24.

[22] Several Purcell works from Lbl Add. 30931–3 were copied by Philip Hayes in Ktp MR 2–5.3 and 4: Hayes annotated some of Flackton's scores and often acknowledged Flackton's ownership of the autographs in his transcriptions.

[23] The primary source of the revised text of *My beloved spake* used for *Works*, XIII (1988), was Ob MS Tenbury 1031, copied *c.* 1705 by Charles Badham. The authority of William Isaack, copyist of Cfm 117, and the possibility that Hayes's exemplar was a revised autograph, might now lead their version to be preferred.

## Table 4.6  Primary manuscript sources of Purcell's symphony anthems

| Composition date | Anthem | Primary source(s) | Probable copying date | Copyist |
|---|---|---|---|---|
| < 1677 | My beloved spake (early version) | Lbl Add. 30932 | 1677 | Henry Purcell |
| | (revised version) | Lbl Add. 50860* | < 10 Dec. 1677 | William Tucker |
| | | Cfm 117 | 1683 | William Isaack |
| | | Ob MS Tenbury 1031 | 1706 | Charles Badham |
| | If the Lord himself (inc.) | Lbl Add. 50860* | < 10 Dec. 1677 | William Tucker |
| | | J-Tn N5/10* | < 10 Dec. 1677 | William Tucker |
| | Praise the Lord ye servants (inc.) | Lbl Add. 50860* | < 10 Dec. 1677 | William Tucker |
| | | J-Tn N5/10* | < 10 Dec. 1677 | William Tucker |
| | | EIRE-Dcc partbooks* | *c.* 1740(?) and later | John Mathews and others† |
| *c.* 1678–9 | Behold now praise the Lord | Lbl Add. 30932 | *c.* 1678–9 | Henry Purcell |
| *c.* 1680–1 | It is a good thing to give thanks | Lbl R.M. 20.h.8 | *c.* 1680–1 | Henry Purcell |
| | O praise God in his holiness | Lbl R.M. 20.h.8 | *c.* 1680–1 | Henry Purcell |
| *c.* 1681–2 | Awake put on thy strength | Lbl R.M. 20.h.8 | *c.* 1690 | mostly London A; Purcell section copied *c.* 1681–2 |
| *c.* 1682–3 | In thee O Lord | Lbl R.M. 20.h.8 | *c.* 1682–3 | Henry Purcell |
| | | Ob MS Mus.c.26 | | Henry Purcell |
| | I was glad | Lbl R.M. 20.h.8 | *c.* 1682–3 | Henry Purcell |
| | | Bu 5001 | | Henry Purcell |
| | My heart is fixed | Lbl R.M. 20.h.8 | *c.* 1682–3 | Henry Purcell |
| | | Bu 5001 | | Henry Purcell |
| | Praise the Lord O my soul and all that is within me | Lbl R.M. 20.h.8 | *c.* 1682–3 | Henry Purcell |
| | The Lord is my light | Lbl R.M. 20.h.8 | *c.* 1682–3 | Henry Purcell |
| | | Bu 5001 | | Henry Purcell |
| *c.* 1683 | I will give thanks unto thee (original version) | Lbl Add. 47845 | *c.* 1683? | John Reading |
| | They that go down to the sea in ships | Lbl Add. 47845 | *c.* 1683? | John Reading |
| | | US-AUS Pre-1700 85 | *c.* 1684–6 | John Gostling |
| | | Lbl R.M. 20.h.8 ∫ | 1685 | Henry Purcell |
| | | Lbl Add. 31445 | 1696 | James Hawkins |
| *c.* 1683–4 | Rejoice in the Lord | Lbl R.M. 20.h.8 | *c.* 1683–4 | Henry Purcell |
| | | Lbl Add. 31445 | 1696 | James Hawkins |
| | | Lbl Add. 17840 | < 1698 | Francis Smith |
| | Why do the heathen | Lbl R.M. 20.h.8 | *c.* 1683–4 | Henry Purcell |
| *c.* 1684–5 | I will give thanks unto thee (revised version) | Lbl R.M. 20.h.8 | *c.* 1684–5 | Henry Purcell |
| | Unto thee will I cry | Lbl R.M. 20.h.8 | *c.* 1684–5 | Henry Purcell |
| < 1685 | I will give thanks unto the Lord‡ | Lcm 2011 | *c.* 1685 | London D |
| | O Lord grant the King a long life‡ | Ob MS Tenbury 1503 | 1715 | John Phipps |
| 1685 | My heart is inditing | Lbl R.M. 20.h.8 | 1685 | Henry Purcell |
| 1687 | Behold I bring you glad tidings | US-AUS Pre-1700 85 | 1687 | John Gostling |
| | | Lcm 2011 | | partly FQ4 |
| 1687–8 | Praise the Lord O my soul O Lord my God | US-AUS Pre-1700 85 | 1688 | John Gostling |
| | | Lbl R.M. 20.h.8 ∫ | 1690 | London A |
| | | Lbl Add. 31445 | 1696 | James Hawkins |

Table 4.6 (*cont.*)

| Composition date | Anthem | Primary source(s) | Probable copying date | Copyist |
|---|---|---|---|---|
| | Thy way O God is holy | US-AUS Pre-1700 85** | 1688 | John Gostling |
| 1688 | Blessed are they that fear the Lord | Lbl Add. 30931 | 1688 | Henry Purcell |
| | O sing unto the Lord | US-AUS Pre-1700 85 | 1688 | John Gostling |
| | | Lbl R.M. 20.h.8 | *c.* 1690 | London A |
| *c.* 1689 | Praise the Lord O Jerusalem | Lbl R.M. 20.h.8 | *c.* 1690 | London A |
| *c.* 1688–90 | My song shall be alway | US-AUS Pre-1700 85†† | *c.* 1688 | John Gostling |
| | | Ob MS Mus.Sch. C.61 | 1690 | Francis Withy |
| | | Och 22 | | Richard Goodson |
| | | Och 1188/9 (string parts) | <1695 | Henry Purcell, Oxford B and a third copyist |
| | | Lbl Add. 17840 | <1698 | Oxford A |

All sources are scores unless indicated otherwise.

* Vocal partbooks.

† One alto partbook in the hand of John Mathews (d. 1799), who attributes the work to Boyce; the other alto and both bass books in the hand of John Phipps (d. 1759). The tenor books are in different unidentified hands.

§ Incomplete.

‡ In Lbl R.M. 20.h.8 index.

** Only source with string parts.

†† With organ accompaniment: other primary sources have string parts.

*Behold now praise the Lord* (Lbl Add. 30932, fols. 121r–125v) visibly belongs to a different stage of Purcell's career, its handwriting in many respects resembling that of Lbl Add. 30930. The secretary 'e' occurs several times but the italic form is more characteristic, and the work was probably composed in late 1678 or early 1679, after *Save me O God*, the earliest Purcell anthem in Cfm 88, but before the majority of his own anthems in that manuscript and the partsongs in Add. 30930. The score in Add. 30932 consists of a six-folio quire of paper, now lacking its final leaf, in which the first three staves (fol. 121r) already contained Michael Wise's catch *When Judith had laid Holofernes to bed* in another hand. Purcell had to cover these staves with a pasteover, so it is possible that he originally intended not to use the first page but to copy the overture on a separate sheet. Whatever his reason for using fol. 121r the result was fortunate, for the reverse of the slip obliterating the catch bears a few autograph bars of Purcell's Three Parts on a Ground in the key of F for recorders.

The main body of the work begins with an anacrusis at the top of fol. 121v and no reference to the preceding symphony on fol. 121r, which is untidily copied and in

Table 4.7 Separate autograph scores of Purcell symphony anthems: Birmingham University, Barber Institute MS 5001; Oxford, Bodleian Library MS Mus.c.26; London, British Library Additional MSS 30931 and 30932

| Title | Manuscript | Dimensions | Watermarks |
|---|---|---|---|
| My beloved spake | Add. 30932, fols. 87–93 | 323 × 226 | foolscap: no countermark |
| Behold now praise the Lord | Add. 30932, fols. 121–5 | 325 × 203 | Amsterdam with factor's mark 'HC' and countermark 'IP' |
| In thee O Lord do I put my trust | Mus.c.26, fols. 10–17 | 320 × 195 | Amsterdam with factor's mark 'HC': no countermark |
| The Lord is my light | Bu 5001, fols. 146–51 | 319 × 197 | Amsterdam with factor's mark 'HC': no countermark |
| I was glad | Bu 5001, fols. 154–9 | 320 × 197 | foolscap with countermark 'IB' |
| My heart is fixed | Bu 5001, fols. 162–7 | 319 × 197 | foolscap with cursive factor's mark 'HC' and countermark 'PB' |
| Blessed are they that fear | Add. 30931, fols. 61–6 | 327 × 208 | foolscap: no countermark |

Rastrology

| | Staves on page | Staves in rastrum | Rastrum span | Rastrum profile |
|---|---|---|---|---|
| Add. 30931, fols. 61–6 | 12 | 6 | 138 | 13.5(11)12.5(12.5)12(13)12.5(13)12(13.5)11.5 |
| Add. 30932, fols. 87–93 | 10 | 5 | 120.5 | 11.5(13)12(16)12(15.5)12.5(15)12 |
| Add. 30932, fols. 121–5 | 12 | 4 | 84.5 | 11.5(13)12.5(12.5)11.5(12)11 |
| Mus.c.26, fols. 10–17 | 12 | 6 | 136.5 | 11.5(13)12.5(12.5)12(12.5)12(13.5)12.5(12.5)12.5 |
| Bu 5001, fols. 146–51 | 12 | 6 | same as Mus.c.26 | |
| Bu 5001, fols. 154–9 | 10 | 5 | 128 | 13(14.5)14.5(14.5)14(16)14(14)13.5 |
| Bu 5001, fols. 162–7 | 12 | 6 | 131.5 | 12(11.5)13(12.5)12(12)12.5(11.5)12.5(10)12.5 |

spite of a compressed layout does not fit on the page: the original conclusion was missing as early as *c.* 1685 when the copy in Lcm 2011 was transcribed from Add. 30932, and the last few bars have been supplied on a pasted extension by Philip Hayes, who slightly adapted material from a subsequent passage.[24] Purcell evidently composed the opening symphony last,[25] though as far as can be seen from rough drafts of anthems composed in the 1680s he did not continue this practice. Lcm 2011 indicates that although *Behold now praise the Lord* was not entered in R.M. 20.h.8 it retained its place in the Chapel Royal repertory.

Preliminary copies survive of four R.M. 20.h.8 anthems: *In thee O Lord do I put my trust* in Ob MS Mus.c.26; and *The Lord is my light, I was glad* and *My heart is*

[24] A copy by Hayes in Ktp MR 2–5.3, pp. 204–16, also contains his completion of the symphony.
[25] We are grateful to Dr Rebecca Herissone for this suggestion.

*fixed* in Bu 5001,[26] a collection of composers' autographs possibly salvaged from the Whitehall fire of 1698 and bound by 1731, when it belonged to John Barker (fl. 1720–1755).[27] All four works were copied into R.M. 20.h.8 *c.* 1682–3 with minimal variation between the draft and fair-copy versions. Ob MS Mus.c.26 is a guardbook containing, amongst other things, Purcell's autographs of the verse anthem *Let mine eyes run down with tears* and the ode *Hail bright Cecilia* (1692): the folios bearing *Let mine eyes* (fols. 4–9) and *In thee O Lord* (fols. 10–17) have an identical paper type and stave ruling, also found in *The Lord is my light* (Bu 5001 fols. 146–51), a coincidence underlining the handwriting evidence of R.M. 20.h.8 that the period 1682–3 saw a concentrated period of activity in Purcell's anthem composition.

Lbl Add. 30931, fols. 61–6, contains Purcell's autograph of *Blessed are they that fear the Lord* composed to celebrate Queen Mary of Modena's pregnancy in January 1688. John Gostling appears to have used it as the source of his own copy in US-AUS Pre-1700 85: on fol. 66v an inscription in William Gostling's hand,[28] similar to John Gostling's in the Austin manuscript, explains the circumstances in which the anthem was composed, and a note by William Flackton on the same page shows that he owned the score by 30 September 1776. The watermark appears on fols. 62, 64 and 66, and although the folios are now individually mounted it seems likely that Purcell worked on successive loose bifolia, as he did in *Of old when heroes thought it base,* Lbl Egerton 2956. The whole manuscript was evidently folded in half horizontally with fol. 66v on the outside.

---

[26] See Iain Fenlon, *Catalogue of the Printed Music and Music Manuscripts before 1801 in the Music Library of the University of Birmingham, Barber Institute of Fine Arts* (London, 1976), 113–14; Watkins Shaw, 'A Collection of Musical Manuscripts in the Autograph of Henry Purcell and Other English Composers, c. 1665–85', *The Library,* 5th series, 14 (1959), 126–31.

[27] A former Chapel Royal choirboy, Barker was appointed organist of Holy Trinity, Coventry, on 20 October 1731; in the same year he signed and dated the back cover of Bu 5001. A volume of harpsichord music in his hand, Lbl Add. 31467, dates from *c.* 1735: manuscript scores at Lichfield Cathedral contain church music by Purcell and the Lincoln organist George Holmes. See Don Franklin, 'Five Manuscripts of Church Music at Lichfield', *RMARC* 3 (1963), 53–8; Nigel Fortune and Iain Fenlon, 'Music Manuscripts of John Browne (1608–91) and from Stanford Hall, Leicestershire', *Source Materials and the Interpretation of Music: a Memorial Volume to Thurston Dart,* ed. Ian Bent (London, 1981), 163, 167n; Zimmerman, *Catalogue,* 464; Spink, *Restoration,* 286.

[28] The hand is identified by Hayes in his copy in Ktp MR 2–5.4, p. 17.

PRINCIPAL NON-AUTOGRAPH SOURCES OF SYMPHONY ANTHEMS

## Two Chapel Royal bass partbooks: London, British Library Additional MS 50860 and Tokyo, Nanki Library MS N5/10

The revised version of *My beloved spake*, together with the more or less fragmentary *If the Lord himself* and *Praise the Lord ye servants*, appears in Lbl Add. 50860, an incomplete Chapel Royal bass book copied by William Tucker (d. 1679) belonging to a set of fifteen books containing 'the Anthems w[i]th Symphonies' for which Tucker's widow Elizabeth was finally paid £15 on 15 February 1685:[29] in 1697 it belonged to William Croft, whose signature appears on the rear flyleaf. In Add. 50860 and a section of his copying in another partbook belonging to the same set, J-Tn N5/10, Tucker invariably gives John Blow the title 'Mr' rather than 'Dr', indicating a date before 10 December 1677 (see Table 4.8). Later additions made to J-Tn N5/10 by other copyists include the chorus of Purcell's verse anthem *Sing unto God*, in the composer's autograph though mistakenly headed 'Sing unto the Lord':[30] presumably this part was entered in 1687, the year of composition given in John Gostling's scorebook US-AUS Pre-1700 85.[31] *Praise the Lord ye servants* also appears in eighteenth-century partbooks at both St Patrick's and Christ Church cathedrals in Dublin:[32] one of the Christ Church alto books was copied by John Mathews, a lay clerk at Durham cathedral from 1764 to 1776 who subsequently moved to Dublin,[33] but three other books are in the earliest hand of the set, probably that of John Phipps (see p. 158).

## London, British Library Additional MS 47845

Lbl Add. 47845 was acquired in 1953 as part of the bequest of E. H. W. Meyerstein.[34] The bookplate of James Kent (1700–76) appears on fol. iv, but the volume is in several hands, none of them Kent's, and consists of a number of once independent

---

[29] *RECM*, V, 272.    [30] See Hugh McLean, 'Blow and Purcell in Japan', *MT* 104 (1963), 702–5.

[31] The partbook seems to have remained in use for some years: various annotations, and a signature on p. 12, were apparently added by Edmund Baker (d. 1765), a Chapel Royal chorister whose voice had changed by 28 December 1710 (*RECM*, II, 106, 148). In 1727 he became organist of Chester Cathedral (Shaw, *The Succession*, 67).

[32] A discovery made by Martin Adams and Kerry Houston.

[33] This set of partbooks is now held by the Representative Church Body Library, Dublin. For Mathews see Crosby, *Catalogue*, 244–5.

[34] See *British Museum Catalogue of Additions to the Manuscripts 1951–1955* (London, 1982), 83, 89.

sections with contrasting paper types and rulings (Table 4.9). Copyist 1 of Add. 47845, who was also responsible for Lbl R.M. 20.h.9, is John Reading,[35] organist of Winchester Cathedral from 1675 to 1681 and of Winchester College from 1681 until his death in 1692; copyist 5 (fols. 55–6) is Daniel Roseingrave, who succeeded Reading at the cathedral.

To judge from the original patterned covers and marbled endpapers preserved in the modern British Library binding the separate quires were brought together in a very fine book, for which a continuous pagination was provided. Some quires date from the 1670s, as ascriptions on fols. 1r and 97v refer to 'Mr' Blow, and all the watermarks could be contemporary with Reading's tenures at Winchester: foolscaps with the countermark 'PB' are described in 1674,[36] while a similar combination with the factor's mark 'AJ' appears in Lbl Add. 33234 of *c.* 1682. The latest paper in Lbl Add. 47845 is the quire between fols. 13 and 19 with a countermark 'RDTI' first used in the 1690s,[37] and binding in the early eighteenth century is indicated by two front endpapers, fols. vi and viii, with a corner watermark consisting of the encircled letters 'BSL'.[38]

The number of symphony anthems in the manuscript suggests a connection with the Chapel Royal (Table 4.10). It is possible that Purcell's duties took him to Winchester between 1682 and 1684, for in 1682 Charles II resolved to spend a month there each autumn before his annual visit to Newmarket and began the construction of a palace left incomplete at his death:[39] musicians certainly accompanied the king on his visits to Winchester[40] and Reading could thus have had the opportunity to obtain copies of the instrumental music in Lbl R.M. 20.h.9 and of the Add. 47845 symphony anthems. The Add. 47845 version of Purcell's *I will give thanks unto thee O Lord* differs from that copied *c.* 1685 in R.M. 20.h.8, which appears to be a later revision, and *They that go down to the sea in ships* might similarly have been composed before 1685, the year usually assigned to it because of the position of the incomplete autograph copy. Hawkins's account of the origin of *They that go down* relates the anthem to an adventure allegedly shared by the king, the Duke of York and John

[35] See Holman, 'Purcell and Roseingrave: a New Autograph', 100; *John Blow: Anthems II*, ed. Bruce Wood, Musica Britannica 50 (London, 1984), 174.

[36] See R. W. Chapman, 'An Inventory of Paper, 1674', *The Library*, 4th series, 7 (1927), 402–8.

[37] Heawood no. 2690.

[38] Four of Heawood's five examples of 'BSL' countermarks, nos. 1676, 2078, 3116 and 3117, date from 1704 or 1705.

[39] Ronald Hutton, *Charles II, King of England, Scotland and Ireland* (Oxford, 1989), 420; John Miller, *Charles II* (London, 1991), 351, 381.

[40] *RECM*, I, 206–7; V, 165.

## Table 4.8 London, British Library Additional MS 50860 and Tokyo, Nanki Library MS N5/10: contents

*1. Copying of William Tucker and his assistants*

| Ascription (from either source) | Title | Add. 50860 folio* | Add. 50860 page* | N5/10 page* |
|---|---|---|---|---|
| Mr: Pell: Humfris | O praise the Lord | 1r | 1 | — |
| Mr: Blow | The kings of Tharsis | — | | 3 |
| Mr: Pell: Humfris | O give thanks | 1v–2r | 2–3 | 4–5 |
| Mr: Pell: Humfris | Thou art my king O God | 2v–3r | 4–5 | 6 |
| Mr: Jo: Blow | When Israel came out of Egypt | 3v– | 6– | 7 |
| Mr: Pell: Humfris | The king shall rejoice | | — | 8 |
| Mr: Jo: Blow | And I heard a great voice | –4r | –11 | 10–11 |
| Mr: Pell: Humfris | Hear my crying O God | 4v | 12 | 9 |
| P:H:W:T:I:B | I will alway give thanks[a] | | — | 12 |
| Mr: Jo: Blow | Arise O Lord | | — | 13 |
| Mr: Will: Turner | O praise the Lord[b] | 5r | 15 | 16 |
| Mr: Pell: Humfries | By the waters of Babylon | 5v–6r | 16–17 | 14–15[c] |
| Mr: John Blow | When the Lord turned again | 6r–6v | 17–18 | — |
| Mr: Hen: Pursell | My beloved spake | 7r–7v | 19–20 | — |
| Mr: Pell: Humfris | Haste thee O God | 8r | 21 | 19 |
| Mr: Pell: Humfris | Rejoice in the Lord | 8v | 22 | 24 |
| Mr: Lock | O clap your hands | 9r | 23 | 20 |
| Mr: Lock[d] | God is gone up | 9v– | 24– | 21 |
| Mr: Blow | Sing we merrily | | — | 22 |
| Mr: Turner | Hold not thy tongue O God | | — | 23 |
| Mr: Jo: Blow | I beheld and lo a great multitude | 10r–10v | 27–28 | 25–26 |
| Mr: Jo: Blow | The Lord is my shepherd | 10v–11r | 28–29 | 26–27 |
| Mr: Hen: Purcell | If the Lord himself | 11v– | 30– | 28 |
| Mat: Locke | God reigneth in the congregation | | — | 29 |
| Mr: Henry Purcell | Praise the Lord ye servants | –12r | –33 | 30–31 |
| Mr: Tho: Tudway | O come let us sing | 12v–13r | 34–35 | [32][e] |
| Mr: Pell: Humfrye | O be joyful | 13v–14r | 36–37 | — |

Pages missing from Add. 50860: 7–10; 13–14; 25–6; 31–2 (original pagination)
Pages missing from N5/10: 1–2; 17–18

*2. Continuation of N5/10 in other hands*

| Ascription | Title | Pages (original) | Modern pencil pagination[f] | Copyist (1–4 unidentified) |
|---|---|---|---|---|
| Mr Purcell | Sing unto God[g] | 32 | 33 | Henry Purcell |
| Mr Turner | O give thanks | 32 | 33 | 1 |
| Dr Blow | The Lord even the most mighty | 30bis–[ ] | 34–35[h] | 2 |
| Mr Tuckers | Lord how long | 31bis | 36 | 3 |
| Dr Child | O sing unto the Lord | 32bis | 37 | 3 |
| Mr Purcell | I was glad | 33 | 38 | 3 |

**Table 4.8** (*cont.*)

| Ascription | Title | Pages (original) | Modern pencil pagination[f] | Copyist (1–4 unidentified) |
|---|---|---|---|---|
| Mr Tucker | I was glad | 34 | 39 | 3 |
| Mr Wise | O praise God in his holiness | 35 | 40 | 3 |
| Dr Blow | O Lord I have sinned | 36 | 41 | 3 |
| Mr Humpheris | Have mercy upon me | – | 42 | 3 |
| Dr Aldridg | O give thanks | – | 43 | 3 |
| Anon. | 'We are his people'[i] | – | 44 | 4 |

Add. 50860: folio, 364 × 228. Watermarks: Angoumois fleur-de-lys with countermark 'HC'.
Rastrology: twelve staves ruled with a four-stave rastrum, span: 94 mm, profile: 12(15)13(14.5)12.5(14)12.5.

N5/10: oblong quarto. Six evenly-spaced staves.

* Original pagination. Works which ended or began on missing pages are indicated thus: 11–; –6.

[a] The 'Club Anthem' by Pelham Humfrey, William Turner and John Blow.

[b] With additions in Add. 50860 in Turner's hand and the autograph inscription 'Wm. Turner'.

[c] Followed by a four-part chant ascribed to 'Mr Tallis' copied in another hand.

[d] Ascription added later in Add. 50860.

[e] Text only, in hand of one of Tucker's assistants: page unnumbered.

[f] Continuation of original pagination as if the previous page had been correctly numbered '32'

[g] Mistakenly entitled 'Sing unto the Lord' by Purcell: the ascription is in another hand.

[h] Pencil p. 35 is unnumbered in the original pagination.

[i] Apparently the chorus of a Jubilate in A minor.

Gostling in the newly built royal yacht *Fubbs*,[41] at face value a near-disaster in which the lives of both the king and the heir apparent were in immediate danger. Yet contemporary chronicles such as Luttrell's *Brief Relation* mention nothing of the kind; the *Fubbs*, moreover, was built in 1682 and Hawkins states that the events he describes took place 'soon after the vessel was launched'.[42] An adventure that might have given rise to the story did in fact occur in the summer of 1682, and although what happened was less obviously dramatic than Hawkins's account it was not without danger and must have been most unpleasant for some of those involved:

[41] Hawkins, *History*, II, 693.

[42] The Duke of York commented favourably on the new yacht's qualities in 1682; see J. P. Kenyon, *The Stuarts* (London, 1966), 141. See also C. M. Gavin, *Royal Yachts* (London, 1932), 59 and Appendix 1(A).

## Table 4.9 London, British Library Additional MS 47845: collation of music folios

| Initial folio of quire | Watermark/countermark | Ruling | Copyist* |
|---|---|---|---|
| 1 | foolscap/— | 1 | 1 |
| 7 | foolscap/— | 1 | 1 |
| 13 | London/'RDTI' | 2 | 2 |
| 20 | Amsterdam/— | 3 | 3 |
| 26 | Foolscap/— | 1 | 1 |
| 32 | Foolscap with 'AJ'/'PB' | 4 | 4 |
| 36 | Foolscap/— | 1 | 1 |
| 38 | Amsterdam/— | 5 | 1 |
| 46 | Amsterdam/— | 6 | 1 |
| 50 | Amsterdam/— | 6 | 1 |
| 54 | Foolscap/'IV' | 7 | 1/5 |
| 58 | Foolscap/'IV' | 7 | 1 |
| 62 | Foolscap/'IV' | 7 | 1 |
| 66 | Foolscap/'IV' | 7 | 1 |
| 70 | Foolscap/'IV' | 7 | 1 |
| 74 | Foolscap/'LM' | 7 | 1 |
| 77 | Foolscap/'LM' | 7 | 1 |
| 80 | Foolscap/'LM' | 7 | 1 |
| 84 | Foolscap/'PB' | 8 | 6 |
| 92 | Foolscap/— | 1 | 1 |
| 96 | Foolscap/— | 1 | 1 |
| 100 | Foolscap/— | 8 | 1 |

Folio, 314 × 205.

Rastrology

| Ruling | Staves on page | Staves in rastrum | Rastrum span | Rastrum profile |
|---|---|---|---|---|
| 1 | 12 | 4 | 82.5 | 11(13)11(13)11.5(12.5)10.5 |
| 2 | 12 | 6 | 135.5 | 11.5(12.5)12.5(12.5)13(11)12(13.5)12.5(12.5)12 |
| 3 | 12 | 6 | 137 | 12(13)11.5(12.5)11.5(13)12.5(12.5)12.5(13)12 |
| 4 | 12 | 6 | 137.5 | 13(12.5)12.5(13)12(13)12(12)12.5(12.5)12.5 |
| 5 | 12 | 6 | 137.5 | 12.5(12)12.5(11)13.5(11)14(11.5)13.5(11)12.5 |
| 6 | 12 | 6 | 138.5 | 13(11)12(13.5)12(13.5)12(13.5)12(13.5)12 |
| 7 | 10 | 5 | 124 | 13(16)12.5(14.5)13(15)13.5(13.5)13.5 |
| 8 | 10 | 5 | 127 | 14(13)14.5(15.5)14(13.5)15(14)13 |

* Identified copyists: 1 = John Reading; 5 = Daniel Roseingrave

## Table 4.10 London, British Library Additional MS 47845: contents

| Folio | Heading or incipit and initial ascription | Terminal ascription |
|---|---|---|
| 1r | Mr Blow's Service in Gamut | |
| 4v | Rejoyce in the Lord | 6v: Pell: Humphry |
| 7r | When Israell came out of Egypt | 12r: John Blow |
| 13r | Thy Mercy O Lord | 19v: Dr John Blow |
| 20r | Hear my voyce O God [from text] | 25v: Dr Blow |
| 26r | O Lord I have sinned | 28r: John Blow |
| 28v | Turn thee unto me O Lord | 29v: John Blow |
| 30r | I will cry unto God | 31v: John Blow |
| 32r | Lord how are they increased [from text] | 35v: Dr Blow |
| 36r | How dost ye City | 37v: John Blow |
| 38r | I will give thanks unto yee O Lord Mr H Pursell | 45v: Mr Henry Pursell |
| 46r | They that goe down to the Sea Mr Purcell | |
| 54r | Behold I bring you glad tidings Mr Purcell | 61v: Mr Henry Pursell |
| 63r*a* | Praise the Lord O my soul Mr Purcell | 72v: Mr Henry Pursell |
| 74r*b* | Hear my prayer O Lord | 78r: William Turner |
| 78v | Canons, 'ML', 'C Gib', anon. | |
| 79v | Canon [anon.], 'Great God' | |
| 80r | Behold now praise the Lord | 82v: William Turner |
| 84r | The earth is the Lord's | [ends 89r without ascription] |
| 92r | Lord what is man | 95r: Wm Turner |
| 96r | O give thanks | 97r: Tucker |
| 97v | Behold how good Mr Blow | 99r: John Blow |
| 100r | O Lord turn thy wrath away from us [Byrd] | |

*a* Fols. 62 and 63 copied in wrong order.
*b* Added at bottom of pages: 74r, a canon ascribed 'W. Gr': 77v–78r a canon ascribed 'ML'.

The King had so bad weather at Sea that he lost the Bowspritt of his owne Yaught, by w[hi]ch the Yaught being in some sorte disabled & not well answering the Helme, the King & Duke quitted her & went on board the Dukes yaucht in w[hi]ch change by ye roughnesse of the Sea they run no small hazard in getting on board. The storme was so greate, that the Yaught rowled so incessantly when they were to eate, that they could neither keepe themselves on their seates nor their meale upon the Table. But Jo: Dillon and one of ye Kings pages were so extreamely sicke yt they needed no meale, And in compassion to them the King sent them ashoare neare Margett from whence they returnd by land.[43]

[43] Ob MS Carte 216, fol. 94, a letter from Lord Longford to the Earl of Arran dated 4 July 1682; cited in Hutton, *Charles II*, 443. Maureen Duffy, *Henry Purcell* (London, 1994), 111, mentions a similar reference in a letter written by James himself.

According to Hawkins, *They that go down* was not performed until after Charles II's death, a claim apparently supported by the incomplete copy in R.M. 20.h.8. But if the anthem reflects the incident in 1682 it is unlikely to have been composed in 1685, and if it was of personal significance to Gostling it is strange that he does not mention its date in US-AUS Pre-1700 85. Composition earlier than 1685 might in any case link *They that go down* to a much more serious event than the king's rough yachting excursion, the tragic loss of the frigate *Gloucester* on 6 May 1682, in which two court musicians were amongst the many who died.[44]

### London, British Library Additional MSS 17840 and 31445

Lbl Add. 17840 and Add. 31445 are the two earliest sources of the inner parts of *Rejoice in the Lord alway*. Add. 17840 (Table 4.11), undoubtedly a stray from Oxford, belonged in the eighteenth century to Philip Hayes: later owners were John Parker, James Bartleman and Vincent Novello, who presented the manuscript to the British Museum on 28 August 1849.

For the most part beautifully written, Lbl Add. 17840 is an exceptionally large volume ruled with an 11.5 mm single-stave rastrum, a characteristic shared with other Oxford manuscripts such as Lbl Add. 17835, Och 11 and Och 12, and all three principal copyists are represented in the Christ Church cathedral partbooks Och 1220–4. The first, Oxford A, is an important scribe who clearly worked under Aldrich's direction and was probably the Christ Church singing-man Charles Husbands, the others being the singing-men Francis Smith (d. 1698) and William Saunders (d. 1729). Smith's Purcell copies are of particular importance: as well as his complete text of *Rejoice in the Lord alway* he provides the primary source for *The Lord is king be the people never so impatient* and his transcription of *Be merciful unto me* may be the earliest one in score (see Table 5.1). Much of Lbl Add. 17840 consists of paper bearing the factor's mark of Abraham Janssen with the cursive countermark 'TJ', perhaps identifying Janssen's son Theodore,[45] similar to a countermark in the score of Purcell's 1692 St Cecilia's Day ode, Ob MS Mus.c.26. The monogram countermark

---

[44] Harold Love, 'The Wreck of the Gloucester', *MT* 125 (1984), 194–5.

[45] 'Theodore' was a Janssen family name shared by one of Abraham's brothers as well as his son. See G. Babinet de Rencogne, *Recueil de documents pour servir à l'histoire de commerce et de l'industrie en Angoumois*, Bulletin de la société archéologique et historique de la Charente, 5th series, 2 (Angoulême, 1880), 67; J. Mathorez, *Les étrangers en France sous l'ancien régime* (Paris, 1919–21), II, 244; Churchill no. 23. Churchill illustrates two examples of the 'TJ' countermark in his nos. 116 (1701) and 240 (1692), but misreads the letters as 'FJ' and ascribes the mark to François Jardel.

of Peter van der Ley, found in some folios between fol. 3 and fol. 14, occurs as early as 1686.[46]

Lbl Add. 31445, mostly the work of the prolific copyist James Hawkins, provides a second early source of the inner parts of *Rejoice in the Lord alway* (Table 4.12). Though there are some variations of ruling, the paper type is identical throughout, its Dutch Lion watermark and Peter van der Ley monogram countermark being consistent with the period *c.* 1696–7 implied by a change in ascription from 'Mr' Turner to 'Dr' Turner and the inclusion, near the end, of a copy of Blow's *I was glad* dated 15 October 1697.[47] Tudway's *Sing we merrily*, fols. 53r–56v, is in the composer's autograph.

### London, Royal College of Music MS 2011

The Royal College of Music acquired Lcm 2011 (Table 4.13) from the Sacred Harmonic Society, to whom it was presented in 1840 by Richard Clark.[48] It is related in paper and rastrology to Lbl Add. 33287 (Table 4.14), with which it shares the principal hand London D and the subordinate copyists 2 and 3, and like Add. 33287 originally consisted of two separate volumes though in Lcm 2011 the division is chronological rather than generic. The entire contents are by Purcell, the first book containing most of his symphony anthems composed between *c.* 1679 and early 1685 and the second *My heart is inditing* and *Behold I bring you glad tidings*: the latter anthem was completed by FQ4, the unidentified copyist of most of the overture in the *Fairy Queen* score Lam 3 (see p. 240). London D's handwriting is exceptionally beautiful, and both Lcm 2011 and Lbl Add. 33287 may have been official collections intended to preserve the large-scale works composed for Charles II's court and chapel.

Apart from *I will give thanks unto the Lord*, which is indexed but not copied in R.M. 20.h.8, Lcm 2011 does not provide a primary source of any anthem, but it casts interesting light on the Chapel Royal repertory at the end of Charles II's reign. *Behold now praise the Lord* was copied from the autograph in Lbl Add. 30932 and certain other works, such as *Rejoice in the Lord alway*, were obviously derived from R.M. 20.h.8. Nevertheless, the order of anthems in Lcm 2011 does not follow that of the great autograph and some appear to have been derived from different sources: *My heart is fixed* is related to the rough autograph in Bu 5001 and *Praise the Lord O my soul and all that is within me* to a lost manuscript.[49] The omission of *I will give*

---

[46] See Heawood no. 151.  [47] See Spink, *Restoration*, 86–7.  [48] King, *Some British Collectors*, 51.

[49] We are grateful to Dr Lionel Pike for bringing the complex relationship between Lcm 2011 and other sources to our attention and for allowing us to use information forthcoming in his revision of *Works*, XIV.

## Table 4.11  London, British Library Additional MS 17840: contents

| Folio | Incipit or heading | Composer | Copyist |
|-------|--------------------|----------|---------|
| 3r | For Sion's sake | Carissimi adapt. Aldrich | Husbands |
| 5v | O pray for the peace of Jerusalem | Carissimi (?) adapt. Aldrich | Husbands |
| 8r | Behold in heav'n | Carissimi (?) adapt. Aldrich | Husbands |
| 10r | Haste thee O Lord | Carissimi adapt. Aldrich | Husbands |
| 12r | O Lord I have heard thy voice | Aldrich | Husbands |
| 15r | Give the King thy judgements | Aldrich | Husbands |
| 17v | Sing unto the Lord | 'Orlando Gibbons' | Husbands |
| 20r | I waited patiently for the Lord | 'Dr Hen: Alldrich' | Husbands |
| 23r | How long wilt thou forget me | 'Mr Chri: Gibbons' | Husbands |
| 24v | Thy beauty O Israel | Wise adapt. Aldrich | Husbands |
| 27r | I will love the Lord | Aldrich | Husbands |
| 30r | My song shall be alway | Purcell | Husbands |
| 33v | Like as the hart | Humphrey | Husbands |
| 35r | O how amiable | Carissimi (?) adapt. Aldrich | Husbands |
| 37r | I will love thee O Lord | 'Mr Bartholamew Isaack' | Husbands |
| 39v | The Lord is King | Aldrich | Husbands |
| 41r | I will exalt thee | anon. | Husbands |
| 43v | Comfort yee my people | Aldrich | Husbands |
| 46v | God is our hope and strength | Aldrich | Husbands |
| 48r | Praise the Lord O ye his servants | Vaughan Richardson | Husbands |
| 50v | Hide not thou thy face | Farrant adapt. Aldrich | Husbands |
| 51v | O praise the Lord | Aldrich | Husbands |
| 52r | I was in the spirit | Blow adapt. Aldrich | Husbands |
| 54v | I am well pleased | Carissimi adapt. Aldrich | Husbands |
| 57r | Behold now praise the Lord | 'Dr Hen. Aldrich' | Husbands |
| 58v | Awake put on thy strength | 'Mr Wise' | Husbands |
| 61r | Open me the gates of righteousness | 'Mr Wise' | Husbands |
| 63r | The Lord is my light | 'Mr Wm Lawes' | Smith |
| 66r | We have heard with our ears | Palestrina adapt. Aldrich | Smith |
| 68r | Hold not thy tongue | Palestrina adapt. Aldrich | Smith |
| 69r | Sing unto the Lord | 'Christofer Gibbons' | Smith |
| 71r | The Lord said unto my Lord | 'Dr Chris: Gibbons' | Smith |
| 73r | O be joyful | Humphrey | Smith |
| 75r | O give thanks | 'H. Purcell' | Smith |
| 79r | Dr Blow's Service in A re | [Blow] | Husbands |
| 85r | Dr Aldrich his Morning Service in A♯ | [Aldrich] | Husbands |
| 87v | Evening Service [in A] | Blow | Smith |
| 90v | Te Deum | 'Mr Hen: Purcell' | Smith |
| 97v | Jubilate | [Purcell] | Smith |
| 103r | Rejoice in the Lord alway | 'Hen Purcell' | Smith |
| 106r | Lord let me know my end | 'Mr Matthew Locke' | Smith |
| 109r | Be mercifull unto me O God | Purcell | Smith |
| 112r | In jury is God known | 'W. N' [William Norris] | Smith |
| 113v | Blessed are those | 'W. N' | Smith |
| 116r | Behold thou hast made my days | Orlando Gibbons | Smith |

**Table 4.11** (*cont.*)

| Folio | Incipit or heading | Composer | Copyist |
|---|---|---|---|
| 118r | Behold how good and joyful | 'Mr W. Norris' | Smith |
| 122r | The Lord is King by Mr Hn: P[a] | [Purcell] | Smith |
| 124v | The souls of the righteous | 'Hn: Hall' | Smith |
| 127v | O Lord my God | 'Mr Humphry' | Smith |
| 130r | O praise the Lord | 'Mr Pelham Humphreys' | Saunders |
| 133v | Be not wroth | Byrd adapt. Aldrich | Saunders |
| 135v | O Lord grant the Queen a long life | Aldrich | Saunders |
| 139r | Blessed be the Lord my strength | 'Dr Blow' | Saunders |
| 144r | Have mercy upon me O God | 'Mr Humphris' | Saunders |
| 146v | O Lord I have sinned | 'Dr Blow' [end, 'Mr John Blow'] | Saunders |
| 149r | Haste thee O God | 'Pelham Humphris' | Saunders |
| 152r | I will love thee | 'Je. Clark' [end, 'Jerry Clark'] | Unidentified[b] |

Folio, 437 × 275. Watermarks: arms of Strasbourg countermarked 'DS' or monogram 'PVL' (fols. 3–14); arms of Strasbourg with cursive factor's mark 'HC' but without countermark (fols. 15–109); arms of Strasbourg with cursive factor's mark 'AJ' and cursive countermark 'TJ' (fols. 110–52).

Rastrology: sixteen staves ruled with a single-stave rastrum of 11.5 mm.

[a] *The Lord is king be the people never so impatient.*
[b] Compare Lbl Add. 17835, fols. 36v–42v and 134r–141v, and one of the hands in Ob MS Mus.Sch. C.135 (R. Goodson, *Janus did ever*, 1704/5).

*thanks unto thee O Lord* suggests that Lcm 2011 was transcribed before Purcell completed the later version of this work in R.M. 20.h.8 and *Awake put on thy strength*, also missing from Lcm 2011, must still have been incomplete.

### Other sources of the symphony anthem version of *My song shall be alway*

As well as Lbl Add. 17840, four more early sources in Oxford libraries contain *My song shall be alway* with its symphonies (Table 4.15). Three are scores: Ob MS Mus.Sch. C.61, Och 22 and Och 766. Och 1188/9, fols. 42–5, is a partly autograph set of string parts.[50] Some of these manuscripts demonstrably originated in Oxford, and it is likely that the symphony anthem version of *My song shall be alway* was performed in that city, where there was a real if sporadic tradition of instrumental anthem accompaniment.[51]

[50] Bruce Wood, 'A Newly Identified Purcell Autograph', *M&L* 59 (1978), 329–32.
[51] Examples include Locke's *O be joyful in the Lord all ye lands*, also in Och 1188/9; his *Ad te levavi oculos meos*, written 'to carry on the Meetinge at the musick schoole. Thursday the 16th Novem[ber] 1665'; and Richard Goodson's *Rejoice in the Lord ye righteous*.

**Table 4.12 London, British Library Additional MS 31445: contents**

| Folio | Incipit or heading | Ascription | Comments |
|---|---|---|---|
| 3r | God spake sometimes in visions | Dr Blow | 1688 |
| 37r | Praise the Lord O my soul | Mr Hen. Purcell | with str. parts |
| 46v | Blessed is the man that feareth the Lord | Mr Purcell 1688 | organ acc. |
| 53r | Sing we merrily | Dr Tudway [index] | in Tudway's hand |
| 57r | Blessed are those that are undefiled | Mr Norris | |
| 62r | Hold not thy tongue O God | Dr Turner [index] | |
| 72v | O sing praises | Mr Turner | |
| 80v | God sheweth me his goodness | Mr Turner | |
| 92r | O praise the Lord | Mr Turner | |
| 98r | Hear O Heav'ns | Mr Humphris | |
| 102r | I am well pleased | Mr Dan: Purcell | |
| 106r | Chanting Evening Service | Ja. Hawkins | |
| 109r | They that go down to the sea in ships | Mr Purcell | |
| 117r | Rejoice in the Lord | Mr Hen: Purcell[a] | |
| 123r | Turn us again O God | Dr Blow | |
| 135v | Deliver me from mine enemies | Dr Turner | |
| 141v | I was glad | Dr Blow[b] | |
| 156v | O give thanks | Mr Purcell | |
| 165r | O sing unto God | Dr Blow | |
| 171r | Praise the Lord ye servants | Mr Phil: Hart | |
| 178r | I will give thanks unto thee | Norris [index] | |
| 186r | God sheweth me his goodness | Mr Norris | |

Folio, 312 × 202. Watermarks: Dutch Lion countermarked with monogram 'PVL'.

Rastrology: twelve staves; fols. 3–50, 150–193/ii ruled with a six-stave rastrum, span: 128.5, profile: 11(12)11(13)11.5(12)12(11)11.5(11.5)11.5; fols. 51–6, 59–61/i, 106–49 ruled with a four-stave rastrum, span: 78, profile: 11.5(11)11.5 (11.5)10.5(11.5)10.5; fols. 57–8, 62–105 ruled with a four-stave rastrum, span: 82, profile: 11(12)10.5(12.5)10.5(13.5)11. Front endpapers: fol. 1, watermark 'Britannia', fol. 2, early cover.

Copyists: James Hawkins; Thomas Tudway (fols. 53r–56v)

[a] 'called the Bell Anthem'.
[b] 'This was made by Dr Blow Oct ye 15 1697 att Hamton town for the opening of St Pauls Cathederall.'

Ob MS Mus.Sch. C. 61 is in the hand of Francis Withy, a singing-man at Christ Church from 1670 until his death in 1727.[52] The assorted contents of the manuscript reflect the diverse activities of a busy professional musician, but in the sequence copied from the back of the volume is a full score of *My song shall be alway* (pp. 73–64) marked 'Sep 9th 90', a date sometimes thought to connect the

---

[52] See Robert Thompson, '"Francis Withie of Oxon" and his Commonplace Book, Christ Church, Oxford, MS 337', *Chelys* 20 (1991), 3–27.

**Table 4.13  London, Royal College of Music MS 2011: contents**

| Page (original) | Folio | Incipit | Copyist | Comments |
|---|---|---|---|---|
| '1st Book' | | | | |
| 1 | 2r | My heart is fixed O God | London D* | |
| 8 | 5v | Praise the Lord O my soul | | |
| 20 | 11v | I will give thanks unto the Lord | | |
| 27 | 15r | Unto thee will I cry | | |
| 37 | 20r | I was glad | | |
| 43 | 23r | Behold now praise the Lord | | |
| 48 | 25v | It is a good thing to give thanks | | |
| 59 | 31r | O praise God in his holiness | | |
| 68 | 35v | In thee O Lord do I put my trust | | |
| 78 | 40v | The Lord is my light | | |
| 86 | 44v | Rejoice in the Lord alway | | |
| 90 | 46v | Why do the heathen | | |
| '2nd Book' | | | | |
| 1 | 50r | My heart is inditing | London D*/2* | hand changes on fol. 62r (p. 25). |
| 36 | 67v | Behold I bring you glad tidings | 3*/FQ4 | hand changes at beginning of fol. 70 (p. 41). |

Folio, 432 × 272. Watermarks: arms of Strasbourg with factor's mark 'AJ' and countermark 'CDG'. (For rastrology see Table 4.14.)

* Hand shared with Lbl Add. 33287: see Table 4.20.

anthem with William III's arrival at Windsor on that day after abandoning the siege of Limerick[53] although William was only passing through on his way to London, without a victory to celebrate, and had no particular liking for elaborate musical services. The manuscript itself is notable for its emphasis on music by Catholic composers including Withy's father John, Christopher Simpson, Polewheele, 'Mr Arnald', Finger and Matteis,[54] and an inscription on the back flyleaf provides evidence that Withy had personal contact with leading musicians of his own time, including former members of James II's Catholic Chapel Royal:

[53] Holman, *Four and Twenty Fiddlers*, 406.

[54] 'Mr Arnald' was presumably 'Mr Arnould', a gentleman of King James II's Catholic chapel: see *RECM*, II, 17, 21. 'Polewheel' was the alias of the Catholic priest George Warham (born 1607, ordained 1633): in view of the Catholic associations of much bass viol music it is possible that the famous 'Polewheele's Ground' has some connection with him. See Godfrey Anstruther, *The Seminary Priests II: Early Stuarts 1603–1659* (Great Wakering, 1975), 249, 337.

**Table 4.14 London, British Library Additional MS 33287 and Royal College of Music MS 2011: rastrology**

| Rastrum | Number of staves | Span | Profile |
|---|---|---|---|
| A | 4 | 88.5 | 12(12.5)13(12.5)12.5(13.5)12.5 |
| B | 5 | 114 | 13(12.5)12.5(13.5)12.5(12.5)13(12.5)12 |
| C | 6 | 140 | 13(13)13(12.5)12.5(13.5)12.5(12.5)13(12.5)12 |

Ruling patterns
Add. 33287, fols. 1–52    A + C + C = 16 staves
Add. 33287, fols. 53–229    A + A + A + A = 16 staves
Lcm 2011, fols 2–49    A + B + A = 16 staves
Lcm 2011, fols. 50–71    A + C + C = 16 staves

**Table 4.15 Sources of the symphony version of *My song shall be alway***

| Source | Format | Dimensions | Paper type |
|---|---|---|---|
| Ob MS Mus. Sch. C.61 | folio | 315 × 203 | foolscap with countermark 'PT'; fols. 1, 19, 31, 33: arms of Amsterdam, no countermark. |
| Och 766 | folio | 323 × 200 | fols. 1–4: foolscap, no countermark; fols. 5–6: Dutch lion with illegible cursive countermark |
| Och 1188/9 | | | |
|   fol. 42 | folio | 330 × 207 | countermark possibly 'PVL' in separate letters |
|   fol. 43 | folio | 327 × 208 | countermark possibly 'BC' |
|   fol. 44 | folio | 327 × 208 | arms of Amsterdam |
|   fol. 45 | folio | 327 × 209 | arms of Amsterdam |

Rastrology

| Source | Staves on page | Staves in rastrum | Rastrum span | Rastrum profile |
|---|---|---|---|---|
| Ob MS Mus. Sch. C.61 | 12 | 6 | 137.5 | 11.5(13.5)12(13.5)12.5(13.5)12(13)12(12)12 |
| Och 766 | 12 | 6 | 129 | 11(12.5)11(13)11(12.5)11(12)11.5(13)11 |
| Och 1188/9 | | | | |
|   fol. 42 | 12 | 6 | 131 | 11.5(12.5)12(13)12(11.5)11(13.5)11.5(12)12 |
|   fols. 43–5 | 12 | 4 | 84 | 13(11)12.5(12)12.5(11)12.5 |

Mr Shore ⎫ July 22d Anna: 1693

Monseur La Rich ⎭ was at Mr G. Luellen Cha[mbers] at

Ch[rist] Ch[urch]. Monse: Diseb plais on ye Base Violin Ex[cellently]

'Mr Shore' was presumably a member of the famous family of trumpeters. 'La Rich' was probably the oboist François le Riche, appointed to the Private Music in 1685; though he was employed on a casual basis under William III, he lost his permanent place with the fall of James II.[55] 'Monse: Diseb' must have been Desabaye, like Arnold a gentleman of James II's Catholic chapel.[56]

The string parts in Och 1188/9, a collection of loose papers connected with Oxford, suggest that Purcell added instrumental sections to an existing work. Most of the opening symphony in the second treble, tenor and bass parts, ending with a cancelled terminal flourish before the *petite reprise*, is in the same hand (Oxford B) as the score of *The Indian Queen* in Lbl Add. 31453, fols. 40–83. This copyist seems to have transcribed the lower parts in Och 1188/9 from a separate score containing only the symphony without a *petite reprise*. Purcell then cancelled his terminal flourish, added the *petite reprise* and provided independent chorus string parts not found in any of the early scores. The first treble part, the work of a third copyist who was clearly aware of the final length of the symphony, may be a replacement of a heavily altered or lost original: it lacks the heading in Purcell's hand found in the other three parts, and its paper and rastrology are also distinctive (see Table 4.15). Och 766 has no distinguishing features that prove an Oxford provenance, but the score in Och 22, pp. 105–15, was copied by the elder Richard Goodson.

### Oxford, Bodleian Library MS Tenbury 1503

Ob MS Tenbury 1503 (Table 4.16) is the primary source of *O Lord grant the king a long life*, the second anthem listed in the index of R.M. 20.h.8 but not copied. A transcription by Philip Hayes survives in Ktp MR 2–5.3, pp. 197–205.[57] In the nineteenth century the manuscript belonged to W. H. Cummings and in 1955 it was

---

[55] One document dating from 1689–97 lists 'La: Rich' amongst the 'Hoboys only for this voyage & not to bee established but to bee payd for attending His Ma[jest]ie into Holland'; *RECM*, II, 40. His initial appointment in 1685, however, was as one of 'Three New [instrumental] Bases' (ibid., 5); it may have been in this capacity that in 1688 he travelled to Windsor as one of the Chapel Royal (ibid., 21).

[56] *RECM*, II, 16, 21.

[57] Fortune, 'A New Purcell Source', 110, suggests that the Tatton copy is independent, but its variants could have been introduced by Hayes as corrections of perceived errors or mistakes and omissions of his own.

acquired by St Michael's College, Tenbury, from J. L. Boston, who had purchased it from the Oxford bookseller Leonard Hyman.[58]

The front cover inscription 'John Phipps His Score Book January the 6 1714:15', practised several times on the last page, seems to belong to the main copyist. John Phipps (d. 1759),[59] a vicar choral at St Patrick's Cathedral, Dublin, from 1720 until 1758,[60] had a career long enough to allow for the considerable development apparent in the handwriting, including changes in the style of the C clef and the letter 'r'. In places another writer has made extensive corrections, and an original foliation beginning with '10' on the first page contains a number of subsequent interruptions, reflecting the removal of several pages. The obscure composer 'Godfry' could be Thomas Godfrey, who served as organist at both Dublin cathedrals in the late 1680s,[61] and a hand similar to Phipps's later work in Ob MS Tenbury 1503 appears in the oldest surviving set of Christ Church, Dublin, cathedral partbooks.[62]

## OTHER AUTOGRAPH COPIES OF ODES

From *Now does the glorious day appear*, the first birthday ode Purcell composed for Queen Mary, the court odes and similar works survive in a variety of sources including three autographs (Tables 4.17 and 4.18). Lbl Egerton 2956, Purcell's working score of the Yorkshire Feast Song, *Of old when heroes thought it base*, was purchased by the British Museum as lot 1391 of W. H. Cummings's sale in May 1917. Although the manuscript was bound or rebound in the nineteenth century, it retains its original quiring structure and clearly consists of eleven bifolia; in contrast to other works, such as the 1692 St Cecilia ode, the paper type is the same throughout and the opening symphony does not appear to have been written separately from the main body of the work.

Much the most important early source of *Hail bright Cecilia*, Purcell's St Cecilia's Day ode for 1692, is the largely autograph score now incorporated in Ob MS Mus.c.26, fols. 21–69. Fols. 21, 68 and 69, each in the hand of a different copyist, no doubt represent repairs made for later revivals of the ode. The overture (fols. 21–5)

---

[58] Correspondence preserved with the manuscript.

[59] A will proved in Dublin in 1759 and destroyed in 1922 was probably his: see Vicars, *Index*, 376.

[60] See Lawlor, *Fasti*, 223, 245. Phipps also held a post at Christ Church, Dublin: see Grindle, *Irish Cathedral Music*, 40, 44.

[61] Shaw, *The Succession*, 410, 419; Grindle, *Irish Cathedral Music*, 223–4.

[62] See n. 33 above: these partbooks also contain works by Godfrey including a setting of *God is our hope and strength*.

## Table 4.16 Oxford, Bodleian Library MS Tenbury 1503: contents

| Folio | Title | Copyist's ascription | Later ascription |
|---|---|---|---|
| 1r | I will sing a new song | Mr Wise | |
| 4v | I will magnify thee | | Tucker [pencil] |
| 7v | O Lord grant the king a long life | Mr Hen: Purcell | |
| 12r | Awake put on thy strength | | Mr Wise |
| 16v | Praise the Lord O my soul O Lord my God | | Dr Croft |
| 24v | Behold thou hast made my days | | Orlando Gibbons |
| 27v | The kings of Tharsis | | Dr Blow |
| 31v | O Lord my God why hast thou forsaken me | Mr. Pell: Humphry | Pelham Humphrey |
| 37r | Above the stars my saviour dwells | | '?Parsons' (pencil: index) |
| 41r | O Lord I have sinned | | Dr Blow |
| 46r | I am well pleased | | Dr Aldrich from Carissimi |
| 54v | Thy word is a lantern | | H. Purcell |
| 60v | Lord how are they increased | | Dr Blow |
| 65v | Sing unto the Lord | Mr Orlando Gibbons | |
| 72r | I will sing unto the Lord as long as I live (inc.) | | Dr Croft |
| 72v | My song shall be alway | Mr Hen: Purcell | |
| 77v | Blessed is the people | | Dr Croft |
| 86r | Praise the Lord O ye his servants | | |
| 91v | O sing unto God (inc.) | Dr Blow's | |
| 92v | O sing unto God | Dr Blow's | |
| 98v | Behold I bring you glad tidings | | Purcell |
| 103v | God is our hope and strength [verse setting in C] | Dr Blow | |
| 112r | O give thanks | | Purcell |
| 120r | I was glad | Mr Purcell | |
| 124r | Hear O heavens | | P. Humphrey |
| 128r | Lord teach us to number our days | | [Humphrey] |
| 132r | We will rejoice in thy salvation | | [Blow] |
| 137v | Like as the hart | | [Humphrey] |
| 142r | Haste thee O God | | P. Humphrey |
| 146v | O be joyful in the Lord | | [Humphrey] |
| 149v | Lift up your heads | | |
| 153v | God is our hope and strength | Godfry | |
| 157r | O clap your hands | | Dr Crofts |
| 161v | This is the day | | |
| 165r | Have mercy upon me O God | | Humphrys [pencil] |

Folio, 316 × 196. Binding: contemporary blind-tooled reversed sheep, 321 × 200. Watermarks: arms of Amsterdam with countermark 'I VILLEDARY' (fols. 1–11, 18–33, 64–93); arms of Amsterdam with countermark 'DM' (fols. 12–17, 34–63, 94–169).

Rastrology: twelve staves ruled with two three-stave rastra; 'VILLEDARY' and some 'DM' paper, span: 59.5, profile: 11(14)12.5(11)11; other 'DM' paper, span: 60, profile: 12.5(13)12(11.5)11.5.

Principal copyist: John Phipps

## Table 4.17 Primary manuscript sources of welcome songs and other odes

| Date | Title | *Lbl R.M.* 20.h.8 *folio* | *Lbl Add.* 33287 *folio* | *Other principal early sources* |
|------|-------|---------------------------|--------------------------|----------------------------------|
| 1680 | Welcome, vicegerent of the mighty king | | | Lbl Add. 22100 |
|      |                                        | | | Lbl Add. 31447 |
| 1681 | Swifter Isis | 245v | 78v | |
| 1682 | What shall be done in behalf of the man | 238r | 148v | |
|      | The summer's absence | 232v | 155r | |
| 1683 | From hardy climes | 207r | 162r | |
|      | Fly bold rebellion | 197v | 130v | |
|      | Welcome to all the pleasures | | 96v | |
| 1684 | From those serene and rapturous joys | 182v | 168v | |
| 1685 | Why are all the muses mute | 166r | 177r | |
| 1686 | Ye tuneful muses | 155r | 198r | |
|      | Raise, raise the voice | | 26v | Lbl R.M. 24.e.5 |
|      |                        | |      | Och 470, 1145 |
| 1687 | Sound the trumpet, beat the drum | 139r | 187v | Lbl Add. 31447 |
|      |                                  |      |      | Cfm 119 |
| 1689 | Celestial music | 125v | 37r | |
|      | Now does the glorious day appear | 116v | | Ob MS Mus.c.28 |
| 1690 | Of old when heroes thought it base | 105v | | Lbl Egerton 2956 |
|      | Arise my muse | 90r | | Ob MS Mus.c.26 |
| 1691 | Welcome glorious morn | | | Lbl Add. 31447 |
|      |                       | | | Lcm 994 |
|      |                       | | | Lbl R.M. 24.e.8 |
| 1692 | Love's goddess sure was blind | | | Lbl Add. 31447 |
|      |                               | | | Lcm 994 |
|      |                               | | | Lbl R.M. 24.e.8 |
|      | Hail bright Cecilia | | | Ob MS Mus.c.26 |
|      |                     | | | Lbl Add. 31447 |
|      |                     | | | Lbl Add. 31448 |
|      |                     | | | Lbl Add. 31453 |
|      |                     | | | Cfm 119 |
| 1693 | Celebrate this festival | | | Ob MS Mus.c.28 |
|      |                         | | | Lbl R.M. 24.e.4 |
|      |                         | | | Lbl Add. 17835 |
|      |                         | | | Lbl Add. 31447 |
|      |                         | | | Och 468–71 |
| 1694 | Great parent, hail | | | Lbl Add. 31447 |
|      |                    | | | Lbl R.M. 24.e.8 |
|      |                    | | | Lcm 994 |
|      | Come ye sons of art | | | Lcm 993 |
| 1695 | Who can from joy refrain | | | Lbl Add. 30934 |
|      |                          | | | Ob MS Mus. c.27* |
|      |                          | | | Lbl Add. 31447 |
|      |                          | | | Cfm 119 |
|      |                          | | | Cfm 684 |

and most of the final chorus (60–7) are on paper marked with a crude arms of Amsterdam and the vertical 'IACH' monogram of Jacob and Adriaan Corneliszoon Honigh:[63] another scribe later replaced the lost or damaged first folio on an unused half-sheet of this paper. From fol. 26 to fol. 59 the watermark is the arms of London, with the factor's mark 'AJ' and the cursive countermark 'TJ'. Apart from the replacement pages at the end all sheets are similarly ruled, but it may be significant that both the overture and the last chorus are on different paper from the rest of the work. A broadly similar pattern appears in the autograph score of *Who can from joy refrain* (see below), so Purcell could have intentionally composed the beginnings and ends of his major odes independently of their central sections or at least have organised his scores so that these passages could easily be separated. The two early secondary sources of *Hail bright Cecilia* are important only for the passages not copied by Purcell in Mus.c.26, though Lbl Add. 31453, fols. 2–37, is in the hand of William Isaack.

Lbl Add. 30934 (see Illus. 1.7) contains five separate scores of odes by Henry Purcell, Daniel Purcell and Jeremiah Clarke, collected by William Croft. The volume as a whole and each individual work have been provided with a title page of unruled paper: fol. 79, which precedes Purcell's autograph copy of *Who can from joy refrain* (fols 80–93), has a countermark consisting of the crowned initials 'GR', dating the compilation of the volume after 1714, when George I came to the throne: it bears Croft's inscription 'The following song was compos'd by ye Famous Mr Hen: Purcell and p[e]rform[e]d upon ye Duke of Gloucesters Birth Day and is the originall score'.

The manuscript is heavily corrected and must be Purcell's first copy, comparable with the anthem autographs in Bu 5001 and Ob MS Mus.c.26. Most of the folios are now individually mounted, but it is still possible to form some impression of the composer's working procedure (Table 4.19). His initial material seems to have been two sheets of paper with an arms of Berne bear watermark, a type unusual in post-Restoration English music sources but also found in Lcm 1144 and in a secondary source of this ode, Ob MS Mus.c.27*:[64] one half-sheet must have been torn out and the remaining three form fols. 82–4. Purcell probably continued on a

---

[63] Churchill no. 18; Voorn, *De papiermolens*, no. 46. According to Voorn the monogram was used from 1675 until *c.*1692.

[64] One mark of the pair has the initial 'M' beneath, offset to one side; the other the letters 'NM', identifying the Berne papermaker Niklaus Malacrida. See Johann Lindt, *The Paper Mills of Berne and their Watermarks, 1465–1859* (Hilversum, 1964), nos. 158–9 and pp. 19–21. This paper must have been made before 1697, when Malacrida is first known to have owned or rented a paper mill.

## Table 4.18 Separate scores of individual odes

| Work | Manuscript | Folios | Format and dimensions | Paper type | Copyist |
|---|---|---|---|---|---|
| Raise, raise the voice | Lbl R.M. 24.e.5 | 1–9 | folio, 324 × 213 (mounted) | (1) foolscap: cursive factor's mark 'HG' (2) foolscap: factor's mark 'AJ'. No countermarks [most sheets very obscure] | London D |
| | Och 1145 | | folio, 328 × 205 | (1) Amsterdam: factor's mark 'AJ'; countermark 'IV' (2) Dutch Lion: factor's mark 'AJ'; countermark 'CDG' | |
| Of old when heroes thought it base | Lbl Egerton 2956 | | folio, 328 × 204 | Amsterdam: factor's mark 'AJ'; countermark 'RC' | Purcell |
| Now does the glorious day appear | Ob MS Mus.c.28 | 19–39 | folio, 322 × 199 | Pro Patria: countermark crowned 'GR' | |
| Arise my muse | Ob MS Mus.c.26 | 71–94 | folio, 325 × 205 | Amsterdam: countermark 'GB' | London A |
| Hail bright Cecilia | Ob MS Mus.c.26 | 21–69 | folio, 325 × 203 | 21–5: Amsterdam: countermark 'IACH' | 21: 1* |
| | | | | 26–59: London: factor's mark 'AJ'; countermark cursive 'TJ' | 22–67: Purcell |
| | | | | 60–7: Amsterdam: countermark 'IACH' | |
| | | | | 68: Dutch Lion | 68: 2* |
| | | | | 69: countermark 'H' | 69: 3* |
| | Lbl Add. 31453 | 2–37 | folio, 325 × 206 (mounted) | Amsterdam: countermark 'HD' | Isaack |
| Celebrate this festival | Ob MS Mus.c.28 | 78–99 | folio, 322 × 208 | Amsterdam: no countermark | Isaack, Walter |
| Who can from joy refrain | Lbl Add. 30934 | 80–93 | folio, 318 × 200 324 × 201 318 × 200 | Amsterdam: countermark 'CS' bear: no countermark Amsterdam: countermark 'DS' | Purcell |
| | Ob MS Mus.c.27* | 27–32 | flat, 321 × 410 | 27, 30: Amsterdam: countermark 'IV' 28, 29: bear 31: Amsterdam: countermark obscure 32: foolscap: countermark 'ID' | Isaack, Walter |
| | Cfm 684 | | flat, 325 × 409 | Amsterdam: countermark 'CS' | Isaack, Walter |

## Table 4.18 (*cont.*)

Rastrology

| Manuscript | Staves on page | Staves in rastrum | Rastrum span | Rastrum profile |
|---|---|---|---|---|
| R.M. 24.e.5, fols. 1–9 | 12 | 6 | 136 | 12(13)12(12)12(12.5)12.5(12.5)12.5(13.5)12.5 |
| Och 1145, fols. 1–2, 7–8; | 12 | 4 | 83.5 | 11(12)11.5(13)11(13)12 |
| fols. 3–6 | 12 | 6 | 131 | 11(11.5)11.5(12.5)12(13)12.5(11.5)12.5(12)12 |
| Egerton 2956 | 12 | 4 | 84 | 12.5(11)12.5(12)12(11.5)12.5 |
| Ob MS Mus.c.28, fols. 19–39 | 12 | 6 | 130 | 11(12.5)11(13.5)11.5(13)10.5(13.5)11(13)11 |
| Ob MS Mus.c.26, fols. 71–94 | 12 | 4 | 81.5 | 11.5(11.5)12.5(11)12.5(11.5)11 |
| Ob MS Mus.c.26, fols. 21–67; | 12 | 6 | 132 | 11(12.5)12.5(13)11(13)11.5(13.5)11(11.5)12 |
| fol. 68; | 12 | 4 | 70.5 | 9.5(11)9.5(11)9.5(11)9.5 |
| fol. 69 | 14 | | | single-stave rastrum of 10.5 mm |
| Add. 31453, fols. 2–37 | 12 | 4 | 81.5 | 11.5(12)11.5(12)11.5(12)11.5 |
| Ob MS Mus.c.28, fols. 78–99 | 12 | 6 | 129 | 11.5(12)12.5(11.5)12(11)13(10)(12)12 |
| Add. 30934, fols. 80–1, 86–7, 91; | 12 | 6 | 133.5 | 12(12.5)12(13)11(12.5)11.5(12.5)12(12.5)11.5 |
| fols. 82–5, 88–90; | 12 | 6 | 131 | 12(12)12(13)12(12.5)11(12)12(12)11 |
| fols. 92–3 | 12 | 6 | 121 | 11.5(9.5)12(10)12(9.5)11.5(10)11.5(11.5)12 |
| Ob MS Mus.c.27*, | | | | |
| fols. 27, 30, 31; | 12 | 4 | 87.5 | 12.5(11)12.5(13.5)13.5(13)12 |
| fols. 28, 29; | 12 | 6 | 134.5 | 13(11)13.5(12.5)12.5(12.5)12.5(12)13(10)12.5 |
| fol. 32 | 12 | 6 | 128 | 11(12)12(11.5)12(12)11.5(12.5)11(12)11 |
| Cfm 684 (rectos) | 12 | 4 | 85 | 11.5(11)12(13)12.5(15)11 |
| (versos) | 12 | 4 | 87 | 12.5(11)12(13)13(14.5)12 |

* Copyists 1–3 in Ob MS Mus.c.26, fols. 21–69 are unidentified.

four-folio quire consisting of one sheet of bear paper and one of Amsterdam countermarked 'CS', all cut down at some stage to the dimensions of the slightly smaller Amsterdam paper. It is not possible to tell whether fols. 89–91 are the remains of a further four-folio quire or of two separate bifolia, but the watermark half-sheet to match fol. 91 has gone. The overture was written on a bifolium of 'CS' paper which, like the central bifolium 86–7, is intact. Purcell organised his work so that the overture and final chorus could conveniently be separated from the rest, perhaps to facilitate the copying of parts or for rehearsal; a similar procedure seems to have been followed for the autograph of the St Cecilia's day ode in Ob MS Mus.c.26 but not in Lbl Egerton 2956, *Of old when heroes thought it base.*

**Table 4.19  London, British Library Additional MS 30934, fols. 80–93: conjectural collation**

| Folio | Watermark or countermark | Comments |
|---|---|---|
| 80 | Amsterdam | bifolium 80–1 intact, containing the overture |
| 81 | 'CS' | |
| 82 | – | |
| 83 | – | |
| 84 | bear | |
| [84/i | lost bear folio] | |
| 85 | – | the whole of this central quire cut down to |
| 86 | Amsterdam | 318 × 200. Bifolium 86–7 intact. |
| 87 | 'CS' | |
| 88 | bear | |
| | | possible alternative collation: |
| [88/i | lost Amsterdam folio] | 89  – |
| 89 | – | 90  bear |
| 90 | bear | 91  'CS' |
| 91 | 'CS' | [91/i lost Amsterdam folio] |
| 92 | 'DS' | shown to be a bifolium by distinctive ruling: contains |
| 93 | Amsterdam | the last chorus |

## PRINCIPAL SOURCES OF ODES IN COPYISTS' HANDS

### London, British Library Additional MS 33287 and Royal Music 24.e.5

Unlike its companion Lcm 2011, which is entirely devoted to Purcell anthems, Lbl Add. 33287 contains music by composers other than Purcell and appears to represent an attempt to collect the complete Stuart court repertory of symphony songs and odes, originally in two distinct books (Table 4.20). It is the only extensive secondary source of Purcell's symphony songs, mostly copied from R.M. 20.h.8 (Table 4.21).

The bulk of both sections of Lbl Add. 33287 is in the hand of London D, who supplied each with a formal index headed 'A Table of all the Songs In this Booke with the Names of those that Composed ym'. Much of the paper, including the whole of the first section, is the same as that of Lcm 2011, with which Add. 33287 also has important rastral connections (see Table 4.14). Much of the manuscript appears to have been copied before binding, as the ends of the original indexes correspond with distinct changes in the character and quality of the musical hand-writing at Purcell's *O what a scene* (fol. 22v) and Blow's *Hail Monarch sprung of race divine* (fol. 138v), the New Year song for 1686. The second section, devoted to court odes, seems to date from 1685 because its third work is Blow's *How does the new born infant year rejoice* composed for 1 January of that year.

Although the texts of Purcell's music in Lbl Add. 33287 are often closely related to R.M. 20.h.8, in general duplicating the autograph's headings and reproducing its omissions, London D and the other copyists sometimes add extra details such as the designation of certain parts for oboe or flute in *Swifter Isis* and the names of performers in *Sound the trumpet*. The two Purcell welcome songs entered in Add. 33287 entirely by subsidiary hands are more likely to be related to an independent autograph than to R.M. 20.h.8, where *Ye tuneful muses* was in any case not copied by Purcell, while amongst the symphony songs *Hark how the wild musicians sing* in the main hand must also, given the number of variants, have been derived from an independent source. The inclusion of *Welcome to all the pleasures* and Blow's *Begin the song* amongst the court odes in Lbl Add. 33287 is confirmation that these Cecilian odes were regarded as part of the court repertory, the Purcell work perhaps being omitted from R.M. 20.h.8 because the score had been printed. Equally significant is the place of Purcell's *Raise, raise the voice* amongst the symphony songs in the manuscript's first section. Here not quite complete, it is the final work added by London D and immediately precedes Purcell's last symphony song, *If ever I more riches did desire* of late 1686 or 1687: *Raise, raise the voice* has sometimes been regarded as a Cecilian ode and assigned to 1683, but its position in Add. 33287 both supports the later date more appropriate on stylistic grounds[65] and indicates that the work was not written for the same purpose as *Welcome to all the pleasures* and *Begin the song*.[66]

London D seems to have compiled Add. 33287 after the death of Charles II, as he amplifies Purcell's headings referring to 'the King' or 'his Majesty' to avoid any ambiguity. He was uncertain of dates as recent as 1683 if they were not given in his sources, and his copying came to an abrupt halt in 1686, for Blow's 1687 New Year song *Is it a dream* is missing and other works dating from 1686 onwards are in different hands. London D left *Why are all the muses mute* and *Raise, raise the voice*

---

[65] See *Works*, X (1990), ix–x; Spink, 'Purcell's Odes', 163–5.

[66] See Holman, *Henry Purcell*, 161: the text of *Raise, raise the voice* in fact refers to Apollo rather than St Cecilia, though it does mention 'sacred Music's holy day'.

## Table 4.20  London, British Library Additional MS 33287: contents

| Folio | Heading or incipit | Ascription | Copyist[a] |
|---|---|---|---|
| 2r | Go Perjur'd man | By Dr John Blow | London D |
| 3v | Whilst on Septimius panting breast | By Dr John Blow | London D |
| 5v | Chear up my freinds | By Mr William Turner | London D |
| 8v | Farewell fair Saint | By Mr William Turner | London D |
| 10v | Hark Damon hark | By Mr Henry Purcell | London D |
| 12r | How pleasant is this flowry Plain | By Mr Henry Purcell | London D |
| 14v | Hark how the wild musitians sing | By Mr Henry Purcell | London D |
| 17v | 'Tis you great Ceres | By Mr William Turner | London D |
| 19v | See where she sitts | By Mr Henry Purcell | London D |
| 21v | Tis not to add new glory's to the Day | By Mr William Turner | London D |
| 22v | Oh what a Scene does entertain my Sight | By Mr Henry Purcell | London D |
| 24v | Soft notes and gently rais'd | By Mr Henry Pursell | London D |
| 26v | Raise, Raise the voice (inc.) | Mr Henry Purcell [index] | London D |
| 31v | If ever I more Riches did desire | Mr Henry Purcell [index] | 2 |
| 37r | Celestial Musick did the Gods inspire (inc.) | [Purcell] | 3, 4 |
| 44v | Hither this way | Mr Henry Purcell | 5 |
| 46v | By Silver Thames's flowry side | | 5 |
| 48r | See from ye silent grove | Dr Pepusch [pencil] | 5 |
| 50v | Tell me Shepherds have you seen | | 5 |
| 51v | The God of Love had lost his Bow | | 5 |
| | [recitative preceding previous song] | | |

[end of first section]

| Folio | Heading or incipit | Ascription | Copyist[a] |
|---|---|---|---|
| 53r | Great Janus. A Birth days song May The 29: 16[79][b] | By Dr John Blow | London D |
| 58r | The Birth of Jove. A Birth days song. May: 29: 16[78] | By Dr John Blow | London D |
| 63r | A New years Song. January the First 1684/5 How does the new-born: &c: | By Dr John Blow | London D |
| 69v | See, Mighty S[i]r: A New years song: January: the First 167[2][c] | By Mr Pelham Humphrys | London D |
| 72r | When from his Throne: A Birth days Song May: 29: 16[72] | By Mr Pelham Humphrys | London D |
| 75r | Dread S[i]r, the Prince of Light. A New years Song. January: the First 16[78] | By Dr John Blow | London D |
| 78v | Swifter Isis Swifter flow. A Welcome Song For the King: 1681 Charles: 2: | By Mr Henry Purcell | London D |
| 84v | Arise Great Monarch. A new years Song January the first 16[82] | By Dr John Blow | London D |
| 89v | Oh Mighty Prince. A new Years Song January the first 16[–][d] | By Mr William Turner | London D |
| 93r | The New Year is Begun. A new Years song January the first 16[80] | By Dr John Blow | London D |
| 96v | A Song perform'd on St Cecilia's Day. November: the: 22th: 1683. Welcome to all the pleasures | By Mr Henry Purcell | London D |
| 103r | A Song Perform'd on St Cecilias Day. November: 22th: 1684. Begin the Song | By Dr John Blow | London D |

Table 4.20 (*cont.*)

| Folio | Heading or incipit | Ascription | Copyist[a] |
|---|---|---|---|
| 112r | Great S[i]r the Joy of all our hearts. A new years Song January the first: 16[81] | By Dr John Blow | London D |
| 118r | My Trembling Song awake arise. A new Years Song January the first 1684 | By Dr John Blow | London D |
| 125r | Dread S[i]r, Father Janus, & c: A new years Song: January the First: 16[83] | By Dr John Blow | London D |
| 130v | A welcome Song p[e]rform'd to King Charles the Second in ye Year 1683 [Fly bold rebellion] | By Mr Henry Purcell | London D |
| 138v | A New years Song perform'd to King James the Second January: first 1686 [Hail monarch sprung of race divine] | By Dr John Blow | London D |
| 148v | A Welcome Song p[e]rform'd before James Duke of York at his Return from Scotland 1682 [What shall be done in behalf of the man] | By Mr Henry Purcell | London D |
| 155r | A Welcome Song perform'd before King Charles the Second: October 21th: 1682 [The summer's absence] | By Mr Henry Purcell | London D |
| 162r | A song performed to George Prince of Denmark upon his Marriage with ye Lady Ann, daughter to James D: of York [1683: From hardy climes] | By Mr Henry Purcell | London D |
| 168v | A Welcome song perform'd to King Charles the Second: Anno: 1684 [From those serene and rapturous joys] | By Mr Henry Purcell | London D |
| 177r | Welcome Song 1685 being the first perform'd to King James the Second [Why are all the muses mute] | Mr Henry Purcell [index] | London D, 2, 5 |
| 187v | Sound the Trumpet 1687 | Mr Henry Purcell [index] | 2, 3 |
| 198r | Ye symphony to yee tunefull mueses begines hear 1686 | Mr Henry Purcell [index] | 2, 3 |
| 209v | Yee Sons of Phebus [New Year, 1688] | Dr John Blow | 2, 3 |
| 221v | [St Cecilia ode 1687; incomplete] | [G. B. Draghi] | 2, 3 |

Folio, 439 × 265. Watermarks: arms of Strasbourg with factor's mark 'AJ' and countermark 'CDG' (fols. 1–52, 58–9, 62–3, 65–9, 72–3, 76–7, 80, 86–7, 89–96, 102–3, 105–8, 110–11, 113–17, 120–4, 126–7, 129–49, 152, 169, 172–81, 184–7, 189–90, 192–6, 200–29); arms of Strasbourg with countermark 'RC' (fols. 53–7, 60, 81–4, 125, 128, 165–8, 170–1); arms of Strasbourg with countermark 'PT' (fols. 61, 64, 70–1, 74–5, 78–9, 85, 88, 97–101, 104, 109, 112, 118–19, 150–1, 153–64, 182–3, 188, 191, 197–9).

Original ink pagination of first section 1–71, extended by early copyists from 72–99.
Original ink pagination of second section 1–338 (= fol. 222r).

Rastrology: see Table 4.14.

[a] Copyists 2–5 unidentified.

[b] Unless otherwise stated incomplete dates are supplied from the chronology in Rosamond McGuinness, *English Court Odes, 1660–1820* (Oxford, 1971), 12–61. In spite of its heading in Add. 33287, *Great Janus though the festival be thine* is evidently a New Year ode: ibid., 16, 46.

[c] The date is given in the index of Robert Veel, *New Court-Songs, and Poems* (London, 1672): see Peter Dennison, *Pelham Humfrey* (Oxford, 1986), 113n.

[d] Before 1685: McGuinness, *English Court Odes*, 18, 49.

**Table 4.21  Primary manuscript sources of symphony songs**

| Work | Lbl R.M. 20.h.8 folio | Lbl Add. 33287 folio | Other early sources |
|---|---|---|---|
| How pleasant is this flowery plain | 226r INV | 12r | Lbl Add. 33235; Add. 33236 |
| We reap all the pleasures | 224r INV | | |
| Hark how the wild musicians sing | 222v INV | 14v | |
| Hark Damon hark | 218r INV | 10v | Lbl Add. 22100; Add. 33234 |
| See where she sits | 209r INV | 19v | B-Bc 1035.g |
| Oh what a scene does entertain | 188r INV | 22v | |
| Soft notes and gently raised | 185v INV | 24v | |
| If ever I more riches did desire | 144v INV | 31v | |

unfinished, entering the former work in the appropriate index but not the latter, which was indexed, though not completed, by hand 2. At first, in *If ever I more riches did desire* (1687), hand 2 sought to emulate the beautiful copying of London D, but thereafter the special character of the manuscript is lost, even in hand 2's unfinished continuation of *Why are all the muses mute*. The subsidiary hands are sometimes difficult to distinguish, but hand 2 seems to have exercised a supervisory role up to 1689, providing the text for the last four works in the manuscript as well as indexing the symphony song he copied and the last three court odes. In the first section of the volume hand 3, supervised by 2 who added some performance directions, managed to copy *Celestial Music* up to just beyond the end of the symphony. Hand 5 belongs to a later owner of the manuscript, who used it to collect secular cantatas including one by J. C. Pepusch and 'Hither this way' from Purcell's *King Arthur* copied from the 1706 edition of *Orpheus Britannicus*, Book I.[67] Hand 5 also added the last page of the 1685 welcome song and hand 4 finished *Celestial Music*. A further scribe, who did not contribute any music, indexed the titles but not the composers of the last few works in the first section and supplied a heading for *Celestial Music* in which the composer's name is left blank.

The first section of Lbl R.M. 24.e.5 (fols. 1–9) contains a complete score of *Raise, raise the voice* in the hand of London D. The name 'Bowen', added in different writing above the treble solo in bar 112, presumably refers to the famous boy singer Jemmy Bowen and implies that a further performance took place during his time as a Chapel Royal chorister between 1692 and 1696.[68]

[67] *Works*, XXVI (1971), xii.      [68] *Works*, X (1990), x, xii.

Sources copied by London A, John Walter and William Isaack:
London, British Library Additional MS 22100
Oxford, Bodleian Library MS Mus.c.26, fols. 71–94
Oxford, Bodleian Library MS Mus.c.28, fols. 78–99
Oxford, Bodleian Library MS Mus.c.27*
Cambridge, Fitzwilliam Museum Music MS 684

The most authoritative group of copyists' sources containing Purcell's odes are those transcribed by identifiable musicians linked to royal establishments either at White-hall or Windsor: John Walter, William Isaack and London A. Most contain later works, but fol. 151v of Lbl Add. 22100, a scorebook copied by Walter,[69] is inscribed 'Mr Dolbins Book Anno Domini 1682/1'.[70] The manuscript's contents (Table 4.22) give the impression that copying was completed well before the old-style period 1681/2, 1 January to 24 March 1682, as it would have made little sense for Walter to omit Purcell's *Swifter Isis* and Blow's *Arise great monarch* if they had been composed before his copying was finished (Illus. 4.2).

Lbl Add. 22100 is the earlier and better of two sources of Purcell's first court ode, the 1680 welcome song *Welcome vicegerent of the mighty king*. The likelihood that the manuscript was copied after Blow's *Great Sir the joy of all our hearts* became available in January 1681 but before March, when Purcell probably composed *Swifter Isis*, has a bearing on *Haste gentle Charon* and *Hark Damon hark*, the two works by Purcell entered shortly before *Venus and Adonis*: both appear in R.M. 20.h.8 after the welcome song *The summer's absence unconcerned we bear*, dated 21 October 1682, and Walter's source for them is likely not to have been R.M. 20.h.8 but earlier, separate autographs. The remaining odes copied by Walter in collaboration with his colleague William Isaack were composed in the 1690s, by which time Walter's handwriting had changed from the refined style of Lbl Add. 22100, and together with other sources imply that an extensive duplicate collection of music for court performances was kept at Windsor. Fols. 78–99 of Ob MS Mus.c.28 (see Table 3.6), a single gathering of twenty-two folios, contain an almost complete score of *Celebrate*

---

[69] See Bruce Wood, 'A Note on Two Cambridge Manuscripts and their Copyists', *M&L* 56 (1975), 309.

[70] Sir Gilbert Dolben (1658–1722), a lawyer, was one of the stewards of the 'Musical Society' responsible for the St Cecilia festivities in London in 1684; his son Sir John Dolben (1684–1756) was a major patron of music in the first half of the eighteenth century. See *DNB*, XV, 189; Donald Burrows, 'Sir John Dolben, Musical Patron', *MT* 120 (1979), 65–7; 'Sir John Dolben's Music Collection', *MT* 120 (1979), 149–51; Richard Charteris, 'Newly Discovered Sources of Music by Henry Purcell', *M&L* 75 (1994), 16–32.

## Table 4.22 London, British Library Additional MS 22100: contents

| Folio | Heading and incipit[a] | Ascription |
|---|---|---|
| 3r | A song to Welcome home his Majesty from Windsor 1680 'Welcome vicegerent of ye Mighty King' | Composed by Mr. Purcell |
| 13v | A song on New years Day 1681 'Great Sir ye joy of all our hearts' | Compos'd by Dr. Jo: Blow |
| 26r | (Song) 'Fair Nymphs yt to ye wanton wind' | Composed by Dr. Blow |
| 30v | Song 'Lord I confess my sin is great' | Jo: Walter |
| 32v | (Awake my Lyre) [heading] | Composed by Dr. Blow |
| 40v | (Go perjur'd man) [heading] | Composed by Dr. Blow |
| 44v | Song 'Ah my soul why so dismay'd' | Composed by Dr. Gibbons |
| 46v | Song 'These two full howres now have I gazing bin' | Composed by Mr. Hall |
| 48v | Song 'A winged harbinger' | Composed by Dr. Blow |
| 54v | A Song for ye Queens Birth Day 'Illustrious day what glory canst y[o]u boast' | Composed by Dr. Blow |
| 56v | Song 'Lucifer celestis' | Composed by Signior Carissimo |
| 59r | A Song for ye 29th of May [1678] 'The Birth of Jove' | Dr. Blow |
| 73v | Song 'As on Euphrates shady banks' | Dr. Blow |
| 77v | A Song upon a Ground 'Scocca pur' | Mr. Baptist [pencil: Mr Baptist Lully] |
| 79r | Song 'Awake fair goddess of this place' | Mr. Hall |
| 81v | Song 'Then from a whirlwind oracle' | Composed by Mr. Lock |
| 84r | Song 'Ah Alexander rowse' | Mr. James Hart |
| 87r | Song 'See where she sitts' | Mr. Turner |
| 89v | A Dialouge 'Allas, allas who has bin here' | Composed by M. Lock |
| 92v | The Despondent Lover's Song[b] 'Divinest Syren, cruell fair' | Composed by Mr. Lock |
| 94r | Song 'Farewell fair saint' | Composed by Mr. Turner |
| 98v | Song 'See O see how ye flowers adorn ye spring' | Compos'd by Mr. Turner |
| 100v | Song 'Awake my lute' | Compos'd by Mr. Turner [102v]: 'Wm Turner' [signature; 102r] |
| 103r | Song: of Devills 'Prepare, prepare new guests draw near' | Mr. Turner |
| 105v | A Dialouge between Saul, Samuel & ye Witch of Endor 'In guilty night' | Compos'd by Mr. Lanear |
| 108r | A Dialouge between Orpheus and Charon 'Hast gentle Charon' | Compos'd by Mr. Purcell |
| 111r | Song 'As on Septimius panting breast' | Composed by Dr. Blow |
| 115v | Song: The Passion 'Enough my muse' | Compos'd by Dr. Blow |
| 117v | Song 'Hark Damon Hark' | Compos'd by Mr. Purcell |
| 120r | Song 'Shall all ye buds' | Dr. Blow |
| 123r | A dance in ye prologue: w[hi]ch was ommitted | |
| 123v | A Masque for ye Entertainment of ye King [Venus and Adonis] | Dr. Blow [in pencil] |

Folio, 363 × 265. Watermarks: Angoumois fleur-de-lys with countermark 'IHS' (fols. 3–47, 83–102, 111–49) Angoumois fleur-de-lys with countermark 'IV' (fols. 48–82; 103–10). Flyleaves: fols. 1, 2, 150, 151, watermark as fols. 3–47, etc.

Rastrology (both paper types): twelve staves ruled with a four–stave rastrum, span: 99; profile: 13(15)14(14.5)14 (15)13.5.

Copyist: John Walter

[a] Headings and incipits are transcribed literally, including Walter's parentheses and punctuation.

[b] The words 'The Despondent Lover's' added by a later hand.

Illus. 4.2  Henry Purcell: *Welcome vicegerent of the mighty king*, copied by John Walter. British Library Add. MS 22100, fol. 4r

*this festival:*[71] the beginning of the overture is missing and the outermost of twelve original sheets has been lost, another score in Isaack's hand, Lbl R.M. 24.e.4, making good the deficiency. Individual singers are named, and on fol. 83r are instructions such as 'one paper' showing how the performing parts are to be laid out.

Isaack and Walter were also jointly responsible for Ob MS Mus.c.27*, a score of *Who can from joy refrain.* The source comprises six sheets extracted in 1939 from Ob MS Mus.c.27 and retaining their earlier folio numbers 27–32: two folios, 28 and 29, have an unusual bear watermark similar to the one in the autograph Lbl Add. 30934, indicating that the copyists drew on the same paper supply as Purcell although the stave ruling is different. Apart from fol. 31, which measures 410 by 321 mm and approximates to its original size, all sheets have been significantly cut down. Cfm 684, copied by William Isaack alone, is a related but more elegantly finished source of the same work retaining, after careful conservation, a patterned and coloured printed paper cover labelled in its right-hand half 'Birth Day song Duke of Gloster H. Purcell 1695'. This cover presumably surrounded the other sheets when they were folded in half for storage. All seven music folios (fols. 2–8) are marked with the Arms of Amsterdam and the countermark 'CS', one of the combinations found in the autograph section of Add. 30934. Cfm 684 was advertised as autograph in W. H. Cummings's sale (23 May 1917; lot 1394), though the manuscript's next owner, Ralph Griffin, realised that it was not in Purcell's hand but 'an extraordinarily exact copy'.[72] A marked difference in rastrology between recto and verso sides of each folio may mean that the paper in Cfm 684 was part of a substantial stock ruled first on one side and then, after the rastrum had begun to show signs of wear, on the other. Both Ob MS Mus.c.27* and Cfm 684 are 'stratigraphic' copies written across the full width of flat sheets of paper with the separate blocks of staves provided for facing pages joined together.

Fols. 71–94 of the composite volume Ob MS Mus.c.26 contain a score of *Arise my muse* copied with unusual care by London A.[73] The inscription 'Richardson book' on fol. 71r perhaps links this manuscript with the organist and former Chapel Royal chorister Vaughan Richardson,[74] and the identification of four

[71] It is possible, as Bruce Wood suggests, that this manuscript was actually the master copy for the first performance (see *Works*, XXIV, pp. xiv–xv), though the same cannot be true of all the scores transcribed by Isaack and Walter.

[72] Griffin's annotations inside the manuscript's front cover. He paid £20 for it at Cummings's sale and gave it to the Fitzwilliam Museum in 1935.

[73] The score's wrapper, now forming fols. 70 and 95, is made out of a violin part from one of Cazzati's Op. 18 sonatas copied on paper similar to that of Lbl R.M. 20.h.9.

[74] Organist of Winchester Cathedral from 1692 to 1729: see Spink, *Restoration*, 366.

singers, 'Boucher', 'Mr Robert', 'Mr Turner' and 'Mr Damascene',[75] suggests that it was copied from a separate autograph connected with the original performance at court. Apart from the incomplete score in R.M. 20.h.8, also by London A, all other sources of *Arise my muse* descend from Ob MS Mus.c.26 by way of the compressed copy in Lbl Add. 31447.[76]

## London, British Library Additional MS 31447

Lbl Add. 31447, copied by FQ4, was part of the large collection purchased by the British Museum from Julian Marshall in 1880–1 and contains no other evidence of ownership. Though unsatisfactory as a musical source, the manuscript is nevertheless of interest as an apparently systematic attempt to collect Purcell's later odes and major theatre works (Table 4.23), and for all its faults is the principal source of the birthday ode of 1691;[77] the inclusion of the much earlier *Welcome vicegerent of the mighty king* (1680) with the heading 'A Welcome Song at ye Princ of Denmark's comeing home' suggests that this work was revived for a ceremony involving Prince George, the husband of Princess Anne. All the music paper in the manuscript is of one type, found also in Ooc Ua 34–37, but the stave ruling from fol. 107 onwards differs from that of preceding folios: the change of rastrum appears to be significant and corresponds with the end of the original index written on fol. 1v. All works copied up to fol. 106 are indexed in a form that gives their key, instrumental and vocal forces, and page reference, the Yorkshire Feast Song, for example, being described thus:

D♯ – Yorkshire Song Vios: Flutes: Haut: Trums: Ketle Drum
2 Tres: 2 Contras: 1 Ten: 2 Bass with Through Bass        29

Works copied on paper with the second ruling are indexed in a slightly different style without a list of parts, and two works omitted from either stage of the original index, the 1690 birthday ode and Purcell's music from *The Libertine*, 'The last piece in the Book', were added to it in another hand. The relationship between contents, stave rulings, original page numberings and the different stages of the index shows that most of the paper ruled with the second rastrum was used first, forming a number of

---

[75] Joseph Bourchier, Anthony Robert, the composer William Turner and Alexander Damascene: *RECM*, II, passim.

[76] *Works*, XI (1993), xiv.

[77] This ode, along with *Arise my muse*, *Love's goddess sure was blind* and *Great parent hail*, seems to have been copied from Lbl Add. 31447 into the later sources Lbl R.M. 24.e.8 and Lcm 994 by James Kent; see *Works*, XI (1993), xiv–xv; Burrows, 'Sir John Dolben's Music Collection'.

**Table 4.23 London, British Library Additional MS 31447: contents**

| Folio | Pages | Heading |
|-------|-------|---------|
| 2r | [1]–[6] | Oedipus |
| 5r | 7–22 | Timon of Athens |
| 13r | 23–33 | Bonduca |
| 18v | 34–90 | King Arthur |
| 47r | 91–98 | Circe |
| 51r | 99–125 | The Indian Queen |
| 65r | 1–28 | St Cecilia's Song 1692 |
| 79r | 29–45 | Yorkshire Song |
| 87r | 45–52 | Du: of Gloucester's Birth-Day's Song |
| 94r | 53–65 | A Wellcom Song 1687 |
| 100r | 65–78 | Celebrate Queen's Birth-Day's Song |

[end of pagination in this series]

| | | |
|-------|-------|---------|
| 107r | 1–9bis | A Welcome Song at ye Princ of Denmark's comeing home [Welcome, vicegerent of the mighty king] |
| 112r | 1–19 | Queen's Birth-day Song 1691 |
| 121v | 20–28 | Queens Birth-days Song 1690 |
| 130r | 29–47 | Queens Birth-Day's Song 1692 |
| 140r | 1–16 | A Commemoration Song Performd att Christ Church in Dublin Jany ye 9 1693/4 |
| 148r | 1–8 | The Libertine |

Large upright quarto, 365 × 257. Watermarks: Angoumois fleur-de-lys with countermark 'IHS/I VILLEDARY'.

Rastrology: twelve staves ruled with four-stave rastra: rastrum 1 (up to fol. 106), span: 90, profile: 12(14.5)12(14.5)12(14.5)11; rastrum 2 (fol. 107 onwards), span: 94, profile: 13(14)13(14.5)13.5(14.5)12.5.

Copyist: FQ4

separate smaller volumes, and was combined later with the two principal series of stage and court music, though *The Libertine*, omitted from the second stage of the index and in fact in the wrong part of the volume, was added last, on blank pages incorporated when the book was bound.

The detailed index indicates that Lbl Add. 31447, with its unusually compressed, sometimes ambiguous, notation in which several parts are often written on one stave, is a file copy intended to enable someone familiar with the music to reproduce individual parts rather than to be an easily legible manuscript. The position of *Who can from joy refrain* before several earlier odes means that copying of most if not all of the second principal section of Add. 31447 took place after

1695, though the odes from fol. 107 onwards might well have been copied previously, and a date in the mid-1690s is not out of the question as a few examples of the full 'I VILLEDARY' countermark found in this manuscript are recorded between 1691 and *c.* 1700.[78]

## London, Royal College of Music MS 993

Lcm 993, pp. 143–80, contains the only surviving complete copy of *Come ye sons of art away*, Purcell's ode for Queen Mary's birthday in 1694. Most of this manuscript, including *Come ye sons of art*, was transcribed by Robert Pindar,[79] according to the title page as the first volume of a more extensive collection: 'Vocal and Instrumental Musick with the Overtures Songs and Chorusses as composed by Mr Henry Purcell Vol. 1st Finished Anno Domini 1765'. The birthday ode is given the incorrect description 'Ode for new years Day 1693/4'. The suspicions aroused by this title are not allayed by the musical text,[80] though the kettledrum part, which has sometimes been considered inauthentic,[81] does appear to be broadly seventeenth-century in character.

## Miscellaneous sources

A few further sources are worthy of mention, though for different reasons cannot be considered of primary importance. Two related manuscripts of *Raise, raise the voice*, a score, Och 1145, and a composite vocal and instrumental bass part copied from it by the elder Richard Goodson, Och 470, fols. 49r–47v INV, provide evidence that a performance took place in Oxford: both sources omit bars 146–9 and have other common variants. An interesting feature of Och 470 not shared with Och 1145 is the addition of a 'Boree' and a minuet, probably composed by Goodson, on slips of paper pasted to fol. 48r. Ob MS Mus.c.28, fols. 19–39, contains a score of *Now does the glorious day appear* in the same eighteenth-century hand as William Norris's St Cecilia ode *Begin the noble song* on fols. 40–63 of the same manuscript. In Ktp MR 2–5.3, pp. 117–32, is an incomplete score of an anonymous ode, *The noise of foreign wars*, copied *c.* 1785 by Philip Hayes: the whole of the four-volume Tatton collection is otherwise devoted to works elsewhere copied by or attributed to

---

[78] See Churchill nos. 27, 363; Heawood no. 1809.

[79] We are grateful to Dr Bruce Wood for confirming that Pindar's signature conforms with the main text hand.

[80] See, for example, Holman, *Henry Purcell*, 186; *Works*, XXIV (1998), xvi–xvii.

[81] Robert King, *Henry Purcell* (London, 1994), 203.

Purcell, so there can be no doubt that Hayes thought this ode was also his composition.[82] Hayes's diligence in hunting down Purcell sources commands respect and it is quite possible that he found his way to an authentic ode which has otherwise failed to survive.

[82] The 'Music in the Tempest as alter'd by Davenant and Dryden', Ktp MR 2–5.3, pp. 133–96, is attributed to Purcell in Ob MS Tenbury 1266, probably Hayes's source for this work as well as *Dido and Aeneas*.

# 5

# *Performing materials from the London sacred establishments and other sacred sources*

Fewer than a third of Purcell's non-concerted anthems are found in Cfm 88. For the remaining works we must turn to performing materials – many connected to the Chapel Royal and Westminster Abbey – and to other miscellaneous sources, including separate autographs, the work of copyists in Purcell's immediate circle and sources produced outside of London, in some cases well after his death. Table 5.1 lists the primary source or sources, together with the probable dates of copying and the copyists, for all of Purcell's full and verse anthems.[1]

## PERFORMING MATERIALS FROM THE CHAPEL ROYAL

### London, British Library Royal Music 27.a.1–8

The partbooks from the Chapel Royal were seen in the late seventeenth century as having a central importance derived not only from their use at the royal court but also from their having been looked upon as a kind of repository of works by the leading composers of the period,[2] who with few exceptions were directly associated with the court. From Charles II's time until the first years of the eighteenth century the Chapel partbooks were given a distinctive, official character through their physical make-up: they were of vellum instead of paper, which would have made

---

[1] For symphony anthems see Table 4.6, pp. 140–1.
[2] See, e.g., Vernon Butcher, *The Organs and Music of Worcester Cathedral* ([Worcester], 1981), 35.

### Table 5.1 Primary manuscript sources of Purcell's full and verse anthems

| Anthem (listed alphabetically) | Primary source(s) | Probable copying date | Copyist |
|---|---|---|---|
| Be merciful unto me | Lbl Add. 30931 | *c.*1690 | Daniel Henstridge |
| | Lbl Add. 17840 | *c.*1692–8 | Francis Smith |
| | Lbl R.M. 27.a.1–5 | *c.*1694–6 | Edward Braddock[a] |
| Blessed be the Lord my strength[b] | Lwa Triforium Set I | 1677 | William Tucker |
| | Y M1(S) | *c.*1677 | Stephen Bing |
| | Cfm 117 | *c.*1679 | William Isaack |
| Blessed is he that considereth the poor | US-AUS Pre-1700 85 | *c.*1698 | John Gostling |
| | Mp BRm370Bp35 | *c.*1698 | John Blow |
| Blessed is he whose unrighteousness is forgiven | Cfm 88 | *c.*1679–81 | Henry Purcell |
| Blessed is the man | US-AUS Pre-1700 85 | *c.*1688–90 | John Gostling |
| Blow up the trumpet in Sion | Lwa Triforium Set I | 1677 | William Tucker |
| | Y M1(S) | *c.*1677 | Stephen Bing |
| Bow down thine ear O Lord | Cfm 88 | *c.*1679–81 | Henry Purcell |
| Give sentence with me | Y M1(S) | *c.*1679 | Stephen Bing |
| Hear me O Lord and that soon[c] | Cfm 88 | *c.*1678–81 | Henry Purcell |
| Hear my prayer O God (inc.) | WO A.3.1–5 | *c.*1684 | unidentified |
| | DRc C27, C28, C34[d] | *c.*1690–5 | Matthew Owen |
| | DRc A25 | *c.*1695–1710 | William Greggs |
| Hear my prayer O Lord (inc.) | Cfm 88 | *c.*1685 | Henry Purcell |
| I was glad (full anthem) | EL 6 | *c.*1705–13 | James Hawkins |
| I will love thee O Lord | Och 22 (chorus only) | *c.*1690 | Richard Goodson |
| | Ob MS Mus.Sch. C.40 | *c.*1698–1716 | Charles Badham |
| I will sing unto the Lord | Lwa Triforium Set I | 1677 | William Tucker |
| | Y M1(S) | *c.*1677 | Stephen Bing |
| | Cfm 117 | *c.*1679 | William Isaack |
| Let God arise | Lwa Triforium Set I | 1677 | William Tucker[e] |
| | Y M1(S) | *c.*1677 | Stephen Bing |
| | Cfm 117 | *c.*1679 | William Isaack |
| Let mine eyes run down with tears | Lwa Triforium Set I | *c.*1682 | unidentified |
| | Ob MS Mus.c.26 | *c.*1682 | Henry Purcell |
| Lord how long wilt thou be angry | Cfm 88 | *c.*1684 | Henry Purcell |
| | US-R M2040/A628/Folio | *c.*1685 | London A |
| Lord who can tell | Lbl R.M. 27.a.1–3, 5–8 | *c.*1676 | William Tucker |
| | Cfm 117 | *c.*1679 | William Isaack |
| O consider my adversity | EL 20 | *c.*1705 | James Hawkins |
| O give thanks | Cfm 152 | 1693 | Henry Purcell |
| | US-AUS Pre-1700 85 | 1693 | John Gostling |
| | Lbl R.M. 27.a.1–6, 8 | *c.*1694–6 | Edward Braddock |
| O God the king of glory | Lwa Triforium Set I | 1677 | William Tucker |
| | Y M1(S) | *c.*1677 | Stephen Bing |
| O God they that love thy name (inc.) | DRc C28, C34 | *c.*1690–5 | Matthew Owen |
| | DRc A33 | *c.*1690–1700 | William Greggs |

## Table 5.1 (*cont.*)

| Anthem (listed alphabetically) | Primary source(s) | Probable copying date | Copyist |
|---|---|---|---|
| O God thou art my God | Lbl R.M. 27.a.1–3, 5, 6 | *c.* 1681–2 | Edward Braddock[f] |
| | Cfm 88 | *c.* 1682–3 | Henry Purcell |
| | Cfm 117 | *c.* 1683–4 | William Isaack |
| O God thou hast cast us out | Cfm 88 | *c.* 1679–81 | Henry Purcell |
| | Cfm 117 | *c.* 1679 | William Isaack |
| O Lord God of hosts | Lbl R.M. 27.a.1,5 | *c.* 1681–2 | Edward Braddock |
| | Cfm 88 | *c.* 1682–3 | Henry Purcell |
| O Lord our governor | Lwa Triforium Set I | 1677 | William Tucker |
| | Y M1(S) | *c.* 1677 | Stephen Bing |
| | Cfm 117 | *c.* 1679 | William Isaack |
| O Lord rebuke me not | DRc C27, C28, C34 | *c.* 1690–5 | Matthew Owen |
| | DRc A25 | *c.* 1695–1710 | William Greggs |
| | LI 2–4 | *c.* 1691–3 | unidentified |
| | Ob MS Tenbury 789 | *c.* 1715 | unidentified |
| O Lord thou art my God | Cfm 88 | *c.* 1684 | Henry Purcell |
| | US-R M2040/A628/Folio | *c.* 1685 | London A |
| O praise the Lord all ye heathen | Y M1(S) | *c.* 1679 | Stephen Bing |
| | DRc A4 | *c.* 1679–81 | Alexander Shaw |
| Out of the deep | Lbl Add. 30931 | *c.* 1685 | Henry Purcell |
| | US-R M2040/A628/Folio | *c.* 1685 | London A |
| Remember not Lord our offences | Cfm 88 | *c.* 1679–81 | Henry Purcell |
| | Cfm 117 | *c.* 1679 | William Isaack |
| Save me O God | Y M1(S) | *c.* 1677 | Stephen Bing |
| | Cfm 117 | *c.* 1679 | William Isaack |
| | Cfm 88 (revised) | *c.* 1678 | Henry Purcell |
| | US-R M2040/A628/Folio (revised) | *c.* 1685 | London A |
| Sing unto God | US-AUS Pre-1700 85 | 1687 | John Gostling |
| | J-Tn N5/10 | *c.* 1687 | Henry Purcell |
| | Lbl R.M. 27.a.1–6, 8 | *c.* 1694–6 | Edward Braddock[g] |
| The Lord is king and hath put on | US-LAuc fC6966/ M4/A627/1700 | after *c.* 1682 | Daniel Henstridge |
| | US-NH Filmer 21 | after *c.* 1698 | Daniel Henstridge |
| The Lord is king be the people never so impatient | Lbl Add. 17840 | *c.* 1692–8 | Francis Smith |
| The Lord is king the earth may be glad | US-AUS Pre-1700 85 | 1688 | John Gostling |
| | Mp BRm370Bp35 | *c.* 1698 | John Blow |
| | Lbl Add. 30931 | 1776 | William Flackton[h] |
| The way of God is an undefiled way | US-AUS Pre-1700 85 | 1694 | John Gostling |
| | Mp BRm370Bp35 | *c.* 1698 | John Blow |
| Thy righteousness O God is very high (inc.) | DRc C28, C34 | *c.* 1690–5 | Matthew Owen |
| | DRc A33 | *c.* 1690–1700 | William Greggs |

**Table 5.1** *(cont.)*

| Anthem (listed alphabetically) | Primary source(s) | Probable copying date | Copyist |
|---|---|---|---|
| Thy word is a lantern | Y M1(S) | *c.* 1690–5 | John Gostling |
| | LI 2–4 | *c.* 1693–4 | unidentified |
| | Lbl R.M. 27.a.1–3, 5–6, 8 | *c.* 1694–6 | Edward Braddock |
| Turn thou us O good Lord | Lbl Add. 30931 | *c.* 1677 | Daniel Henstridge |
| Who hath believed our report | Lbl Add. 30932 | *c.* 1674–5 | Henry Purcell |

[a] Braddock's copies in Lbl R.M. 27.a.1–6 and 8 may involve the work of several assistants; see below.

[b] Two other early sources are Lbl Add. 30932, fols. 157–60, a copy in the hand of Daniel Henstridge made probably by 1680, and Lbl Add. 34203, an organbook in the hand of George Loosemore (d. 1682).

[c] This anthem is a reworking of a previously composed sacred partsong in Lbl Add. 30930.

[d] Information on copyists and dates of Durham sources are from Crosby, *Catalogue.*

[e] With corrections in Purcell's hand in the alto partbook.

[f] John Church replaced Braddock's copy of this anthem in 27.a.3 and 27.a.6.

[g] John Church replaced Braddock's copy of this anthem in 27.a.1.

[h] A note in Flackton's hand (fol. 78r) implies that this is a diplomatic copy of a now-lost draft autograph; a further note on fol. 78v is dated 1776 (see Chapter 2, pp. 76–7 and n. 66).

them significantly more expensive to produce.[3] The durability of the vellum leaves may have also contributed to the ongoing practice of cannibalising older books when new sets were being made, so that in some cases individual leaves were still in use a hundred or more years after they were first copied. Fifteen of the 102 Chapel Royal partbooks deposited in the British Museum in 1927[4] survive to form the 'first' set, Lbl R.M. 27.a.1–15, largely copied by John Church, gentleman of the Chapel Royal from 1697 to 1740 and an expert calligrapher who may have developed his skills as an apprentice to John Playford.[5] Only R.M. 27.a.1–8 are of concern here: in these books Church included several layers of earlier leaves all copied before 1700. Of these eight, the main six vocal partbooks (decani and subdecani books for countertenor, tenor and bass) are Lbl R.M. 27.a.1–3, 5, 6 and 8.[6] Shaw's

[3] For example, the 1672 treasurer's book from Westminster Abbey records a payment 'for Parchment to make a Ledger Booke 120 skins at 9*d* each 4*l.*10*s.*0*d*' (Lwa WAM 33705, fol. 5v). By comparison a ream (consisting of twenty twenty-four-sheet quires) of high-quality paper of the type found in Cfm 88 was priced at £1–14–0 in 1674; see R. W. Chapman, 'An Inventory of Paper, 1674', *The Library*, 4th series, 7 (1927), 404.

[4] Not part of the Royal Music Library entrusted to the Museum by George V in 1911, the partbooks were catalogued with the 'Royal Music' prefix only in 1958. Our discussion of Lbl R.M. 27.a.1–8 is much indebted to Margaret Laurie, 'The Chapel Royal Part-Books', in *Music and Bibliography: Essays in Honour of Alec Hyatt King*, ed. Oliver Neighbour (New York and London, 1980), 28–50; and Watkins Shaw, 'A Contemporary Source of English Music of the Purcellian Period', *AcM* 31 (1959), 38–44.

[5] Robert Thompson, 'Manuscript Music in Purcell's London', *EM* 23 (1995), 611–13.

[6] These six books, formerly Lbl R.M. 23.m.1–6, are the ones catalogued in Shaw, 'A Contemporary Source', 38–44.

and Laurie's descriptions of the construction of these books require little further comment:

> It was apparently about the year 1705 that these books were built up around the leaves surviving from some older books. Evidently these were arranged to correspond approximately with their original position, and then the books were made up with new vellum pages. There is, however, no correspondence between one book and another as to what old leaves each contains.[7]

> After Church had selected the old pages required and interspersed them with new, he was faced with a considerable amount of making good, for he had to copy not only beginnings and ends where they ran over into rejected pages but in many cases one or more complete parts as well.[8]

The older material Church incorporated consisted principally of the work of William Tucker and Edward Braddock, both gentlemen of the Chapel Royal since at least 1661.[9] They were aided at times by subordinate copyists, Tucker by two assistants who copied texts only and Braddock by several different hands, some visibly immature, who in places emulated certain aspects of Braddock's own writing. Table 5.2 provides a running inventory of one partbook, R.M. 27.a.1, the countertenor decani book, exemplifying the various layers present in these books and showing that Church indeed found it necessary to redo part of the work of earlier copyists. Table 5.3 provides an index to Tucker's and Braddock's copying in the main six books and R.M. 27.a.4.[10]

Tucker's copying was completed by about 1677: Blow is always styled 'Mr' and fourteen of the twenty-two items in Tucker's hand in various of the main six books are also listed in the 'Catalogue of Severall Services & Anthems . . . transcribed into the Books of His Ma[jes]ties Chappell Royall since Anno 1670 to Midsumer 1676', dating from 1 August 1676, and surviving amongst payment warrants in the Lord Chamberlain's papers.[11] Tucker copied nine of the last ten anthems named in the

---

[7] Ibid., 38.   [8] Laurie, 'Chapel Royal Part-Books', 36.

[9] Braddock also served as clerk of the cheque from 1688. See *RECM*, I, 51; David Baldwin, *The Chapel Royal: Ancient and Modern* (London, 1990), 423–4. On the identification of Tucker's hand see Watkins Shaw, 'A Cambridge Manuscript from the English Chapel Royal', *M&L* 42 (1961), 264; on Braddock's hand see Laurie, 'Chapel Royal Part-Books', 32.

[10] Table 5.3 is based on that in Shaw, 'A Contemporary Source', 43–4.

[11] *RECM*, I, 162–4; listed are the titles and composers of sixty-five anthems and nineteen services (or individually listed canticles), with John Blow, William Child, William Tucker and Michael Wise appearing most frequently. For the corresponding payment from the treasurer's accounts ('To Doctor Will[ia]m Holder, Subdeane of his Ma[jes]ties Chappell Royall, for transcribing into bookes of his Ma[jes]ties Chappell Royall severall Anthems and Services in the space of 6 yeares ended at Midsumer 1676, by Warr[an]t dated the first of Aprill 1676: £64. 10s. 0d.') see *RECM*, V, 146. Holder, as subdean, would have been in a position of musical authority at the Chapel, though he seems not to have been directly involved in the copying of the partbooks.

## Table 5.2 London, British Library Royal Music 27.a.1: contents

Copyists: A = William Tucker and assistants
B = Edward Braddock and assistants
C = John Church

| Item | Page (orig.) | Title | Ascription | Copyist |
|------|------|-------|-----------|---------|
| 1 | 1 | O how amiable | Mr Jo: Blow | A |
| 2 | 3 | Lord teach us to number our days | Mr Pell: Humfrye | A |
| 3 | 4 | Hear O heavens | Mr Pell: Humphrys | A |
| 4 | 6 | O Lord thou hast searched me out | Mr Jo: Blow | A |
| 5 | 7 | 'Dr Childs in A re' | [Child] | A + C |
| 6 | 9 | I am well pleased | Dr Aldrich | C |
| 7 | 10 | Lord thou hast been our refuge | Dr Turner | C |
| 8 | 10 | Save me O God | Dr Blow | C |
| 9 | 10 | O God wherefore art thou absent | Dr Blow | C |
| 10 | 11 | Awake, awake put on thy strength | Mr Wise | C |
| 11 | 12 | Thy way O God | Mr Henry Purcell | C |
| 12 | 13 | O praise the Lord | [Weldon] | C |
| 13 | 14 | I will call upon the Lord | [Blow] | C |
| 14 | 14 | The Lord is full of compassion | Mr Clarke | C |
| 15 | 14 | I was glad | Mr Purcell | C |
| 16 | 15 | Out of the deep | Dr Aldrich | C |
| 17 | 15 | The Lord is my strength | Mr Clarke | C |
| 18 | 16 | Thou O Lord hast heard | Dr Tudway | C |
| 19 | 16 | O sing unto the Lord | Mr Croft | C |
| 20 | 17 | The Lord hear thee | Mr Blow | A |
| 21 | 18 | Haste thee O God | Pell: Humfris | A |
| 22 | 19 | O Lord rebuke me not | Dr Childs | A |
| 23 | 20 | Like as the hart | Pell: Humfris | A |
| 24 | 21 | 'Mr Blow: Ser: in G' | [Blow] | A + C |
| 25 | 26 | Call to remembrance | Alterd from Farrant by Dr Aldrich | C |
| 26 | 27 | Hide not thou thy face | Alter'd [Farrant–Aldrich] | C |
| 27 | 28 | Praise the Lord O my soul | Mr Jere: Clarke | C |
| 28 | 29 | Lord thou art become gracious | John Church | C |
| 29 | 30 | Righteous art thou O Lord | John Church | C |
| 30 | 31 | O Lord God of my salvation | Mr William Croft | C |
| 31 | 32 | O clap your hands | Mr William Croft | C |
| 32 | 33 | The earth is the Lord's | Mr Wm Croft | C |
| 33 | 34 | I will sing unto the Lord | Mr William Croft | C |
| 34 | 36 | O Lord rebuke me not | Mr Croft | C |
| 35 | 37 | I will magnify thee O God | Mr Croft | C |
| 36 | 38 | O Lord I will praise thee | Alterd from Italian by Dr Aldrich [Carissimi] | C |
| 37 | 39 | I was glad | [Croft] | C |
| 38 | 40 | Not unto us Lord | Translated by Dr Aldrich [Farrant and H. Lawes] | C |

## Table 5.2 (*cont.*)

| Item | Page (orig.) | Title | Ascription | Copyist |
|------|------|-------|------------|---------|
| 39 | 41 | Bow thine ear | Mr Bird | C |
| 40 | 42 | O praise the Lord all ye heathen | Mr Croft | C |
| 41 | 43 | O Lord God of my salvation | Mr William Croft | C |
| 42 | 44 | We have a strong city | Dr Aldrich | C |
| 43 | 46 | Out of the deep | Mr Croft | C |
| 44 | 48 | 'Dr Aldrich in E' | [Aldrich] | C + A |
| 45 | 57 | Lord who can tell | Mr Henry Purcell | A |
| 46 | 57 | 'Mr Alldridg in G' | [Aldrich] | A |
| 47 | 63 | Lord let me know mine end | Mr Lock | A |
| 48 | 64 | O give thanks | Will: Tucker | A |
| 49 | 64 | Turn thy face from my sins | John Church | C |
| 50 | 66 | I will give thanks | Mr Croft | C |
| 51 | 66 | 'Dr Aldrichs in A♮♯' | [Aldrich] | C |
| 52 | 72 | Sing unto God | Mr Hen: Purcell | C |
| 53 | 73 | Deus misereatur [Service in A] | Mr Aldrich | B |
| 54 | 74 | 'Mr Pursell's Service in B♭' | [Purcell] | B |
| 55 | 81 | O God thou art my God | [Purcell] | B |
| 56 | 82 | O Lord God of hosts | Mr Henry Purcell | B |
| 57 | 84 | Benedicite [Service in B♭] | Mr Henry Purcell | B |
| 58 | 87 | Bow down thine ear | Mr Clarke | C |
| 59 | 88 | I will sing a new song | Mr Wise | B |
| 60 | 90 | Behold how good and joyful | [Wise] | B |
| 61 | 91 | O Lord rebuke me not | Mr Weldon | C |
| 62 | 92 | 'Mr Purcells even[in]g service' | [Purcell] | B |
| 63 | 97 | Unto thee O Lord | J. Church | C |
| 64 | 97 | O Lord my God | Mr Pelham Humphrys | C |
| 65 | 98 | 'Dr Child's Service in D♯' | [Child] | C |
| 66 | 103 | O Lord God of our salvation | Seignior Pallestrina | C |
| 67 | 104 | Behold thou hast made my days | Dr Orlando Gibbons | C |
| 68 | 105 | Deliver us O Lord | Mr Croft | C |
| 69 | 106 | 'Mr Richard Farrant's High Service' | [Farrant] | C |
| 70 | 110 | Sing unto the Lord | Mr Croft | C |
| 71 | 110 | Blessed is the people | Mr Croft | C |
| 72 | 111 | Plead thou my cause | Dr Tudway | C |
| 73 | 111 | Ponder my words | Mr Weldon | C |
| 74 | 111 | Praise the Lord ye servants | Mr Weldon | C |
| 75 | 112 | Thy beauty O Israel | Mr Wise | C |
| 76 | 112 | Behold I bring you glad tidings | [Purcell] | C + B |
| 77 | 115 | Be merciful unto me O God | Mr Purcell | B |
| 78 | 118 | O give thanks | Mr Purcell | B |
| 79 | 124 | We will rejoice in thy salvation | [Blow] | B |
| 80 | 129 | O sing unto God | [Blow] | B |
| 81 | 133 | O be joyful | [Blow] | B |
| 82 | 138 | Thy word is a lantern | [Purcell] | B |

## Table 5.2 (*cont.*)

| Item | Page (orig.) | Title | Ascription | Copyist |
|------|------|-------|------------|---------|
| 83 | 141 | Why do the heathen | [Blow] | B |
| 84 | 144 | O God thou hast cast us out | Mr Purcell | B + C |
| 85 | 145 | They that go down to the sea | Mr Hen: Purcell | C |
| 86 | 146 | 'Dr Benjamin Roger's Service in D♯' | [Rogers] | C |
| 87 | 148 | O Lord grant the king | Mr Croft | C |
| 88 | 150 | We will rejoice | [Croft] | C |
| 89 | 151 | My song shall be alway | Mr Henry Purcell | C |
| 90 | 152 | Give ear O Lord | Dr Henry Aldrich | C |
| 91 | 153 | I will alway give thanks | Mr Croft | C |
| 92 | 154 | The Lord is my strength | Mr Croft | C |
| 93 | 154 | Let God arise | Mr Davis | C |
| 94 | 155 | I have set God always before me | Mr Goldwin | C |
| 95 | 156 | Hear my prayer O Lord | Dr Croft | C |
| 96 | 156 | Hear my crying O God | Mr Weldon | C |
| 97 | 158 | God is gone up | Dr Croft | C |
| 98 | 160 | Lord what love have I | Dr Croft | C |
| 99 | 161 | By the waters of Babylon | [Aldrich] | B |
| 100 | 162 | God is our refuge | Dr Aldrich | C |
| 101 | 163 | It is a good thing | Mr H. Pur[cell] | C |
| 102 | 163 | For Zion's sake | Altered from Charissimi by Dr Aldrich | C |
| 103 | 164 | Hear my crying O God | Mr Croft | C |
| 104 | 164 | Let my complaint come before thee | Mr Croft | C |
| 105 | 165 | How long wilt thou forget me | Mr Clar[ke] | C |
| 106 | 165 | I will love thee O Lord | Mr Clark[e] | C |
| 107 | 166 | O Lord my God | J: Church | C |
| 108 | 167 | Praise the Lord O my soul | Mr Croft | C |
| 109 | 167 | Behold now praise the Lord | Dr Croft | C |
| 110 | 168 | I will give thanks | J: Church | C |
| 111 | 169 | I waited patiently | Mr Croft | C |
| 112 | 170 | Rejoice in the Lord | Mr Weldon | C |
| 113 | 170 | O praise the Lord ye that fear him | Mr John Weldon | C |
| 114 | 171 | I will love thee | Mr Clarke | C |
| 115 | 172 | 'Church's Service in F faut' | [Church] | C |
| 116 | 176 | We have heard with our ears | [Palestrina–Aldrich] | C |
| 117 | 178 | The king shall rejoice | Mr Weldon | C |
| 118 | 178 | The Lord hath appeared for us | Dr Croft | C |
| 119 | 179 | In thee O Lord | Mr John Weldon | C |
| 120 | 180 | Praise the Lord O my soul | Dr William Croft | C |
| 121 | 180 | O God thou art my God | Dr Green | C |
| 122 | 181 | Blessed is he that considereth | [Wise] | C |
| 123 | 182 | O Lord give ear | Dr Green | C |
| 124 | 182 | Let God arise | Dr Green | C |
| 125 | 183 | My soul truly waiteth | Dr Green | C |

Table 5.2 (*cont.*)

| Item | Page (orig.) | Title | Ascription | Copyist |
|------|------|-------|-----------|---------|
| 126 | 184 | I will seek unto God | Dr Maurice Green | C |
| 127 | 184 | Hear my prayer | Dr Green | C |
| 128 | 185 | O praise the Lord ye that fear him | Dr Croft | C |
| 129 | 186 | We wait for thy loving kindness | Dr William Croft | C |
| 130 | 187 | O Lord thou hast searched me out | Dr Croft | C |
| 131 | 188 | The Lord is king | Dr Croft | C |
| 132 | 188 | Acquaint thyself with God | Dr Green | C |
| 133 | 188 | O be joyful | Dr Croft | C |
| 134 | 189 | O how amiable | Dr Green | C |
| 135 | 190 | Sing unto God O ye kingdoms | Dr Croft | C |
| 136 | 191 | I will magnify thee | Dr Green | C |
| 137 | 192 | I will give thanks | Dr Green | C |
| 138 | 192 | The king shall rejoice | Dr Green | C |
| 139 | 193 | Rejoice | Mr Gates | C |
| 140 | 194 | Lord how long wilt thou be angry | Dr Green | C |
| 141 | 195 | Hear my prayer O Lord | Mr Strowde | C |
| 142 | 196 | Behold I bring you glad tidings | Dr Maurice Green | C |
| 143 | [197] | Praise the Lord O my soul | Dr Green | C |
| 144 | [198] | O give thanks | Dr Green | C |

Vellum leaves throughout, 324 × 235.

Rastrology: nine staves per page; ruled with various single-stave rastra.

'Catalogue' and the works copied but not listed, including Purcell's *Lord who can tell,* must have been produced in the period immediately after 1 August. The copying of Braddock and his assistants exists in two distinct layers: the first (Table 5.2, items 53–62, with two insertions from Church) includes the Deus misereatur from Aldrich's Service in A, ascribed to 'Mr' Aldrich (Aldrich received his doctorate in 1682), and the various parts of Purcell's Service in B♭, interspersed amongst two anthems each by Purcell and Wise. Laurie's date of *c.* 1681–2 for this layer seems very appropriate not only on account of the Aldrich ascription but also because Purcell's service was composed no later than September 1682[12] and must have been added to the Chapel books immediately. The second Braddock layer may be the remains of a much larger copying project carried out in the 1690s (Table 5.2, items 76–84): the surviving portions are mainly devoted to works of Blow and Purcell and include nine of the latter's anthems (see Table 5.3; only the bass decani book, R.M. 27.a.3,

[12] Lwa WAM 33717, fol. 5v.

## Table 5.3 Copying by William Tucker and Edward Braddock in the Chapel Royal partbooks, London, British Library Royal Music 27.a.1–8

The following six books comprise the earliest extant set of vocal partbooks:

| | |
|---|---|
| contratenor decani | 27.a.1 |
| contratenor subdecani | 27.a.5 |
| tenor decani | 27.a.2 |
| tenor subdecani | 27.a.6 |
| bass decani | 27.a.3 |
| bass subdecani | 27.a.8 |

The treble subdecani book, 27.a.4, does not in its present state derive from the above set. It does, however, contain copies by Braddock that were still in use in the early nineteenth century, interspersed with layers of much later vintage. The Braddock material, with the exception of an unidentified fragment by Adrian Batten, is entirely concordant with other Braddock copying from the main set and is noted in the rightmost column here (new foliation). The fragmentary bass partbook, 27.a.7, is entirely in Tucker's hand and was never cannibalised into a later book. Its contents are listed in Table 5.4.

In the following table each work is located by means of the initial page number:

| | |
|---|---|
| regular type | Tucker and assistants |
| italics | Braddock and assistants |
| C | in John Church's hand in that partbook |
| — | not found in that partbook |

| composer/title | 27.a.1 | 27.a.5 | 27.a.2 | 27.a.6 | 27.a.3 | 27.a.8 | 27.a.4 |
|---|---|---|---|---|---|---|---|
| **ALDRICH, HENRY** | | | | | | | |
| Service in G | 57 | 52 | 59 | 44 | 58 | 50 | |
| Service in e | 48 | 43/49 | 53 | 41 | 55 | 49 | |
| *Deus misereatur in A* | *73* | — | — | — | — | — | |
| *By the waters of Babylon* | *161* | *149* | *204* | *118* | *185* | *133* | *25r* |
| **AMNER, JOHN** | | | | | | | |
| Come hither and hearken (incomplete) | — | 43 | — | — | — | — | |
| **BLOW, JOHN** | | | | | | | |
| *Morning and Evening Service in G | 21 | 21 | 32 | C | 25 | C | |
| Communion Service (triple time) in G | — | *143* | — | *113* | *173* | *126* | |
| Sanctus and Gloria in G | — | *146* | — | *108* | *181* | *122* | |
| *O be joyful* | *133* | *129* | *183* | *106* | *154* | *115* | |
| *O God wherefore art thou absent | C | C | 45 | C | C | C | |
| *O how amiable | 1 | 1 | 1 | C | C | C | |
| *O Lord thou hast searched me out | 6 | 3 | 6 | 3 | 4 | 4 | |
| *O sing unto God* | *129* | C | C | *106* | *151* | *115* | |
| *Save me O God | C | C | 46 | C | C | C | |

## Table 5.3 (*cont.*)

| composer/title | 27.a.1 | 27.a.5 | 27.a.2 | 27.a.6 | 27.a.3 | 27.a.8 | 27.a.4 |
|---|---|---|---|---|---|---|---|
| The Lord hear thee | 17 | 13 | 25 | C | C | 15 | |
| We will rejoice in thy salvation | 124 | 125 | C | 105 | 147 | 114 | 18v |
| Why do the heathen | 141 | 133 | 186 | 107 | 161 | 116 | |
| CHILD, WILLIAM | | | | | | | |
| *Morning and Communion Service in a† | 7 | 5 | C | 4 | C | 9 | |
| *Te Deum in e | — | — | 48 | — | C | — | |
| *O Lord rebuke me not | 19 | — | — | — | 24 | — | |
| FARRANT, RICHARD/arr. ALDRICH | | | | | | | |
| Call to remembrance | C | 147 | C | 116 | 183 | 132 | 24r |
| Hide not thou thy face | C | 148 | 203 | 117 | 184 | 133 | 24v |
| HUMFREY, PELHAM | | | | | | | |
| Haste thee O God | 18 | 14 | 25 | C | 23 | 16 | |
| *Hear O heavens | 4 | 4 | 7 | 3 | 6 | C | |
| *Like as the hart | 20 | 19 | 31 | C | 24 | C | |
| *Lord teach us to number our days | 3 | 1 | 3 | C | 3 | 3 | |
| The king shall rejoice | — | 140 | — | 109 | 170 | 123 | |
| LOCKE, MATTHEW | | | | | | | |
| Lord let me know mine end | 63 | 57 | 64 | 96 | C | 55 | |
| LOOSEMORE, HENRY | | | | | | | |
| Praise the Lord O my soul | — | — | 161 | — | 133 | — | |
| PURCELL, HENRY | | | | | | | |
| Morning and Evening Service in B♭ | 74/84/92 | 77/86 | 73/83 | C | C | C | |
| Be merciful unto me | 115 | 123 | 165 | C | 138 | C | 16v |
| Behold I bring you glad tidings | 112 | C | 162 | C | 134 | C | 16v |
| I was glad | C | C | C | C | 129 | C | 15r |
| Lord who can tell | 57 | 51 | 58 | 43 | 56 | 49 | |
| O give thanks | 118 | 124 | 169 | 105 | 143 | 113 | 17v |
| O God thou art my God | 81 | 79 | 86 | C | C | — | |
| O God thou hast cast us out | 144 | 136 | C | C | 164 | 117 | 15v |
| O Lord God of hosts | 82 | 80 | — | — | — | — | |
| Sing unto God | C | 144 | 197 | 114 | 175 | 128 | 23v |
| They that go down to the sea | C | 138 | C | 108 | 166 | 118 | |
| Thy way O God is holy | C | C | C | C | 123 | C | |
| Thy word is a lantern | 138 | 132 | 184 | 107 | 158 | 116 | |

**Table 5.3** (*cont.*)

| composer/title | 27.a.1 | 27.a.5 | 27.a.2 | 27.a.6 | 27.a.3 | 27.a.8 | 27.a.4 |
|---|---|---|---|---|---|---|---|
| TUCKER, WILLIAM | | | | | | | |
| *O give thanks | 64 | 58 | 66 | — | — | 56 | |
| TURNER, WILLIAM | | | | | | | |
| *Lord thou hast been our refuge | C | 11 | C | C | C | C | |
| WISE, MICHAEL | | | | | | | |
| *Awake, awake put on thy strength | C | 63 | C | C | C | C | |
| Behold how good and joyful | *90* | *85* | — | — | — | — | |
| I will sing a new song | *88* | *85* | — | — | — | — | |
| ANONYMOUS | | | | | | | |
| The Lord is my shepherd (inc.) | — | — | 68 | — | — | — | |

* Listed in the 'Catalogue of Severall Services & Anthems' added to the Chapel Royal books from 'Anno 1670 to Midsumer 1676' (*RECM*, I, 162–4). The 'Catalogue' includes a service by Aldrich without indication of key, which in all likelihood refers to one of the two services found in these partbooks.
† Only 27.a.5 contains both services.

includes all nine on the original leaves). Laurie has pointed out that several of the works in this layer were composed, according to John Gostling's dates in US-AUS Pre-1700 85, in the late 1680s and 1690s, and has suggested that this copying may have spanned from *c.* 1693 to the time when Church inherited responsibility for the books, *c.* 1697–1702.[13] A payment to Ralph Battle, William Holder's successor as subdean of the Chapel Royal, on 16 November 1694, for the transcribing of fifty-four anthems[14] may represent part of this layer of copying, Battle presumably having official oversight for Braddock's work just as Holder did for Tucker's.

Two further partbooks from the first set, Lbl R.M. 27.a.4 and 27.a.7, while not corresponding broadly with the main six books, contain seventeenth-century copying. R.M. 27.a.4 is a treble subdecani book which came into its present state in the nineteenth century, the latest of several inscriptions at various points in the book being dated 1847. Newer paper at each end surrounds old vellum, in much poorer condition here than in the main six partbooks, mostly in the hand of Church but with a few pages of Braddock's work still intact. The vellum pages contain eleven anthems of which ten, including six by Purcell, are concordant with the second Braddock layer

[13] Laurie, 'Chapel Royal Part-Books', 35.     [14] *RECM*, II, 141; VIII, 288.

## Table 5.4 London, British Library Royal Music 27.a.7: contents

| Page (orig.) | Title | Ascription |
|---|---|---|
| 9 | *Magnificat [in a] | [Child] |
| 10 | *'Dr Childs ser: in A re' | [Child] |
| 10 | *Lord thou hast been our refuge | Mr William Turner |
| 11 | The Lord hear thee | Mr John Blow |
| 12 | Haste thee O God | Mr Pell: Humfrys |
| 13 | *O Lord rebuke me not | Dr Child |
| 13 | *Like as the hart | Mr Pell: Humfris |
| 14 | *'Mr Blow's ser: in Gamut' | Mr Jo: Blow |
| 20 | Remember not Lord | Mr Jo: Amner |
| 21 | Behold how good and joyful | Mr Hutchinson |
| 23 | 'Mr Blows Holy, holy' [in G] | Mr John Blow |
| 24 | *O God wherefore art thou absent | Mr Jo: Blow |
| 25 | *Save me O God | Mr io: Blow |
| 26 | *'Dr Child's Ser: in E Flat' | Dr Child |
| 31 | Come hither and hearken | Mr Jo: Amner |
| 32 | 'Mr Alldridg in E' | [Aldrich] |
| 38 | Lord who can tell | Mr Henry Purcell |
| 38 | 'Alldridg in G' (incomplete) | [Aldrich] |

Vellum leaves throughout, 324 × 235.

Rastrology: nine staves per page; ruled with a single-stave rastrum, span: 15.5.

Copyist: William Tucker

*Listed in the 'Catalogue of Severall Services & Anthems' added to the Chapel Royal books from 'Anno 1670 to Midsumer 1676' (*RECM*, I, 162–4). The 'Catalogue' includes a service by Aldrich without indication of key, which in all likelihood refers to one of the two services found in these partbooks.

of the main six books (see Table 5.3). R.M. 27.a.7, a fragmentary bass partbook, is the only uncannibalised manuscript amongst R.M. 27.a.1–8 and is entirely in the hand of Tucker, with original pagination from 9 to 38 (Table 5.4). It includes thirteen of the twenty-two items in Tucker's hand in the six main partbooks (including Purcell's *Lord who can tell*), Blow's Sanctus in G (in Braddock's hand in the main six), and three additional items: Child's Service in E♭, John Amner's *Remember not Lord* and John Hutchinson's *Behold how good and joyful.*

The Chapel Royal partbooks, while for most works providing an incomplete record, are of unquestioned value as Purcell sources, even beyond what Watkins Shaw called their '"association" interest', being the very books from which some of Purcell's liturgical works were performed at the Chapel Royal at a time when he himself 'supervised the performances'.[15] Tucker's copies of Purcell's *Lord who can*

---

[15] Shaw, 'A Contemporary Source', 38.

*tell* (though lacking the soprano) are easily the earliest of this anthem, which because it exists in the oldest sections of these manuscripts must have been composed *c.* 1676 or before. (The earliest complete text is that of William Isaack in Cfm 117, copied *c.* 1679.) Of similar value are Braddock's copies of the Service in B♭, which together with those in Lwa Triforium Sets I and II (there also the work of copyists in Braddock's circle) provide the earliest texts, though not collectively complete; and Braddock's copies of *O God thou art my God* and *O Lord God of hosts* probably predate the autographs in Cfm 88. For four of the nine Purcell anthems copied by Braddock in the 1690s (*Behold I bring you glad tidings, O give thanks, Sing unto God* and *Thy way O God is holy*) the Chapel Royal partbooks provide early corroborative texts for the primary sources in US-AUS Pre-1700 85. Braddock's copy of *Be merciful unto me* is one of the earliest of this anthem (see Table 5.1), and his copy of *Thy word is a lantern*, save the even less complete texts in LI 2–4 and Y M1(S), is the only one that can be dated with some certainty before 1700.

### Cambridge, Fitzwilliam Museum Music MS 152

Cfm 152 contains the fragmented remains of one or more Chapel Royal organ-books:[16] its identified copyists were members of the Chapel, and all of the works in the earliest layers are also found in the Chapel Royal 'Catalogue' of 1676 (see Table 5.5).[17] The manuscript was apparently part of the founder's bequest at the Fitzwilliam, though unusually it does not bear Fitzwilliam's signature, and there is no evidence of any earlier ownership. Shaw suggests that the various layers of Cfm 152 'came to be bound together in the eighteenth century at a time when each had reached a state of some decrepitude, in order that as much further use as possible might be had from them',[18] but given which works have survived complete in Cfm 152 a more probable explanation is that it was brought together by an eighteenth-century collector intent on saving autograph manuscripts of major composers. This would account for the presence of so many incomplete works, always limited to one side of a page, surrounding material written by the more famous hands. Nonetheless, we get a sense here, lacking from the vocal partbooks Lbl R.M. 27.a.1–8, of composers and copyists working in close proximity: Purcell writing on the reverse of a

---

[16] Shaw, 'A Cambridge Manuscript', 263–7.

[17] *RECM*, I, 162–4. There are two correlations in the ordering of the anthems in Cfm 152 and the 'Catalogue': Tucker's *O give thanks* and Batten's *Hear my prayer O God* appear consecutively in both, as do Tucker's *Praise the Lord ye servants* and Blow's *O Lord I have sinned* and *Lord how are they increased*.

[18] Shaw, 'A Cambridge Manuscript', 266.

## Table 5.5 Cambridge, Fitzwilliam Museum Music MS 152: contents

| Page | Folios | Title | Ascription | Copyist |
|------|--------|-------|------------|---------|
| 53 | 1r | Nunc Dimittis in F (inc.) | Orlan[do] Gibbons | Edward Braddock |
| 54 | 1v–2r | Sanctus and Gloria in G | [Blow] | Henry Purcell[a] |
| [5]6 | 2v–5r | O give thanks | HPurcell 1693 | Henry Purcell[b] |
| 62 | 5v | My song shall be alway (inc.) | [Purcell] | John Church |
| [break in original pagination] | | | | |
| 123 | 6r | *Credo in e (inc.) | Mr Pellham Humfrey | unidentified 1 |
| 124 | 6v–9r | *Evening Service in e | Pell: Hum: | Pelham Humfrey |
| [break in original pagination][c] | | | | |
| 200 | 9v–10r | *O give thanks | Will: Tucker | unidentified 2 |
| 202 | 10v–11r | *Hear my prayer O God | Mr Batten | unidentified 3 |
| 204 | 11v | *The earth is the Lord's | Dr Child | William Tucker |
| [break in original pagination] | | | | |
| 18[9] | 12r | Praise the Lord O my soul (inc.) | Mr Jeremiah Clark[e] | John Church |
| 190 | 12v–13r | Sanctus and Gloria in b | W[m]: Croft | William Croft[d] |
| 192 | 13v–15r | Unto thee O God | Wm: Crof[t] | William Croft |
| [1]96 | 15v | I will love thee (inc.)[e] | [Clarke] | John Church |
| [break in original pagination] | | | | |
| 221 (197)[f] | 16r | *Praise the Lord ye servants (inc.) | Will: Tucker | William Tucker |
| 223 (198) | 16v–17v | *O Lord I have sinned | John Blow | John Blow |
| 226 (201) | 18r–19r | *Lord how are they increased | John Blow | John Blow |
| 229 | 19v | *My heart is fixed (inc.) | [Tucker] | William Tucker |
| [break in original pagination] | | | | |
| 231 | 20r | The Lord is my strength | Mr Clarke | John Church |
| 232 | 20v–21r | O praise the Lord all ye heathen | W[m]: Cr[oft] | William Croft |
| 234 | 21v | We have a strong city (inc.) | [Aldrich] | John Church |

Oblong quarto, 202 × 310; each folio is now mounted in its own paper frame. Watermarks: Angoumois fleurs-de-lys; countermarks: fols. 1–4, 'IHS/AI'; fols. 12–15 and 20–1, 'IV'.

Rastrology

| Folios | Staves on page | Staves in rastrum | Rastrum span | Rastrum profile |
|--------|----------------|-------------------|--------------|-----------------|
| 1–4 | 6 evenly spaced† | 3 | 78 | 16.5(15)16(13)17.5 |
| 5 | 8 in 4 systems | 2 | 29.5 | 9.5(10.5)9.5 |
| 6–11 | 6 evenly spaced† | 3 | 83.5 | 16(18)16.5(16.5)16.5 |
| 12–15 | 6 evenly spaced† | 3 | 78.5 | 17(15)16(13)17.5 |
| 16–19 | 6 evenly spaced† | 3 | 83.5 | same as fols. 6–11 |
| 20–21 | 6 evenly spaced† | 3 | 78.5 | same as fols. 12–15 |

* Listed in the 'Catalogue of Severall Services & Anthems' added to the Chapel Royal books from 'Anno 1670 to Midsumer 1676' (*RECM*, I, 162–4).
† Six-line staves.

[a] Additional text on fol. 2r in a different hand.
[b] On fol. 2v '1693' was added later and may not be in Purcell's hand. Additions on fol. 3v in a different hand. On fol. 4v Purcell provides the bass line only; another scribe has added a C clef on the top stave. Completion of *O give thanks* on fol. 5r is entirely in John Church's hand and is ascribed 'Mr Henry Purcell'.
[c] Humfrey's service runs to p. 129; p. 200 is the verso of p. 129.
[d] Additions on fol. 13r in John Church's hand.        [e] Inscribed 'Thanksgiving Anthem for forcing the Lines'.
[f] A second, apparently later pagination appears at this point (given in parentheses); p. 223 is the verso of p. 221.

sheet copied by Braddock, and Blow and Tucker (and later Croft and Church) working contemporaneously.

The oldest material in Cfm 152 is in two distinct layers, fols. 6–11 and 16–19, consisting of paper of the same type and ruled with the same three-stave rastrum (see Table 5.5). The presence of Blow's autograph of *O Lord I have sinned*, composed in 1670, and especially the handwriting of Pelham Humfrey (who died in 1674) suggest a date in the early 1670s for these layers. Fols. 1–4 are the next oldest, consisting of an incomplete copy of Orlando Gibbons's Nunc dimittis in F, in Braddock's hand, and Blow's Sanctus and Gloria in G and Purcell's *O give thanks*, both in Purcell's hand, the latter completed by John Church on an inserted folio (which also contains the beginning of *My song shall be alway*). The two works in Purcell's hand are also found amongst the 1690s Braddock material in Lbl R.M. 27.a.1–6 and 8 and were probably copied in both sources some time in or just after 1693, when *O give thanks* was composed. (The inscribed date of '1693' in Cfm 152 may have been added by someone other than Purcell, the more authoritative dating for *O give thanks* being Gostling's in US-AUS Pre-1700 85.) The newest material in Cfm 152 consists of two layers, with identical stave-rulings, in the handwriting of Croft and Church (fols. 12–15 and 20–1), which include an incomplete copy of Jeremiah Clarke's *I will love thee . . . it is God*, composed in 1705.

Cfm 152's chief importance as a Purcell source derives from the autograph of *O give thanks*. There are enough similarities with the copies in US-AUS Pre-1700 85 and Lbl R.M. 27.a.1–6 and 8 to suggest that all three descended from the same draft autograph,[19] though in Cfm 152 Purcell went well beyond his exemplar in adding copious figuring and occasional dynamic indications in the verses, both of which point to the manuscript's use in performance. The lack of textual incipits and the omission of any material for the right hand in most of the verses may indicate that Purcell knew he himself would be at the organ. At a later time someone filled in part of the missing material, replicating the floridity of the solos rather cumbersomely.

.

---

[19] The two non-autograph sources share a number of features such as a clear reading of the chorus in bars 30–41 with a similar tempo indication: 'brisk time' in US-AUS Pre-1700 85 and 'brisker' in Lbl R.M. 27.a.1–6 and 8. See *Works*, XXIX (1960), 88–107, 196–8; and *The Gostling Manuscript* (facsimile edn), intro. by Franklin B. Zimmerman (Austin and London, 1977), 78–86 INV.

PERFORMING MATERIALS FROM WESTMINSTER ABBEY, ST PAUL'S
CATHEDRAL AND RELATED SOURCES

## London, Westminster Abbey MSS Triforium Set I

The two partbooks of Lwa Triforium Set I (alto cantoris '1A' and tenor cantoris '4')
came to the attention of modern scholars in 1972, when they were found amongst
old music books apparently stored in the triforium at Westminster Abbey since the
retirement of Frederick Bridge, organist from 1882 to 1918.[20] Unlike the cannibalised Chapel Royal partbooks, large sections of these two books have remained
unaltered since the 1670s, when they were copied by William Tucker,[21] who was a
minor canon at the Abbey as well as a gentleman of the Chapel Royal. The original
paper in both books, fols. 2–79 in the alto and 2–80 in the tenor (modern foliation),
is all of the same type (Angoumois fleur-de-lys with 'IHS/IP' countermark) with
largely similar stave-rulings (see Table 5.6). Nearly all of this paper was used by
Tucker and must represent the remains of a substantial copying project for which he
was paid £20 in two £10 instalments in 1677 (see Table 5.7). Tucker's consistent
styling of Blow as 'Mr' further indicates that all of his work was completed by
December 1677. The remaining old pages left uncopied by Tucker (fols. 72v–79v in
the alto and 63v–80v in the tenor) were filled, completely in the alto and partially in
the tenor, by copyists working within a few years of Tucker's death in 1679: Stephen
Bing (see the discussion of Y M1(S) below), who also copied Blow's Te Deum in E
Minor on fol. 1 in both books (a later insertion on different paper),[22] Edward
Braddock (Master of the Choristers at the Abbey from 1670 to 1708) and three
unidentified scribes working under Braddock's supervision.[23] Several correction slips

[20] The various manuscript partbooks were organised into sets by Margaret Laurie; see Ian Cheverton,
'English Church Music of the Early Restoration Period, 1660–ca.1676' (Ph.D. thesis, University of
Wales, Cardiff, 1984), 386.

[21] As in the Chapel Royal partbooks with the assistance of two copyists who at times provide the texts.

[22] Bing's copying in these books probably corresponds to the 1679 payment record (see Table 5.7; the 1676
payment is not a possibility since the titles in Bing's hand refer to 'Dr' Blow): Bing's work in the two
extant books occupies four pages per book, which would be consistent with the reference to '29 Sheets and
23 Staves' (i.e., just over thirty-one pages) in the payment record if Bing copied the same material in a
complete set of eight books.

[23] Like the assistants working for Braddock in the Chapel Royal partbooks these copyists at times emulate his
hand: in the canticles from Purcell's Service in B♭ unidentified 1 (see Table 5.6) alternates between a
roughly formed C clef similar to Braddock's and a more naturally formed version. Braddock also seems to
have checked over the work of unidentified 3: in the latter's copy of 'Dr Blow's Triple Creed in Gamut',
Braddock has added some additional directs (his are distinctly different from those of the main hand); see,
e.g., fol. 79r (alto) and fol. 70r (tenor).

## Table 5.6 London, Westminster Abbey MSS Triforium Set I: contents

| Item | Folios[a] | Title | Ascription | Copyist |
|------|--------|-------|------------|---------|
| 1 | 1r/1r | 'Dr Blow's Te Deum to his Benedicite Service' | [Blow] | Bing[b] |
| 2 | 2r/2r | Benedicite Service in e | Mr Blow | Tucker |
| 3 | 5r/5v | 'Dr Childs Flat Ser: in E' | [Child] | Tucker |
| 4 | 5v/8v | 'Dr Childs Service in A re' | Dr Child | Tucker |
| 5 | 9r/12r | I will sing unto the Lord | Mr Hen: Pursell | Tucker |
| 6 | 9v/12v | 'Dr Childs Ser: in E:♯' | Dr Child | Tucker |
| 7 | 12r/14v | O God the king of glory | Mr He: Pursell | Tucker |
| 8 | 12v/15r | O Lord God of hosts | Mr Will: Turner | Tucker |
| 9 | 13r/15v | Benedicite Service in F | Will: Tucker | Tucker |
| 10 | 16v/20r | O clap your hands | Mr Will: Tucker | Tucker |
| 11 | 17v/20v | O God wherefore art thou absent | Mr Blow | Tucker |
| 12 | 18r/21r | O give thanks | Will: Tucker | Tucker |
| 13 | 18v/22r | 'Farrant's high Service' | [R. Farrant] | Tucker |
| 14 | 23v/26r | God is our hope and strength | Mr Iohn Blow | Tucker |
| 15 | 24r/27r | The Lord hear thee | Mr Iohn Blow | Tucker |
| 16 | 24v/27r | 'Mr Pell: Humfrys Service in E' | [Humfrey] | Tucker |
| 17 | 28v/32r | Save me O God | Mr Iohn Blow | Tucker |
| 18 | 29r/32r | 'Mr Blows Serv: in G' | Mr Io: Blow | Tucker |
| 19 | 32r/35v | Service in e | Mr Hen: Alldridg | Tucker[c] |
| 20 | 36r/40v | If the Lord himself[d] | Mr Hen: Alldridg | Tucker |
| 21 | 37r/39r | Evening Service in D | Mr Io: Ferrabosco | Tucker |
| 22 | 38r/40r | Evening Service in C | Mr Will: Tucker | Tucker |
| 23 | 39v/41r | O praise God in his holiness | Mr Wise | Tucker |
| 24 | 39v/42r | Thou art my king O God | Dr Child | Tucker |
| 25 | 40r/42r | Behold how good and joyful | Dr Child | Tucker |
| 26 | 40v/66r | O Lord my God | Mr Pell: Humfrey | Tucker |
| 27 | 40v/66r | 'Dr Childs Evening Ser: in A re' | Dr Child | Tucker |
| 28 | 42r/67v | By the waters of Babylon | P. Humfrey | Tucker |
| 29 | 42v/68r | O Lord rebuke me not | Dr Child | Tucker |
| 30 | 43v/42v | O be joyful | Mr Humfris | Tucker |
| 31 | 44r/43r | Not unto us O Lord | Mr Lock | Tucker |
| 32 | 44v/43v | I am well pleased | Will: Tucker | Tucker |
| 33 | 44v/— | O Lord rebuke me not (text only) | Dr Wm Child | Tucker assistant |
| 34 | 45r/44r | I will magnify thee O God | Will: Tucker | Tucker |
| 35 | 45r/44r | Awake up my glory | Mr Wise | Tucker |
| 36 | 45v/44v | Behold how good and joyful | Mr Blow | Tucker |
| 37 | 45v/45r | I was glad | Will: Tucker | Tucker |
| 38 | 46r/45v | Let God arise | Mr Will Laws | Tucker |
| 39 | 46r/— | Comfort ye my people | Will: Tucker | Tucker |
| 40 | 46v/46r | Rejoice in the Lord | Mr Pell: Humfris | Tucker |
| 41 | 46v/46v | This is the day | Will: Tucker | Tucker |
| 42 | 47r/47v | Lord how long wilt thou be angry | Wm Tucker | Tucker[e] |
| 43 | 47v/47v | How are the mighty fallen | Wise: Will: Tucker[f] | Tucker |
| 44 | 48v/48r | Turn thee unto me O Lord | Mr Blow | Tucker |

## Table 5.6 (*cont.*)

| Item | Folios[a] | Title | Ascription | Copyist |
|------|-----------|-------|-----------|---------|
| 45 | 49r/49r | Wherewithal shall a young man | Will: Tucker | Tucker |
| 46 | 49v/49v | O Lord our governor | Hen: Pursell | Tucker |
| 47 | 50r/50r | My heart is fixed | Will: Tucker | Tucker |
| 48 | 50v/50v | Sing we merrily | Mr John Blow | Tucker |
| 49 | 50v/52r | The earth is the Lord's | Dr Child | Tucker |
| 50 | 51r/51v | I will alway give thanks | W: Turnor: P: Humfris: Jo: Blow | Tucker |
| 51 | 51r/52v | I beheld and lo a great multitude | Dr Rogers | Tucker |
| 52 | 51r/53r | O clap your hands | Dr Rogers | Tucker |
| 53 | 52r/53v | Haste thee O God | Mr Pell: Humfris | Tucker |
| 54 | 52v/54v | Have mercy upon me O God | Mr Pell: Humfris | Tucker |
| 55 | 53r/55r | The Lord said unto my Lord | Dr Gibbons | Tucker |
| 56 | 53v/56r | Blow up the trumpet | Mr Henry Purcell[g] | Tucker |
| 57 | 54v/57r | O Lord I have sinned | Mr Jo: Blow | Tucker |
| 58 | 55r/58r | Let God arise | Mr Henry Purcell | Tucker/ Purcell[h] |
| 59 | 55v/58v | Christ rising | Mr Jo: Blow | Tucker |
| 60 | 55v/59v | Blessed be the Lord my strength | Mr Henry Purcell | Tucker |
| 61 | 56r/62v | Hear O heavens | Mr Pell: Humfris | Tucker |
| 62 | 56v/60v | O how amiable | Mr Jo: Blow | Tucker |
| 63 | 57r/61v | Lord thou hast been our refuge | Mr Turner | Tucker |
| 64 | 57r/63v | Unto thee O Lord | Will: Tucker | Tucker |
| 65 | 57v/64r | Behold God is my salvation | Mr Tudway | Tucker |
| 66 | 58v/64v | Lord teach us to number our days | Mr Pell: Humfrys | Tucker |
| 67 | 59r/65v | O Lord thou hast searched me out | Mr John Blow | Tucker |
| 68 | 59v/69r | Lord how are they increased | Mr Jo: Blow | Tucker |
| 69 | 60r/69v | O give thanks | Mr Pell: Humfrye | Tucker |
| 70 | 61v/70v | Like as the hart | Mr Pell: Humfrye | Tucker |
| 71 | 62r/71r | O Lord I have loved | Tho: Tomkins | Tucker |
| 72 | 62v/71r | The king shall rejoice | Mr Jo: Tomkins | Tucker |
| 73 | 63r/72r | Let my complaint | [Batten][i] | Tucker |
| 74 | 63v/72v | 'Dr Blow's Kyrie & Creed' in G | [Blow] | Bing |
| 75 | 64v/73v | Prepare ye the way | Mr Wise | Braddock |
| 76 | 65r/74v | 'Mr Purcell's Benedicite in B♭'[j] | [Purcell] | unidentified 1 |
| 77 | 69r/— | Let mine eyes run down with tears | Mr Purcell | unidentified 1 |
| 78 | 69v/79v | I was glad | Mr Henry Purcell | unidentified 2[k] |
| 79 | 69v/— | Commandments in G | [Blow] | unidentified 3 |
| 80 | 70r/79r | 'Dr Blow's Triple Creed in Gamut' | Dr Blow | unidentified 3 |
| 81 | —/80r | 'Rogers in A'[l] | [Rogers] | |
| 82 | 71r/— | 'Mr Birds Service' in d | [Byrd] | |
| 83 | 76r/— | 'Dr Aldrich in Gamut' | [Aldrich] | |
| 84 | 80r/— | 'Dr Nares Service in F' | [Nares] | |
| 85 | 84r/— | Sing unto the Lord | Dr Greene | |
| 86 | 85r/— | God is our hope and strength | Dr Greene | |
| 87 | 86r/— | 'Dr Nares in Gamut' | [Nares] | |

**Table 5.6** (*cont.*)

| Item | Folios[a] | Title | Ascription | Copyist |
|------|-----------|-------|------------|---------|
| 88 | 87r/— | Hear O Lord | Mr King | |
| 89 | 88v/— | Keep we beseech thee | Mr Travers | |
| 90 | 89r/— | O praise God in his holiness | Mr Woodward | |
| 91 | 89v/— | Not unto us Lord | Dr Aldrich [arr. from R. Farrant and H. Lawes] | |
| 92 | 90r/— | My God my God | Mr John Reynolds | |
| 93 | 90v/— | Wherewithal shall a young man | Mr Cook | |
| 94 | 91r/— | O praise God in his holiness | Mr Cook | |
| 95 | 91v/— | Blessed be the Lord | Mr Hall | |
| 96 | 92r/— | Sing unto the Lord | Dr Croft | |
| 97 | 92v/— | Give the king thy judgements | Dr Ayrton | |
| 98 | 93v/— | Bow down thine ear | Dr Ayrton | |
| 99 | 95r/— | O praise God in his holiness | Mr John Weldon | |
| 100 | 95v/— | Lord how long wilt thou be angry | Dr Greene | |
| 101 | 96v/— | Praise the Lord O my soul | R. Creighton | |
| 102 | 97v/— | 'Sanctus–Aldrich in Gamut' | [Aldrich] | |

Folio, tenor cantoris (TC) 335 × 218, alto cantoris (AC) 326 × 218. Watermarks (early paper only: TC, fols 2–80; AC, fols. 2–79): Angoumois fleur-de-lys; countermark 'IHS' (backwards 'S') with 'IP'. Fol. 1 in both books (added by Bing): Angoumois fleur-de-lys in TC; 'IHS/HC' in AC.

Rastrology (TC, fols. 2–80; AC, fols. 2–79): nine staves per page; ruled with four-stave (span: 123; profile: 17(17.5)17(18.5)17.5(18)17.5) and single-stave rastra (span: 17.5), most commonly with two blocks of four staves at the top in TC and at the bottom in AC; there are several pages at various points in TC that vary from the norm.

[a] Lwa Triforium Set I comprises partbooks 'Tenor Cantoris 4' (TC) and 'Alto Cantoris 1A' (AC); the sequence of this inventory, the quoted titles and the ascriptions are based on TC. Modern foliation is given for both books, that of TC first.

[b] With correction slips in John Church's hand in AC.

[c] Fol. 33 has been repaired in TC, probably by John Church.

[d] Inscribed 'Jan. 30' in TC.

[e] Fol. 47 has been repaired in TC, probably by John Church.

[f] This may be Tucker's arrangement of Wise's *Thy beauty O Israel.* The work is elsewhere attributed to Aldrich (see Crosby, *Catalogue*, 236), though Aldrich's autograph of his arrangement in Och 16 is different, using Wise's original text. The anthem is simply ascribed 'Mr Wise' in AC.

[g] A later hand has added '1681' in TC.

[h] There are corrections in Purcell's hand in AC, fol. 58v.

[i] This anthem is ascribed to 'Tho: Tomkins' in TC but is correctly ascribed to 'Adrian Batten' in AC.

[j] Includes all four alternative canticles.

[k] In John Church's hand in AC.

[l] The remaining works were copied by various eighteenth- and nineteenth-century copyists active after John Church. The final item, Aldrich's Sanctus in G, was added in blue pencil.

## Table 5.7 Payments for music books and copying at Westminster Abbey, 1660–1700

| Year[a] | WAM[b] | Payee | Text |
|---|---|---|---|
| 1661 | 33695 | John Playford | 'To John Playford for a sett of Mr Barnards collections of services and Anthemes conteyning tenn Bookes in ffolio bound in rough Leather with one Quire of Ruled Paper xiii*l* x*s* and for the Loane of another sett for foure or five Sundayes and for Portage and carrying them x*s* in all xiiii *l*' (fol. 5r) |
| | | Henry Purcell Sr | 'To Henry Purcell for Bookes of Services for the choristers i*l*' (fol. 5r) |
| 1662 | 33696 | Christopher Gibbons | 'To Christopher Gibbon for Organ Bookes v*l*' (fol. 5v) |
| 1673 | 33706 | Stephen Bing | 'To Steph[e]n Bing for ruled papyr for a set of Quirebookes ii*l*' (fol. 6r) |
| | | Stephen Crespion | 'To Stephen Crispen Chaunter for 4 new Comon prayer bookes at 11*s* 6*d* each – 46*s* and for 16 Quire of ruled papyr for ye Quire 20*s* and for large Ruled papyr for ye Organ booke 8*s*. In all iii*l* xiiii*s*' (fol. 6r) |
| | | | 'To him more for bynding 8 Service Bookes at 3*s* 6*d* each. 28*s* and for binding one Organ booke 4*s*. In all xxxii*s*' (fol. 6v) |
| 1675 | 33709 | Thomas Kequick | 'To Tho: Kequick for binding of viii fol[i]o bookes of Services and Anthems of the Choire xxxii*s*' (fol. 6r) |
| 1676 | 33710 | William Willis | 'To William Willis for an Organ booke viii*s*' (fol. 5v) |
| | | Stephen Bing | 'To Mr Bing for Books for ye Church for ye last year 1675 then omitted xxxii*l* 1*s* vi*d*' (fol. 5v) |
| | | Henry Purcell | 'To Henry Pursell for pricking out two bookes of organ parts v*l*' (fol. 5v) |
| 1677 | 33712 | William Tucker | 'To Mr Tucker for Coppying out some Musick bookes for the use of the Church x*l*' (fol. 5v) |
| | | | 'To him more on the like Occasion x*l*' (fol. 5v) |
| 1679 | 33714 | Stephen Bing | 'To Mr Bing for writing 29 Sheets and 23 Staves xxxviii*s*' (fol. 6r) |
| 1681 | 33716 | ? | 'Paid for mending the Bookes of the Choire x*s*' (fol. 5v) |
| 1682 | 33717 | ? | 'Paid for writing mr Purcells Service & Anthems xxx*s*' (fol. 5v) |
| 1683 | 33718 | ? | 'Paid for pricking & mending ye Church Books xx*s*' (fol. 5v) |

Table 5.7 (*cont.*)

| Year[a] | WAM[b] | Payee | Text |
|---|---|---|---|
| 1684 | 33719 | Charles Taylour | 'To Charles Taylour for writing & Pricking an Anth[e]m in the Church Bookes xx*s*' (fol. 5r) |
| 1688 | 33722 | ? | 'Paid for a Sett of Service Bookes for ye Choire v*l* xiii*s*' (fol. 5v) |
| | | Henry Purcell | 'Paid mr Purcell for makeing ye Service Bookes x*l*' (fol. 5v) |
| | | ? | 'Paid to the Stationer for binding ye Service Bookes lviii*s* vi*d*' (fol. 5v) |
| 1690 | 33724 | Edward Braddock | 'Paid Mr Bradock for new binding eight comon Prayer Books for the Choire & for writeing & Pricking fforty Sheets of Paper iii*l* x*s*' (fol. 6r) |
| 1693 | 33727 | Edward Braddock | 'Paid to Mr Bradock Master of the Choristers for entring eight Anthems iiii*l*' (fol. 5r) |
| | 47671 | Edward Braddock | receipt corresponding to the above entry: |
| | | | 'Received then of Dr: Birch treasurer ffor writing and pricking of eight Anthems with ye organ part into a new sett of books ffor Westminster Abby at ten shillings an Anthem for the sum of foure pound I say received by me Edw: Braddocke 4*l* 0 0' |
| 1696 | 33729 | Edward Braddock | 'To Mr Bradock for book's & for writing & Pricking ym for the Choire iii*l* ii*s* v*d*' (fol. 5r) |
| 1700 | 33732 | Edward Braddock | 'To Mr Braddock for writing & pricking Books for ye Choire xiii*l* viii*s*' (fol. 5v) |
| | 47681 | Edward Braddock | invoice and receipt corresponding to the above entry, various information ordered here chronologically: |
| | | | 'Mr Braddock his bill for writing ye Services & Anthems for the Choire 13*l* 8*s* 0*d* Certifyed by Dr Birch ac[coun]t[?] A[nn]o 1700' |
| | | | 'ffor writing and pricking of thirty services into ye too trebles of ye Decany sides at 2 shilling a service 3*l*-0*s*-0*d* |
| | | | ffor writing and pricking of a hundred Anthems into ye too books of ye Decany side at six pence each Anthem 2-10-0 |
| | | | ffor writing and pricking the same services into ye too treble books of ye Cantoris side 3-0-0 |

**Table 5.7** (*cont.*)

| Year[a] | WAM[b] | Payee | Text |
|---|---|---|---|
| | | | ffor writnig [sic] and pricking the same Anthems into ye too treble Books of ye Cantoris side 2-0-0 |
| | | | ffor twelve quire of ruled paper 1-4-0 |
| | | | ffor binding the four books 1-4-0 |
| | | | sum 13/-8-0' |
| | | | 'March 1st 1700 Rec[eive]d of the Reverand Dr Willis by Mr Needham the sume of thirteen pounds eight shillings 13/8s in discharge of the bill with in mentioned – Edw: Braddock' |
| | | | 'Nov 22. 1700 When I was Subdean I ordered the makeing of these books w[hi]ch were judged also necessary to the Choir by others whom I consulted Witnes mine hand Pet: Birch' |

[a] Annual salaries and other routine payments relating to music are omitted. The treasurer's books from 1664, 1686, 1695 and 1698 are missing.
[b] Westminster Abbey Muniments.

in the books were added by John Church, who seems to have taken charge of performing materials at the Abbey as well as the Chapel Royal in the early eighteenth century, but the rest of the old pages in the tenor book were copied much later, apparently in the 1730s or after.[24] Newer paper was added in the eighteenth and nineteenth centuries, in the alto book a single gathering accommodating Benjamin Rogers's Service in A, and in the tenor book enough paper to allow the completion of James Nares's Service in F and the addition of a further eighteen works.

Lwa Triforium Set I is significant for the chronology of Purcell's early anthems. Tucker's copying provides the earliest source of six works (*I will sing unto the Lord, O God the king of glory, O Lord our governor, Blow up the trumpet in Sion, Let God arise* and *Blessed be the Lord my strength*) which must have been composed by 1677 and were probably copied from Purcell's original composing scores: the direct, if limited, involvement of Purcell in the transcription of his works is proven by his correction of Tucker's copy of *Let God arise* in the alto partbook (fol. 58v). Certain traits of Purcell's handwriting in this correction – particularly the secretary 'e' which he abandoned in the late 1670s – suggest that it was made at or shortly after the time of

[24] Cheverton notes that the service by Byrd was 'copied by James Chelsum between 1734 and 1741' ('English Church Music', 390).

199

Illus. 5.1 Henry Purcell: *Let God arise*, copied by William Tucker with autograph alterations. Westminster Abbey Triforium Set I, alto cantoris partbook, fol. 58v

copying (Illus. 5.1). Tucker's copies were also the source from which Bing made some substantial additions to his personal partbooks Y M1(S) in *c.* 1677–9, including all six Purcell anthems, suggesting that a record of these works as they were transmitted from Purcell to Tucker, lacking only the organ part, survives complete in Bing's transcriptions.

The remaining Purcell copies in Lwa Triforium Set I, including the alternative canticles to the Service in B♭, *Let mine eyes run down with tears* and *I was glad*, copied by two different scribes in Braddock's circle, correspond to the 1682 payment record 'for writing mr Purcells Service & Anthems' (Table 5.7). The regular canticles were apparently copied at the same time in a different set of books: Lwa Triforium Set II consists of a single tenor decani partbook which came into its present form in the eighteenth century as the result of cannibalisation by Church

but in the 1670s and early 1680s probably belonged to a distinct set containing service music and older anthems. The earliest copying in Triforium Set II is entirely in Stephen Bing's hand and, if there are no missing payment records, must date from 1675 (see Table 5.7 under 1676), the rest being the work of Church and later copyists apart from the remainder of Purcell's service (fols. 63v–67v) in the hand of another Braddock-circle scribe.[25] This is on the same type of paper as Bing's copying (also the same, though with different stave-rulings, as the original paper in Triforium Set I), indicating that Bing left a number of pages blank in the original book from which Triforium Set II survives, as Tucker did in Triforium Set I, and that copying was continued in both sets on the unused pages in the early 1680s immediately after Bing's contributions. The fact that no individual payee was named in the 1682 record may mean that the work was carried out by more than one scribe under Braddock's supervision. A 1682 date of copying for *Let mine eyes run down with tears* and *I was glad* in Triforium Set I indicates that the former is closely contemporary with the autograph in Ob MS Mus.c.26 (discussed later in this chapter) and that the latter came into a kind of dual existence as a symphony anthem and organ verse anthem almost from the start, as the autograph of the string version of *I was glad* in Lbl R.M. 20.h.8 dates from *c.* 1682–3.

Nothing has apparently survived of Purcell's own copying for the Abbey (see Table 5.7): the two organ books for which he was paid £5 in 1676 – unless his autograph organ score of Blow's *God is our hope and strength* in the guardbook Och 554 is somehow a stray from the Abbey – and a large copying project devoted to service music, reflected in three adjacent entries in the 1688 treasurer's book, one of which has Purcell being paid for 'making ye Service Bookes'. This is a curious locution given the numerous, more specific references to 'writing' or 'pricking' elsewhere in the payment records, and possibly Purcell oversaw the project but was not involved as a copyist. In any case, the extant books of Lwa Triforium Sets I and II provide no evidence of the activities of copyists working in the late 1680s and 1690s, and the next set of extant books (Lwa Triforium Set III) begins with Church's copying.

## York Minster MSS M1(S)

The set of eight partbooks Y M1(S), copied mainly by Stephen Bing with later additions by John Gostling, has long been viewed as an important source not only of Restoration music but of a broader sacred repertory dating back to the late sixteenth

---

[25] For a partial inventory of Lwa Triforium Set II see ibid., 391–2.

century.[26] Consisting of medius, countertenor, tenor and bass books for the cantoris and decani sides,[27] Y M1(S) contains approximately 300 compositions, including several unique (or nearly unique) copies of works ranging from Orlando Gibbons to Purcell. The set passed from John Gostling to his son William and was sold as lot 82 (of the first day) in the sale of William Gostling's music collection in 1777,[28] subsequently forming lot 168 in the Hayes brothers' sale in 1798.[29] Its whereabouts immediately thereafter are unknown, though it has been in the York Minster Library since at least 1850.[30]

The early history of Y M1(S) is closely linked to the career of Stephen Bing,[31] who became a minor canon at St Paul's Cathedral by 1641 and was reappointed in 1661 as senior cardinal, the second-ranking minor canon. The cathedral was badly damaged in the Great Fire of 1666, and though attempts were made to continue choral services in some fashion[32] the minor canons were permitted to seek other appointments: in 1667 Bing became senior vicar choral at Lincoln Cathedral, a post he held until 1672, when he returned to London as a lay vicar at Westminster Abbey, all the time remaining a minor canon at St Paul's, collecting his fees there until his death in 1681. He began the partbooks, a file-copy set not intended for use in performance, in or just before 1669, starting with a group of services which include 'Mr Ben Rogers Short Sharp Service' and, several works later, 'Dr Rogers's Service in Gamut', acknowledg-

[26] Watkins Shaw, *The Bing–Gostling Part-books at York Minster: a Catalogue with Introduction* (Croydon, 1986); Cheverton, 'English Church Music', 507–16; David Griffiths, *A Catalogue of the Music Manuscripts in York Minster Library* ([York], 1981), 1–20; Robert Francis Ford, 'Minor Canons at Canterbury Cathedral: the Gostlings and their Colleagues' (Ph.D. thesis, University of California at Berkeley, 1984), 258–76 (though a valuable study, we do not agree with aspects of Dr Ford's chronology for these books or with his statement that a few loose scraps of music kept with Y M1(S) are in the same hand as the copy of Wise's *Prepare ye the way* in Lwa Triforium Set I, which Ford identifies as Charles Taylour: Wise's anthem is undoubtedly in Braddock's hand and the scraps are in a different hand). See also Jonathan P. Wainwright, *Musical Patronage in Seventeenth-Century England: Christopher, First Baron Hatton (1605–1670)* (Aldershot, 1997), 52–114; and Sarah Boyer and Jonathan Wainwright, 'From Barnard to Purcell: the Copying Activities of Stephen Bing', *EM* 23 (1995), 620–48.
[27] The library of York Minster has numbered the individual books from 1 to 8, beginning with the medius cantoris and ending with the bass decani (this numbering is used herein); Shaw's numbers (*Bing–Gostling Part-books*) begin with the medius decani book; thus his book 1 is the library's book 5, etc.
[28] *A Catalogue of the Scarce, Valuable and Curious Collection of Music, Manuscript and Printed, of the Reverend and Learned William Gostling* ([London], 1777), 13.
[29] *A Catalogue of the Very Curious and Valuable Music Library of Antient and Modern Compositions . . . Collected . . . by the Late W. and P. Hayes, Doctors in Music, Oxon* (London, [1798]); the description on p. 12 begins 'Anthems, in 8 Parts, from the Collection of the late Mr. Gosling'.
[30] David Griffiths, 'The Music in York Minster', *MT* 123 (1982), 637.
[31] Shaw, *Bing–Gostling Part-books*, 5–7; Cheverton, 'English Church Music', 507–10; Ford, 'Minor Canons at Canterbury', 258–61; Wainwright, *Musical Patronage*, 99–113.
[32] Spink, *Restoration*, 295–8.

ing the D.Mus. conferred on Rogers at Oxford on 8 July 1669. Bing loosely laid out the books in several sections according to numbers of voices and genre, and for the most part worked continuously within each section, though at times he went back and filled in unused spaces. Other items copied early on include a group of older anthems derived from Barnard's *First Book of Selected Church Musick* and, as Bing's inscription in the medius decani reads, 'A Collection of such Anthems for verses as have bin made at Lincoln in ye years [16]68, 69 & 70' (fol. 83r).

The ordering of the pieces within the sections of Y M1(S) suggests that there was a gap of several years in the 1670s when little was copied: in some sections works from Barnard or the Lincoln group are followed almost immediately by other items concordant with Tucker's material in Lwa Triforium Set I. Bing apparently had access to Tucker's books at both the Abbey and the Chapel Royal: there are numerous notes in Bing's hand indicating he compared his readings of works previously copied against those in the London sources, and other notes suggesting he copied directly from them. At various points the ordering between Y M1(S) and Triforium Set I indicates an immediate relationship: for example, the following group of nine anthems, given here as they appear in the medius decani of Y M1(S), are in nearly the same order in Triforium Set I. The item number from the latter source (see Table 5.6) is given here in parentheses.

| | | |
|---|---|---|
| Purcell | Blessed be the Lord my strength, fol. 79v | (60) |
| Humfrey | Hear O heavens, fol. 79v | (61) |
| Blow | O how amiable, fol. 79v | (62) |
| Turner | Lord thou hast been our refuge, fol. 79v | (63) |
| Tudway | Behold God is my salvation, fol. 79v | (65) |
| Humfrey | Lord teach us to number our days, fol. 80r | (66) |
| Humfrey | O give thanks, fol. 80r | (69) |
| Humfrey | Like as the hart, fol. 80r | (70) |
| Blow | O Lord thou hast searched me out, fol. 80v | (67) |

Bing's transcriptions from Triforium Set I must have been made just after the completion of Tucker's copying in 1677, for none of the works by 'Mr' Blow in Tucker's hand are ascribed to 'Dr' Blow by Bing. There are, however, two works in Y M1(S) which Bing ascribes to 'Dr' Blow: the Te Deum in E Minor and the 'Second Commandments & Creed in Gamut' (in triple metre). These both occur amongst the final additions in Bing's hand, preceded anywhere from one to three works before in the various books by the first Commandments and Creed to 'Mr' Blow's Service in

G. Bing's two additions to Lwa Triforium Set I, probably made in 1679, are in fact the Te Deum in E Minor and the first Commandments and Creed (Table 5.6, items 1 and 74), there both ascribed to 'Dr' Blow. This implies that Bing's last copies in his partbooks date from some time between December 1677 and the time of his final work for the Abbey, so although the absolute terminus must remain Bing's death in November 1681 it is possible he added nothing further to Y M1(S) after *c.* 1679. The books remained unbound until about this time: not only are occasional pages folded to match the mostly uniform size of the remaining stock, but all of the flyleaves (several of which Gostling later ruled with staves) and some of the pages containing Bing's later copying display the arms of Amsterdam watermark with the 'AI' countermark of Abraham Janssen, indicating a date of manufacture in the 1670s.[33] The books could not have been bound any later than April 1679, since Bing recorded on the front pastedown in the bass cantoris his presence at the opening of a 'Mr Airsdens will' on the 28th of that month.

The importance of Bing's transcriptions in Y M1(S) of the six Purcell anthems also copied by Tucker in 1677 in Lwa Triforium Set I has already been mentioned, but three more Purcell anthems are also in Y M1(S) in Bing's hand: *Give sentence with me* (the unique copy),[34] *O praise the Lord all ye heathen* and *Save me O God* (see Table 5.8). The first two of these, like the two works Bing ascribed to 'Dr' Blow, fall amongst the last of Bing's entries in Y M1(S), and thus a date of *c.* 1679 for their copying is reasonable. The date of Bing's copy of *Save me O God*, in an unrevised version earlier than the autograph in Cfm 88, is more difficult to place: in several of the books it follows immediately after his copies from Lwa Triforium Set I, in one of them – the medius decani – on the same page as a work ascribed to 'Mr Blow'. But in the medius and bass cantoris books it appears on the same page as one of the 'Dr' Blow items, an inconsistency explained by Bing's practice of sometimes copying parts of services in different places to avoid wasting space. In the medius cantoris, for example, Bing copies 'Mr Aldridgs Benedicite' on fol. 52v and then – two pages and seven anthems later – provides 'The Rest of Mr Aldridg's Service'. Thus the proximity of *Save me O God* to the Triforium Set I concordances is likely the more important factor in dating Bing's copy, which may be from 1677, just after his transcriptions from the Abbey books.

---

[33] The paper containing Bing's earlier copying features several different watermarks, three of which are unusual in music manuscripts of slightly later vintage: the pillars (resembling Heawood no. 3496, though with the initials 'APO'), the horn and a form of the fleur-de-lys on a shield simpler than the Angoumois fleur (similar to Heawood no. 1666).

[34] Eric Van Tassel, 'Purcell's "Give Sentence"', *MT* 118 (1977), 381–3.

# Table 5.8 Works by Purcell in York Minster MSS M1(S)

KEY:

| | |
|---|---|
| 1 = medius cantoris | 5 = medius decani |
| 2 = contratenor cantoris | 6 = contratenor decani |
| 3 = tenor cantoris | 7 = tenor decani |
| 4 = bass cantoris | 8 = bass decani |

Works are located in each book by means of modern folio/original page.

| title | 1 | 2 | 3 | 4 | 5 | 6 | 7 | 8 | copyist |
|---|---|---|---|---|---|---|---|---|---|
| Service in B♭ | 61v/106 | 60r/111 | 51v/92 | 52v/96 | 60v/112 | 48v/88 | 62r/103 | 46v/86 | Gostling |
| Behold I bring you glad tidings | 55v/94 | — | 86v/158 | — | — | 60v/110 | — | 57v/108 | Gostling |
| Blessed be the Lord my strength | — | — | — | — | 79v/150 | 105r/199 | 98r/177 | 101v/196 | Bing |
| Blow up the trumpet in Sion | 77v/138 | 79r/149 | 73r/131 | 77v/146 | 87v/166[a] | 103v/196 | 97r/175 | 101r/195 | Bing |
| Give sentence with me | 83v/150 | 97r/185 | 78v/142 | 82v/150 | — | — | — | — | Gostling |
| I was glad | — | 97v/185bis | 81r/147 | — | 113r/213 | — | — | 55v/104 | Gostling |
| I will sing unto the Lord | 59v/102 | 72v/136 | 59v/108 | 50r/91 | 69v/130 | 72r/133 | 61r/101 | 68v/130 | Bing |
| Let God arise | — | — | — | — | 111r/209 | 104r/197 | 97v/176 | 101v/195 | Bing |
| O give thanks | — | — | 84v/154 | — | 82r/155 | 59r/109 | — | 56v/106 | Gostling |
| O God the king of glory | — | — | — | — | 62v/116 | 56v/104 | 56r/91 | 55v/104 | Bing |
| O God thou art my God | 85v/154 | 74r/139 | 86r/157[b] | 69v/130 | — | — | — | — | Gostling |
| O God thou hast cast us out | 86v/156 | 98v/187 | 89r/163 | 51v/94[c] | — | — | — | — | Gostling |
| O Lord our governor | 75v/134 | 90v/172 | — | 75v/142 | 109v/206 | 100r/189 | 93v/168 | 96r/185 | Bing |
| O praise the Lord all ye heathen | — | — | 78v/142 | — | 113r/213 | 108r/205 | 102r/185 | 108v/210 | Bing |
| Save me O God | 56v/96 | 67v/126 | — | 50v/92 | 70v/132 | 73r/135 | 61v/102 | 68v/130 | Bing |
| Thy way O God is holy | — | — | 56r/101 | — | 79r/149 | 58r/107 | — | 70r/133 | Gostling |
| Thy word is a lantern | 87r/157 | — | — | — | 64v/118 | — | 72r/138 | 87r/157 | Gostling |

Folio, 305 × 195.

[a] There is a also a separate correction slip in Bing's hand for this anthem, bound into the book, now fol. 89.

[b] Gostling copied the tenor part twice; see also fol. 88r/p. 161.

[c] See also fol. 71r/p. 133.

It is not known how Y M1(S) came into John Gostling's hands, though there are several possibilities. Gostling became a minor canon at St Paul's in January 1682,[35] and Bing's partbooks may have remained at the cathedral after his death; alternatively, the books may have gone to Canterbury, where Bing was buried[36] and Gostling was also a minor canon from 1675. Whatever actually happened, Gostling added nothing to the books until the 1690s. All of his additions display his later tendency to form minims and semibreves in a teardrop shape, a characteristic of his hand not apparent before *c.* 1693, when he began to prepare performing materials for the opening of the new St Paul's[37] using Y M1(S) and some older St Paul's service books copied by Bing as his main exemplars. Gostling's copying in the extant St Paul's partbooks (discussed below) is closely modelled on Bing's calligraphic style, and from the mid-1690s on Gostling retained the teardrop-shaped notes in his other manuscripts.[38] In certain respects Gostling's copies of Purcell's works in Y M1(S) are less important than Bing's (Table 5.8): they show some signs of carelessness and several are also found in Gostling's scorebook, US-AUS Pre-1700 85, where they were probably copied from draft autographs. But all of Gostling's Purcell additions to Y M1(S) are concordant with the work of the Braddock circle in Lbl R.M. 27.a.1–6 and 8, and Gostling may have transcribed most of these from the Chapel Royal partbooks, suggesting at a minimum that his readings in Y M1(S) deserve attention when other extant London performing materials provide only a partial text.

### Other Gostling copies: the St Paul's and Tenbury partbooks

Y M1(S) gives little measure of John Gostling's extensive activities as a copyist, which spanned from the 1670s at Canterbury Cathedral (evidence of this work survives only in payment records) through the St Paul's project of the 1690s and on to the apparently more personal collections, Ob MSS Tenbury 797–803 and 1176–82, of *c.* 1705–15; some of his final copying was again for Canterbury, several partbooks extant there containing works in his hand copied as late as 1720.[39] The scale of the St Paul's project is reflected in a 1699 payment of £80 to Gostling for eight partbooks and two organbooks of anthems and two further organbooks of services; presumably this work took place over the previous several years and was at least partially complete

---

[35] Shaw, *Bing–Gostling Part-books*, 9.  [36] Ford, 'Minor Canons at Canterbury', 260, 569.
[37] The choir opened for services in December 1697.
[38] See also the discussion of US-AUS Pre-1700 85 in Chapter 2.
[39] Ford, 'Minor Canons at Canterbury', 177–82, 214–16, 253–304 and passim.

by December 1697.[40] The four partbooks of Lsp A2 (countertenor, tenor and bass decani, and bass cantoris) contain the remains of the original set,[41] and fragments of one of the anthem organbooks exist in Cfm 669, a mostly eighteenth-century manuscript partly made up of earlier leaves.[42] Not mentioned in the 1699 payment record is a set of service books completed by Gostling at about the same time but started before 1677 by Stephen Bing,[43] now Lsp A1, of which the countertenor and tenor decani books survive. Gostling seems to have had sole charge for creating the repertory for the new cathedral and was given special authority for the task by Bishop Henry Compton,[44] so it is no surprise that Gostling's copying in Lsp A1, A2 and Cfm 669 overlaps tremendously with other materials he had at hand: of more than 150 items he entered in surviving St Pauls books only twelve are not found in either Y M1(S) or US-AUS Pre-1700 85. While providing a valuable record of the place of Purcell's works in the repertory, the St Paul's manuscripts have less textual import-ance as Purcell sources than earlier Gostling copies (Table 5.9): of the Service in B♭ and the eleven anthems contained in Lsp A1, A2 and Cfm 669, only three works (*Be merciful unto me*, *Let mine eyes run down with tears* and *Lord who can tell*) are not concordant with Y M1(S) or US-AUS Pre-1700 85.

Similar relationships exist amongst Gostling's later manuscripts: Ob MSS Ten-bury 1176–82, a set of fair copies in four partbooks and three organbooks, compiled *c.* 1705 to *c.* 1715, seem to have been envisioned as a retrospective set, with items taken first from earlier sources such as US-AUS Pre-1700 85 and subsequently from Ob MSS Tenbury 797–803 (which were Gostling's second set of file-copies, copied *c.* 1710–15, and mostly limited to an eighteenth-century repertory) and Gostling's second scorebook, US-Cn Case 7A/2, compiled *c.* 1705 to *c.* 1715.[45] While the Tenbury sets and the second scorebook all seem to have been Gostling's personal

[40] Arthur T. Bolton and H. Duncan Hendry, eds., *Photographic Supplement of St. Paul's Cathedral and Part III of the Building Accounts from October 1st, 1695 to June 24th, 1713*, The Wren Society 15 (Oxford, 1938), 55.

[41] The identification of the early sets of St Paul's partbooks as 'A1', 'A2' and 'B' comes from an unpublished list of music manuscripts in the cathedral library, prepared by Richard Andrewes in 1969.

[42] Cfm 669 was given to the Fitzwilliam Museum in 1919 by Ralph Griffin and was previously owned by W. H. Cummings. Two pieces of the original leather covers, now mounted on the modern binding, are both stamped 'St. P. C.'.

[43] The extant payment record, dated 22 January 1677, 'To Mr Bing in full of his bill for a sett of service books £7–19–7' is in Lg 25707, p. 100; cited in Wainwright, *Musical Patronage*, 108.

[44] W. Sparrow Simpson, *Registrum Statutorum et Consuetudinum Ecclesiae Cathedralis Sancti Pauli Lon-dinensis* (London, 1873), 282–3.

[45] The Tenbury sources are inventoried in Edmund H. Fellowes, *The Catalogue of Manuscripts in the Library of St. Michael's College, Tenbury* (Paris, 1934), 165–7, 254–7. For a discussion and inventory of US-Cn Case 7A/2 see Ford, 'Minor Canons at Canterbury', 288–94, 893–9.

## Table 5.9  John Gostling's copies of works by Purcell in the St Paul's and Tenbury partbooks

KEY:

| | |
|---|---|
| Lsp A1 | London, St Paul's Cathedral MSS A1 Partbooks |
| Lsp A2 | London, St Paul's Cathedral MSS A2 Partbooks |
| Cfm 669 | Cambridge, Fitzwilliam Museum Music MS 669 (formerly a St Paul's organbook) |
| T 797 | Oxford, Bodleian Library MSS Tenbury 797–803 |
| T 1176 | Oxford, Bodleian Library MSS Tenbury 1176–82 |
| x | work is found in the manuscript(s)[a] |
| * | also in US-AUS Pre-1700 85 |
| † | also in Y M1(S) in Stephen Bing's hand |
| ∫ | also in Y M1(S) in John Gostling's hand |

| | Lsp A1 | Lsp A2 | Cfm 669 | T 797 | T 1176 |
|---|---|---|---|---|---|
| Service in B♭∫ | x | | | | |
| Funeral Sentences* | | | | | x |
| Be merciful unto me | | x | | | |
| Blessed are they that fear the Lord* | | | | | x |
| Blessed is he that considereth the poor* | | | | | x |
| Blessed is the man* | | | | | x |
| It is a good thing to give thanks* | | | | | x |
| I was glad*∫ | | x | | | |
| I will sing unto the Lord† | | x | x | x | |
| Let God arise† | | x | | | |
| Let mine eyes run down with tears | | x | | | |
| Lord who can tell | | x | | | |
| My song shall be alway* | | x | | | |
| O give thanks*∫ | | x | | | |
| O God thou art my God∫ | | | | | x |
| O God thou hast cast us out∫ | | | | | x |
| O sing unto the Lord* | | | | | x |
| Praise the Lord ... O Lord my God* | | | | | x |
| Save me O God*† | | | | | x |
| Sing unto God* | | x | | | |
| The Lord is king the earth may be glad* | | | | | x |
| The way of God is an undefiled way* | | | | | x |
| They that go down to the sea* | | x | | | |
| Thy way O God is holy*∫ | | x | | | |
| Why do the heathen | | | | | x |

[a] For full inventories see Robert Francis Ford, 'Minor Canons at Canterbury Cathedral: the Gostlings and their Colleagues' (Ph.D. thesis, University of California at Berkeley, 1984), 868–84; and Edmund H. Fellowes, *The Catalogue of Manuscripts in the Library of St Michael's College, Tenbury* (Paris, 1934), 165–7, 254–7. Ford incorrectly assigns all of the early copying in Lsp A1 to Gostling. The books were in fact begun by Stephen Bing; see Watkins Shaw, *The Bing–Gostling Part-books at York Minster: a Catalogue with Introduction* (Croydon, 1986), 112–4.

items and can be identified with lots in the sale catalogue of William Gostling's music collection,[46] there is an interesting relationship between Tenbury 1176–82 and the Lsp A2 partbooks: Gostling consistently avoided transcribing works in the Tenbury set which he had already copied in Lsp A2 (see Table 5.9), suggesting that Tenbury 1176–82 were intended for St Paul's and were produced both as file-copies and exemplars for future performing materials. Only Ob MSS Tenbury 1176–82, of these later manuscripts, can be considered a significant, though for the most part secondary, Purcell source, containing twelve anthems and the Funeral Sentences (Table 5.9); Ob MSS Tenbury 797–803 and Cfm 669 include only *I will sing unto the Lord*, and there is no Purcell in US-Cn Case 7A/2. Ten of the thirteen works in Tenbury 1176–82 are concordant with US-AUS Pre-1700 85, and two of the remaining three (*O God thou art my God* and *O God thou hast cast us out*) are amongst Gostling's additions to Y M1(S): the only Purcell anthem in Tenbury 1176–82 for which an earlier copy in Gostling's hand does not survive, *Why do the heathen*, may descend from the autograph in Lbl R.M. 20.h.8 or the closely related copy in Lcm 2011. *Why do the heathen* and other Purcell symphony anthems are arranged for organ in Tenbury 1176–82, providing textual evidence of contemporary organ accompaniments and indicating Gostling's intention to bring Purcell's symphony anthems – minus strings – into the active repertory.

## Manchester Central Library MS BRm370Bp35

Mp BRm370Bp35 contains thirteen organ parts copied by John Blow on originally unbound or loosely stitched sheets copied stratigraphically across their full width, a method which enlarges the oblong format common in organ parts to its limit (Table 5.10). Discoloration of fol. 12v suggests it was once the outside, though the right half is darker than the left, together with other evidence of creasing indicating that the collection was folded to normal folio size: some attempt must have been made to keep the pages in order, as several works extend from one sheet to the next. The existing binding was carried out for Henry Watson, who donated his music library to the city of Manchester in 1902, and there is no evidence of prior ownership.[47] The second

---

[46] *Catalogue . . . William Gostling*, 5, 12–13; lots 2 and 83 (both from the first day of the sale) are probably Ob MSS Tenbury 1176–82 and 797–803 respectively, and one of the two books described in lot 79 (also first day) is US-Cn Case 7A/2. Subsequent owners of the Tenbury sets include Highmore Skeats, W. J. Porter and Joseph Warren; see Fellowes, *Catalogue*, 165, 254; and Ford, 'Minor Canons at Canterbury', 486.

[47] King, *Some British Collectors*, 85.

**Table 5.10  Manchester Central Library BRm370Bp35: contents**

| Item | Folio | Title | Ascription | Item in Ob MSS Tenbury 1176-82 |
|------|-------|-------|------------|-------------------------------|
| 1 | 1r | The Lord is king the earth may be glad | [Blow] | |
| 2 | 2r | Lord remember David | [Blow] | 40 |
| 3 | 3r | Blessed is he that considereth the poor | [Purcell] | |
| 4 | 3v | The way of God is an undefiled way | [Purcell] | 41 |
| 5 | 4v | Funeral Sentences | Mr Purcell | 42 |
| 6 | 5r | The Lord is king the earth may be glad | Mr Purcell | 43 |
| 7 | 6v | Blessed are they that fear the Lord | Mr Purcell | 44 |
| 8 | 7v | Praise the Lord . . . O Lord my God | Mr Purcell | 46 |
| 9 | 8v | It is a good thing to give thanks | Mr Purcell | |
| 10 | 9v | O sing unto the Lord . . . for he hath done | Jo: Blow | 47 |
| 11 | 10r | Bring unto the Lord | J. Blow | 45 |
| 12 | 11r | O sing unto the Lord | Mr Purcell | 49 |
| 13 | 12r | Thy mercy O Lord | Jo: Blow | 48 |

Folio (copied stratigraphically), 329 × 413. Watermarks: Dutch Lion with countermark 'AI'.

Rastrology (sheets are ruled for normal folio use): twelve staves per page, ruled with a four-stave rastrum, span: 81.5; profile: 11(13)10.5(13.5)10.5(12.5)10.5.

Copyist: John Blow

work in the collection, Blow's *Lord remember David*, is reliably dated 1698 by Gostling in US-AUS Pre-1700 85, and a period of copying beginning in the late 1690s suggests that the organ parts were prepared for the newly reopened St Paul's (where Blow was Master of the Choristers from 1687 to 1703): they display striking relationships of text and order with a group of anthems in Ob MSS Tenbury 1176–82 (items 40–9; see Table 5.10) and seem to have been available to Gostling when he was copying these books.[48]

Blow's efforts in Mp BRm370Bp35 perhaps even came at Gostling's request: every work in Mp BRm370Bp35 is also in US-AUS Pre-1700 85, and it is possible that Blow used Gostling's scorebook as a copy-text, providing several new organ arrangements (including ones for four of Purcell's symphony anthems: *Blessed are they that fear the Lord, Praise the Lord . . . O Lord my God, It is a good thing to give thanks* and

[48] Some of the relationships between the two sources are charted in *Works*, XVII (1996), xvi–xvii, 229–30; XXVIII (1959), 187; and other relevant volumes. See also Lionel Pike, 'Alternative Versions of Purcell's *Praise the Lord, O My Soul: O Lord My God*', in *Irish Musical Studies 5*, ed. Patrick F. Devine and Harry White (Dublin, 1996), 272–80. Item numbers from Ob MSS Tenbury 1176–82 are those given in Fellowes, *Catalogue*, 255.

*O sing unto the Lord*), which Gostling in turn used in Ob MSS Tenbury 1176–82. Beyond its value in providing evidence of Blow's thoughts on accompaniment, Mp BRm370Bp35 provides early corroborative texts for three verse anthems for which US-AUS Pre-1700 85 is the primary source: *The way of God is an undefiled way, The Lord is king the earth may be glad* and *Blessed is he that considereth the poor*. Gostling's copy of the last of these is not much earlier than Blow's, having been added to US-AUS Pre-1700 85 in *c.* 1698.

## THE SOURCES OF THE SERVICE IN B♭

All but one of the early principal sources of the Service in B♭ are discussed elsewhere: Cfm 117 in Chapter 2; Lbl R.M. 27.a.1–3, 5, 6 and 8, and Lwa Triforium Sets I and II in this chapter; and Lbl R.M. 20.h.9, copied by John Reading in the 1680s, in Chapter 7.[49] Remaining is Purcell's autograph composing score of the Benedicite in Ob MS Mus.a.1. This consists of a single bifolium of super royal paper (530 × 740 mm) which was ruled for a folio book, Purcell connecting most of the staves in order to copy stratigraphically (see Table 5.11). On the reverse of a large correction slip ruled with the same four-stave rastrum as the main bifolium is the opening of Monteverdi's *Cruda Amarilli* in Purcell's hand, untexted save for the incipit.[50] Purcell's handwriting throughout Ob MS Mus.a.1 displays the italic 'e' and secretary 'r', features dating from *c.* 1679–81 and thus suggesting that the Service in B♭ was composed some time before the September 1682 Westminster Abbey payment record for the copying of Purcell's service (see Table 5.7), which has served as a terminus for its date of composition. (By late 1682 Purcell was beginning to use the italic 'r' in his handwriting.) If there was any gap between the composition of the regular canticles and the alternative set including the Benedicite (described in some sources as Purcell's 'First' and 'Second' services) the earliness of Ob MS Mus.a.1 suggests it was minimal.[51]

Beyond these sources are several slightly later ones with relatively good lines of

---

[49] We are grateful to Dr Margaret Laurie for her advice regarding several of the sources of the Service in B♭.

[50] Franklin B. Zimmerman, 'Purcell and Monteverdi', *MT* 99 (1958), 368–9; see also Rebecca Herissone, 'Purcell's Revisions of his own Works', in *Purcell Studies*, 62–3.

[51] The evidence of the recently discovered St Paul's bass partbook Lsp 43.D, which probably came into its present state no later than the early 1680s, may add weight to the argument that there was some short interval between the composition of the regular and alternative sets: Lsp 43.D includes both sets of canticles separated by nine other services and copied by different hands. See Boyer and Wainwright, 'From Barnard to Purcell', 635–8.

**Table 5.11 Separate autograph scores of service music, full and verse anthems*[a]*** (including works by other composers)

| Title | Manuscript | Dimensions | Watermarks |
|---|---|---|---|
| Funeral Sentences | Lbl Add. 30931, fols. 81–4 | 326 × 206 | foolscap/no countermark |
| Who hath believed our report | Lbl Add. 30932, fols. 94–8 | 324 × 227 | foolscap/'PB' countermark |
| Service in B♭ (Benedicite) | Ob MS Mus.a.1 | 530 × 740* | Angoumois fleur-de-lys/'IHS/IM' countermark |
| Let mine eyes run down with tears*[b]* | Ob MS Mus.c.26, fols. 4–9 | 320 × 195 | arms of Amsterdam with 'HC'/no countermark |
| Out of the deep | Lbl Add. 30931, fols. 67–70 | 329 × 209 | foolscap/no countermark |
| By the waters of Babylon (by Pelham Humfrey) | Lbl Add. 30932, fols. 52–5 | 320 × 197 | foolscap/no countermark |
| God is our hope and strength (by John Blow: organ score) | Och 554, fol. 3 | 328 × 425* | foolscap/'CDG' countermark |
| Miserere mei Domine (by John Bull)*[c]* | Ord–Dart MS, location unknown | '9 in by 14 in' | unknown |
| Lord thou art become gracious (by Daniel Roseingrave) | Och 1215, no. 1*[d]* | 325 × 415* | arms of Amsterdam/'VDL' monogram countermark |

Rastrology

| Manuscript | Staves on page | Staves in rastrum | Rastrum span | Rastrum profile |
|---|---|---|---|---|
| Add. 30931, fols. 81–4 | 12 | 4 | 78.5 | 10(13)10(12.5)10.5(12.5)10 |
| Add. 30932, fols. 94–8 | 10 | 5 | 122.5 | 13.5(14)13.5(15)12.5(14.5)12(15)12.5 |
| Ob Mus.a.1 | 16 | 4 | 109.5 | 14.5(16)16(16.5)15.5(15.5)15.5 |
| Ob Mus.c.26, fols. 4–9 | 12 | 6 | 136.5 | 11.5(13)12.5(12.5)12(12.5)12(13.5)12.5(12.5)12.5 |
| Add. 30931, fols. 67–70 | 12 | 3 | 60 | 11.5(12.5)11.5(13)11.5 |
| Add. 30932, fols. 52–5 | 12 (2 × 6) | 3 | 57 | 11.5(12)11(11.5)11 |
| Och 554, fol. 3 | 10 | 5 | 128 | 12(16.5)12.5(16)13(16)13(16.5)13*[e]* |
| Ord–Dart MS | 14 | — | — | — |
| Och 1215, no. 1 | 12 | 6 | 137 | 12.5(11)13.5(11)13(12)14(12.5)12.5(11.5)13 |

\* Copied stratigraphically on a single bifolium ruled for normal folio use: measurements are for the entire sheet.

*[a]* This table excludes Purcell's symphony anthems; for similar information on those works see Table 4.7.

*[b]* Copied stratigraphically across openings; dimensions given are per folio.

*[c]* All information derives from Thurston Dart, 'Purcell and Bull', *MT* 104 (1963), 30–1.

*[d]* In a folder of loose pages.     *[e]* Five-line staves to which Purcell added a sixth, freehand line.

filiation: John Gostling's copies (Y M1(S) and Lsp A1) and several partbooks and organbooks from Eton College and St George's Chapel, Windsor, especially WRch 11–13 and 57. Only one source of the service named thus far contains all of the regular and alternative canticles with all voices present: William Isaack's file-copy score in Cfm 117. But Isaack initially copied only incipits of the literary text, later going back and providing a rather sparse underlay, and he scored the music in large, irregular bar-lengths, giving little sense of the work's metrical character. Och 38, however, provides a complete score of the service in the hand of John Walter, another Windsor copyist with close ties to Purcell. Walter may have based his copy on that in Cfm 117: both sources show evidence of revision from the version found in the Chapel Royal and Abbey sources, and Walter's hand is seen in several editorial annotations to Isaack's copy in Cfm 117.[52] Och 38, devoted entirely to Purcell's service, displays the late version of Walter's hand, suggesting that the copying took place *c.* 1700 (see Illus. 5.2 and Appendix 1, pp. 314–15), a date well supported by paper type: arms of Amsterdam watermark with 'IV' (pp. 1–15) and 'CB' (pp. 17–63) countermarks. Unlike Isaack, Walter provides a complete underlay and regular and appropriate barring throughout.

## OTHER SEPARATE AUTOGRAPHS OF SACRED WORKS

In addition to Ob MS Mus.a.1 and the separate autographs of symphony anthems discussed in Chapter 4 (see Table 4.7), there are several other separate autographs of Purcell's sacred music and four copies in his hand of sacred works by other composers. These manuscripts (Table 5.11) include three of Purcell's earliest autographs: the unrevised version of the Funeral Sentences (missing the opening movement 'Man that is born of a woman') in Lbl Add. 30931, *Who hath believed our report* (Illus. 5.3) in Lbl Add. 30932 and Purcell's copy of Pelham Humfrey's *By the waters of Babylon* (see Illus. 1.1) also in Add. 30932. All three feature the hook-shaped bass clef, which Purcell abandoned by 1678 if not one or two years earlier; the handwriting is visibly youthful; and the anthem texts reveal that Purcell was a poor speller, a situation improving in slightly later sources. The only other autograph of similar vintage is US-NHb Osborn 515, which contains several instrumental basses in Purcell's hand, including 'The Stairre Case Overture in B me' (see Chapter 7). It is difficult to imagine that any of these date from much later than *c.* 1675, and the possibility that one or more dates from the early 1670s cannot be ruled out. Slightly later autographs produced before the end of 1677, such as *My beloved spake* in Add. 30932 (see Illus. 1.5) or the organ arrangement of Blow's *God is our hope and strength* in Och 554 (Illus. 5.4), have a strikingly more mature appearance. There is also at times a noticeable musical immaturity in the very early autographs: the Funeral

---

[52] For instance, Walter has added the indication 'full' at several points in Cfm 117; see, e.g., fol. 302r INV.

Illus. 5.2 Henry Purcell: Service in B♭, copied by John Walter. Christ Church, Oxford, Mus. 38, p. 25

Illus. 5.3  Henry Purcell: *Who hath believed our report*, autograph. British Library Add. MS 30932, fol. 94v

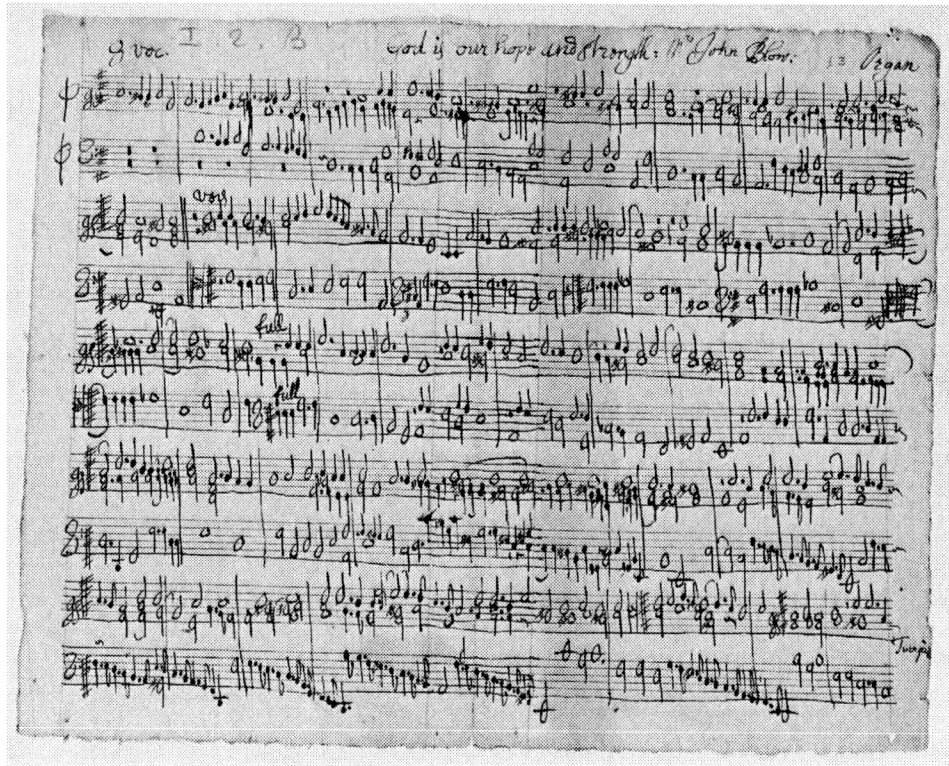

Illus. 5.4. John Blow: organ part of *God is our hope and strength*, copied by Purcell. Christ Church, Oxford, Mus. 554, fol. 3r

Sentences reveal some misconceptions about counterpoint,[53] and the arrangement of *By the waters of Babylon* incorporates an organ reduction vastly less competent than the Blow organ part in Och 554. Unfortunately, there is no external evidence to assist in the dating of these early autographs, though Bruce Wood has argued convincingly that Purcell's first working of the Funeral Sentences was created to complete a set composed by Henry Cooke, possibly for Cooke's own funeral in 1672 or Humfrey's in 1674.[54]

Of later vintage are the autographs of *Let mine eyes run down with tears* in Ob MS Mus.c.26[55] and *Out of the deep* in Lbl Add. 30931. We suggested above that the copy

[53] Robert Shay, 'Purcell's Revisions to the Funeral Sentences Revisited', *EM* 26 (1998), 457–67.

[54] Bruce Wood, 'The First Performance of Purcell's Funeral Music for Queen Mary', in *Performing the Music*, 73–6.

[55] Paper type and stave-rulings for the Ob MS Mus.c.26 copy of *Let mine eyes* are identical to other autograph material in the same guardbook; see Chapter 4, pp. 142–3.

of *Let mine eyes* in Lwa Triforium Set I was part of a group of Purcell's works added to the Abbey partbooks by September 1682, a date further corroborated by the evidence of the autograph: Purcell's hand exhibits the italic 'e' and a transition between the secretary and italic 'r'; the italic 'r' incidence here is 12.4 per cent, a roughly similar percentage to the October 1682 welcome song *The summer's absence* (10.3 per cent incidence) in Lbl R.M. 20.h.8, suggesting that *Let mine eyes* was composed not long before being copied into the Abbey books. While several of these separate autographs may represent working drafts, that of *Let mine eyes* provides the most compelling evidence of Purcell's propensity for revision, containing five correction slips, some of which include sketch material for the same work on the reverse of the finished slips, indicating that there were three stages of activity all in close proximity.[56] The autograph of *Out of the deep* exhibits the italic 'r' throughout, thus placing it in 1685 or after: the work's only concordance is in US-R M2040/A628/Folio (see Chapter 1), a scorebook compiled by London A and completed in the mid-1680s.

A reasonably large proportion of Purcell's early copying, especially taking into account his editorial work in Cfm 88, is devoted to the works of other composers. It is thus not surprising that among the separate autographs are works by such figures as Blow or Humfrey; the reasons for copying works by John Bull and Daniel Rosein-grave are not so obvious, though Purcell may have made other such copies (which now no longer survive) of lesser-known works for various personal or professional reasons. Purcell's organ arrangement of Humfrey's symphony anthem *By the waters of Babylon* in Lbl Add. 30932 (see Illus. 1.1), one of the four earliest Purcell autographs, may date from before Humfrey's death and could have been produced when Humfrey was Purcell's primary composition instructor. The organ score of Blow's *God is our hope and strength* in the guardbook Och 554 (Illus. 5.4), only recently identified as being in Purcell's hand, comes from a slightly later phase of his career, handwriting characteristics suggesting *c.* 1675–6, and may be connected with his copying for the Abbey in 1676, when he was paid £5 for 'pricking out two bookes of organ parts' (see Table 5.7).[57]

Purcell's copy of John Bull's ten-part canon on the plainsong *Miserere mei Domine* is certainly the most unusual item in this group. All that is known of this autograph

[56] Herissone, 'Purcell's Revisions', 63–5, 70–80; *Works*, XXIX (1960), 1–18, 191.

[57] Only the last few bars of this organ part are on the verso: Purcell may have recopied it to eliminate the awkward page-turn, thus ensuring the survival of the sheet now in Och 554. On the connection between Purcell's copies of Blow's *God is our hope and strength* in Och 554 and Cfm 88, see Chapter 2, p. 39.

derives from a brief article by Thurston Dart, fortunately with the relevant material illustrated.[58] The manuscript, described by Dart as a scorebook of twenty-four folios and flyleaves (which contain music) stitched into a vellum cover, was owned by Samuel Butler, Henry Festing Jones, Boris Ord and Dart himself, though its present whereabouts are unknown. It also contains fantazias by Orlando Gibbons and John Coprario, and on the flyleaves a dialogue by Nicholas Lanier and three madrigals by Monteverdi, including *Cruda Amarilli*. Bull's *Miserere* features Purcell's italic 'e' and secretary 'r', and must have been transcribed *c.* 1679–81, during the period when he produced, amongst other things, the Benedicite in Ob MS Mus.a.1: he may have made a copy of *Cruda Amarilli* from the Ord–Dart manuscript on paper from the same stock as he used for Ob MS Mus.a.1, later cutting it into a correction slip for the Benedicite. In all probability the *Miserere* was the only item in the Ord–Dart manuscript in Purcell's hand, though the collection casts important light upon his knowledge of earlier music.

Last of this group of separate autographs is the single-sheet copy of Daniel Roseingrave's anthem *Lord thou art become gracious* in Och 1215, like Och 554 a guardbook of unrelated items.[59] Only the music hand here is Purcell's, the title and text incipits being added by Roseingrave himself, organist and Master of the Choristers at Winchester Cathedral from 1681 to 1692. The circumstances of his collaboration with Purcell may never be known, but it is most likely to have taken place between 1682 and 1684, when Charles II made annual visits to Winchester:[60] a close musical connection between Whitehall and Winchester is implied by Lbl Add. 47845 and R.M. 20.h.9, and the paper type of the score in Och 1215 closely resembles that of John Blow's New Year odes for 1681 and 1682, *Great Sir the joy of all our hearts* and *Arise great monarch* in Bu 5001, fols. 41 and 32. *Lord thou art become gracious* is written on a bifolium ruled for normal use with the staves connected freehand across the gap, and in this case the stratigraphic layout, which halves the number of clefs and line ends, was probably adopted for speed and ease of copying.

---

[58] Thurston Dart, 'Purcell and Bull', *MT* 104 (1963), 30–1.

[59] Peter Holman, 'Purcell and Roseingrave: a New Autograph', in *Purcell Studies*, 94–105. The only other known copies of *Lord thou art become gracious* are in the so-called Winchester Organbook, US-BE 751, where it appears in Roseingrave's hand, and Lbl R.M. 20.h.9, a scorebook in the hand of another Winchester musician, John Reading.

[60] Holman ('Purcell and Roseingrave', 105) suggests that Purcell may have copied the score in London to send to Roseingrave in Winchester.

OTHER NON-AUTOGRAPH MANUSCRIPTS OF SACRED WORKS

This final section of Chapter 5 encompasses a miscellany of for the most part unrelated manuscripts, most of these containing only one or at most a few Purcell copies which can be considered primary or early corroborative texts.

### Oxford, Christ Church Mus. 22

The scorebook Och 22, bound in the eighteenth century as part of the collection of Richard Goodson II, seems to have come together in at least three distinct stages. The newest material in the volume (pp. 133 to the end), mostly in the hand of Goodson II, is not of importance here. More significant is the material up to p. 131 (pp. 132–3 is an inserted sheet of unruled paper containing an early table of contents), which is almost entirely in the hand of Richard Goodson I and includes his copies of Purcell's Funeral Sentences, in their middle version (one of the two earliest copies of this version, the other being Daniel Henstridge's in US-LAuc fC6966/M4/A627/1700),[61] and the chorus ('They prevented me') from the anthem *I will love thee O Lord*, which survives complete only in a later and problematic source: Charles Badham's scorebook Ob MS Mus.Sch. C.40 (see Table 5.12). (Both Henstridge's and Badham's scorebooks are discussed below.)

Goodson I's contributions to Och 22 fall into two sections, identifiable through changes in handwriting, paper type and stave-rulings. The material copied up to p. 59 represents an early phase of Goodson's work completed before Blow's 1677 doctorate and possibly at the time of Goodson's first adult musical appointment in Oxford in 1675. His handwriting in this section is in many respects close to Edward Lowe's, so perhaps Goodson was consciously emulating Lowe's hand at a time when Lowe was his mentor. Goodson's second section is marked by a change in paper type at p. 60 (a recto) and the appearance of his regular mature hand. This section actually begins on p. 59 (the last page of the earlier paper type) which had been left unused. The first two works of this second section, Blow's *Jesus seeing the multitude* and Henry Cooke's *Turn thou us O good Lord*, cannot have been added after too long a gap: the ascription to the first of these is partially cut off, but

[61] On the middle version of the Funeral Sentences, see Robert Ford, 'Purcell as his own Editor: the Funeral Sentences', *Journal of Musicological Research* 7 (1986), 47–67; Shay, 'Purcell's Revisions to the Funeral Sentences Revisited', 457–67; and Henry Purcell, *Funeral Sentences with March and Canzona for the Funeral of Queen Mary*, ed. Christopher Hogwood (Oxford, 1995).

## Table 5.12 Oxford, Christ Church Mus. 22, pp. 1–131: contents

| Page | Title | Ascription |
|---|---|---|
| 1 [ = verso] | O Lord I have sinned | Mr John Blow |
| 7 | The Lord said unto my Lord | Dr Gibbons |
| 12 | Who shall separate us | Mr Math: Lock |
| 17 | Lord how are they increased | M[r] J[ohn] Bl[ow]* |
| 22 | 'Mr John Blow's Te Deum' in e | Mr John Blow |
| 27 | 'Mr Blow's Service in A' | Finis Mr Blow's in A |
| 45 | How doth the city | By Mr John Blow |
| 50 | Teach me O Lord | Dr Gibbons |
| 53 | Gloria patri in A | Mr John Blow |
| 55 | I will cry unto thee | Mr John Blow |
| 59 | Jesus seeing the multitudes | M[r] J[ohn] Bl[ow]* |
| 66 | Turn thou us O good Lord | Capt: Henry Cooke |
| 69 | Turn thee unto me O Lord | [Blow] |
| 73 | Funeral Sentences | [Purcell] |
| 80 | Like as the hart | [Humfrey] |
| [86–7 blank] | | |
| 88 | I will love thee O Lord (chorus only) | [Purcell] |
| 89 | O Lord I have heard | [Aldrich] |
| 97 | I will love thee O Lord | [Aldrich] |
| 105 | My song shall be alway | [Purcell] |
| 115 | O how amiable | [?Carissimi–Aldrich] |
| 120 | The Lord is king | [Aldrich] |
| 123[–131] | Not unto us O Lord | Mr Matt: Lock |

Folio, 346 × 223.

Watermarks and rastrology (12 staves per page throughout)

| Pages | Watermark/countermark | Staves in rastrum | Rastrum span | Rastrum profile |
|---|---|---|---|---|
| [0]–59 | Angoumois fleur-de-lys/'HG' | 4 | 93.5 | 12(15)13(14.5)12.5(14)12.5 |
| 60–83, 88–115, 120–1 and 126–7 | Angoumois fleur-de-lys/'IHS/ET' | 4 | 94.5 | 11.5(15)13(14.5)13(15)12 |
| 84–7 | simple fleur-de-lys/'DS' | 4 | 94 | 13(13)14(14)13(14.5)13 |
| 116–19 | Angoumois fleur-de-lys/'IHS/IC' | 3 | 64.5 | 11.5(14)12(15)11.5 |
| 122–5 and 128–31 | Angoumois fleur-de-lys/'AI' | 3 | 64.5 | 11.5(14)12(15)11.5 |

Copyist: Richard Goodson I (except pp. 80–5 added by two later hands)

* Ascription partially cut off.

enough of it is visible to indicate that Goodson ascribed the work to 'Mr' Blow. Thereafter the character of Och 22 changes considerably: Goodson left all but Locke's *Not unto us O Lord* unascribed, and there are other signs of haste such as partially texted choruses. Humfrey's *Like as the hart*, coming just before the chorus to Purcell's *I will love thee O Lord*, is not in Goodson's hand and was added later, initially on pages Goodson left blank presumably to accommodate the additional sections of the Purcell anthem. There were in fact not enough blank pages for the Humfrey, and so a second interloper added a bifolium of newer paper, pp. 84–7 (simple fleur-de-lys watermark with 'DS' countermark), using only pp. 84–5 to complete the work. Three works beyond the incomplete Purcell anthem is his symphony anthem *My song shall be alway*, which survives in several other Oxford manuscripts including Francis Withy's scorebook Ob MS Mus.Sch. C.61, where it is dated 1690; to judge from its position in John Gostling's scorebook US-AUS Pre-1700 85 the work cannot have been composed much before 1688.[62] This all suggests that the unascribed works Goodson added to Och 22 came rather intermittently over a period of years. While Goodson's copies of the incomplete *I will love thee O Lord* and the middle version of the Funeral Sentences are of primary importance, the precise dates he entered these works in Och 22 can only be surmised between the extremes of *c.* 1677 and 1690.

### Daniel Henstridge's Purcell manuscripts

It is not surprising that a number of important Purcell manuscripts survive in the handwriting of Daniel Henstridge given his seventy-year career (1666–1736) as organist in Gloucester, Rochester and Canterbury. He provides the only sources for two Purcell anthems: *The Lord is king and hath put on*, in the scorebook US-LAuc fC6966/M4/A627/1700 and the partbook fragment US-NH Filmer 21, and *Turn thou us O good Lord*, in Lbl Add. 30931. In addition, Henstridge's transcriptions of *Be merciful unto me* and *Blessed be the Lord my strength* in Lbl Add. 30931–2 are early, and his score of the Funeral Sentences in their middle version (also in the Los Angeles scorebook) may be the oldest extant copy.

---

[62] See Chapter 2, p. 76, and Chapter 4, pp. 153–7.

## Table 5.13 University of California at Los Angeles, William Andrews Clark Memorial Library MS fC6966/M4/A627/1700: contents

COPYISTS
Henstridge I    Daniel Henstridge, old G clef
Henstridge II   Daniel Henstridge, new G clef

| Page | Title | Ascription(s) | Copyist |
|------|-------|---------------|---------|
| 1 | O Lord God of my salvation | Dr Blow | Henstridge I |
| 6 | 4-part instrumental work [?] | Dr Jo: Blow | Henstridge I |
| 8 | O Lord I have sinned | Dr Blow | Henstridge I |
| 15 | Awake, awake put on thy strength | Mr Wise | Henstridge I |
| 22 | I will magnify thee | Mr Wm Turner | Henstridge I |
| 26 | Funeral Sentences | Mr Henry Pursell, Mr Henry Purcell | Henstridge I |
| 33 | Praise the Lord O my soul | Dr Wm Child | Henstridge I |
| 35 | Blessed is he | Mr Wise | Henstridge I |
| 40 | Turn thee unto me | Dr Blow | Henstridge I |
| 44 | How are the mighty fallen | Mr Wise | Henstridge I |
| 50 | The Lord hear thee | Mr Tudway | Henstridge I/II |
| 62 | Quare fremuerunt gentes | Mr Tudway Bachelor in Musicke | Henstridge II |
| 74 | Lord how are they increased | Dr Blow | Henstridge II |
| 80 | Give ear O Lord | Dr Aldrige | Henstridge II |
| 84 | The Lord is king and hath put on | Mr H. Purcel* | Henstridge II |
| 87 | Out of the deep | Dr Aldrige | Henstridge II |
| 90 | O be joyful in the Lord | Mr Humpris* | Henstridge II |
| 95 | 6-part chant | [?] | Henstridge II |
| 96 | O praise God in his holiness (inc.) | [?] | Henstridge II |
| 96 | 6-part chants 'The 2d & 3d will serve for a double-tune' | By the subchanter of yorke Mr Nalson | Henstridge II |
| 98 | Christ being raised | Dr Blow | Henstridge II |
| 104 | O praise the Lord | Mr Humphreys, Pellham Humfreys | Henstridge II |
| 112 | I said in the cutting off of my days | Dr Blow, Dr Jo: Blow | Henstridge II |
| 121 | O give thanks | Mr Humphreys | Henstridge II |
| 131 | The kings of Tharsis | Dr Jo: Blow | Henstridge II |
| 138 | I will hearken | Dr John Blow | Henstridge II |
| 147 | O give thanks | Dr Blow | Henstridge II |
| 160 | I will alway give thanks | Composed by Mr Humphreys, Dr Blow & Mr Turner | Henstridge II |
| 166 | Behold how good and joyful | Dan:ll Henstridge | Henstridge II |
| 170 | O give thanks | Dr Aldrich* | Henstridge II |
| 174 | O sing unto the Lord | Mr Nich: Wotton | unidentified I |
| 178 | I was glad | Mr Purcell | Henstridge II |
| 184 | I waited patiently | Dr Blow | Henstridge II |
| 189 | I will love thee O Lord | Mr John Church | unidentified II |
| 200 | Praise the Lord O my soul | Finis Mr Church | unidentified II |
| 210 | Ponder my words O Lord | Dr Blow | Henstridge II |
| 216 | This is the day | Mr Baptist [Draghi] | Henstridge II |
| 230 | Blessed is the man (chorus only) | Mr Purcell | Henstridge II |

**Table 5.13**  (*cont.*)

| Page | Title | Ascription(s) | Copyist |
|---|---|---|---|
| 230 | Thy way O God (chorus only) | [Purcell] | Henstridge II |
| 231 | Bring unto the Lord | Blow* | Henstridge II |
| 238 | Thy hands have made me | Dr Blow | Henstridge II |
| 241 | Hear O heavens (inc.) | [Humfrey] | Henstridge II |

[manuscript inverted]

| Page | Title | Ascription(s) | Copyist |
|---|---|---|---|
| 264 | How art thou fallen | [Blow] | Henstridge II |
| 261 | See O see how the flowers | [Turner] | Henstridge II |
| 259 | 4-part instrumental work | [?] | Henstridge II |
| 258 | Sonata (Z.790) | [Purcell] | Henstridge II |
| 250 | Sonata (Z.791) (inc.) | [Purcell] | Henstridge II |
| 249 | Behold God is my salvation | [?] | Henstridge II |

Folio, 369 × 238. Watermark: Angoumois fleur-de-lys with 'PSAB' countermark. Rastrology: twelve staves per page, ruled with a four-stave rastrum.

* Ascription not in Henstridge's hand.

The scorebook US-LAuc fC6966/M4/A627/1700 (Table 5.13)[63] came into William Gostling's collection presumably after Henstridge's death – Gostling's bookplate is on the back pastedown – and can be tentatively identified as one of the volumes listed in lot 80 (first day) in the sale of Gostling's collection.[64] Henstridge compiled the manuscript over a fairly broad period, initiating the project during his Rochester tenure but after December 1677, as the first three works in the volume are ascribed to 'Dr' Blow. In the first ten works and part of the eleventh Henstridge's G clefs are of the unusual pattern he used before *c.*1682, when he adopted a more conventional

[63] In the early 1960s US-LAuc fC6966/M4/A627/1700 was in the collection of Theodore Finney deposited at the University of Pittsburgh music library; see Theodore M. Finney, 'A Manuscript Collection of English Restoration Anthems', *JAMS* 15 (1962), 193–9; Finney, 'A Group of English Manuscript Volumes at the University of Pittsburgh', in *Essays in Musicology in Honor of Dragan Plamenac on his 70th Birthday*, ed. Gustave Reese and Robert J. Snow (Pittsburgh, 1969; repr. New York, 1977), 21–48; and Richard Charteris, 'A Checklist of the Manuscript Sources of Henry Purcell in the University of California, William Andrews Clark Memorial Library, Los Angeles', *Notes* 52 (1995), 411–12. Finney sold his collection in 1970, selected English manuscripts including the Henstridge scorebook going to the William Andrews Clark Memorial Library at the University of California at Los Angeles. The balance of Finney's collection, including a large number of non-English items, went to the University of Texas at Austin, where they are now in the Harry Ransom Humanities Research Center. Of the items Finney catalogued in 'A Group of English Manuscript Volumes' numbers 1–3, 6 and 9–12 are currently in Los Angeles, while 4–5 and 7–8 are in Austin.

[64] *Catalogue . . . William Gostling*, 12; though attributed to the hand of John Gostling in the catalogue, the composers listed, including 'Baptist' (Draghi), are all present in US-LAuc fC6966/M4/A627/1700.

form.[65] An early 1680s date of inception is further supported by the evidence of paper type: Angoumois fleur-de-lys watermark with a rare 'PSAB' countermark also found in a handful of other important Purcell sources of similar vintage.[66] Of the pre-*c*. 1682 items in US-LAuc fC6966/M4/A627/1700 the most significant for present purposes is Purcell's Funeral Sentences (Illus. 5.5): because the work is found here amongst the 'early G clef' copying, Henstridge's score can be dated with greater precision than Richard Goodson's in Och 22 and is possibly the earlier of the two. Later additions to the scorebook, some added by other copyists, include works by Nicholas Wooton, whose anthems would not have been entered before Henstridge's 1698 arrival in Canterbury (where Wooton was Henstridge's predecessor as organist), and John Church. On pp. 96–7 are several chants ascribed to 'the subchanter of yorke Mr Nalson'. Valentine Nalson only became the York subchanter in 1708, a fact that would seem to disrupt the chronological flow of the volume, but these chants follow an incomplete and unascribed anthem, *O praise God in his holiness*, and thus could have been added on blank pages at a later date.

US-LAuc fC6966/M4/A627/1700 also provides the only complete source of *The Lord is king and hath put on*. The work's attribution to Purcell has been questioned because the ascription 'Mr H. Purcel' is not in Henstridge's hand and appears to be a later addition, but another Henstridge copy of the same anthem has recently come to light: US-NH Filmer 21 is a loose bifolium from a countertenor partbook, containing Aldrich's *Out of the deep* (ending only) and *Give ear O Lord*, and Purcell's *The Lord is king and hath put on*, here ascribed 'Mr Hen: Purcell' by Henstridge.[67]

The unique *Turn thou us O good Lord* is found amongst numerous scores copied by Henstridge in the Flackton Collection, Lbl Add. 30931–3. This item (Add. 30931, fols. 79–80) predates most of Henstridge's other Purcell transcriptions: not only does it use his earlier G clef, but it is inscribed 'Mr Hen. Pursoll of Westminster', suggesting some unfamiliarity with the composer. Only Henstridge's copies of *Turn thou us O good Lord* and *Blessed be the Lord my strength* exhibit this spelling of Purcell's name; before he changed the formation of his G clef he used both 'Pursell' and

---

[65] This dating is based on a similar changeover in clef in Henstridge's manuscript songbook Cfm 118 (see Chapter 7), occurring just before ascriptions to Henry Aldrich change from 'Mr' to 'Dr'; Aldrich received his D.D. in 1682.

[66] Finney, 'A Manuscript Collection', 194; for further information on the 'PSAB' countermark, see Table 7.6 and the discussion of Lbl R.M. 20.h.9 in Chapter 7 below.

[67] Robert Ford, 'The Filmer Manuscripts: a Handlist', *Notes* 34 (1977–8), 821. Another item in US-NH Filmer 21 is a chant with the text 'O Be joyfull &c' in the same hand as Nicholas Wooton's *O sing unto the Lord* in US-LAuc fC6966/M4/A627/1700, suggesting that Filmer 21 has a Canterbury provenance and was thus produced in 1698 or after.

Illus. 5.5  Henry Purcell: Funeral Sentences copied by Daniel Henstridge. University of California at Los Angeles, William Andrews Clark Memorial Library MS fC6966/M4/ A627/1700, p. 26

'Purcell', stabilising at the latter spelling *c.* 1682. Since *Blessed be the Lord my strength* was in the Abbey partbooks by 1677, both of these early copies could date from about that year.

### The sources of the funeral music for Queen Mary

The principal manuscripts of Purcell's Funeral Sentences, surviving in three versions dating from the early 1670s to the early 1680s, have all been discussed above, in this chapter or in Chapter 2. It remains to survey the sources for his unrelated funeral music of 1695, a setting of 'Thou knowest Lord the secrets of our hearts', intended to complete Thomas Morley's Funeral Sentences, which in Purcell's day lacked that sentence (Morley's 'Thou knowest Lord' was later rediscovered), and an instrumental march and canzona, all written for the obsequies of Mary II.[68]

None of the principal sources for the 1695 'Thou knowest Lord' have particularly close ties to the composer: the earliest – *c.* 1700–5 – are those in the anthem scorebook Lbl Add. 31444, fol. 208 (in the hand of James Hawkins, bound together with Purcell's printed *Te Deum & Jubilate* of 1697), and Och 794, a volume comprising three printed items (the *Te Deum & Jubilate* and *Harmonia Sacra*, Books I and II) and two inserted pages of manuscript containing 'Thou knowest Lord' (inscribed 'Mr Hen: Purcells Part of the Buriall Song'), a separate organ part for the same work and an open score of the funeral march (but no canzona). Och 794 comes from the collection of Richard Goodson II (though the manuscript folios are not in his or his father's hand), and paper type (arms of Amsterdam watermark and a misformed 'AI' countermark) suggests a date of transcription not long after 1700. A related copy of 'Thou knowest Lord' is in Och 1246, a tenor partbook from Christ Church: on p. '20d' is the bass part copied by Goodson II in the tenor clef with octave adjustments to keep the part in the tenor range and transposed up a tone to cadence on A. A note on the bottom of the page, now substantially cut off, appears to match the inscription in Och 794. A slightly later but well-known copy is Thomas Tudway's in Lbl Harley 7340, volume 4 (dating from 1717) of his six-volume collection prepared for Edward Harley. It is from Tudway that we learn that 'Thou knowest Lord' was 'accompanied w[i]th flat, Mournfull Trumpets' (fol. 264v), and his preface to the same volume includes a lengthy description of the work given as part of a defence of old-fashioned church music (fol. 3r). While most other extant sources derive from the printed copy

---

[68] Wood, 'The First Performance', 61–81; Wood, ed., *A Purcell Anthology* (Oxford, 1995), 22–3, 103–4; Hogwood, ed., *Funeral Sentences with March and Canzona.*

of Purcell's 'Thou knowest Lord' provided in William Croft's *Musica Sacra*, Book I (London, 1724), two relatively late manuscripts provide this sentence in its original context, amongst Morley's Funeral Sentences: Ob MS Tenbury 859 of *c.* 1720, where the entire work is attributed to 'Dr: Morley', and Lbl Add. 5054 of *c.* 1750, a copy in the hand of Henry Needler, attributed in the table of contents to 'Tho: Morley and Hen: Purcell', though here Croft's final sentence (unattributed) stands in for Morley's.[69] The sources of the march and canzona are a much simpler affair: only Ooc Ua 37 (see Chapter 6 and Table 6.3), one of four Oriel College scorebooks in the hand of London E who collaborated closely with Daniel Purcell *c.* 1696–1702, contains both pieces; and the only other manuscript to preserve the march in its original version is Och 794, all other copies deriving from the version in *The Libertine*.

## James Hawkins's scorebooks

James Hawkins, organist at Ely from 1683 to 1729, was easily one of the most prolific copyists of the late seventeenth and early eighteenth centuries. While he is responsible for several extant partbooks, his great interest seems to have been in collecting works in score: over fifteen of his scorebooks survive amongst the Ely music manuscripts,[70] and several more have found their way into other collections, such as Lbl Add. 31444–5 and Ob MS Tenbury 1504.[71] Hawkins seems to have had unusually good access to items from the London circle, a point underscored by the fact that two Purcell anthems – *O consider my adversity* and the full anthem version of *I was glad* – survive only in his scorebooks. Hawkins in fact made three different copies of *O consider my adversity*, in EL 12, 19 and 20. That in EL 12 (pp. 331–46), a volume opening with Handel's 'Utrecht' Te Deum of 1713, is in all likelihood a copy from EL 20 (pp. 116–29), which is probably the earliest of the three sources, though an attribution to 'Dr' Tudway places it not before 1705. The copy in EL 19 (pp. 61–73), a manuscript dated 1718 at the end of the volume, stems from a different exemplar, suggesting that Hawkins at various points encountered two different versions of this anthem, both now lost.[72] Why Hawkins would make three copies of the same work is not immediately clear, though Spink notes that he was a 'compulsive

---

[69] Wood, 'The First Performance', 79–81.

[70] The numbering of the Ely sources in W. E. Dickson, *A Catalogue of Ancient Choral Services and Anthems Preserved Among the Manuscript Sources and Part-Books in the Cathedral Church of Ely* (Cambridge, 1861), is still in use, though they are now deposited at the University Library, Cambridge.

[71] The best overview of Hawkins's copying activities is in Spink, *Restoration*, 84–7; see also 237–53.

[72] See *Works*, XXIX (1960), 195–6.

copyist',[73] and a reprimand from the Dean and Chapter in 1693, that Hawkins 'shall not be allow[e]d any bill for pricking' without prior approval,[74] suggests that the recopying of works may have come in the name of potential remuneration.

The attribution of the full anthem *I was glad* to Purcell rests on a strong circumstantial case made by Bruce Wood,[75] for the only known copy of the work is in Hawkins's hand in EL 6 (pp. 210–20), where it is ascribed to 'Dr Blow' in the table of contents. Wood's argument rests on the evidence of Sandford's *History of the Coronation of . . . James II*: Sandford describes the performance and provides the text (Psalm 122, verses 1 and 4–7 with the Gloria patri) of a 'full Anthem' by 'Mr Hen. Purcel', sung as the introit at the coronation by the Westminster Abbey choir.[76] The text Sandford provides does not match that of Purcell's symphony anthem version of *I was glad* (Psalm 122, verses 1–6), which Wood rightly notes would have been unwieldy sung in procession, but does match that of the setting in EL 6, which is indeed a full anthem, and which could have effectively been sung on the move. The work itself is remarkably inventive, which might help to point to Purcell as the composer, though it may belittle Blow's abilities too much to rule out that he was capable of such music. There is nothing else in EL 6 itself that might help to resolve this matter, though it should be noted that Hawkins left most of the works in the volume unascribed on the scores; the presence of several paper types implies that the compilation took place over some years in the early eighteenth century (*I was glad* is on some of the later paper: Pro Patria watermark and 'IV' countermark); and it is thus possible that in creating the table of contents, which could not have been made until the volume was complete, Hawkins's memory failed in correctly identifying all the composers. Beyond its unique copy of *I was glad*, EL 6 is also of importance in providing the only concordance for Purcell's earliest version of the Funeral Sentences (pp. 172–7).

## Other early eighteenth-century scorebooks

Several other early eighteenth-century scorebooks also figure prominently as Purcell sources, attesting to the important role of sometimes relatively minor collector-copyists. Charles Badham, a minor canon at St Paul's from 1698 to 1716, preserved a

---

[73] Spink, *Restoration*, 84.     [74] Cited in ibid., 84; see also Shaw, *The Succession*, 101–2.

[75] Bruce Wood, 'A Coronation Anthem – Lost and Found', *MT* 118 (1977), 466–8; see also Henry Purcell, *I was glad*, ed. Bruce Wood (Borough Green, 1977).

[76] Francis Sandford, *A History of the Coronation of the Most High, Most Mighty, and Excellent Monarch, James II* (London, 1687); cited in Wood, 'A Coronation Anthem', 467.

number of Purcell's works in his scorebooks, which include Ob MSS Mus.Sch. C.38–40, B.7 and Tenbury 1031 and 1258. His copies have frequently been described as 'corrupt' or 'defective',[77] comments not wholly undeserved for he seems to have strayed often from his copy texts. But Badham's transcription of *My beloved spake* in Tenbury 1031 is both significant and reliable (see p. 139, n. 23), and in one instance his efforts provide the only complete copy of a Purcell anthem, that of *I will love thee O Lord* in Mus.Sch. C.40, the only other sources being Och 22, containing just the final chorus (see above), and a bass partbook at Gloucester Cathedral.[78] Presumably Badham's scorebooks date from his tenure at St Paul's, though Mus.Sch. C.40 may be one of the earlier ones: the paper bears the Angoumois fleur-de-lys watermark and 'IHS' countermark, which are encountered less frequently after 1700, and Aldrich is the latest composer represented.

John Cooper, a vicar choral at York Minster from 1715 to 1728, produced several scorebooks of sacred music which eventually found their way into the collection of another singing-man, William Knight, who in turn bequeathed them to his York music colleagues; they apparently remained in the residence of the vicars choral, rather than in the Minster itself, thus avoiding destruction in the fire of 1829, and finally came to reside in the Minster library thereafter.[79] Of greatest significance amongst Cooper's books is Y M14/2(S), containing the earliest score of Purcell's Evening Service in G Minor, with the Gloria of the Nunc dimittis inscribed 'Composed by Mr Rosengrave Junior',[80] probably the son of the Daniel Roseingrave whose anthem Purcell copied in Och 1215. The fact that a 1712 payment record 'to Mr Bardon . . . for pricking Mr Purcells Evening Service in G.♭.'[81] also survives at York lends additional authority to the work's attribution to Purcell, which has sometimes been doubted, though the paucity of early source material is a matter not easily explained. The remains of Bardon's efforts, which presumably consisted of transcription into the Minster partbooks, may be DRc M170, a bass partbook with a York provenance (Cooper's hand is also in evidence).[82]

Another of Cooper's scorebooks, Y M8(S), provides one of the earliest complete texts of *Thy word is a lantern*: several seventeenth-century partbooks contain this work, including Y M1(S) (Gostling's hand); Lbl R.M. 27.a.1–3, 6 and 8 (Braddock's

[77] See, e.g., *Works*, XXVIII (1959), 194–5; Spink, *Restoration*, 84.
[78] Used in the Purcell Society Edition to supply the bass verses; see *Works*, XXVIII (1959), 194–5.
[79] Griffiths, 'Music in York Minster', 635–6.
[80] Griffiths, *Catalogue of the Music Manuscripts in York Minster*, 82.   [81] Cited in ibid., 230.
[82] Crosby, *Catalogue*, 85–6; see also Anthony Ford, 'A Purcell Service and its Sources', *MT* 124 (1983), 121–2.

hand); LI 2–4; and WO A.3.1, 3 and 4; but collectively these do not provide the entire anthem. For the work's completion one or more of several eighteenth-century scorebooks must be considered, such as Y M8(S), Ob MSS Tenbury 1504 (the work of James Hawkins), 1503 (a volume dated 1715 and belonging to John Phipps of Dublin; see Chapter 4) and 789 (*c.* 1715 and associated with Peterborough).[83] Tenbury 789 similarly provides a score of *O Lord rebuke me not*, which survives incomplete in the pre-1700 performing materials DRc C27, C28, C34 and A25; and LI 2–4 (see Table 5.1).

### Performing materials from the provinces

The importance of provincial partbooks and organbooks as Purcell sources should be clear from the several mentioned in the preceding sections, including items from Canterbury (US-NH Filmer 21), Durham, Gloucester, Lincoln, Oxford, Worcester and York (DRc M170). It remains to mention three Purcell anthems (which to greater or lesser degrees survive incomplete) only known today through their preservation in cathedral performing materials: *Hear my prayer O God, O God they that love thy name* and *Thy righteousness O God is very high*. Not surprisingly, manuscripts from Durham Cathedral figure in all three of these works: Durham seems to have established comparatively high standards of manuscript preservation from an early time.[84] The sources of *Hear my prayer O God* include four Durham items: the bass partbooks DRc C27, C28 and C34, copied *c.* 1690–5 by Matthew Owen, and more helpfully the organbook A25, copied *c.* 1695–1710 by William Greggs. Copies at Worcester – the partbooks WO A.3.1–5 (bass, countertenor, tenor, countertenor and bass, respectively) – may be slightly earlier: the work appears in all five books but only WO A.3.2 and 5 contain parts produced *c.* 1684, an early example of a Purcell anthem finding its way into a provincial repertory.[85] There is a partial eighteenth-century score of *Hear my prayer O God* in Lbl Add. 17820, but aside from some variant readings it does not assist in the anthem's completion. The other two anthems (*O God they that love thy name* and *Thy righteousness O God is very high*) survive exclusively in three Durham sources: the bass partbooks DRc C28 and C34, and the organbook A33, another volume in the hand of Greggs, *c.* 1690–1700, which unfortunately provides no evidence of the inner parts for these short full anthems.

---

[83] Spink, *Restoration*, 333–4; see also *Works*, XXXII (1959, rev. 1967), 185–7; and Wood, ed., *A Purcell Anthology*, 103, 105.

[84] See Crosby, *Catalogue*, ix–x and passim; information on copyists and dates of Durham sources derive entirely from Crosby.     [85] Cheverton, *English Church Music*, 429–39; cf. *Works*, XXVIII (1959), 193.

# 6

# *Music for the theatre*

Purcell's career as a theatre composer from 1689 onwards produced no major scorebooks comparable to the great autographs of his earlier years. Printed editions provide the main sources of *Dioclesian* and of Purcell's contributions to the three parts of *Don Quixote*,[1] but apart from the partial autograph of *The Fairy Queen*, a few songs transcribed into the Gresham autograph and a movement in *The Gordian Knot Unty'd* adapted from the suite in G in Lbl Add. 30930 the rest of Purcell's theatre music exists only in non-autograph copies of varying authority. Sources of songs and instrumental movements detached from their theatrical origin are dealt with in Chapter 7, the present chapter being concerned with 'complete' manuscripts of dramatic works in the scribal or repertorial groups listed below:

1.  *Dido and Aeneas*: Ob MS Tenbury 1266; Ktp MR 2–5.3, pp. 1–72
2.  *The Fairy Queen*: Lam 3, Lbl Add. 62671
3.  The 'London E' group: Ooc Ua 34–37; Lam 21 (*King Arthur*), 24 (*Bonduca, Oedipus, Timon of Athens*); Lbl Add. 5337, fols. 2r–21v (*Timon of Athens*), Add. 31447; Cfm 87 (*Circe*)
4.  The 'Chapel Royal' group: Lbl Add. 5333, Add. 31449, Add. 31452, R.M. 24.e.13; Lcm 2230; Cfm 119; US-NYp Drexel 4285.6 (*Oedipus*)
5.  The 'Thames valley' group: Lbl Add. 31453 (*The Indian Queen*); CH Cap. VI/I/I (*Timon of Athens*)
6.  Miscellaneous primary sources: Lbl Add. 5337, fols. 27–42 (*Bonduca*); Ob MS Mus.c.27 (*Theodosius*); Cfm 683; Ob MS Tenbury 785
7.  Other sources: Ob MS Tenbury 1278 (*The Indian Queen*); F-Pc Rés. F. 202 (*King Arthur*)

---

[1] Dates of performance and publication of these works were as follows: *Dioclesian* 1690/1691; *Don Quixote* Parts 1 and 2 1694/1694; *Don Quixote* Part 3 1695/1696. See *Don Quixote: the Music in the Three Plays of Thomas Durfey* (facsimile edn), intro. by Curtis A. Price, MLE A2 (Tunbridge Wells, 1984). *Orpheus Britannicus*, I, provides the best source of Purcell's only contribution to Part 3, 'From rosy bowers'.

SOURCES OF *DIDO AND AENEAS*

Oxford, Bodleian Library MS Tenbury 1266
Knutsford, Tatton Park MR 2–5.3, pp. 1–72

The origins of *Dido* are disputed. The one near-certain fact is that it was performed in 1689 by pupils at a girls' boarding school belonging to Josias Priest, a distinguished dancer and choreographer who worked with Purcell on major projects such as *King Arthur*,[2] but its evident relationship to John Blow's court masque *Venus and Adonis*, subsequently presented at Priest's school in 1684, has led to well-founded arguments that *Dido* might also have followed the same path.[3] No new light is cast on the controversy by the principal musical sources, both dating from the mid-eighteenth century or later, Ob MS Tenbury 1266 and its derivative or close relative Ktp MR 2–5.3, pp. 1–72, copied by Philip Hayes *c.* 1785.[4]

The words of the opera can be found in two sources much earlier than the extant music manuscripts. A folio libretto was printed for the school performance that probably took place in 1689: *An Opera Perform'd at Mr. Josias Priest's Boarding-School at Chelsey. By Young Gentlewomen. The Words Made by Mr. Nat. Tate. The Musick Composed by Mr. Henry Purcell.* This libretto presents *Dido and Aeneas* in three acts of roughly equal length preceded by a prologue: its act divisions do not correspond with the musical sources and no music has survived for the prologue or for six lines of text at the end of Act II, scene 2.[5] In 1700 a reordered and revised version of the 1689 libretto was incorporated in a quarto edition of *Measure for Measure or Beauty the Best Advocate As it is Acted at the Theatre in Lincoln's-Inn-Fields. Written Originally by Mr Shakespear: And now very much Alter'd; with Additions of several Entertainments of Musick*, an adaptation by Charles Gildon. In 1704 the opera was again produced at the Lincoln's Inn Theatre, this time as an 'afterpiece' following a play.[6] The broad outline of the

---

[2] See Chapter 1, n. 25.

[3] See, for example, Bruce Wood and Andrew Pinnock, '"Unscarr'd by turning times"? The Dating of Purcell's Dido and Aeneas', *EM* 20 (1992), 372–90; Curtis A. Price, 'Dido and Aeneas: Questions of Style and Evidence', *EM* 22 (1994), 115–25.

[4] See Nigel Fortune, 'A New Purcell Source', *MR* 25 (1964), 109–13. Two distinguished editors of *Dido* have concluded that Hayes's score was not derived from Tenbury but is a more critical copy of a common original: see Margaret Laurie, *Works*, III (1979), x; Ellen T. Harris, *Henry Purcell's* Dido and Aeneas (Oxford, 1987), 46.

[5] Lcm I.A.20 is the unique copy.

[6] *The Daily Courant*, 29 January 1704: the play was *The Anatomist* (by Edward Ravenscroft, 1697) with 'an additional Masque of Aeneas and Dido, composed by the late Mr Henry Purcell' to be performed that day. *The Anatomist* already included a masque, *The Loves of Mars and Venus*, with music by Finger and Eccles.

**Table 6.1  Oxford, Bodleian Library MS Tenbury 1266: contents**

| Section | Work | Pagination |
|---------|------|------------|
| [1] | Dioclesian | unpaginated |
| [2] | Ode for the Duke of Gloucester's Birth Day | unpaginated |
| [3] | Ode for Queen Mary's Birth Day [Celebrate this festival] | 1–34 |
| [4] | Musick in the Tempest by Mr Henry Purcell | 1–64 |
| [5] | The Loves of Aeneas and Dido Set Mr Henry Purcell | 1–79 |

Section 5: folio, 453 × 279. Watermarks: arms of Strasbourg (bend) with countermark 'J WHATMAN'.

Rastrology: sixteen staves ruled with an eight-stave rastrum, span: 161.5, profile: 10(11.5)10.5(11.5)9.5 (11.5)10(12)10(11.5)10(11.5)10(12)10.

Tenbury and Tatton manuscripts probably derives from the 1704 performance, the only one in which there is any likelihood that the prologue was not included.[7]

In Ob MS Tenbury 1266 *Dido* is the last of five sections (Table 6.1). Each has separate pagination, or no pagination at all, and the score of *Dido* differs from the rest of the volume in paper type, stave ruling and handwriting. The 'J WHATMAN' countermark resembles other examples dating from the last decades of the eighteenth century,[8] so the score may be little earlier than the Tatton manuscript, its authority depending on the faithful copying of an earlier exemplar evidenced by the use of old-fashioned conventions such as the C2 tenor violin clef instead of the modern viola C3, 'incomplete' key signatures and flats or sharps instead of natural signs.[9] Further early sources of the ground 'Ah! Belinda' exist in the first book of *Orpheus Britannicus* (1698) and DRc D9; single-sheet editions of 'Fear no danger' and 'Come away fellow sailors' were published in connection with the 1700 *Measure for Measure*;[10] and an instrumental version of the former song and the prelude to the

---

*The Daily Courant*, 7 April 1704, advertised *The Man of Mode* (George Etheredge's 1676 play) with 'the Masque of Aeneas and Dido in several Musical Entertainments compos'd by . . . Henry Purcell', to be performed on 8 April. See Michael Tilmouth, 'A Calendar of References to Music in Newspapers Published in London and the Provinces (1660–1719)', *RMARC* 1 (1961), 53, 54. *The Anatomist* was also performed on 17 February 1704 with '4 musical entertainments' one of which was *The Loves of Mars and Venus*; if the other 'entertainments' were by Purcell, they were probably the three acts of *Dido*. See Harris, *Henry Purcell's* Dido, 48n.

[7]  See Eric Walter White, 'New Light on Dido and Aeneas', in Holst, ed., *Henry Purcell*, 14–34; Harris, *Henry Purcell's* Dido, 63.

[8]  Compare the countermark to Heawood no. 104 (1784).

[9]  These features are modernised in Ktp MR 2–5.3.

[10]  *Fear no danger to ensue* (Zimmerman, *Catalogue*, 496); *The Saylors Song*, Set by Mr Henry Purcell Sung by Mr Wiltshire, in the Play call'd *Measure for Measure* and exactly engraved by Tho: Cross (Zimmerman, *Catalogue*, 497).

latter appear in the partbooks Cmc F.4.35 (1–5), copied early in the eighteenth century by Charles Babel.[11]

A second group of sources of *Dido* related to libretti from Academy of Ancient Music concerts in 1774, 1784 and 1787[12] consists of the scores Lbl Add. 15979, fols. 2r–62r, and Add. 31450, fols. 57r–116r; a further score, US-Ws W.b.539; and Lam 25, a set of parts dated 1787.[13] These manuscripts belong to the same *stemma* as Ob MS Tenbury 1266, lacking music for the prologue and the end of Act II, but differ in the allocation of parts, a large number of minor details, and the drastic truncation of Aeneas's A minor recitative to provide a brief modulatory passage leading to the Bb opening of Act III. Although their modified version of the work was published by the Musical Antiquarian Society in 1841, the manuscripts of this second group have no value as independent sources but merely reflect a late eighteenth-century enthusiasm for 'improving' upon Purcell.[14]

## SOURCES OF *THE FAIRY QUEEN*

### London, Royal Academy of Music MS 3
### London, British Library Additional MS 62671

The *Fairy Queen* score Lam 3, the only major source of any of Purcell's theatre works to contain autograph passages (Table 6.2),[15] is probably the file copy made for the first series of performances in 1692[16] and mislaid after the 1693 revival.[17] The

---

[11] See Rebecca Herissone, 'The Magdalene College Partbooks: Origins and Contents', *RMARC* 29 (1996), 47–95. Babel's version of 'Fear no danger' interchanges the inner string parts and transposes the viola part up an octave, a procedure that might derive from an authentic set of accompanying string parts.

[12] Harris, *Henry Purcell's Dido*, 125–6.

[13] Another score, J-Tn N4/41, combines elements from both groups of manuscripts; Harris, *Henry Purcell's Dido*, 46, 129–31.

[14] Compare changes made by Arne to *King Arthur*: see Ellen T. Harris, 'King Arthur's Journey into the Eighteenth Century', in *Purcell Studies*, 268–9.

[15] Our identification of Purcell's hand in Lam 3 corresponds closely with that given by Curtis A. Price, *Henry Purcell and the London Stage* (Cambridge, 1984), 330, although the extent of the involvement of FQ2 (Price's 'scribe C') is not recognised there.

[16] For the association of Lam 3 with the 1692 rather than the 1693 performance see Bruce Wood and Andrew Pinnock, '*The Fairy Queen*: a Fresh Look at the Issues', *EM* 21 (1993), 44–62.

[17] *The Flying Post*, 9–11 October 1701: 'The Score of Musick for the Fairy Queen, set by the late Mr Henry Purcel and belonging to the Patentees of the Theatre-Royal in Covent Garden, London, being lost upon his Death; Whoever shall bring the said Score, or a true Coppy thereof, first to Mr Zachary Baggs, Treasurer of the said Theatre, shall have twenty guinea's for the same.' A similar advertisement appeared in *The London Gazette*, 16–20 October 1701, offering a proportion of the 20 guineas for any one or more acts of the opera.

manuscript seems to have remained lost until at least 1728,[18] but inscriptions at the front of the volume identify two later owners: William Savage (1720–89), who studied with Pepusch and from 1748 to 1773 was Master of the Choristers at St Paul's Cathedral, and his pupil R. J. S. Stevens (1757–1837), organist of the Charterhouse and the Temple Church and Gresham Professor of Music.[19]

The greater part of the score is the work of a single competent scribe, FQ1, who seems to have transcribed existing manuscripts containing most of the work apart from introductory and incidental instrumental movements (Illus. 6.1). He left space for these sections and for a few other passages, such as the 'Dance for the 4. Seasons of the year' (fols. 79v–81r) for which no more than a heading was provided. Comparable omissions occur in Lbl R.M. 20.h.8 and smaller gaps in FQ1's copying similarly reflect Purcell's characteristic working methods: the discontinuous bass line of 'Ye gentle spirits' on fols. 42v–43v, for instance, is reminiscent of the autographs of *What a sad fate* and *Since from my dear* in the Gresham songbook, and the incomplete Dance for the Haymakers (fol. 47r) lacks inner parts in the same way as certain works in Lbl Add. 30930 and R.M. 20.h.8. FQ1's confidence about the number of pages to be left for missing movements, together with the fact that sections copied later in other hands fit in more or less exactly to the spaces he allowed, strongly suggests that he was working from autograph material in which Purcell had left blank pages, but FQ1 does not seem to have collaborated closely with the composer and never finished sections Purcell had started. Purcell apparently added passages unfinished when his original score was handed over to FQ1, working with an assistant, FQ2, who copied the chaconne occupying three folios at the reverse of the manuscript: the same hand, distinguishable by G and C clefs different from Purcell's and directs with a prominent ascender, often appears in the Second Music and the act tunes, especially in inner parts, and adds a few titles to sections copied by FQ1 (Illus. 6.2).[20] The First Music was entrusted to the obviously inexperienced FQ3. The manuscript's most problematic passage is from folios 97r to 100r, 'Sure the dull God', copied in evident haste: all literary text and much of the music is in Purcell's autograph, but in places the notation of certain parts seems to be either in a rough form of FQ2's writing or in

[18] Roger North's statement in 'Memoires of Musick' (1728) that *King Arthur* was 'unhappyly lost' must, given the number of extant manuscripts of that work, confuse it with *The Fairy Queen*: see John Wilson, *Roger North on Music* (London, 1959), 353.

[19] Shaw, *The Succession*, 182; *DNB*, XVIII, 1119.

[20] Wood and Pinnock, '*The Fairy Queen*', 46, regard FQ2 as a variant form of Purcell's own writing, added at a later date. There are marked similarities, but the consistency of FQ2 suggests that it is in fact a separate hand modelled on Purcell's.

Table 6.2 London, Royal Academy of Music MS 3, *The Fairy Queen*: sections entirely or partly copied by Purcell

| Works, XII (1968) pages | Movement | Lam 3 folios | Feature (k-s = key signature; t-s = time signature) | Copyist |
|---|---|---|---|---|
| 1–3 | First Music: Prelude | 1v–2v | title: 'Prelude' | HP |
| | | | vn 1 and bass: bar 4 beats 3–4 (on extended staves: inner parts blank) | HP |
| | Air, bars 1–10 | | title: 'Aire' | FQ2 |
| | | | clefs, k-s, t-s of first system | FQ3 |
| | | | other notation of first system | FQ2 |
| | | | clefs, k-s of second system | HP |
| | | | outer parts of second system*ᵃ* | HP |
| | | | inner parts of second system | FQ2 |
| 7 | Air, bars 11–20 | 3v | first system: clefs and k-s of outer parts; notation of vn 1 | HP |
| | | | lower parts | FQ2 |
| | | | second system: all parts except vn 2 | HP |
| | | | vn 2 | FQ2 |
| 8–9 | Rondeau | 3v–4r | title: 'Roundeaux' | HP |
| | | | t-s '3' in all parts | HP |
| | | | all directs in first system | FQ2 |
| | | | outer parts | HP |
| | | | inner parts | FQ2 |
| | | | repeat directions | HP |
| 10–14 | Overture | 4r–5v | title: 'Overture' | HP |
| | | | rubrics: 'Trumpets' and 'violins' | HP |
| | | | clefs, k-s, t-s | HP |
| | | | trumpet parts, bars 1–3 | HP |
| | | | vn 1 bars 1–2 | HP |
| | | | vn 2; va bar 3 | HP |
| | | | bass bars 1–4 | HP |
| 34–5 | First Act Tune | 20v | title: 'first Act Tune' | HP |
| | | | first system: clefs, k-s, t-s | HP |
| | | | outer parts | HP |
| | | | inner parts | FQ2 |
| | | | all directs in first system | FQ2 |
| 65 | Dance for the Followers of Night | 35v | title: 'For Followers of ye Night' | FQ2 |
| 67–8 | second Act Tune | 36r | title: 'Aire' | FQ2 |
| 73–5 | Symphony while the swans come forward | 40r | title: 'Overture' | FQ2 |
| 102–3 | Third Act Tune: Hornpipe | 54v | title: '3d Act Tune' | HP |
| | | | outer parts | HP |
| | | | all clefs of second system; all terminal flourishes | HP |
| | | | inner parts | FQ2 |
| | | | all directs in first system | FQ2 |

## Table 6.2 (*cont.*)

| Works, XII (1968) pages | Movement | Lam 3 folios | Feature (k-s = key signature; t-s = time signature) | Copyist |
|---|---|---|---|---|
| 140–3 | See, see my many-coloured fields | 76r | bar 1: rubric 'Violins' | HP |
| | | 76v | vn parts (but not clefs) from bar 26 | HP |
| | | 77r–77v | bass, including clef, from bar 33 | HP |
| | | | all parts, including text, from bar 38 to bass direct at end of bar 62 | HP |
| 147 | Fourth Act Tune | 81v | title: 'Aire' | FQ2 |
| | | | outer parts | HP |
| | | | inner parts | FQ2 |
| | | | all directs in first system | FQ2 |
| 149–51 | Thrice happy lovers | 82v–83r | bar 1: k-s, rubric 'Juno'; bars 1–27: clefs | FQ1 |
| | | | all other music and text | HP |
| | | | bars 45–6: corrected vocal part | HP |
| 185–90 | Sure the dull God | 97r | all parts from last quaver of bar 5 | HP |
| | | 97v | bars 16–25: all clefs, k-s, vocal parts and text | HP |
| | | | string parts | FQ2 |
| | | 98r | bars 26–9: all clefs except soprano, bass, bc | FQ2 |
| | | | soprano, bass, bc clefs | HP |
| | | | vocal parts and text | HP |
| | | | string parts | FQ2 |
| | | 98v | bars 30–6 beat 2: all clefs | HP |
| | | | Vocal parts and text, bc | HP |
| | | | upper string parts | FQ2 |
| | | 99r | bars 36 beat 3–44: all clefs | HP |
| | | | rubrics: 'Cho', sop. 1, bc | HP |
| | | | 'Cho', all other parts | FQ2 |
| | | | vocal treble in chorus | HP |
| | | | other parts in chorus | FQ2 |
| | | 99v | bars 45–8 beat 2: all clefs | HP |
| | | | vocal treble, bc | HP |
| | | | other parts | FQ2 |
| | | 100r | bars 48 beat 3–52: vocal treble 1, bc | HP |
| | | | all other parts | FQ2 |
| — | — | 107r | 'Finis' | HP |

Folio, 378 × 238. Watermarks: countermark monogram 'PVL' only.

Rastrology: twelve staves ruled with a four-stave rastrum, span: 98, profile: 14(13)14.5(13.5)15.5(13)15.

*The outer parts and final two bars of the inner parts of this movement were initially sketched by Purcell in pale brown ink, later covered in darker notation by himself and FQ2.

Illus. 6.1 Henry Purcell: trio 'They shall be as happy' from *The Fairy Queen*, copied by FQ1. Royal Academy of Music, London, MS 3, fol. 104v

Illus. 6.2  Henry Purcell: the First Music from *The Fairy Queen*, partly autograph and partly copied by FQ2. Royal Academy of Music, London, MS 3, fol. 3v

the hand of yet another assistant. The work of all three copyists FQ1–FQ3 was subject to some degree of checking and revision by Purcell or FQ2, but the unfinished overture was filled in rather later by FQ4 from the version without trumpets in *Ayres, Compos'd for the Theatre.* FQ4 may have had the scorebook in his possession around the time when the Theatre Royal was looking for it, and his involvement deepens the mystery of its disappearance (see Illus. 6.4).

All of Lam 3's 165 folios consist of one type of paper, marked only with the countermark monogram 'PVL'. Most of the volume is bound in regular quires and more than fifty folios are unused; a fragment of the old spine bearing the title 'OP FAIRE QUEEN' is preserved in the modern binding. The number of watermarked and unmarked folios in each quire usually corresponds exactly, showing that odd pages have not been torn out, but three watermarked folios between fols. 101 and 105 lack their unmarked partners, which may have contained an earlier version of the chaconne lying between the present fols. 104 and 105. This suggestion is supported by details of notation: the trio 'They shall be as happy' ends on 104v with both a terminal flourish and a calligraphic pattern apparently used by FQ1 as an examination mark, inexplicable if the trio was meant to lead at once to the chorus based on the same material;[21] the rubric 'chorus' at the end of the trio has been partially erased, removing some of the adjacent stave; and the chorus begins at the top of fol. 105r as if it were a new movement, repeating a time signature redundant unless something different once separated the chorus from the trio.

Fols. 4–37 of Lbl Add. 62671 (formerly British Council MS Op. 45) contain a number of movements from *The Fairy Queen*, mostly derived from printed sources available in the early eighteenth century but including a copy of the overture, complete with trumpet parts, independent of the 1697 *Ayres*. Although the front endpapers bear the countermark 'J WHATMAN', suggesting that the volume's binding and continuous pagination date from the mid-eighteenth century at the earliest, the movements from *The Fairy Queen* are copied on distinctive mould-stained paper with a bend watermark which would not preclude an earlier date. The paper, and some archaic details of notation, suggest that the manuscript represents an attempt made shortly after 1700 to collect as much material from the lost *Fairy Queen* as could be found.[22]

---

[21] On this basis Anthony Lewis's placement of the dance in *Works*, XII (1968) is correct. For a different view see Wood and Pinnock, '*The Fairy Queen*', 55, 57.

[22] See Price, *Henry Purcell and the London Stage*, 331–6.

THE LONDON E GROUP OF SOURCES

Oxford, Oriel College MSS Ua 34–37
London, Royal Academy of Music MSS 21, 24
London, British Library Additional MSS 5337, fols. 2r–21v, 31447
Cambridge, Fitzwilliam Museum Music MS 87

London E, who was responsible for four related scorebooks in the library of Oriel College, Oxford, and several further manuscripts containing music by Purcell and other composers (Tables 6.3 and 6.4), seems to have been at work between 1696, the date of *Pausanias* (Ob MS Tenbury 1175), and 1702, when Leveridge's music for *Macbeth* (Cfm 87, fols. 26r–46r) was performed on 25 November.[23] His elegant calligraphy is not always accurate, but in Lbl Add. 30934 and Add. 31461 he collaborates closely with Daniel Purcell, taking over from the composer in sections of what are otherwise autograph scores (Illus. 6.3). Tenbury 1175, of little importance as a source of music by Henry Purcell, underlines the relationship between London E and Daniel Purcell: the whole of this large manuscript is a single bound volume, and the end of the London E section on p. 79 is followed by a work in Daniel Purcell's autograph, the trumpet song *Arise great dead* from Act V of Richard Steele's *The Funeral, Or, Grief A-la-mode* (1702).[24]

A flyleaf of the *King Arthur* score Lam 21 is inscribed 'The Booke of John Townsend Junr',[25] the same name appearing on the first page of music paper along with the date '1698/9' and the signatures of the later owners 'Savage' and 'R. J. Stevens Charterhouse 1817'. Certain textual details suggest derivation from a theatre file copy resembling the Lam 3 *Fairy Queen*, with rather more care than is apparent in the related source Ooc Ua 35: in bar 9 of 'Woden, first to thee' Lam 21 contains the direction 'single' for the string parts, a feature shared only with the authoritative Ob MS Tenbury 785, and at the end of 'I call, I call' Lam 21 uniquely provides the direction 'Exeunt omnes', a rare indication in a score of *King Arthur* that what follows

---

[23] Robert Ford suggests that London E may have been employed as a copyist or engraver by the publisher John Walsh, because some of the printed theatre parts in the series *Harmonia Anglicana* (1701–6) and the Queen's Theatre act music in Lbl g.15 are engraved in a style resembling his handwriting: see 'Osborn MS 515: a Guardbook of Restoration Instrumental Music', *FAM* 30 (1983), 175–6. There is certainly a general similarity, but London E's distinctive clefs do not appear in the prints even though they seem pre-eminently suitable for engraving.

[24] See Shirley Strum Kenny, ed., *The Plays of Richard Steele* (Oxford, 1971), 96; Curtis A. Price, *Music in the Restoration Theatre* (Ann Arbor, 1979), 171.

[25] John Townsend was possibly related to James Townsend, a Chapel Royal choirboy whose voice changed in 1690: *RECM*, II, 33–4.

## Table 6.3  Sources of Purcell copied by London E

| Folios | Original pagination | Heading or incipit | Ascription |
|--------|--------------------|--------------------|------------|
| **1. Ooc Ua 34** | | | |
| 2r–10v | [1]–18 | The Musick of Oedipus | Mr Hen: Purcell |
| 12r–31v | [1]–40 | Timon of Athens | By Mr HP |
| 32r–46v | [1]–30 | The Musick of Bonduca | Mr H. Purcell |
| Large upright quarto, 368.5 × 257. | | | |
| **2. Ooc Ua 35** | | | |
| 1–86 | [1]–169 | K. Arthur an Opera | By H.P. |
| Large upright quarto, 374 × 262. | | | |
| **3. Ooc Ua 36** | | | |
| 2r–17r | [1]–31 | The Musick in the Tragedy of Circe | by Mr H. Purcell |
| 18r–75r | | The Opera of the Indian Queen | by Mr HP |
| Large upright quarto, 373 × 262. | | | |
| **4. Ooc MS Ua 37** | | | |
| | [1]–40 | The D[uke] of Glouc[ester]s Birthday Song | By Mr Hen: Purcill |
| | [1]–64 | The Yorkshire Song | By Mr Hen Purcil |
| | [1]–3 | The Queens Funerall March Sounded before her Chariot | Mr H Purcel |
| Large upright quarto, 372 × 265. | | | |
| **5. Lam 21** | | | |
| | 1–[196] | K: Arthur An Opera | H Purcell* |
| Folio, 314 × 197. | | | |
| Binding: contemporary inlaid gilt-tooled calf (rebacked), 322 × 203. | | | |
| **6. Lam 24** | | | |
| 1r–27v | [1]–54 | Cantata | Del Bravissimo Stradella |
| | | ['Chi dira che nel veleno' (C minor); | |
| | | 'Deh sgorgate in questo' (D minor); | |
| | | 'Furie del Nero tartaro' (D major); | |
| | | 'Festeggia mio core' (A minor; inc)] | |
| 28r–46v | [1]–38 | The Music of Bonduca | by Mr H Purcell |
| 48r–59v | [1]–24 | The Musick of Oedipus | By Mr Hen Purcell |
| 60r–89v | [1]–60 | The Musick of Timon of Athens | By Mr Hen Purcell |
| 90r–101r | [1]–23 | Benedictus Dominus | Del Bravissimo Stradella |
| 102r–118v | 67–100 | [Cantatas] | [Stradella] |
| | | 'Godi, godi gia bila alma mia' | |
| | | 'Vando venni' | |
| | | 'Dulce Auretta' | |
| | | 'Fulminato han furie' | |
| | | 'Una valta al fin saziatecci' | |
| | | 'Rivolgi gl'occhi' | |
| | | 'Invisibile al mio core' | |
| Folio, 307 × 191. | | | |

## Table 6.3  (*cont.*)

| Folios | Original pagination | Heading or incipit | Ascription |
|---|---|---|---|
| **7. Lbl Add. 5337** | | | |
| 2r–21v | [1]–40 | [Timon of Athens] | |
| Folio: 324 × 204. | | | |
| **8. Cfm 87** | | | |
| 1v–11v | 2–22 | Circe | |
| Folio, manuscript withdrawn for conservation. | | | |
| **9. Ob MS Tenbury 1175, pp. 1–79** | | | |
| | 1–21 | The Duke of Glocest[er's] Birth day Musick | Henry Purcell* |
| | [23]–37 | The Musick in the Play ['When night her purple veil'; unlikely to be by Henry Purcell] | H.P. |
| | 39–57 | Musick in the last Act of the Indian Queen [in fact the concluding masque by Daniel Purcell] | Hen. Purcel* |
| | 59–69 | Musick in the Opera of Cynthia and Endymion | By Mr D[anie]ll Purcell 1696 |
| | 71–9 | Musick in the Tragedy of Pausanius | By Mr D. Purcell |
| Folio, 367 × 265. | | | |
| **10. US-NHb Osborn 515** | | | |
| 15r–16v | | [Incidental music to Timon: bass part only] | Mr Henry Purcell |
| Folio, 318 × 201. | | | |

Watermarks and rastrology

1–4. Oriel College manuscripts: all have twelve staves per page, ruled with a four-stave rastrum.
Ua 34: fleur-de-lys on shield with countermark 'IHS/IVILLEDARY'.
Rastrum span: 91, profile: 11.5(14.5)12.5(14)12.5(13.5)12.
Ua 35, fols. 1–42: fleur-de-lys on shield with factor's monogram 'GVH' and countermark 'IHS/IVILLEDARY'.
Rastrum span: 91.5, profile: 12(14)12.5(14)13(14)12.5.
Ua 35, fols. 43–86: paper as in Ua 34.
Rastrum span: 92, profile: 10.5(15.5)11.5(15)12(15)12.
Ua 36 and 37: paper and rastrology as in Ua 35, fols. 43–86.

5. Lam 21
pp. 1–4: Dutch Lion with countermark 'ID'.
pp. 5–128: arms of Amsterdam with countermark monogram 'SH'.
pp. 129–68: foolscap with factor's mark 'HC' and countermark 'CDG'.
pp. 169–[196]: Dutch Lion with countermark 'HD'.
Four flyleaves at either end: large central watermark largely concealed in the binding.

All pages have twelve staves ruled with a six-stave rastrum:
pp. 1–4 and 129–68: rastrum span: 130, profile: 11(12.5)11.5(11)12(12.5)11.5(12)11.5(12)11.
pp. 5–128: rastrum span: 123.5, profile: 11.5(12)11.5(11)11.5(11)11(11)10.5(11.5)10.5.
pp. 169–[196]: rastrum span: 130.5, profile: 12.5(11.5)12.5(11.5)12(12)12(11.5)12(12)11.5.

**Table 6.3** (*cont.*)

6. Lam 24

fols. 1–47, 54–61, 94–101: arms of Amsterdam with countermark monogram 'PVL'.
fols. 48–53, 72–89: Dutch Lion with countermark cursive 'HD'.
fols. 62–71: arms of Amsterdam with countermark 'DP'.
fols. 90–3, 102–19: Dutch Lion with countermark monogram 'PVL'.

All pages have twelve staves except fols. 28r and 60r, which belong to specially ruled bifolia with the top four staves of the first recto omitted for decorative headings.

| Folios | Staves in rastrum | Rastrum span | Rastrum profile |
|---|---|---|---|
| 1–27, 90–3, 102–19 | 4 | 83 | 11.5(12)12(11.5)12(11.5)12 |
| 28–9, 60–1, 94–101 | 4 | 82 | 11(12)11.5(12)11.5(12)12 |
| 30–47, 54–4, 62–71 | 6 | 126.5 | 11(11)12(11)12(12)13(10)11.5(12)11 |
| 48–53, 72–89 | 4 | 80 | 11(11.5)11(12.5)11(12)10.5 |

7. Lbl Add. 5337, fols. 2–21

Lion, not of traditional Dutch pattern, with countermark 'GOB'; compare Heawood no. 3158, dated 1698. Twelve staves ruled with a six-stave rastrum, span: 130.5, profile: 11.5(11.5)12(11.5)12(12)12.5 (11.5)13(9.5)12.5.

8. Cfm 87: unavailable

9. Ob MS Tenbury 1175

Angoumois fleur-de-lys with countermark 'LVG'. Sixteen staves ruled with a four-stave rastrum, span: 71, profile: 10(10)10(10)10(11)10.

10. US-NHb Osborn 515, fols. 15–16

Dutch Lion with countermark 'IW'. Twelve staves ruled with a four-stave rastrum, span: 83, profile: 11(13.5)11(13)10.5(13)11.

*ascription not in London E's hand

is in fact another scene. Lam 21 is the primary 'complete' source of *King Arthur*, possibly connected to one of the revivals that took place between 1692 and 1699,[26] but even so must be several stages removed from Purcell's original and contains serious faults, for example in 'Come if you dare'[27] and in the first main cadence of 'Our natives not alone appear'.[28] The division in this manuscript, Ooc Ua 35 and Lbl Add. 31447 of the first and second stanzas of 'How happy the lover' between Acts IV and V must result from a failure to appreciate that an instruction such as 'The end of

[26] See *Works*, XXVI (1971), viii.
[27] Laurie, 'The "Cambury" Purcell Manuscript', in *Irish Musical Studies 5*, ed. Patrick F. Devine and Harry White (Dublin, 1996), 262–71; *Works*, XXVI (1971) 178–9.
[28] *Works*, XXVI (1971), 203.

**Table 6.4 Music by composers other than Purcell copied by London E**

| Manuscript | Headings, titles and attributions |
| --- | --- |
| Lg G.Mus 458 | St Caecilias Song for the Yeare 1698 By Mr Dan: Purcell |
| Lcm 988 | Daniel Purcell: *The Grove, or Love's Paradise* (1700) |
| Lcm 989 | A Song on the Anniversary of Her Royal Highness Princess Ann of Denmarke Composed by Daniell Purcell Anno 1697/8 |
| Lbl Add. 30934 fols. 39v–50r | Daniel Purcell, Song on her Royal Highness Birth Day Feb:6th 1699/1700 [part] |
| Lbl Add. 31461 fols. 52v–53r | Chorus of Daniel Purcell, *I will sing unto the Lord* |
| Cfm 87 | |
| fols. 26r–43r | The Musick of Macbeth sett by Mr Leveridge [1702] |
| fols. 44r–77r | The Musick in the Opera of the Rivall Queens [Daniel Purcell and Godfrey Finger: 1701] |
| fols. 78r–122v | The Musick of the Virgin Prophetess by Mr Finger [1701] |
| fols. 123r–170r | Mr Dan[ie]ll Purcells Prize Musick [from Congreve's *The Judgement of Paris*, 1701] |
| US-NHb Osborn 515 fols. 17r–18r | Daniel Purcell: unidentified theatre suite [bass part only] |

See also Table 6.3 for works incorporated in bound volumes with music by Henry Purcell.

the 4th Act' added to an earlier source meant that the rest of the passacaglia was to be cut.[29]

Ooc Ua 34–37, acquired in 1786 as part of the bequest of Edward, fifth Lord Leigh, are interrelated in paper type, rastrology and binding and represent a systematic attempt to collect Purcell's dramatic music and other late works. Though copied on large, good-quality paper (with the exception of Ooc Ua 35, fols. 1–42, all of a single type), the books are roughly cut and folio dimensions vary considerably: both kinds of paper were made by Jean Villedary, whose full surname appears in the countermark in a manner more characteristic of the eighteenth than the seventeenth century.[30]

The Oriel scores provide important sources of *King Arthur* (Ooc Ua 35) and *The Indian Queen* (Ooc Ua 36, fols. 18–75). Ooc Ua 35, like Lam 21 and Lbl Add. 31447, seems mainly to represent an uncritical transcription of an existing theatre score, though 'You say 'tis love', omitted from Lam 21, probably came from a

[29] See Andrew Pinnock, 'King Arthur Expos'd: a Lesson in Anatomy', in *Purcell Studies*, 255–6.
[30] A few examples nevertheless date from the 1690s: see Lbl Add. 31472, a source of continental music copied in Oxford by Francis Smith (d. 1698), and Churchill nos. 27 (1691); 363 (1694).

Illus. 6.3  Daniel Purcell: a section of *Song on her Royal Highness Birth Day* (1700), partly autograph and partly in the hand of London E. British Library Add. MS 30934, fol. 43r

separate manuscript.[31] For *The Indian Queen*, Ooc Ua 36 provides an almost complete copy including Daniel Purcell's Act V masque. In Ismeron's recitative 'Ye twice ten hundred deities' bars 12–17 are given in a distinctive version otherwise found only in Lbl Add. 31453, where they were later altered to conform with other sources; bars 13–15 lack harmonic direction, the bass moving in semibreves from B♮ to G and back again, and appear to have been adapted to permit a climactic G above middle C at the beginning of bar 15. This clumsy change was probably introduced when Ismeron was performed by a singer other than Richard Leveridge, with whom the role was closely associated and whose range does not seem to have extended so high.[32] Apart from the omission of overtures and act music usual in 'complete' sources of the dramatic operas, Ooc Ua 36 lacks the Act IV song 'They tell us that you mighty powers above' originally performed by Letitia Cross:[33] the four-part instrumental arrangement of the song is present (fols 50v–51r), but precedes the direction 'The end of the 3d Act', and the first section of the fifth act up to Daniel Purcell's masque is designated as 'The IIIIth Act'. Lbl Add. 31447, copied by FQ4 (Illus. 6.4), consists of paper identical with the main type of Ooc Ua 34–37, and the rastrum used for fols. 2–107 resembles that of Ua 34.[34] The contents of the first section of Add. 31447 (fols. 2r–64r, originally paginated [1]–125) correspond exactly with Ooc Ua 34–36, and readings are often strikingly similar,[35] though in some cases it appears more likely that the two sources are parallel than that one was copied from the other. The identity of paper type between the Oriel collection and Add. 31447 strongly suggests that all five manuscripts date from the same period, and FQ4's consistent use of natural signs perhaps points to copying in the first decade of the eighteenth century rather than *c.* 1696–1702 as implied by London E's datable manuscript work.[36]

---

[31] This dialogue, headed in the word-book 'SONG by Mr. *HOWE*', was not part of Dryden's text and does not always appear in the same place in the music manuscripts. Dr Margaret Laurie points out that its tonal progression from G minor to G major confirms that it belongs where it is printed, between 'Fairest Isle' in B♭ and the C major of the conclusion.

[32] Olive Baldwin and Thelma Wilson, 'Purcell's Stage Singers', in *Performing the Music*, 280.

[33] According to the unauthorised *The Songs in The Indian Queen: as it is now Compos'd into an Opera. By Mr Henry Purcell* (London, 1695), *Orpheus Britannicus*, II (London, 1702) and Lbl Add. 31453: see *Works*, XIX (1994), xiii, 171. See also Baldwin and Wilson, 'Purcell's Stage Singers', 124–5.

[34] For further details of Lbl Add. 31447 see pp. 173–5.

[35] A close textual relationship between Ooc Ua 34–36 and Lbl Add. 31447 is noted in *Works*, II (1994), xiv–xv; XIX (1994), xxvii; XXVI (1971), xi.

[36] The natural sign was introduced to England in *Musica Oxoniensis* (1698), a small collection of songs by Richard Goodson and John Weldon published by Francis Smith and Peter de Walpergen.

Illus. 6.4  Henry Purcell: the Frost Scene from *King Arthur*, copied by FQ4. British Library
Add. MS 31447, fol. 33r

## THE 'CHAPEL ROYAL' GROUP OF SOURCES

London, British Library Additional MSS 5333, 31449, 31452
London, British Library Royal Music 24.e.13
London, Royal College of Music 2230
Cambridge, Fitzwilliam Museum Music MS 119

Many of Purcell's major stage works appear in manuscripts in three interrelated hands directly or indirectly linked with the court and Chapel Royal: London A; the composer William Croft; and a collaborator with Croft, London F.[37] All three appear in Lbl Add. 31452, where London A entered the last work in the score, Jeremiah Clarke's *Barbadoes Song*,[38] and compiled a table of contents on fol. iii$^v$, featuring his usual idiosyncratic spelling (Table 6.5): if London A is to be identified with Francis Pigott the manuscript must have been copied between 1696, the date of Blow's *Hail thou infant year*, and 1704 (Table 6.6).

The most extensive copying by Croft in this group of manuscripts occurs in Lbl Add. 5333, which contains scores of *King Arthur*, the Yorkshire Feast Song and *The Libertine* (Table 6.7). All the copied music paper in the volume is of a single type, but its collation, in large quires corresponding to significant sections of music, shows that Croft and London F worked on loose sheets in the same way as in Lcm 2230. Titles and annotations were inserted on double sheets of plain paper, or on music paper of a different kind from the rest of the volume. Though the collation shows that its contents are intact, Lbl Add. 5333 contains a drastically shortened version of Acts IV and V omitting 'Two daughters of this aged stream', the second stanza of 'How happy the lover' and everything between 'Round thy coast' and the Grand Chorus. Like Lcm 2230, Lbl Add. 5333 may well date from the seventeenth century: the countermark 'DS' occurs in Lbl Add. 17840, which was substantially complete before 1698 and at the end of Purcell's autograph of *Who can from joy refrain*, Lbl Add. 30934, fols. 80–93.[39]

---

[37] London F's hand in Lcm 2230 and Cfm 119 has been mistakenly identified with that of William Isaack: see Lionel Sawkins, '*Trembleurs* and Cold People: How Should they Shiver?', in *Performing the Music*, 253; Bruce Wood, 'A Note on Two Cambridge Manuscripts and their Copyists', *M&L* 56 (1975), 308–12.

[38] Thomas F. Taylor, *Thematic Catalog of the Works of Jeremiah Clarke* (Detroit, 1977), 31–3. The Lbl Add. 31452 copy is incomplete; the score in Lcm 1106 is also in the hand of London A.

[39] D-Hs ND VI 3103 was apparently copied from Add. 5333 in the eighteenth century: it contains the same three works but has cross-references to *Orpheus Britannicus* for published movements. See Richard Charteris, 'Newly Discovered Sources of Music by Henry Purcell', *M&L* 75 (1994), 16–32.

### Table 6.5 London, British Library Additional MS 31452: original table of contents, fol. iii[v]

| | | |
|---|---|---|
| Maske | Mr HP | 1 |
| [pencil: Mask in Timon of Athens] | | |
| Duke of Gloster's Berth day | HP | 33 |
| Bonduca | HP | 60 |
| Oedipus | HP | 83 |
| Dr Blows Opera | Dr B | 105 |
| [pencil: Welcome ev'ry guest] | · | |
| A Bearth Day Song | dr B | 155 |
| [pencil: Hail thou infant year] | | |
| Barbadoes Song [inc] | Mr JC | 178 |
| [pencil: Bring Sheaperds bring the Kids | Dr Blow | 137] |

### Table 6.6 London, British Library Additional MS 31452: contents

| Folios | Contents and inscriptions | Copyist |
|---|---|---|
| i | Bookplate of 'James Kent, Trin. Coll. Camb' pasted to modern flyleaf | |
| ii | Bookplate of Julian Marshall pasted to modern flyleaf | |
| iii[v] | Original table of contents (see Table 6.5) | London A |
| iv | signature: 'Ja: Kent' | |
| 1r–14v | 'Masque in Timen of Athens by Mr Henry Purcell' | London F |
| 14/i–14/ii | [unused] | |
| 15r–28r | 'Ode for the Duke of Gloster's birth day' | London F |
| 28v–39v | 'Bonduca by Mr Henry Purcell' | London F |
| 40r–46r | Oedipus 'Mr Henry Purcell' | London F |
| 46/i–46/ii | unused | |
| 47r–54r | Welcome, welcome every guest [index: Dr Blow] | Croft |
| 54v–61r | The nymphs of the wells [index: Dr Blow][a] | Croft |
| 61/i | [unused: arms of Strasbourg watermark] | |
| 62r–70r | Bring shepherds bring the kids [index, pencil: Dr Blow] | Croft |
| 71r–82r | Hail thou infant year [index: Dr Blow] | Croft |
| 82v–100r | Barbadoes Song [index: J[eremiah] C[lark]] | London A |

Folio, 379 × 241. Watermarks: Angoumois-style fleur-de-lys with countermark 'AA'.

Rastrology: twelve staves ruled with a four-stave rastrum, span: 97, profile: 14(13)14(14)14(13)15.

[a]Covered by the ascription 'Dr Blows Opera' on fol. iii[v].

**Table 6.7 London, British Library Additional MS 5333: contents**

| Folio | Contents and inscriptions | Copyist |
|---|---|---|
| 1r [unruled] | Pasted label bearing signatures 'Wm Croft'; 'Ja: Kent' | |
| 2r [unruled] | Signature: 'Wm Croft' | |
| 3r | 'The Opera of King Arthur Compos'd by ye Late famous Mr H. Purcell who Departed this life Novem: ye 22d 1695 in ye 37th year of his age' | Croft |
| 4r–18v | King Arthur: Act I | London F |
| 19r–34r | King Arthur: Act II | Croft |
| 35r–46v | King Arthur: Act III | London F |
| 47r–50v | King Arthur: Act IV (Passacaglia only) | Croft |
| 50v–56v | King Arthur: Act V | London F |
| 57r–61v | The Libertine | London F |
| 61/i–ii | unused | |
| 62r [unruled] | 'A Song compos'd by Mr H: Purcell for ye Yorkshire Feast Anno Dñi [—]' | |
| 62/i | unused | |
| 63r–83r | Yorkshire Feast Song | Croft |

Folio, 360 × 230. Watermarks: crude fleur-de-lys on shield without countermark (fols. 1, 2, 62); fleur-de-lys without shield countermarked 'H' (fols. 3, 3/i, 4/i, 4/ii, ruled paper not used for music, 4/i, 4/ii misplaced); fleur-de-lys without shield countermarked 'DS' (all other music pages). Collation: A–C² (fols. 3–4/ii); D¹² (fols. 5–16); E² (fols. 17–18; end of Act I); F¹⁶ (fols. 19–34; Act II); G¹² (fols. 35–46; Act III); H¹⁰ (fols. 47–56; Acts 4 and 5); I⁸ lacking 1 (fols. 57–61/ii; *The Libertine*); J² lacking 1 (fol. 62); K²⁴ lacking 1 (fols. 62/i–83; Yorkshire Feast Song)

Rastrology: twelve staves ruled with a four-stave rastrum, span: 96.5, profile: 14.5(13)14.5(12.5)14(13.5) 14.5.

Lcm 2230 consists of five discrete sections (Table 6.8); the third of these contains no music, although a heading, mostly cut off when the book was bound, was written at the top of fol. 62r. All sections but the second, which is made up of two quires, are a single quire of manuscript paper: copying always begins on the second or a subsequent folio, probably because extra sheets had to be wrapped around a quire started normally on the first recto to allow each work to be completed. The papers of the first section, the Blow *Te Deum and Jubilate*, and the fourth section, Act II of *The Indian Queen*, are identical, and the watermarks of the unused music pages are the same as those of three of the unruled pages inserted between the music quires. The manuscript's 'ID' and 'SH' monogram papers also appear in London E's *King Arthur* score Lam 21, dated '1698/9', and Croft's inscription on the second flyleaf shows that binding took place before the end of 1700. As in Lbl Add. 5333 Croft and London F worked together, Croft contributing a single page to the first section otherwise in

## Table 6.8  London, Royal College of Music MS 2230: contents

| Folios | Contents and ascription | Copyist |
|---|---|---|
| [ii] | Inscription 'Wm Croft's Booke 1700' | |
| 1r–27v | *Te Deum and Jubilate* Dr John Blow [preceded by three unused music pages] | London F: 27r and text of 27v, Croft |
| 28–28/i | unruled | |
| 29 | ruled: unused | |
| 30r–60v | *Great Quire of Heaven* Dr Blow | London F |
| 61 | unruled | |
| 62–81 | ruled: unused, but heading cut off on 62r | |
| 82 | ruled: unused | |
| 83r–91v | *The Indian Queen* Act II | Croft |
| 92 | ruled: unused | |
| 93r–99r | *The Indian Queen* Act V | London F |

Folio, 313 × 199. Binding: contemporary inlaid blind-tooled calf, 319 × 200.

Watermarks

| 1. | fols. 1–27 and three preceding folios: Dutch Lion with countermark 'ID' (as section 4) |
|---|---|
| 2. | fols. 29–60: arms of Amsterdam with countermark 'VHS' |
| 3. | fols. 62–81: arms of Amsterdam with countermark 'HD' |
| 4. | fols. 82–91: Dutch Lion with countermark 'ID' (as section 1) |
| 5. | fols. 92–9: arms of Amsterdam with countermark monogram 'SH' |

front flyleaves, i–ii; rear flyleaf: foolscap with countermark monogram 'HK'
unruled folios, 28, 28/i, 61: arms of Amsterdam with countermark 'HD' as fols. 62–81

Rastrology: twelve staves, ruled with six-stave rastra

| Paper | Rastrum span | Rastrum profile |
|---|---|---|
| 1, 4 | 130 | 11(12)11.5(12)11.5(12)12(11)11.5(12.5)11 |
| 2 | 122.5 | 11(11.5)11(11.5)11.5(11)11(11)11(11)10.5 |
| 3 | 126 | 11.5(11.5)11.5(12.5)11(11.5)11.5(12.5)11(10.5)11 |
| 5 | 123.5 | 10.5(11.5)10.5(11)11(11)11.5(11)11(12)11.5 |

London F's hand.[40] The large scorebook Cfm 119 (Table 6.9), entirely by London F, is a major collection of Purcell's works possibly dating from after 1706;[41] in *The Indian Queen*, Cfm 119 is the only manuscript to contain a text of 'Ye twice ten hundred deities' related to the second edition of *Orpheus Britannicus*, Book I (1706), the first publication to include the string parts of this song. For *King Arthur* the two

---

[40] Fol. 27r: he also wrote the text of fol. 27v.
[41] Contrary to J. A. Fuller-Maitland and A. H. Mann, *Catalogue of Music in the Fitzwilliam Museum, Cambridge* (London, 1893), 73, Croft's hand does not appear in Cfm 119.

## Table 6.9 Cambridge, Fitzwilliam Museum Music MS 119: contents

| Pages | Headings, comments and incipits |
| --- | --- |
| 1–55 | A Song Sett by Mr Henry Purcell For St Caecelias Feast [*Hail bright Cecilia*]; 'Finis Mr Henry Purcell for ye 22 of Frebruary 1695' [p. 55] |
| 56–85 | A Song Sett for ye Yorkshire Feast by Mr Henry Purcell |
| 86–102 | Masque in Timen of Athens |
| 103–42 | Musick in ye Iindian Queen Opera |
| 143–8 | [unused] |
| 148bis–215 | The Opera of King Arthur by Mr Henry Purcell |
| 216–33 | A Song for ye Duke of Gloster's birth Day July ye 24: 1695 |
| 234–42 | Musick in Oedipus |
| 243–56 | Musick in Bonduca |
| 257–64 | The Libertine |
| 265–82 | A Song for King James birth day/by Mr Henry Purcell ['Sound ye Trumpett Beat ye Drum'] |
| 283–6 | [unused] |

Folio, 397 × 264. Watermarks: elongated fleur-de-lys on shield with countermark 'IV'.
Rastrology: sixteen staves ruled with a four stave rastrum, span: 80, profile: 10.5(12)10.5(12.5)10.5(12)11.5.
One flyleaf at either end: watermark simple fleur-de-lys.

Copyist: London F

---

'Chapel Royal' sources seem to descend from the same faulty original material as the 'London E' group.

Lbl Add. 31449 is one of three related dramatic opera manuscripts in which music copied by London A is combined with an acting text in a different hand: the others are Lbl Add. 15318, a score of *The Island Princess* (1699), and Lcm 862, Finger's *The Virgin Prophetess* of 1701. Although both music and text pages in Lbl Add. 31449 are made of similar paper marked with a simple fleur-de-lys and the initials 'CDG', the watermarks are not identical and the ruled and unruled papers came from a different stock (Table 6.10). The attempt to interleave text and music was not wholly successful, much of the text of Act II, for example, preceding the music it should follow: the text hand also copied the prologue and the recitative section of 'Ye twice ten hundred deities', although both are set to music, and gave a cue for a song at the beginning of Act III (fol. 32v) for which no music is apparently provided. Lbl Add. 31449 differs from all other early scores of Purcell's theatre music except Lam 3 in including all the introductory, dance and act music, but a few of the instrumental movements are suspect: the final section of the Act II symphony is clearly corrupt; a dance given at the end of Act II is probably by Daniel Purcell, and another at the beginning of Act III is a poor arrangement of an air from the Second Music in *The*

### Table 6.10  London, British Library Additional MS 31449: paper and rastrology

Folio, 362 × 234. Watermarks: simple fleur-de-lys with countermark 'CDG'; different watermark pairs in ruled and unruled pages. Endpaper (fol. 69/i): cursive monogram countermark.
Rastrology: sixteen staves ruled with a four-stave rastrum, span: 72, profile: 9.5(11)10(11)10(10.5)9.5.

Copyist: London A

*Fairy Queen.* Lbl Add. 31449 has been regarded as the earliest source of *The Indian Queen*, perhaps dating from a revival in 1696 for which Daniel Purcell's masque was written,[42] but certain features may suggest a slightly later date: a number of text pages in Lbl Add. 15318 are made of the same paper type as those of Lbl Add. 31449 and the cast list on fol. 1r identifies James Bowen, who played the God of Dreams, as 'Mr Bowen' rather than 'the boy' although the part is definitely for a treble. Bowen appeared as an adult singer in a concert at York Buildings in May 1698 and took a countertenor part in *The Island Princess*.[43]

Two further Purcell stage works survive in London A's hand. A score of the masque from *Timon of Athens* is bound into Lbl R.M. 24.e.13 as pp. 62–110 and paginated internally 1–49: the two treble singers are named as 'George' and 'Jacob';[44] and on p. 101 the bass part of 'Come let us agree' is headed 'Lev:', presumably identifying Richard Leveridge. A preceding six-folio quire of eighteenth-century paper (pp. 51–61) contains a title page and an incomplete, probably spurious, overture. US-NYp Drexel 4285.6 is a score of the music from *Oedipus*.[45]

## THE 'THAMES VALLEY' MANUSCRIPTS

### London, British Library Additional MS 31453
### Chichester, West Sussex Record Office MS Cap. VI/I/I

Two significant early sources of Purcell's dramatic music can be linked with Oxford or the musical establishments of St George's Chapel, Windsor, and the nearby Eton

---

[42] *Works*, XIX (1994), xiii. Daniel Purcell's masque is datable from *Deliciae Musicae...With the Additional Musick to the Indian Queen, by Mr. Daniel Purcell, as it is now Acted at His Majesties Theatre . . . The First Book of the Second Volume* (London, 1696); this publication was advertised in *The Post Boy* on 3 March 1696.

[43] Baldwin and Wilson, 'Purcell's Stage Singers', 124.

[44] One of the trebles may have been George Pack: see *Works*, II (1994), x, xiii.

[45] The University of London Library holds a photocopy.

College. CH Cap. VI/I/I (see pp. 121–3 and 260–1) was started by John Walter before 1680 and belongs to the 'Court' group of song sources, but amongst material added in another hand after Walter was appointed organist and *informator choristarum* at Eton is a copy of *Timon of Athens* related to the Chapel Royal group. The guardbook Lbl Add. 31453 contains two scores with evident Windsor connections: William Isaack's copy of *Hail bright Cecilia*, and Blow's *Venus and Adonis* copied by John Walter. Fols. 40–83 contain *The Indian Queen* copied by Oxford B, who assisted Purcell in writing out parts for *My song shall be alway* in Och 1188/9 (Table 6.11): the manuscript includes the Act V masque headed, in a different hand, 'Additional Act by Mr Daniel Purcel (Mr Henery Purcell being dead)'. Bars 12–17 of 'Ye twice ten hundred deities' were originally given in the modified version found in Ooc Ua 36 but were subsequently corrected to conform with the 'Chapel Royal' sources: this alteration must have been made before the period 1702–7 during which *The Indian Queen* was transcribed from Lbl Add. 31453 into John Dolben's manuscript now D-Hs ND VI 3101[46] by the Oxford copyist William Saunders.

MISCELLANEOUS PRIMARY SOURCES

London, British Library Additional MS 5337, fols. 27–42
Oxford, Bodleian Library MSS Mus.c.27; Tenbury 785
Cambridge, Fitzwilliam Museum Music MS 683

Four manuscripts which do not fall into the groups outlined above are very early sources of the music they contain. The score of *Bonduca* (1695) incorporated in Lbl Add. 5337 as fols. 27–42 (Table 6.12) is written in a hand of distinctly seventeenth-century appearance. A four-folio quire in the guardbook Ob MS Mus.c.27 headed 'Songs in Theodosia by Mr Hen: Purcell' contains the ceremonial scene from Act I of *Theodosius* (1680), for some of which this manuscript is the only early source (Table 6.13). Both sheets of paper have fleur-de-lys watermarks consistent with a date *c.* 1680, the first with the complex monogram countermark 'PSAB' and the second 'IHS/ET'. The pages show signs of considerable wear and tear, and fol. 33 has been extended by pasting a large piece of paper to its lower half to enable the whole chorus 'Prepare, prepare the rites begin' to be copied on one side, 33r.

Cfm 683 and Ob MS Tenbury 785, identical in paper type and ruling, are

---

[46] *Works*, XIX (1994), xxvii.

### Table 6.11  London, British Library Additional MS 31453, fols. 40–83: paper and rastrology

Folio, 325 × 200. Watermarks: arms of Amsterdam without countermark.
Rastrology: twelve staves ruled with a six-stave rastrum, span: 131, profile:
11.5(12.5)12(11.5)12.5(11.5)13(10)12(12)11.5.

Copyist: Oxford B

### Table 6.12  London, British Library Additional MS 5337, fols. 27–42: paper and rastrology

Folio, 331 × 204. Watermarks: Dutch Lion with countermark 'AI'.
Rastrology: twelve staves ruled with a six-stave rastrum, span: 128.5, profile:
11.5(11.5)11.5(11.5)12(12)11.5(12)11(12)11.

### Table 6.13  Oxford, Bodleian Library MS Mus.c.27, fols. 33–6: paper and rastrology

Folio, 361 × 234 (fol. 34, the only intact and unextended folio). Watermarks: Angoumois fleurs-de-lys countermarked with complex monogram 'PSAB' (fols. 33–4) or with 'IHS/ET' (fols. 35–6).
Rastrology (both papers): fourteen staves: twelve ruled with a four-stave and two with a two-stave rastrum; four-stave rastrum, span: 87, profile: 12.5(12)13(12.5)13(11.5)13; two-stave rastrum, span: 38, profile: 13(12)12.5.

survivors from a larger volume in which the former constituted pp. 115–72 and the latter continued from p. 173.[47] As well as most of the first act of *King Arthur* they contain other theatre music in performing order, including songs as well as instrumental movements (Table 6.14), and are probably related to productions in 1690 and 1691. Ob MS Tenbury 785 is the best source of its *King Arthur* passage, and the copyist's abrupt termination of his work on fol. 24r, at the end of bar 122 in 'Come if you dare', is as unfortunate as it is inexplicable. On fol. 24v an incomplete score of Bassani's *Ave verax honor* begins, in a different music hand but with the text written by the *King Arthur* scribe; from fol. 27r a much later copyist added further Purcell movements, using recto sides only. The poor quality of the paper, characteristic of earlier Dutch imports used in England, supports the date in the early 1690s suggested by the repertory copied in the principal hand.

[47] Laurie, 'The "Cambury" Purcell Manuscript'.

OTHER SOURCES

Oxford, Bodleian Library MS Tenbury 1278
Paris, Bibliothèque du Conservatoire MS Rés. F. 202

Two further sources of dramatic music cast light upon the early history of the music they contain. Ob MS Tenbury 1278, comprising two bifolia stitched into a cover, is a bass part copied for Richard Leveridge in *The Indian Queen*: it includes the complete chorus bass line, as well as the solo sections for the High Priest in Act V and for Hymen in Daniel Purcell's masque, but not the solos for Envy or the conjurer Ismeron, although Leveridge certainly took the latter role in the performance represented by Lbl Add. 31449 and single-sheet prints of 'The Conjurers Song' identify him as its singer.[48] Lbl Add. 31449 may date from *c.*1698, and Ob MS Tenbury 1278 could belong to a previous performance rather than to a later revival: if another singer took the part of Ismeron in the earliest productions, the extended range of 'Ye twice ten hundred deities' given in Ooc Ua 36 and originally copied in Lbl Add. 31453 is more readily explicable.[49] Leveridge's assumption of the role at a later date might have caused the return to Purcell's original version in Add. 31449, where the part of Ismeron is assigned to Leveridge in the *Dramatis Personae*, and in a correction to Add. 31453.[50]

Vincent Novello bought F-Pc Rés. F. 202, a score of *King Arthur*, at Samuel Picart's sale in 1848,[51] a previous owner, who had inscribed the title page verso on 2 December 1805, being one D[anie]l Mumford of 10 Greville Street, Hatton Garden. In certain respects, such as the shortening of the Act IV passacaglia, it resembles the 'Chapel Royal' sources, although its details are generally closer to the London E group. F-Pc Rés. F. 202 includes an unfinished setting of 'St George', the first verse of text for the final chorus,[52] though the omission of this passage from other early

---

[48] The earlier of two single-sheet songs linking 'Ye twice ten hundred deities' with Leveridge is *The Conjurers Song in The Indian Queen, Set by Mr Henry Purcell and Sung by Mr Leveridge* [*c.*1700?], probably derived from the version in *Orpheus Britannicus*. See *Works*, XIX (1994), xxx.

[49] *Works*, XIX (1994), xvi.

[50] Amongst Purcell's identified theatre bass singers only John Bowman had a range corresponding to the altered 'Ye twice ten hundred deities', but Bowman left the United Company before the production of *The Indian Queen*; see Baldwin and Wilson, 'Purcell's Stage Singers', 123, 275–81.

[51] Lbl S.C. Puttick & Simpson 6(1).

[52] See *Works*, XXVI (1971), 205. In F-Pc Rés. F. 202 'St George' lacks the entire bass part: the complete setting included in Edward Taylor's edition for the Musical Antiquarian Society (1843) did not come from US-LAuc fP985/M4/K52/bound, which gives a version of 'St George' derived from the following chorus like that in Ob MS Tenbury 338.

## Table 6.14  Cambridge, Fitzwilliam Museum Music MS 683 and Oxford, Bodleian Library MS Tenbury 785: contents

| Folios | Headings, incipits and ascriptions |
| --- | --- |

**Cfm 683**

| | |
| --- | --- |
| 1r | The Song Sung at ye Yourkshire feast 1689    Compos'd by Mr Pur[cell] |
| 23v | The Musick in ye play call'd Amphitrion. Set by Mr Purcell    1st Musick |
| 23v | 2d Musick; 24r: 'play this last Tune againe after the Prologue' |
| 24v | Overture |
| 25v | 1st Act Tune |
| 25v | 2d Act Tune |
| 26r | Song in the 3d Act for Mr Bowman 'Caelia that I once was Blest' |
| 26v | 3d Act Tune |
| 27r | Song in ye 4th Act for Mrs Butler 'Iris I sigh and hourely dye' |
| 27v | Dance for Tinkers |
| 27v | A Dialogue between Thirses and Iris Sung by Mr Bowman and Mrs Butler 'Fair Iris and her Swain' |

**Ob MS Tenbury 785**

| | |
| --- | --- |
| 1r | 4th Act Tune [from *Amphitryon*] |
| 1v | The Musick in ye distres[se]d Innocence or the Princess of Persia    Mr Purcell |
| 1v | first Musick |
| 2r | 2d Musick |
| 2v | Overture |
| 3v | 1st Act Tune |
| 3v | [2nd] Act Tune |
| 4r | 3d Act Tune |
| 4v | 4th Act Tune |
| 5r | The Musick in the Comedy call'd the Gordian Knot Unty'd    Mr Purcell |
| 5r | 1st Musick 'Chacone' |
| 6r | 2d Musick [Air] |
| 6r | Minuet |
| 6v | Overture |
| 8r | 1st Act Tune |
| 8v | 2d Act Tune 'Rondeau' |
| 9r | 3d Act Tune |
| 9v | 4th Act Tune 'Lilli Burlero' |
| 10r | an Overture in Sr Anthony Love or ye Rambling Lady    Mr Purcell |
| 11r | 1st Song    The Prelude    'over to the Song' |
| 11v | 'Persuing Beauty Men descry' |
| 12v | Dialogue 'No more sr no more Ile enquire' |
| 13v | 3d Song 'In vain Clemene you bestow' |
| 14v | Ground [in E minor][a] |
| 15v | The Musick in K-Arthur or the British Worthey    Mr Purcell [Act I, inc.] |
| 24v | Ave verax honor    Battista Bassani [inc.] |
| 26v | unused |

[from here on copying continues in a much later hand, usually on recto sides of folios only]

**Table 6.14** (*cont.*)

| Folios | Headings, incipits and ascriptions |
|---|---|
| 27r | Jigg in the married Beau |
| 28v | Minuet in Bonduca |
| 29r | Overture in King Arthur [in D minor] |
| 37r | Fugue in the Indian Queen |
| 40r | [Minuet] in Bonduca |
| 42r | Overture in the Virtuous Wife |
| 43r | 2d Overture in the Fairy Queen |
| 46r | Preludio in the Fairey Queen |
| 49r | [Minuet] In the Old Bachelor |

Folio, 320 × 205 (Cfm 683); 320 × 202 (Ob MS Tenbury 785). Watermarks: arms of Amsterdam without countermark.

Rastrology: twelve staves ruled with a six-stave rastrum, span: 131, profile: 12(11.5)12.5(11)12.5(13)12 (12)11.5(11.5)11.

*ª*Attributed to John Eccles in *The Division Violin*, II (1693) and in Lbl Add. 35043.

sources is evidence that it was provided by a different composer. Some sections, such as the four-part symphony to 'Fairest Isle' and the duet 'You say 'tis love', have affinities with early printed editions,[53] but Rés. F. 202 reveals no consistent pattern of relationship either with printed sources or with other manuscripts and, like the 'Chapel Royal' group, appears to represent an attempt to improve upon unsatisfactory existing material. The hand of Rés. F. 202 looks broadly contemporary with that of Croft's collaborator, London F, and the layout of the fourteen staves on each page, drawn by a six-stave and a two-stave rastrum, also suggests a date within fifteen years or so of Purcell's death rather than later in the eighteenth century.

[53] *Works*, XXVI (1971), 200–1. The 'Fairest Isle' symphony shares errors in bars 18 and 21 with *Ayres* (1697); bars 11 and 12 of 'You say 'tis love' have the word-setting of *Deliciae Musicae* (1696) and *Orpheus Britannicus* (1698).

# 7

# *Vocal, keyboard and instrumental music*

## Manuscript sources of vocal chamber music

Apart from the autograph scores Lbl Add. 30930 and R.M. 20.h.8, significant manuscripts of vocal chamber music fall into three well-defined categories. R.M. 20.h.8 stands at the centre of a 'Court' group of sources linked with Whitehall or Windsor (Table 7.1). A second group was copied by identified Oxford musicians (Table 7.4), and a third appears to be associated with the southeastern corner of England, in particular the London Inns of Court and the cathedral cities of Rochester and Canterbury (Table 7.7).

### THE 'COURT' GROUP OF SOURCES

Chichester, West Sussex Record Office MS Cap. VI/I/I
Oxford, Bodleian Library MS Mus.c.28, fols. 100–24
Brussels, Koninklijk Conservatorium MS 1035.g
London, Guildhall Library MS Safe 3

No music from R.M. 20.h.8 appeared in print during the reign of Charles II, and the derivative manuscript B-Bc 1035.g was not copied until *c.*1690. R.M. 20.h.8 is therefore the primary source for much of Purcell's small-scale vocal music up to 1685, though isolated early concordances show that it sometimes contains revisions of existing work rather than new compositions.

The earliest contents of CH Cap. VI/I/I are the songs at either end of the volume, copied by John Walter before he took up his appointment at Eton College (see Table 3.13 and pp. 121–3 above) and therefore part of the 'Court' group of vocal music

**Table 7.1 The 'Court' group of sources**

| Manuscript | Copyists of songs and vocal ensembles | Comments |
|---|---|---|
| Lbl R.M. 20.h.8 | Purcell; London A | major autograph source |
| B-Bc 1035.g | | Purcell works often copied from R.M. 20.h.8: *c.* 1690 |
| CH Cap. VI/I/I | John Walter | songs copied *c.* 1677–80 |
| Lg Safe 3 | Purcell | autograph songs, 1692–5 |
| Ob MS Mus.c.28, fols. 100–24 | John Walter | *c.* 1680 |

sources. *Sleep, Adam, sleep* and *What hope for us remains now he is gone*, Purcell's elegy for Matthew Locke, may well date from the time of Locke's death in 1677, the secretary forms of the lowercase 'e' and 'r' found in these songs apparently representing an early form of Walter's handwriting which underwent a transformation similar to Purcell's.[1] The remaining Blow and Purcell songs were transcribed around 1680, the year identified in the manuscript's title page inscription and the heading of *She loves and she confesses too*, as was Walter's score of Purcell's sacred partsongs, Ob MS Mus.c.28, fols. 100–24 (see pp. 104–6).

Most of B-Bc 1035.g (Table 7.2) is in a single unidentified hand, though a second copyist transcribed two songs from *Amphitryon* (1690) on the initial music page at the reverse. The manuscript was copied from either end, the two sequences of sacred and secular music fortuitously meeting on p. 54 with exactly the required amount of space available. Subsequently the book was rebound, inverting the pages copied from the back so that all the music is the same way up: in the process, the conclusion of *If prayers and tears* on p. 54 INV was separated from the rest of the work and was recopied on the final flyleaf in an eighteenth-century English hand which also added some annotations on the front flyleaf. Stave ruling throughout is in two blocks of six separated by a wide gap in which an extra stave has often been added. Most of the Purcell compositions from *While you for me alone had charms* onwards have headings similar to those in Lbl R.M. 20.h.8 and usually seem to have been copied from the autograph, but printed concordances, and a reference on p. 42 to the coronation of William and Mary, point towards a date after 1689. *It must be done my soul*, the first of three songs on texts by John Norris (1657–1711) attributed to Francis Bragge, is plausibly ascribed to Purcell in Bu 5002. Purcell set Norris's *The Aspiration* in

---

[1] A similar example of Walter's hand appears in the first few pages of an incomplete score of Blow's *Venus and Adonis*, Lbl Add. 31453, fols. 152r–159r. This manuscript appears to have been started before Walter's complete copy of *Venus* in Lbl Add. 22100.

## Table 7.2 Brussels, Koninklijk Conservatorium MS 1035.g: contents

| Page | Headings and incipits | Attribution | Scoring | Text attribution; comments |
|------|----------------------|-------------|---------|----------------------------|
| 1 | Psal:122 ver.1.2.: 'Laetatus sum' | — | S,bc | |
| 2–3 | Psal:71. Part ye First.: 'I to thy wings for refuge fly' | Mr Math: Lock[a] | S,B,bc | 'Mr Sands's para[phrase]' |
| 4–5 | Psal:71. part ye 2d.: 'Now in the winter of my Years' | Mr Math: Lock | S,B,bc | 'Mr Sandys' |
| 6–7 | Psal:137. First part.: 'As on Euphrates Shady banks' | Mr Math: Lock | S,B,bc | 'Mr Sandys' |
| 8–9 | Psal:137. part:2d: 'Remember Edom Lord' | Mr Lock | S,B,bc | 'Mr Sandys. paraph[rase]' |
| 10–11 | Psalm.96.: 'New composed ditties sing' | Mr Lock | S,B,bc | |
| 12–13 | Psalm.93.: 'Now great Jehovah reigne's' | Mr Lock | S,B,bc | |
| 14–15 | Ex Psal.105.: 'Cantate Dominum' | Mr Lock | S,B,bc | 'Buchanan' |
| 16–17 | Ex Psal:55.: 'Lord to my pray'rs incline thine ear' | Mr Lock | S,B,bc | 'Sandys: paraph[rase]' |
| 18–19 | Ex Psal:55.: 'My pray'rs shall w[i]th: ye Suns uprise ascend' | Mr Lock | S,B,bc | |
| 20–1 | Ex Hymno Hildeberti Cenomunensis: 'Urbs Coelestis urbs beata' | Mr Lock | S,B,bc | |
| 22–3 | Ex Epistola quadam Sti: Augustini: 'Quid faciemus' | Mr Lock | S,B,bc | |
| 24–5 | Cant: cap:2: ver: 8:10;11;12;13: 'Vox dilecti' | Mr Lock | S,B,bc | |
| 26–8 | The Meditation: 'It must be done my soul' | Mr Fra Bragge | B,bc | 'Mr Norris' |
| 29–31 | The Arrest: 'Whither so fast fond Passion' | Mr Fra: Bragge | B,bc | 'Mr Norris' |
| 32–3 | The Conquest: 'In Pow'r or wisdom to contend with Thee' | Mr Bragge | B,bc | 'Mr Norris' |
| 34–5 | Cant: cap.5. ver.8,9,16.: 'I charge you O daughters of Jerusalem' | Mr Mich: Wise | S,B,bc | |
| 35–7 | A Paraphrase on the 84 Psalm: 'O how pleasant and how fair' | Mr Mat: Lock[b] | S,bc | |
| 38–41 | Part of the 84 Psalm: 'O how amiable' | Mr Peter Isaac | S,[bc] | incomplete |
| 42–9 | Anthem at the Coronacon of King William and Queen Mary: 'The Lord God is a sun and shield' | Dr Blow | A,T,B, satb | |
| 50–1 | Part of the 25th Psalm: 'Unto thee O Lord' | Sigr: Vesi | S,bc | |
| 52–4 | Part of the 122 Psalm: 'O pray for ye peace of Jerusalem' | Dr Blow | S,satb,bc | |

[manuscript inverted]

| Page | Headings and incipits | Attribution | Scoring | Text attribution; comments |
|------|----------------------|-------------|---------|----------------------------|
| 1 | 'For Iris I sigh and hourly dye'[c] | [Purcell] | S,bc | |
| | 'Celia that I once was blest' | [Purcell] | | |
| 2–3 | Nestor: 'Nestor who did to thrice mans age'[d] | Mr Purcell | S,B,bc | |
| 4–5 | Song for 2 voices: 'Let Hector Achilles and each brave commander' | Mr Purcell | S,B,bc | |
| 6 | 'Begin the Song! Your Instruments advance!' | [Blow] | CT,bc[e] | |
| 7 | 'Bring gentlest thoughts' | [Blow] | CT,bc | |
| 8–9 | 'Hark how the wakened strings resound' | [Blow] | CT,T,bc[f] | |
| 10–12 | The 9th Ode of Horace Imitated. A Dialogue 'While you for me alone had Charms' | Mr Purcell | S,B,bc | |
| 12–15 | A Dialogue between Charon and Orpheus: 'Hast gentle Charon' | Mr Purcell | B,B,bc | |
| 16–26 | Mr Cowley's Complaint: 'In a deep visions Intellectual scene' | Mr Purcell | S,S,B,bc | |
| 27–31 | The Concealment: 'No, to w[ha]t purpose' | Mr Purcell | S,B,bc | 'Mr Cowley' |
| 32–5 | Weeping: 'See where she sits'[g] | Mr Purcell | S,B,bc | 'Mr Cowley'; '2 Violins vid: Simp: Book' |
| 36–40 | Sighs for King Charles the second: 'If pray[e]rs and tears' | Mr Purcell | S,bc | |

[a] In Cfm 163 this and the following eleven works are ascribed to Silas Taylor, probably correctly. See R. E. M. Harding, *A Thematic Catalogue of the Works of Matthew Locke* (Oxford, 1971), 30–4.
[b] In *Cantiones Sacrae*, 1674.
[c] These two songs, from *Amphitryon* (1690), are copied in a different hand from the rest of the manuscript.
[d] This and the following song were published in *Comes Amoris*, III (1689).
[e] This and the following song are copied here with the vocal part an octave higher in the treble clef.
[f] Copied here with both vocal parts an octave higher in the treble clef; expanded from the version published in 1684.
[g] The heading 'Weeping' does not appear in Lbl R.M. 20.h.8 but was used by Pietro Reggio for his setting of the same text published in 1680.

*Harmonia Sacra* of 1688, incorrectly describing the poet as 'of Wadham College, Oxon': he actually belonged to Exeter College before being elected to a fellowship at All Souls,[2] but one Francis Bragge who matriculated at Wadham in 1680 perhaps introduced Purcell to Norris's poetry and composed the second and third Norris settings in B-Bc 1035.g.

The songbook Lg Safe 3 belonged to Gresham College by 1872[3] but was not identified as an autograph until 1911:[4] from 1837 to 1863 the Gresham music professorship was held by the Purcell scholar Edward Taylor, who could hardly have overlooked the manuscript's importance, so it must have been acquired between 1863 and 1872.[5] The watermarks are identical with a pair in the trio sonata set Ob MSS Mus.Sch. E.400–403 (*c*.1685),[6] but the first music Purcell copied is from *The Fairy Queen* (1692), the delay between paper manufacture and use confirming that he acquired the volume as a bound manuscript book. Several songs are unique and others appear in distinctive readings: most are for solo soprano and continuo (Table 7.3), vocal parts originally intended for other voices sometimes simply being written out an octave higher though more often this upward shift of the melody is combined with a downward transposition of the song as a whole. A few duets retain vocal bass parts at their original pitch but in the alto and bass duet *Now the maids and the men* both voices are written out in the treble clef a minor seventh higher than the original; other duets, such as *Turn then thine eyes*, are more or less extensively altered to become soprano solos. A number of continuo parts are completely absent, included only when the voice is silent, or added at a later date in different-coloured ink from the voice part.

These incomplete texts imply that Purcell himself played from the manuscript, and together with its distinctive repertory suggest that it might have been copied in connection with his court employment in the 1690s. In one private concert for Queen Mary, according to Hawkins, he accompanied the singers Arabella Hunt and John Gostling,[7] and the Gresham songbook's soprano solos and soprano and bass duets could have provided some of the music they performed. The book seems to

---

[2] *DNB*, XLI, 132–4.

[3] *Catalogue of Books and Music in the Library of Gresham College* (London, 1972), 46. The entire Gresham collection was placed in the care of the Corporation of London in November 1958 and transferred to the Guildhall Library.

[4] See *Henry Purcell: the Gresham Autograph* (facsimile edn), intro. by Margaret Laurie and Robert Thompson (London, 1995); William Barclay Squire, 'An Unknown Autograph of Henry Purcell', *MA* 3 (1911–12), 6.

[5] An item described as 'H. Purcell. Songs. Contemporary MS' was offered for sale by the London auctioneers Puttick and Simpson on 20 November 1862 and bought by Alfred Whittingham, an Oxford Street music dealer; Lbl S.C. Puttick and Simpson 84(2), lot 141.

[6] One corresponds with Heawood no. 1784, dated 1683.    [7] Hawkins, *History*, II, 564n.

Table 7.3  London, Guildhall Library MS Safe 3 (Gresham autograph songbook): contents[a]

| Folios | Incipit | Source/earliest concordance[b] | Date[c] | Transposition key[d] | voice[e] |
|---|---|---|---|---|---|
| 1r–3v | Now ye maids & ye men[f] | The Fairy Queen | 2/5/92 | F –2 | both+10 |
| 4r–5v | Thus ye Gloomy World | The Fairy Queen | 2/5/92 | B♭ –2 | +10 |
| 5v–6v | Come all yee songsters | The Fairy Queen | 2/5/92 | B♭ –2 | +10 |
| 6v–7r | May ye God of Witt | The Fairy Queen | 2/5/92 | B♭ –2 | +10 |
| 7v–8r | Heark how all things | The Fairy Queen | 2/5/92 | | |
| 8v–10r | Thrice happy Lovers | The Fairy Queen | 2/5/92 | | |
| 10v–11v | I look'd & saw | The Indian Emperor | c. 12/91 | | |
| 12r–12v | Now ye Night is chac'd away | The Fairy Queen | 2/5/92 | | |
| 13r–14r | Hark th'Ecchoing Air | The Fairy Queen | 2/5/92 | | |
| 14r–15r | Turn then thine eyes[g] | The Fairy Queen | 2/5/92 | | |
| 15v–16r | No no poor suff'ring heart | Cleomenes | 4/92 | | |
| 16r–17v | In vain 'gainst Love | Henry the Second | 8/11/92 | | |
| 17v–18r | Yes Daphne in yo[u]r Face | The Fairy Queen | 2/5/92 | | +12 |
| 18v–19v | Corrinna is divinely fair | GJ12/92 | [1/93] | | |
| 19v–20r | Thus to a ripe consenting maid | The Old Bachelor | 3/93 | | |
| 20v–22r | Tis Natures voice | Hail bright Cecilia | 22/11/92 | D –3 | +9 |
| 22v–23r | Thou tuns't this World | Hail bright Cecilia | 22/11/92 | | |
| 23v–24v | The Fife and all ye Harmony of war | Hail bright Cecilia | 22/11/92 | A –5 | +7 |
| 25r–25v | Aprill who till now | Celebrate this festival | 30/4/93 | c –4 | +8 |
| 25v–26r | Departing thus/I envy not | Celebrate this festival | 30/4/93 | | |
| 26v–27r | Kindly treat Maria's day | Celebrate this festival | 30/4/93 | B♭ –2 | –2 |
| 27v–29r | Ah! Cruel Nymph | | | | |
| 29v–34r | Behold ye Man[h] | The Richmond Heiress | 4/93 | | |
| 34v–35v | I see she fly's me | Aurung–Zebe | | | |
| 36r–37r | I love & I must*[i] | | | | |
| 37v–39r | Come let us leave ye Town[j] | The Fairy Queen | 2/5/92 | | |
| 39v–40r | Not all my torments* | | | | |
| 40v–42r | Fair Cloe my Breast[k] | 6BM1692 | [3/3/92] | | |
| 43r | [unused] | | | | |
| 43v–44r | What can wee poor Females doe[l] | 5CAm1694 | [14/12/93] | | |
| 44v–46r | Celia [Cynthia] frowns | The Double Dealer | 11/93 | | |
| 46v–48r | What a sad fate[m] | | | | |
| 48v–50r | When first I saw | Dioclesian [revival] | [c. 2/94] | | |
| 50v–51r | Since from my Dear† | Dioclesian [revival] | [c. 2/94] | | |
| 51v–52r | Sawny is a bonny Lad | GJ1–2/94 | 25/1/94 | | |
| 52v–53r | Leave these useless Arts[n] | Epsom Wells | | | |
| 53v–55r | I sigh'd and own'd my Love | The Fatal Marriage | 2/94 | | |
| 55v–56r | There's not a Swain[o] | Rule a Wife; GJ4/94 | [10/4/94] | | |
| 56v–57r | Strike ye Violl | Come ye sons of art | 30/4/94 | a –5 | +7 |
| 57v–58r | Olinda in ye Shades unseen* | | | | |
| 58v–59r | I fain wo'd be free*† | | | | |
| 59v | I burn [beginning of text][p] | | | | |
| 60r | [unused] | | | | |
| 60v–61r | Ah how sweet it is to love† | Tyrannic Love; DM1695 | [6/5/95] | | |
| 61v–65v | Let ye dreadfull Engines† | Don Quixote Part 1 | 5/94 | | +12 |
| 66r | [unused] | | | | |
| 66v–67r | Lucinda is bewitching fair† | Abdelazar | 1/4/95 | | |
| 67v–68v | Whilst I w[i]th grief†[q] | The Spanish Fryar; DM1695 | [6/5/95] | | |

## Table 7.3 (*cont.*)

| Folios | Incipit | Source/earliest concordance[b] | Date[c] | Transposition | |
|--------|---------|-------------------------------|---------|---------------|---|
| | | | | key[d] | voice[e] |
| 69r | [unused] | | | | |
| 69v–70r | Ah! w[ha]t paines*† | | | | |
| 70v–72r | Tis vain to fly [D. Purcell][r] | 5TM1696 | [2/2/96] | | |
| 72v–73r | What ungratefull Devil [D. Purcell] | Love's last shift | 1/96 | | |
| 73v–75v | [unused] | | | | |
| 77v–76r | Since Cloris the powers†[j] [Courteville] | | | | |

Key to printed concordances

| 6BM1692 | *The Banquet of Music*, Book 6 (advertised 3/3/1692) |
| 5CAm1694 | *Comes Amoris*, Book 5 (advertised 14/12/1693) |
| DM1695 | *Deliciae Musicae* [vol. I], Book 1 (advertised 6/5/1695) |
| GJ | *The Gentleman's Journal* (followed by month and year). Many issues appeared at least a month late. |
| 5TM1696 | *Thesaurus Musicus*, Book 5 (advertised 22/2/1696) |

Oblong quarto, 282 × 212. Watermarks: Angoumois fleur-de-lys with factor's initials 'HC' and countermark 'IP' (resembling Heawood no. 1784).

Rastrology: six staves ruled with a three-stave rastrum, span: 79.5, profile: 15(16)16.5(15.5)16.5.

All songs are for solo soprano and continuo unless otherwise described in the notes below.

* Unique to this manuscript.

† Incomplete: usually lacking all or part of the basso continuo.

[a] This table is mostly derived from that compiled by Margaret Laurie in *Henry Purcell: the Gresham Autograph* (facsimile edn, London, 1995), xii–xiii.

[b] 'Earliest concordances' are given only when they offer evidence of the date of composition.

[c] Dates are of known first performances of major works; those in square brackets are derived from earliest printed sources.

[d] The key named is that in the Gresham songbook: the transposition is measured in semitones down from the key in the complete original work.

[e] Transposition in semitones up or down from the original pitch of the vocal line.

[f] Originally for alto and bass: notated here with both parts in the treble clef. Headed 'Dialogue'. The Gresham version is closer to the print bound with most extant copies of *Some Select Songs as they are Sung in the Fairy Queen* (1692) than to the full score Lam 3: see Bruce Wood and Andrew Pinnock, '*The Fairy Queen*: a Fresh Look at the Issues', *EM* 21 (1993), 49–51.

[g] Originally for S,S,bc.

[h] Headed 'A Dialouge between a Mad Man & Mad Woman'; S,B,bc.

[i] Headed 'Bell Barr': no explanation has been found for this title.

[j] S,B,bc.

[k] S,B,bc.

[l] S,bc; this solo version appears in 5CAm1694 but a duet setting was published in *Orpheus Britannicus*, II (1702).

[m] In A minor, 3/2 time. A radically different version in C minor, 3/4 time, appears in *Orpheus Britannicus*, I (1698).

[n] S,bc: a version for S,B,bc also exists.

[o] An arrangement of the Hornpipe from the First Music in *The Fairy Queen*, in E minor. Early printed editions give the song in G minor, the key of the original hornpipe.

[p] The words 'I burn' appear in Purcell's hand six times beneath the first stave, after which someone else has written four more repetitions and the words 'no more'. The tenfold repetition occurs in John Eccles's 'I burn my Brain consumes to Ashes' in the second part of *Don Quixote*, and it is to this song that the heading of 'Whilst I with grief' on fol. 67v refers.

[q] Headed 'On Mrs Bracegirdle Singing (I Burn &c) in ye play of Don Quixote'.

[r] This and the following song are in Daniel Purcell's hand.

[s] Copied with the manuscript reversed in an unidentified hand.

have been Purcell's own property and for a time to have remained in his family, as two songs near the end were composed and copied by Daniel Purcell.

## THE 'OXFORD' SOURCES

Oxford, Christ Church Mus. 350
Birmingham University, Barber Institute of Fine Arts MS 5002
London, British Library Additional MS 30382

The Oxford manuscripts listed in Table 7.4 contain a number of songs and duets by Purcell, often in apparently early copies. Although no Purcell sources exist in his hand, the Chapel Royal organist Edward Lowe (d. 1682) was probably responsible for introducing much of Purcell's music to Oxford:[8] a few years later, many of the identified Oxford copyists and local composers were members of a music club that met at the Mermaid Tavern, and it is likely that Purcell's compositions were often performed there.[9]

Much the most important of the Oxford sources is Bu 5002 (Tables 7.5 and 7.6), predominantly the work of two main copyists: the first is unknown but the second, responsible for pp. 113–79, is identifiable as Edward Hull, whose work in this manuscript seems to be earlier than his recorded activity at Christ Church in the early 1690s. The elder Richard Goodson, Lowe's successor as Professor of Music and, in due course, as organist of Christ Church, contributed a setting of *All things are hushed* on pp. 86–7, perhaps his own work; Ralph Palmer, composer of *I will magnify thee* beginning on p. 180, was an acquaintance of the younger Richard Goodson in the early eighteenth century, for the first page of the keyboard manuscript Och 1177 bears his inscription 'Mr Palmer hath borrowed Ye folio book of Lessons and Overtures of my Father's writing & others'. The modern binding of Bu 5002 may contain the pages of originally separate books, as the present pp. 94–138 were numbered 1–36 (folios from 1 to 9 and pages from 10 to 36) and there is no obvious reason why pp. 1–93, 139–88 and 189–257 should not also have been distinct volumes, but the whole collection is related and broadly contemporary: several paper types as well as the two principal hands appear in more than one section, and both the paper and the first attribution to

[8] Lowe appears to have been active and in good health until shortly before his death: Och 1127 contains parts in his usual firm and legible hand for Aldrich's act song *Conveniunt doctae sorores*, performed on 7 July 1682. See Peter Holman, 'Original Sets of Parts for Restoration Concerted Music', in *Performing the Music*, 271.

[9] Margaret Crum, 'An Oxford Music Club, 1690–1719', *BLR* 9 (1973–8), 83–99.

**Table 7.4 The 'Oxford' group of sources**

| Manuscript | Copyists | Comments |
|---|---|---|
| Bu 5002 | (1) unidentified | *c.* 1678–85 |
| | (2) Richard Goodson | |
| | (3) Edward Hull | |
| Och 350 | Richard Goodson | *c.* 1675–1690 |
| Lbl Add. 30382 | Henry Bowman | *c.* 1675–85? |
| Ob MS Mus.Sch. C.61 | Francis Withy | *c.* 1687–92 |
| Lbl Add. 31460 | (1) Henry Bowman | before 1678 |
| | (2) Edward Hull | |
| | (3) Richard Goodson | |
| | (4) William Husbands | before 1693 |
| | (5) Charles Husbands (?) | before 1692 (?) |
| Lbl Add. 33234 | Charles Morgan | *c.* 1680–5 |
| Lbl Add. 33235 | Simon Child (?) | before 1693 |
| J-Tn 0-1-54 | Edward Hull | |

Paper, rastrology and copyists of principal sources

Bu 5002: see Table 7.6

Och 350: oblong quarto, 149 × 232. Binding: contemporary blind-tooled calf, 155 × 236. Watermarks: Angoumois fleur-de-lys without countermark. Rastrology: six staves ruled with a three-stave rastrum, span: 49; profile: 9.5(11)10(9)9.5. Copyist: Richard Goodson.

Lbl Add. 30382: folio, 307 × 199. Various arms of Amsterdam and foolscap watermarks. Rastrology: ruled as required without a rastrum. Copyist: Henry Bowman.

'Mr' Blow are consistent with an origin in the late 1670s. The headings of Purcell's works differ from those of Lbl R.M. 20.h.8, and there are many minor differences of literary and musical texts: in *Silvia, thou brighter eye of night*, for example, the autograph contains simplified continuo parts in bars where Bu 5002 duplicates the vocal bass, a contrast corresponding to that between Purcell's autograph of his sacred partsongs in Lbl Add. 30930 and the earlier copy by Blow in Och 628. *Go tell Aminta*, however, resembles Lbl R.M. 20.h.8 rather than Bowman's copy in Lbl Add. 30382.

Och 350 is entirely in the hand of the elder Richard Goodson: ascriptions up to p. 106 are to 'Mr' Blow, so three-quarters of the manuscript had been copied by 1678, though subsequent additions were made over a lengthy period. *Urge me no more* (pp. 109–13), the first of the two Purcell songs in the book, follows shortly after the last ascription to 'Mr' Blow; never published, this song appears to have been copied by John Walter in CH Cap. VI/I/I around 1680 (see above) as part of the 'Court' repertory. A third early source, Lbl Add. 33234, is closely related to Och 350.

**Table 7.5 Birmingham University, Barber Institute of Fine Arts MS 5002: contents**

| Pages | Headings and incipits | Ascription | Earliest print | Date of autograph in Lbl R.M. 20.h.8 |
|-------|----------------------|------------|----------------|--------------------------------------|
| [First section] | | | | |
| 1–3 | Hercules and the Serpents 'The big-limb'd babe' | [Pietro Reggio] | Reg1680 | |
| 4–7 | Acme and Septimius 'As on Septimius panting breast' | Mr John Blow | | |
| 8–11 | 'Go perjured man' | Dr Blow | | |
| 12–13 | A song 'Alas how barbarous' | Mr Pursel | | |
| 14–23 | 'Awake my lyre' | Dr Blow | | |
| 24–9 | Chorus of Nymphs & Shepherds 'Fair nymph that to the water went' | Dr Blow | | |
| 30–7 | 'How pleasant is this flow'ry plain' | Mr Purcel | | 1682–3 |
| 38–41 | Strephon and Dorrinda 'Has yet your Breast no pitty' | H.P. | 1BM1688*a* | |
| 42–3 | Sappho's Complaint 'Beneath a dark and melancholy grove'*b* | H.P. | | |
| 44–54 | Mr Cowley's Complaint 'In a deep vision's intellectual scene'*c* | H.P. | | 1683 |
| 55–7 | 'Amongst the shades' | H.P. | 4TM1687 | 1682–3 |
| 57–9 | 'Above the tumults of a busy state' | H.P. | | 1682–3 |
| 60–1 | An Hymn 'Arise my darkened melancholy soul' | Dr John Blow | | |
| 62–3 | A Religious Elegy 'With sick and famish'd eyes' | H.P. | HS1688 | 1682–3 |
| 64–6 | Job's Curse 'Let the night perish' | H.P. | HS1688 | 1682–3 |
| 67–9 | An Elegy 'Silvia thou brighter eye of night' | H.P. | | 1683–4 |
| 70–1 | An Elegy 'Alexis, dear Alexis' | Dr Blow | | |
| 72–3 | An Hymn 'O Lord since I experienced have'*d* | H.P. | | |
| 74–6 | A penitential Hymn 'Great, good and just' | H.P. | HS1688 | |
| 77–9 | On the Crucifixion 'The earth trembled' | H.P. | HS1688 | |
| 79–84 | A prayer in an Anthem 'Plunged in the confines of despair' | Hen. Purcell | | |
| 86–7 | 'All things are hush'd' | [Richard Goodson]*e* | | |
| 88–93 | O give thanks unto the Lord (inc.)*f* | Dr Blow | | |
| [second section] | | | | |
| 94–103 | O Praise the L[or]d | Pelham Humphrey | | |
| 104–12 | I said in the cutting off of my days | Dr Blow | | |
| 113–24 | Hear my Crying O God | Pelham Humfrey | | |
| 124–38 | The Lord is my Sheapheard | Dr Blow | | |
| [third section] | | | | |
| 139–40 | [unused] | | | |
| 141–6 | An Anthem 'Since God so tender a regard' | Mr Henry P[urcell] | | |
| 147–52 | An Anthem 'When on my sick bed' | Henry Purcell | | |

## Table 7.5 (*cont.*)

| Pages | Headings and incipits | Ascription | Earliest print | Date of autograph in Lbl R.M. 20.h.8 |
|---|---|---|---|---|
| 153–7 | An Anthem out of Job 'O I'm sick of life' | [Purcell] | | |
| 158–72 | O give thanks unto the Lord | Pel. Humfreys | | |
| 173–9 | The Kings of tharsis | Dr Blow | | |
| 180–1 | Anthem 'I will magnify thee'ᵍ | Ralph Palmer Esq. | | |
| 182 | [instrumental piece] | | | |
| 183–6 | The Meditation 'It must be done my soul' | H.P. | | |
| 186–8 | Musick, Loves spokesman 'Go tell Aminta' | Hen. Purcell | OB1706 | 1683–4 |
| [fourth section] | | | | |
| 189–90 | [unused] | | | |
| 191–7 | 'Audite sancti' | Segnior Charissimi | | |
| 198–203 | 'Who shall separate us' | Mr Math. Lock | | |
| 204–9 | Salve Regina | [Monferrato] | | |
| 210–13 | 'Anima mea liquefacta est' | [Marini] | | |
| 214–19 | 'Plage tua Domine' | Felice Sances | | |
| 220–5 | 'O Domine guttae' | Felice Sances | | |
| 226–8 | 'Amante che dite' | [Carissimi] | | |
| 229–32 | 'Allume delle stelle' | [Monteverdi] | | |
| 232–5 | 'Tu dormi ah crudo core' | [Monteverdi] | | |
| 236–9 | 'Parlo misero O taccio' | [Monteverdi] | | |
| 240 | 'Gloria patri et filio' | Dr Blow | | |
| 241 | 'Dite O cieli se crudeli' | | 2BM1688 | |
| 242 | 'Gloria patri et filio' | Mat. Locke | | |
| 243–8 | 'Bone Jesu verbum patris' | | | |
| 249–51 | 'Regina celi laetare' | | | |
| 252–5 | 'Lucifer celestis' | Signir Charissimi | | |
| 256 | 'Anima mea suspira' (inc.) | | | |

Key to printed concordances

| 1BM1688 | [Henry Playford], *The Banquet of Musick . . . The First Book* |
|---|---|
| 2BM1688 | [Henry Playford], *The Banquet of Musick . . . The Second Book* |
| HS1688 | [Henry Playford], *Harmonia Sacra* |
| OB1706 | Henry Purcell, *Orpheus Britannicus . . . the second edition* |
| Reg1680 | Pietro Reggio, *Songs* |
| 4TM1687 | [Henry Playford], *The Theater of Music . . . The Fourth and Last Book* |

Copyist of pp. 113–79: Edward Hull

ᵃThe only manuscript concordance is Lbl Add. 33234.

ᵇA less complete version is in Lbl Add. 19759.

ᶜAn earlier version than in Lbl R.M. 20.h.8.

ᵈUnique.

ᵉAttributed to Blow, presumably by association with the following work, in the manuscript's modern index, this piece is in Goodson's hand and may be assumed to be his composition. Another anonymous setting of similar words, also copied by Goodson, appears in Och 1154, section G.

ᶠPages are evidently missing after p. 93, the last of the first section.

ᵍProbably in Palmer's own hand.

## Table 7.6 Birmingham University, Barber Institute of Fine Arts MS 5002: paper and rastrology

Folio, 367 x 228/238. Page numbers are taken from the recto side of each folio. Two successive pages bear the number 86, so rectos from the second '86' onwards have even page numbers. All watermarks are Angoumois fleurs-de-lys; all pages have twelve staves ruled with four-stave rastra.

1. Factor's mark 'HC', countermark 'LR' (pp. 3, 5, 77–85, 140–56, 162). Rastrum span: 96.5, profile: 13(14.5)14(14.5)13(14)13.5. Similar paper and rulings are found in Och 620, pp. 134–[161], a score of music by Coprario in the hand of the elder Richard Goodson.

2. Countermark 'IHS' (pp. 1, 7, 11, 13, 25, 31, 33–41, 47). Rastrum: as paper 1. Found in the first book only, often in gatherings with paper types 1, 3 or 4.

3. Countermark 'IHS/ET' (pp. 9, 15, 17–23, 27, 29). Rastrum span: 95, profile: 11.5(15.5)12.5(15)13 (15)12. Found in the first book only. Similar paper and rulings are found in Och 22.

4. Countermark monogram 'PSAB' (pp. 43, 45, 49–75, 158, 160, 164–79, 191–255). Rastrum span: 98, profile: 14(14)13.5(14.5)13(15)13.5. Similar watermarks are found in Ob MSS Mus.Sch. C.20–23, which bear Lowe's inscription 'the paper & binding of these 4 Books cost 9s 6d the 1st of May 1680'.

5. Factor's mark 'AJ', countermark 'CDG' (pp. 86–92, 114–38, 181, 187, 257). Rastrum span: 103, profile: 14(14.5)15(15.5)14.5(15)15. The predominant paper type of the second book. The paper must date from before 1683, the year of de George's death.

6. Countermark 'HC' (pp. 94–100, 110, 112, 183, 185). Rastrum span: 93, profile: 12(15)13(14.5)12.5 (14)12.5. Similar paper and rulings occur in the first section of Och 22.

7. Factor's mark 'HC', no countermark (pp. 102–8). Rastrum span: 98, profile: 14(15)14(14.5)14(13.5) 13.5. Found in the second book.

Goodson's copy of the second Purcell song in Och 350, *From silent shades* (pp. 121–7), was not derived from the fourth book of *Choice Ayres* (1683).

Lbl Add. 30382 is in the hand of Henry Bowman, whose *Songs for 1, 2 & 3 Voyces* were engraved in Oxford and issued in 1677 according to the title page although a second title page gives the year 1678.[10] The manuscript contains two Purcell duets: *Go tell Aminta* (fols. 36r–37v), copied in Lbl R.M. 20.h.8 in 1683 or 1684, has a large number of distinctive variants, in contrast to Bu 5002 which in this instance resembles the autograph; *In some kind dream* (fols. 35r–36v), which precedes *Go tell Aminta* in Add. 30382, was not entered in Lbl R.M. 20.h.8 until 1685. Close contact between Bowman and Lowe is demonstrated by Bowman's contributions to Act music during Lowe's professorship,[11] so it is more than possible that Bowman

---

[10] Bowman describes himself as 'Philo-Musicus', suggesting that he was not a professional musician. A second edition of the *Songs* was published by Richard Davis in 1679. See Ian Spink, *English Song, Dowland to Purcell* (London, 1974), 144, 154, 224, 265.

[11] Examples include *My Lesbia* in Ob MS Mus.Sch. C.120, a song composed for the 'Act' or degree ceremony on 11 July 1680 though for some reason not performed. See Holman, 'Original Sets', 15, 266,

acquired these songs from Lowe and that they were therefore composed before 1682, some years earlier than the date indicated by their position in the autograph.

### Other Oxford sources

A few Oxford manuscripts not of the first importance as Purcell song sources are nevertheless of considerable interest. Francis Withy's score book Ob MS Mus.Sch. C.61, already mentioned in connection with *My song shall be alway* (see pp. 153–7), contains the song *Fly swift ye hours* published in *The Banquet of Musick*, VI (1692). The copy in Mus.Sch. C.61 and another in Lbl Add. 33236 do not seem to descend from this print or its immediate exemplar, and Withy's annotations show that *Fly swift ye hours* must have been added to Mus.Sch. C.61 between September 1690 and July 1692. Lbl Add. 33234 is a large collection of sacred and secular vocal music commenced *c.* 1682 by Charles Morgan (*c.* 1660–1738) of Magdalen College, Oxford:[12] most of the Purcell works it contains occur in other early sources and sometimes reflect the existence of versions older than the surviving autograph. Lbl Add. 33235 belonged in 1757 to Philip Hayes, who acquired it from the widow of Simon Child, a singing-man at Christ Church, Oxford, from 1688 to early 1694 and organist of New College from 1702 until his death in 1731.[13] Similarities between Child's signatures in the Christ Church disbursement books, his inscriptions in Add. 33235 and the manuscript's main text hand suggest that he might have been its principal copyist, though a few pages, including the first work, the beginning of the second, and part of fol. 123v, are in the distinctive hand of William Husbands, who succeeded Lowe as organist of Christ Church in 1682, and confirm that most if not all of the manuscript was complete by 1693, when Husbands left Oxford for Hereford. Another of Child's manuscripts, Lbl Add. 31460, was largely copied by Henry Bowman, but the Purcell works are in the hands of Edward Hull or Oxford A: they are generally related to *Harmonia Sacra* of 1688, though *Let the night perish* follows readings already in the Oxford manuscript repertory rather than those of the 1688 print and the figuring of some songs differs

270. For other manuscripts in Bowman's hand see Andrew V. Jones, *The Motets of Carissimi* (Ann Arbor, 1982), II, 148, 178.

[12] Charles Morgan was a choirboy at Christ Church, Oxford, from 1670 to 1677 and a singing-man at the same college until 1681; after taking the degree of B.A. from Magdalen he served as a lay clerk there from 1681 to 1725. He was a member of the Mermaid Tavern music society and it is likely that Add. 33234 contains some of the club's repertory. See Crum, 'An Oxford Music Club', and *Hearne*, VII, 205; Bloxam, *Register*, II, 78, 249.

[13] See *Hearne*, X, 462; Crum, 'An Oxford Music Club'; Shaw, *The Succession*, 390.

considerably from the published version. J-Tn 0–1–54, a varied collection of vocal music in score copied by Hull,[14] shares the duet *In some kind dream* with Bowman's score Lbl Add. 30382. In the nineteenth century the manuscript belonged to W. H. Cummings[15] and before him to Joseph Warren, who in May 1833 had found it, used as a scrapbook for printed song sheets, at a barber's shop in Lambeth.[16] Unfortunately a number of pages were seriously damaged either by the overpasting of the song sheets or Warren's efforts to remove them, including those bearing *In some kind dream* and *Hence fond deceiver*.

THE 'SOUTHEASTERN' GROUP OF SOURCES

London, Royal College of Music MS 1119
London, British Library Additional MSS 19759, 29397
Cambridge, Fitzwilliam Museum Music MS 118

These four manuscript songbooks (Table 7.7) contain extensive interconnected repertories of songs and catches, only a small proportion of which are by Purcell (Table 7.8). Lcm 1119 has evident connections with the Inner Temple; Cfm 118 and Add. 29397 are linked either by Daniel Henstridge's handwriting or the presence of works by the minor composers Charles Wren[17] and John Vanderheighden[18] to the Kentish cathedrals.

[14] A page is illustrated in *Nanki Music Library* [an illustrated exhibition catalogue] (Tokyo, 1967), 41. In *Catalogue of Rare Books and Notes: the Ohki Collection, Nanki Music Library* (Tokyo, 1970), this manuscript is listed as N4/39.

[15] It formed lot 1401 in Cummings's sale: see *Catalogue of the Famous Musical Library of Books, Manuscripts, Autograph Letters, Musical Scores etc., the Property of the Late W. H. Cummings* (London, 1917). The British Library copy is S.C. Sotheby 1240.

[16] The details are given by Warren in an annotation in the manuscript: they are summarised in Zimmerman, *Catalogue*, 481.

[17] Charles Wren (d. 1678), was a choirboy at Canterbury Cathedral. By 1672 he was organist of Rochester, but moved in 1673 to Gloucester Cathedral. See Shaw, *The Succession*, 121, 235; Spink, *Restoration*, 260–1, 336.

[18] John Vanderheighden (d. 1681) was a clerk at Magdalen College, Oxford, from 1673 to 1680 and a chaplain from 1680 to 1681. He then became a minor canon of Canterbury Cathedral, in his home town, but must have died very soon after his appointment and was buried in the cloisters on 26 May 1681. He composed two vocal works in Cfm 118 and on fol. 8r of the keyboard manuscript Lbl Add. 22099 'A German air' is attributed to 'Heyden'. See Foster, *Alumni*, IV, 1533; Robert Hovenden, ed., *The Register Booke of Christnings, Marriages and Burialls within the Precinct of the Cathedrall and Metropoliticall Church of Christe of Canterburie* (London, 1878), 126; Robert F. Ford, 'Minor Canons at Canterbury Cathedral: the Gostlings and their Colleagues' (Ph.D. thesis, University of California at Berkeley, 1984), 126–32.

### Table 7.7 The 'southeastern' group of sources

| Manuscript | Probable date | Comments |
|---|---|---|
| Lcm 1119 | *c.* 1683–92 | probably connected with the Inner Temple |
| Lbl Add. 19759 | *c.* 1681–5 | 'Charles Campelman his book June ye 9 1681' |
| Lbl Add. 29397 | *c.* 1682–8 | |
| Cfm 118 | *c.* 1678–84 | mostly in Henstridge's hand |

Dimensions, watermarks and rastrology

Lcm 1119: folio, main music section 306 × 191.
Watermarks: arms of Amsterdam with countermark 'RM' (fols. 4–9, 11, 14, 23–24/ii); foolscap with countermark 'LM' (fols. 10, 12–13, 15–22). Twelve staves ruled with a six-stave rastrum, span: 138.5, profile: 12.5(11)13.5(11.5)14(11)14(11)13.5(12)14.

Lbl Add. 19759: folio, 313 × 202.
Watermarks: foolscap without countermark. Twelve staves ruled with a six-stave rastrum, span: 138, profile: 13(11)13(11.5)14(11)14(11)14(11.5)13.5 (compare Lcm 1119).

Lbl Add. 29397: narrow oblong duodecimo, 63 × 157.
Watermarks: arms of Amsterdam without countermark. Four staves ruled with a four-stave rastrum, span: 44, profile: 6(6)7(5.5)6(6)7.

Cfm 118: folio, 295 × 194. Binding: contemporary blind tooled distressed calf, 302 × 205, rebacked.
Watermarks: foolscap with countermark 'CB' (pp. 1–78, 81–2, i.e. most copied pages); foolscap with countermark 'IV' (pp. 79–80; 85 onwards). Ten staves ruled with five-stave rastra: 'CB' paper, span: 124, profile: 13(14)13.5(15)13(14.5)12.5(15.5)13; 'IV' paper, span: 126, profile: 12(15.5)13(16)13.5(15.5)13 (14.5)13.5.

The provenance of Lcm 1119 is established by its opening pages. On fol. 1r, a sheet of music paper with the countermark 'IV', the manuscript's main hand has written 'A Coppy of the old Measures in ye Inner Temple'. Directions for performing these dances continue on fol. 2r, a plain sheet of posthorn writing paper, and on its reverse, on what would have been the outermost surface if the sheet was folded into four, is this inscription:

> The old Measures of the Inner Temple London as they were first begun and taught
> by Robert Holeman a dancing: Master before 1640 and continued ever since in the
> Inner-Temple-Hall                                     Mr Butler Buggins

Some of the songs copied in the same hand date from well into the 1680s or later, so the prefatory folios cannot have been written by Buggins himself, Master of the Revels at the Inner Temple from 1672 to 1675, who died in 1678.[19] The volume may

---

[19] F. A. Inderwick, ed., *A Calendar of the Inner Temple Records*, II (London, 1898), 268, 271, 289, 327; III (London, 1901), 10, 20, 41, 63, 71, 79, 89, 94, 108. C. H. Ridge, ed., *Index to Wills Proved in the Prerogative Court of Canterbury, 1676–85* (London, 1948), 54.

## Table 7.8 Songs and catches by Purcell in sources of the 'southeastern' group

| *Title* | *Lcm 1119 fol.* | *Add. 19759 fol.* | *Add. 29397 fol.* | *Cfm 118ᵃ p.* | *Earliest print* | *Other early MS concordances* |
|---|---|---|---|---|---|---|
| A thousand several ways I tried | 7v | 30v | | 83 | CA1684 | |
| Alas how barbarous | | | | 36 | | Lbl Add. 33234; Bu 5002 |
| Beneath a dark and melancholy grove | | 30v | | | | Bu 5002 |
| Come honest sexton take thy spade^b | | 6v | | | HS1688 | |
| Drink on till night be spent [catch] | | | 47r | | 2PMC1686 | |
| From silent shades | | | 71r | 78 | CA1683 | Lbl Add. 33234; Och 350 |
| Great Apollo and Bacchus [catch] | | | 44r | | | |
| Here's that will challenge all the fair [catch]^c | 6r | 15v | | | MC1673 | |
| How delightful's the life of an innocent swain | | 31v | | | | |
| How peaceful the days^d | | 13r | | | CA1679 | |
| Let the grave fools [catch] | | 14v | | | CC1685 | |
| My wife has a tongue [catch] | | | 67r | | CC1685 | |
| O! Solitude | | | 50r | | TM1687 | Lbl R.M. 20.h.8 |
| She loves and she confesses too | | | 68v | 74 | CA1683 | Lbl Add. 33234; CH Cap. VI/I/I |
| She who my poor heart possesses | | 35r | | | CA1683 | |
| Since the Duke is returned [catch]^e | | 39v | | | CC1685 | |
| Since women so false and so jiltish are grown [catch] | | 40r | | | | |
| Sir Walter enjoying his damsel [catch] | | | 46r | | 2PMC1701 | |
| 'Tis easy to force to the water your horse [catch] | | 26r | | 9 | CC1685 | |
| To all lovers of music [catch] | | | 56r | | CAm1687 | |
| To thee and to a maid [catch] | | | | 82 | CC1685 | |
| 'Twas women made me love [catch]^f | | | | 43 | CC1685 | |
| We sing to him whose wisdom formed the ear | | 37v | | | HS1688 | |
| When Strephon found his passion vain | 4r | | | | CA1683^g | |
| Who but a slave | | | | 54 | | |
| Who comes there [catch] | | 30v | | | CC1685 | |
| Why so serious, why so grave [S only] | 14r | | | | | |
| Would you know how we meet [catch] | 17r | | | | 2TM1685 | |
| Young John the gardener [catch]^h | | 39r | 23r | | NC1683 | |

Key to printed concordances

| | |
|---|---|
| CA1679 | [John Playford], *Choice Ayres and Songs . . . The Second Book* |
| CA1683 | [John Playford], *Choice Ayres and Songs . . . The Fourth Book* |
| CA1684 | [John Playford], *Choice Ayres and Songs . . . The Fifth Book* |
| CAm1687 | [John Carr and Samuel Scott], *Comes Amoris . . . The First Book* |
| CC1685 | [John Playford], *Catch that Catch Can* |
| HS1688 | [Henry Playford], *Harmonia Sacra* |
| MC1673 | [John Playford], *The Musical Companion . . . The First Book* |
| NC1683 | [D. Brown and T. Benskin], *The Newest Collection of the Choicest Songs* |
| 2PMC1686 | [John Playford], *The Second Book of the Pleasant Musical Companion* |
| 2PMC1701 | enlarged edition of 2PMC1686 |

**Table 7.8** (*cont.*)

Key to printed concordances (*cont.*)

| | |
|---|---|
| 2TM1685 | [Henry Playford and Robert Carr], *The Theater of Music . . . The Second Book* |
| TM1687 | [Henry Playford], *The Theater of Music . . . The Fourth and Last Book* |

Only the earliest printed and manuscript concordances are listed.

[a] The catch *Once in our lives* in Cfm 118, p. 2, is not Purcell's but the setting by Michael Wise published in CC1685.

[b] Really by Matthew Locke.

[c] Perhaps by one of Purcell's older relatives.

[d] In C minor: in CA1679 anonymous and in A minor.

[e] The text probably refers to the return of the Duke of York from Scotland in June 1682.

[f] This catch is not here attributed to Forcer, as stated in Zimmerman, *Catalogue*, 126, but is at the top of a page which ends with Forcer's *My life is now a burden grown*.

[g] Lcm 1119 is clearly independent of the 1683 print.

[h] All sources listed here give this catch in B♭, but the two manuscripts are not identical. Later sources are in C.

once have contained other material, for the first manuscript music page is numbered '26', although the songs themselves begin a new sequence from '1'. They include two catches and three solo songs ascribed to Purcell, one of them unique: *Why so serious, why so grave*, lacking its bass part.

On fol. 1r of Lbl Add. 19759 is the inscription 'Charles Campelman his Book June ye 9 1681', followed by another, in a different hand, 'God give him grase 1682', but it has proved impossible to identify Campelman or to establish a provenance for the manuscript. Apart from three songs added in the eighteenth century most of the copying is in Campelman's hand and was probably carried out between 1681 and 1685. Few of the songs have bass parts, but the source is more important than it at first appears, for fols. 18r–18v contain the melodies of seven songs by John Banister from Crowne's court masque *Calisto*:[20] these songs, and others by Staggins, Banister and Cambert, imply a link with court musical circles and a reason for the inclusion of Purcell's unpublished *Beneath a dark and melancholy grove* (fol. 30v) together with an attributed version of *How peaceful the days* significantly different from that printed anonymously in *Choice Ayres* of 1679.

The small oblong duodecimo Lbl Add. 29397 seems from its concordances to have been copied between 1682 and 1688. On fols. 58r–56r INV is a second treble part to Wise's *Old Chiron thus preached* attributed to 'D.Hens[tridge]'; the ascrip-

[20] Holman, *Four and Twenty Fiddlers*, 366–73.

tion appears to be autograph, and in any case the added part provides a link with Rochester. A further connection is provided by *Mine own Sabina* (fols. 15v–16r), by Charles Wren, Henstridge's predecessor as organist at Rochester: the song was published anonymously in *Choice Ayres* of 1673, but the attribution must have been supplied from another source or through personal knowledge.

Cfm 118 is bound with three Playford prints, Henry Lawes's *Select Ayres and Dialogues* of 1669 and the *Choice Ayres* of 1675 and 1679, and is likely to have been compiled between 1680 and 1685 as an extension of this printed repertory: an attribution to 'Mr' Aldrich on p. 7 changes to 'Dr' Aldrich by pp. 76 and 77 in acknowledgement of his doctorate conferred in 1682. Only two composers are not generally given the formal titles 'Mr' or 'Dr', Daniel Henstridge and John Vander-heighden, and most of the manuscript appears to be in Henstridge's hand, changing near the end to a later style incorporating a conventional contemporary G clef in place of the distinctive form used in Henstridge's earlier manuscripts.[21] At the time when Cfm 118 must have been copied, Henstridge was organist of Rochester Cathedral. Another hand appears on the first few pages and then intermittently throughout the rest of the volume, sometimes providing text or clefs in collaboration with Henstridge: this copyist, who cannot have been Vanderheighden (d. 1681), made annotations throughout the three prints now bound with Cfm 118.

## Manuscript sources of keyboard music

### HARPSICHORD OR VIRGINAL MUSIC

Much of Purcell's harpsichord music was published in *The Second Part of Musick's Hand-maid* of 1689, 'carefully Revised and Corrected by . . . Mr Henry Purcell', and the posthumous *A Choice Collection of Lessons* issued by Frances Purcell in 1696.[22] Manuscript sources nevertheless show that, as its title implies, *A Choice Collection* was a selection from a body of harpsichord music built up over a number of years. The

---

[21] Examples of Henstridge's hand in Lbl Add. 30931–2 confirm that he was the copyist of Cfm 118: his signature appears on Add. 30932, fols. 153r, 153v and 155v, and his copy of *Turn thou us good Lord*, Add. 30931, fols. 79v–80r, illustrates not only the early G clef found in Cfm 118 but also the idiosyncratic spelling 'Mr Hen. Pursoll'. See also pp. 221–6.

[22] See Henry Purcell, *Eight Suites*, and Purcell, *Miscellaneous Keyboard Pieces*, ed. Howard Ferguson, 2nd edn (London, 1968).

suites of contrasting movements in printed editions and early manuscripts might therefore be better seen as occasional groupings made for particular publications, pupils or colleagues rather than as definitive and complete multi-sectional works:[23] this individuality extends to textual detail, and the readings of Purcell's keyboard autograph Lbl MS Mus.1 differ significantly both from *A Choice Collection* and from other early manuscript sources.

Himself a keyboardist, Purcell must have worked his way through a considerable quantity of music composed by his elders and contemporaries; in turn, his own compositions provided teaching material for a younger generation, and it is not surprising that some manuscripts contain works by Purcell and other composers without any sign that the copyist knew who had actually written them.[24] The jig that concludes Purcell's A minor suite in Lbl MS Mus.1 serves to illustrate both the complex history of Purcell's harpsichord music and the uncertainty that surrounds some attributions. Anonymous in all sources, it appears on fols. 8v–9r of Ob MS Mus.Sch. E.399, a keyboard collection inscribed at the reverse 'Elizabeth Nodes her Book August 8th 1681' and 'Mrs Beety Nodes her book March the 10 1682'. The main copyist, possibly Francis Forcer,[25] was also responsible for US-NH Filmer 15, dated '1677/8', and for an almand in US-NH Filmer 17 which in MS Mus.Sch. E.399 forms a pair with the jig. The contents of Mus.Sch E.399 include several concordances with Filmer 15 and are generally consistent with a date no later than 1682. Both the musical quality of the A minor jig and its inclusion in Lbl MS Mus.1 point towards Purcell as its composer, but the Bodleian source shows the movement being transcribed without acknowledgement well before the accepted date of any of Purcell's attributed harpsichord works (Illus. 7.1 and 7.2).

---

[23] See Robert Klakowich, 'Seventeenth-Century English Keyboard Autographs', *JRMA* 121 (1996), 135: 'it is misleading for cataloguers [of composers such as Purcell, Blow or Draghi] to designate a numerical succession of "suites" as "Suite no. 1", "Suite no. 2", etc., as if to preserve the sanctity of a unified group where such unity never existed in the mind of the composer'. With this reservation, we shall continue to use the word 'suite' as a convenient shorthand.

[24] Even apparent autographs do not guarantee authorship. The prelude which begins Purcell's C major suite in Lbl MS Mus.1 is a metrical version of an anonymous unmeasured prelude found in duplicate copies in the 'La Pierre' manuscript F-Pn Rés. Vmd. MS 18 and in Lbl Add. 39569: see Robert Hill, 'A Keyboard Prelude in C major by Henry Purcell: Three Newly Located Concordances' (published electronically 1997, http://dioptra.com/earmus/purcell/purcell.html).

[25] Robert Ford, 'The Filmer Manuscripts: a Handlist', *Notes* 34 (1977–8), 820.

Illus. 7.1 Henry Purcell: jig in A minor, autograph. British Library MS Mus.1, fol. 10r

### Two primary manuscript sources: London, British Library MS Mus.1 and Oxford, Christ Church Mus. 1177

The partly autograph manuscript now Lbl MS Mus.1 (Table 7.9) was acquired by the British Library in late 1994.[26] Music in Purcell's hand occupies no more than twelve folios at one end of the volume, the rest, copied from the other end, containing possibly autograph movements by Giovanni Battista Draghi (*c*. 1640–1708), who had settled in London by 1667. Several pieces are signed with the initial 'B', and on the first page of the 'Purcell end' (now fol. 1r) is a brief passage of recitative-like music in C minor, in the same hand as Draghi's keyboard works, setting the words of what might have been his address: 'In Bedford Street over against ye Cross Keys Tavern at ye signe of ye Catt – Baptist'. No other evidence that Draghi lived at the Cat in

---

[26] For further details of the manuscript and its recent history see Curtis Price, 'Newly Discovered Autograph Keyboard Music of Purcell and Draghi', *JRMA* 120 (1995), 77–102; Christopher Hogwood, 'A New English Keyboard Manuscript of the Seventeenth Century: Autograph Music by Purcell and Draghi', *BLJ* 21 (1995), 161–75; and *Henry Purcell: the Newly-Discovered Autograph Manuscript of Harpsichord Music*, Sotheby's sale catalogue (1994).

Illus. 7.2 Henry Purcell: jig in A minor, possibly copied by Francis Forcer. Bodleian Library MS Mus.Sch. E.399, fol. 8v

Bedford Street has been found and two manuscripts in a different hand, Lcm 1106, fols. 29r–74r, and part of Cfm 652, also have a claim to be regarded as his autograph,[27] but Lbl MS Mus.1 is at the very least an independent source containing four previously unknown movements.

With its elegantly tooled calf binding, consistent paper type and regular quiring the manuscript seems characteristic of the good-quality bound manuscript books offered for sale by the Playfords (see p. 18) and as such is likely to have belonged to a pupil or an amateur player rather than to a professional. Fols. 43r and 43v contain what appear to be a beginner's first attempts at musical notation, and some of the music copied by Purcell is obviously teaching material, three elementary pieces being followed by nine keyboard versions of theatre works[28] interrupted on fols. 4r–5r by one of the seventeenth century's most popular keyboard studies, Orlando Gibbons's G major prelude from *Parthenia*. The remaining eight movements form

---

[27] Klakowich, 'Seventeenth-Century English Keyboard Autographs', 133–4.

[28] Not necessarily derivative transcriptions as it cannot be proved which came first: see Price, 'Newly Discovered Autograph Keyboard Music', 90–3.

## Table 7.9  London, British Library MS Mus.1: contents

*THE 'PURCELL END'*

| Folios[a] | | Work | Z no. | Keyboard concordances[b] and comments |
|---|---|---|---|---|
| *A* | *B* | | | |
| 43r | 1v | Prelude, C | — | previously unknown |
| 42v | 2r | [Minuet], C | — | previously unknown |
| 42v | 2r | [Air], C | — | previously unknown |
| 42r | 2v | [Minuet from *The Double Dealer*] | T676 | Cfm 653 |
| 42r | 2v | ['Thus happy and free' from *The Fairy Queen*] | 629/44 | unique keyboard version |
| 41v | 3r | [Hornpipe from *The Old Bachelor*] | T685 | Cfm 653 |
| 41r | 3v | [Air from *The Double Dealer*] | 592/9 | in C, not B♭; unique keyboard version |
| 40v–39v | 4r–5r | Prelude, G [Orlando Gibbons] | | from *Parthenia* |
| 39r | 5v | [Hornpipe from *The Fairy Queen*] | 629/1b | En Inglis 94 MS 3343 |
| 38v | 6r | [Hornpipe], A | — | attributed to John Eccles in *Apollo's Banquet* (1701) and Ob MS Tenbury 1508 |
| 38r | 6v | [Trumpet Minuet from *The Virtuous Wife*] | 611/8 | unique keyboard version |
| 37v | 7r | [Air from *The Virtuous Wife*][c] | 611/9 | Lbl Add. 39569; Ob MS Tenbury 1508; En Inglis 94 MS 3343 |
| 37r | 7v | [Minuet from *The Virtuous Wife*] | 611/7 | US-LAuc M678/M4/ H295/1710/Bound |
| 36v | 8r | Prelude, a | 663/1 | CCL1696 |
| 36r–35v | 8v–9r | [Almand], a | 663/2 | CCL1696; Och 1177; F-Pc Rés. 1186 bis, Part 1 |
| 35r | 9v | Corant, a | 663/3 | CCL1696; Och 1177; F-Pc Rés. 1186 bis, Part 1 |
| 34v | 10r | [Jig], a | — | Ob MS Mus.Sch. E.399; Cfm 653 |
| 34r | 10v | Prelude, C | — | F-Pn Rés. Vmd. MS 18; Lbl Add. 39569: see p. 277, n. 24 |
| 33v–34r | 11r–10v | [Almand], C[d] | 666/2 | CCL1696; Cfm 653 |
| 33r | 11v | [Corant], C | 666/3 | CCL1696; 2MHM1689; Cfm 653 |
| 32v | 12r | Sarraband, C | 666/4 | CCL1696; 2MHM1689; Cfm 653; Och 46 |

## Table 7.9 (*cont.*)

*THE 'DRAGHI END'*

| Folios A | B | Work [all untitled] | Kl. no.[c] | Concordances |
|---|---|---|---|---|
| 1r–1v | 43v–43r | Rough attempts at musical notation | | |
| 2r | 42v | Unused | | |
| 2v–3r | 42r–41v | Prelude, g | 13 | SSSL1707 |
| 3v–5r | 41r–39v | Almand, g | 14 | SSSL1707 |
| 5v–6v | 39r–38r | Corant, g | 15 | SSSL1707 |
| 7r–8v | 37v–36r | Air, g | — | |
| 9r–10r | 35v–34v | Jig, g | 18 | SSSL1707 |
| 10v–11r | 34r–33v | Prelude, A | — | |
| 11v–13r | 33r–31v | Almand, A | 20 | SSSL1707 |
| 13v–14v | 31r–30r | Corant, A | 21 | SSSL1707 |
| 14v–15v | 30r–29v | Saraband, 'Slow', A | 22 | SSSL1707 |
| 15v–16v | 29r–28r | Movement in 3/8, A | — | |
| 16v–18v | 28r–26r | Jig, A | 23 | SSSL1707 |
| 18v–19r | 26r–25v | Prelude, c | 45 | US-Wc M21/M185/Case |
| 19v–20v | 25r–24r | 'ye double of ye prelude' | 45 | Ob MS Mus.Sch. E.397[f] |
| 20v–22v | 24r–22r | Almand, c | 46 | Ob MS Mus.Sch. E.397; US-Wc M21/M185/Case |
| 23r–24r | 21v–20v | Air, c | 49 | Ob MS Mus.Sch. E.397; US-Wc M21/M185/Case |
| 24v–27v | 20r–17r | Toccata-like work, G | — | |
| 28r–30r | 16v–14v | Almand, G | 8 | SSSL1707 |
| 30v–32r | 14r–12v | The Hunting Tune, G | 12 | SSSL1707 |

Key to printed concordances:

CCL1696    *A Choice Collection of Lessons*

2MHM1689 *The Second Part of Musick's Hand-maid*

SSSL1707    G. B. Draghi, *Six Select Sutes of Lessons for the Harpsicord*

Oblong quarto, 207/8 × 273. Binding: contemporary blind-tooled calf (including original spine), 213 x 278. Watermarks: arms of Strasbourg; no countermark to one member of the mould pair, the other countermarked 'IHS/PB'.

Rastrology: six six-line staves ruled with a two-stave rastrum, span: 48.5, profile: 17(15)17.

[a] Published descriptions of this manuscript refer to different systems of foliation. Sequence A is that applied to the newly discovered source by Robert Spencer and followed in Curtis A. Price, 'Newly Discovered Autograph Keyboard Music of Purcell and Draghi', *JRMA* 120 (1995), 81–3, 98. Foliation B is the current British Library sequence beginning at the 'Purcell End'. The Sotheby's sale catalogue of 1994 used separate sequences starting at either end.

[b] Printed and significant early manuscript concordances only.

[c] Later known as 'La Furstenberg' in Continental sources.

[d] The concluding bars of this movement are copied at the foot of the preceding page.

[e] Number in Giovanni Battista Draghi, *Harpsichord Music*, ed. Robert Klakowich (Madison, 1986). Works without a number were previously unknown.

[f] The double is preceded in Ob MS Mus.Sch. E.397 by the last few bars of the prelude, which appears to have occupied a page now torn out: Kl. nos 45, 46 and 49 may well have been copied into E.397 from Lbl MS Mus.1. See Robert Klakowich, 'Seventeenth-Century English Keyboard Autographs', *JRMA* 121 (1996), 133.

suites in A minor and C major corresponding to those later published in *A Choice Collection*, but in place of the printed A minor saraband is a jig that also appears anonymously in Ob MS Mus.Sch. E.399 and Cfm 653 and the C major suite has a different prelude (see p. 277, n. 24). Concordances and handwriting suggest that Purcell's copying was carried out after 1690, but the manuscript's paper, with an arms of Strasbourg watermark and rather small 'IHS/PB' countermark, probably dates from before 1682 and the order in which the two copyists entered music in the manuscript is therefore uncertain.[29] The overall progression of difficulty certainly implies that Purcell's contribution came first, but the manuscript's paper type points to an opposite interpretation and the absence of any early concordances of the Draghi movements does not of itself prove that they were copied after the Purcell.[30]

By far the most significant non-autograph manuscript source of Purcell's harpsichord music is Och 1177, copied as far as fol. 6r by Edward Lowe and continued by Richard Goodson.[31] At first (fols. 6v–10r) Goodson modelled his hand on Lowe's, adding anonymous movements if anything simpler than the pieces by Portman, La Barre, Gibbs, Bryne and Lowe himself that form the attributed initial contents of the volume: this material might date from *c.* 1675, shortly after the end of Goodson's time as a choirboy. More complex music follows, and on fols. 15v–16r a verse for organ by 'Dr' Blow shows that Goodson must have reached this point after December 1677. The sequence of pieces beginning at the front of the manuscript ends with a prelude in C by Blow which also appears in Cfm 653 (p. 18) and other sources. Most of the longer works in the volume, which include movements by Draghi, Locke, Blow, Purcell and 'Mr Disiner',[32] are copied from the reverse (fols. 41r–17v: see Table 7.10), though the music itself provides no obvious explanation for this arrangement.

[29] Uneven wear on the upper and lower edges of the binding suggests that for many years the Purcell music was considered to be the 'right way up', perhaps simply because the easier material was used more frequently.

[30] Price, 'Newly Discovered Autograph Keyboard Music', 102.

[31] Candace Bailey, ed., *Late-Seventeenth-Century English Keyboard Music: Oxford, Bodleian Library MS Mus.Sch. D.219; Oxford, Christ Church, Mus. MS 1177*, Recent Researches in the Music of the Baroque Era 81 (Madison, 1997).

[32] Gerhard Disiner or Diessener appears to have been a court musician in Kassel from *c.* 1660 to 1673: see William S. Newman, *The Sonata in the Baroque Era*, 3rd edn (New York, 1972), 226–7. A few works appear in English sources, notably *Melothesia* (1673). On 27 November 1684 *The London Gazette* contained an advertisement for his *Kitharapaideia, or a Book of Lessons for the Harpsichords*, but no example of this volume is known.

The Purcell suite movements in Och 1177 were not all copied at the same time. The two movements closely related to *A Choice Collection*, the prelude in G (fol. 29v)[33] and 'Saraband to the lessons before, in A' (fols. 23r–22v), share a distinctive style of handwriting and were evidently transcribed into the manuscript as additions to existing Purcell material: the prelude, written in a compressed manner uncharacteristic of Goodson, occupies a single page that had been left blank so the following almand in G could be copied on a single opening. Much of the manuscript could have been copied before binding, and the original, highly distinctive, Purcell suite movements beginning on the first verso (fol. 29r INV) of a six-folio gathering could well be earlier than the C minor ground transcribed from *Ye tuneful muses* of 1686 on fols. 32r–31v[34] and the arrangement of Lully's Italian ground-bass song *Scocca pur tutti* on fols. 31r–30r, which in any case is independent of *Musick's Hand-maid* (1689).[35]

If Richard Goodson is to be identified with 'R.G.', author of an elegy printed in the second book of *Orpheus Britannicus* (1702), he claimed personal friendship with Purcell:

> And now farewell! nor fame, nor love, nor art,
> Nor tears avail! – we must for ever part!
> For ever! Dismal accent! What alone!
> But that can tell our loss, or reach our moan!
> What term of sorrow preference dare contend?
> What? but the tenderest dearest name of – friend!

In the early 1680s Goodson copied three sonatas and the five-part Fantazia upon One Note from Purcell's autograph Lbl Add. 30930 into Och 3 and Och 620. This demonstrable connection with Purcell means that the variant Purcell movements in Och 1177 are highly likely to descend from an authoritative source (Illus. 7.3).[36]

### Other sources of Purcell's harpsichord music

Many further manuscripts contain harpsichord music by Purcell, but in several, such as Lbl Add. 31465 and 52363, B-Bc XY 15139Z and the 'Wild Court' volume, US-LAuc D173/M4/H295/1690/bound, the Purcell movements are

[33] See Purcell, *Eight Suites*, ed. Ferguson, 29. Goodson seems to have realised the inaccuracy of the print after the first six bars and checked for mistakes before continuing.

[34] See Robert Klakowich, '*Scocca pur*: Genesis of an English Ground', *JRMA* 116 (1991), 73–6.

[35] Ibid.; Purcell is suggested as a possible arranger of the keyboard version.

[36] As is suggested in *Eight Suites*, ed. Ferguson, 24–5.

## Table 7.10 Oxford, Christ Church Mus. 1177: contents of reverse sequence

| Folios | Key | Heading | Ascription | Concordances[a] |
|---|---|---|---|---|
| 41r–40v | d | Almaine | [Draghi] | |
| 40r | d | Corant | [Draghi] | |
| 39v | d | Sarabant | Sgr Batis [Draghi] | |
| 39r–38v | G | Almand | Mr Mat: Lock | Add. 31403, fol. 57v; Add. 31465, fol. 43v |
| 38r–37v | G | Corant | Dr Blow | Add. 31403, fol. 56v; Add. 31465, fol. 43v |
| 37r | | [incomplete work] | | |
| 36r–35v | D | Almaine | Dr Jo: Blow | |
| 34r–33v | d | Almaine | Dr Jo: Blow | |
| 32r–31v | c | [Ground] | [Purcell] Z.T681 | Cfm 653, p. 30 |
| 31r–30r | c | [Ground 'Scocca pur']<sup>b</sup> | | 2MHM1689 |
| 29v | G | Prelude | Mr H. Purcell Z.662/1 | CCL1696 |
| 29r–28v | G | Allmand | Mr Purcell Z.662/2 | CCL1696 |
| 28r–27v | G | Corant | [Purcell] Z.662/3 | CCL1696 |
| 27r–26v | a | [Saraband] | Mr H: Purcell Z.654<sup>c</sup> | |
| 26v–25v | D | Trumpett Almond | | Add. 31403, fol. 58v |
| 24v | a | Prelude | [Purcell] | |
| 24r | a | Almand | [Purcell] Z.663/2 | Cfm 653, p. 16; F-Pc Rés.1186 bis Part 1, fol. 44r; Lbl MS Mus.1 |
| 23v | a | Corant | [Purcell] Z.663/3 | Cfm 653, p. 16; F-Pc Rés.1186 bis Part 1, fol. 44v; Lbl MS Mus.1 |
| 23r | d | [Almain] | [Draghi/Blow]<sup>d</sup> | SSSL1707 |
| 23r–22v | a | Saraband to the lessons before, in A | [Purcell] Z.663/4 | |
| 22r–20v | G | Morlake Ground | Dr Blow | 2MHM1689; Add. 31403, fol. 61v; F-Pc Rés.1186 bis Part 1, fol. 38v |
| 20r–18v<sup>e</sup> | g | Ground | Dr Blow | Cfm 653, p. 26 |
| 18v | C | Ground | Mr Disiner | |
| 18r–17v | b | [Ground] | | |

Key to printed concordances
CCL1696    *A Choice Collection of Lessons*
2MHM1689    *The Second Part of Musick's Hand-maid*
SSSL1707    G. B. Draghi, *Six Select Sutes of Lessons for the Harpsicord*

Folio, 326 × 207. Contemporary limp vellum covers preserved within modern binding, now cut down to 323 × 206. Watermark: arms of Amsterdam with ornate countermark consisting of a plant or branch between two pillars, or the letters 'II', the whole surrounded by a wreath surmounted by a fleur-de-lys.<sup>f</sup>

Rastrology: eight six-line staves ruled with a four-stave rastrum: span: 120.5, profile: 16.5(18)16(19.5)16.5(17)16.5.<sup>g</sup>

Copyist: Richard Goodson I

**Table 7.10 (*cont.*)**

*ᵃ* Primary sources only; for full details of concordances see Candace Bailey, ed., *Late-Seventeenth-Century English Keyboard Music: Oxford, Bodleian Library MS Mus.Sch. D.219; Oxford, Christ Church, Mus. MS 1177* (Madison, 1997), 100–3.

*ᵇ* Possibly arranged by Purcell; see Robert Klakowich, '*Scocca pur*: Genesis of an English Ground', *JRMA* 116 (1991), 73–6.

*ᶜ* Clearly attributed to Purcell, but the somewhat unimaginative divisions may be by Goodson.

*ᵈ* The early manuscripts B-Bc XY 15139Z and Lbl Eg. 2959 attribute this movement to Blow, though it was published as Draghi's in *Six Select Sutes*.

*ᵉ* On fol. 19v is the cancelled line of text 'How blest are shepherds how happy their', from *King Arthur* (1691). This has no connection with any of the music in the manuscript.

*ᶠ* The same watermarks appear in Och 1176.

*ᵍ* As in Och 1176.

mainly or entirely transcribed from printed sources.[37] Two volumes copied by Charles Babel, Lbl Add. 39569 and Ob MS Tenbury 1508, appear to be based on the printed editions but include extra ornamentation.[38] Table 7.11 lists manuscripts which contain Purcell movements clearly independent of the 1689 and 1696 publications.[39]

Och 1176, mainly in Edward Lowe's hand and sharing its paper type and ruling with Och 1177, is essentially a book of organ voluntaries by Orlando Gibbons, Christopher Gibbons and John Hingeston, to which Goodson's few additions (fols. 14r–16r) are largely unrelated. They include a copy of Purcell's C major almand Z.665/2 differing in a few details from the version published in *Musick's Hand-maid* but resembling that of Och 1179, another manuscript known to have been in Oxford in the late seventeenth century. In the extensive early eighteenth-century keyboard book Cfm 653 the suite in C seems to have come more or less directly from *A Choice Collection*[40] but pp. 89–91 contain a distinctive suite in G: the copyist later added the

---

[37] See *Eight Suites*, ed. Ferguson, 24; Peter Holman, 'A New Source of Restoration Keyboard Music', *RMARC* 20 (1986–7), 53–7; Robert Klakowich, 'Harpsichord Music by Purcell and Clarke in Los Angeles', *Journal of Musicology* 4 (1985–6), 171–90.

[38] *Eight Suites*, ed. Ferguson, 24. The hand of Charles Babel (fl. *c.* 1700) is identifiable through a signature in Ob MS Mus.Sch. E.393: he copied Lbl Add. 39569 and Ob MS Tenbury 1508 for his son William (*c.* 1690–1723), and also the instrumental partbooks Cmc F.4.35 (1–5) described below. See Hawkins, *History*, II, 826; *London, British Library MS Add. 39569 ('Babell MS')* (facsimile edn), intro. by Bruce Gustafson (New York and London, 1987); Rebecca Herissone, 'The Magdalene College Partbooks: Origins and Contents', *RMARC* 29 (1996), 47–95.

[39] Other early sources not of primary importance for their Purcell content include CDp M.C.I.39(j) and US-Cn VM2.3 E58r. See Malcolm Boyd, 'Music Manuscripts in the Mackworth Collection at Cardiff', *M&L* 54 (1973), 133–41; Richard Charteris, 'Some Manuscript Discoveries of Henry Purcell and his Contemporaries in the Newberry Library, Chicago', *Notes* 37 (1980), 7–13; Bruce Gustafson, *French Harpsichord Music of the Seventeenth Century* (Ann Arbor, 1979).

[40] *Eight Suites*, ed. Ferguson, 25.

Illus. 7.3  Henry Purcell: unique prelude to the keyboard suite in A minor, copied by the elder
Richard Goodson. Christ Church, Oxford, Mus. 1177, fol. 24v INV

published corant and saraband Z.660/3 and 4. The almand and corant in A minor, like the jig concordant with Lbl MS Mus.1, descend from manuscript rather than printed sources; the same two movements also appear alongside music attributed elsewhere to William Croft in F-Pc Rés. 1186 bis Part 1, where they are unlikely to have been copied before the mid-1690s. Lbl Add. 31403, a large keyboard volume commenced *c.* 1633 by Edward Bevin,[41] contains organ and harpsichord music added some fifty or more years later, mostly by Daniel Henstridge:[42] much of his hand-writing resembles that of Cfm 118 (*c.* 1681–5), but Purcell's harpsichord preludes in C major and G minor immediately precede the overture to William Croft's *Laurus cruentas* of 1713 and look as though they belong to a later stage in Henstridge's career. In another hand is a version of Purcell's G minor suite Z.661, anonymous and with a different prelude replacing the one published in 1696 (fols. 35r–36r). US-LAuc M678/M4/H295/1710/bound mainly contains transcriptions of theatre pieces, one, a keyboard setting of a minuet from *The Virtuous Wife*, concordant with the autograph Lbl MS Mus.1.[43]

En Inglis 94 MS 3343 is possibly the work of the London organist Philip Hart, whose name is not given the formal title 'Mr' in any of fourteen attributions: the hand is not the same as in his established autograph Lbl Add. 32161, fols. 84v–85r, but the two manuscripts could be separated by some forty years and the apparent signatures are strikingly similar. One flyleaf inscription 'Essex Deane 1695' identi-fies a son of Sir Anthony Deane (*c.* 1626–1721), Commissioner of the Royal Navy,[44] and another records that in 1719 Sir Anthony gave the book to Diana Gostlin.[45] The manuscript's contents are more likely to have been copied *c.*1695

[41] Son of Elway Bevin: see Robert Ford, 'Bevins, Father and Son', *MR* 43 (1982), 104–8.

[42] Further organ parts, voluntaries, didactic examples and exercises, often incomplete or in pencil, were added by eighteenth-century hands.

[43] See Klakowich, 'Harpsichord Music', 183–5.

[44] Essex Deane (b. 25 April 1682) was a son of Sir Anthony's second marriage. See Gwilym Beechey, 'A New Source of Seventeenth-Century Keyboard Music', *M&L* 50 (1969), 278–89; Percival Boyd: 'Inhabitants of London' (MS at Society of Genealogists, London); William Musgrave, *Obituary Prior to 1800, as far as Relates to England Scotland and Ireland*, 6 vols. (London, 1899–1901), II, 160; Joseph Foster, ed., *London Marriage Licences, 1521–1869* (London, 1887), 391; W. Bruce Bannerman, ed., *The Registers of St Olave Hart Street, London, 1563–1700* (London, 1916).

[45] Diana Gostlin (d. 1747) was a sister of Francis Gosling (d. 1768), a member of the Stationers' Company and a partner in Gosling, Bennett and Gosling, bankers to the East India Company. Diana Gosling married Robert Wynne of Garthewin, Denbighshire, in whose family En Inglis 94 MS 3343 remained for many years. See Boyd, 'Inhabitants'; J. Burke, *A Genealogical and Heraldic History of the Commoners of Great Britain and Ireland*, 4 vols. (London, 1833–8), III, 646–7; Musgrave, *Obituary*, II, 160; Lucy S. Sutherland, *The East India Company in Eighteenth-Century Politics* (Oxford, 1952), 102, 105, 117, 125; Beechey, 'A New Source'.

Table 7.11 Other primary manuscript sources of harpsichord music by Purcell

| Manuscript | Title | Page or folio | Comments |
|---|---|---|---|
| Cfm 653 | Almand, a, Z.663/2 | p. 16 | unascribed |
| | Corant, a, Z.663/3 | p. 16 | unascribed |
| | Air, C, Z.T683 | p. 19 | unascribed: a version of the hornpipe in B♭ from *Abdelazar* |
| | Trumpet March, C, Z.T698 | p. 20 | unascribed: from *The Indian Queen* |
| | Ground, c, Z.T681 | p. 30 | |
| | Hornpipe, e, Z.T685 | p. 57 | from *The Old Bachelor* |
| | Air, d, Z.T676 | p. 77 | from *The Double Dealer* |
| | [Prelude], a, Z.652[a] | p. 81 | unascribed |
| | Jigg, a | p. 88 | |
| | Minuit, a, Z.650 | p. 88 | |
| | Prelude, G, Z.660/1 | p. 89 | |
| | Almand [with divisions], G, Z.643[b] | p. 90 | |
| | Corant, G, Z.644[c] | p. 91 | |
| | Air [duple time], G, Z.641 | p. 91 | |
| | Minuet, G, Z.651 | p. 95 | |
| | Overture, D, Z.T691[d] | p. 96 | from *Timon of Athens* |
| | Chacone, g, Z.T680 | p. 101 | unascribed: from *Timon of Athens* |
| | Jigg, g, Z.T686 | p. 103 | unascribed: from *Abdelazar* |
| | Overture, C | p. 106 | unascribed: from *Bonduca* |
| | Prelude, C, Z.666/1 | p. 107 | unascribed |
| | Almand, C, Z.666/2 | p. 108 | unascribed |
| | Corant, C, Z.666/3 | p. 109 | unascribed |
| | Sarabrand, C, Z.666/4 | p. 109 | unascribed |
| | Corant, [Saraband], G, Z.660/3, 4 | p. 110 | |
| | [Overture], d | p. 114 | unascribed: from *King Arthur* |
| Och 46 | Saraband, C, Z.666/4 | fol. 65r | |
| | A Ground in Gamut set by Mr Purcel, g, Z.645 | fol. 64r | |
| | [Britons strike home], Z.574/2 | fol. 62v | from *Bonduca* |
| Och 1176 | [Almand], C, Z.665/2 | fol. 14r | copied by Richard Goodson |
| Och 1179 | [Almand], C, Z.665/2 | p. 21 | copied by FQ4 |
| Add. 31403 | Prelude, g | fol. 35r | Suite in g, Z.661, with alternative prelude |
| | Almaine, g, Z.661/2 | fol. 35v | |
| | Corrant, g, Z.661/3 | fol. 36r | |
| | Sarraband, g, Z.661/4 | fol. 36r | |
| | Prelude, C, Z.666/1 | fol. 37v | copied by Daniel Henstridge |
| | Prelude, g, Z.661/1 | fol. 38r | copied by Daniel Henstridge |
| En Inglis 94 MS 3343 | Brittans Strike Home, Z.574/2 | fol. 19v | tunes from *Bonduca*: MS possibly |
| | [Song tune], Z.574/3 | fol. 20v | copied by Philip Hart |

## Table 7.11 (*cont.*)

| Manuscript | Title | Page or folio | Comments |
|---|---|---|---|
| | A Tune, Z.574/4 | fol. 21v | |
| | [Hornpipe], Z.574/5 | fol. 22v | |
| | A Tune, Z.574/6 | fol. 23v | |
| | A Tune, Z.574/7 | fol. 24r | |
| | Tune, Z.574/8 | fol. 24v | |
| | A Tune, Z.574/9 | fol. 25v | 'The End of ye: Sett By: Mr: Henry Purcell' |
| | A Tune, Z.611/9 | fol. 27v | 'Mr: Henry Purcell': from *The Virtuous Wife* ('La Furstenberg', in a) |
| | Sebell, Z.T678 | fol. 29v | |
| | [Hornpipe], Z.629/1b | fol. 54v | from *The Fairy Queen* |
| | [Decorated version of Z.574/6] | fol. 60v | Mr: Hen: Purcell |
| F-Pc Rés. 1186 bis Part 1 | Almand, a, Z.663/2 | fol. 44r | |
| | Corant, a, Z.663/3 | fol. 44v | |
| US-LAuc M678/M4/ H295/1710/ bound | ["Twas within a furlong of Edinboro' town', Z.605/2] | fol. 1r | *The Mock Marriage*; ascr. Clarke in Lbl Add. 22099 |
| | [Trumpet Tune, called the Cibell, Z.T678] | fol. 2r | |
| | [Hornpipe], Z.T683 | fol. 4v | from *Abdelazar* |
| | [Minuet], Z.632/5 | fol. 5r | from *Timon of Athens*: unique transcription |
| | [Jig], Z.T686 | fol. 5v | from *Abdelazar* |
| | [Prelude], Z.665/1 | fol. 12r | in D, amongst movements by R. King |
| | [A New Ground], Z.T682 | fol. 15v | |
| | [Trumpet Tune], Z.T698 | fol. 34v INV | |
| | [Hornpipe], Z.628/18 | fol. 31v INV | from *King Arthur*: unique transcription |
| | [Ground], c, Z.681 | fol. 24r INV | |
| | [Minuet], Z.611/7 | fol. 22r INV | from *The Virtuous Wife*: in Lbl MS Mus.1 |
| US-Wc M21/ M185/Case | Overture, Z.T691 (632/1) | p. 53 | from *Timon of Athens* |
| | [Air], Z.574/6 | p. 96 | from *Bonduca*: MS copied by London A |

[a] Considered by Ferguson to be spurious: see Henry Purcell, *Miscellaneous Keyboard Pieces*, ed. Howard Ferguson, 2nd edn (London, 1968), 36.
[b] The almand (Z.660/2) of the printed Suite in G with spurious divisions: ibid.
[c] Considered 'doubtful' by Ferguson: ibid., 28.
[d] Also in Lbl Add. 41205; Hirsch III.472; US-NYp Drexel 5609; US-Wc M21/M185/Case.

than in 1719: they include two concordances with Lbl MS Mus.1, an arrangement of the *Fairy Queen* hornpipe and the common-time tune from *The Virtuous Wife*,[46] and a sequence of movements from *Bonduca* in the same order as in *Ayres for the Theatre* of 1697.

The argument for identifying the copyist of US-Wc M21/M185/Case, London A, with the Chapel Royal organist Francis Pigott is strengthened by this manuscript's contents,[47] which include six toccatas and a sonata by Italian composers such as Bernardo Pasquini and Fabrizio Fontana and five extracts from sonatas by Kuhnau as well as several works by Draghi. The continental music copied here by London A is evidence that a similar repertory passed through Purcell's hands, possibly including the toccata in A (Z.D229) attributed to him in the organ books Lbl Add. 31446 and Add. 34695 (see below).[48] These two sources, in which the toccata appears in closely related readings, come from northeastern England and the work might have been taken to Durham by Purcell's pupil Robert Hodge in 1693.

### SOURCES OF ORGAN MUSIC

Many of Purcell's authenticated organ works were copied by provincial musicians unconnected with the Chapel Royal (Table 7.12). An extract from an auction catalogue attached to the modern front cover of Lbl Add. 31446 claims that the book once contained 'the Autograph of "George Holmes his Book" 1698 at my Lord Bishop of Durham's'; Holmes (*c.* 1680–1721) began his career at Durham[49] and there is no reason to doubt that he was the copyist of the manuscript, which includes the toccata in A, Z.D229, and the single organ version of the voluntary in D minor. Lbl Add. 31468, an organ book containing a few harpsichord pieces, is

---

[46] Possibly an arrangement by Purcell of an existing melody: the tune became well known in France during the eighteenth century under the title 'La Furstenberg', and for some reason was not included with other movements from *The Virtuous Wife* in *Ayres* (1697). See Guy Oldham, '"La Furstenberg" and Purcell', *Recherches sur la musique française classique* 3 (1963), 39–41.

[47] See *Washington, D.C., Library of Congress MS M21.M185 Case* (facsimile edn), intro. by Alexander Silbiger (London and New York, 1987).

[48] The toccata appears without attribution in Lbl Add. 24313, an undoubtedly English manuscript also containing five toccatas by Michelangelo Rossi (d. 1656); in Lbl Add. 39569, copied by Charles Babel, its first part is used anonymously as the prelude to a suite in A (fols. 4v–6r). See Gloria Rose, 'Purcell, Michelangelo Rossi and J. S. Bach: Problems of Authorship', *AcM* 40 (1968), 203–19.

[49] Holmes was a chorister at Durham Cathedral from 1688 to 1694 and subsequently became organist to the Bishop of Durham: from 1705 until his death he was organist of Lincoln Cathedral. See Crosby, *Catalogue*, 175; Shaw, *The Succession*, 161; Spink, *Restoration*, 65–8, 286–9.

## Table 7.12  Sources of Purcell's organ music

| Manuscript | Format | Dimensions | Watermarks | Works and ascriptions |
|---|---|---|---|---|
| Lbl Add. 31446 | oblong quarto | 235 × 358 | Angoumois-style† fleur-de-lys, with countermark monogram 'PVL' (?) | 'Toccato by Mr Hen: Purcell', fols. 5v–9r[a] [Voluntary, d], Mr H. Purcell, fols. 9v–10v |
| Lbl Add. 31465 | oblong sexto | 120 × 240 | simple fleur-de-lys with countermark 'CDG' | 'A Vers' (in F, Z.716), fols. 21v–22r |
| Lbl Add. 31468 | oblong quarto | 186 × 260 | Angoumois-style† fleur-de-lys, with countermark 'LVG' (?) | Prelude, a, Z.652, fols. 7v–8r* 'A Volantary for ye Duble Organ by Mr Henry Percell', fols. 24v–27r |
| Lbl Add. 34695 | oblong quarto | 223 × 331 | Angoumois fleur-de-lys with countermark 'IV' | Voluntary, G, Z.720, fols. 13v–14r Prelude, g, Z.661/1, fols. 14v–15r Prelude, G, Z.662/1, fols. 15v–16r Prelude, C, Z.666/1, fols. 16v–17r [Voluntary on Psalm 100], Mr Henry Purcell, fols. 27v–28v* 'Toccato by Mr Hen: Purcell', fols. 41v–45r[b] Prelude, a, Z.652, fols. 57v–58r* |
| Och 1179 | folio | 285 × 181 | posthorn | [Voluntary] 'In C', Z.717, p. 38 [Almand], C, Z.665/2, p. 21 |

Rastrology

| Source | Staves on page | Staves in rastrum | Rastrum span | Rastrum profile |
|---|---|---|---|---|
| Lbl Add. 31446 | 6§ | 3 | 84 | 17.5(15.5)16.5(17)17 |
| Lbl Add. 31465[c] | 4§ | 1 | 14.5 | |
| Lbl Add. 31468 | 6§ | 3 | 66.5 | 13.5(13.5)13(13.5)12.5 |
| Lbl Add. 34695 | 6§ | 1 | 14.5 | |
| Och 1179 | 8§ | 4 | 102.5 | 13.5(16)14(16.5)13.5(15.5)13.5 |

\* Probably not by Purcell.

† The countermarks suggest that these papers are Dutch.

§ Six-line staves.

[a] Ascription repeated at end.

[b] Ascription added later, though apparently in the main hand.

[c] Fols. 2–6, which include instructions 'for playing on a continued Bass' from *Melothesia*, are ruled differently without the use of a rastrum, though the paper itself is the same as that of the rest of the volume.

entirely in the hand of William Davis, whose inscription 'Will. Davis Ejus Liber' appears on the reverse flyleaf.[50] From 1693 Davis was a lay clerk of Worcester Cathedral, where he later became Master of the Choristers: his manuscript is unlikely to date from much after 1700 and is the unique source of 'A Volantary for ye Duble Organ by Mr Henry Purcell' (fols. 24v–27r). Lbl Add. 31465 and Add.

[50] Spink, *Restoration*, 395–8.

34695 are in the hand of Nicholas Harrison, a professional copyist at work in northeastern England,[51] whose name appears on fol. 1v of the former manuscript. The paper and handwriting of both volumes clearly belong to the eighteenth century: Add. 34695 is the only source of the Voluntary in G, Z.720, and Add. 31465, primarily a collection of harpsichord music, of the Verse in F, Z.716. The imperfect text of the Voluntary in C, Z.717, was copied by FQ4 in Och 1179, which belonged to George Lluellen (1668–1739).[52]

## Miscellaneous sources of instrumental music

The printed editions of Purcell's sonatas and *A Collection of Ayres, Compos'd for the Theatre* constitute primary sources of the majority of Purcell's instrumental compositions, but several manuscripts nevertheless appear to be of the first importance. A few pages of the guardbook US-NHb Osborn 515 contain some of Purcell's earliest surviving autographs, and the scorebook Lbl R.M. 20.h.9 seems to have a close connection with the composer. Four sources of theatre music, Lcm 1144 and 1172, Lbl Add. 30839 and 39565–7 (a set of four partbooks), and Cmc F.4.35 (1–5) reflect a later stage of Purcell's career and are at least partly independent of the published *Ayres* of 1697. A further manuscript, Y M15(S), is the unique source of Purcell's 'Trumpet Sonata'.

### New Haven, Yale University, Beinecke Rare Book and Manuscript Library, Osborn MS 515

US-NHb Osborn 515 is a guardbook containing bass parts of music varying from consort works by Jenkins and Lawes to theatre tunes of the 1690s.[53] It must have

---

[51] A bill at Durham Cathedral dated 18 November 1709 states that Harrison lived in Gateshead: see Crosby, *Catalogue*, 244.

[52] George Lluellen was a son of the Buckinghamshire physician and author Martin Lluellen. According to Hawkins he was a page of the back stairs at the court of Charles II, where he became acquainted with Purcell; after the king's death he studied at Merton College and Christ Church, Oxford. In 1705 he became rector of Pulverbatch in Shropshire. Lluellen was credited by Hawkins with having preserved copies of a number of Purcell songs incorporated in the second edition of *Orpheus Britannicus*. See Hawkins, *History*, II, 749n; Burney, *History*, II, 394n; Foster, *Alumni*, III, 921, s.v. Llewellyn; *DNB*, XI, 1320, s.v. Lluelyn, Martin.

[53] A comprehensive description is in Robert Ford, 'Osborn MS 515: a Guardbook of Restoration Instrumental Music', *FAM* 30 (1983), 174–84. See also Alan Browning, 'Purcell's "Stairre Case Overture"', *MT* 121 (1980), 768–9; Gloria Rose, 'A New Purcell Source', *JAMS* 25 (1972), 230–6.

belonged to a set of at least five volumes, as it includes some five-part movements by Dietrich Becker, and was bound *c*. 1700 because the latest section, consisting of theatre tunes from *Timon of Athens* and unidentified music by Daniel Purcell, is in the hand of London E, active around the turn of the century. The compiler of the collection, who was also the copyist of much of the music, provided an index on the first flyleaf verso and added ascriptions at various points throughout the volume.

Several features of Osborn 515 suggest Kentish provenance. One folio is in the hand of a scribe associated elsewhere with Sir Robert Filmer,[54] of East Sutton, Kent, and another is an autograph of Robert Wren, lay clerk and organist of Canterbury Cathedral from 1671 to 1691.[55] Fols. 2 and 3, in the compiler's hand, contain the bass of two examples from Athanasius Kircher, *Musurgia Universalis* (Rome, 1650) and identify Osborn 515 with part of lot 13 (second day) in William Gostling's auction catalogue of 1777: 'Jenkins's, Purcell's, &c. &c. Sonatas and Overtures, with Kircher's extolled Sonata, MS.'[56]

Apart from the later *Timon of Athens* movements, the manuscript contains ten movements either definitely ascribed to Purcell by the compiler or likely to be his because of their context (Table 7.13), including six unique autograph movements written in a hand resembling that of the early Funeral Sentences in Lbl Add. 30931: the stave ruling of one of the autograph folios, fol. 9, is the same as that of fol. 1, the bass part of Locke's Curtain Tune from *The Tempest* (1674). In the later eighteenth century Osborn 515 and its companions passed through the hands of Philip Hayes, who transcribed a score of the Purcell 'Stairre Case Overture' from them at the end of Ktp MR 2–5.3: by this time one volume, containing the overture's tenor part, was missing, though as well as the two treble books and the surviving string bass there was a separate basso continuo.[57] In 1814, when the set formed lot 633 of Charles Burney's sale, there were three volumes[58] and W. H. Cummings, whose bookplate appears in the manuscript, owned only the surviving bass book.

---

[54] US-NH Filmer 7; see Ford, 'Osborn MS 515', 175.
[55] Ibid., 175, and Spink, *Restoration*, 209–10.    [56] Ford, 'Osborn MS 515', 176.
[57] Browning, 'Purcell's "Stairre Case Overture"', 769; see also *Works*, XXXI (1990), 76–8, 122–3. Hayes sometimes supplied missing continuo lines in his transcriptions, but he is unlikely to have invented the distinctive continuo bass of this movement.
[58] *Works*, XXXI (1990), xiv–xv.

**Table 7.13  New Haven, Beinecke Rare Book and Manuscript Library, Osborn MS 515: music by Purcell**

| Folios | Heading or description | Copyist | Comments |
|---|---|---|---|
| 9r | Pavana | Purcell | separate movements; both in F minor |
| | Allegro [time signature 31 = 9/4] | | |
| 10r | Chacone | compiler | appears in *The Gordian Knot Unty'd* (1691) |
| 11r | 'a.4.' [French overture in C with concluding 'grave'] | compiler | |
| 11v | [untitled piece in B minor, apparently an almand, copied at the bottom of the page] | compiler | no ascription in text; possibly covered by index ascription '4. Pavans & Chicones. Hen. Purcel.' |
| 15r–16v | [incidental music from *Timon of Athens*] | London E | |
| 19r | The Stairre Case Overture in B me | Purcell | |
| 20r | A Pavin | Purcell | not in fact a pavan but a tripartite movement in F minor containing a section in triple time |
| 20r | Prelude [B minor] | compiler | not ascribed to Purcell; possibly connected to the almand in B minor on fol. 11v |
| 20v | Overture | Purcell | separate movements in C |
| | Allegro | | major |

Folio guardbook of varied material

| Folios | Dimensions | Watermark |
|---|---|---|
| 9 | 318 × 202 | faint countermark 'IB' (possibly 'PB') |
| 10 | 313 × 200 | unusual Dutch Lion with factor's mark 'HC' |
| 11–12 (bifolium?) | 318 × 198 | foolscap (fol. 12) |
| 15–16 (bifolium) | 318 × 201 | Dutch Lion (fol. 15); countermark 'IW' (fol. 16) |
| 19–20 (bifolium?) | 318 × 203 | foolscap (fol. 19); countermark 'CDG' (fol. 20) |

Rastrology

| Folios | Staves on page | Staves in rastrum | Rastrum span | Rastrum profile |
|---|---|---|---|---|
| 9 | 10 | 5 | 120 | 11.5(15)12.5(15.5)12(14.5)12(15)12 |
| 10 | 12 | 1 | 11.5 | 11.5 |
| 11–12 | 10 | 5 | 117 | 13(13.5)13.5(12.5)13(14)12.5(12)13 |
| 15–16 | 12 | 4 | 83 | 11(13.5)11(13)10.5(13)11 |
| 19–20 | 10 | 5 | 128 | 12(16)13(15.5)14(15.5)14(15)13 |

## London, British Library, Royal Music 20.h.9

A range of circumstantial evidence establishes that the principal copyist of R.M. 20.h.9 (Table 7.14) was John Reading, organist of Winchester Cathedral from 1675 to 1681 and of Winchester College from the latter year until 1692 (Illus. 7.4). The canon attributed to 'John Reading' written at the foot of fols. 6v–7r is the only work given an ascription without a formal title, and the same hand appears in US-BE 751, a manuscript of undoubted Winchester provenance,[59] as well as Lbl Add. 47845. Perhaps as a result of the court's visits to Winchester between 1682 and 1684 (see p. 145), Reading had access to substantial Purcell works not in general circulation, to canonic exercises Purcell might have written during the study of polyphony that gave rise to the fantazias and, to judge from the annotations on fols. 108v and 110v, to the familiar gossip of court musicians.

The manuscript's fleur-de-lys watermark and elaborate 'PSAB' countermark seem to date from around 1680. They occur in paper ruled identically to R.M. 20.h.9 in Bu 5002 and Lbl Add. 33235; similar paper with a different rastrology forms some folios of Ob MSS Mus.Sch. C.20–23, a set of parts copied by Edward Lowe and annotated 'the paper & binding of thes 4 Bookes cost 9s 6d the 1st of May 1680'.[60] It has been argued that the second work in the reverse sequence, Purcell's five-part overture in G minor, must have been composed after 1687, when Draghi's St Cecilia ode started a fashion for Italianate five-part string writing,[61] but although the work is undoubtedly Italian rather than French in scoring, with two violin parts in the treble clef, it is a French overture in style until it reaches its coda of sustained minims. The contrapuntal complexity of its central imitative section links it to the fantazias,[62] and supports the date *c.*1682–5 indicated for R.M. 20.h.9 by other evidence.

In the bass partbook US-NH Filmer 8, pp. 95–7, the G minor overture is followed by five dances,[63] forming a suite with an overall attribution to Purcell: a triple-time air in rondo form, a bourrée, two further triple-time dances and a 'jigg'. This work must have been broadly comparable to the incomplete four-part suite in G in Lbl Add. 30930, fols. 54r–52v INV (see Tables 3.2 and 3.4), in which the bass of the

---

[59] See Peter Holman, 'Purcell and Roseingrave: a New Autograph', in *Purcell Studies*, 100.

[60] A further occurrence of the watermark and countermark is in US-LAuc fC6966/M4/A627/1700: see Theodore M. Finney, 'A Manuscript Collection of English Restoration Anthems', *JAMS* 15 (1962), 193–9.

[61] Holman, *Henry Purcell*, 66.    [62] Adams, *Henry Purcell*, 106.

[63] See Ford, 'The Filmer Manuscripts', 818.

## Table 7.14 London, British Library R.M. 20.h.9: contents

| Folios | Heading or incipit | Ascription and comments |
|---|---|---|
| 1r–1v | [Canon] 4 in 2 Arsin per Thesin 'Gloria Patri'*a** | Mr Henry Pursell |
| 1v–2r | 'Miserere' 4 in 2* | Mr Henry Pursell |
| 2r | 'God is gone up with a merry noise'* | '7: parts by Mr Henry Pursell' |
| 2v–5v | O how Amiable | Dr Blow |
| 6r–17v | Sing unto ye Lord O ye Saints of his*b* | Dr Blow |
| 6v–7r | A Cannon of 4:in:2: Arsin and Thesin | John Reading |
| 18r–20v | Lord thou art become gracious | Mr Rosingrave |
| 21r–25r | Sing we Merrily | Dr Blow [without symphonies] |
| 25v–37r | Service in B:flatt [Te deum; Benedictus; Commandments; Creed] | Mr Purcell |
| 37v–40v | [Service in B♭: Magnificat; Nunc dimittis]*c* | [Purcell] Untitled; anonymous; textless. In an eighteenth-century hand |

[manuscript inverted]

| | | |
|---|---|---|
| 121r–118r | 3 parts upon a Ground play'd 2 notes higher for F[lutes]† | Mr Henry Pursell [in D, i.e. transposed for violins] |
| 117v–115r | 5 parts; Overture [G minor] | Mr Henry Pursell |
| 114v–113v | Overture [D minor]* | Mr Henry Pursell |
| 113r–112r | Overture [G major]* | Mr Henry Pursell |
| 111v–111r | Duo | |
| 110v–109r | 'Dragon'; 'This peice of Musick was Christ'ned Draggon at New Markett 1679'*d* | |
| 108v–108r | 'Seignor Givano Battista Vately Symphony w[hich] M[r] Nich. Staggins produced as his owne May 29th 1679'*e* | [G. B. Vitali] |
| 108r–105r | A Sonata of 3 parts | Dr Blow |
| 105r–103r | [Sonata] | Senior Giovana Battista [Vitali] Op. 5 no. 8, 'La Guidoni' |
| 102v–99r | [Piece for violin, viola da gamba and bc]*f* | |
| 98v–52r | Sonatas of three Parts with a Through-Base | Henry Purcell 'Aged 25 in ye Yeare 1683' Sonata primo [etc.] |
| 52r–41r | Sonnata Prima Mr Young's three parts [etc.: three more sonatas, the last incomplete]*g* | [William] Young |

Folio, 365 × 233. Binding: contemporary vellum, 370 × 240. Watermarks: Angoumois fleur-de-lys countermarked monogram 'PSAB'; original front flyleaves, watermark posthorn with monogram 'GVH' factor's mark.

Rastrology: twelve staves ruled with a four-stave rastrum, span: 99, profile: 13(15)14(14)14(15)13.5.

Copyist: John Reading

---

* Unique Purcell source.

† Only complete source of a Purcell work.

*a* Followed on fol. 1v by a five-bar passage illustrating the treatment of suspensions.

*b* Incomplete, as in all other sources.

*c* Several leaves were torn out between fols. 37 and 38, presumably before the textless Magnificat was copied.

*d* 'Dragon', the 'top horse of England' was a racehorse belonging to Charles II: see *CSPD 1682*, 456.

*e* See Holman, *Four and Twenty Fiddlers*, 300–2.

*f* See Mark Caudle, 'The English Repertory for Violin, Bass Viol and Continuo', *Chelys* 6 (1975–6), 70.

*g* Ibid., 74. Two leaves appear to have been torn out between fols. 40 and 41, so the last sonata may once have been complete.

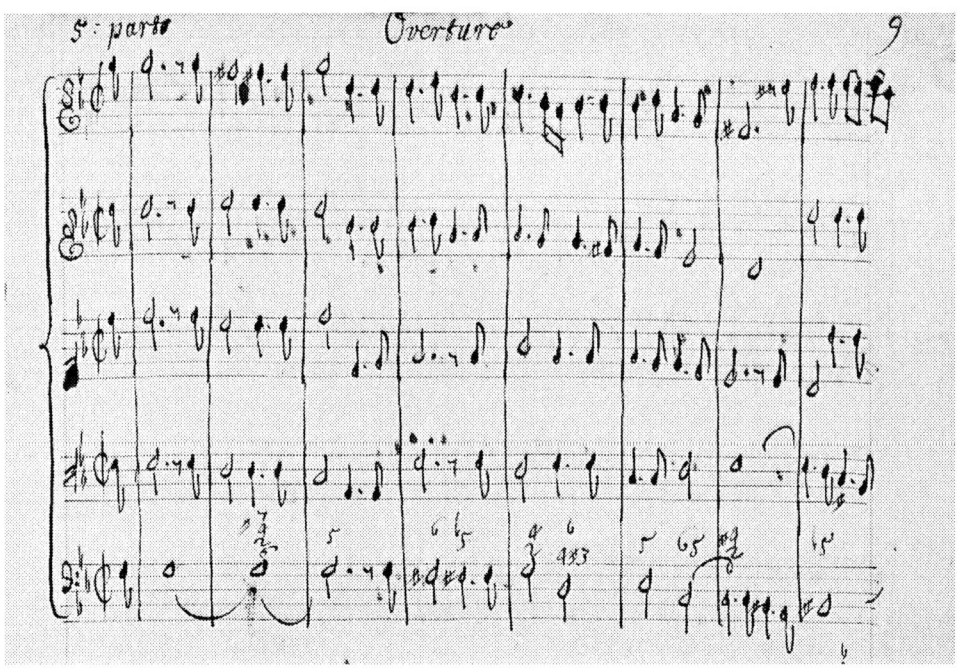

Illus. 7.4  Henry Purcell: overture in G minor, copied by John Reading. British Library R.M. 20.h.9, fol. 117v

concluding 6/4 jig is the popular song 'Hey boys, up go we'. In the 1686 ode *Ye tuneful muses* the same melody appears both as the bass of a vocal solo and as a violin obbligato and a full version of the jig serves as a ritornello,[64] but the suite in Lbl Add. 30930 was probably written first: 'Hey boys, up go we' became widely popular after Thomas D'Urfey adapted it, with explicit reference to the Exclusion Crisis, in his play *The Royalist* (1682),[65] and a contemporary broadside with the same tune is headed 'Good York and Albany: or, the Loyal Welcome to his Royal Highness on his Return from Scotland'.[66]

Purcell's original setting of 'Hey boys, up go we' may therefore date from 1682, around the same time as the ode *What shall be done in behalf of the man*, which

---

[64]  See Westrup, *Purcell*, 178–80.

[65]  Claude M. Simpson, *The British Broadside Ballad and its Music* (New Brunswick, 1966), 305. Stanza 6 begins 'The Whigs shall rule *Committe-chair* / Who will such laws invent / As shall Exclude the Lawful *Heir* / By *Act of Parliament*': see (for example) Thomas D'Urfey, *Wit and Mirth: or Pills to Purge Melancholy*, 6 vols. (London 1719–20), II, 286.

[66]  D'Urfey, *Wit and Mirth*, III, 306: the heading of yet another broadside with the same tune, 'An Excellent New Hymne to the Mobile exhorting them to Loyalty', has obvious associations with the 'mobile crowd' of *What shall be done in behalf of the man*.

similarly celebrated the Duke of York's homecoming; conversely, if the ritornello from *Ye tuneful muses* was the earlier version of the jig, Lbl Add. 30930 might be expected to retain its 6/8 notation, inner parts and other minor variants. Both the G major and G minor suites, in a single key throughout and unlikely to be sets of theatre tunes, could have been composed in the early 1680s for the Twenty-Four Violins, but an altered version of the air from the G major suite was included in *The Gordian Knot Unty'd* (1690)[67] and other movements originally composed for the court perhaps survive unacknowledged in the *Ayres* published in 1697.

London, Royal College of Music MSS 1144 and 1172
London, British Library Add. MSS 30839 and 39565–7
Cambridge, Magdalene College MS F.4.35 (1–5)

Four early manuscript sources provide unique or independent texts of theatre movements by Purcell. The two volumes of Lcm 1144 are the survivors of an original set of at least four books, copied on loose sheets by a number of different hands and assembled using plain sheets of Amsterdam paper with the countermark 'ISRB' as dividers between the different works. In a few places music was copied on these pages, including some movements from *King Arthur* scored from the 1697 *Ayres* beginning on fol. 5v of 1144a, but otherwise the theatre suites by Purcell (Table 7.15), though arranged in key rather than performing order, are independent of the 1697 *Ayres*.[68] The rest of the identifiable music was written for plays produced in the period 1695–1700, which is also consistent with the watermarks in the Purcell parts. Apart from the *King Arthur* score all the movements by Purcell are in a single hand also responsible for other material including Daniel Purcell's music for *Love's Paradise* of 1700 and are mostly written on uniformly ruled Amsterdam paper in which one member of the mould pair is countermarked 'IW' and the other has no countermark.[69] The name 'Elizabeth Sharp' appears on fol. 22v of 1144b.

The only score amongst the early theatre-music manuscripts is Lcm 1172,[70] all

[67] Holman, *Henry Purcell*, 66.
[68] See *Works*, XIX (1994), xxv. Music ascribed to *The Double Dealer* on fol. 7 of each book is not by Purcell. A suite from *The Double Marriage* (fols. 38r and 50r) is probably by Louis Grabu: see Holman, *Henry Purcell*, 193; Curtis A. Price, *Henry Purcell and the London Stage* (Cambridge, 1984), 14.
[69] Compare Churchill no. 34 (1698).
[70] See *Instrumental Music for London Theatres, 1690–99: Royal College of Music MS 1172* (facsimile edn), intro. by Curtis Price, MLE A3 (Withyham, 1987). Though we disagree with Price's conclusion about the purpose of the manuscript, his information about the plays for which the music was written is invaluable. See also Curtis A. Price, *Music in the Restoration Theatre* (Ann Arbor, 1979); Price, 'Eight "Lost" Restoration Plays "Found" in Musical Sources', *M&L* 58 (1977), 294–303.

**Table 7.15  London, Royal College of Music MS 1144: parts of theatre suites by Purcell**

| Work | 1144a folios | 1144b folios | Watermark/countermark |
|---|---|---|---|
| The Rival Sisters | 34r–35r | 46r–47r | Amsterdam/— (1144a) |
| | | | Amsterdam/'IW' (1144b) |
| The Fairy Queen | 40r–43v | 53r–55bisr | Amsterdam/'IP' |
| The Moor's Revenge | 44r–45v | 56r–57v | Bear/— |
| The Husband's Revenge*ᵃ* | 48r–49r | 62r–63r | Amsterdam/— (1144a) |
| | | | — (1144b fol. 62); 'IP' (1144b fol. 63)*ᵇ* |
| The Indian Queen | 50r–51v | 66r–67r | Amsterdam/— |
| Bonduca | 52r–53r | 70r–71r | Amsterdam/— (1144a) |
| | | | Amsterdam/'IW' (1144b) |
| Timon | 54r–55r | 74r–75r | Amsterdam/'IW' |

Guardbook of originally unbound parts, folio: Purcell material 322–30 × 205–10.

Rastrology

| Work | Staves on page | Staves in rastrum | Rastrum span | Rastrum profile |
|---|---|---|---|---|
| The Rival Sisters | 12 | 6 | 131 | 12(11.5)12(12)11.5(12)12.5(11)12(11)11.5 |
| The Fairy Queen | 12 | 6 | 137 | 12.5(11)12.5(13 5)12(13)12(13.5)12(13.5)11.5 |
| The Moor's Revenge | 10 | 5 | 125 | 14(14)12(16)12.5(15.5)14(14)12.5 |
| The Husband's | 12 | 6 | 131 | 12(11.5)12(12)11.5(12)12.5(11)12(11)11.5 (1144a) |
| Revenge | 12 | 6 | 136 | 12(11.5)12(13)12(13)12(13)12(13)12 (1144b fol. 62) |
| The Indian Queen; | 12 | 6 | 131 | 12(11.5)12(12)11.5(12)12.5(11)12(11)11.5 |
| Bonduca; Timon | | | | |

*ᵃ The Old Bachelor.*

*ᵇ*Lcm 1144b, fol. 63, is a slip of paper 87 × 213, not conjunct with fol. 62, bearing the countermark 'IP'.

except the last folio in the hand of London A and a strikingly unusual source in both content and format. Apparently containing the G minor section of a very large collection of theatre movements by different composers, the manuscript consists of flat sheets displaying a variety of watermarks and rulings (Table 7.16). Although the copyist often indicates the source of the movements in Lcm 1172, if only by cryptic abbreviations of a play's title, it seems unlikely that the scores were copied for theatrical use, even as archival material: almost every production had its own introductory and act music,[71] and there is no evidence of these tunes being recycled to the extent implied by the size of the collection in Lcm 1172. The separation of

---

[71] *Instrumental Music for London Theatres*, vii.

## Table 7.16 London, Royal College of Music MS 1172: contents

| Folio | Watermark | Countermark | Ruling | Contents, ascription and comments[a] |
|---|---|---|---|---|
| 1 | Amsterdam | IV | 1 | 1r–2v: overture and act tunes by J. Paisible ('Mr |
| 2 | Foolscap | T | 2 | Peaceable') for *Oroonoko* (1695) |
| 3 | Dutch Lion | PVL* | 3 | 3r: 'Overture in ye Vertuous Wife'; 'B'; 'HP' |
| | | | | 3v: '1 Act Tune Vertuous Wife'; 'B'; 'Mr HPur' |
| | | | | 3v: 'Old Batchelder'; 'HP'[b] |
| 4 | Dutch Lion | PVL* | 3 | 4r–4v: three act tunes (Z.570/6, 7 and 9) from *Abdelazer*; 'Mr H. Purcell' |
| 5 | Towers | — | 4 | 5r–5v: 'A Ground in Timen of Athens'; 'Courtin Tune' (Z.632/20); 'Mr Hen. Purcell' |
| 6 | Dutch Lion | PVL* | 3 | 6r–6v: '1st Lesson' [etc.]; 'Loves last shift'; 'Mr Peasable' |
| | | | | 6v: minuet, anon. |
| 7 | Dutch Lion | PVL* | 3 | 7r–9r: overture and airs; 'Younger Brother'; 'Mr Morgan' |
| 8 | Dutch Lion | PVL* | 3 | [First air on fol. 8r headed 'Mr HPurcells Farewell Tune'] |
| 9 | Dutch Lion | PVL* | 3 | 9v: '2nd Lesson in Bonduca' (Z.574/8); 'HP'; [minuet, Z.574/9]; 'HP' |
| 10 | Amsterdam | IV | 1 | 10r: two airs; 'Mock Maridge'; 'Mr Morgan' |
| | | | | 10v–11r: overture and minuet: 'Titus Andronicus'; 'Mr Cl[arke]' |
| 11 | Towers | — | 5 | 11v: 'Psiche 3d Act'; 'Minuet Pisiche 4th Act'; 'Mr Morgan' |
| 12 | Towers | — | 5 | 12r–14v: ground and airs from 'Fled'; 'Mr Farmer' |
| 13 | Towers | — | 5 | |
| 14 | Dutch Lion | HP | 6 | |
| 15 | Amsterdam | ID | 6 | 15r–15v: overture; 'Antony & Cleopatra'; 'Mr Clarke' |
| 16 | Amsterdam | SH* | 5 | 16r–16v: [act tunes] 'In a wife for Any man'; 'Mr J. Clarke' |
| | | | | 16v: 'Pulchanello In ye Vertuous Wife' [vn 1 only][c] |
| 17 | Towers | — | 7 | 17r–18v: overture and airs; 'Matchless'; 'Mr Morgan' |
| 18 | Towers | — | 4 | |
| 19 | Amsterdam | SH* | 6 | 19r: 'Cupids Dance In Sinthia & Indem' [i.e. *Cinthia and Endimion*] |
| | | | | 19v: three dances; [1] 'in ye Spanish Wives'; [2] 'Rehersall' [3] unidentified [2 and 3 vn 1 only] |
| 20 | Lion | HP | 6 | 20r: overture; 'Lust'; 'Amadis'; 'Mr Lully' |
| | | | | 20v: 'Moors Dance'; 'Henry ye 8th' [vn 1 only] |
| | | | | 20v: 'Lady Wartons Faer well'; 'Cleopatre'; 'Clarke' |
| 21 | Amsterdam | HD | 3 | 21r: 'Lust'; 'Lully' |
| | | | | 21r: 'Fled'; 'Farmer' |
| | | | | 21v: three airs; 'Alas'; 'Farmer' |
| 22 | Amsterdam | IW | 3 | 22r–22v: '2d Musicke In ye Lost Lover' [etc.]; 'My Lord Byron' |
| 23 | Amsterdam | HD | 3 | 23r–25v: overture and airs; 'Humourus Liftenant'; 'Mr Gorten' |
| 24 | Amsterdam | HD | 3 | |

## Table 7.16 (*cont.*)

| Folio | Watermark | Countermark | Ruling | Contents, ascription and comments[a] |
|---|---|---|---|---|
| 25 | Lion | ID | 8 | |
| 26 | Amsterdam | HD | 3 | 26r: 'Virtuous Wife' [Z.611/2]; 'Mr HP' |
| | | | | 26r: 'Horn Pipe K Ar 3d Act'; 'Mr HP' |
| | | | | 26v: 'R O Princ of Persia' [Purcell; Z.577/6] |
| | | | | 26v–27v: overture and airs 'in ye Gordian Knott'; 'HP' |
| 27 | Amsterdam | HD | 3 | |
| 28 | Amsterdam | HD | 3 | 28r–28v: gigue and two other dances from *Amadis* [Lully] |
| 29 | Dutch Lion | ID | 8 | 29r–29v: 'Overture in ye Rivall Sisters' [Purcell]; at end, 'Redgly'[d] |
| 30 | Amsterdam | IV | 9 | 30r–30v: act tunes, etc.; 'Mourning Brid'; 'Finger' |
| 31 | Dutch Lion | HD | 10 | 31r: two airs; 'Mr D Pur' |
| | | | | 31v: 'Synthia'; 'Mr D P' |
| | | | | 31v–32r: airs; 'Farewell'; 'Mr Finger' |
| 32 | Amsterdam | IV | 11 | 32v–35v: overture and airs 'In ye Island Princes'; 'Mr J. Clarke' |
| | | | | 34v (at foot): 'Dance in Valentinian' |
| | | | | 35r (at foot): 'Jigg'; 'Mr Peasable' |
| | | | | 35v (at foot): 'Minuet in Don quixet' [vn 1 only] |
| 33 | Dutch Lion | HD | 11 | |
| 34 | Dutch Lion | HD | 8 | |
| 35 | Dutch Lion | — | 8 | |
| 36 | Amsterdam | I GAUDIN | 8 | 36r–37v: airs by Lully from various works |
| | | | | 36v (at foot): 'Dance in A Woman' [vn 1 only] |
| 37 | Amsterdam | I GAUDIN | 8 | |
| 38 | Amsterdam | ? cursive | 8 | 38r: 'Overture in Mr P Opera'; 'Mr H. Purcell'[e] |
| | | | | 38v: three movements, two by Lully headed 'Dance Labe'; the third, anon., 'Entre Dance Labe'.[f] |
| 39 | Dutch Lion | ID | 8 | 39r–39v: 'Spanish Wives'; 'Mr Peasable' |
| 40 | Amsterdam | VHS | 11 | 40r–40v: 'Del Concerti Grosso Del Sr Archangelo Corelli'[g] |
| 41 | Amsterdam | HP* | 3 | 41r–42v: overture and airs, some marked 'Pleasure'; 'Mr Peasable' |
| 42 | Amsterdam | — | 3 | |
| 43 | Dutch Lion | ? | 12 | 43r: '1st Act Tune in ye Fairy Queen'; 'Mr HP' |
| | | | | 43r: [air; 'Pleasure']; 'Mr P' [i.e. Paisible]. The same tune appears on fol. 47r. |
| | | | | 43v: two airs; 'Mr Orme' |
| 44 | Amsterdam | HP* | 3 | 44r–44v: 'Chacone Armida' and dances [vn 1 and bass only]; [J. Eccles] |
| 45 | Amsterdam | HP* | 3 | 45r: 'The Gloster' [vn 1 and bass only]; [Paisible] |
| | | | | 45v: two rigaudons |
| 46 | Foolscap | PVL* | 13 | 46r: 'Princes' [Paisible] |
| | | | | 46v: 'Round O Gloucester'; 'Mr Lenton' |
| | | | | 46v: 'Wives Victory' |
| 47 | Amsterdam | PVL* | 13 | 47r: 'Entry' [anon]; 'Pleasure'; 'Mr Peasable' |

## Table 7.16 (*cont.*)

| Folio | Watermark | Countermark | Ruling | Contents, ascription and comments[a] |
|---|---|---|---|---|
| 48 | Amsterdam | IW | 13 | 47v–48v: overture and airs; 'Mr WR' |
| 49 | ?Strasbourg | — | 14 | 49r–49v: ground |

Rastrology

| Ruling | Staves on page | Staves in rastrum | Rastrum span | Rastrum profile |
|---|---|---|---|---|
| 1 | 12 | 6 | 129.5 | 11.5(12)11(12)12(12)11.5(12.5)11.5(11.5)11 |
| 2 | 12 | 6 | 120 | 11(11)10.5(11)11(10)11(11)11.5(10.5)11 |
| 3 | 12 | 6 | 131 | 11.5(11.5)12(12)12(12)12.5(11.5)12.5(11)12 |
| 4 | 12 | 6 | 128 | 11.5(11.5)11.5(12)12.5(11)12(12)11.5(11)11 |
| 5 | 12 | 6 | 131 | 11(13)11(12.5)12(12.5)11.5(12.5)11(13)11 |
| 6 | 12 | 6 | 129 | 11.5(10)12(12)11.5(12)11.5(11.5)13(11.5)11 |
| 7 | 12 | 4 | 83.5 | 11.5(12)12(12.5)11(13)11 |
| 8 | 12 | 6 | 130.5 | 12(10.5)13(11)12.5(11)12(11)13(10.5)12 |
| 9 | 12 | 6 | 122.5 | 12(10)13(10.5)11.5(10)11.5(10.5)12(10.5)11 |
| 10 | 12 | 6 | 132 | 12(11.5)12.5(11.5)13(11)13.5(10.5)12.5(11.5)12.5 |
| 11 | 12 | 6 | 123 | 10.5(11)11.5(11)11(11)11.5(11.5)11.5(11.5)11 |
| 12 | 12 | 6 | 126 | 12(10.5)12(10.5)12(11)12(11)11.5(11)11.5 |
| 13 | 12 | 6 | 129 | 11(12)12(11.5)12(12)12(11.5)12(11)11.5 |
| 14 | 12 | 4 | 73 | 10.5(11.5)9.5(12)9.5(11)9 |

\* Monogram countermark

[a] For comprehensive discussion of the manuscript's contents see *Instrumental Music for London Theatres, 1690–1699: Royal College of Music MS 1172* (facsimile edn), intro. by Curtis Price, MLE A3 (Withyham, 1987), vii–xvi.
[b] In fact an act tune from *The Double Dealer*, Z.592/8.
[c] Not by Purcell: see *Instrumental Music*, ix.
[d] The overture is the same as that of *Love's goddess sure was blind*. John Ridgley, one of the court violinists, may have borrowed this movement and composed the remaining dances in Lcm 1144: see Holman, *Henry Purcell*, 225. Alternatively, 'Redgly' may be identifiable with 'Mr WR', the composer of some movements on fols. 47v–48r.
[e] This overture has been linked with *The Tempest* and, more plausibly, with the lost prologue to *Dido and Aeneas*: see *Instrumental Music*, ix–x; Margaret Laurie, 'Did Purcell set *The Tempest*?', *PRMA* 90 (1963–4), 43–57. In his index to Lbl Add. 31452, however, London A used the word 'opera' in the sense of 'works': see Table 6.5.
[f] Anthony L'Abbé, a French dancer: see *Instrumental Music*, x.
[g] A spurious attribution: see *Instrumental Music*, x.

movements in different keys would be inconvenient if a particular set of tunes was to be recopied for a revival, but mixed suites by various composers were compiled for non-theatrical purposes in collections such as Cmc F.4.35 (1–5) and the sheets now bound in Lcm 1172 perhaps represent preliminary editorial work for a similar project.

The four partbooks Lbl Add. 30839 and Add. 39565–7 may have been copied by a French musician, as headings in sometimes faulty French such as 'Overture de Mr Pourselle' (fol. 41v) and 'Suit de la reine de la inde' (fol. 43v) suggest, though the set's repertory is essentially English. There are many references to flutes, oboes and trumpets, and the books evidently belonged to an ensemble with several wind players, if not to a wind band. The partbooks might have been compiled for Princess Anne's band,[72] which included oboists such as Thomas Chevalier[73] and other musicians with French names, and probably date from shortly after 1695. They include movements by Purcell from all four major semi-operas and *Bonduca* as well as the instrumental movements from *Timon of Athens*, here untitled and ascribed either explicitly or by implication to James Paisible: the ordering of the Purcell pieces does not relate closely to the published *Ayres* of 1697 or to the similar though independent manuscript sets in Lcm 1144. Two movements on fol. 43r of the second treble and tenor books headed 'marche funeralle Tollet' and 'autre marche Mr Paisible' are the oboe-band marches for Queen Mary's funeral published in *The Sprightly Companion*,[74] and link the partbooks even more firmly with a wind ensemble.

In the partbooks Cmc F.4.35 (1–5), Purcell's movements lose all connection with their theatrical origins.[75] Almost all the music in this collection, beautifully copied by Charles Babel,[76] is anonymous and unidentified, and is usually organised into suites of pieces by different composers: just over forty movements have a part for trumpet. A theatre musician as well as a professional copyist, Babel seems to have had access to good sources of some important Purcell works: the Cibell for trumpet and strings, more widely known in a keyboard version; the G minor overture also in Lcm 1172; and arrangements of 'Fear no danger' and 'Come away fellow sailors' from *Dido and Aeneas*. Personal marks in one of the set's two Strasbourg bend paper types, the factor's initials 'LVG' and the full name 'I VILLEDARY' support the date shortly after 1700 appropriate for the collection's repertory.

---

[72] See Michael Tilmouth, 'English Chamber Music, 1675–1720' (Ph.D. thesis, University of Cambridge, 1960), 383.

[73] See, for example, *RECM*, II, 65.

[74] See Bruce Wood, 'The First Performance of Purcell's Funeral Music for Queen Mary', in *Performing the Music*, 63–6.

[75] See Herissone, 'The Magdalene College Partbooks'.     [76] See n. 38 above.

## York Minster MS M15(S)

The six folios of Y M15(S) are the only source of the 'Sonata by Mr Hen: Purcell' for trumpet and strings, possibly the overture of the lost 1694 birthday ode *Light of the world*.[77] The paper has a Pro Patria watermark countermarked 'IV' consistent with the eighteenth-century character of the main copyist's hand, the presence of natural signs and an erased C3 clef, altered to the old-fashioned C2, in the tenor violin part of the first system. The score was evidently based on a defective set of parts, leading to a number of problems in the transcription and the annotation 'Wants a barr' in the second violin part of the last movement. Some sections have been heavily corrected, and two passages are rewritten in a different but apparently contemporary hand on smaller, separate pieces of the main paper.

[77] Michael Tilmouth, 'The Technique and Form of Purcell's Sonatas', *M&L* 40 (1959), 109–21.

# APPENDIX 1

## *Identified copyists and early owners*

The purpose of this appendix is to provide background information about significant individuals mentioned in the text or tables, especially those who appear several times. No references are given for well-known historical figures and major composers.

**BADHAM, Charles** (fl. 1698–1715): singer and copyist

A minor canon at St Paul's from 1698 to 1715, Badham preserved a number of Purcell's works in his scorebooks, which include Ob MSS Mus.Sch. B.7 and C.38–40, Tenbury 1031 and Tenbury 1258. On the whole his copies are less reliable, though his score of *My beloved spake* in Tenbury 1031 has long served as the copy-text for the revised version of that anthem, and his transcription of *I will love thee O Lord* in Mus.Sch. C.40 is the only complete text.
(George Hennessy, *Novum Repertorium Ecclesiasticum Parochiale Londinense, or London Diocesan Clergy Succession from the Earliest Time to the Year 1898* (London, 1898), 66; Spink, *Restoration*, 84)

**BING, Stephen** (*c.* 1618–81): singer and copyist

The long career of the prolific copyist Stephen Bing has been detailed in several recent studies. His file-copy partbooks Y M1(S) provide early transcriptions of several Purcell anthems including the unique source of *Give sentence with me*.
(Eric Van Tassel, 'Purcell's "Give Sentence"', *MT* 118 (1977), 381–3; Robert F. Ford, 'Minor Canons at Canterbury Cathedral: the Gostlings and their Colleagues' (Ph.D. thesis, University of California at Berkeley, 1984), 258–76; Watkins Shaw, *The Bing–Gostling Part-books at York Minster: a Catalogue with Introduction* (Croydon, 1986); Pamela Willetts, 'Stephen Bing: a Forgotten Violist', *Chelys* 18 (1989), 3–17; Sarah Boyer and Jonathan Wainwright, 'From Barnard to Purcell: the Copying Activities of Stephen Bing', *EM* 23 (1995), 620–48; Jonathan P. Wainwright, *Musical Patronage in Seventeenth-Century England: Christopher, First Baron Hatton (1605–1670)* (Aldershot, 1997), 52–114)

**BRADDOCK, Edward** (d. 1708): singer, choirmaster and copyist

A gentleman of the Chapel Royal from 1660, Braddock also served as clerk of the cheque from 1688. He was additionally Master of the Choristers at Westminster Abbey from 1670. From the evidence of the extant Chapel Royal partbooks, Lbl R.M. 27.a.1–6 and 8, Braddock appears to

have been the main copyist at the Chapel in the 1680s and 1690s; and payment records at the Abbey indicate that he had similar responsibilities there (see Table 5.7).
(Edward F. Rimbault, ed., *The Old Cheque-Book or Book of Remembrance of the Chapel Royal from 1561 to 1744* (London, 1872; repr. New York, 1966), 210 and passim; Margaret Laurie, 'The Chapel Royal Part-books', in *Music and Bibliography: Essays in Honour of Alec Hyatt King*, ed. Oliver Neighbour (New York and London, 1980), 28–50; *BDM*)

**FLACKTON, William** (*c.* 1710–98): bookseller, music publisher and musician

The son of John Flackton, a bricklayer, William Flackton traded as a bookseller in Canterbury. A few compositions survive in manuscripts at Canterbury Cathedral, where he was a chorister from 1718 to 1726; later he was organist of Faversham parish church. Flackton's main claim to musical fame is the valuable collection of unbound manuscript music he assembled, now Lbl Add. 30931–3, which includes a number of Purcell autographs.
(H. R. Plomer, G. H. Bushnell and E. R. M. Dix, *A Dictionary of the Printers and Booksellers who were at work in England, Scotland and Ireland from 1726 to 1735* (Oxford, 1932), 94; Spink, *Restoration*, 208)

**FORCER, Francis** (*c.* 1650–1705): organist and composer

Francis Forcer was a chorister at Durham Cathedral and then organist to the Bishop of Durham. In 1669 he went to London, where he held organist's posts at Dulwich College (1669–71), St Giles Cripplegate (*c.* 1673–6) and St Sepulchre Holborn (1676–1705): in 1697 he acquired a share in the lease of Sadler's Wells.

There is some circumstantial evidence that Forcer belonged to Purcell's circle in the late 1670s. An extended ground-bass composition appears in US-NYp Drexel 5061, an important source of Purcell fantazias, and Ob MS Mus.Sch. E.399 contains the A minor jig found in the autograph Lbl MS Mus.1, copied in a hand plausibly advanced as Forcer's on the basis of an apparent signature in US-NH Filmer 17; the same hand and signature also occur in US-NH Filmer 15, dated '1677/8'. Further keyboard works attributed to Forcer are in London A's manuscript US-Wc M21/M185/Case and in Lbl Add. 31403, copied by Daniel Henstridge.
(Robert Ford, 'The Filmer Manuscripts: a Handlist', *Notes* 34 (1977–8), 814–25; Dawe, *Organists*, 98; Crosby, *Catalogue*, 148; Spink, *Restoration*, 232–3)

**GATES, Bernard** (*c.* 1685–1773): singer and choirmaster

One of the last of John Blow's students as a child of the Chapel Royal, Gates became a gentleman of the Chapel in 1708 and Master of the Children in 1727. He also served from 1711 as lay vicar at Westminster Abbey, becoming Master of the Choristers there in 1741. He retired from his positions of authority in 1757, remaining on the lists of the choirs at the Chapel and the Abbey until his death. Purcell's scorebook Cfm 88 is inscribed 'N.5. B. Gates, 13th: Jan[uar]y: 1727/8', though the exact circumstances of Gates's ownership are unclear.
(Rimbault, ed., *The Old Cheque-Book*, 228; *Grove*, VII, 183–4; David Baldwin, *The Chapel Royal: Ancient and Modern* (London, 1990), 426, 431; *BDM*)

**GOODSON, Richard** (I) (b. *c.* 1655; d. Great Tew, Oxon., 13 Jan. 1718): organist, composer and copyist, Professor of Music at Oxford

**GOODSON, Richard** (II) (1688–1741): organist, Professor of Music at Oxford

Richard Goodson was a choirboy at Christ Church, Oxford, from 1667 and a singing-man from 1675. He succeeded Edward Lowe as Heather Professor of Music on 19 July 1682 and by 1683 had been appointed organist of New College, resigning in 1692 to become organist of Christ Church. Manuscripts in his hand include significant Purcell sources such as Och 3, 22, 350 and 620. His copies of three sonatas in Och 3 and the Fantazia upon One Note in Och 620 were made from the autograph and suggest personal contact with the composer. As professor of music from 1682 he was responsible for organising the weekly meetings of the Music School, and he also belonged to the distinguished music club at the Mermaid Tavern.

The younger Richard Goodson succeeded his father as professor and as organist of Christ Church. Like his father he was an industrious copyist, though none of the Purcell sources in his hand is of the first importance. He bequeathed a substantial music library to Christ Church, detailed by J. B. Malchair in Lcm 2125; a note inside the cover of Och 617 leaves no doubt that Goodson II, not his father, was the benefactor.

(*Hearne*, VI, 130; *Wood*; H. E. Salter, ed., *Surveys and Tokens* (Oxford, 1923), 186, 221; Margaret Crum, 'Early Lists of the Oxford Music School Collection', *M&L* 48 (1967), 23–34; Crum, 'An Oxford Music Club, 1690–1719', *BLR* 9 (1974), 83–99; T. A. Trowles, 'The Musical Ode in Britain, *c.* 1670–1800' (Ph.D. thesis, University of Oxford, 1992); Shaw, *The Succession*, 211; Peter Holman, 'Original Sets of Parts for Restoration Concerted Music at Oxford', in *Performing the Music*, 9–19, 265–71; Rebecca Herissone, 'The Theory and Practice of Composition in the English Restoration Period' (Ph.D. thesis, University of Cambridge, 1996))

**GOSTLING, John** (*c.* 1650–1733): singer and copyist

A renowned singer for whom Purcell very likely composed many of his virtuosic bass solos, Gostling was a minor canon at Canterbury from 1674, a gentleman of the Chapel Royal from 1679 (succeeding William Tucker) and a minor canon at St Paul's from 1683, rising to subdean there in 1689. Many of his scores of Purcell anthems in US-AUS Pre-1700 85 are primary sources, and he seems to have created singlehandedly several sets of performing materials for the opening of the new St Paul's in 1697.

(Hawkins, *History*, II, 693; W. Sparrow Simpson, *Registrum Statutorum et Consuetudinum Ecclesiae Cathedralis Sancti Pauli Londinensis* (London, 1873), 282–3; Franklin B. Zimmerman, 'Anthems of Purcell and Contemporaries in a Newly Rediscovered "Gostling Manuscript"', *AcM* 41 (1969), 55–70; Ford, *Minor Canons at Canterbury*; Shaw, *The Bing–Gostling Part-books*; *BDM*)

**HAWKINS, James** (d. 1729): organist, composer and copyist

James Hawkins was organist of St John's College, Cambridge, in 1681–2 and then of Ely Cathedral from 1682 until his death in 1729. He had probably been a choirboy at Worcester Cathedral. His copying of earlier and contemporary music in manuscripts at Ely (now deposited in Cambridge University Library) and Lbl Add. 31444–5 went far beyond the requirements of his duties, and he was responsible for two primary and a number of relatively early secondary sources of anthems by Purcell.

(Shaw, *The Succession*, 101–2, 362; Spink, *Restoration*, 84–7, 243–53)


**HAYES, Philip** (1738–97): organist, Professor of Music at Oxford

Together with his brother William, Philip Hayes accumulated one of the greatest eighteenth-century English music libraries. A copy of its sale catalogue, published *c.* 1798 by Smart's Music Warehouse, survives as British Library C.61.h.1(11): lot 1, 'Anthems, Odes, Canons and Dido and Eneas . . .' now forms the four volumes of Ktp MR 2–5. These scores, in the hands of Hayes and the Chapel Royal copyist Thomas Barrow (d. 1789), are mostly derived from known autographs but in a few cases offer evidence of good sources extant in the late eighteenth century and now lost. Hayes's interest seems to have been primarily musical rather than antiquarian, for having transcribed the contents of Lbl R.M. 20.h.8 into Ktp MR 2–5.1 and 2 he gave the autograph to King George III; similarly, Lbl Add. 30930 seems to have passed through his hands some time after 1757, when he used it to correct passages in Lbl Add. 33235, but later in the century is found in the possession of other collectors.

(King, *Some British Collectors*, 110, 128; Nigel Fortune, 'A New Purcell Source', *MR* 25 (1964), 109–13; Alan Browning, 'Purcell's "Stairre Case Overture"', *MT* 121 (1980), 768–9; Laurie, 'The Chapel Royal Part-books'; *Works*, XVII (1994), xvii–xviii)


**HENSTRIDGE, Daniel** (d. 1736): organist, copyist and composer

Daniel Henstridge was successively organist of the cathedrals of Gloucester (1666–73), Rochester (1673–99) and Canterbury (1699–1736, though after 1718 his appointment was nominal). An active copyist and a competent composer of church music, he received his early training at New College, Oxford, rather than the Chapel Royal.

(Shaw, *The Succession*, 235–6; Spink, *Restoration*, 207–9, 260, 336)


**HODGE, Robert** (d. 1709): organist, singer, composer and copyist

A choirboy at Exeter Cathedral, Robert Hodge presumably showed exceptional promise because on 6 October 1683 the Dean and Chapter agreed to send him to study 'with Dr Blow or some other person of the King's Chapel'. In fact his teacher was Purcell, with whom he must have worked until January 1687, when he became a probationary vicar choral at Wells. A letter from Purcell to the Dean of Exeter dated 2 November 1686, reproduced in Westrup, *Purcell*, suggests that Hodge boarded at Purcell's house: he might possibly be identified with London B, the anonymous copyist of all or part of the welcome songs for 1685 and 1686.

Hodge remained at Wells from 13 January 1687 until mid-1690, becoming organist in 1688. He was briefly a lay clerk at Durham, where two incomplete anthems survive in DRc C34, and from April 1693 until his death he held various appointments at the two Dublin cathedrals. Of particular significance is a payment made in 1698 for bringing several anthems and services from

England and transcribing them for St Patrick's. He was buried on 26 May 1709, and a will proved in Dublin in that year, destroyed in 1922, was probably his.
(Vicars, *Index*, 233; Lawlor, *Fasti*, 218, 243, 250; Zimmerman, *Life*, 136; Crosby, *Catalogue*, 175; Grindle, *Irish Cathedral Music*, 28, 32–3; Shaw, *The Succession*, 288, 420; Westrup, *Purcell*, plate facing p. 81)

**HULL, Edward** (fl. *c*. 1690): singer and copyist

Edward Hull was a singing-man at Christ Church, Oxford, from mid-February 1690 to late April 1692. The disbursement book for 1692 records two payments to him for copying anthems, his distinctive signature leaving no doubt that the anthem *Behold in heaven*, arranged by Aldrich possibly from Carissimi, in Och 1220–4 is in his hand. Hull was responsible for the score of Purcell's 1683 sonatas in Och 39 and for J-Tn 0–1–54: his hand also appears in Och 7, Och 411–13, Och 1246 and Bu 5002. He was a member of the music club at the Mermaid Tavern.
(Crum, 'An Oxford Music Club')

**HUSBANDS, Charles** (bapt. Windsor, 11 December 1670; d. 23 February 1692?): singer, copyist and organist

**HUSBANDS, William** (bapt. Windsor, 5 March 1665; d.1701): singer, copyist, composer and organist

Charles Husbands, whose father of the same name was a gentleman of the Chapel Royal, is listed as a Christ Church chorister from 1677 to 1684 but from 1682 to 1687 was a child of the Chapel Royal. He became a singing-man at Christ Church in 1688, and a marginal note in the disbursement book for 1690 shows that he was paid as organist for nine weeks in the third quarter, no doubt taking over from his brother William (below) who had been promoted to the superior rank of chaplain. His death in 1692 is implied by information in Wood's *Colleges and Halls* describing a stone in the Christ Church Divinity Chapel amongst the Lowe family tombs bearing the inscription 'CH Org. ob Feb 23 1691 aet. 21': this passage, however, was added by John Gutch for the publication of Wood's manuscript in 1786 and the Christ Church registers do not refer to Husbands's death or burial.

In the first quarter of 1691 a payment of 15s to 'the Organist for pricking Anthems for the Quire' is signed by Charles Husbands. The sequence of payments in the disbursement books and the order of works in the cathedral partbooks Och 1220–4 strongly suggests that Charles was the copyist of *Thy beauty O Israel*, arranged by Aldrich from Michael Wise, and Locke's *O give thanks*. The same hand (Oxford A) appears in other Oxford sources as well as in Lbl Add. 17835 and Add. 17840. Husbands's signature is not a completely convincing match with the text hand and Oxford A was responsible for the parts of Aldrich's *Dum mosa torpet sanguine Gallico* (Ob MS Mus.Sch. C.121), which bear the heading 'Act Song for 93', the year after Charles Husbands's supposed death. Nevertheless, it is difficult to believe that Oxford A and the copyist of the anthems in Och 1220–4 for which Charles Husbands was apparently paid in 1691 are not one and the same:

Oxford A gives way in several manuscripts to Francis Smith, who was paid for copying in the Christ Church partbooks between 1693 and 1696, and it is possible that either the Christ Church memorial stone or Gutch's transcription of it was a year or two adrift.

Charles Husbands's elder brother William was a chorister at Christ Church, Oxford, from 1673 to 1682 and then served as organist until 1690. From 1692 until 1701 he was a vicar choral of Hereford Cathedral and vicar of St John's in that city. His idiosyncratic hand appears in a number of Christ Church sources though no Purcell copying can be attributed to him.
(Anthony Wood, *The History and Antiquities of the Colleges and Halls in the University of Oxford with a Continuation to the Present Time by the Editor, John Gutch* (Oxford, 1790), 504; F. T. Havergal, *Fasti Herefordenses* (Edinburgh, 1869), 98; Crum, 'An Oxford Music Club'; Ian Cheverton, 'English Church Music of the Early Restoration Period' (Ph.D. thesis, University of Wales, Cardiff, 1985), II, 380; Shaw, *The Succession,* 211)

**ISAACK, 'Barnabas'** (mentioned in 1682): organist

**ISAACK, Bartholomew** (22 September 1661 – 1709): organist and composer, probably to be identified with Barnabas Isaack

**ISAACK, Peter** (*c.* 1655–94): singer and organist

**ISAACK, William** (1650–1703): singer and copyist

The Isaack family of musicians were sons of an older William Isaack. 'Barnabas' Isaack, organist of St John's College, was granted university privileges at Oxford on 14 July 1682. Such privileges, often extended to college employees who were not Oxford graduates, were the equivalent of civic freedom. The name 'Barnabas' appears in no other context, although the annual accounts of St John's mention 'Mr Isaack' in 1680, 1681 and 1684. A Venite chant attributed to 'B. Izaack' on fol. 4v of Och 437, an organ book associated with St John's, is essentially the same as 'Mr Bartholomu Isac his double tune' transcribed by Francis Withy on p. 19 of Ob MS Mus.Sch. D.217, and in Och 337 Withy makes several references to 'Isaack', on p. 110 identifying him as 'Mr Bartho I'. These coincidences suggest that Withy's colleague, and the St John's organist, may in fact have been Bartholomew (b. 1661), so the granting of privileges in 1682 may have been related to the approach of his twenty-first birthday.

Whether or not he is to be identified with Barnabas Isaack, Bartholomew Isaack was a Chapel Royal chorister whose voice had changed by 6 December 1676, when Blow began to be paid £30 yearly for 'keeping' him and, no doubt, continuing his training. From 1684 to 1687 Isaack held a vicar choral's post at one or both of the Dublin cathedrals and he re-emerges in 1705 as organist of St Saviour, Southwark. The inclusion of works by Bartholomew Isaack in US-NYp Drexel 5061, a major source of Purcell's fantazias, suggests that he was a member of Purcell's immediate circle *c.* 1680.

Peter Isaack, brother of Bartholomew, was a Chapel Royal choirboy until 1670. From 1672 until 1687 he served in the choir at St Patrick's Cathedral, Dublin, so it is unlikely that he copied US-NYp Drexel 5061, as has been suggested. He then spent a few years at Salisbury, returning to Dublin in 1691 or 1692 to be organist of both cathedrals. He died in Chester on his way home from a visit to England and his will, now destroyed, was proved in Dublin in 1694.

William Isaack, elder brother of Bartholomew and Peter, held posts at Eton College and St George's Chapel, Windsor. He was a prolific and capable copyist responsible for a number of important sources including Purcell's *Who can from joy refrain* in Cfm 684 and *Hail bright Cecilia* in Lbl Add. 31453, fols. 2–37. *Celebrate this festival* in Ob MS Mus.c.28, fols. 78–99, and another score of *Who can from joy refrain*, Ob MS Mus.c.27*, were copied in collaboration with John Walter, whose annotations also appear in Isaack's great collection Cfm 117. Both Isaack and Walter contributed to the Eton College organ books WRec 299, vols. I and II.

(Foster, *Alumni*; Vicars, *Index*, 246; Lawlor, *Fasti*, 250; E. H. Fellowes, *The Vicars or Minor Canons of His Majesty's Free Chapel of St George in Windsor Castle* (Windsor, 1945); E. H. Fellows and E. R. Poyser, eds., *The Baptism, Marriage and Burial Registers of St George's Chapel, Windsor* (Windsor, 1957); Shelagh Bond, ed., *The Chapter Acts of the Dean and Canons of Windsor* (Windsor, 1966); Bruce Wood, 'A Note on Two Cambridge Manuscripts and their Copyists', *M&L* 56 (1975), 308–12; Dawe, *Organists*, 38, 65; *RECM*, I, 166; Peter Holman, 'Bartholomew Isaack and "Mr Isaack" of Eton: a Confusing Tale of Restoration Musicians', *MT* 128 (1987), 381–5; Grindle, *Irish Cathedral Music*, 27–8, 31–2; Francis Knights, 'The History of the Choral Foundation of St John's College, Oxford', *MT* 131 (1990), 444–7; Shaw, *The Succession* 411, 419; Robert Thompson, '"Francis Withie of Oxon" and his Commonplace Book, Christ Church, Oxford, MS 337', *Chelys* 20 (1991), 3–27; Spink, *Restoration*; *BDM*)

## KENT, James (1700–76): organist, composer and copyist

James Kent left the Chapel Royal on 30 March 1717, and soon afterwards was appointed organist of Finedon, Northamptonshire, where Sir John Dolben, subdean of the Chapel Royal, had presented a magnificent organ to the parish church of his family estate. In 1731 Kent became organist of Trinity College, Cambridge: early in 1738 he moved on to Winchester Cathedral, where he held office until 1774.

Kent is significant as both a copyist and a collector of music. Manuscripts he owned include Lbl Add. 5333 and Add. 31452, which he seems to have acquired from Croft and used as sources for some of the Purcell works he copied in Lcm 994–6, part of John Dolben's collection. Other music was apparently transcribed from Lbl Add. 31447.

(Donald Burrows, 'Sir John Dolben's Music Collection', *MT* 120 (1979), 149–51; Shaw, *The Succession*, 299–300, 367)

## LOWE, Edward (*c*. 1610–82): organist and composer, Professor of Music at Oxford

From around the time of the Restoration until his death Edward Lowe was organist of Christ Church, Oxford, and of the University, Professor of Music at Oxford and one of the three organists of the Chapel Royal. Purcell succeeded him in the last of these posts in 1682. A title in

Lowe's hand is written on the reverse of Och 554, fol. 3, an organ part of Blow's *God is our hope and strength* written out by Purcell in or before 1677, and it is possible that Lowe was indirectly responsible for many of the early Purcell sources in Oxford libraries. The distinctive version of Purcell's Funeral Sentences copied by Richard Goodson I in Och 22 may well have been provided for Lowe's burial in the Divinity Chapel of the cathedral.
(*RECM*, I, V; Shaw, *The Succession*, 210–11; *BDM*)


**PIGOTT, Francis** (d. 1704): organist, composer and copyist

Francis Pigott, recorded as a Chapel Royal choirboy from 1678 until Michaelmas 1683, was probably related to George and Francis Piggot, who in the early 1660s were members of the Old Jewry Music Society in London. The younger Francis Pigott became organist of Magdalen College, Oxford, in January 1686 and was then described as 'Mr Pygott, the Organist of St John's'. There is no independent evidence that Pigott ever held such a post, though he seems to have had family connections with St John's as one George Pigott, son of Francis of London, was a student there. 'Barnabas' Isaack, organist of St John's in 1682, can probably be identified with Bartholomew Isaack, who took up appointments in Dublin in late 1684 or early 1685, and Pigott may well have gone to Oxford at that time. He returned to London in 1688 as organist of the Temple Church, to play the Father Smith organ championed by Purcell and Blow in a protracted contest against one built by Renatus Harris and demonstrated by Draghi. In 1695 he succeeded Purcell as organist of the Chapel Royal, though because Purcell's place as a gentleman of the Chapel was given to the singer Alexander Damascene his appointment was 'extraordinary' until 24 March 1697, when he was sworn into a full organist's place on the death of William Child. He collaborated with Blow, Croft and Clarke in publishing *A Choice Collection of Ayres for the Harpsichord* (London, 1700) and an anthem, *I was glad*, is in the Gostling scorebook US-AUS Pre-1700 85.

Pigott's Chapel Royal background and subsequent selection as Purcell's successor suggest that he might be identified with the copyist London A, whose work indicates an especially close involvement with Purcell and other Chapel Royal organists (see Table 4.4). His somewhat variable signatures in Middle Temple records show striking similarities to London A's text hand, in particular the forms of the capital 'F' and 'P' and the lowercase 'g' and 'i'.
(Rimbault, ed., *The Old Cheque Book*, 21, 25; Bloxam, *Register*, II, 198–9; Foster, *Alumni*, III, 1163; F. A. Inderwick, ed., *A Calendar of the Inner Temple Records*, III (London, 1901), 248, 265 and passim; C. H. Hopwood, ed., *A Calendar of the Middle Temple Records* (London, 1903), 183 and passim; Zimmerman, *Catalogue*, 414, 470; Ian Spink, 'The Old Jewry "Musick-Society": a 17th-Century Catch Club', *Musicology* 2 (1965–7), 35–41; Dawe, *Organists*, 132–3; *RECM*, I, 183, 186, 206, 208, 211; Shaw, *The Succession*, 9–10, 382)


**READING, John** (*c.* 1645–92): organist, composer and copyist

Reading held posts at Lincoln Cathedral (junior vicar and poor clerk 1667, Master of the Choristers 1670) and Chichester (organist 1674–5) before moving to Winchester, where he was

organist of the cathedral from 1675 to 1681 and of Winchester College from 1681 until his death. Even if, as is possible, he was an unrecorded Chapel Royal chorister in the years 1660–7, his path and Purcell's could have crossed only briefly. The close knowledge of Purcell's music reflected by manuscripts copied by Reading, Lbl Add. 47845 and R.M. 20.h.9, probably stems from contact in the early 1680s.
[Shaw, *The Succession*, 76, 160, 298–9; Spink, *Restoration*, 363–5)

**ROSEINGRAVE, Daniel** (d. 1727): organist and composer

Daniel Roseingrave was successively organist of Gloucester Cathedral (1679–81), Winchester Cathedral (1681–92), Salisbury Cathedral (1692–8) and of both cathedrals in Dublin (St Patrick's 1698–1719; Christ Church 1698–1727). He is stated by Hawkins to have been 'educated in the Chapel Royal and a fellow-disciple of Purcell'; though this claim cannot be corroborated, a close relationship with Purcell is suggested by a copy in Purcell's hand of Roseingrave's *Lord thou art become gracious* now in Och 1215. Roseingrave's own writing appears in US-BE 751 and Lbl Add. 47845.
(Hawkins, *History*, II, 771; Grindle, *Irish Cathedral Music*, 28–9, 32; Shaw, *The Succession*, 299, 411, 420–1; Spink, *Restoration*, 364–5; Peter Holman, 'Purcell and Roseingrave: a New Autograph', *Purcell Studies*, 94–105)

**SAUNDERS, William** (b. *c.* 1667; bur. St Cross, Oxford, 7 Jan. 1729): singer and copyist

A singing-man at Christ Church from 1694 to 1729, Saunders was employed as a copyist there and at New College. Hearne states that he had also been a singing-man at St John's and comments that although he died poor he was 'by profession a Pricker of Musick, & got formerly abundance of money by it'. The Mermaid Tavern music club hired material from him. Saunders's variable hand, identifiable by relating the Christ Church disbursement books to Och 1220–4, occurs in a number of other Oxford manuscripts, including Lbl Add. 17835 and Add. 17840, where he takes over from Francis Smith, and D-Hs ND VI 3101. No Purcell source copied by Saunders is of primary importance.
(*Hearne*, V, 189; X, 84; Crum, 'An Oxford Music Club'; Richard Charteris, 'Newly Discovered Sources of Music by Henry Purcell', *M&L* 75 (1994), 16–32. The unknown copyist 'X' tentatively identified as Saunders in Andrew V. Jones, *The Motets of Carissimi* (Ann Arbor, 1982), I, 83–6, in fact represents the hands of Charles Husbands and Francis Smith.)

**SMITH, Francis** (bapt. St Mary the Virgin, Oxford, 14 Nov. 1672; bur. St Mary the Virgin, 20 Aug. 1698): singer and copyist

Francis Smith was a choirboy at Christ Church, Oxford, from 1681 to 1690 and then a singing-man until his death. He was paid for copying in the 'Church Books' (i.e. Och 1220–4) in 1695 and 1696, and his music hand can be identified from his signatures in the Christ Church disbursement books. Other work included sections of Och 48, Och 53 and Lbl Add. 17835, Add. 17840 and Add. 31472, in many cases following material copied by Oxford A. In 1698 Smith and the typecutter Peter de Walpergen issued *Musica Oxoniensis,* a book of songs by Richard Goodson and John Weldon featuring the very beautiful 'second Walpergen' movable typeface.

Administration of Smith's estate was granted to his father Francis Smith, glover, Simon Child (the organist of New College) and one Charles Dowson on 1 September 1698 (Oxfordshire Record Office, MS Wills Oxon 174/3/41). The accompanying inventory reveals something of the circumstances of a young Oxford musician and shows that Smith was an artist and engraver as well as a singer. He was part-owner of the second Walpergen type-fount, his share at that time being worth £15. For some reason the administration was not properly carried out in 1698 and new documents were prepared in late 1714 and early 1715: these list Smith's share of the Walpergen fount, by then worth less than £6, in some detail.
(D. W. Krummel, *English Music Printing, 1553–1700* (London, 1975), 136–7)


**TUCKER, William** (1622?–79): singer, composer and copyist

Possibly a son of Edmund Tucker, organist of Salisbury Cathedral, William Tucker became a minor canon at Westminster Abbey and a gentleman of the Chapel Royal shortly after the Restoration. His handwriting, identifiable from signatures in the Westminster Abbey Precentor's Book 1660–72 (Lwa WAM 61228A), establishes that a number of Purcell anthems were composed no later than 29 February 1679: in the year ending at Michaelmas 1677 he received £20 for copying at Westminster Abbey (Lwa WAM 33712, fol. 5v), almost certainly for the partbooks of the now incomplete Triforium Set I. His hand also appears in the Chapel Royal bass partbooks Lbl Add. 50860 and J-Tn N5/10, the survivors of a set for which his widow Elizabeth was paid £15 on 15 February 1685, in the fragmentary Chapel Royal organ book Cfm 152, and in the earliest layers of the Chapel Royal partbooks Lbl R.M. 27.a.1–8.
(Rimbault, ed., *The Old Cheque Book*; J. L. Chester, *The Marriage, Baptismal and Burial Registers of the Collegiate Church or Abbey of St Peter, Westminster* (London, 1876); Watkins Shaw, 'A Cambridge Manuscript from the English Chapel Royal', *M&L*, 42 (1961), 263–7; Laurie, 'The Chapel Royal Part-books'; *RECM*, I, V; Shaw, *The Succession*; Spink, *Restoration*; *BDM*)


**WALTER, John** (d. 1708): organist, choirmaster and copyist

Warrants to provide for 'John Waters, late child of the Chapel Royal' were issued on 26 February 1677. From 1681 he was a lay clerk at St George's Chapel, Windsor, and organist and *informator choristarum* of Eton College. In 1693 and 1694 he sent the talented Eton chorister John Weldon to study with Purcell. Some of the earlier Purcell sources copied by Walter suggest that he was a close friend of Purcell and a member of his personal, as well as professional, musical circle.

Walter's hand changed markedly in the course of his career. His earliest work, found in the first two Purcell songs in CH Cap. VI/I/I and at the beginning of his *Venus and Adonis* score in Lbl Add. 31453, has features in common with Purcell's early hand. By the early 1680s Walter had adopted italic text and a delicate, slightly mannered, music notation, both exemplified by his later work in CH Cap. VI/I/I, the large scorebook Lbl Add. 22100 and the Purcell sacred partsongs in Ob MS Mus.c.28, fols. 100–23. A group of manuscripts copied around the end of the century display a rather more straightforward, though still neat and legible, style: these include a score of Purcell's Service in B♭, Och 38, and the music from *Don Quixote* in Ob MS Mus.c.28, fols. 3r–18v. Ob MS Mus.c.27* and Ob MS Mus.c.28, fols. 78–99, dating from a similar period, were copied in collaboration with William Isaack. Both hands also appear in WRec 299, vols. I and II. (Montague R. James, 'Organs and Organists in the College Accounts', *Etoniana* 24 (22 October 1919), 369–76; Roderick Williams, 'Manuscript Organ Books in Eton College Library', *M&L* 41 (1960), 358–9; Wood, 'A Note on Two Cambridge Manuscripts'; *RECM*, I, 144–5, 169; Shaw, *The Succession*, 375)

# APPENDIX 2

## *Unidentified copyists*

The unidentified copyists listed below either contributed to partly autograph sources or were responsible for more than one significant manuscript.

### FQ1–FQ4

Three of the four copyists other than Purcell represented in the *Fairy Queen* score Lam 3 are known only from this source (see pp. 235–40): it therefore seemed helpful if inconsistent to label all four with reference to *The Fairy Queen* rather than to add them to the series London A–F. FQ4, however, whose role in Lam 3 is by far the least significant, copied several other sources including the latter part of the keyboard manuscript Och 1179; John Blow's St Cecilia's Day ode for 1700 in Lcm 1097, fols. 125r–134v; the latest additions to Lcm 2011; and the whole of the extensive Purcell collection Lbl Add. 31447. In spite of inaccuracy and a highly compressed layout, this last manuscript is a primary source of *Love's goddess sure was blind*.

**London A**: see PIGOTT, Francis (Appendix I)

**London B**: see HODGE, Robert (Appendix I)

### London C

The unidentified hand which copied the greater part of Purcell's ode *Celestial Music* (composed in 1689) in Lbl R.M. 20.h.8 is different from that of the welcome songs for 1685 and 1686 (London B). It is unlikely to have belonged to Hodge, who left London by early 1687 and is more likely to be identified with London B. Most of the choristers who left the Chapel Royal between 1684 and 1688 can also be ruled out: William Norris (warrants dated 3 June 1686) because he had gone to Lincoln; Charles Husbands (warrants dated 23 November 1687) and Vaughan Richardson (warrants dated 17/18 June 1688) because their hands are at least tentatively identified elsewhere. (*RECM*, II, 8, 9, 16, 19, 20; Spink, *Restoration*, 282)

## London D

London D was the first and principal copyist of two major anthologies, Lbl Add. 33287 and Lcm 2011, and transcribed one Purcell score apparently intended as performing material, *Raise, raise the voice* in Lbl R.M. 24.e.5. The larger sources are beautifully but uncritically copied, many works such as *Behold now praise the Lord* and *Rejoice in the Lord alway* being obviously derived from extant, to some extent imperfect, autographs. R.M. 24.e.5, in contrast, is the primary source of *Raise, raise the voice*.
(*Works*, X (1990), xii, xv)

## London E

London E was a close collaborator of Daniel Purcell, contributing passages in Lbl Add. 30934 and Add. 31461 to what are otherwise autograph scores. Like Daniel, he seems not to have been connected with the Chapel Royal, and his Purcell manuscripts sometimes reflect a tradition divergent from that handed down through Chapel copyists such as William Croft. Contemporary works in his hand date from the period 1696–1702 (see Tables 6.3 and 6.4).

## London F

In contrast to London E, London F collaborated with William Croft and worked within the Chapel Royal tradition. His work appears in Lbl Add. 5333, Lbl Add. 31452 and Lcm 2230, all of which probably date from around the turn of the century, and the rather later Cfm 119 (see Tables 6.5–6.9).

**Oxford A**: see HUSBANDS, Charles (Appendix I)

## Oxford B

This copyist's link with Oxford is tenuous, based on the assumption that the string parts of *My song shall be alway* to which he contributed, now in Och 1188/9, were produced for use in that city. His score of *The Indian Queen* forms fols. 40–83 of Lbl Add. 31453, a guardbook containing material in the hands of William Isaack and John Walter, and may therefore have been copied at Windsor or Eton. Oxford B's work in Och 1188/9 places him amongst the handful of copyists who demonstrably collaborated closely with Purcell.

# SELECT BIBLIOGRAPHY

(For abbreviated periodical titles see pp. xviii–xix)

## BOOKS AND ARTICLES

Adams, Martin. *Henry Purcell: the Origins and Development of his Musical Style*. Cambridge, 1995.

Allsop, Peter. 'Problems of Ascription in the Roman *Simfonia* of the Late Seventeenth Century: Colista and Lonati', *MR* 50 (1989): 34–44.

Arkwright, G. E. P. *Catalogue of Music in the Library of Christ Church, Oxford*, 2 vols. London, 1915–23.

'Purcell's Church Music'. *MA* 1 (1909–10): 63–72, 234–48.

Ashbee, Andrew, ed. *Records of English Court Music*, 9 vols. Snodland (I–IV), 1986–91; Aldershot (V–IX), 1991–6.

Ashbee, Andrew, and David Lasocki, assisted by Peter Holman and Fiona Kisby. *A Biographical Dictionary of English Court Musicians, 1485–1714*, 2 vols. Aldershot, 1998.

Aston, Peter. 'George Jeffreys'. *MT* 110 (1969): 772–6.

'Tradition and Experiment in the Works of George Jeffreys'. *PRMA* 99 (1972–3): 105–15.

Baldwin, David. *The Chapel Royal: Ancient and Modern*. London, 1990.

Baldwin, Olive, and Thelma Wilson. 'Purcell's Stage Singers'. In *Performing the Music of Henry Purcell*, ed. Michael Burden, 105–29 and 275–81. Oxford, 1996.

Beechey, Gwilym. 'A New Source of Seventeenth-Century Keyboard Music'. *M&L* 50 (1969): 278–89.

Berg, W. E. J. *De réfugiés in de Nederlanden na der herroeping van het Edict van Nantes*. Amsterdam, 1845.

Bloxam, J. R., ed. *A Register of the Presidents, Fellows, Demies ... and other Members of Saint Mary Magdalen College in the University of Oxford, from the Foundation of the College to the Present Time*, 8 vols. Oxford, 1853–85.

Boithias, J.-L., and C. Mondin. *Les moulins à papier et les anciens papetiers d'Auvergne*. Nonette, 1981.

Bolton, Arthur T., and H. Duncan Hendry, eds. *Photographic Supplement of St Paul's Cathedral and Part III of the Building Accounts from October 1st, 1695 to June 24th, 1713*. The Wren Society 15. Oxford, 1938.

Bond, Shelagh. *The Chapter Acts of the Dean and Canons of Windsor, 1430, 1523–1672*. Windsor, 1966.

Boyd, Malcolm. 'Music Manuscripts in the Mackworth Collection at Cardiff'. *M&L* 54 (1973): 133–41.

Boyer, Sarah, and Jonathan Wainwright. 'From Barnard to Purcell: the Copying Activities of Stephen Bing'. *EM* 23 (1995): 620–48.

Bridge, J. Frederick. 'Purcell's Birthplace and Residences'. *MT* 36 (1895): 733–5.

'Purcell's Editors'. *Musical News* (23 May 1903): 486–7.

Briquet, Charles Moïse. *Les Filigranes. Dictionnaire historique des marques du papier dès leur apparition vers 1282 jusqu'en 1600* (facsimile edn), ed. Allan Stevenson, 4 vols. Amsterdam, 1968.

*British Museum Catalogue of Additions to the Manuscripts, 1951–1955.* London, 1982.

Browning, Alan. 'Purcell's "Stairre Case Overture"'. *MT* 121 (1980): 768–9.

Bumpus, John S. *A History of English Cathedral Music, 1549–1889,* 2 vols. London, [1908].

Burnet, Gilbert. *History of his own Time* [Oxford, 1833], ed. Martin Joseph Routh et al., 6 vols. Hildesheim, 1969.

Burney, Charles. *A General History of Music from the Earliest Ages to the Present Period (1789),* 2 vols., ed. Frank Mercer. London, 1935; repr. New York, 1957.

Burrows, Donald. 'Sir John Dolben, Musical Patron'. *MT* 120 (1979): 65–7.

'Sir John Dolben's Music Collection'. *MT* 120 (1979): 149–51.

Butcher, Vernon. *The Organs and Music of Worcester Cathedral.* [Worcester], 1981.

Campbell, Margaret. *Henry Purcell, Glory of his Age.* London, 1993.

Carter, Harry. *A History of the Oxford University Press I: to the Year 1780.* Oxford, 1975.

*Catalogue of the Famous Musical Library of Books, Manuscripts, Autograph Letters, Musical Scores, etc., the Property of the Late W. H. Cummings.* London, 1917.

*Catalogue of Rare Books and Notes: the Ohki Collection, Nanki Music Library.* Tokyo, 1970.

*A Catalogue of the Scarce, Valuable and Curious Collection of Music, Manuscript and Printed, of the Reverend and Learned William Gostling.* [London], 1777.

*A Catalogue of the Very Curious and Valuable Music Library of Antient and Modern Compositions ... Collected ... by the Late W. and P. Hayes, Doctors in Music, Oxon.* London, [1798].

*Catalogue of the W. H. Cummings' Collection in the Nanki Music Library.* Tokyo, 1925.

Caudle, Mark. 'The English Repertory for Violin, Bass Viol and Continuo'. *Chelys* 6 (1975–6): 69–75.

Chapman, R. W. 'An Inventory of Paper, 1674'. *The Library,* 4th series, 7 (1927): 402–8.

Charteris, Richard. 'A Checklist of the Manuscript Sources of Henry Purcell's Music in the University of California, William Andrews Clark Memorial Library, Los Angeles'. *Notes* 52 (1995): 407–21.

'Matthew Hutton (1638–1711) and his Manuscripts in York Minster Library'. *GSJ* 28 (1975): 2–6.

'Newly Discovered Sources of Music by Henry Purcell'. *M&L* 75 (1994): 16–32.

'Some Manuscript Discoveries of Henry Purcell and his Contemporaries in the Newberry Library, Chicago'. *Notes* 37 (1980): 7–13.

Chester, J. L. *The Marriage, Baptismal and Burial Registers of the Collegiate Church or Abbey of St Peter, Westminster.* London, 1876.

Cheverton, Ian. 'English Church Music of the Early Restoration Period, 1660–c.1676'. Ph.D. thesis, University of Wales, Cardiff, 1984.

Churchill, W. A. *Watermarks in Paper in Holland, England, France, etc., in the XVII and XVIII Centuries, and their Interconnection.* Amsterdam, 1935.

Cohen, Selma Jeanne. 'Theory and Practice of Theatrical Dancing'. *Bulletin of the New York Public Library* 63 (1959): 541–54. [Reprinted in Ifan Kyrle Fletcher, Selma Jeanne Cohen and Roger Lonsdale. *Famed for Dance: Essays on the Theory and Practice of Theatrical Dancing in England, 1660–1740,* 22–33. New York, 1960.]

Coleman, D. C. *The British Paper Industry, 1495–1860.* Oxford, 1958.

Corp, Edward T. 'The Exiled Court of James II and James III: a Centre of Italian Music in France, 1689–1712'. *JRMA* 120 (1995): 216–31.

'The Musical Manuscripts of "Copiste Z"'. *Revue de Musicologie* 84 (1998): 37–62.

Crosby, Brian. *A Catalogue of Durham Cathedral Music Manuscripts.* Oxford, 1986.

Crum, Margaret. 'Early Lists of the Oxford Music School Collection'. *M&L* 48 (1967): 23–34.

'An Oxford Music Club, 1690–1719'. *BLR* 9 (1974): 83–99.

Dadelsen, Georg von. *Beiträge zur Chronologie der Werke Johann Sebastian Bachs.* Tübinger Bach-Studien 4–5. Trossingen, 1958.

Daniel, Ralph T., and Peter le Huray. *The Sources of English Church Music, 1549–1660*, 2 vols. London, 1972.

Dart, Thurston. 'Purcell and Bull'. *MT* 104 (1963): 30–1.

Dawe, Donovan. *Organists of the City of London.* Padstow, 1983.

Day, C. L., and E. B. Murrie. 'Playford v. Pearson'. *The Library*, 4th series, 17 (1937): 427–47.

Dennison, Peter. *Pelham Humfrey.* Oxford, 1986.

Dickson, W. E. *A Catalogue of Ancient Choral Services and Anthems Preserved Among the Manuscript Sources and Part-Books in the Cathedral Church of Ely.* Cambridge, 1861.

Dillen, J. G. van, ed. *Bronnen tot de geschiedenis van het bedrijfsleven en het gildewezen van Amsterdam*, 3 vols. The Hague, 1929–74.

Dodd, Gordon, ed. *Thematic Index of Music for Viols.* London, 1980–92.

Duffy, Maureen. *Henry Purcell.* London, 1994.

Fellowes, Edmund H. *The Catalogue of Manuscripts in the Library of St Michael's College, Tenbury.* Paris, 1934. [Supplements and 2nd edn by Watkins Shaw published as reel 1 of *The Music Collection of St Michael's College, Tenbury: Part One, Unpublished English and Continental Music Manuscripts before 1650.* Brighton, 1981.]

*The Vicars or Minor Canons of His Majesty's Free Chapel of St George in Windsor Castle.* Windsor, 1945.

Fellowes, Edmund H., and E. R. Poyser. *The Baptism, Marriage and Burial Registers of St George's Chapel, Windsor.* Windsor, 1957.

Fenlon, Iain. *Catalogue of the Printed Music and Music Manuscripts before 1801 in the Music Library of the University of Birmingham, Barber Institute of Fine Arts.* London, 1976.

Finney, Theodore M. 'A Group of English Manuscript Volumes at the University of Pittsburgh'. In *Essays in Musicology in Honor of Dragan Plamenac on his 70th Birthday*, ed. Gustave Reese and Robert J. Snow, 21–48. Pittsburgh, 1969; repr. New York, 1977.

'A Manuscript Collection of English Restoration Anthems'. *JAMS* 15 (1962): 193–9.

Firth, C. H., and R. S. Rait, eds. *Acts and Ordinances of the Interregnum, 1642–1660*, vol. II, *Acts and Ordinances from 9th February, 1649, to 16th March, 1660.* London, 1911; repr. Holmes Beach, 1972.

Ford, Anthony. 'A Purcell Service and its Sources'. *MT* 124 (1983): 121–2.

Ford, Robert. 'The Filmer Manuscripts: a Handlist'. *Notes* 34 (1978): 814–25.

'Minor Canons at Canterbury Cathedral: the Gostlings and their Colleagues'. Ph.D. thesis, University of California at Berkeley, 1984.

'Osborn MS 515: a Guardbook of Restoration Instrumental Music'. *FAM* 30 (1983): 174–84.

'Purcell as his own Editor: the Funeral Sentences'. *Journal of Musicological Research* 7 (1986): 47–67.

Fortune, Nigel. 'The Domestic Sacred Music'. In *Essays on Opera and English Music in Honour of Sir Jack Westrup*, ed. F. W. Sternfeld et al., 62–78. Oxford, 1975.

'A New Purcell Source'. *MR* 25 (1964): 109–13.

Fortune, Nigel, and Iain Fenlon. 'Music Manuscripts of John Browne (1608–91) and from Stanford Hall, Leicestershire'. In *Source Materials and the Interpretation of Music: a Memorial Volume to Thurston Dart*, ed. Ian Bent, 155–68. London, 1981.

Fortune, Nigel, and Franklin B. Zimmerman. 'Purcell's Autographs'. In *Henry Purcell, 1659–1695: Essays on his Music*, ed. Imogen Holst, 106–21. London, 1959.

Foster, Joseph. *Alumni Oxonienses: the Members of the University of Oxford, 1500–1714*, 4 vols. Oxford, 1891; repr. Nendeln, 1968.

Foster, Joseph, ed. *London Marriage Licences, 1521–1869*, from excerpts by the late Colonel Chester. London, 1887.

*The Register of Admissions to Gray's Inn, 1521–1889*. London, 1889.

Fuller-Maitland, J. A., and A. H. Mann. *Catalogue of the Music in the Fitzwilliam Museum, Cambridge*. London, 1893.

Gavin, Charles Murray. *Royal Yachts*. London, 1932.

Gibson, Strickland, and John Johnson, eds. *The First Minute Book of the Oxford University Press, 1668–1756*. Oxford, 1943.

Godfrey, W. H. *London County Council Survey of London*, IV. London, 1913.

Green, M. A. E., et al., eds. *Calendar of State Papers, Domestic Series ... Preserved in the State Paper Department of Her Majesty's Public Record Office*. London, 1860–.

*Gresham Music Library: a Catalogue of the Printed Books and Manuscripts Deposited in Guildhall Library*. London, 1965.

Griffiths, David. *A Catalogue of the Music Manuscripts in York Minster Library*. [York], 1981.

'The Music in York Minster'. *MT* 123 (1982): 633–7.

Grindle, W. H. *Irish Cathedral Music: a History of Music at the Cathedrals of the Church of Ireland*. Belfast, 1989.

Gustafson, Bruce. *French Harpsichord Music of the Seventeenth Century*, 3 vols. Ann Arbor, 1979.

Harding, Rosamund E. M. *A Thematic Catalogue of the Works of Matthew Locke*. Oxford, 1971.

Harris, Ellen T. *Henry Purcell's* Dido and Aeneas. Oxford, 1987.

'King Arthur's Journey into the Eighteenth Century'. In *Purcell Studies*, ed. Curtis Price, 257–89. Cambridge, 1995.

Havergal, Francis Tebbs. *Fasti Herefordenses*. Edinburgh, 1869.

Hawkins, John. *A General History of the Science and Practice of Music*, 2 vols. London, 1853; repr. New York, 1963.

Heal, Ambrose. *The English Writing-Masters and their Copy-Books, 1570–1800: a Biographical Dictionary & a Bibliography*. London, 1931; repr. Hildesheim, 1962.

[Hearne, Thomas.] *Remarks and Collections of Thomas Hearne*, ed. C. E. Doble et al., 11 vols. Oxford, 1885–1921.

Heawood, Edward. *Watermarks, Mainly of the 17th and 18th Centuries*. Hilversum, 1950.

Hector, L. C. *The Handwriting of English Documents*, 2nd edn. London, 1966.

Hennessy, George. *Novum Repertorium Ecclesiasticum Parochiale Londinense, or London Diocesan Clergy Succession from the Earliest Time to the Year 1898*. London, 1898.

*Henry Purcell: the Newly-Discovered Autograph Manuscript of Harpsichord Music*. Sotheby's sale catalogue. London, 1994.

Herissone, Rebecca. 'The Magdalene College Partbooks: Origins and Contents'. *RMARC* 29 (1996): 47–95.

'Purcell's Revisions of his own Works'. In *Purcell Studies*, ed. Curtis Price, 51–86. Cambridge, 1995.

'The Theory and Practice of Composition in the English Restoration Period'. Ph.D. thesis, University of Cambridge, 1996.

Herne, Samuel. *Domus Carthusiana; or, an Account of the Most Noble Foundation of the Charter-House near Smithfield in London*. London, 1677.

Highfill, Philip H., Jr, Kalman A. Burnim and Edward A. Langhans. *A Biographical Dictionary of Actors, Actresses, Musicians, Dancers, Managers, and Other Stage Personnel in London, 1660–1800*, 16 vols. in progress. Carbondale and Edwardsville, 1973–.

Hogwood, Christopher. 'A New English Keyboard Manuscript of the Seventeenth Century: Autograph Music by Purcell and Draghi'. *BLJ* 21 (1995): 161–75.

'Thomas Tudway's History of Music'. In *Music in Eighteenth-Century England: Essays in Honour of Charles Cudworth*, ed. Christopher Hogwood and Richard Luckett, 19–47. Cambridge, 1983.

Holman, Peter. 'Bartholomew Isaack and "Mr Isaack" of Eton: a Confusing Tale of Restoration Musicians'. *MT* 128 (1987): 381–5.

*Four and Twenty Fiddlers: the Violin at the English Court, 1540–1690*. Oxford, 1993.

*Henry Purcell*. Oxford, 1994.

'A New Source of Restoration Keyboard Music'. *RMARC* 20 (1986–7): 53–7.

'Original Sets of Parts for Restoration Concerted Music at Oxford'. In *Performing the Music of Henry Purcell*, ed. Michael Burden, 9–19, 265–71. Oxford, 1996.

'Purcell and Roseingrave: a New Autograph'. In *Purcell Studies*, ed. Curtis Price, 94–105. Cambridge, 1995.

Hopwood, C. H., ed. *A Calendar of the Middle Temple Records*. London, 1903.

Hovenden, Robert, ed. *The Register Booke of Christnings, Marriages and Burialls within the Precinct of the Cathedrall and Metropoliticall Church of Christe of Canterburie*. London, 1878.

Hughes, Anselm. 'Music of the Coronation over a Thousand Years'. *PRMA* 79 (1952–3): 81–100.

Hughes-Hughes, Augustus. *Catalogue of Manuscript Music in the British Museum*, 3 vols. London, 1906–9.

'Henry Purcell's Handwriting'. *MT* 37 (1896): 81–3.

Hunter, Dard. *Papermaking: the History and Technique of an Ancient Craft*, 2nd edn. London, 1957.

Hutton, Ronald. *Charles II: King of England, Scotland and Ireland*. Oxford, 1989.

Inderwick, F. A., ed. *A Calendar of the Inner Temple Records*, 5 vols. London, 1896–1936.

Irving, John A. 'Matthew Hutton and York Minster MSS M.3/1–4(S)'. *MR* 44 (1983): 163–77.

James, Montague R. 'Organs and Organists in the College Accounts'. *Etoniana* 24 (22 October 1919): 369–76.

Jander, Owen. 'Staff-Liner Identification: a Technique for the Age of Microfilm'. *JAMS* 20 (1967): 112–16.

Jeffery, Peter Grant. 'The Autograph Manuscripts of Francesco Cavalli'. Ph.D. thesis, Princeton University, 1980.

Jones, Andrew V. *The Motets of Carissimi*, 2 vols. Ann Arbor, 1982.

Jones, J. R. *Country and Court: England 1658–1714*. London, 1978.

Keates, Jonathan. *Purcell*. London, 1995.

Kenyon, John Philipps. *The Stuarts: a Study in English Kingship*. London, 1966.

King, A. Hyatt. *Some British Collectors of Music, c.1600–1960*. Cambridge, 1963.

King, Robert. *Henry Purcell*. London, 1994.

Klakowich, Robert. 'Harpsichord Music by Purcell and Clark in Los Angeles'. *Journal of Musicology* 4 (1986): 171–90.

'*Scocca pur*: Genesis of an English Ground'. *JRMA* 116 (1991): 63–77.

'Seventeenth-Century English Keyboard Autographs'. *JRMA* 121 (1996): 132–5.

Klenz, William. *Giovanni Maria Bononcini of Modena*. Durham, NC, 1962.

Knights, Francis. 'The History of the Choral Foundation of St John's College, Oxford'. *MT* 131 (1990): 444–7.

Kobayashi, Yoshitake. *Die Notenschrift Johann Sebastian Bachs: Dokumentation ihrer Entwicklung*. Neue Bach-Ausgabe, 9th series, II. Kassel, 1989.

Krummel, D. W. *English Music Printing, 1553–1700*. London, 1975.

Lacomb, Henri. 'Guez de Balzac, fabricant de papier de l'Angoumois'. In *Contribution à l'histoire de la papeterie en France*, X, 72–89. Grenoble, 1945.

Lafontaine, Henry Cart de, ed. *The King's Musick*. London, 1909.

Laurie, Margaret. 'Did Purcell set *The Tempest*?'. *PRMA* 90 (1963–4): 43–57.

'The "Cambury" Purcell Manuscript'. In *Irish Musical Studies 5: the Maynooth International Musicological Conference 1995, Selected Proceedings Part Two*, ed. Patrick F. Devine and Harry White, 262–71. Dublin, 1996.

'The Chapel Royal Part-books'. In *Music and Bibliography: Essays in Honour of Alec Hyatt King*, ed. Oliver Neighbour, 28–50. New York and London, 1980.

Lawlor, Hugh Jackson, ed. *The Fasti of St Patrick's, Dublin*. Dundalk, 1930.

Le Huray, Peter. Review of *The Gostling Manuscript*. *MT* 118 (1979): 585–6.

Lindt, Johann. *The Paper Mills of Berne and their Watermarks, 1465–1859*. Hilversum, 1964.

Love, Harold. 'The Wreck of the Gloucester'. *MT* 125 (1984): 194–5.

Luttrell, Narcissus. *A Brief Historical Relation of State Affairs from September 1678 to April 1714*, 6 vols. Oxford, 1857.

M., S. M. 'The House of James F. Drake'. *Antiquarian Bookman* (24 January 1966): 292–3.

Madan, Falconer, et al. *A Summary Catalogue of Western Manuscripts in the Bodleian Library at Oxford*, 7 vols. Oxford, 1895–1953.

Manning, Robert. 'Revisions and Reworkings in Purcell's Anthems'. *Soundings* 9 (1982): 29–37.

Marx, Hans Joachim. *Die Überlieferung der Werke Archangelo Corellis: Catalogue raisonné*. Cologne, 1980.

Mathorez, J. *Les étrangers en France sous l'ancien régime*, 2 vols. Paris, 1919–21.

McGuinness, Rosamond. *English Court Odes, 1660–1820*. Oxford, 1971.

McGuinness, Rosamond, and H. Diack Johnstone. 'Concert Life in England I'. In *The Blackwell History of Music in Britain, IV: The Eighteenth Century*, ed. H. Diack Johnstone and Roger Fiske, 31–95. Oxford, 1990.

McKie, William. 'Music in the Abbey'. In *A House of Kings: the History of Westminster Abbey*, ed. Edward Carpenter, 416–45. London, 1966.

McLean, Hugh. 'Purcell and Blow in Japan'. *MT* 104 (1963): 702–5.

Miller, John. *Charles II*. London, 1991.

Miserandino-Gaherty, Cathy. 'The Codicology and Rastrology of GB-Ob Mus.Sch. MSS c.64–9: Manuscripts in Support of Transmission Theory'. *Chelys* 25 (1996–7): 78–87.

Morehen, John. 'The Sources of English Cathedral Music, *c*.1617–*c*.1644'. Ph.D. thesis, University of Cambridge, 1969.

Mould, Clifford. *The Musical Manuscripts of St George's Chapel, Windsor Castle*. Windsor, 1973.

Newman, William S. *The Sonata in the Baroque Era*, 3rd edn. New York, 1972.

Ogg, David. *Europe in the Seventeenth Century*, 9th edn. London, 1971.

Oldham, Guy. '"La Furstenberg" and Purcell'. *Recherches sur la musique française classique* 3 (1963): 39–41.

Pike, Lionel. 'Alternative Versions of Purcell's *Praise the Lord, O My Soul: O Lord My God*'. In *Irish Musical Studies 5*, ed. Patrick F. Devine and Harry White, 272–80. Dublin, 1996.

Pinnock, Andrew. 'King Arthur Expos'd: a Lesson in Anatomy'. In *Purcell Studies*, ed. Curtis Price, 243–56. Cambridge, 1995.

Plath, Wolfgang. 'Beiträge zur Mozart-Autographie II: Schriftchronologie 1770–1780'. *Mozart-Jahrbuch* (1976–77): 131–73.

Playford, John. *An Introduction to the Skill of Musick*, 12th edn, rev. Henry Purcell. London, 1694; repr. (intro. by Franklin B. Zimmerman) New York, 1972.

Plomer, H. R., et al. *A Dictionary of the Printers and Booksellers who were at work in England, Scotland and Ireland from 1726 to 1735*. Oxford, 1932.

Porter, Stephen. 'Henry Purcell and the Charterhouse: Composer in Residence'. *MT* 139 (1998): 14–17.

Price, Curtis. '*Dido and Aeneas*: Questions of Style and Evidence'. *EM* 22 (1994): 115–25.

'Eight "Lost" Restoration Plays "Found" in Musical Sources'. *M&L* 58 (1977): 294–303.

*Henry Purcell and the London Stage*. Cambridge, 1984.

*Music in the Restoration Theatre*. Ann Arbor, 1979.

'Newly Discovered Autograph Keyboard Music of Purcell and Draghi'. *JRMA* 120 (1995): 77–111.

Ralph, Richard. *The Life and Works of John Weaver*. New York, 1985.

Rencogne, G. Babinet de. *Recueil de documents pour servir à l'histoire de commerce et de l'industrie en Angoumois*. Bulletin de la société archéologique et historique de la Charente, 5th series, II. Angoulême, 1880.

Ridge, C. Harold, et al., eds. *Index of Wills Proved in the Prerogative Court of Canterbury*, 10 vols. London, 1893–1948.

Rimbault, Edward F., ed. *The Old Cheque-Book or Book of Remembrance of the Chapel Royal from 1561 to 1744*. London, 1872; repr. (intro. by Elwyn A. Wienandt) New York, 1966.

Rohrer, Katherine T. '"The Energy of English Words": a Linguistic Approach to Henry Purcell's Method of Setting Texts'. Ph.D. thesis, Princeton University, 1980.

Rose, Gloria. 'Purcell, Michelangelo Rossi and J. S. Bach: Problems of Authorship'. *AcM* 40 (1968): 203–19.

'A New Purcell Source'. *JAMS* 25 (1972): 230–6.

Sadie, Stanley, ed. *The New Grove Dictionary of Music and Musicians*, 20 vols. London, 1980.

Sawkins, Lionel. '*Trembleurs* and Cold People: How Should They Shiver?'. In *Performing the Music of Henry Purcell*, ed. Michael Burden, 243–64. Oxford, 1996.

Scoville, Warren Candler. *The Persecution of Huguenots and French Economic Development, 1680–1720*. Berkeley and Los Angeles, 1960.

Searle, Arthur. 'Julian Marshall and the British Museum: Music Collecting in the Later Nineteenth Century'. *BLJ* 11 (1985): 67–87.

Semmens, Richard. 'Dancing and Dance Music in Purcell's Operas'. In *Performing the Music of Henry Purcell*, ed. Michael Burden, 180–96. Oxford, 1996.

Shaw, Watkins [=H. or Harold Watkins Shaw]. 'The Autographs of John Blow'. *MR* 25 (1964): 85–95.

    *The Bing–Gostling Part-books at York Minster: A Catalogue with Introduction.* Croydon, 1986.

    'A Cambridge Music Manuscript from the English Chapel Royal'. *M&L* 42 (1961): 263–7.

    'A Collection of Musical Manuscripts in the Autographs of Henry Purcell and Other English Composers, c.1665–85'. *The Library*, 5th series, 14 (1959): 126–31.

    'A Contemporary Source of English Music of the Purcellian Period'. *AcM* 31 (1959): 38–44.

    'John Blow's Anthems'. *M&L* 19 (1938): 429–42.

    Review of *The Gostling Manuscript. M&L* 60 (1979): 487–90.

    *The Succession of Organists of the Chapel Royal and the Cathedrals of England and Wales from c.1538.* Oxford, 1991.

Shaw, William A., ed. *Calendar of Treasury Books,* 1685–1689, III. London, 1923.

Shay, Robert. 'Purcell as Collector of "Ancient" Music: Fitzwilliam MS 88'. In *Purcell Studies,* ed. Curtis Price, 35–50. Cambridge, 1995.

    'Purcell's Revisions to the Funeral Sentences Revisited'. *EM* 26 (1998): 457–67.

Sheppard, F. H. W., ed. *London County Council Survey of London,* XXXI. London, 1963.

Shute, John D. 'Anthony à Wood and his Manuscript Wood D.19(4) at the Bodleian Library, Oxford: an Annotated Transcription'. Ph.D. thesis, International Institute for Advanced Studies, Clayton, Missouri, 1979.

Siddons, James. 'Nanki Ongaku Bunko (Nanki Music Library)'. In *Directory of Music Research Libraries,* vol. IV (= RISM C4), ed. Rita Benton, 138–40. Kassel, 1979.

Simmons, J. S. G. *Addenda and Corrigenda to Heawood's Watermarks.* Amsterdam, 1970.

Simpson, Claude M. *The British Broadside Ballad and its Music.* New Brunswick, 1966.

Simpson, W. Sparrow. *Registrum Statutorum et Consuetudinum Ecclesiae Cathedralis Sancti Pauli Londinensis.* London, 1873.

Spink, Ian. *English Song, Dowland to Purcell.* London, 1974.

    'The Old Jewry "Musick-Society": a 17th-Century Catch Club'. *Musicology* 2 (1965–7): 35–41.

    'Purcell's Odes: Propaganda and Panegyric'. In *Purcell Studies,* ed. Curtis Price, 145–71. Cambridge, 1995.

    *Restoration Cathedral Music, 1660–1714.* Oxford, 1995.

[Squire, William Barclay]. 'The King's Music: Loan to the British Museum'. *The Times* (13 February 1911): 8.

    'An Unknown Autograph of Henry Purcell'. *MA* 3 (1911–12): 5–17.

Steele, Robert. *Tudor and Stuart Proclamations.* Oxford, 1910.

Stephen, Leslie, et al. *The Dictionary of National Biography,* 22 vols. and supplements. London and Oxford, 1917–.

Stevenson, Allan. *The Problem of the Missale Speciale.* London, 1967.

    'Watermarks are Twins'. *Studies in Bibliography* 4 (1951–2): 57–92.

Taylor, Thomas F. *Thematic Catalog of the Works of Jeremiah Clarke.* Detroit, 1977.

Thompson, Robert. '"Francis Withie of Oxon" and his Commonplace Book, Christ Church, Oxford, MS 337'. *Chelys* 20 (1991): 3–27.

    *The Glory of the Temple and the Stage: Henry Purcell (1659–1695).* London, 1995.

    'Manuscript Music in Purcell's London'. *EM* 23 (1995): 605–18.

    'Purcell's Great Autographs'. In *Purcell Studies,* ed. Curtis Price, 6–34. Cambridge, 1995.

Review of Margaret Campbell, *Henry Purcell: Glory of his Age. Chelys* 22 (1993): 49–50.

'The Sources of Locke's Consort "for seaverall freinds" '. *Chelys* 19 (1990): 16–44.

'The Sources of Purcell's Fantasias'. *Chelys* 25 (1996–7): 88–96.

Tilmouth, Michael. 'A Catalogue of References to Music in Newspapers Published in London and the Provinces (1660–1719)'. *RMARC* 1 (1961); *RMARC* 2 (1962): 1–15.

'English Chamber Music, 1675–1720'. Ph.D. thesis, University of Cambridge, 1960.

'The Technique and Form of Purcell's Sonatas'. *M&L* 40 (1959): 109–21.

'James Sherard, an English Amateur Composer'. *M&L* 47 (1966): 313–22.

Trowles, Tony A. 'The Musical Ode in Britain, *c*.1670–1800'. Ph.D. thesis, University of Oxford, 1992.

Tyson, Alan. *Mozart: Studies of the Autograph Scores.* Cambridge, Mass., 1987.

Urquhart, Margaret. 'Was Christopher Simpson a Jesuit?'. *Chelys* 21 (1992): 3–26.

Van Tassel, Eric. 'Fitzwilliam Museum, MS Mu 88: Score in the Hand of Henry Purcell'. In *Cambridge Music Manuscripts, 900–1700,* ed. Iain Fenlon, 170–4. Cambridge, 1982.

'Music for the Church'. In *The Purcell Companion,* ed. Michael Burden, 101–99. London, 1994.

'Purcell's "Give Sentence"'. *MT* 118 (1977): 381–3.

Vast, Henri. *Les grands traités du règne de Louis XIV,* 3 vols. Paris, 1893–9.

Venn, John and J. A. *Alumni Cantabrigienses. A Biographical List of all Known Students, Graduates and Holders of Office at the University of Cambridge,* 10 vols. Cambridge, 1922–54.

Vicars, Arthur Edward. *Index to the Prerogative Wills of Ireland, 1536–1810.* Dublin, 1897.

Voorn, Henk. *De papiermolens in de provincie Noord-Holland.* Haarlem, 1960.

Wainwright, Jonathan P. *Musical Patronage in Seventeenth-Century England: Christopher, First Baron Hatton (1605–1670).* Aldershot, 1997.

Wasson, Joan. 'Three Corelli Attributions in an Eighteenth Century Manuscript of Trio Sonatas'. M.A. thesis, University of Chicago, 1966.

Wessely-Kropik, Helene. *Lelio Colista, ein Römischer Meister vor Corelli: Leben und Umwelt.* Vienna, 1961.

Westrup, J. A. *Purcell,* rev. Nigel Fortune. London, 1980; repr. (intro. by Curtis Price) Oxford, 1995.

'Purcell's Parentage'. *MR* 25 (1964): 100–3.

Whalley, Joyce Irene. *The Pens Excellencie: a Pictorial History of Western Calligraphy.* New York, 1980.

White, Eric Walter. 'New Light on "Dido and Aeneas"'. In *Henry Purcell, 1659–1695: Essays on his Music,* ed. Imogen Holst, 14–34. London, 1959.

Willetts, Pamela. 'Stephen Bing: a Forgotten Violist'. *Chelys* 18 (1989): 3–17.

Williams, Roderick. 'Manuscript Organ Books in Eton College Library'. *M&L* 41 (1960): 358–9.

Wolf, Jean K. and Eugene K. 'Rastrology and its Use in Eighteenth-Century Manuscript Studies'. In *Studies in Musical Sources and Style: Essays in Honor of Jan LaRue,* ed. Eugene K. Wolf and Edward H. Roesner, 237–91. Madison, 1990.

Wood, Anthony. *The History and Antiquities of the Colleges and Halls in the University of Oxford.* Oxford, 1790.

*The Life and Times of Anthony Wood, Antiquary, of Oxford, 1632–1695, Described by Himself,* ed. Andrew Clark, 5 vols. Oxford, 1891–1900.

Wood, Bruce. 'A Coronation Anthem – Lost and Found'. *MT* 118 (1977): 466–8.

'The First Performance of Purcell's Funeral Music for Queen Mary'. In *Performing the Music of Henry Purcell,* ed. Michael Burden, 61–81. Oxford, 1996.

'John Blow: Anthems with Orchestra'. Ph.D. thesis, University of Cambridge, 1977.

'A Newly Identified Purcell Autograph'. *M&L* 59 (1978): 329–32.

'A Note on Two Cambridge Manuscripts and their Copyists'. *M&L* 56 (1975): 308–12.

'Only Purcell e'er shall equal Blow'. In *Purcell Studies*, ed. Curtis Price, 106–44. Cambridge, 1995.

'Purcell's Odes: a Reappraisal'. In *The Purcell Companion*, ed. Michael Burden, 200–53. London, 1994.

Review of *The Gostling Manuscript*. *EM* 9 (1981): 117–20.

Wood, Bruce, and Andrew Pinnock. '*The Fairy Queen*: a Fresh Look at the Issues'. *EM* 21 (1993): 44–62.

'"Unscarr'd by turning times"? The Dating of Purcell's *Dido and Aeneas*'. *EM* 20 (1992): 372–90.

Zimmerman, Franklin B. 'Anthems of Purcell and Contemporaries in a Newly Rediscovered "Gostling Manuscript"'. *AcM* 41 (1969): 55–70.

*Henry Purcell 1659–1695: an Analytical Catalogue of his Music*. London, 1963.

*Henry Purcell, 1659–1695: his Life and Times*, 2nd edn. Philadelphia, 1983.

'A Newly Discovered Anthem by Purcell'. *MQ* 45 (1959): 302–11.

'Purcell and Monteverdi'. *MT* 99 (1958): 368–9.

'Purcell's Handwriting'. In *Henry Purcell, 1659–1695: Essays on his Music*, ed. Imogen Holst, 103–5. London, 1959.

'Purcell's "Service Anthem" *O God thou art my God* and the B-Flat Major Service'. *MQ* 50 (1964): 207–14.

## MODERN EDITIONS AND FACSIMILES OF MUSIC

Bailey, Candace, ed. *Late-Seventeenth-Century English Keyboard Music: Oxford, Bodleian Library MS Mus.Sch. D.219; Oxford, Christ Church, Mus. MS 1177*. Recent Researches in the Music of the Baroque Era 81. Madison, 1997.

Barnard, John, ed. *The First Book of Selected Church Musick, Consisting of Services and Anthems, such as are now used in the Cathedrall, and Collegiat Churches of this Kingdome*, 10 partbooks. London, 1641; repr. (intro. by John Morehen) Farnborough, Hants., 1972.

Blow, John. *Anthems II: Anthems with Orchestra*, ed. Bruce Wood. Musica Britannica 50. London, 1984.

*Anthems III: Anthems with Strings*, ed. Bruce Wood. Musica Britannica 64. London, 1993.

*Coronation Anthems, Anthems with Strings*, ed. Anthony Lewis and Harold Watkins Shaw. Musica Britannica 7. London, 1953; rev. edns 1969, 1986.

Boyce, William, ed. *Cathedral Music*, 3 vols., rev. Joseph Warren. London, 1849.

Byrd, William. *The English Anthems*, ed. Craig Monson. The Byrd Edition 11. London, 1983.

Clarke, Jeremiah, Richard Leveridge and Daniel Purcell. *The Island Princess: British Library Add. MS 15318* (facsimile edn), intro. by Curtis A. Price and Robert D. Hume. Music for London Entertainment C2. Tunbridge Wells, 1985.

Draghi, Giovanni Battista. *Harpsichord Music*, ed. Robert Klakowich. Recent Researches in the Music of the Baroque Era 56. Madison, 1986.

Gostling, John, comp. *The Gostling Manuscript* (facsimile edn), intro. by Franklin B. Zimmerman. Austin and London, 1977.

*Instrumental Music for London Theatres, 1690–99: Royal College of Music, London, MS 1172* (facsimile edn), intro. by Curtis Price. Music for London Entertainment A3. Withyham, 1987.

Locke, Matthew. *Melothesia.* London, 1673; repr. New York, 1975.

*The Rare Theatrical: New York Public Library, Drexel MS 3976* (facsimile edn), intro. by Peter Holman. Music for London Entertainment A4. London, 1989.

Lonati, Carlo Ambrogio. *Simfonie a3,* 3 vols., ed. Peter Allsop. Crediton, 1988–.

*London, British Library MS Add. 39569 ('Babell MS')* (facsimile edn), intro. by Bruce Gustafson. New York, 1987.

[Playford, Henry, ed.] *Harmonia Sacra.* Book I: London, 1688; 2nd edn 1703; repr. 1714, 1726 (repr. Ridgewood, 1966). Book II: London, 1693, 2nd edn 1714; repr. 1726 (repr. Ridgewood, 1966).

*The Theater of Music,* 4 books. London, 1685–7; (facsimile edn), intro. by Robert Spencer. Music for London Entertainment A1, Tunbridge Wells, 1983.

[Playford, John, ed.] *Choice Ayres, Songs and Dialogues,* 5 books. London, 1673–84; (facsimile edn in 2 vols.), intro. by Ian Spink. Music for London Entertainment A5a and b. London, 1989.

Purcell, Henry. *Eight Suites,* ed. Howard Ferguson, 2nd edn. London, 1968.

*Funeral Sentences with March and Canzona for the Funeral of Queen Mary,* ed. Christopher Hogwood. Oxford, 1995.

*The Gresham Autograph* (facsimile edn), intro. by Margaret Laurie and Robert Thompson. London, 1995.

*I was glad,* ed. Bruce Wood. Borough Green, 1977.

*Miscellaneous Keyboard Pieces,* ed. Howard Ferguson, 2nd edn. London, 1968.

*Orpheus Britannicus,* 2 books. London, 1698–1702; 2nd edn 1706–11; 3rd edn 1721, repr. Ridgewood, 1965.

*A Purcell Anthology,* ed. Bruce Wood. Oxford, 1995.

*The Works of Henry Purcell:*

    II   *Timon of Athens,* ed. Ian Spink. London, 1994.

    III   *Dido and Aeneas,* ed. Margaret Laurie. Borough Green, 1979.

    V   *Twelve Sonatas in Three Parts,* ed. Michael Tilmouth. Sevenoaks, 1976.

    VII   *Ten Sonatas in Four Parts,* ed. Michael Tilmouth. Sevenoaks, 1981.

    X   *Three Odes for St Cecilia's Day,* ed. Bruce Wood. London and Sevenoaks, 1990.

    XI   *Birthday Odes for Queen Mary Part I,* ed. Bruce Wood. London and Sevenoaks, 1993.

    XII   *The Fairy Queen,* ed. J. S. Shedlock, rev. Anthony Lewis. London, 1968.

    XIII   *Sacred Music Part I: Eight Early Anthems,* ed. Peter Dennison. London and Sevenoaks, 1988.

    XIV   *Sacred Music Part II,* ed. Peter Dennison. Borough Green, 1973.

    XV   *Welcome Songs I,* ed. Ralph Vaughan Williams. London, 1905.

    XVII   *Sacred Music Part III: Seven Anthems with Strings,* ed. Lionel Pike. London, 1996.

    XIX   *The Indian Queen,* ed. Margaret Laurie and Andrew Pinnock. London, 1994.

    XXIII   *Services,* ed. Alan Gray. London, 1923.

    XXV   *Secular Songs for Solo Voice,* ed. Margaret Laurie. Borough Green, 1985.

    XXVI   *King Arthur,* ed. Margaret Laurie. London, 1971.

    XXVIII   *Sacred Music Part IV: Anthems,* ed. Anthony Lewis and Nigel Fortune. London, 1959.

    XXIX   *Sacred Music Part V: Anthems,* ed. Anthony Lewis and Nigel Fortune. London, 1960.

XXX     *Sacred Music Part VI: Songs and Vocal Ensemble Music*, ed. Anthony Lewis and Nigel Fortune. London, 1965; repr. 1993.

XXXI    *Fantazias and Miscellaneous Instrumental Music*, ed. Thurston Dart, rev. Michael Tilmouth et al. London and Sevenoaks, 1990.

XXXII   *Sacred Music Part VII: Anthems and Miscellaneous Church Music*, ed. Anthony Lewis and Nigel Fortune. London, 1959; rev. edn 1967.

Purcell, Henry, and John Eccles. *Don Quixote: the Music in the Three Plays of Thomas Durfey* (facsimile edn), intro. by Curtis Price. Music for London Entertainment A2. Tunbridge Wells, 1984.

*Washington, D.C., Library of Congress MS M21.M185 Case* (facsimile edn), intro. by Alexander Silbiger. New York, 1987.

# INDEX OF MANUSCRIPTS IN TABLES

Including comments and footnotes

| MANUSCRIPT | TABLES |
|---|---|
| B-Bc 1035.g | 4.5, 4.21, 7.1, 7.2 |
| B-Bc XY 15139Z | 7.10 . |
| EIRE-Dcc partbooks | 4.6 |
| F-Pc Ré. 1186 bis Part 1 | 7.9–7.11 |
| F-Pn Ré. Vmd. MS 18 | 7.9 |
| GB | |
| Bu 5001 | 3.1, 4.6, 4.7 |
| Bu 5002 | 3.1, 4.5, 7.4-7.6, 7.8 |
| Cfm 87 | 6.3, 6.4 |
| Cfm 88 | 2.1–2.3, 2.5, 2.7, 5.1 |
| Cfm 117 | 2.3, 2.4, 4.6, 5.1 |
| Cfm 118 | 7.7, 7.8 |
| Cfm 119 | 4.17, 6.9 |
| Cfm 152 | 5.1, 5.5 |
| Cfm 163 | 7.2 |
| Cfm 652 | 3.3 |
| Cfm 653 | 7.9–7.11 |
| Cfm 669 | 5.9 |
| Cfm 683 | 6.14 |
| Cfm 684 | 4.17, 4.18 |
| CH Cap. VI/I/I | 3.3, 3.13, 7.1, 7.8 |
| DRc A4, A25, A33, C27–8, C34 | 5.1 |
| En Inglis 94 MS 3343 | 7.9, 7.11 |
| EL 6, 20 | 5.1 |
| Lam 3 | 6.2, 7.3 |
| Lam 21 | 6.3 |
| Lam 24 | 6.3 |
| Lbl Add. 5333 | 6.7 |
| Lbl Add. 5337 | 6.3, 6.12 |
| Lbl Add. 15318 | 4.4 |
| Lbl Add. 17835 | 4.11, 4.17 |
| Lbl Add. 17840 | 4.6, 4.11, 5.1 |
| Lbl Add. 19759 | 7.5, 7.7, 7.8 |
| Lbl Add. 22099 | 4.5, 7.11 |
| Lbl Add. 22100 | 4.5, 4.17, 4.21, 4.22 |
| Lbl Add. 29397 | 4.5, 7.7, 7.8 |
| Lbl Add. 30382 | 4.5, 7.4 |

# INDEX OF RASTRAL MEASUREMENTS

This index lists rastra of more than one stave in the manuscripts described in the tables above, in ascending order first of number of staves and then of rastrum span. The variability of rastral measurements means that the information must be treated with caution, but some striking similarities appear, for example between reference nos. 75, 77 and 78 or 86 and 87. Rastrum profiles may of course be read in either direction.

| Ref. | No. of staves | Span | Profile | Source | Table |
|---|---|---|---|---|---|
| 1 | 2 | 29.5 | 9.5(10.5)9.5 | Cfm 152 | 5.5 |
| 2 | 2 | 36 | 12(12.5)11.5 | Lbl Add. 33236 | 3.9 |
| 3 | 2 | 38 | 13(12)12.5 | Ob MS Mus.c.27, fols. 33–6 | 6.13 |
| 4 | 3 | 49 | 9.5(11)10(9)9.5 | Och 350 | 7.4 |
| 5 | 3 | 57 | 11.5(12)11(11.5)11 | Lbl Add. 30932, fols. 52–5 | 5.11 |
| 6 | 3 | 59.5 | 11(14)12.5(11)11 | Ob MS Tenbury 1503 | 4.16 |
| 7 | 3 | 60 | 11.5(12.5)11.5(13)11.5 | Lbl Add. 30931, fols. 67–70 | 5.11 |
| 8 | 3 | 60 | 12.5(13)12(11.5)11.5 | Ob MS Tenbury 1503 | 4.16 |
| 9 | 3 | 60.5 | 12(12.5)12.5(12.5)11.5 | Lbl Add. 33236 | 3.9 |
| 10 | 3 | 64.5 | 11.5(14)12(15)11.5 | Och 22 | 5.12 |
| 11 | 3 | 74 | 14.5(15)14.5(15)15 | US-NYp Drexel 5061 | 3.8 |
| 12 | 3 | 79.5 | 15(16)16.5(15.5)16.5 | Lg Safe 3 | 7.3 |
| 13 | 4 | 44 | 6(6)7(5.5)6(6)7 | Lbl Add. 29397 | 7.7 |
| 14 | 4 | 70.5 | 9.5(11)9.5(11)9.5(11)9.5 | Ob MS Mus.c.26, fol. 68 | 4.18 |
| 15 | 4 | 71 | 10(10)10(10)10(11)10 | Ob MS Tenbury 1175 | 6.3 |
| 16 | 4 | 72 | 9.5(11)10(11)10(10.5)9.5 | Lbl Add. 31449 | 6.10 |
| 17 | 4 | 73 | 10.5(11.5)9.5(12)9.5(11)9 | Lcm 1172 | 7.16 |
| 18 | 4 | 76.5 | 11(10)11.5(10.5)12(10)11.5 | Cu 959 | 3.12 |
| 19 | 4 | 78 | 11.5(11)11.5(11.5)10.5(11.5)10.5 | Lbl Add. 31445 | 4.12 |
| 20 | 4 | 78.5 | 10(13)10(12.5)10.5(12.5)10 | Lbl Add. 30931, fols. 81–4 | 5.11 |
| 21 | 4 | 80 | 10.5(12)10.5(12.5)10.5(12)11.5 | Cfm 119 | 6.9 |
| 22 | 4 | 80 | 11(11.5)11(12.5)11(12)10.5 | Lam 24 | 6.3 |
| 23 | 4 | 81 | 11(11.5)12(11.5)12(11.5)11.5 | US-AUS Pre-1700 85 | 2.6 |
| 24 | 4 | 81.5 | 11.5(12)11.5(12)11.5(12)11.5 | Lbl Add. 31453, fols. 2–37 | 4.18 |
| 25 | 4 | 81.5 | 11(13)10.5(13.5)10.5(12.5)10.5 | Mp BRm370Bp35 | 5.10 |
| 26 | 4 | 81.5 | 11.5(11.5)12.5(11)12.5(11.5)11 | Ob MS Mus.c.26, fols. 71–94 | 4.18 |
| 27 | 4 | 82 | 11(12)11.5(12)11.5(12)12 | Lam 24 | 6.3 |
| 28 | 4 | 82 | 11(12)10.5(12.5)10.5(13.5)11 | Lbl Add. 31445 | 4.12 |
| 29 | 4 | 82 | 11.5(11.5)12.5(11.5)12(11)12 | US-AUS Pre-1700 85 | 2.6 |
| 30 | 4 | 82 | 11.5(12)12(12)11.5(12)11 | US-AUS Pre-1700 85 | 2.6 |
| 31 | 4 | 82 | 11.5(11.5)12.5(10.5)12.5(11.5)12 | US-AUS Pre-1700 85 | 2.6 |
| 32 | 4 | 82.5 | 11(13)11(13)11.5(12.5)10.5 | Lbl Add. 47845 | 4.9 |
| 33 | 4 | 82.5 | 12(12)11.5(13)11.5(12)11 | Ob MS Mus.Sch. E.400 | 3.11 |
| 34 | 4 | 82.5 | 11(12)11.5(12.5)12(12)11.5 | US-AUS Pre-1700 85 | 2.6 |
| 35 | 4 | 83 | 11(13.5)11(13)10.5(13)11 | US-NHb Osborn 515 | 7.13 |
| 36 | 4 | 83 | 11.5(12)12(12.5)10.5(12.5)12 | US-AUS Pre-1700 85 | 2.6 |
| 37 | 4 | 83 | 12.5(12.5)11.5(13)11.5(11.5)10.5 | US-AUS Pre-1700 85 | 2.6 |
| 38 | 4 | 83.5 | 11(13.5)10.5(13)13(13)11 | Lbl Add. 30930 | 3.4 |
| 39 | 4 | 83.5 | 11.5(12)12(12.5)11(13)11 | Lcm 1172 | 7.16 |
| 40 | 4 | 83.5 | 12(12.5)11(13)11.5(12)11.5 | Ob MSS Mus.Sch. E.401–403 | 3.11 |

| Ref. | No. of staves | Span | Profile | Source | Table |
|---|---|---|---|---|---|
| 41 | 4 | 83.5 | 11(12)11.5(13)11(13)12 | Och 1145 | 4.18 |
| 42 | 4 | 83.5 | 11(12)11.5(13)11(12.5)12.5 | US-AUS Pre-1700 85 | 2.6 |
| 43 | 4 | 84 | 12.5(11)12.5(12)12(11.5)12.5 | Lbl Egerton 2956 | 4.18 |
| 44 | 4 | 84 | 13(11)12.5(12)12.5(11)12.5 | Och 1188/9 | 4.15 |
| 45 | 4 | 84 | 11(12)11.5(13)11.5(12.5)12.5 | US-AUS Pre-1700 85 | 2.6 |
| 46 | 4 | 84.5 | 11.5(13)12.5(12.5)11.5(12)11 | Lbl Add. 30932, fols. 121–5 | 4.7 |
| 47 | 4 | 85 | 12(13)12(13)11(13)11.5 | Bu 5001, fols. 172–4 | see p.104 |
| 48 | 4 | 85 | 11.5(11)12(13)12.5(15(11) | Cfm 684 | 4.18 |
| 49 | 4 | 85 | 12(13)11.5(12.5)11.5(13)11 | Lbl R.M. 20.h.8 | 4.1 |
| 50 | 4 | 85 | 11(12.5)12(12.5)12(13)12 | Lbl Add. 33236 | 3.9 |
| 51 | 4 | 85.5 | 12.5(12)13(12.5)12(11.5)12 | US-AUS Pre-1700 85 | 2.6 |
| 52 | 4 | 86 | 12(13)11.5(13)11(13)11 | CH Cap. VI/I/I | 3.13 |
| 53 | 4 | 87 | 12.5(11)12(13)13(14.5)12 | Cfm 684 | 4.18 |
| 54 | 4 | 87 | 12.5(12)13(12.5)13(11.5)13 | Ob MS Mus.c.27, fols. 33–6 | 6.13 |
| 55 | 4 | 87.5 | 12.5(11)12.5(13.5)13.5(13)12 | Ob MS Mus.c.27* | 4.18 |
| 56 | 4 | 88.5 | 12(12.5)13(12.5)12.5(13.5)12.5 | Lbl Add. 33287 and Lcm 2011 | 4.14 |
| 57 | 4 | 90 | 12(14.5)12(14.5)12(14.5)11 | Lbl Add. 31447 | 4.23 |
| 58 | 4 | 91 | 11.5(14.5)12.5(14)12.5(13.5)12 | Ooc Ua 34 | 6.3 |
| 59 | 4 | 91.5 | 12(14)12.5(14)13(14)12.5 | Ooc Ua 35, fols. 1–42 | 6.3 |
| 60 | 4 | 92 | 12(15)12.5(15)11(14.5)12 | Cfm 117 | 2.4 |
| 61 | 4 | 92 | 10.5(15.5)11.5(15)12(15)12 | Ooc Ua 35, fols. 43–86 | 6.3 |
| 62 | 4 | 93 | 13(14.5)13(13.5)12(14.5)12.5 | Cfm 117 | 2.4 |
| 63 | 4 | 93 | 12(15)13(14.5)12.5(14)12.5 | Bu 5002 | 7.6 |
| 64 | 4 | 93.5 | 12(15)13(14.5)12.5(14)12.5 | Och 22 | 5.12 |
| 65 | 4 | 94 | 13(14)13(14.5)13.5(14.5)12.5 | Lbl Add. 31447 | 4.23 |
| 66 | 4 | 94 | 12(15)13(14.5)12.5(14)12.5 | Lbl Add. 50860 | 4.8 |
| 67 | 4 | 94 | 13(13)14(14)13(14.5)13 | Och 22 | 5.12 |
| 68 | 4 | 94.5 | 11.5(16)11(16)12(17)11 | Cfm 117 | 2.4 |
| 69 | 4 | 94.5 | 11.5(15)13(14.5)13(15)12 | Och 22 | 5.12 |
| 70 | 4 | 95 | 11.5(15.5)12.5(15)13(15)12 | Bu 5002 | 7.6 |
| 71 | 4 | 96.5 | 14.5(13)14.5(12.5)14(13.5)14.5 | Lbl Add. 5333 | 6.7 |
| 72 | 4 | 96.5 | 13(14.5)14(14.5)13(14)13.5 | Bu 5002 | 7.6 |
| 73 | 4 | 97 | 14(13)14(14)14(13)15 | Lbl Add. 31452 | 6.6 |
| 74 | 4 | 98 | 14(13)14.5(13.5)15.5(13)15 | Lam 3 | 6.2 |
| 75 | 4 | 98 | 14(14)13.5(14.5)13(15)13.5 | Bu 5002 | 7.6 |
| 76 | 4 | 98 | 14(15)14(14.5)14(13.5)13.5 | Bu 5002 | 7.6 |
| 77 | 4 | 99 | 13(15)14(14.5)14(15)13.5 | Lbl Add. 22100 | 4.22 |
| 78 | 4 | 99 | 13(15)14(14)14(15)13.5 | Lbl R.M. 20.h.9 | 7.14 |
| 79 | 4 | 103 | 14(14.5)15(15.5)14.5(15)15 | Bu 5002 | 7.6 |
| 80 | 4 | 104 | 13.5(16.5)14(15.5)14(16.5)14 | US-NYp Drexel 5061 | 3.8 |
| 81 | 4 | 109.5 | 14.5(16)16(16.5)15.5(15.5)15.5 | Ob MS Mus.a.1 | 5.11 |
| 82 | 4 | 123 | 17(17.5)17(18.5)17.5(18)17.5 | Lwa Triforium Set I | 5.6 |
| 83 | 5 | 104.5 | 11.5(11)11.5(11.5)12(11)12(12)12 | Lcm 1144 | 7.15 |
| 84 | 5 | 107 | 11(12)12(12)11.5(13)11(13)11 | Och 628 | 3.5 |
| 85 | 5 | 107 | 11(11.5)12(12)11.5(13)11.5(12.5)12 | US-R M2040/A628/Folio | 2.7 |
| 86 | 5 | 108 | 11(13.5)11(13)10.5(14)11(14)10 | Cfm 88 | 2.1 |
| 87 | 5 | 109 | 12(13)12(13)11(14)11(13)11 | Och 628 | 3.5 |
| 88 | 5 | 114 | 13(12.5)12.5(13.5)12.5(12.5)13(12.5)12 | Lcm 2011 | 4.14 |
| 89 | 5 | 117 | 13(13.5)13.5(12.5)13(14)12.5(12)13 | US-NHb Osborn 515 | 7.13 |
| 90 | 5 | 120 | 11.5(15)12.5(15.5)12(14.5)12(15)12 | US-NHb Osborn 515 | 7.13 |

| Ref. | No. of staves | Span | Profile | Source | Table |
|---|---|---|---|---|---|
| 91 | 5 | 120.5 | 11.5(13)12(16)12(15.5)12.5(15)12 | Lbl Add. 30932, fols. 87–93 | 4.7 |
| 92 | 5 | 122.5 | 13.5(14)13.5(15)12.5(14.5)12(15)12.5 | Lbl Add. 30932, fols. 94–8 | 5.11 |
| 93 | 5 | 122.5 | 12.5(14)13(13.5)12.5(16.5)12(16.5)12 | US-R M2040/A628/Folio | 2.7 |
| 94 | 5 | 123.5 | 13(15.5)13(16)13(13)13.5(13)13.5 | US-R M2040/A628/Folio | 2.7 |
| 95 | 5 | 124 | 13(16)12.5(14.5)13(15)13.5(13.5)13.5 | Lbl Add. 47845 | 4.9 |
| 96 | 5 | 124 | 13(14)13.5(15)13(14.5)12.5(15.5)13 | Cfm 118 | 7.7 |
| 97 | 5 | 125 | 14(14)12(16)12.5(15.5)14(14)12.5 | Lcm 1144 | 7.15 |
| 98 | 5 | 125.5 | 13(14.5)14(16.5)13(13.5)13.5(13.5)14 | US-R M2040/A628/Folio | 2.7 |
| 99 | 5 | 126 | 12(15.5)13(16)13.5(15.5)13(14.5)13.5 | Cfm 118 | 7.7 |
| 100 | 5 | 127 | 14(13)14.5(15.5)14(13.5)15(14)13 | Lbl Add. 47845 | 4.9 |
| 101 | 5 | 128 | 12(16)13(15.5)14(15.5)14(15)13 | US-NHb Osborn 515 | 7.13 |
| 102 | 5 | 128 | 13(14.5)14.5(14.5)14(16)14(14)13.5 | Bu 5001, fols. 154–9 | 4.7 |
| 103 | 5 | 128 | 12(16.5)12.5(16)13(16)13(16.5)13 | Och 554, fol. 3 | 5.11 |
| 104 | 6 | 120 | 11(11)10.5(11)11(10)11(11)11.5(10.5)11 | Lcm 1172 | 7.16 |
| 105 | 6 | 121 | 11.5(9.5)12(10)12(9.5)11.5(10)11.5(11.5)12 | Lbl Add. 30934, fols. 80–93 | 4.18 |
| 106 | 6 | 122.5 | 12(10)13(10.5)11.5(10)11.5(10.5)12(10.5)11 | Lcm 1172 | 7.16 |
| 107 | 6 | 122.5 | 11(11.5)11(11.5)11.5(11)11(11)11(11)10.5 | Lcm 2230 | 6.8 |
| 108 | 6 | 123 | 10.5(11)11.5(11)11(11)11.5(11.5)11.5(11.5)11 | Lcm 1172 | 7.16 |
| 109 | 6 | 123.5 | 11.5(12)11.5(11)11.5(11)11(11)10.5(11.5)10.5 | Lam 21 | 6.3 |
| 110 | 6 | 123.5 | 10.5(11.5)10.5(11)11(11)11.5(11)11(12)11.5 | Lcm 2230 | 6.8 |
| 111 | 6 | 126 | 12(10.5)12(10.5)12(11)12(11)11.5(11)11.5 | Lcm 1172 | 7.16 |
| 112 | 6 | 126 | 11.5(11.5)11.5(12.5)11(11.5)11.5(12.5)11(10.5)11 | Lcm 2230 | 6.8 |
| 113 | 6 | 126.5 | 11(11)12(11)12(12)13(10)11.5(12)11 | Lam 24 | 6.3 |
| 114 | 6 | 128 | 11.5(11.5)11.5(12)12.5(11)12(12)11.5(11)11 | Lcm 1172 | 7.16 |
| 115 | 6 | 128 | 11(12)12(11.5)12(12)11.5(12.5)11(12)11 | Ob MS Mus.c.27* | 4.18 |
| 116 | 6 | 128.5 | 11.5(11.5)11.5(11.5)12(12)11.5(12)11(12)11 | Lbl Add. 5337, fols. 27–42 | 6.12 |
| 117 | 6 | 128.5 | 11(12)11(13)11.5(12)12(11)11.5(11.5)11.5 | Lbl Add. 31445 | 4.12 |
| 118 | 6 | 129 | 11.5(10)12(12)11.5(12)11.5(11.5)13(11.5)11 | Lcm 1172 | 7.16 |
| 119 | 6 | 129 | 11(12)12(11.5)12(12)12(11.5)12(11)11.5 | Lcm 1172 | 7.16 |
| 120 | 6 | 129 | 11.5(12)12.5(11.5)12(11)13(10)(12)12 | Ob MS Mus.c.28, fols. 78–99 | 4.18 |
| 121 | 6 | 129 | 11(12.5)11(13)11(12.5)11(12)11.5(13)11 | Och 766 | 4.15 |
| 122 | 6 | 129.5 | 11.5(12)11(12)12(12)11.5(12.5)11.5(11.5)11 | Lcm 1172 | 7.16 |
| 123 | 6 | 130 | 11(12.5)11.5(11)12(12.5)11.5(12)11.5(12)11 | Lam 21 | 6.3 |
| 124 | 6 | 130 | 11(12)11.5(12)11.5(12)12(11)11.5(12.5)11 | Lcm 2230 | 6.8 |
| 125 | 6 | 130 | 11(12.5)11(13.5)11.5(13)10.5(13.5)11(13)11 | Ob MS Mus.c.28, fols. 19–39 | 4.18 |
| 126 | 6 | 130.5 | 12.5(11.5)12.5(11.5)12(12)12(11.5)12(12)11.5 | Lam 21 | 6.3 |
| 127 | 6 | 130.5 | 11.5(11.5)12(11.5)12(12)12.5(11.5)13(9.5)12.5 | Lbl Add. 5337, fols. 2–21 | 6.3 |
| 128 | 6 | 130.5 | 12(10.5)13(11)12.5(11)12(11)13(10.5)12 | Lcm 1172 | 7.16 |
| 129 | 6 | 131 | 12(11.5)12.5(11)12.5(13)12(12)11.5(11.5)11 | Cfm 683 and Ob MS Tenbury 785 | 6.14 |
| 130 | 6 | 131 | 12(12)12(13)12(12.5)11(12)12(12)11 | Lbl Add. 30934, fols. 80–93 | 4.18 |
| 131 | 6 | 131 | 11.5(12.5)12(11.5)12.5(11.5)13(10)12(12)11.5 | Lbl Add. 31453, fols. 40–83 | 6.11 |
| 132 | 6 | 131 | 12(11.5)12(12)11.5(12)12.5(11)12(11)11.5 | Lcm 1144 | 7.15 |
| 133 | 6 | 131 | 11(13)11(12.5)12(12.5)11.5(12.5)11(13)11 | Lcm 1172 | 7.16 |
| 134 | 6 | 131 | 11.5(11.5)12(12)12(12)12.5(11.5)12.5(11)12 | Lcm 1172 | 7.16 |
| 135 | 6 | 131 | 11(11.5)11.5(12.5)12(13)12.5(11.5)12.5(12)12 | Och 1145 | 4.18 |
| 136 | 6 | 131 | 11.5(12.5)12(13)12(11.5)11(13.5)11.5(12)12 | Och 1188/9 | 4.15 |
| 137 | 6 | 131.5 | 12(11.5)13(12.5)12(12)12.5(11.5)12.5(10)12.5 | Bu 5001, fols. 162–7 | 4.7 |
| 138 | 6 | 131.5 | 13(10)13.5(10.5)13.5(10.5)13.5(11)13(9.5)13 | Lcm 1144 | 7.15 |
| 139 | 6 | 132 | 10(13.5)11.5(13.5)11(13.5)11(13)12(13)11 | Lbl Add. 30930 | 3.4 |

| Ref. | No. of staves | Span | Profile | Source | Table |
|---|---|---|---|---|---|
| 140 | 6 | 132 | 12(11.5)12.5(11.5)13(11)13.5(10.5)12.5(11.5)12.5 | Lcm 1172 | 7.16 |
| 141 | 6 | 132 | 11(12.5)12.5(13)11(13)11.5(13.5)11(11.5)12 | Ob MS Mus.c.26, fols. 21–67 | 4.18 |
| 142 | 6 | 133.5 | 12(12.5)12(13)11(12.5)11.5(12.5)12(12.5)11.5 | Lbl Add. 30934, fols. 80–93 | 4.18 |
| 143 | 6 | 134.5 | 13(11)13.5(12.5)12.5(12.5)12(13)13(10)12.5 | Ob MS Mus.c.27* | 4.18 |
| 144 | 6 | 135.5 | 11.5(12.5)12.5(12.5)13(11)12(13.5)12.5(12.5)12 | Lbl Add. 47845 | 4.9 |
| 145 | 6 | 136 | 12(13)12(12)12(12.5)12.5(12.5)12.5(13.5)12.5 | Lbl R.M. 24.e.5, fols. 1–9 | 4.18 |
| 146 | 6 | 136 | 12(11.5)12(13)12(13)12(13)12(13)12 | Lcm 1144 | 7.15 |
| 147 | 6 | 136.5 | 11.5(13)12.5(12.5)12(12.5)12(13.5)12.5(12.5)12.5 | Bu 5001, fols. 146–51 | 4.7 |
| 148 | 6 | 136.5 | 11.5(13)12.5(12.5)12(12.5)12(13.5)12.5(12.5)12.5 | Ob MS Mus.c.26, fols. 4–9 | 5.11 |
|  |  |  |  | Ob MS Mus.c.26, fols. 10–17 | 4.7 |
| 149 | 6 | 137 | 12(13)11.5(12.5)11.5(13)12.5(12.5)12.5(13)12 | Lbl Add. 47845 | 4.9 |
| 150 | 6 | 137 | 12.5(11)12.5(13.5)12(13)12(13.5)12(13.5)11.5 | Lcm 1144 | 7.15 |
| 151 | 6 | 137 | 12.5(11)13.5(11)13(12)14(12.5)12.5(11.5)13 | Och 1215 no. 1 | 5.11 |
| 152 | 6 | 137.5 | 13(12.5)12.5(13)12(13)12(12)12.5(12.5)12.5 | Lbl Add. 47845 | 4.9 |
| 153 | 6 | 137.5 | 12.5(12)12.5(11)13.5(11)14(11.5)13.5(11)12.5 | Lbl Add. 47845 | 4.9 |
| 154 | 6 | 137.5 | 12.5(11)13.5(12.5)13(11.5)14(12)12.5(11.5)13 | Ob MS Mus.c.28, fols. 100–24 | 3.6 |
| 155 | 6 | 137.5 | 11.5(13.5)12(13.5)12.5(13.5)12(13)12(12)12 | Ob MS Mus.Sch. C.61 | 4.15 |
| 156 | 6 | 138 | 13(11)13(11.5)14(11)14(11)14(11.5)13.5 | Lbl Add. 19759 | 7.7 |
| 157 | 6 | 138 | 13.5(11)12.5(12.5)12(13)12.5(13)12(13.5)11.5 | Lbl Add. 30931, fols. 61–6 | 4.7 |
| 158 | 6 | 138.5 | 13(11)12(13.5)12(13.5)12(13.5)12(13.5)12 | Lbl Add. 47845 | 4.9 |
| 159 | 6 | 138.5 | 12.5(11)13.5(11.5)14(11)14(11)13.5(12)14 | Lcm 1119 | 7.7 |
| 160 | 6 | 140 | 13(13)13(12.5)12.5(13.5)12.5(12.5)13(12.5)12 | Lbl Add. 33287 and Lcm 2011 | 4.14 |
| 161 | 8 | 161.5 | 10(11.5)10.5(11.5)9.5(11.5)10(12)10(11.5)10(11.5)10(12)10 | Ob MS Tenbury 1266 | 6.1 |

Six-line staves

| Ref. | No. of staves | Span | Profile | Source | Table |
|---|---|---|---|---|---|
| 162 | 2 | 48 | 17(15)17 | Lbl MS Mus.1 | 7.9 |
| 163 | 3 | 66.5 | 13.5(13.5)13(13.5)12.5 | Lbl Add. 31468 | 7.12 |
| 164 | 3 | 78 | 16.5(15)16(13)17.5 | Cfm 152 | 5.5 |
| 165 | 3 | 78.5 | 17(15)16(13)17.5 | Cfm 152 | 5.5 |
| 166 | 3 | 83.5 | 16(18)16.5(16.5)16.5 | Cfm 152 | 5.5 |
| 167 | 3 | 84 | 17.5(15.5)16.5(17)17 | Lbl Add. 31446 | 7.12 |
| 168 | 4 | 102.5 | 13.5(16)14(16.5)13.5(15.5)13.5 | Och 1179 | 7.12 |
| 169 | 4 | 120.5 | 16.5(18)16(19.5)16.5(17)16.5 | Och 1176/7 | 7.10 |

# INDEX OF WORKS MENTIONED IN THE TEXT

# INDEX OF MANUSCRIPTS MENTIONED IN THE TEXT

# INDEX OF WATERMARK TYPES AND PERSONAL MARKS IN PAPER MENTIONED IN THE TEXT

See also Index of Names for identified papermakers and merchants.

Printed in the United Kingdom
by Lightning Source UK Ltd.
120096UK00001B/43